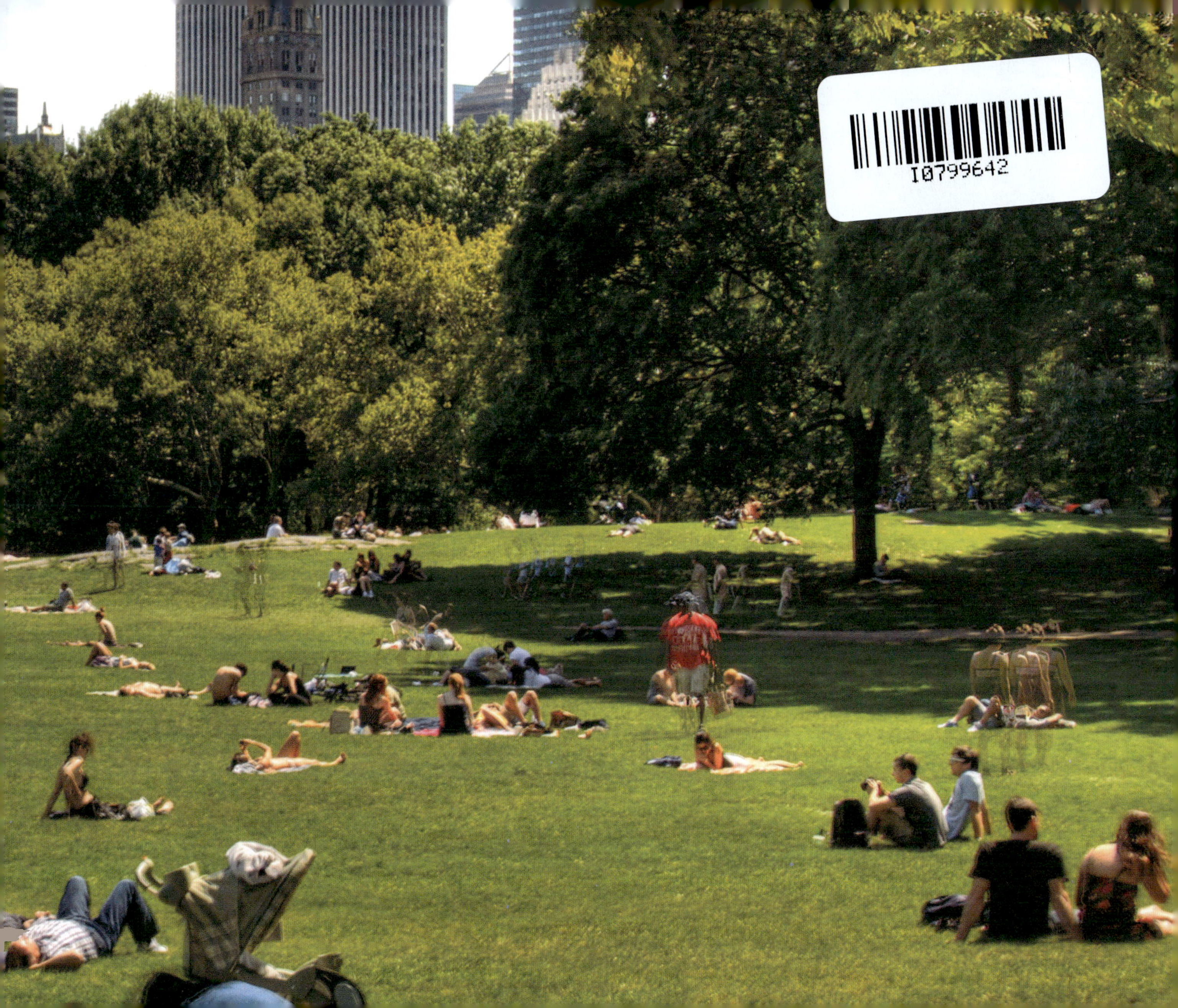

GABRIELA KOGAN

New York NON-STOP

A Photographic Album

UNIVERSE

GABRIELA KOGAN is a leading contemporary graphic designer and a book packager focused on the identity of cities. Her latest book about New York, **NEW YORK: A PHOTOGRAPHIC ALBUM**, also published by Rizzoli/Universe, has become a classic in the bookstores of the city.

Long before understanding the special love that New York City inspires, you get the sense that there is something unique and attractive about this city. Trying to grasp that certain something is one way to try to understand the passion it incites. It's almost as if, by fathoming the origin of that feeling, we can feel like a part of the city itself.

The soul of New York lies in its multiple expressions and that is where we must look for it. It lies in the traces left by all those who built the city as they built their own lives. The city's skyscrapers, traditions, foods, businesses, and landscapes are nothing if not the embodiment of life stories. They are the result of dreamers that came to these shores with old suitcases bearing a scent of pain and farewell, who found in New York a fertile terrain in which these dreams could come true and grow with the city itself.

New York is the shared life of those hundreds of thousands of individual dreams. It is a city that we love the way we love a person, a city whose suffering we bear, a city we grow with, a city from whose ashes we ourselves are reborn.

Because there are so many distinct views of New York, to describe and convey its soul required a great many pairs of eyes, a great many lovers of the city who had once tried to capture in an image a sliver of that which cannot be captured because it is everywhere.

To make this book, I had the privilege of getting in touch with others who love the city like I do. And, unlike other objects of affection, I can honestly state that this love grows the more it is shared.

I am astonished and touched by the invisible ties forged by social networks when there is a common cause, which is why I would like to offer my deepest thanks to all the people who, from the farthest corners of the world, lent me images to try to tell this story. I would also like to thank those generous souls who shared their images according to the terms of Creative Commons. This experience has shown me that something different is happening in the world, that a new way of seeing things is taking shape.

We are bound by a love of New York and the desire to convey this, because we know that it is an honor to be able to tell the story of New York.

I am still surprised when I come upon the same images in the photo albums of different people, people I don't know. These are windows from which to look out on the city I love.

I am overjoyed when I find the same image photographed by many different people. I know that this image holds a bit of the soul of New York we are all looking for.

One of New York's traits is abundance and a celebration of it. There is enough of New York for everyone. And anyone—from the native New Yorker to the passing visitor—who has had the New York experience has something different to say about what the city has given them. And therein lies this book: the abundance of New York in images that, though seemingly disorganized, have an underlying meaning which is what allows us to understand, to taste, and to delve into the city we so love.

Of course, New York is much more than these images. Each one of us knows what is not expressed in these pages, and so we keep looking for it, photographing it in order to arrive at a more thorough and personal description of our beloved city. The soul of New York takes a different shape in the heart of each person who loves it.

The 362 images in this book inspire happiness because they assure us that there is something we do understand, something that, once grasped, is in our heart forever.

Can the spirit of New York be conveyed? I think it can, and this is my attempt to do so.

To Edith Wharton, Nora Ephron and Carrie Bradshaw,
who are, to a large degree, responsible for my love of the city...

To everyone who loves New York and tirelessly searches for its soul.

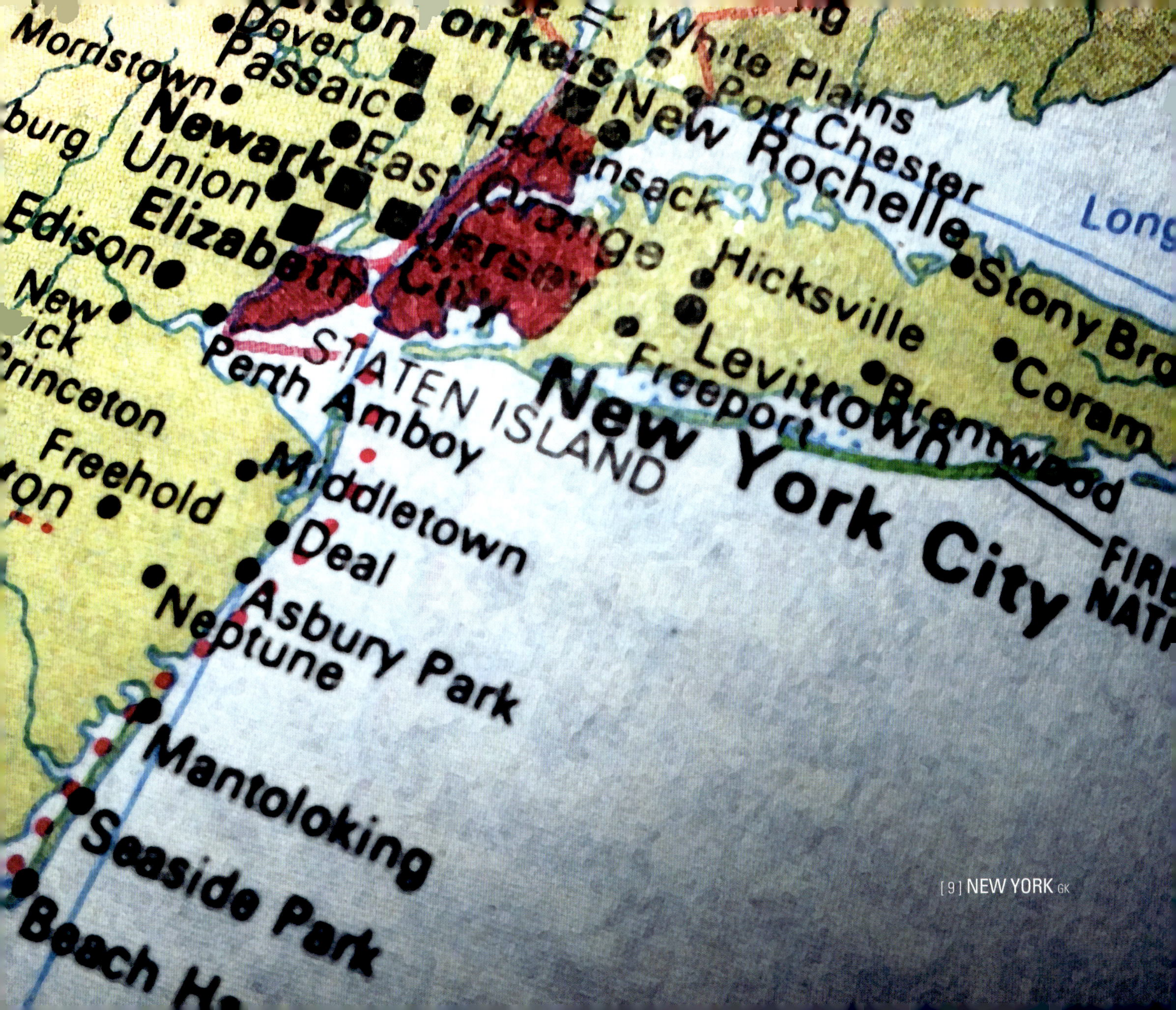
Dover
Morristown
Passaic
Newark
Union
Elizabeth
Edison
East Orange
Hackensack
Jersey City
White Plains
Port Chester
New Rochelle
Hicksville
Levittown
Freeport
Brentwood
Coram
STATEN ISLAND
Perth Amboy
Princeton
Freehold
Middletown
Deal
Asbury Park
Neptune
Mantoloking
Seaside Park
New York City

[10] ELLIS ISLAND STEVE MALPASS

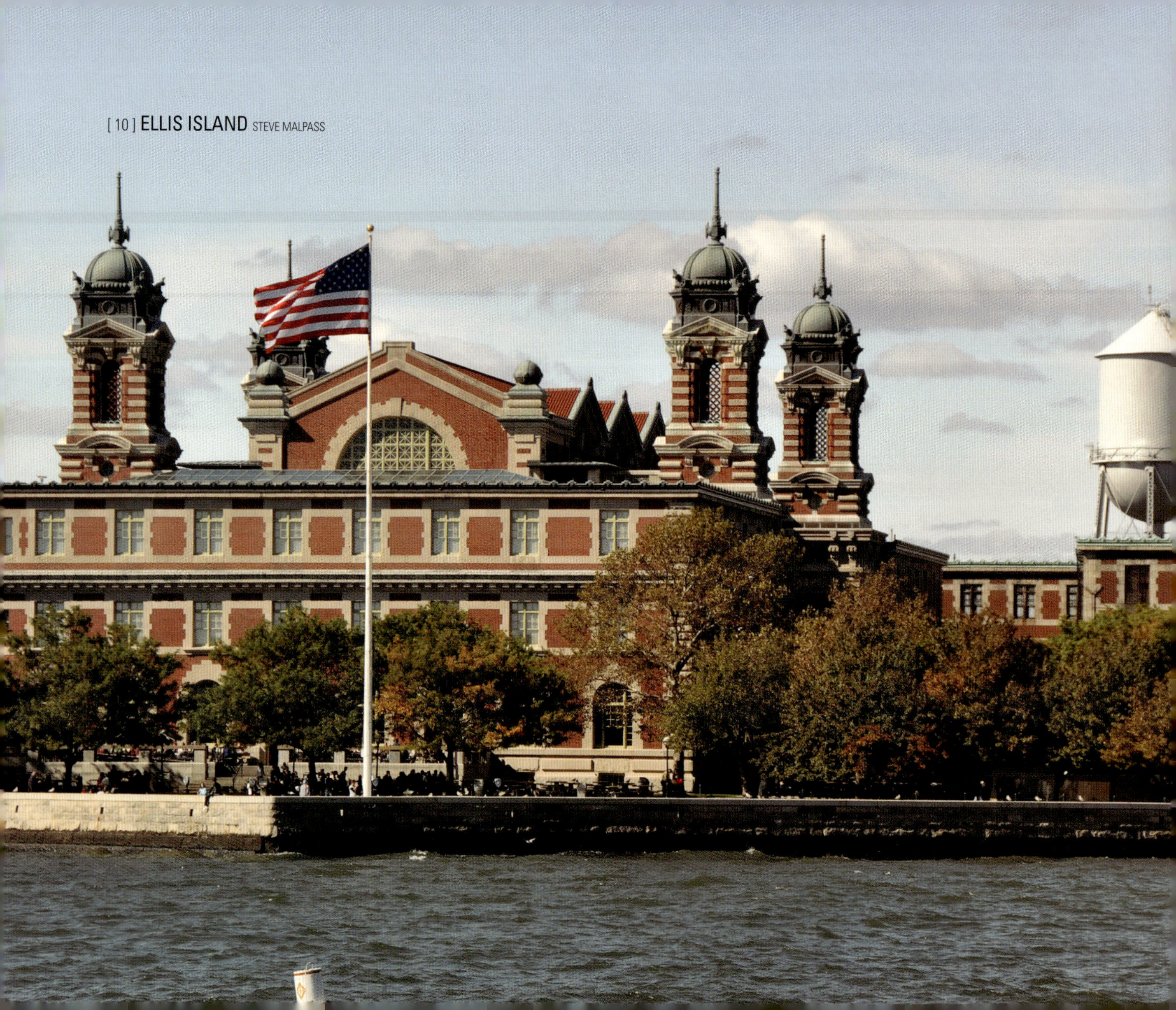

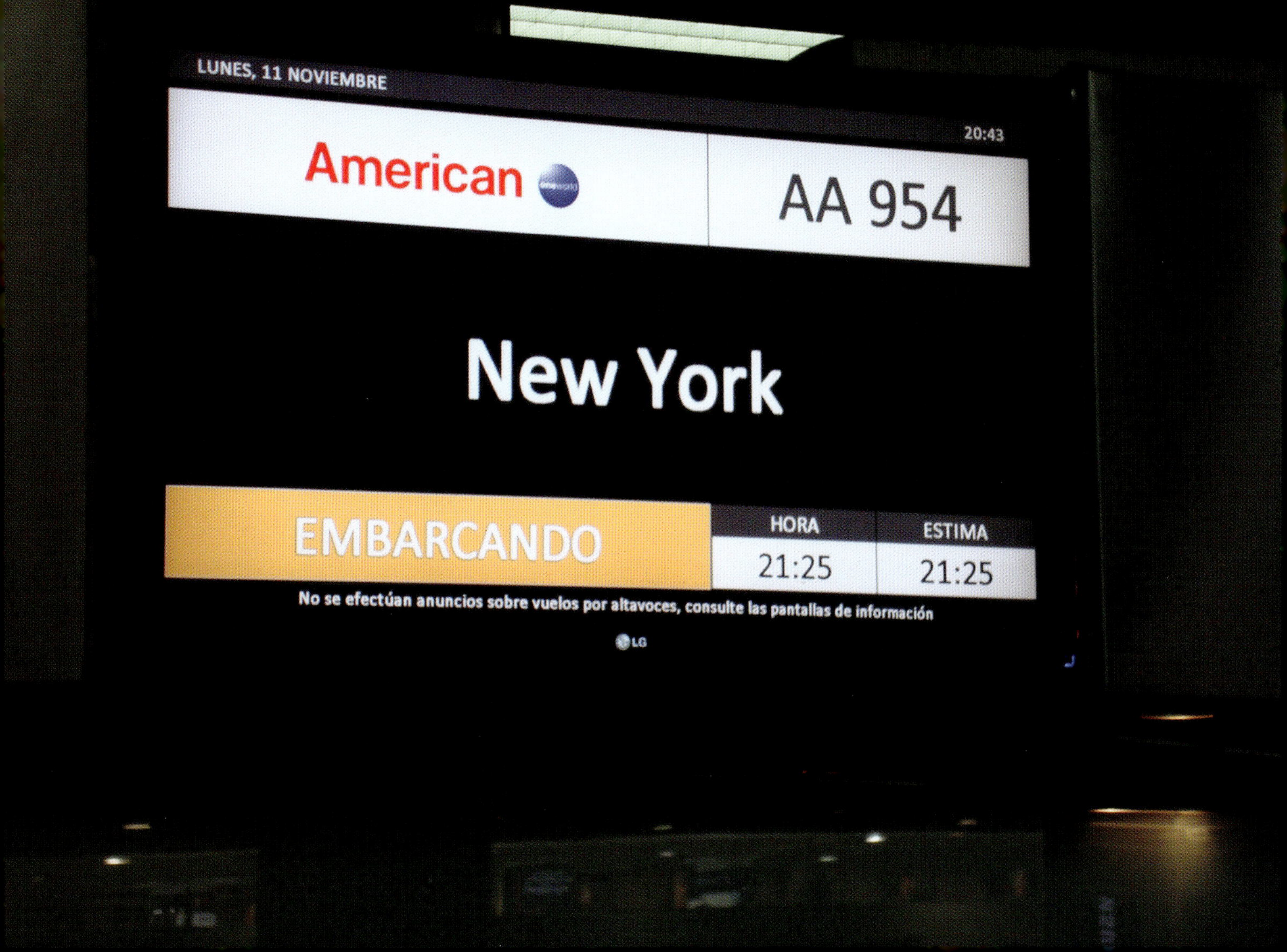
LUNES, 11 NOVIEMBRE
20:43
American
AA 954
New York
EMBARCANDO
HORA
21:25
ESTIMA
21:25
No se efectúan anuncios sobre vuelos por altavoces, consulte las pantallas de información
LG

[12] **JFK TAG** STEVE MALPASS

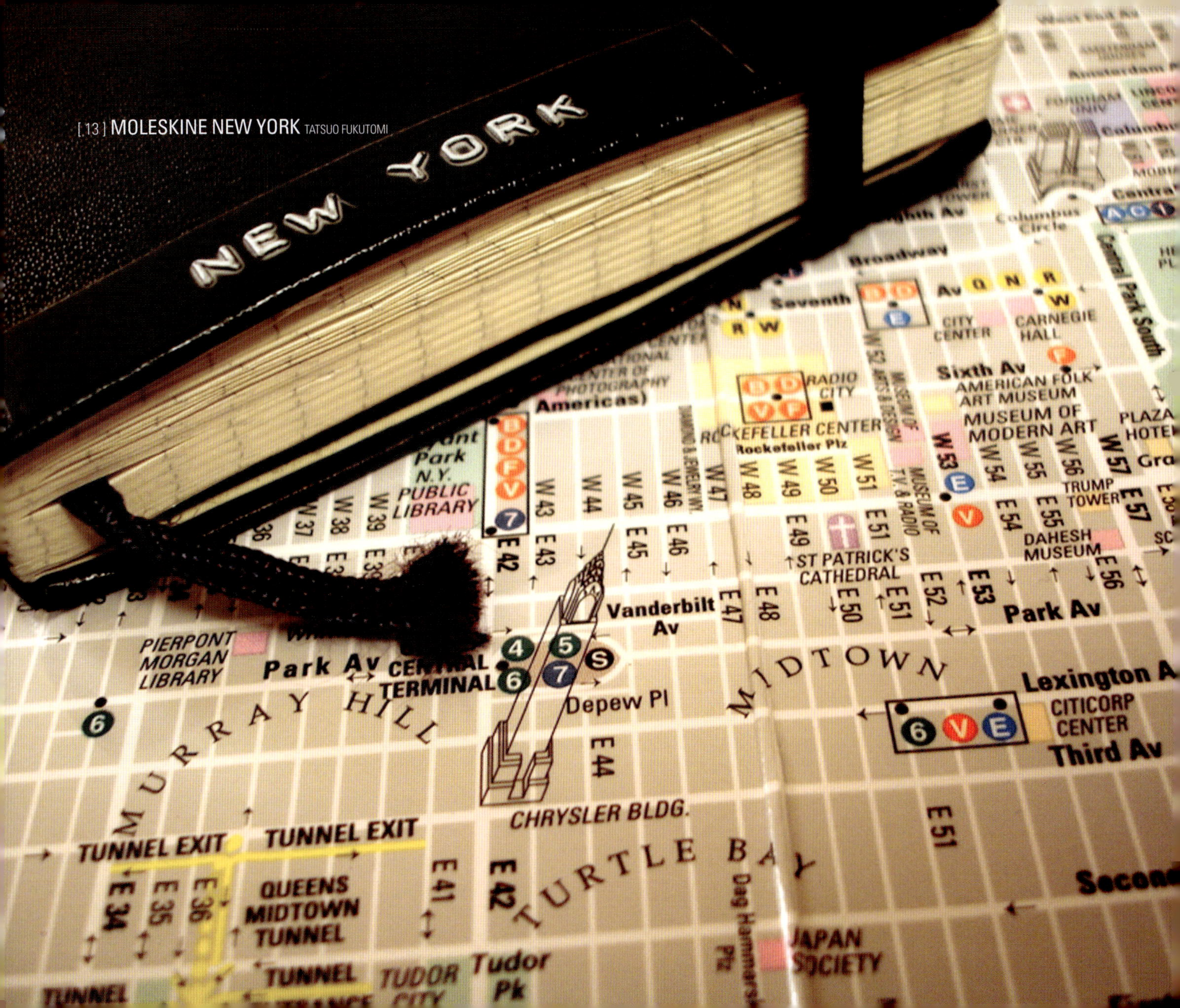

[13] MOLESKINE NEW YORK TATSUO FUKUTOMI

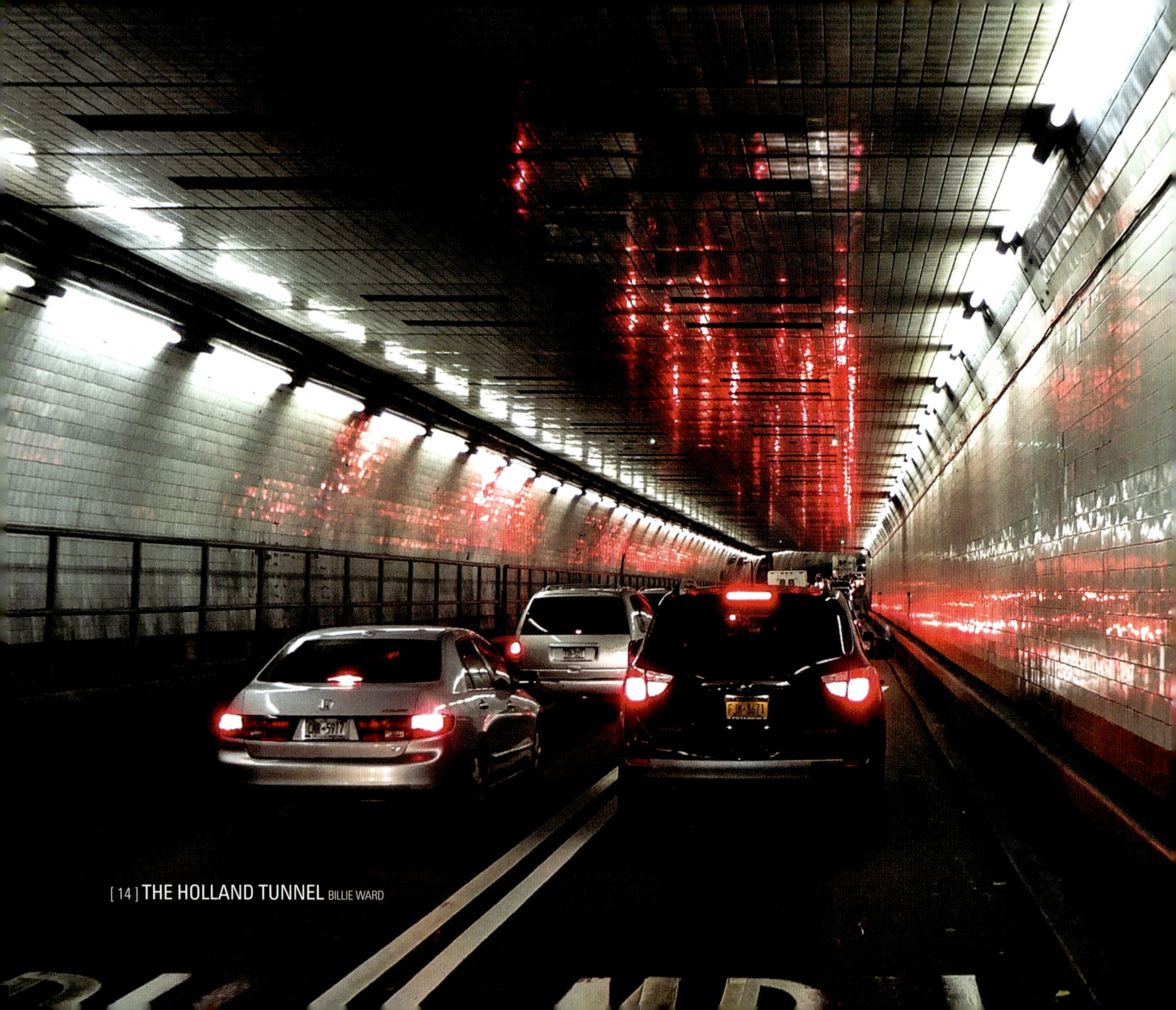

[14] THE HOLLAND TUNNEL BILLIE WARD

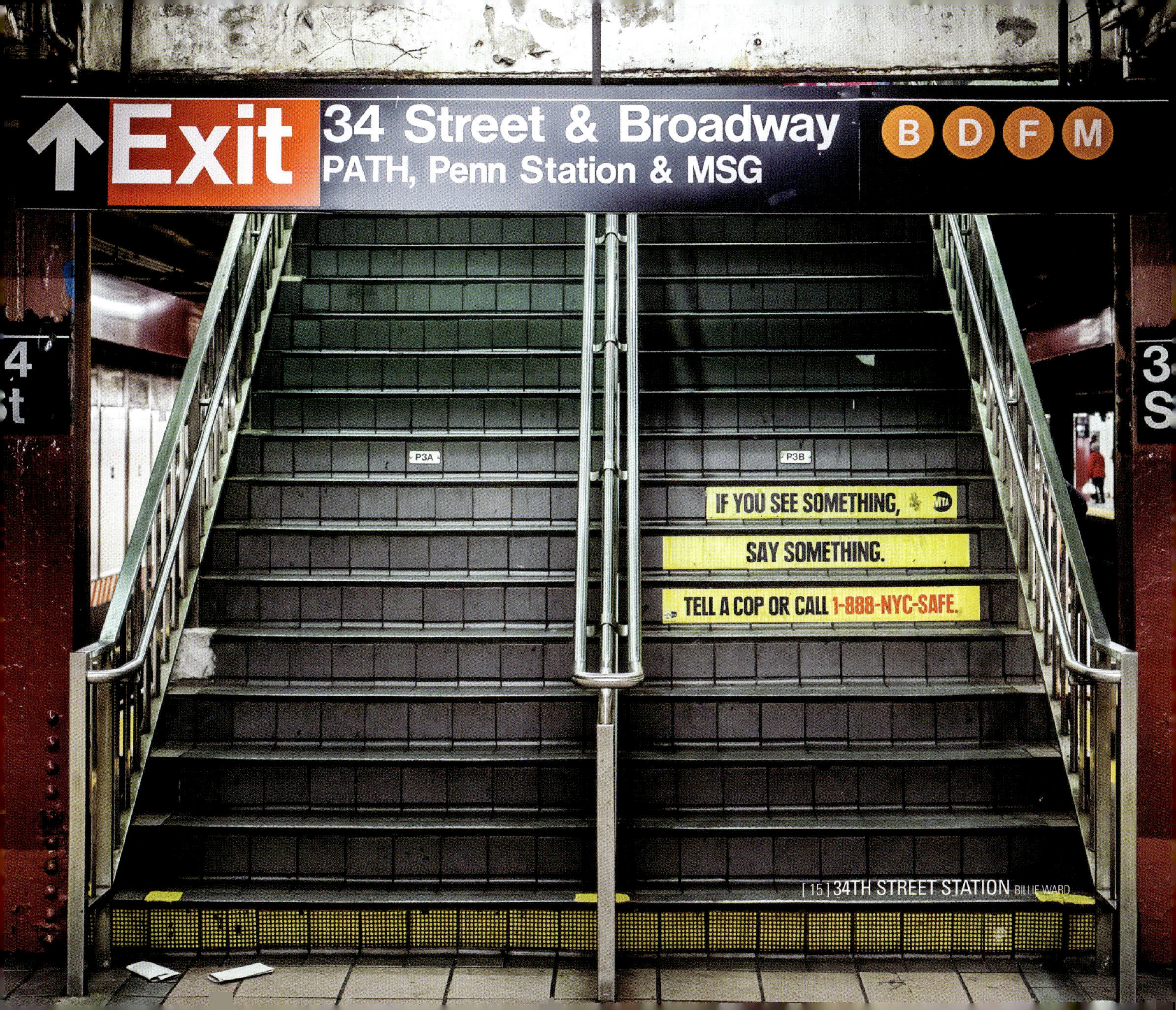

[15] 34TH STREET STATION BILLIE WARD

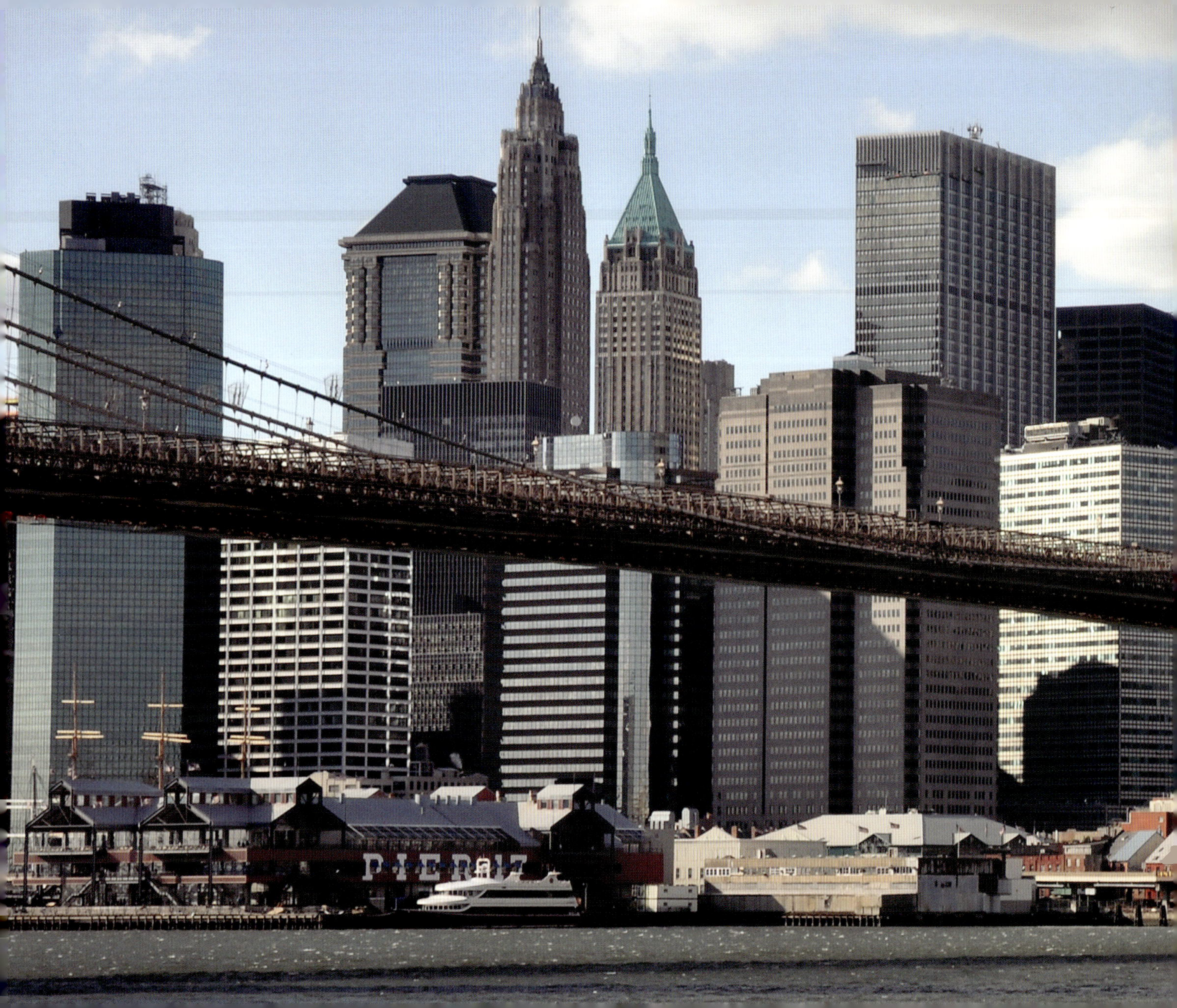
PIER 17

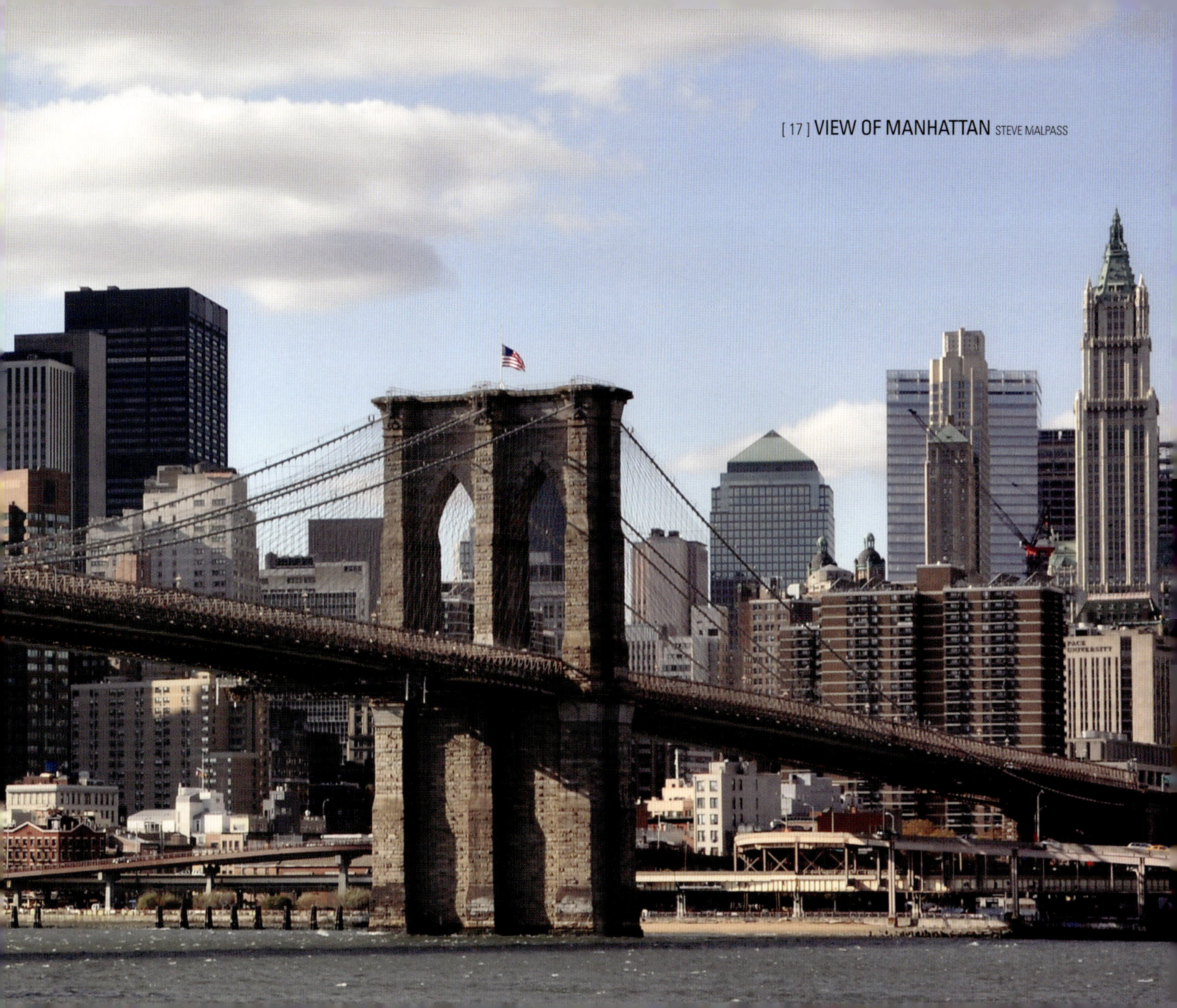

[17] VIEW OF MANHATTAN STEVE MALPASS

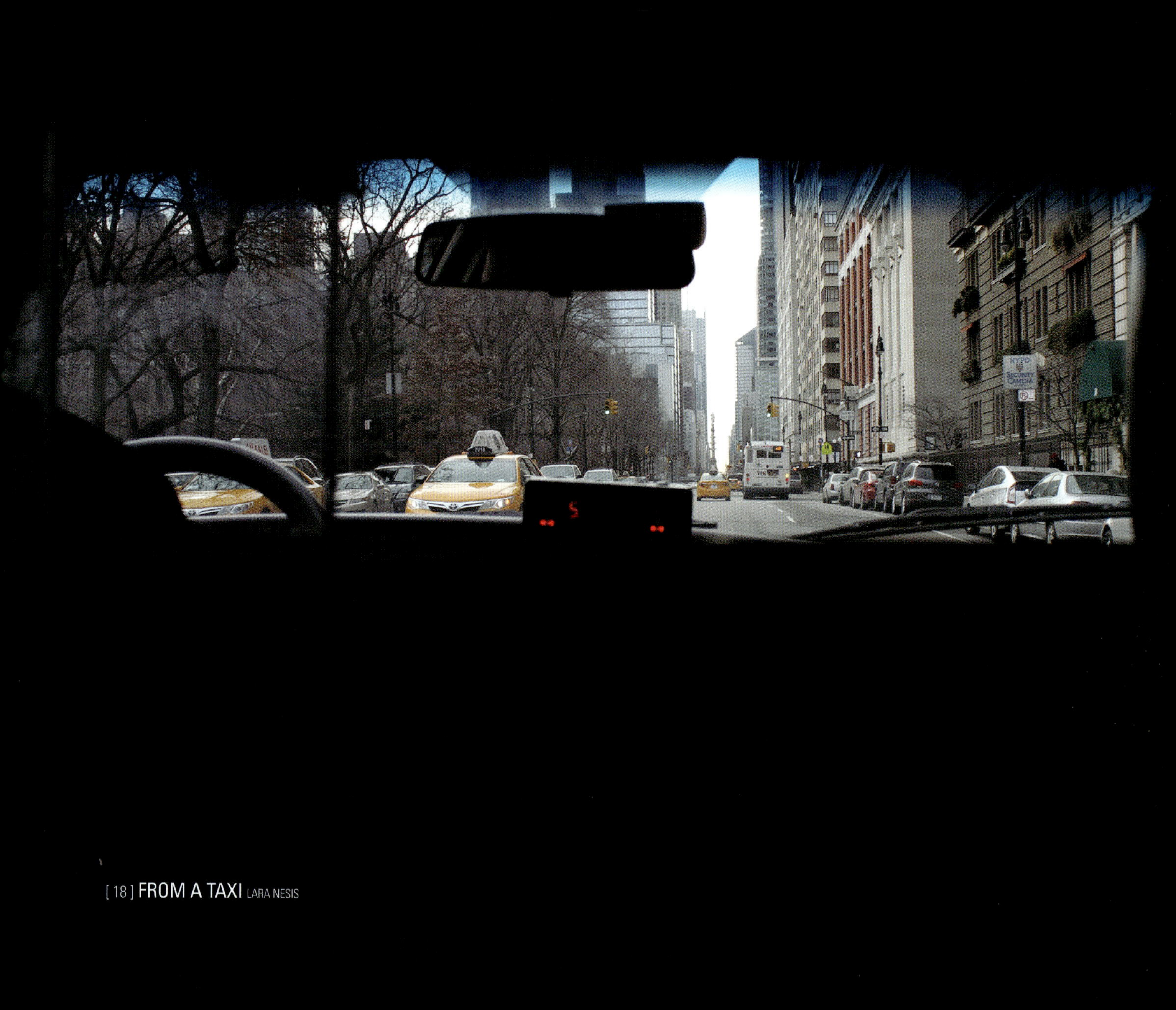

[18] FROM A TAXI LARA NESIS

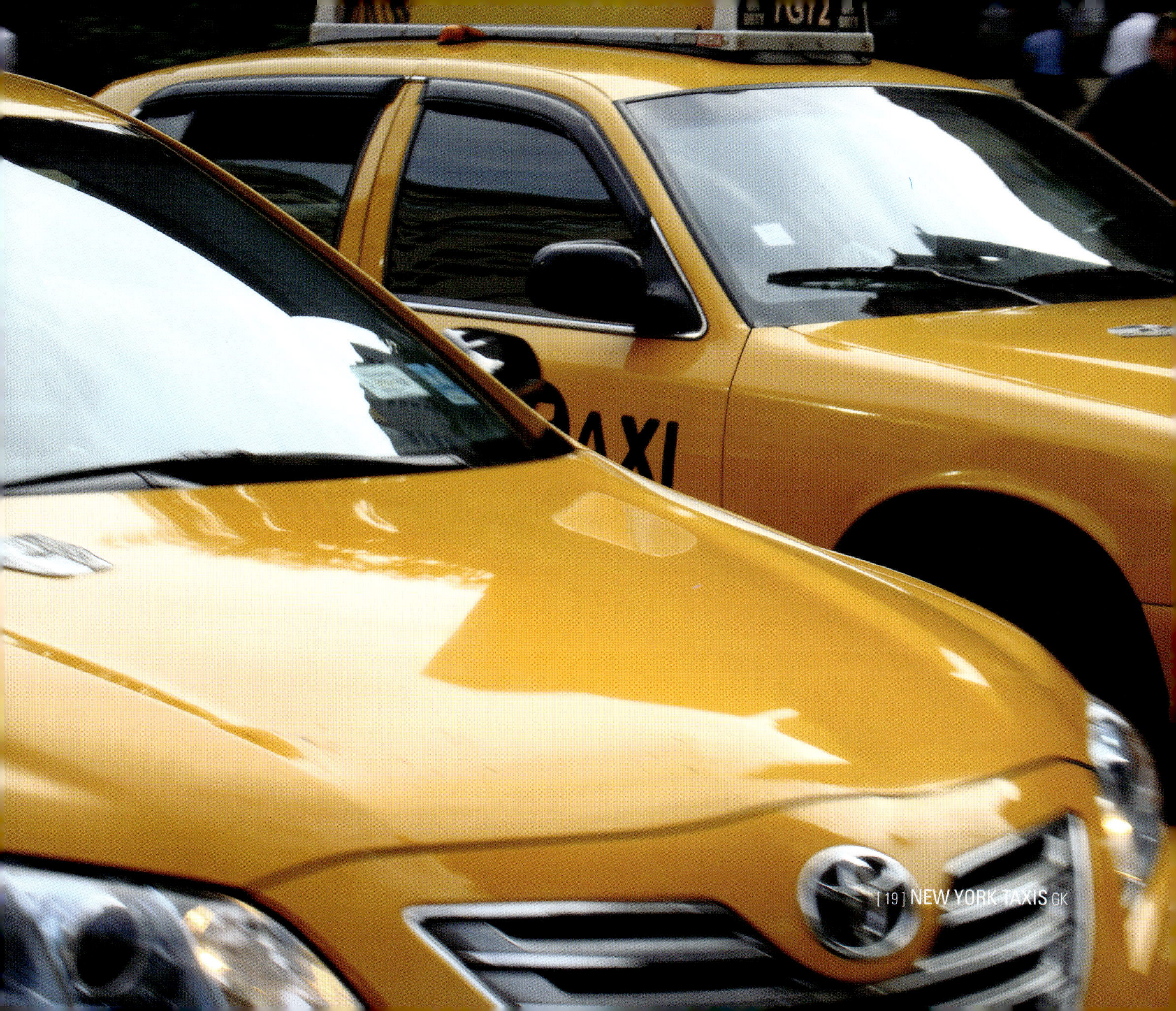

[19] NEW YORK TAXIS GK

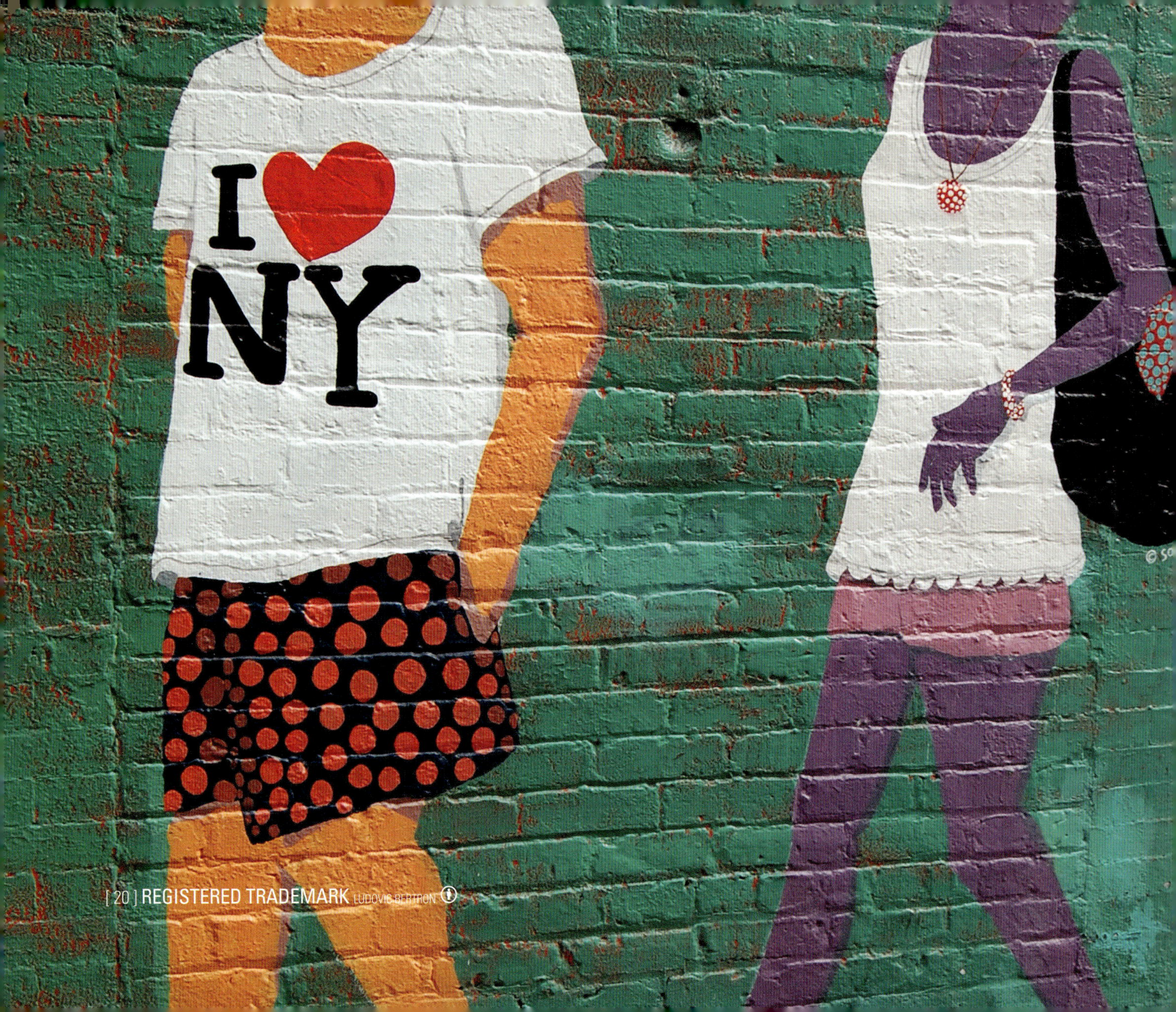

[20] REGISTERED TRADEMARK LUDOVIC BERTRON

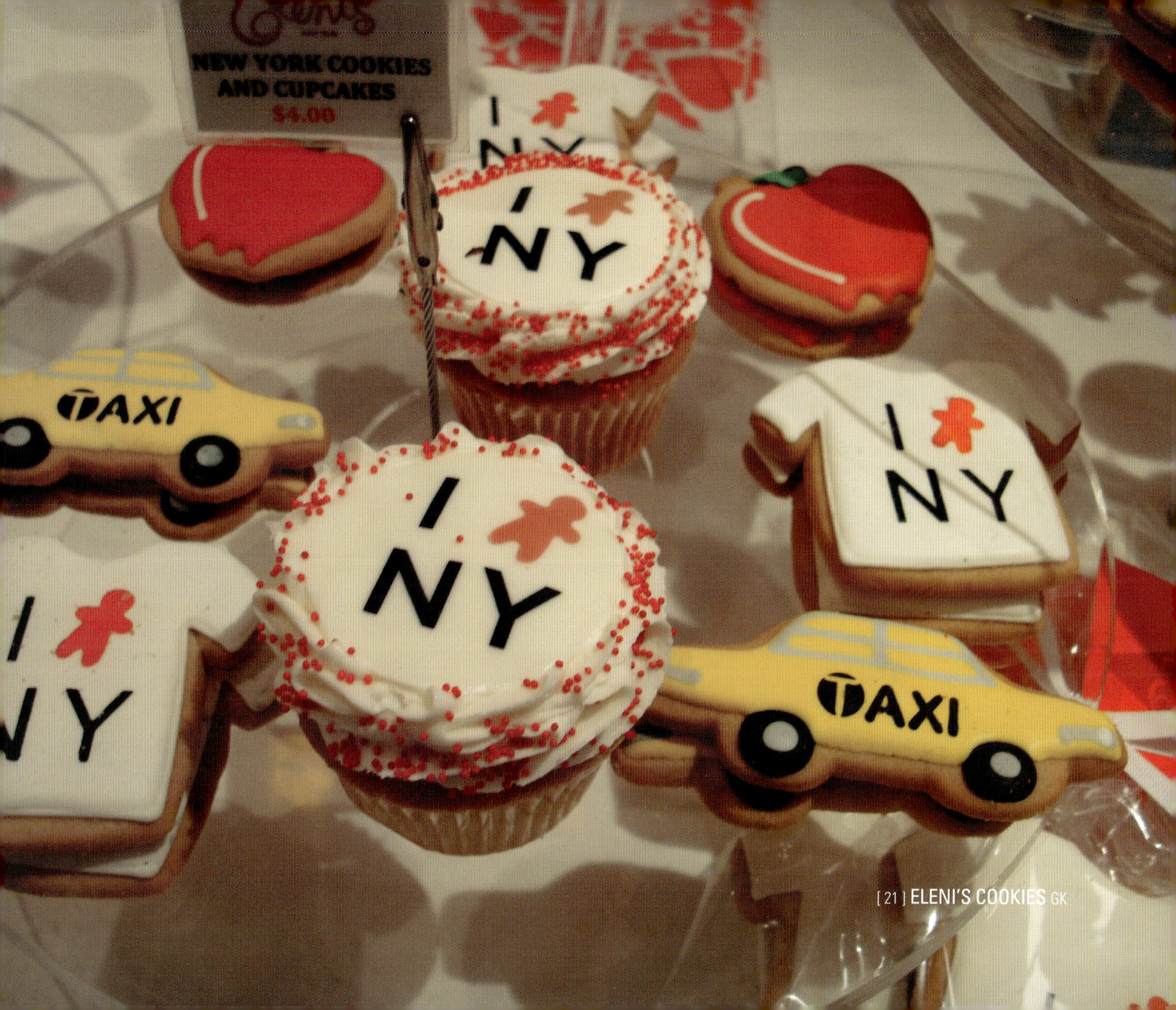

[21] ELENI'S COOKIES GK

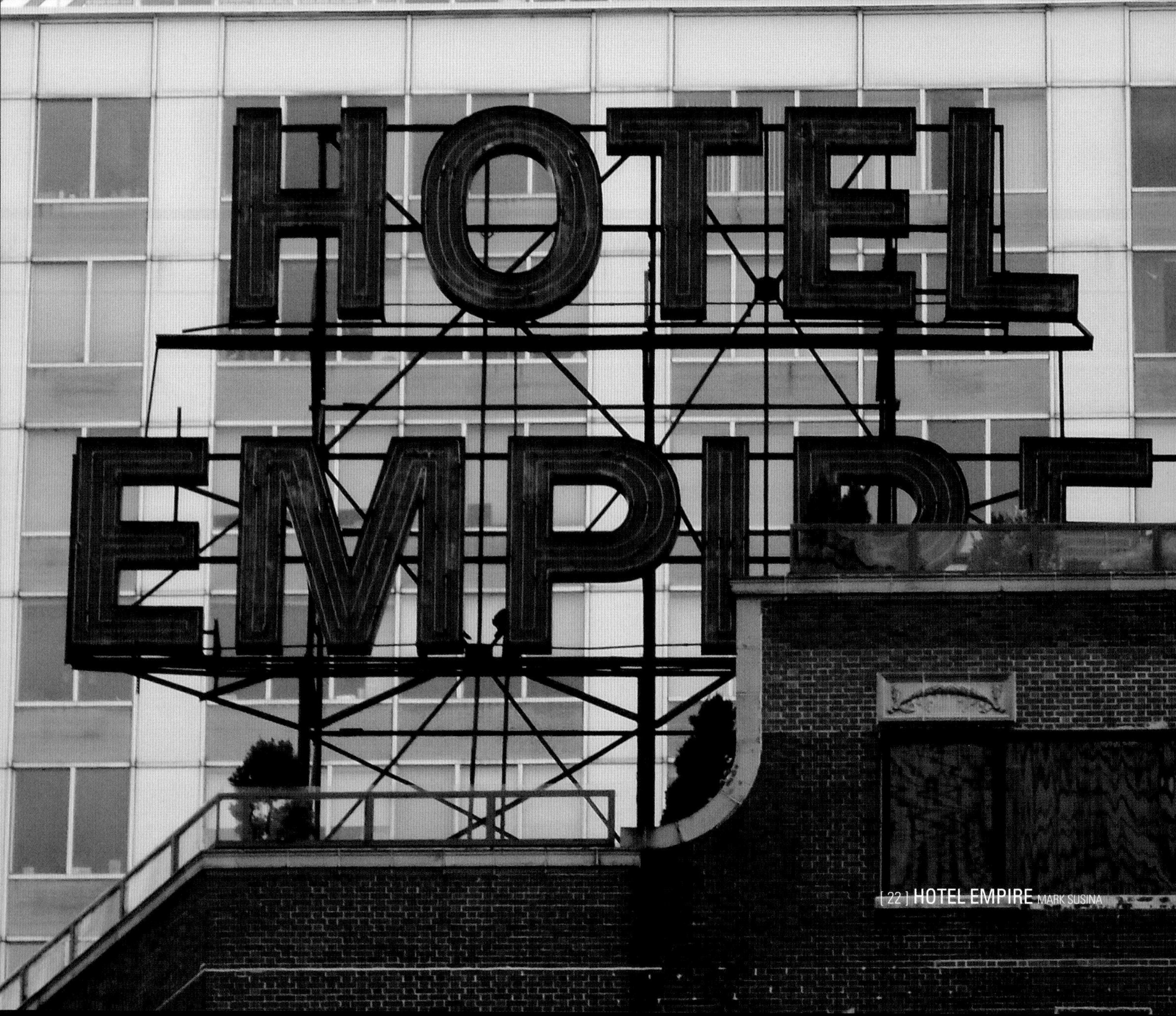

[22] HOTEL EMPIRE MARK SUSINA

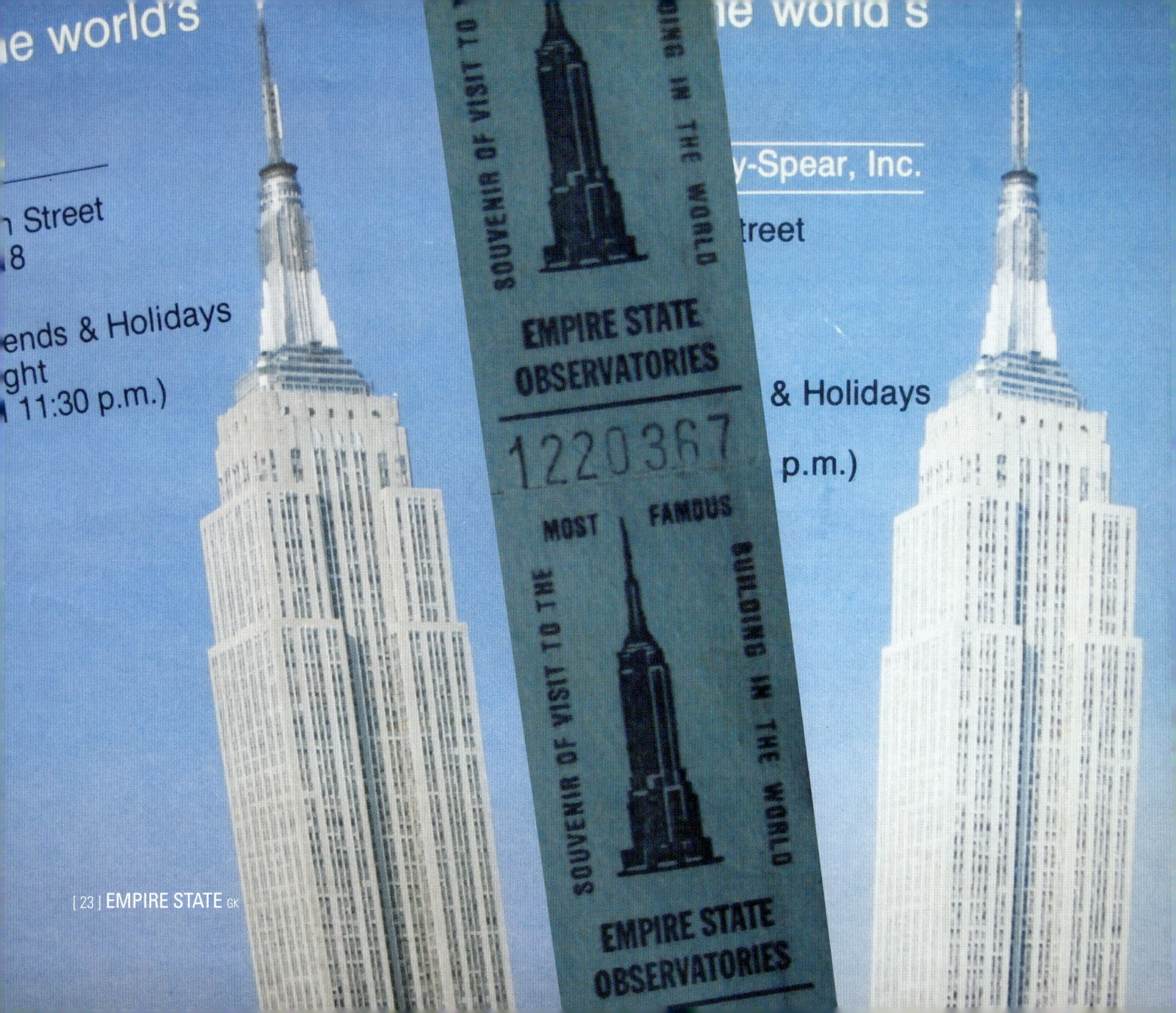
e world's
n Street
ends & Holidays
ght
11:30 p.m.)
SOUVENIR OF VISIT TO THE MOST FAMOUS BUILDING IN THE WORLD
EMPIRE STATE OBSERVATORIES
1220367
SOUVENIR OF VISIT TO THE MOST FAMOUS BUILDING IN THE WORLD
EMPIRE STATE OBSERVATORIES
y-Spear, Inc.
treet
& Holidays
p.m.)

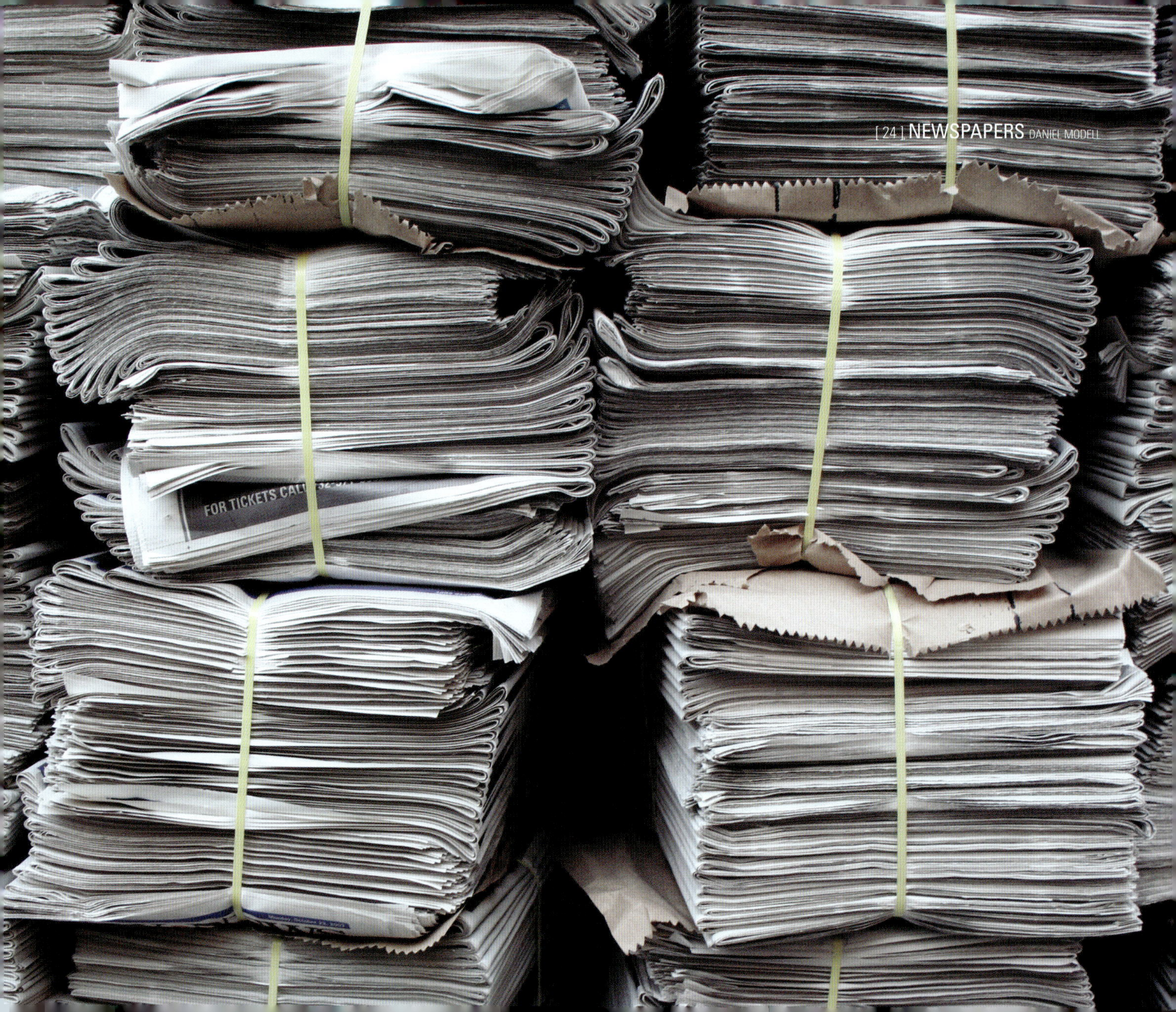

[24] NEWSPAPERS DANIEL MODELL

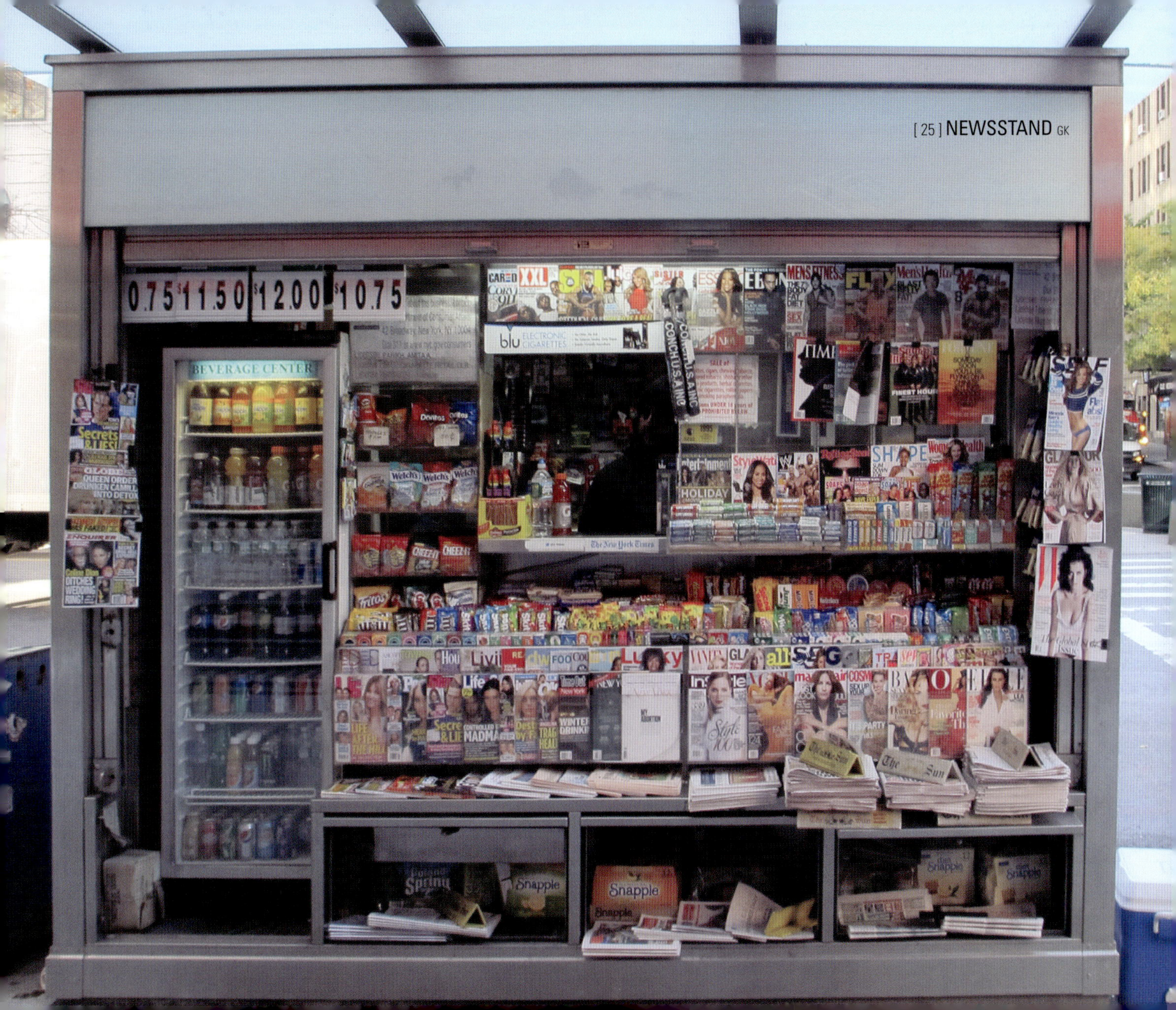

[25] NEWSSTAND GK

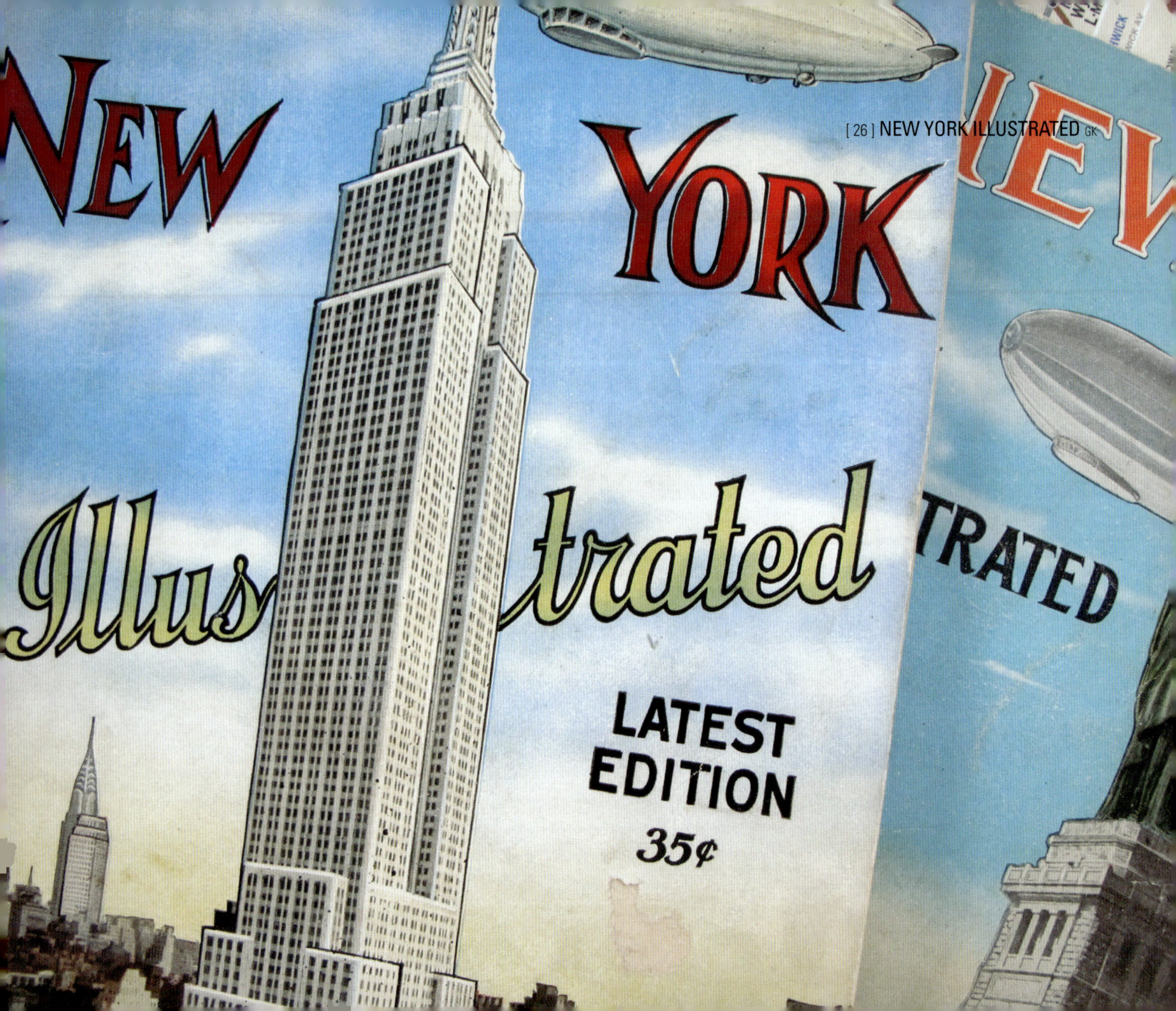
New York Illustrated
LATEST EDITION
35¢
TRATED

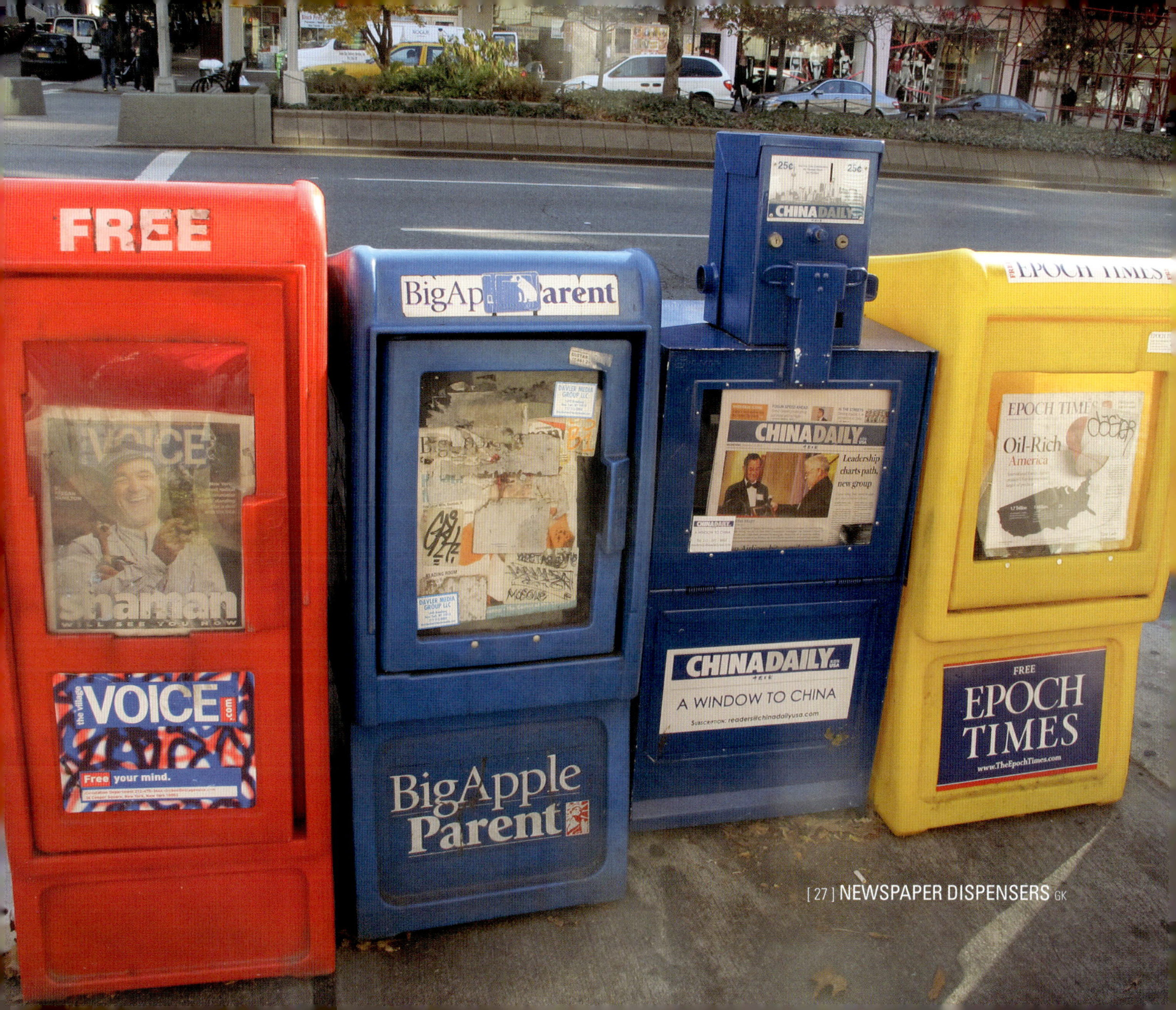

[27] NEWSPAPER DISPENSERS GK

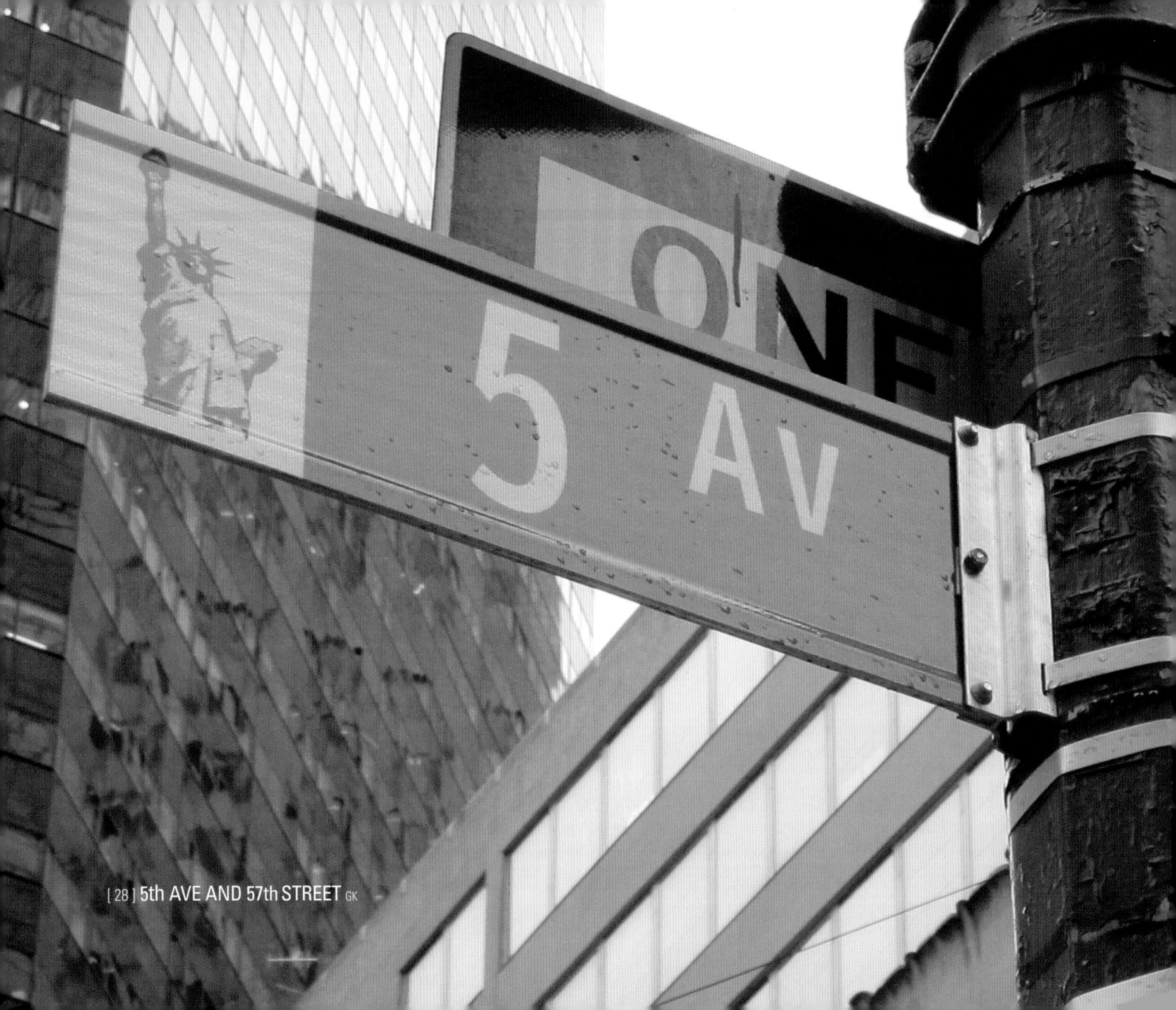

[28] 5th AVE AND 57th STREET GK

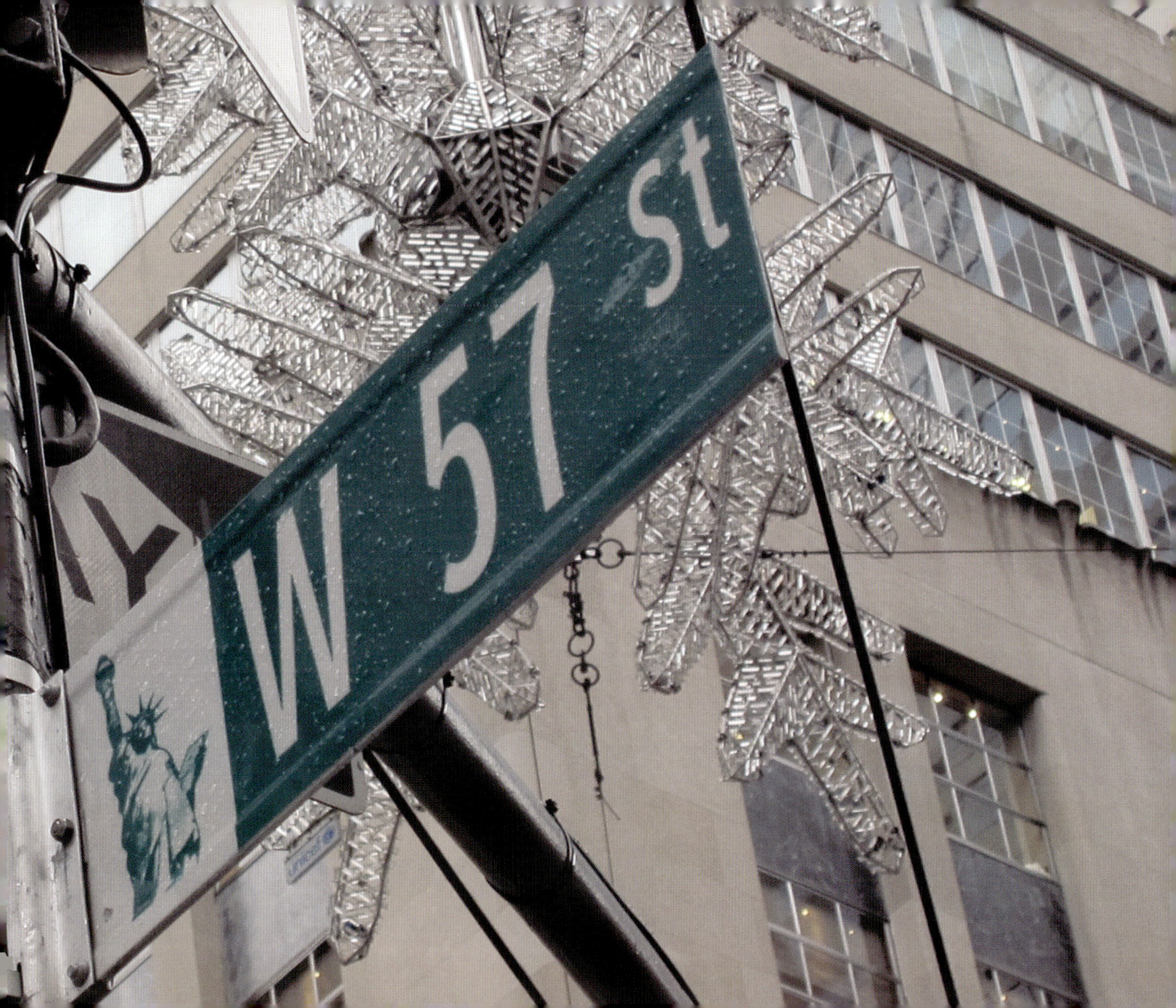
W 57 St

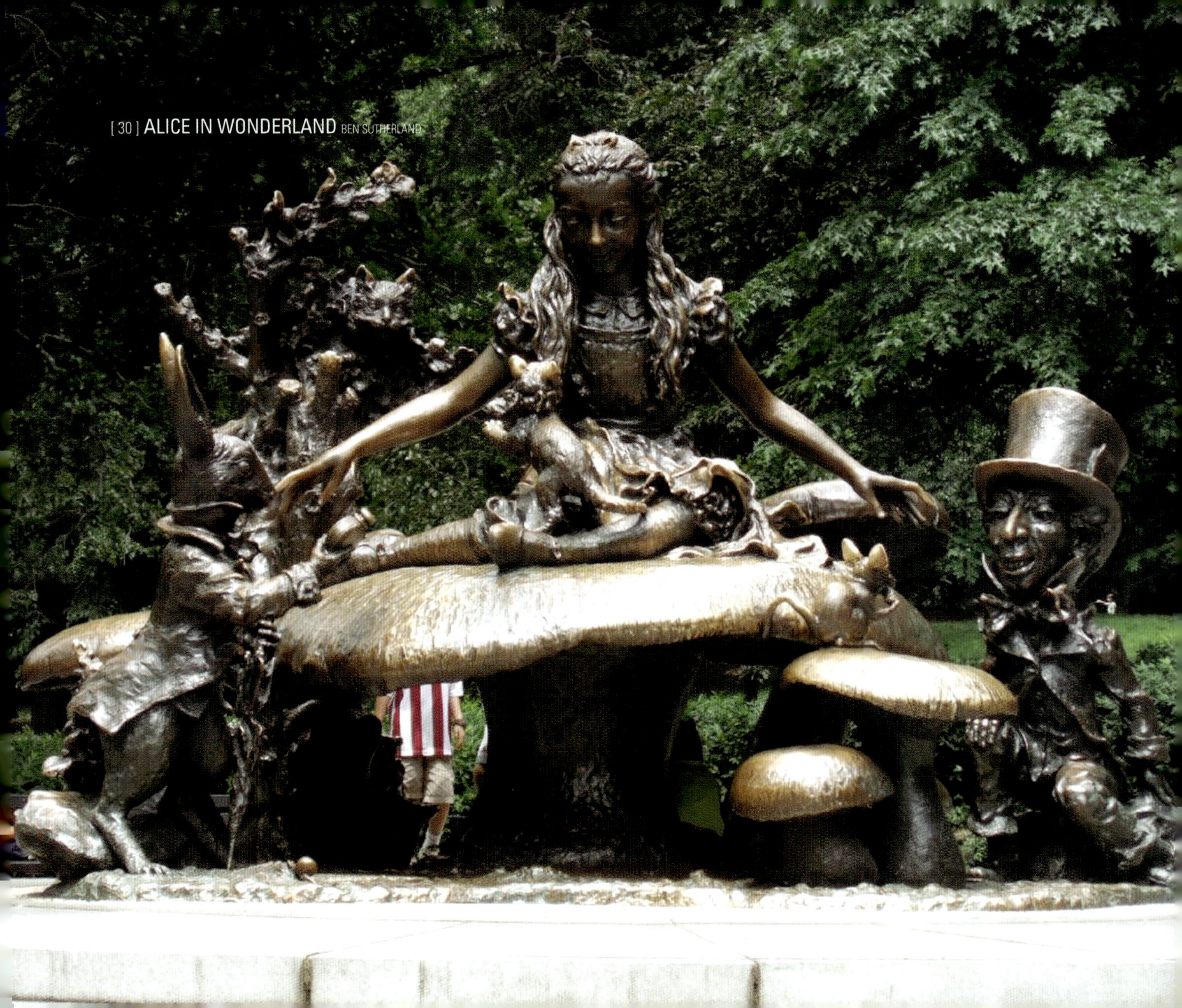
[30] ALICE IN WONDERLAND BEN SUTHERLAND

[31] THE PLAZA HOTEL / APPLE STORE ROB BOUDON

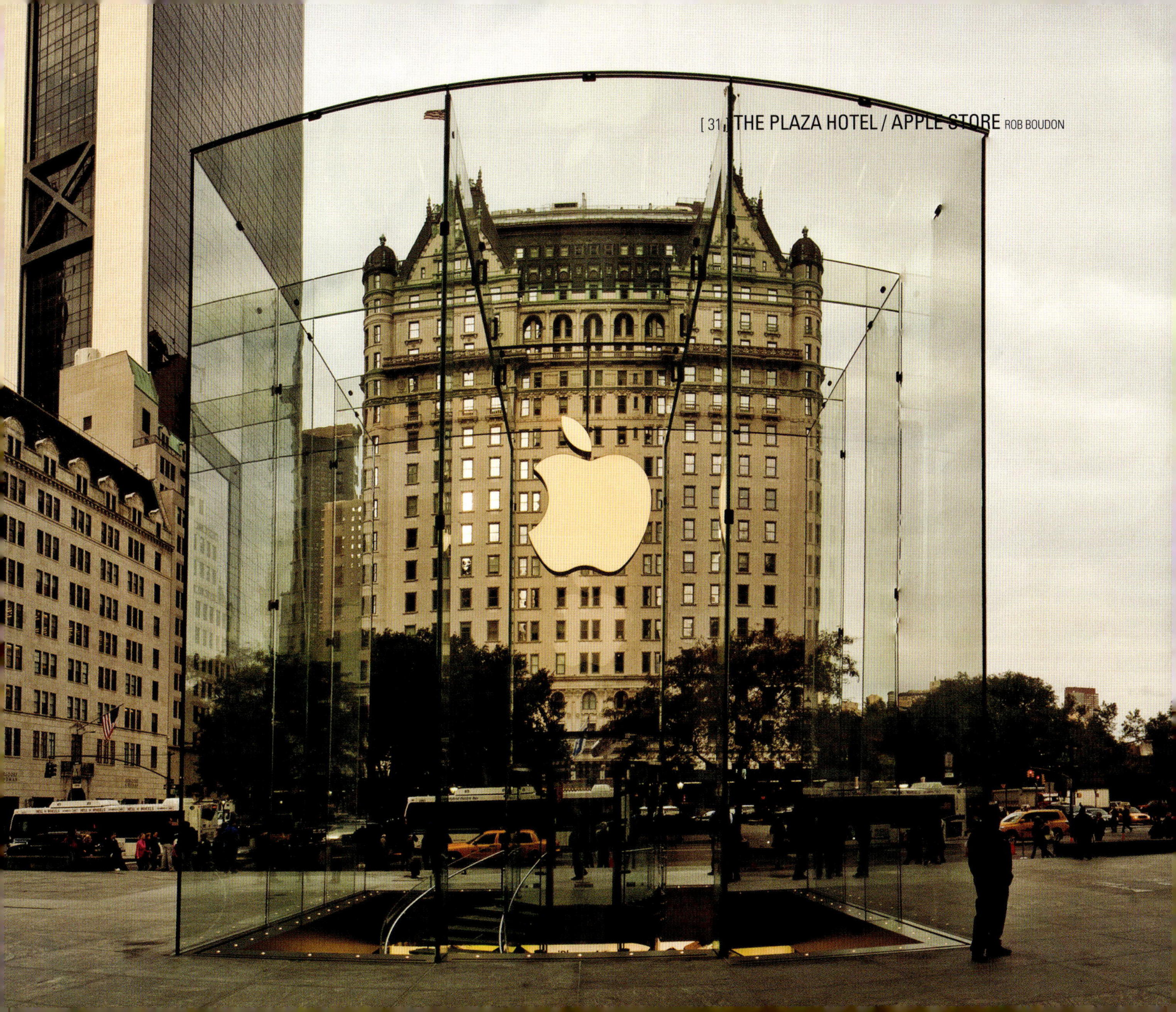

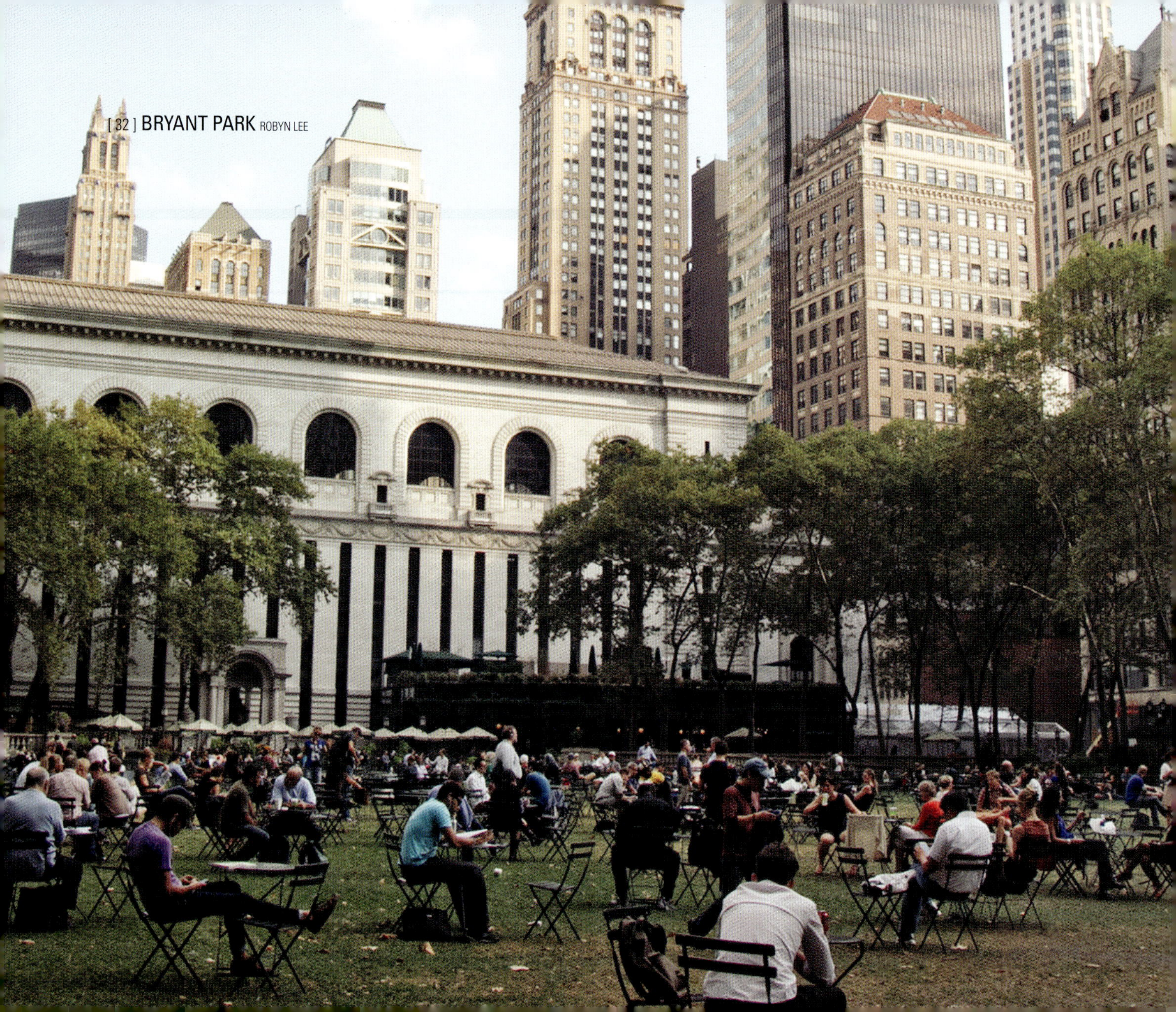

[32] BRYANT PARK ROBYN LEE

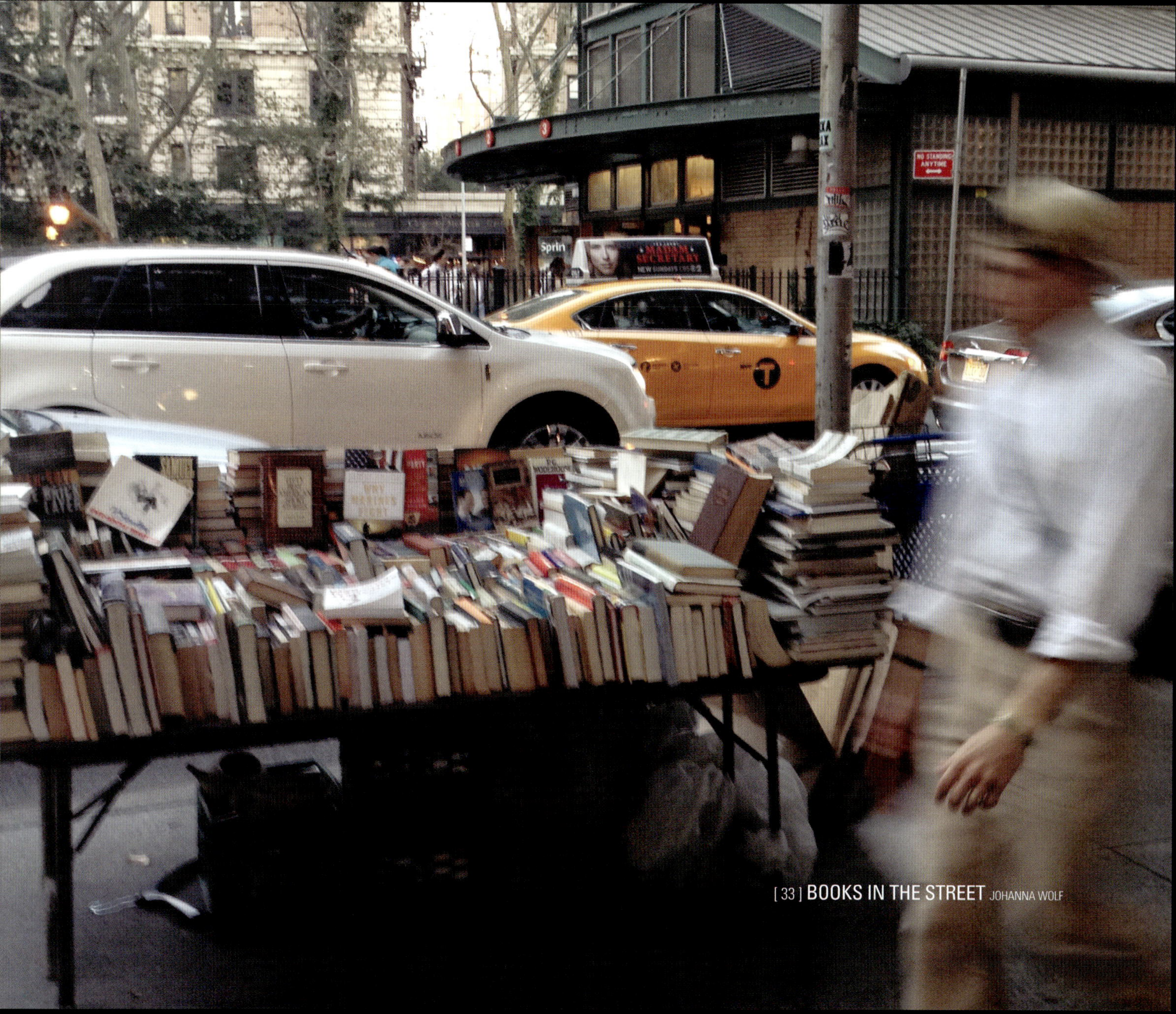

[33] **BOOKS IN THE STREET** JOHANNA WOLF

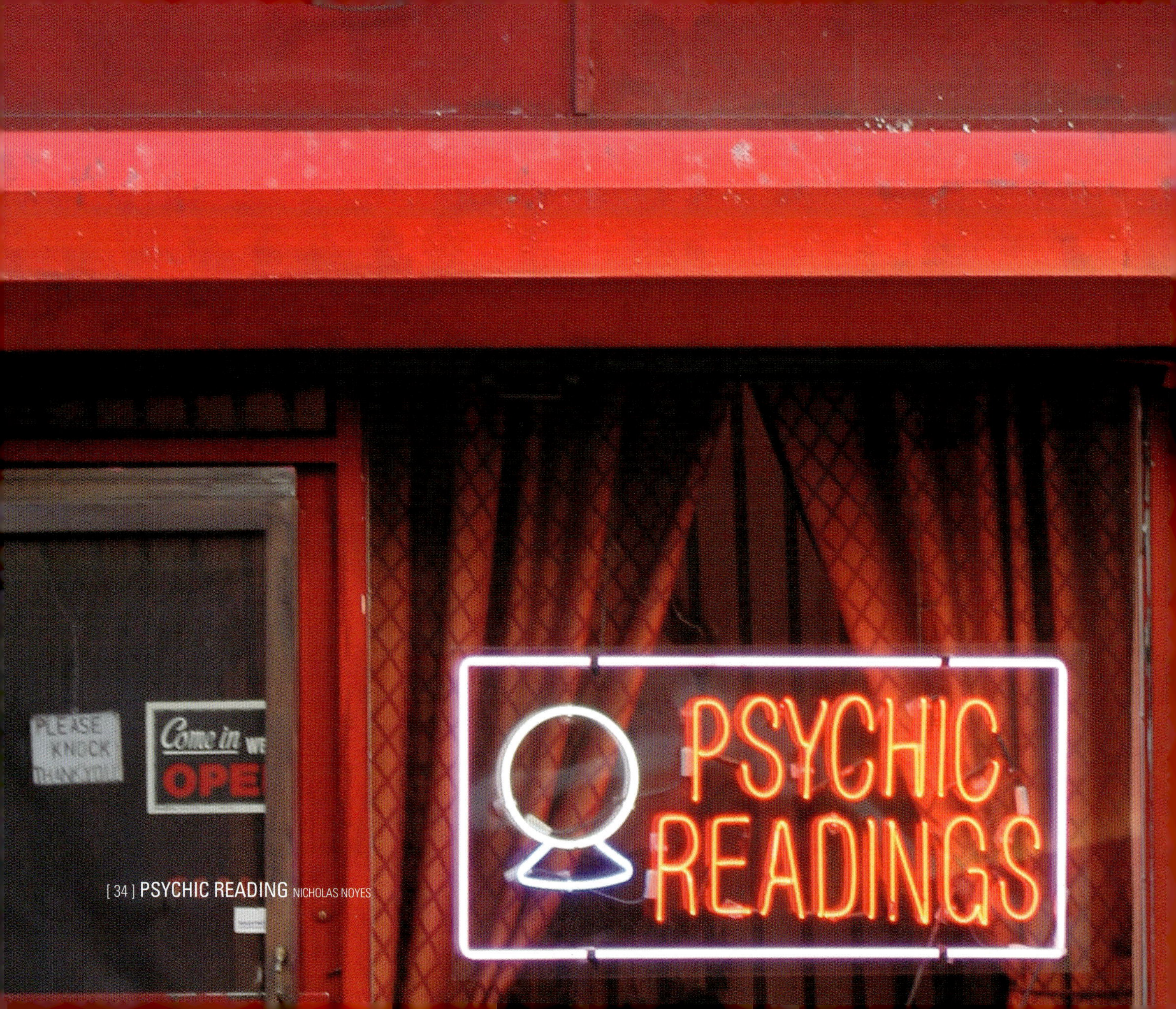

[34] PSYCHIC READING NICHOLAS NOYES

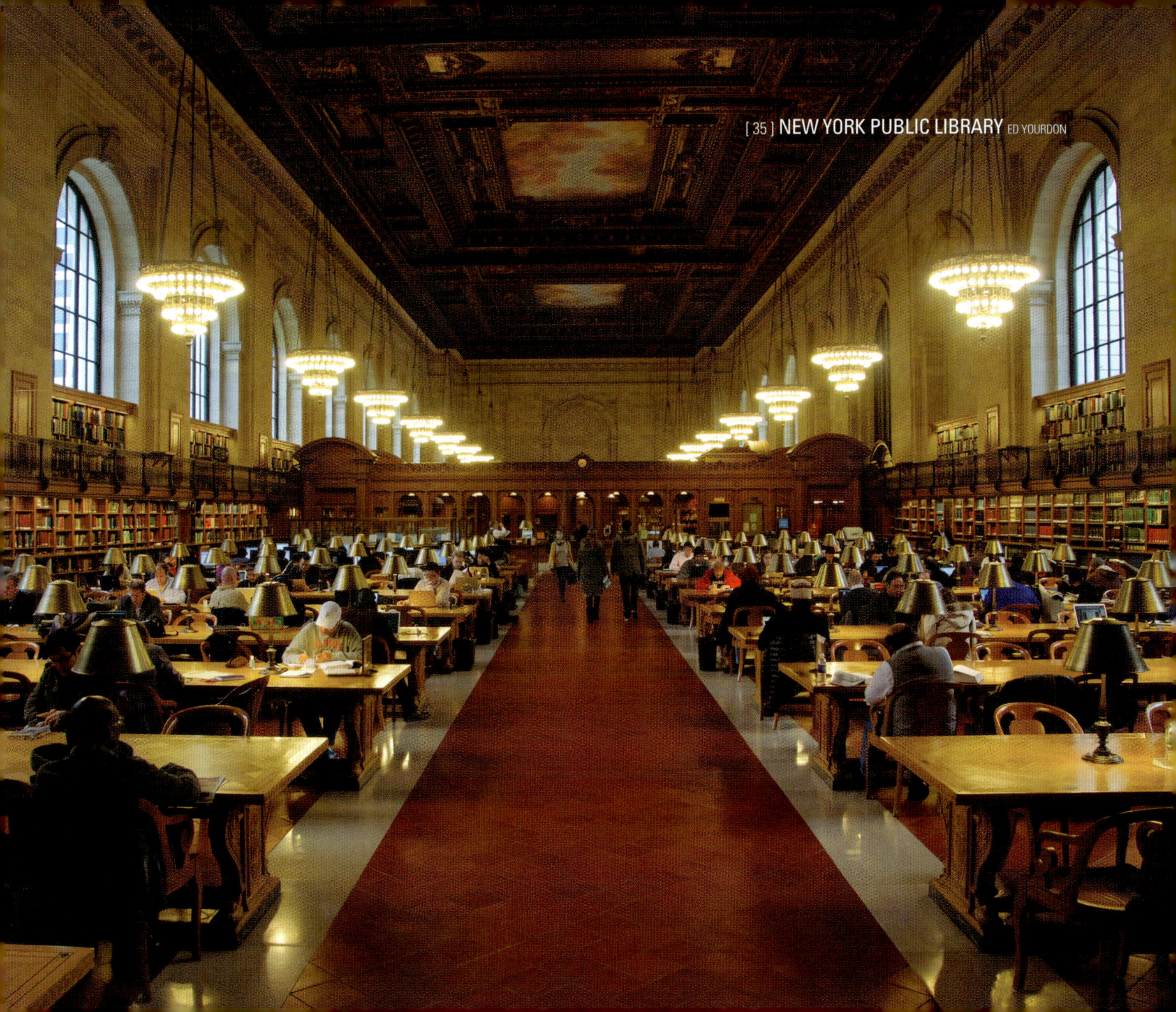

[35] NEW YORK PUBLIC LIBRARY ED YOURDON

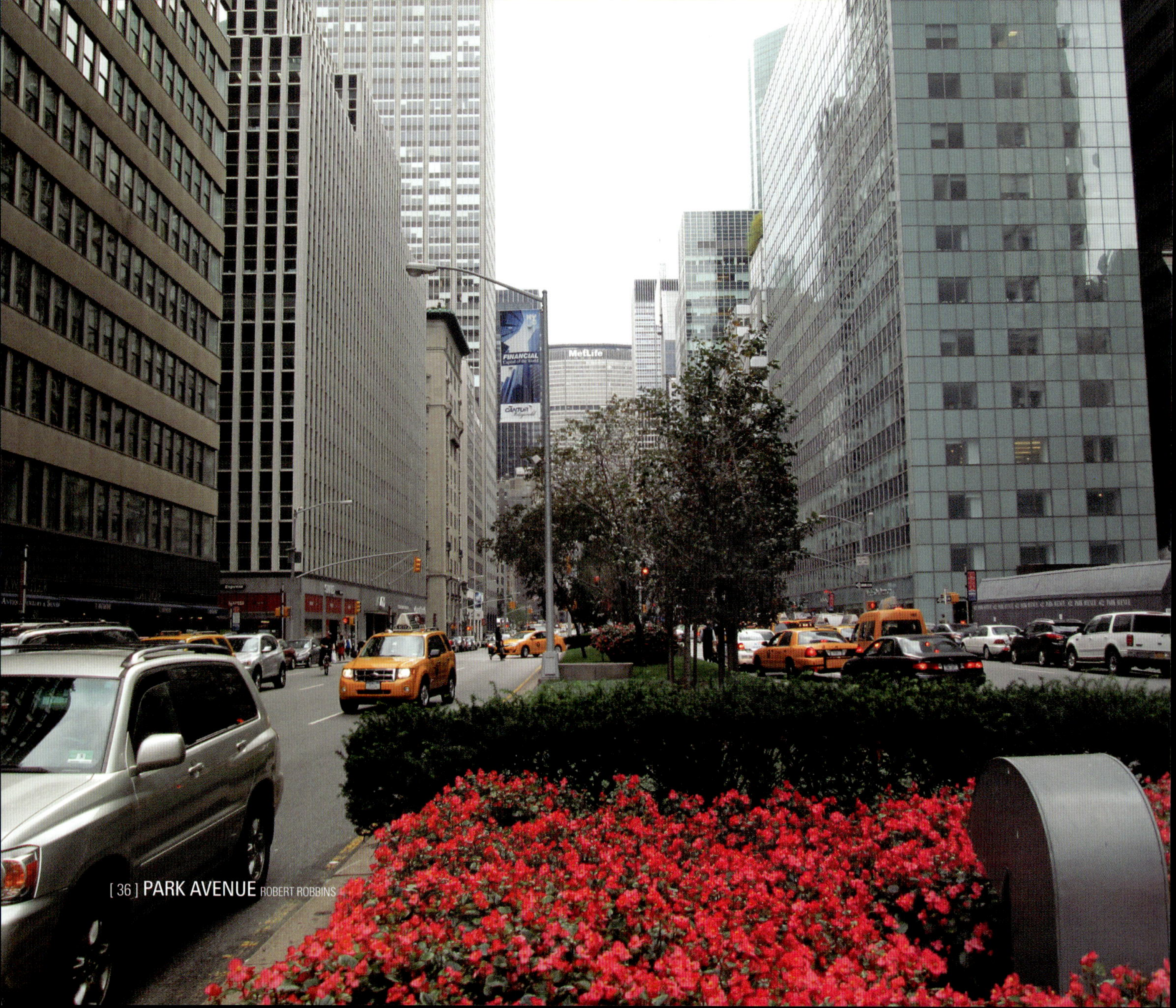

[36] PARK AVENUE ROBERT ROBBINS

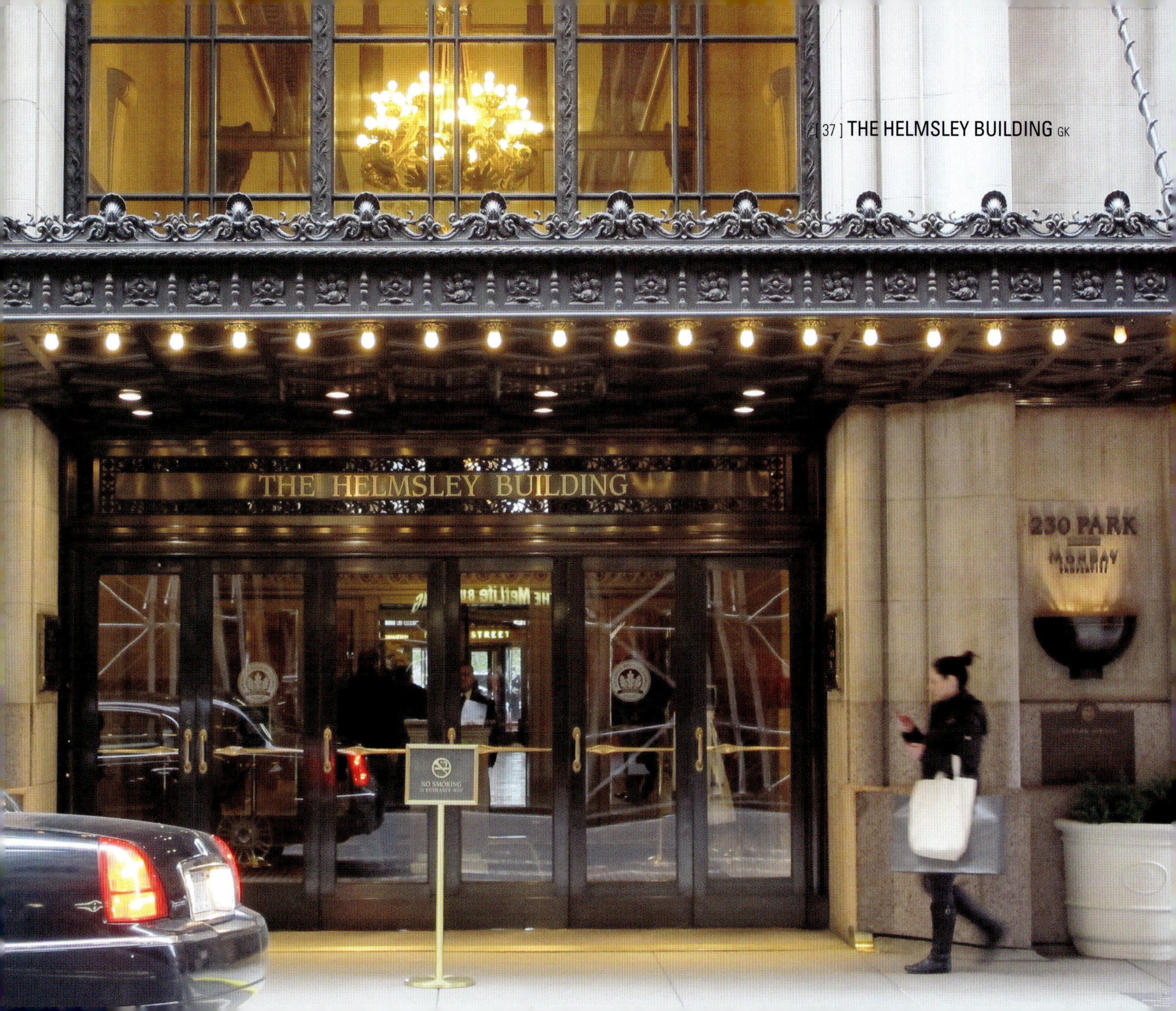

[37] THE HELMSLEY BUILDING GK

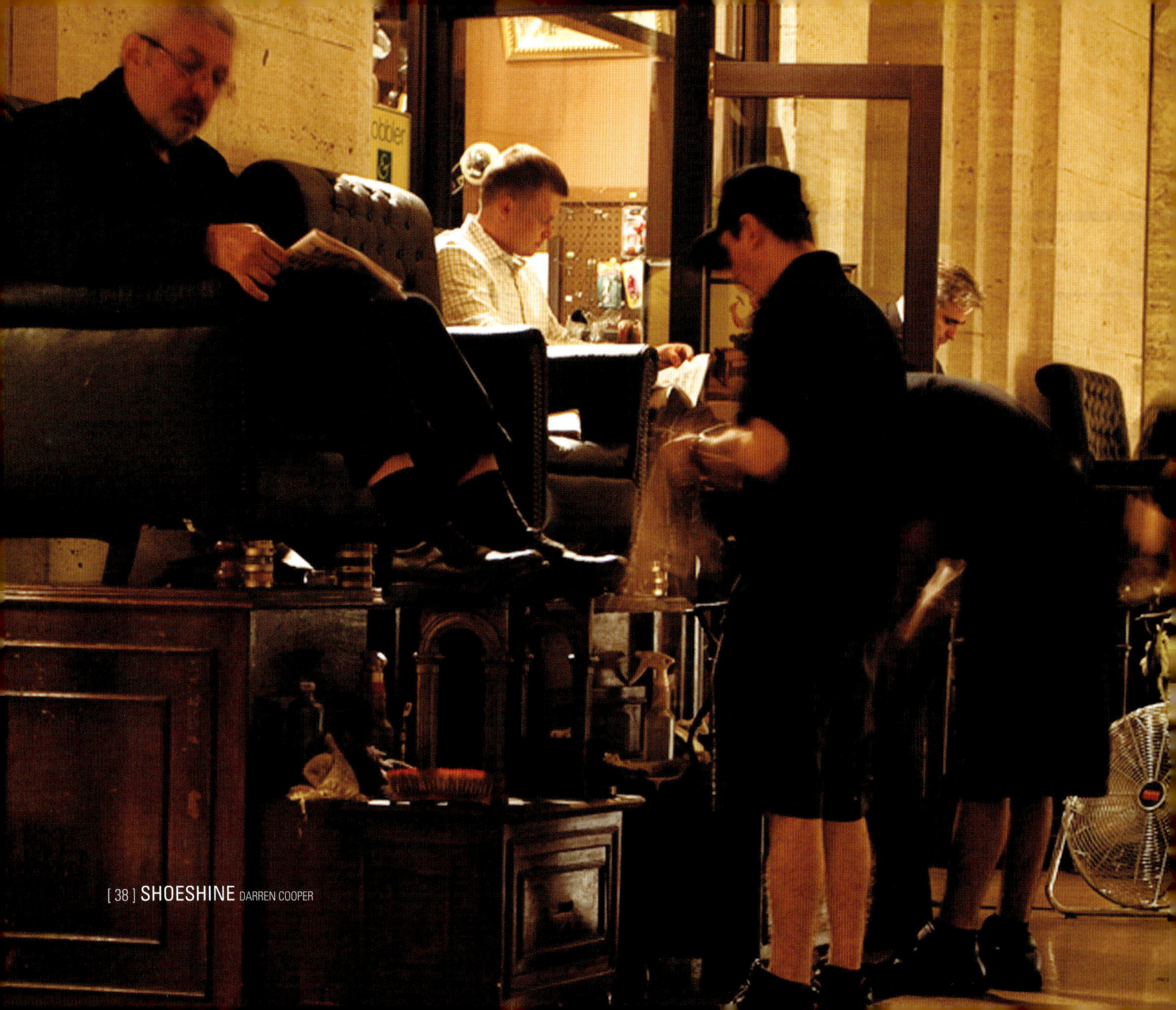

[38] SHOESHINE DARREN COOPER

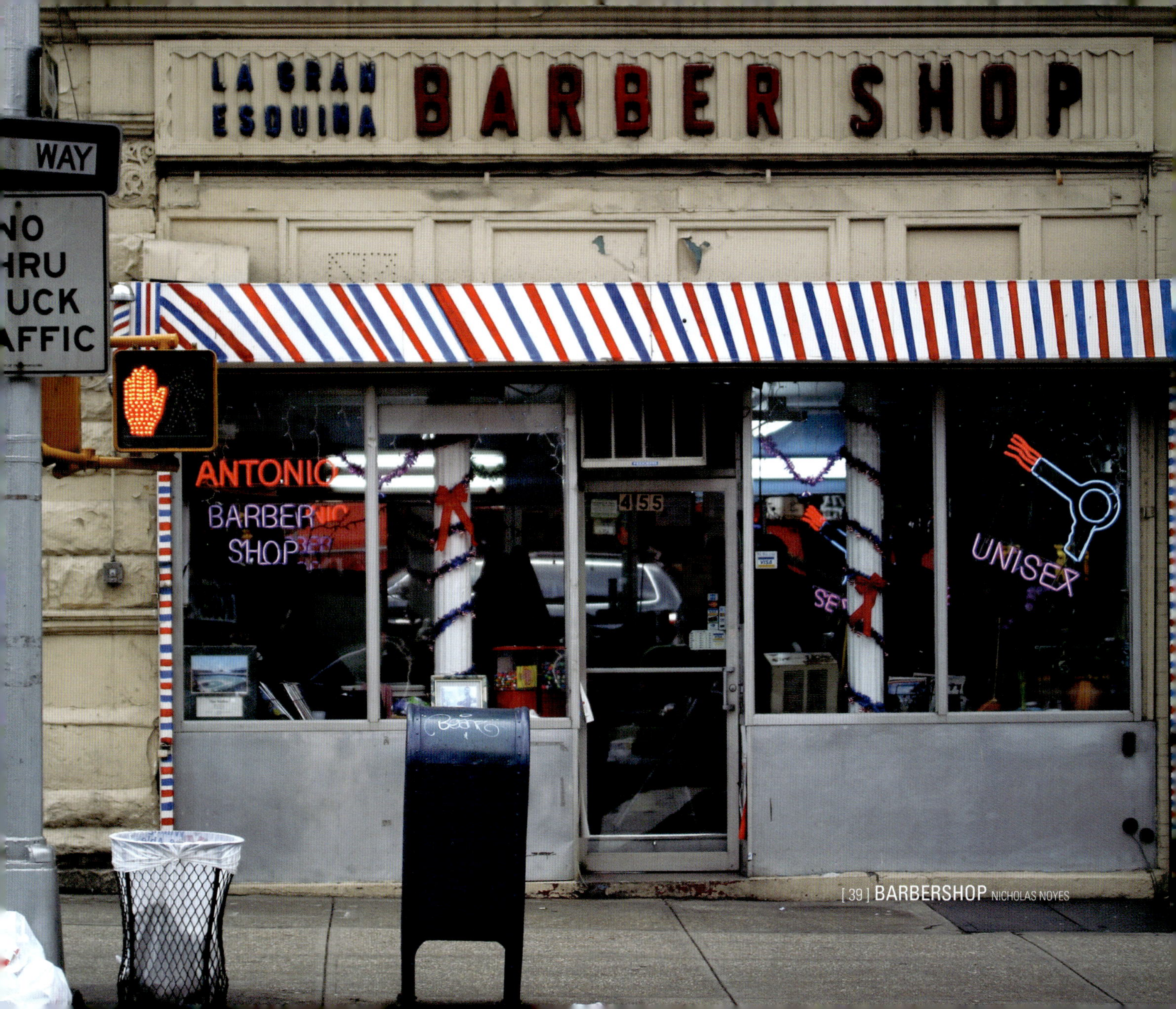

[39] **BARBERSHOP** NICHOLAS NOYES

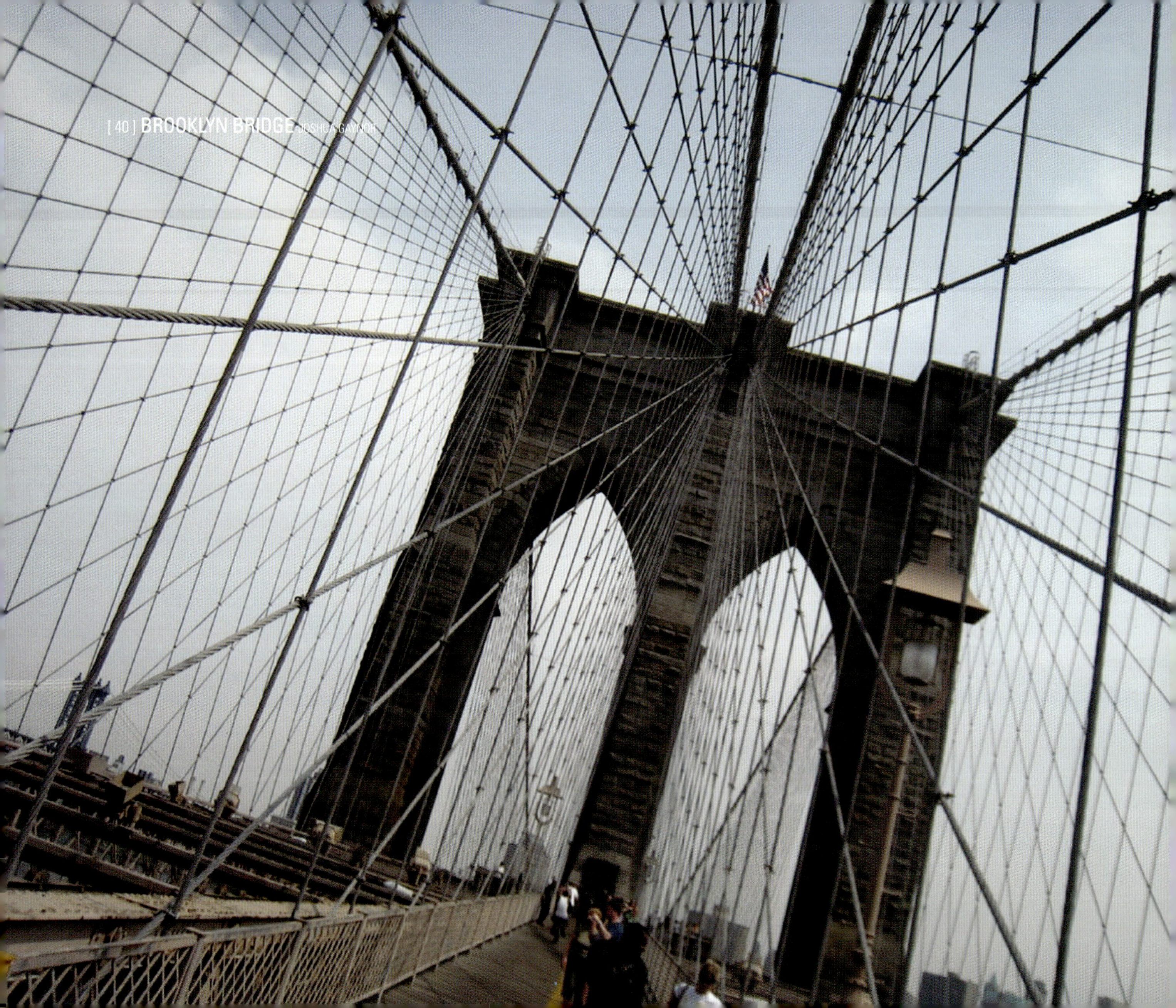

[40] BROOKLYN BRIDGE JOSHUA GAYNOR

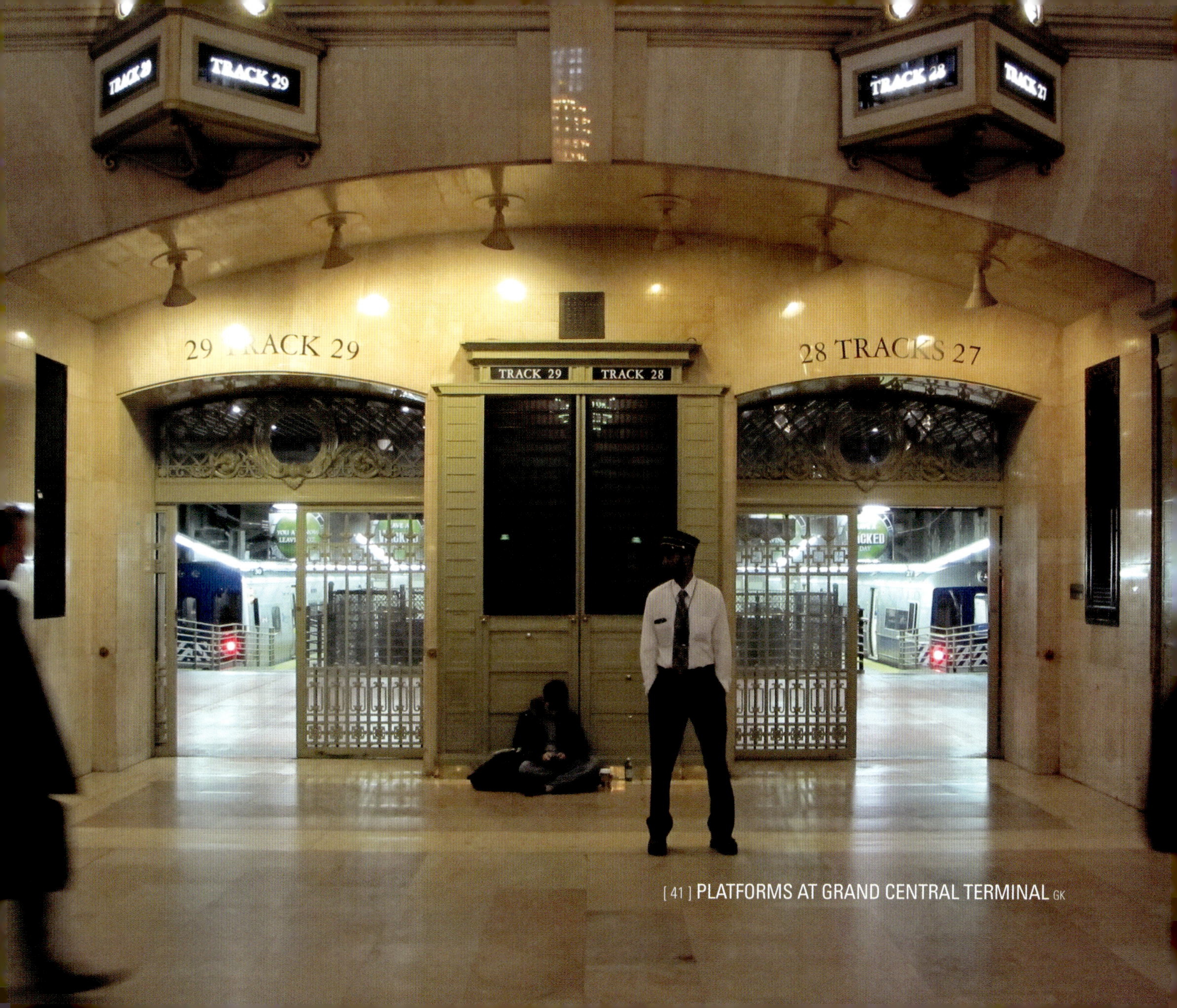

[41] PLATFORMS AT GRAND CENTRAL TERMINAL GK

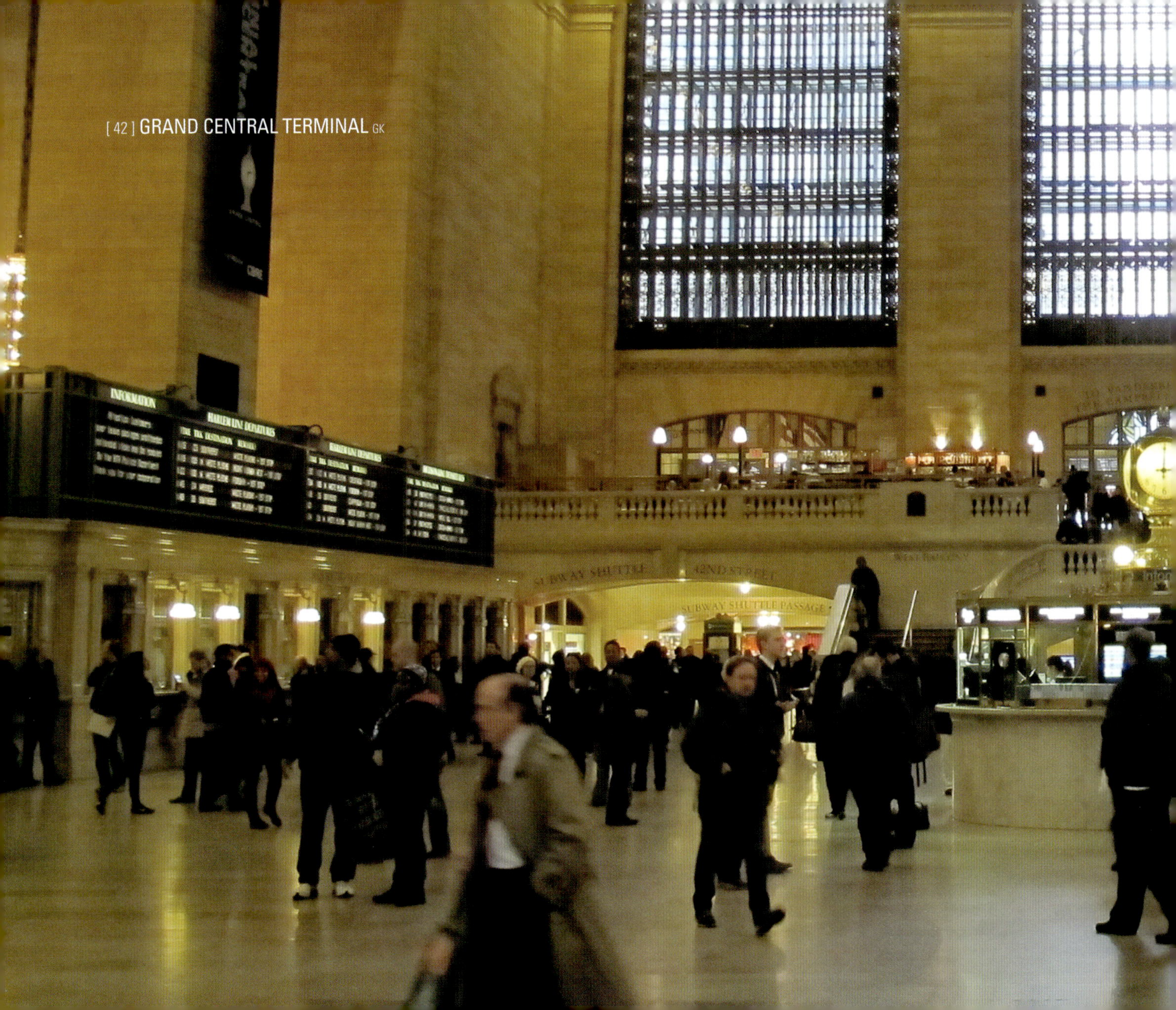

[42] GRAND CENTRAL TERMINAL GK

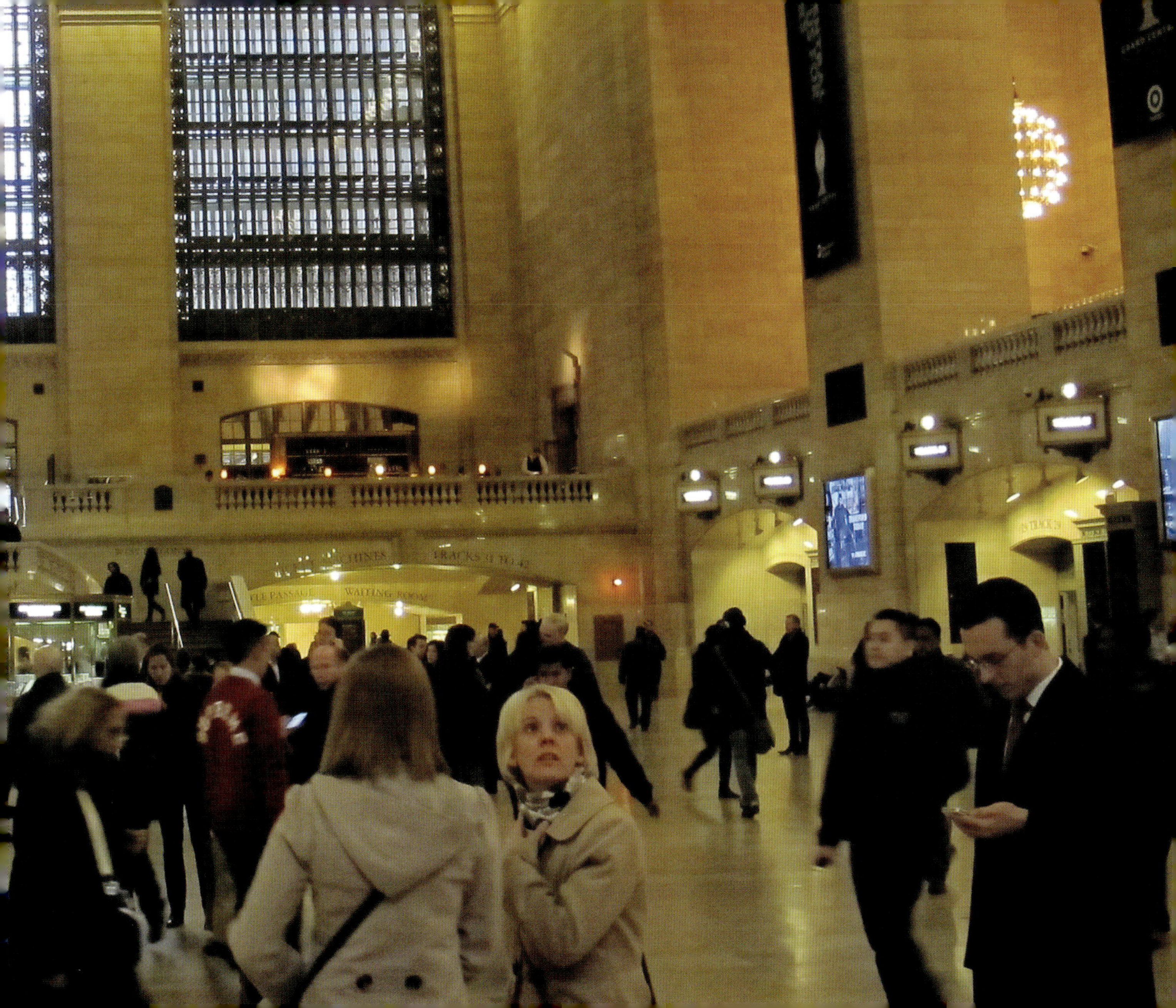

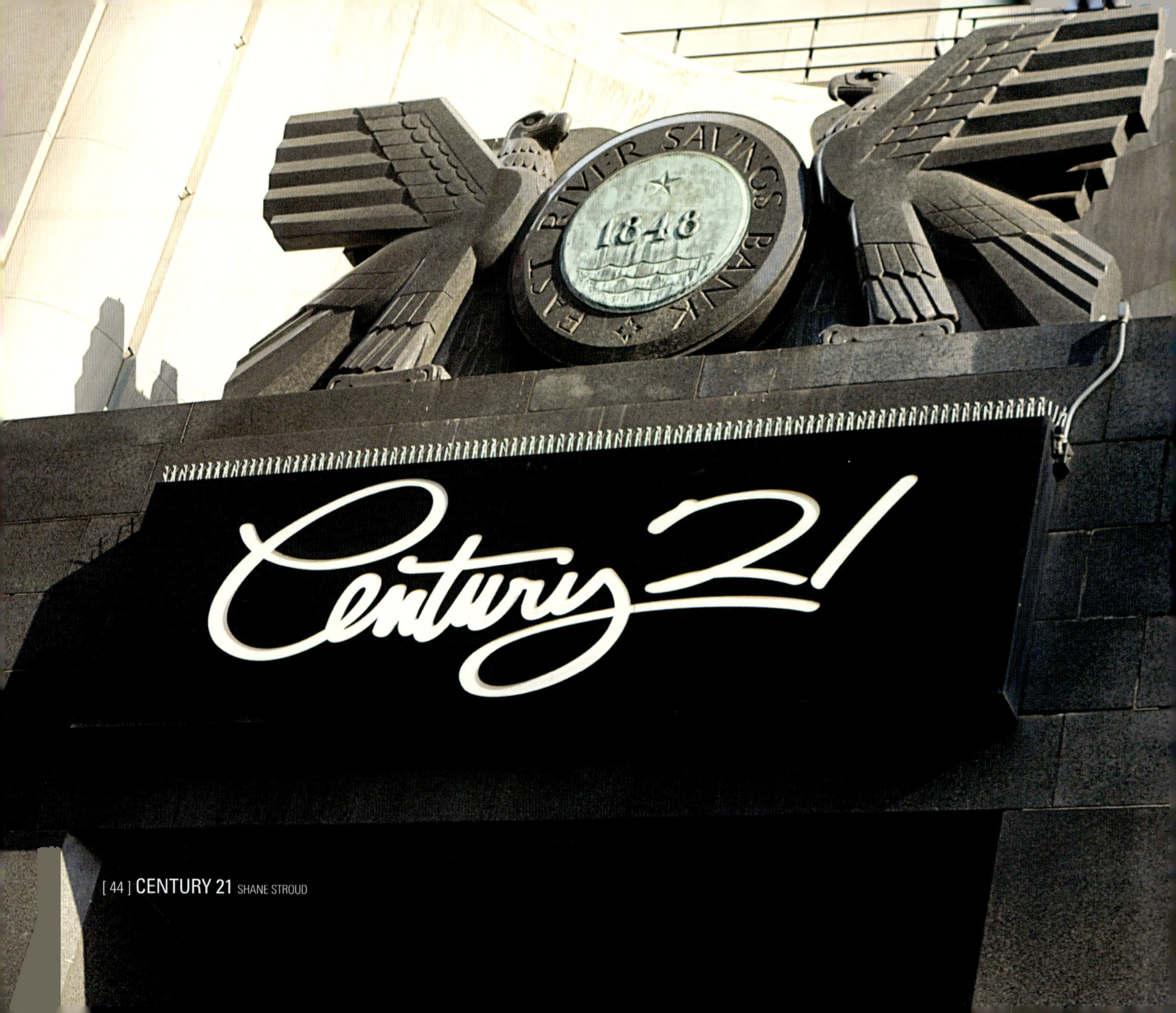
EAST RIVER SAVINGS BANK
1848
Century 21

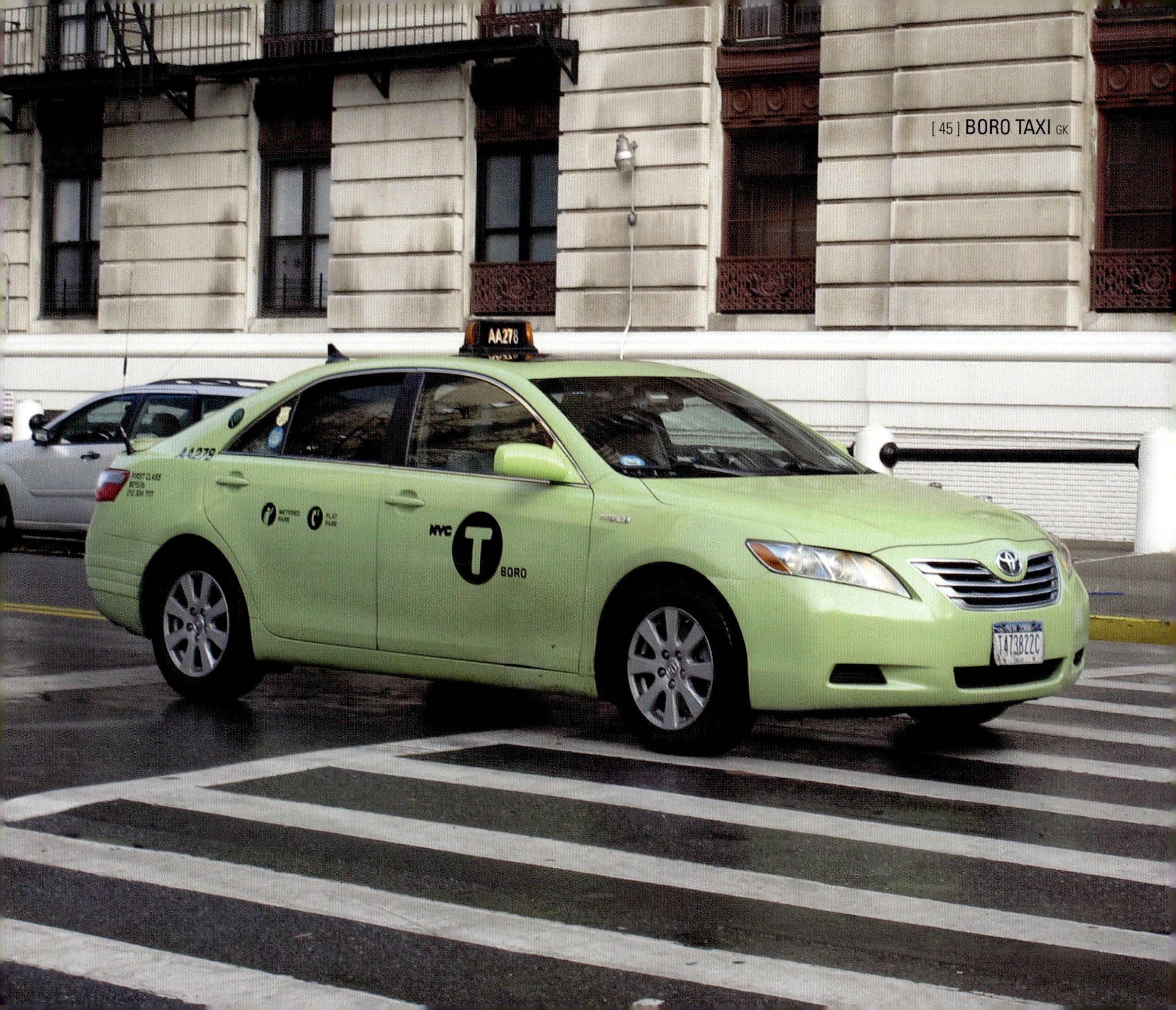

[45] BORO TAXI GK

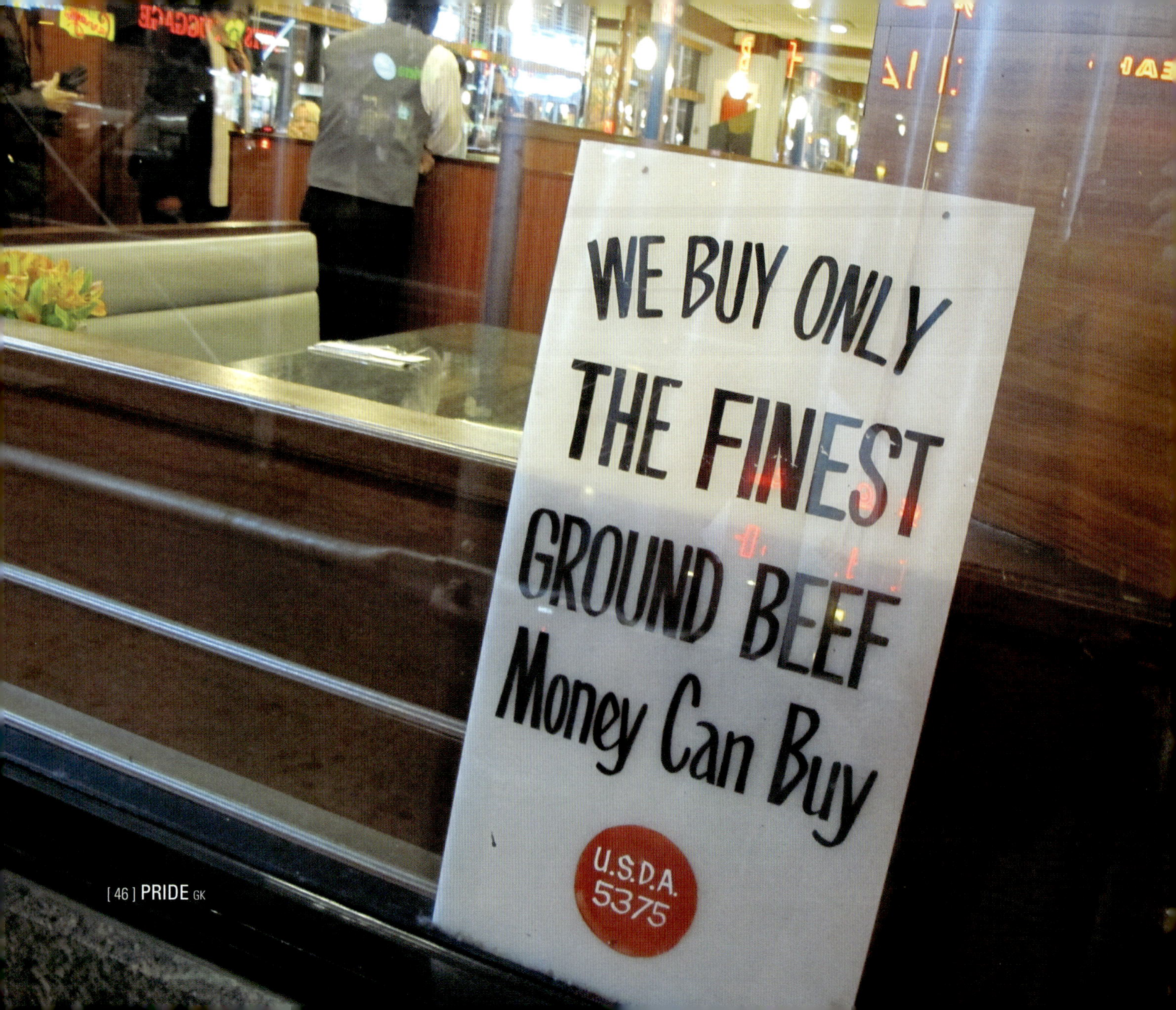
WE BUY ONLY
THE FINEST
GROUND BEEF
Money Can Buy
U.S.D.A.
5375

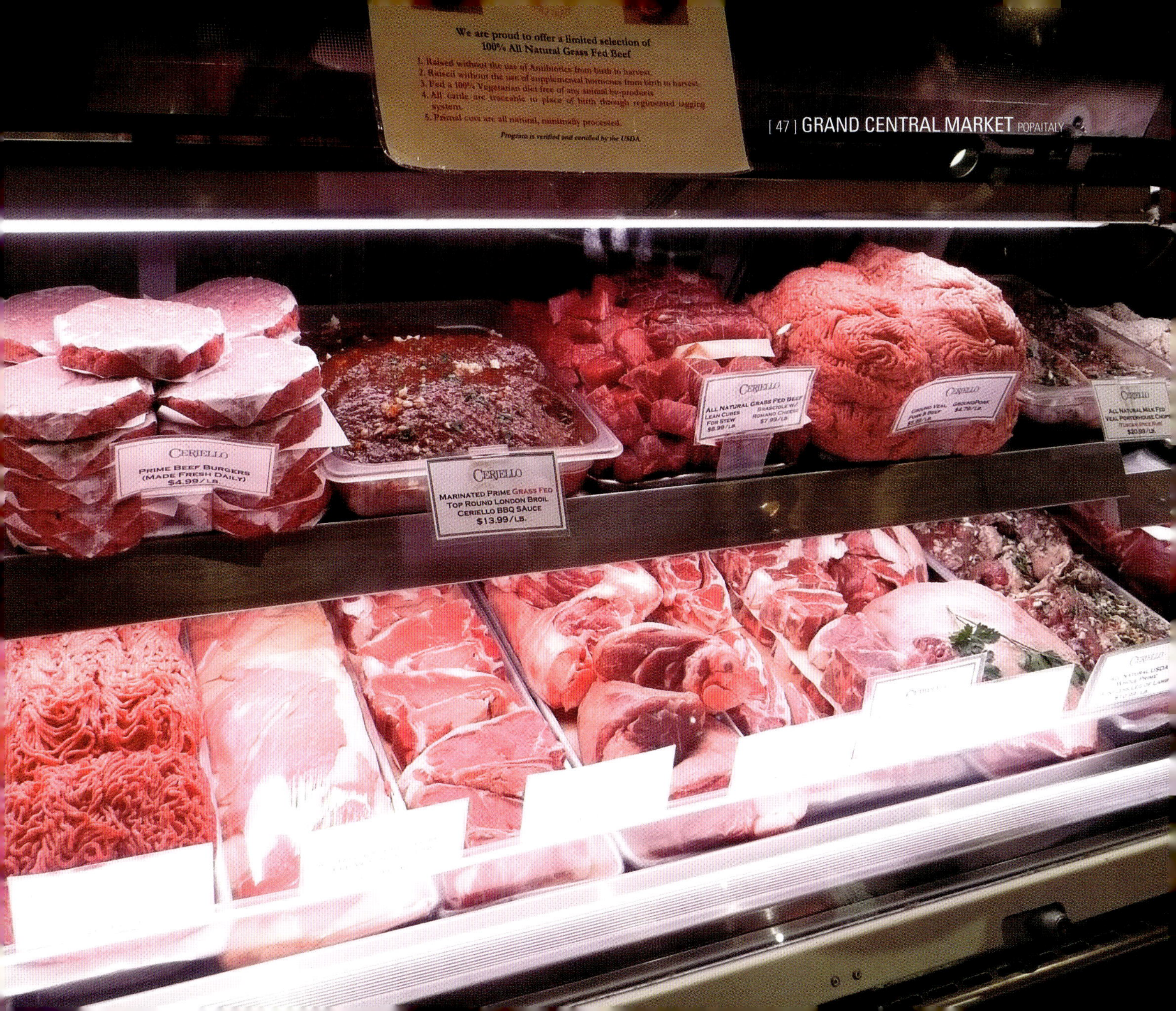
We are proud to offer a limited selection of
100% All Natural Grass Fed Beef
1. Raised without the use of Antibiotics from birth to harvest.
2. Raised without the use of supplemental hormones from birth to harvest.
3. Fed a 100% Vegetarian diet free of any animal by-products
4. All cattle are traceable to place of birth through regimented tagging system.
5. Primal cuts are all natural, minimally processed.
Program is verified and certified by the USDA.
CERIELLO
PRIME BEEF BURGERS
(MADE FRESH DAILY)
$4.99/LB.
CERIELLO
MARINATED PRIME GRASS FED
TOP ROUND LONDON BROIL
CERIELLO BBQ SAUCE
$13.99/LB.
CERIELLO
ALL NATURAL GRASS FED BEEF
LEAN CUBES FOR STEW
$8.99/LB.
BRASCIOLE W/ ROMANO CHEESE
$7.99/LB.
CERIELLO
GROUND VEAL PORK & BEEF
GROUNDPORK
$4.79/LB.
CERIELLO
ALL NATURAL MILK FED
VEAL PORTERHOUSE CHOPS
TUSCAN SPICE RUB
$20.99/LB.

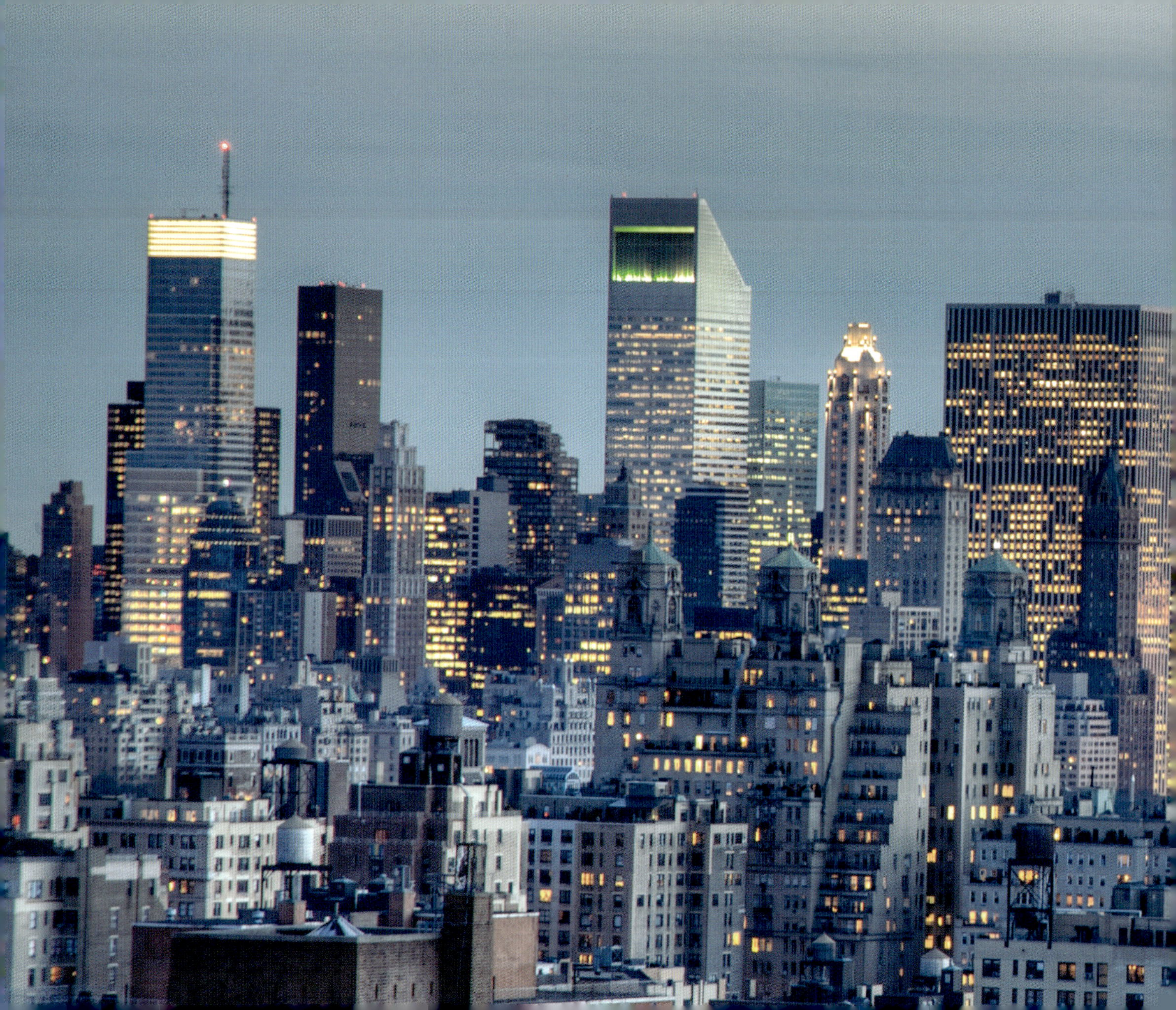

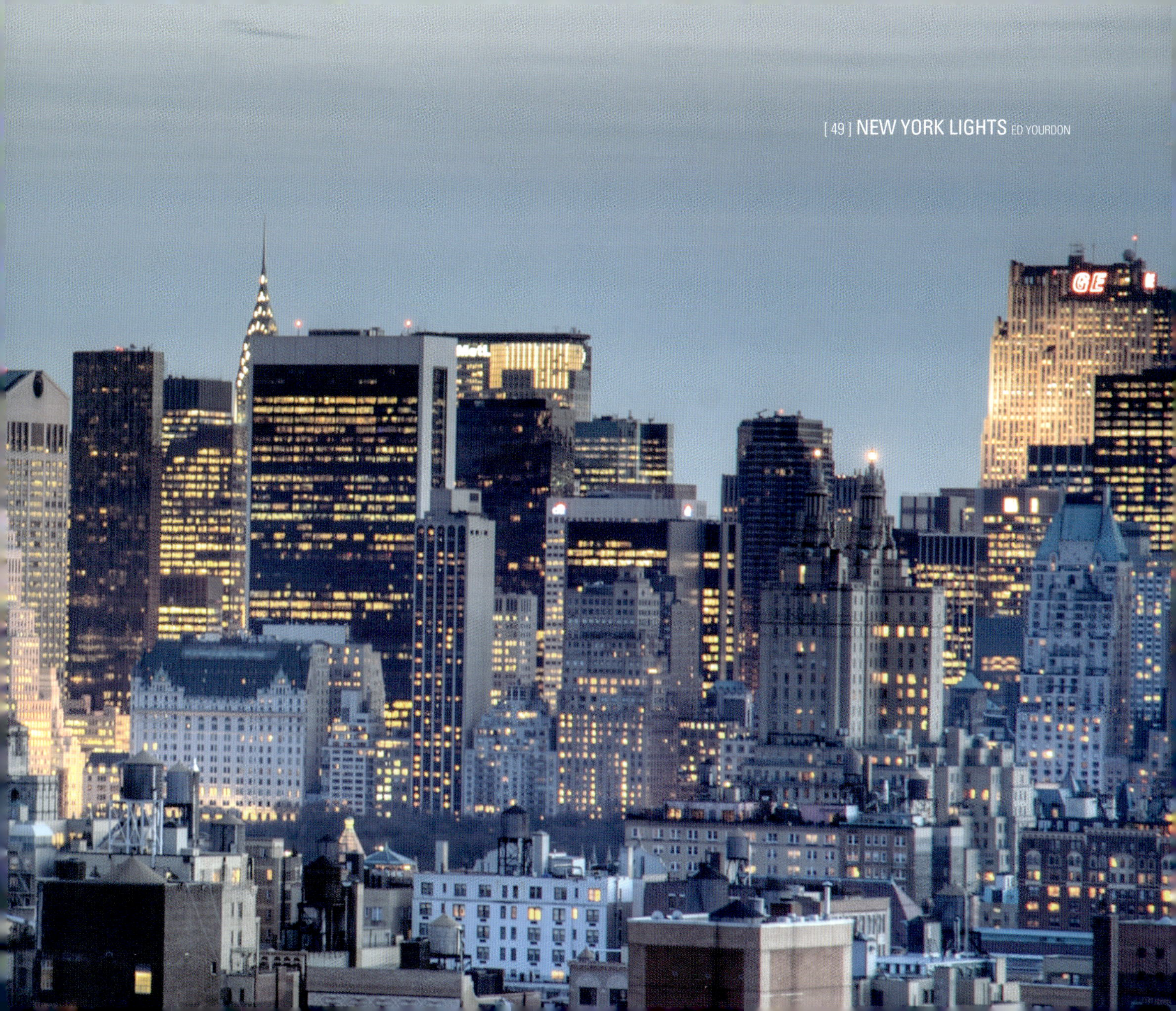

[49] NEW YORK LIGHTS ED YOURDON

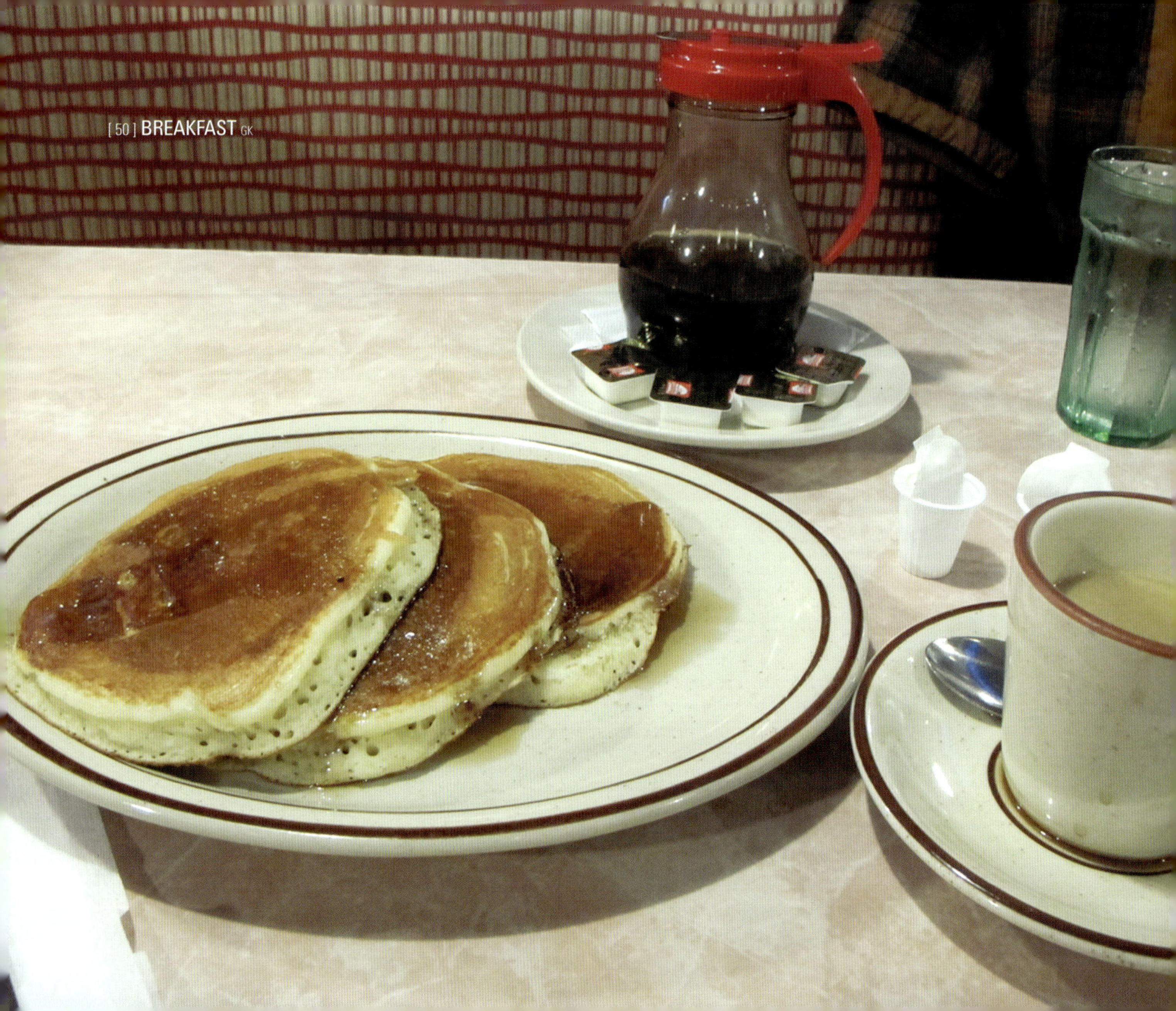

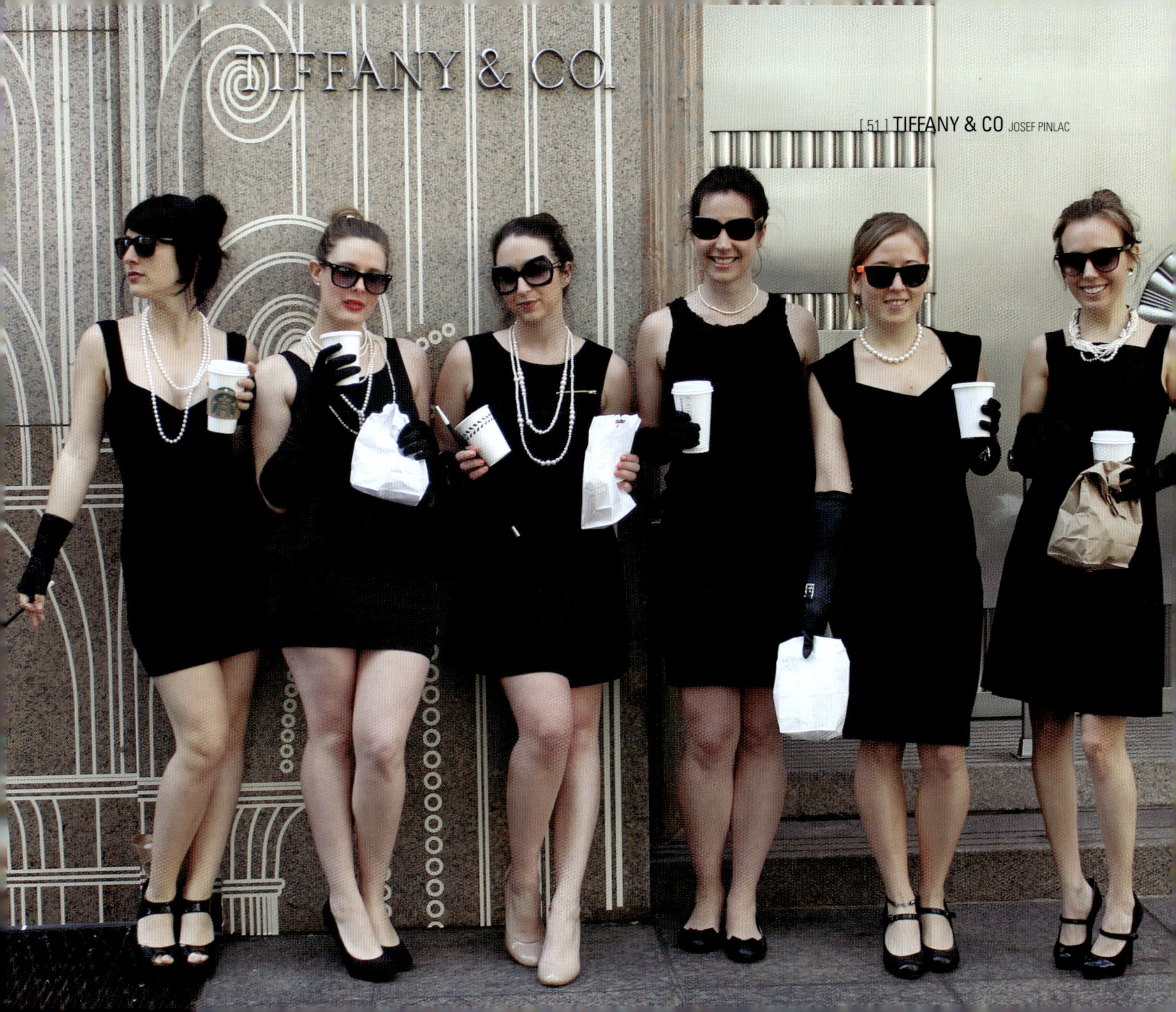

[51] TIFFANY & CO JOSEF PINLAC

[52] THE JUILLIARD SCHOOL BILLIE WARD

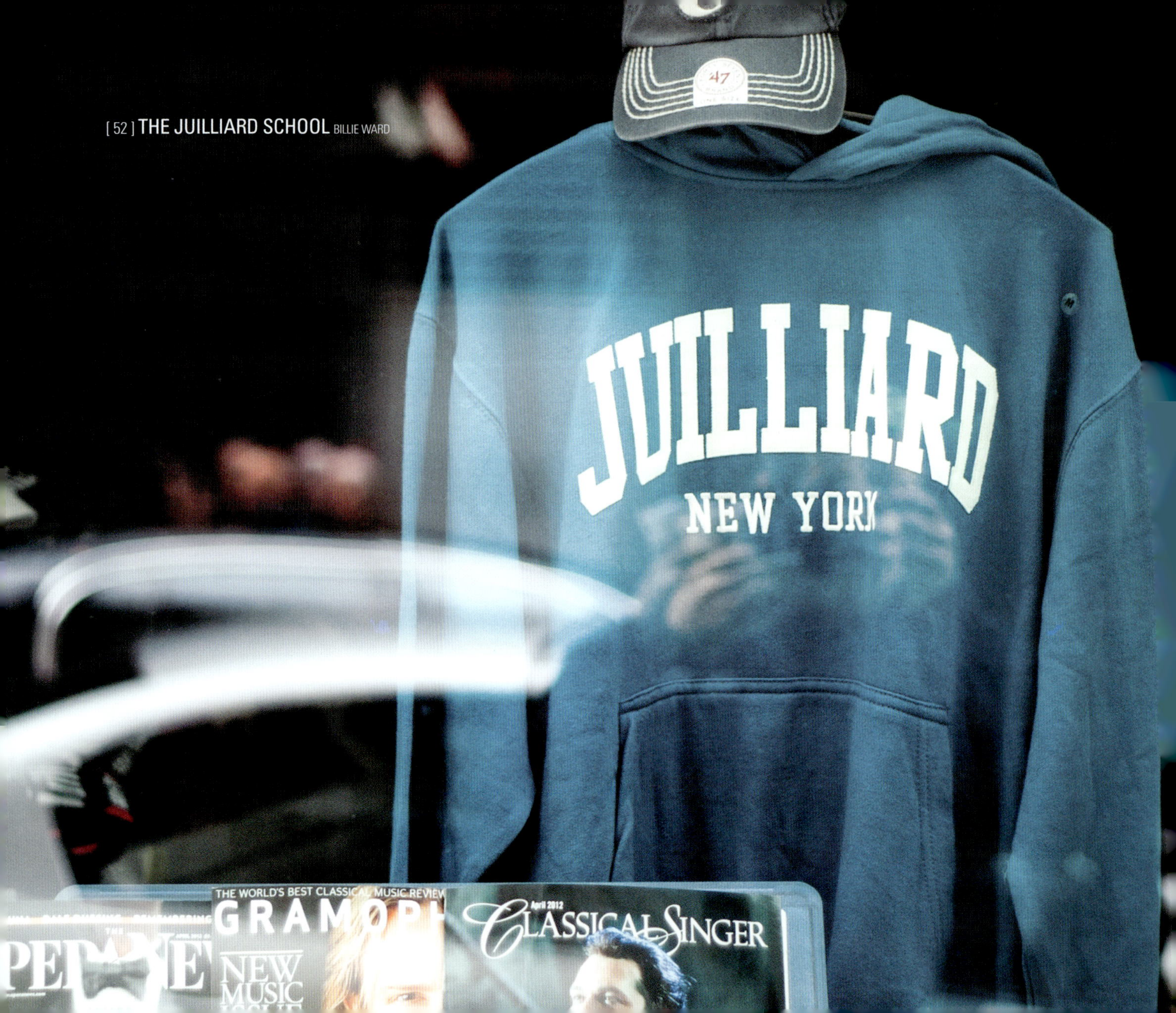

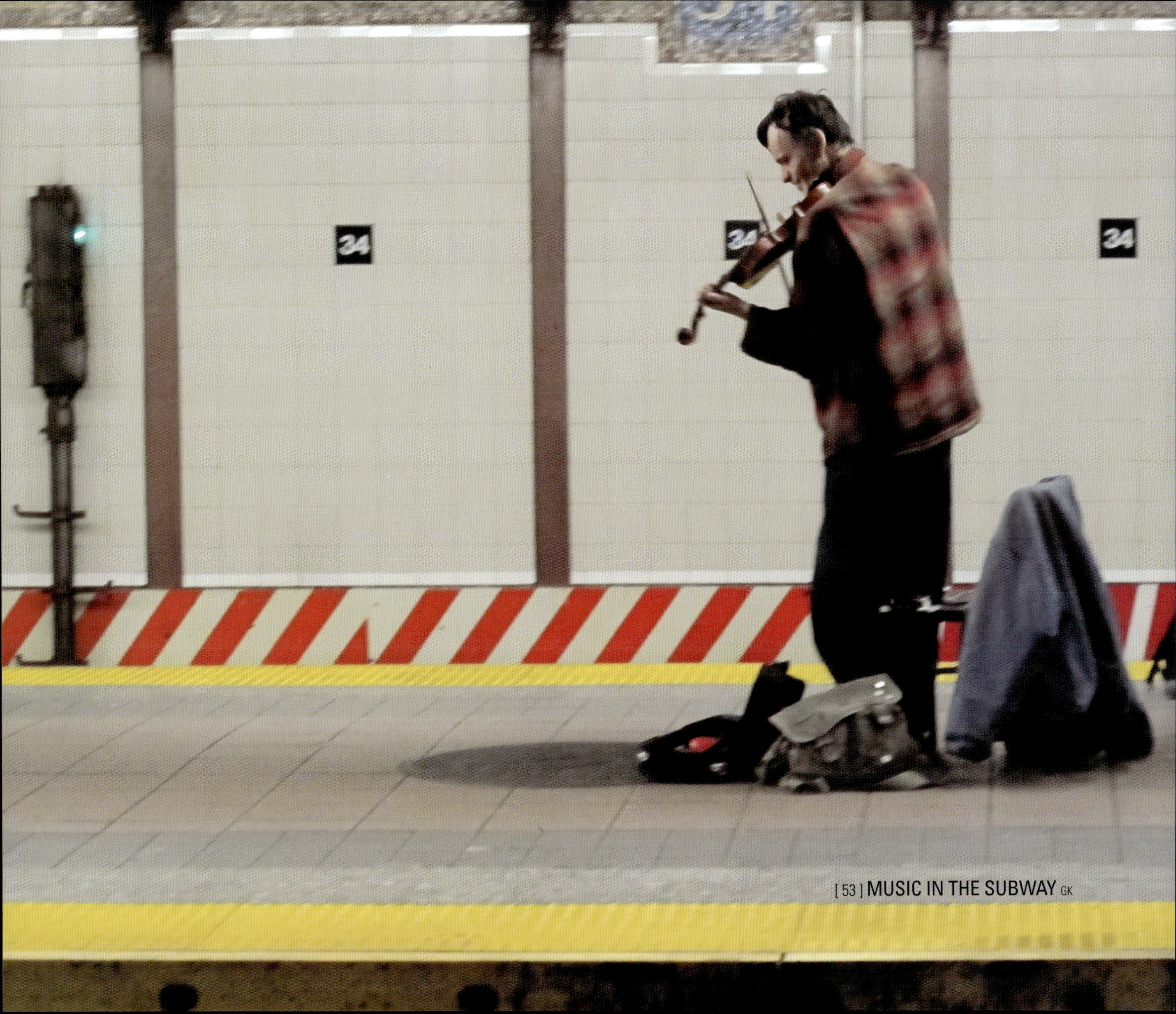

[53] MUSIC IN THE SUBWAY GK

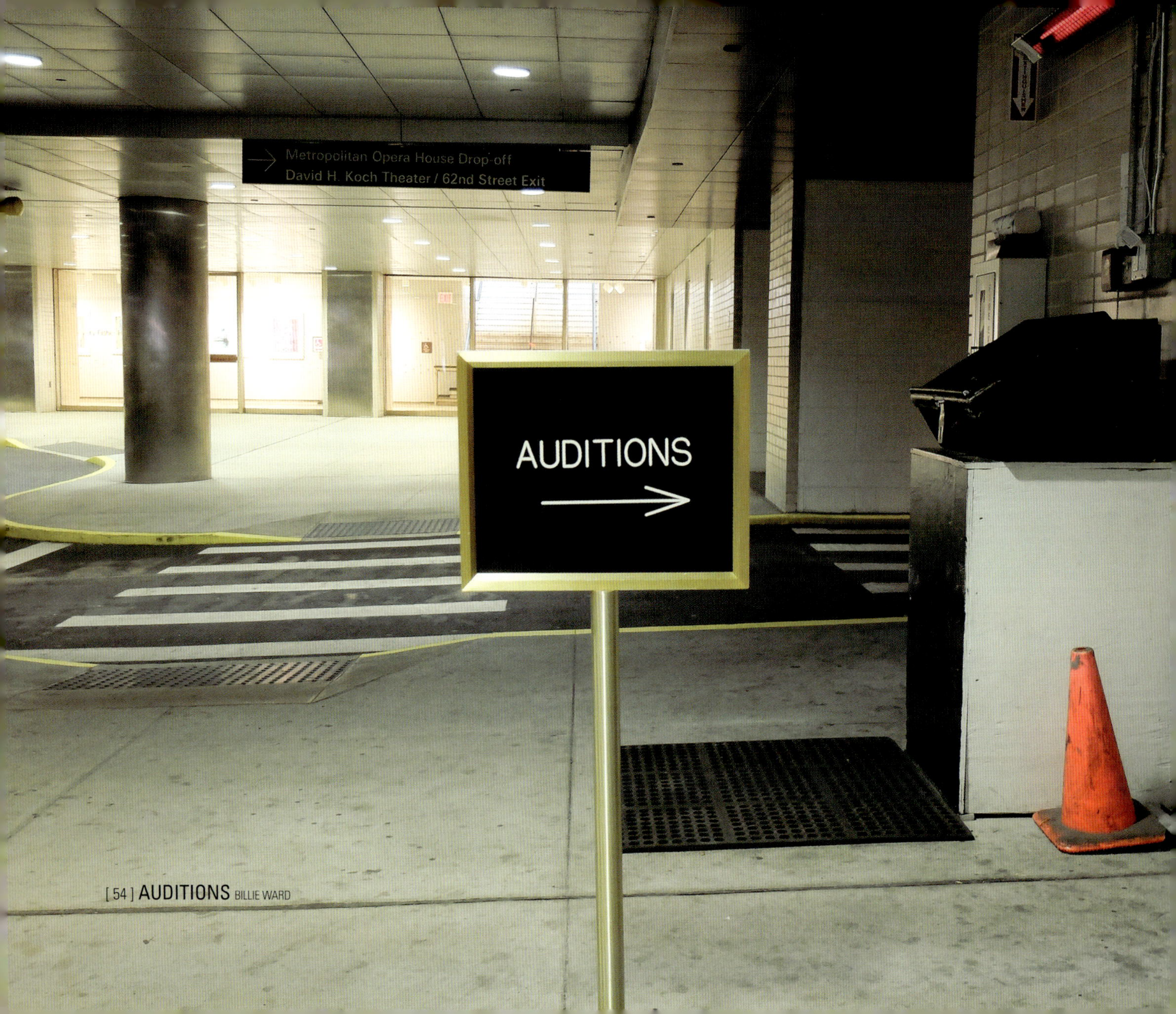

[54] AUDITIONS BILLIE WARD

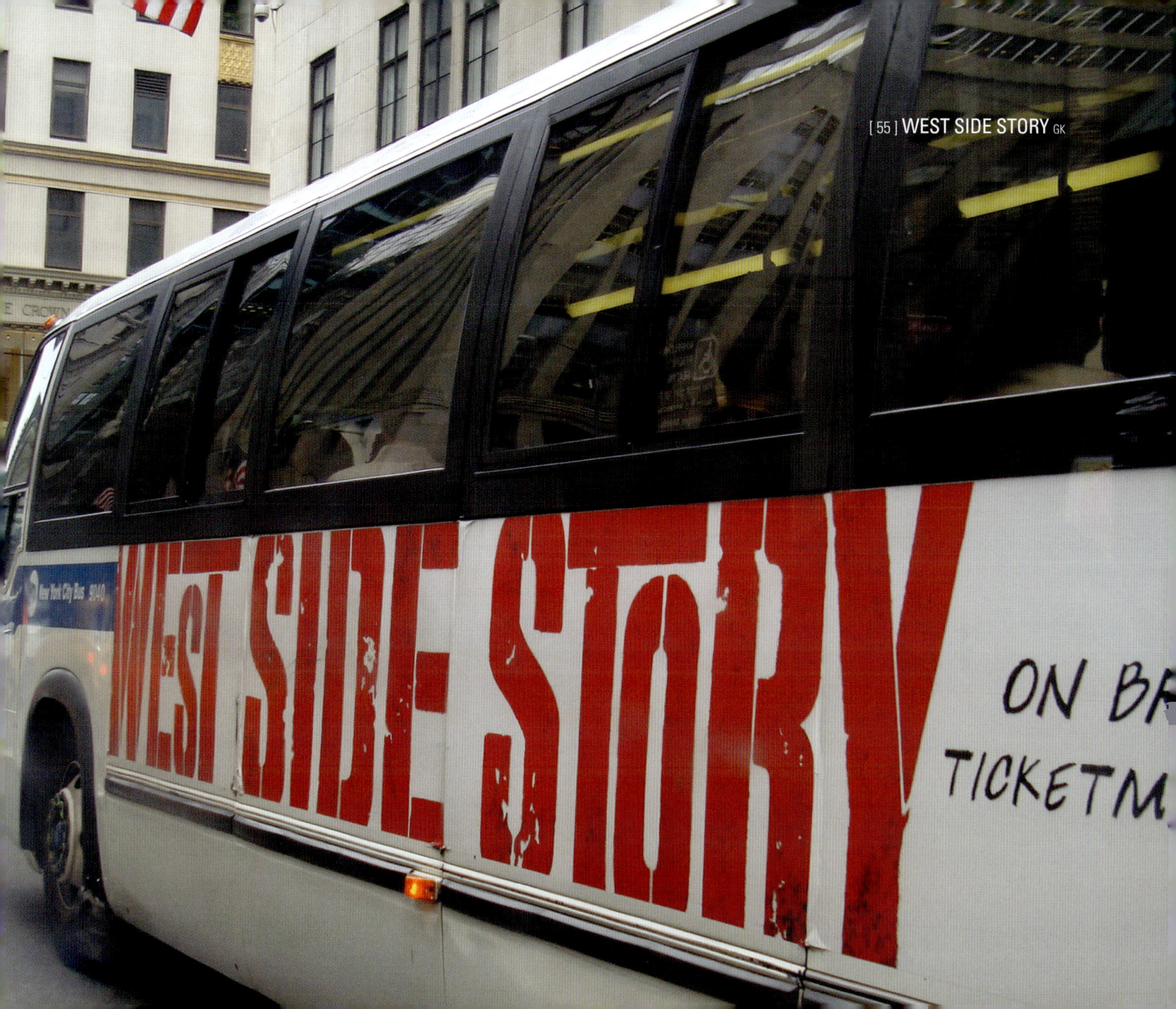

[55] WEST SIDE STORY GK

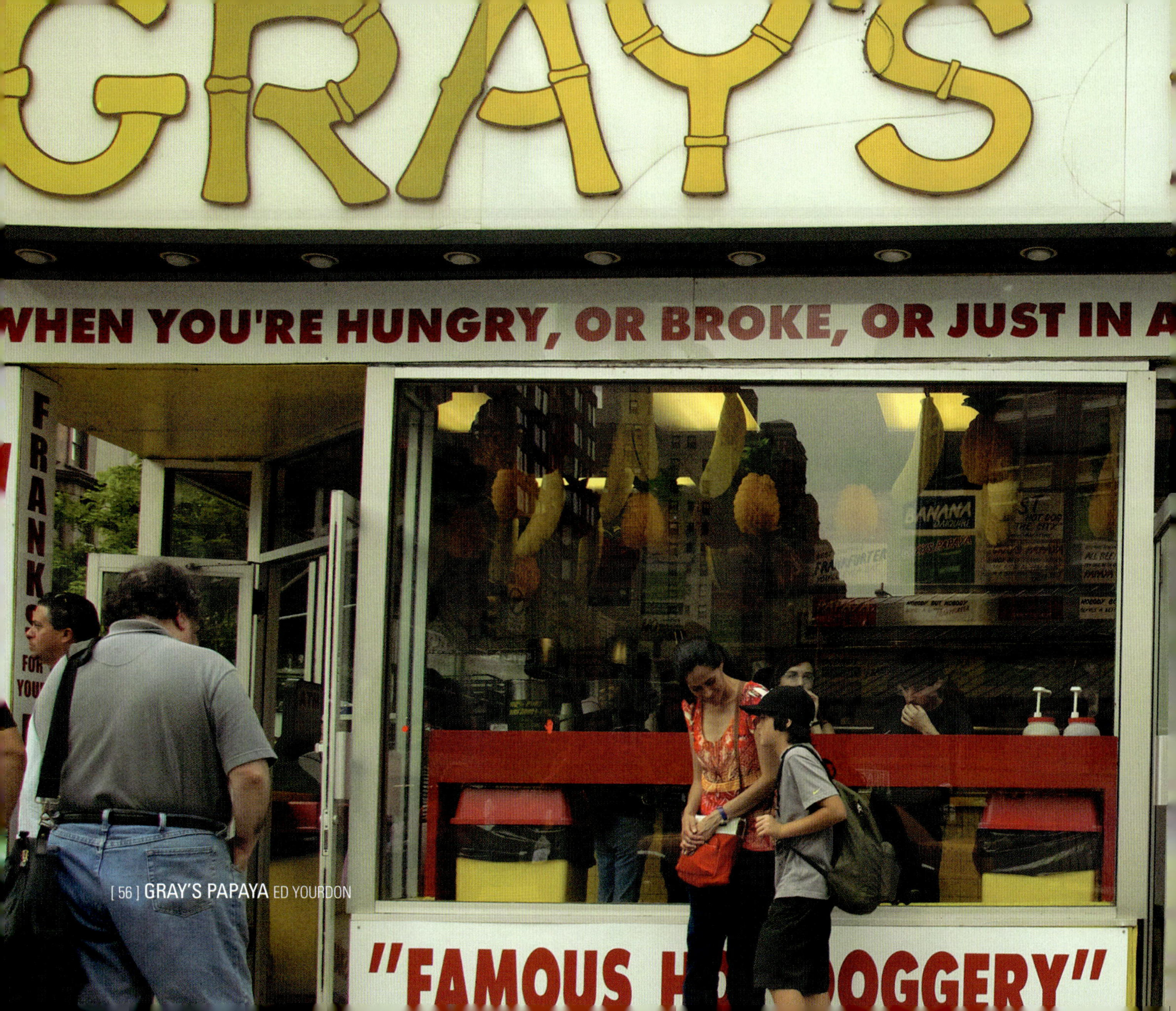

[56] GRAY'S PAPAYA ED YOURDON

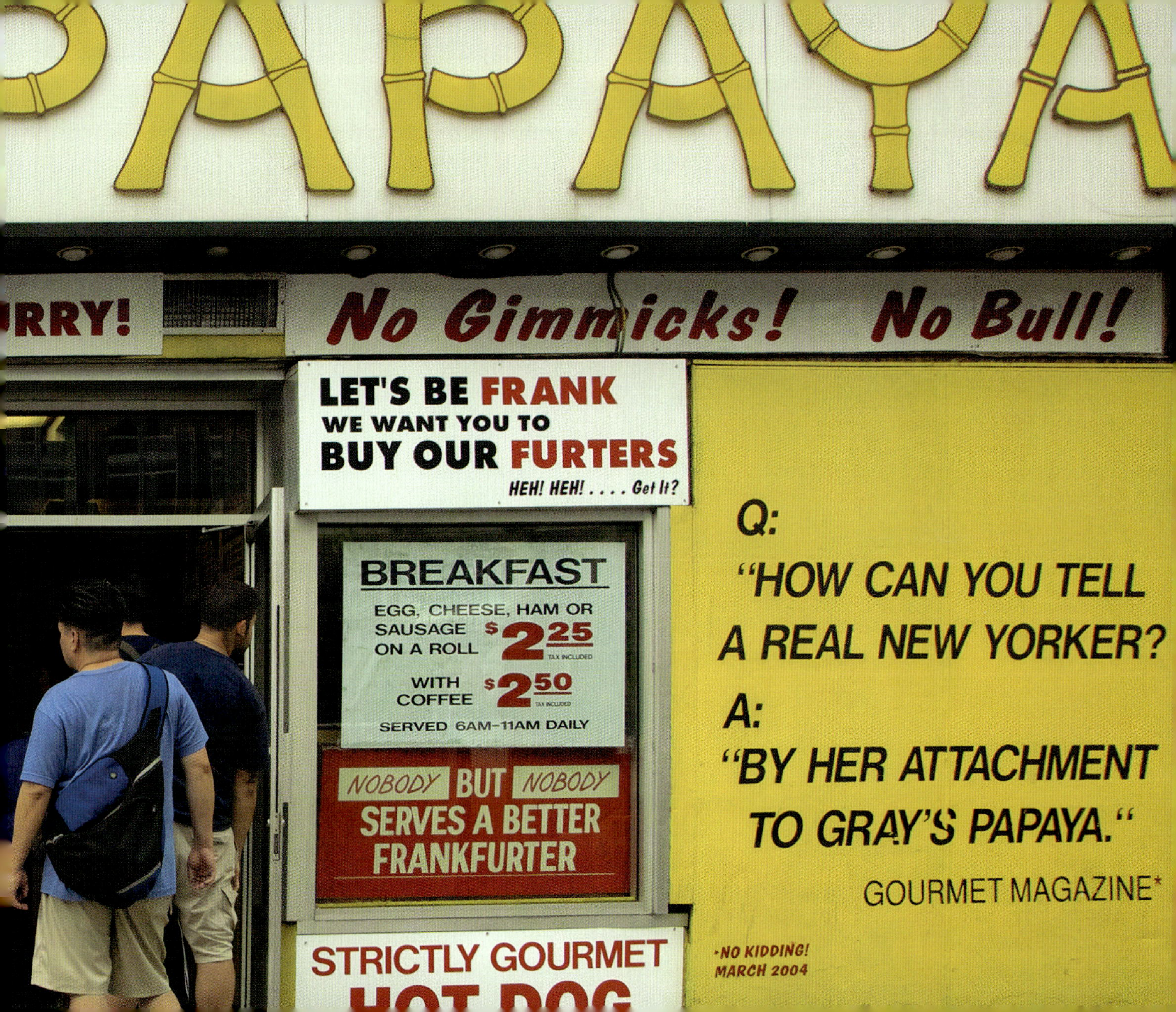
PAPAYA
RRY!
No Gimmicks! No Bull!
LET'S BE FRANK
WE WANT YOU TO
BUY OUR FURTERS
HEH! HEH! . . . . Get It?
BREAKFAST
EGG, CHEESE, HAM OR
SAUSAGE
ON A ROLL
$2.25
TAX INCLUDED
WITH
COFFEE
$2.50
TAX INCLUDED
SERVED 6AM–11AM DAILY
NOBODY BUT NOBODY
SERVES A BETTER
FRANKFURTER
STRICTLY GOURMET
Q:
"HOW CAN YOU TELL
A REAL NEW YORKER?
A:
"BY HER ATTACHMENT
TO GRAY'S PAPAYA."
GOURMET MAGAZINE*
*NO KIDDING!
MARCH 2004

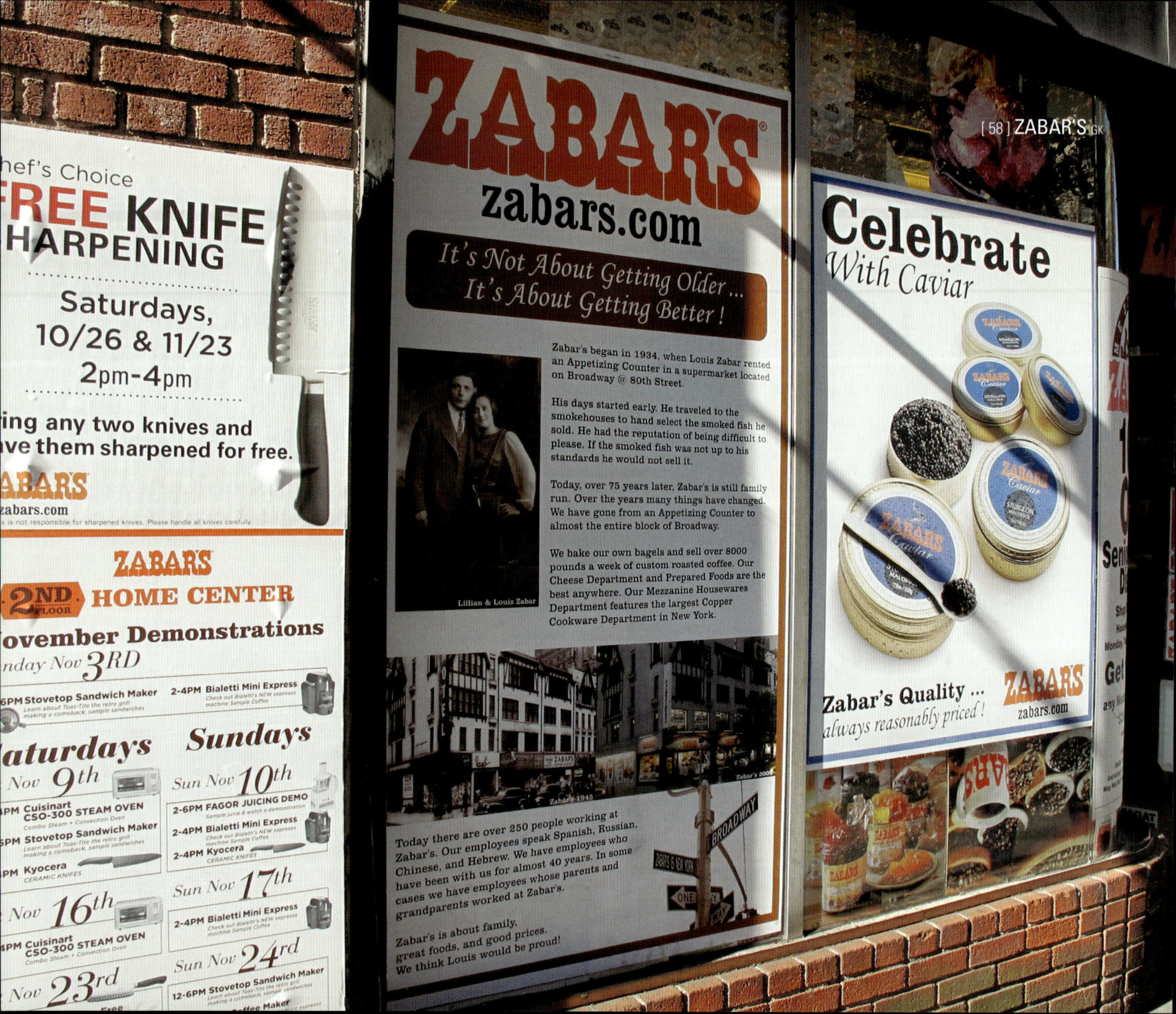
hef's Choice
FREE KNIFE
HARPENING
Saturdays,
10/26 & 11/23
2pm-4pm
ing any two knives and
ave them sharpened for free.
zabars.com
ZABAR'S
2ND FLOOR HOME CENTER
ovember Demonstrations
nday Nov 3RD
6PM Stovetop Sandwich Maker
2-4PM Bialetti Mini Express
aturdays
Sundays
Nov 9th
Sun Nov 10th
PM Cuisinart CSO-300 STEAM OVEN
2-6PM FAGOR JUICING DEMO
5PM Stovetop Sandwich Maker
2-4PM Bialetti Mini Express
2-4PM Kyocera
PM Kyocera
Sun Nov 17th
Nov 16th
2-4PM Bialetti Mini Express
PM Cuisinart CSO-300 STEAM OVEN
Sun Nov 24th
Nov 23rd
12-6PM Stovetop Sandwich Maker
ZABAR'S®
zabars.com
It's Not About Getting Older ...
It's About Getting Better !
Zabar's began in 1934, when Louis Zabar rented an Appetizing Counter in a supermarket located on Broadway @ 80th Street.
His days started early. He traveled to the smokehouses to hand select the smoked fish he sold. He had the reputation of being difficult to please. If the smoked fish was not up to his standards he would not sell it.
Today, over 75 years later, Zabar's is still family run. Over the years many things have changed. We have gone from an Appetizing Counter to almost the entire block of Broadway.
We bake our own bagels and sell over 8000 pounds a week of custom roasted coffee. Our Cheese Department and Prepared Foods are the best anywhere. Our Mezzanine Housewares Department features the largest Copper Cookware Department in New York.
Lillian & Louis Zabar
Zabar's 1945
Zabar's 2008
BROADWAY
ONE WAY
Today there are over 250 people working at Zabar's. Our employees speak Spanish, Russian, Chinese, and Hebrew. We have employees who have been with us for almost 40 years. In some cases we have employees whose parents and grandparents worked at Zabar's.
Zabar's is about family, great foods, and good prices. We think Louis would be proud!
Celebrate
With Caviar
Zabar's Quality ...
always reasonably priced !
ZABAR'S
zabars.com

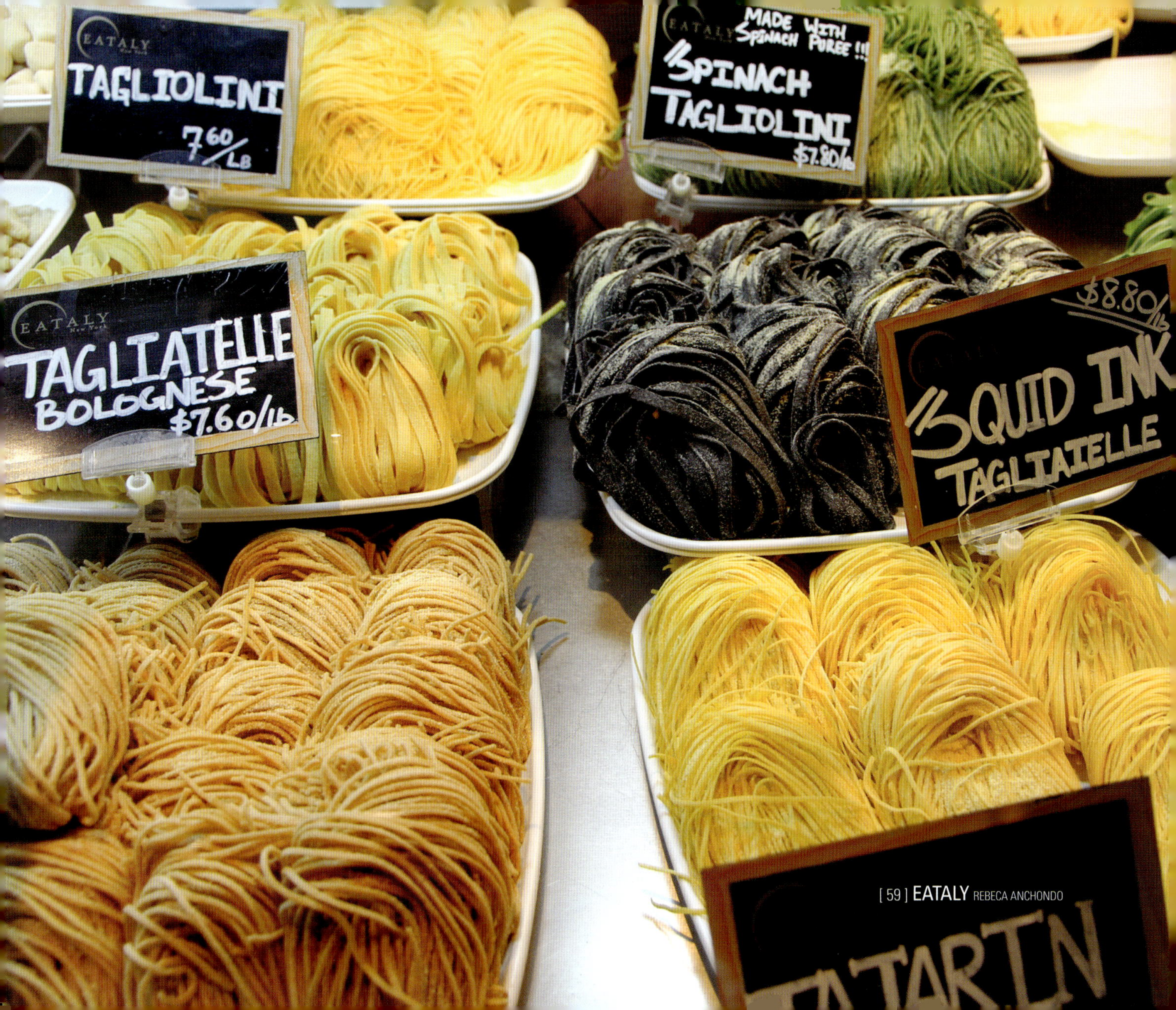
EATALY New York
TAGLIOLINI
7.60/LB
MADE WITH SPINACH PUREE!!!
SPINACH TAGLIOLINI
$7.80/lb
TAGLIATELLE BOLOGNESE
$7.60/lb
$8.80/lb
SQUID INK
TAGLIAIELLE

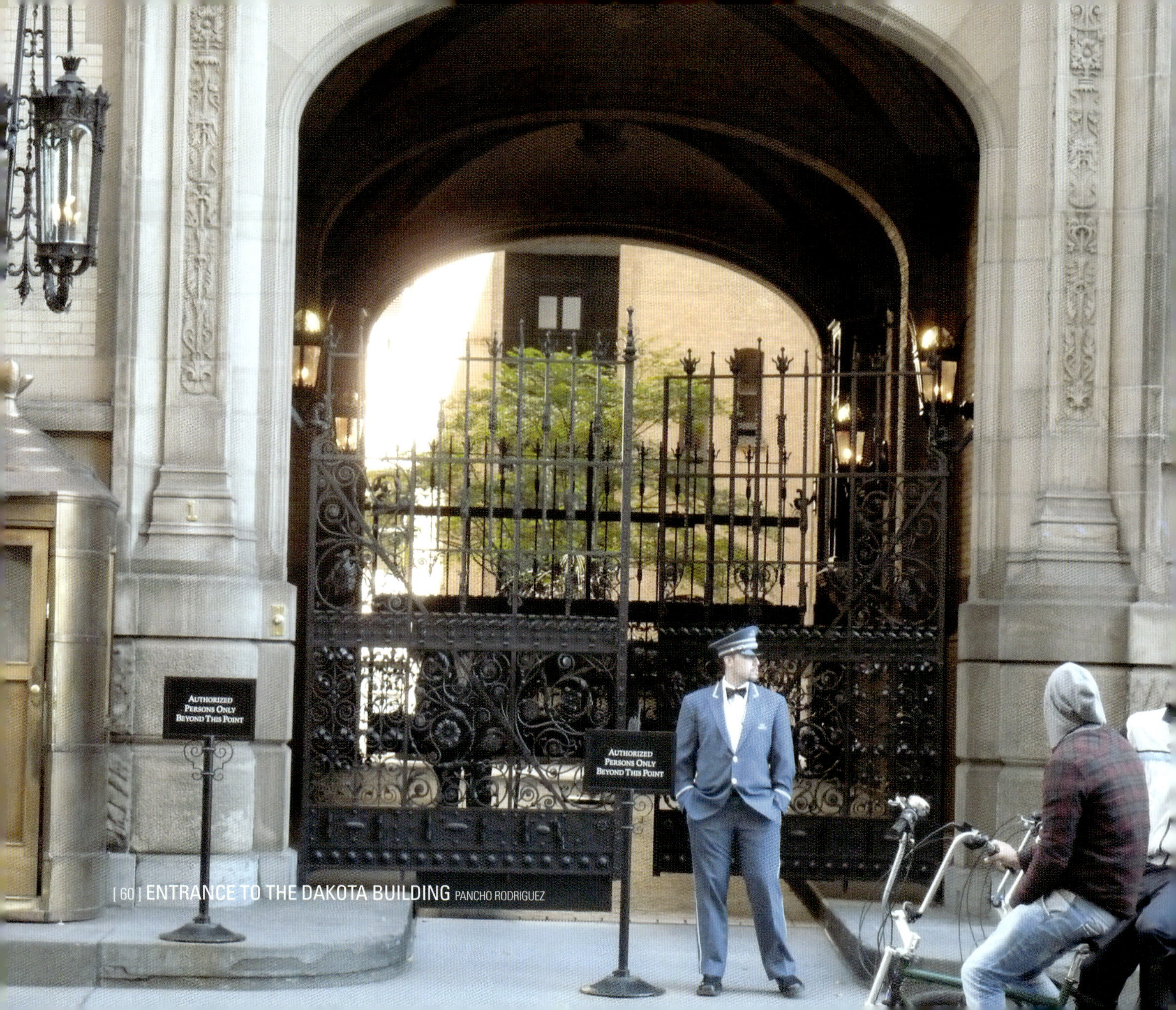

[60] ENTRANCE TO THE DAKOTA BUILDING PANCHO RODRIGUEZ

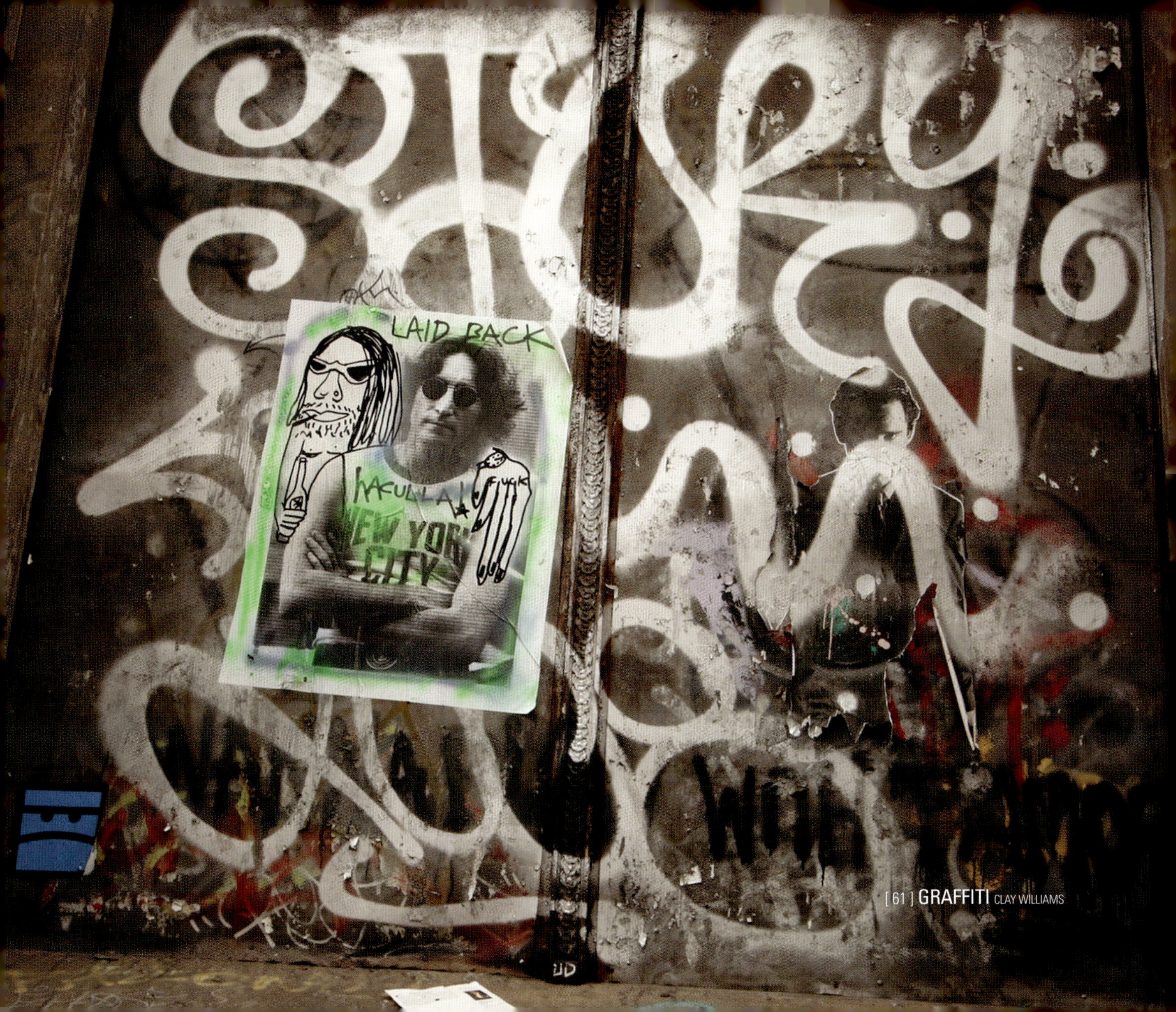

[61] GRAFFITI CLAY WILLIAMS

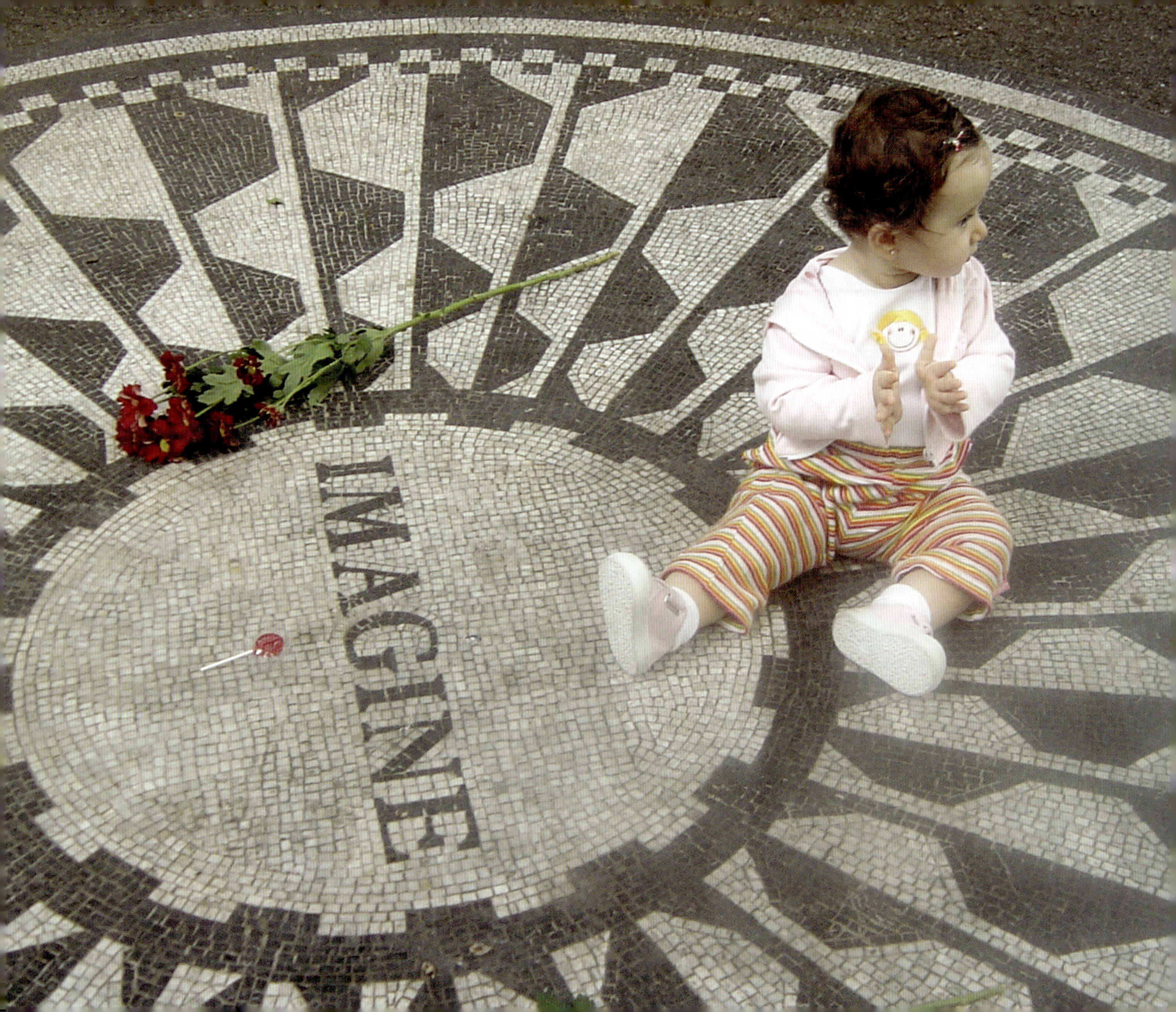
IMAGINE

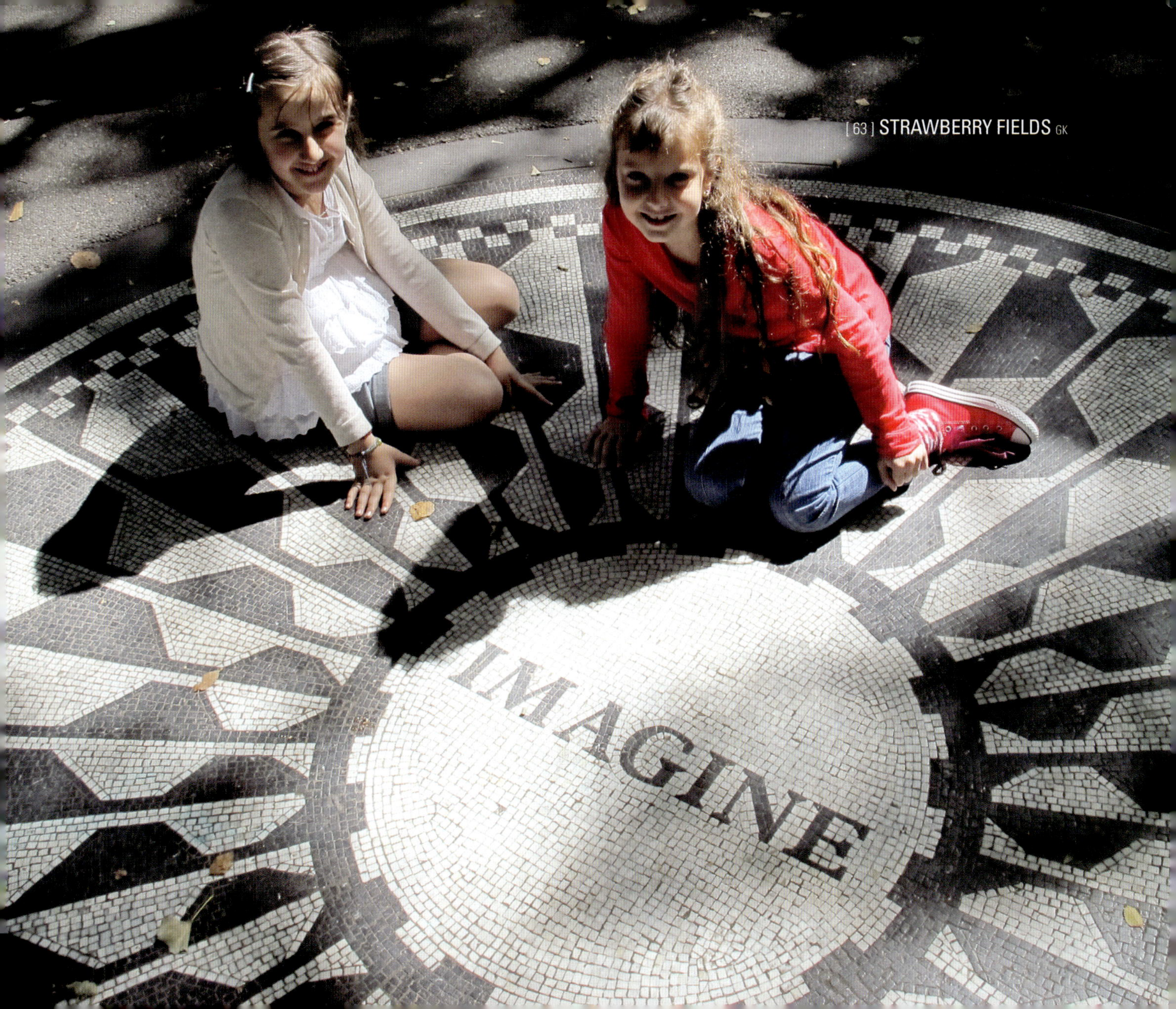

[63] STRAWBERRY FIELDS GK

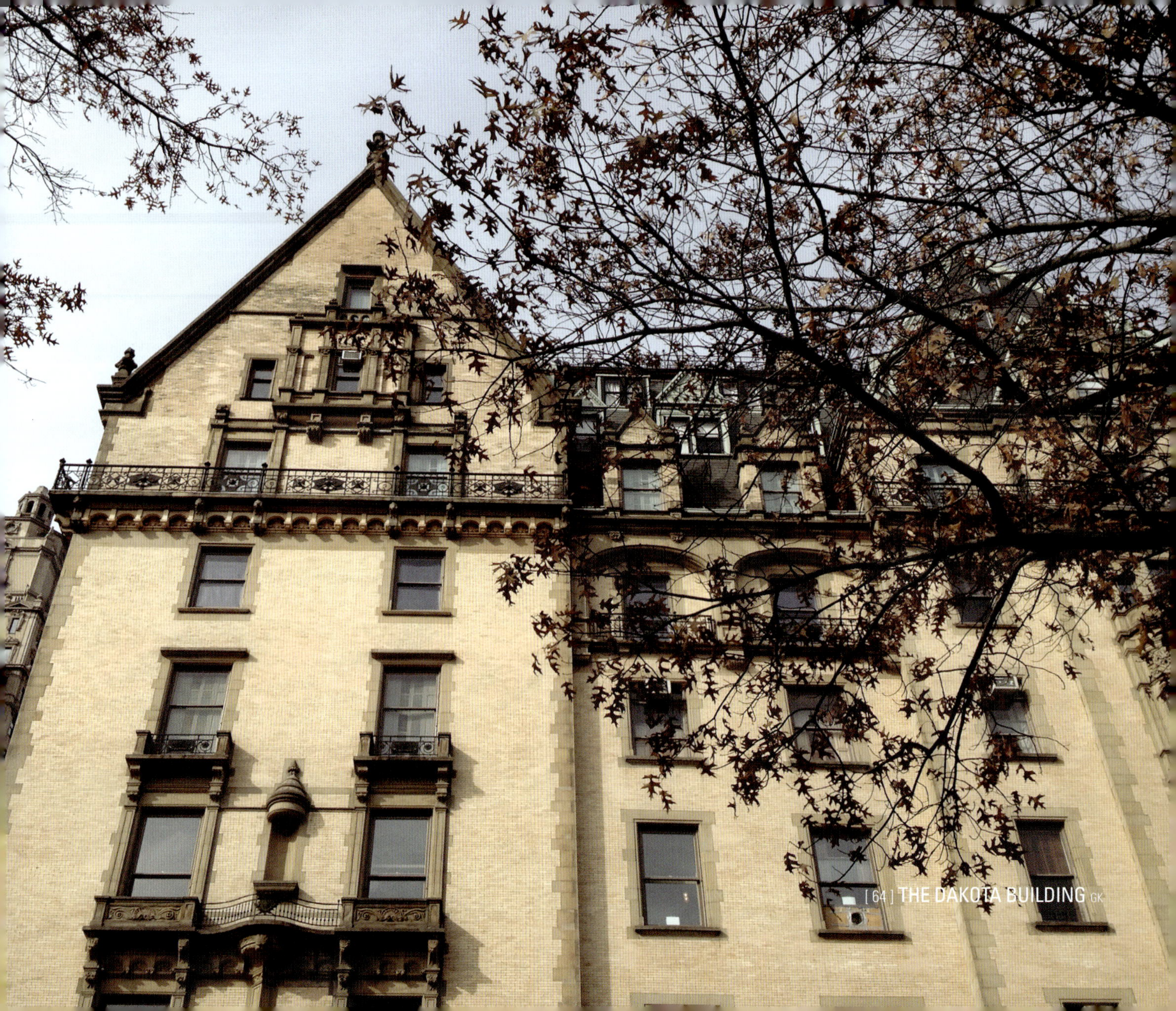

[64] THE DAKOTA BUILDING GK

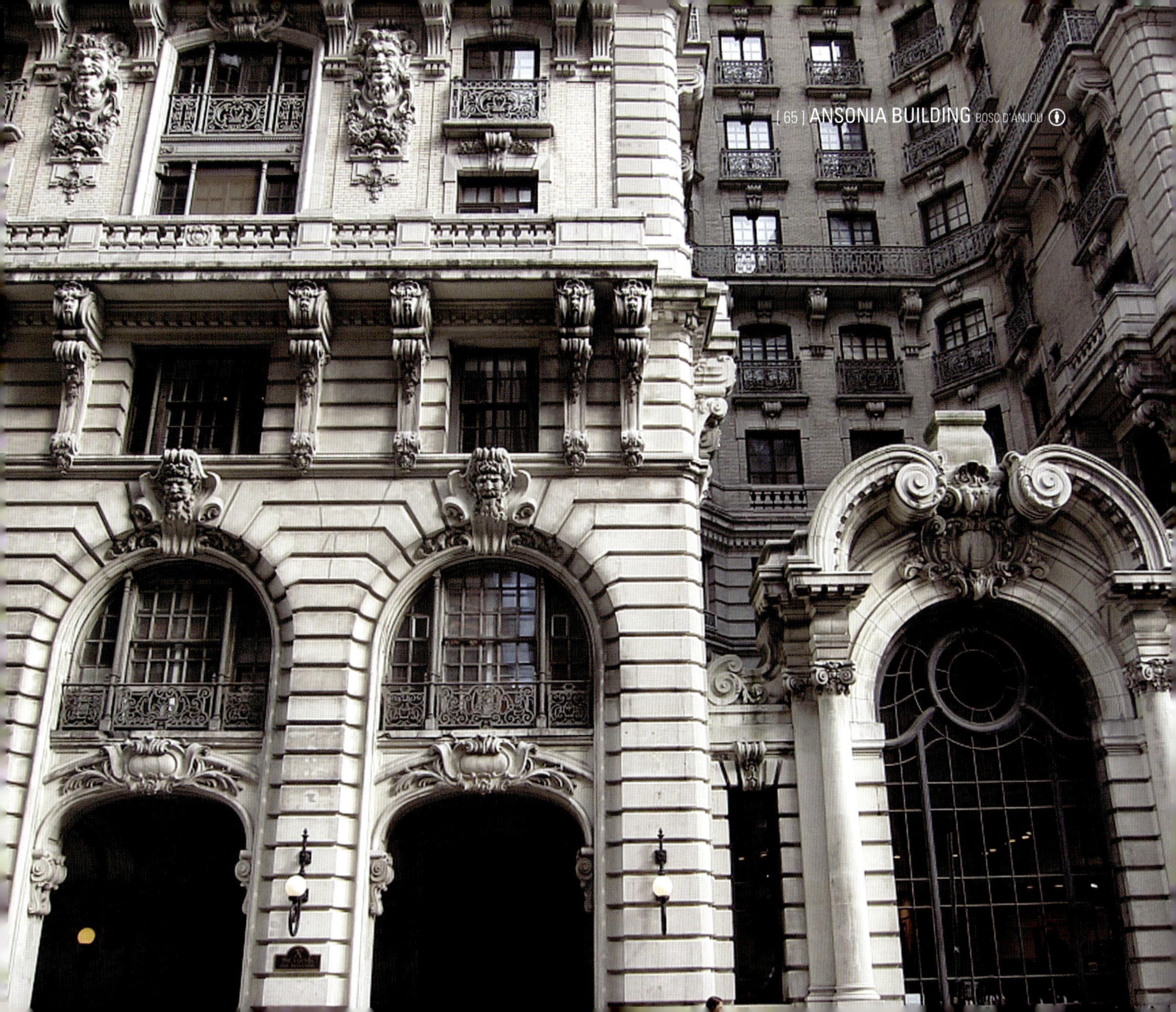

[65] ANSONIA BUILDING BOSC D'ANJOU

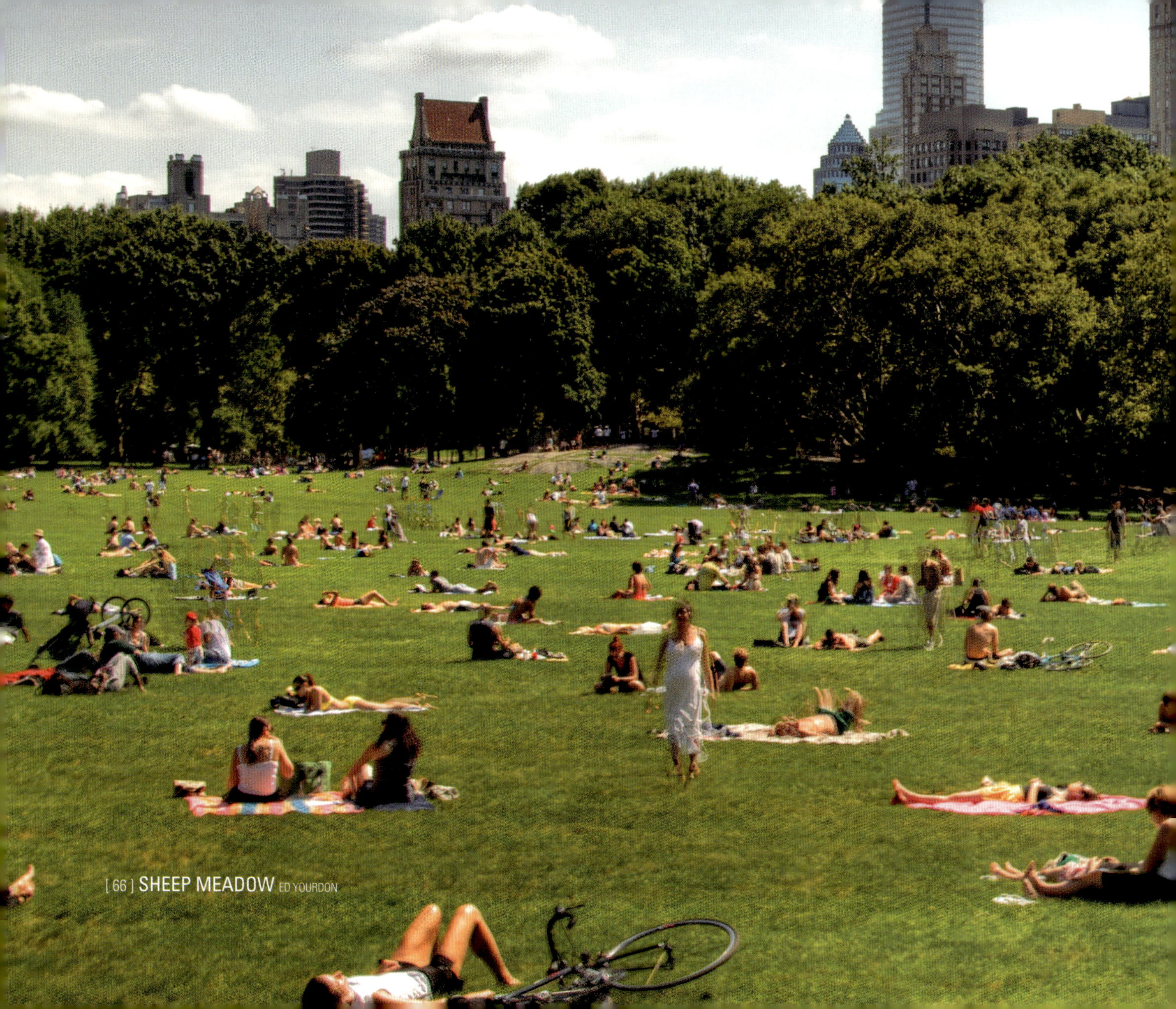

[66] SHEEP MEADOW ED YOURDON

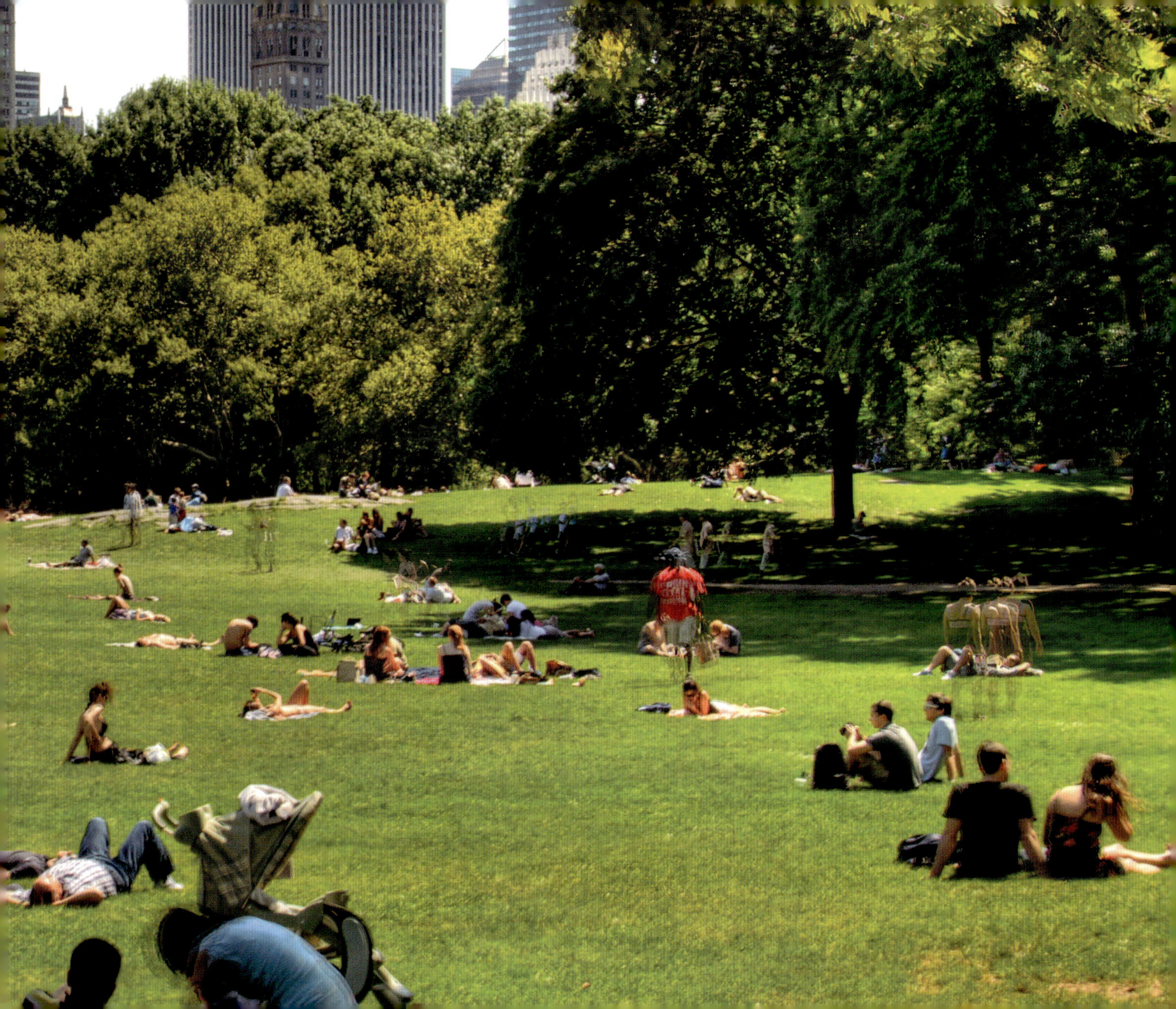

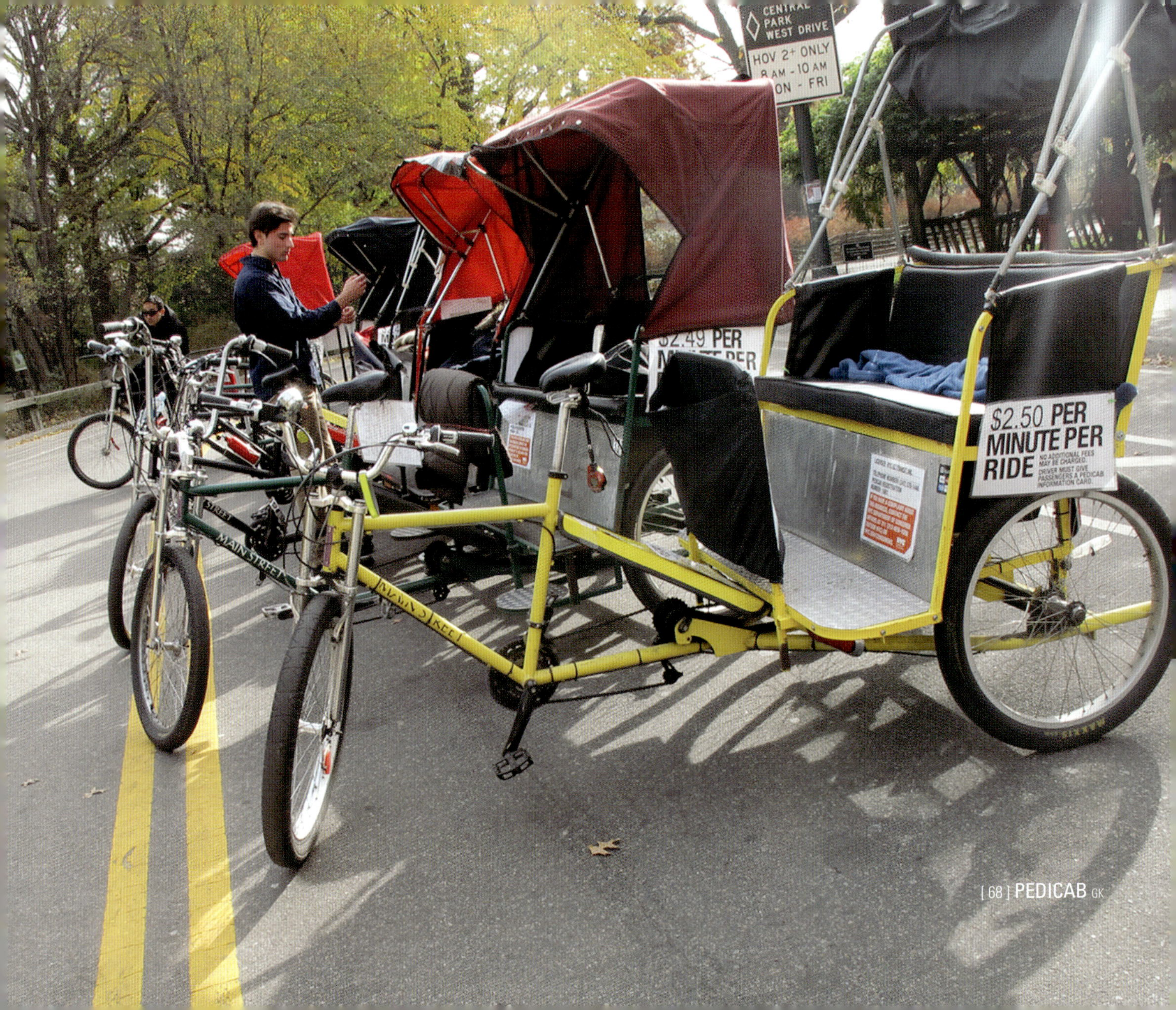

[68] PEDICAB GK

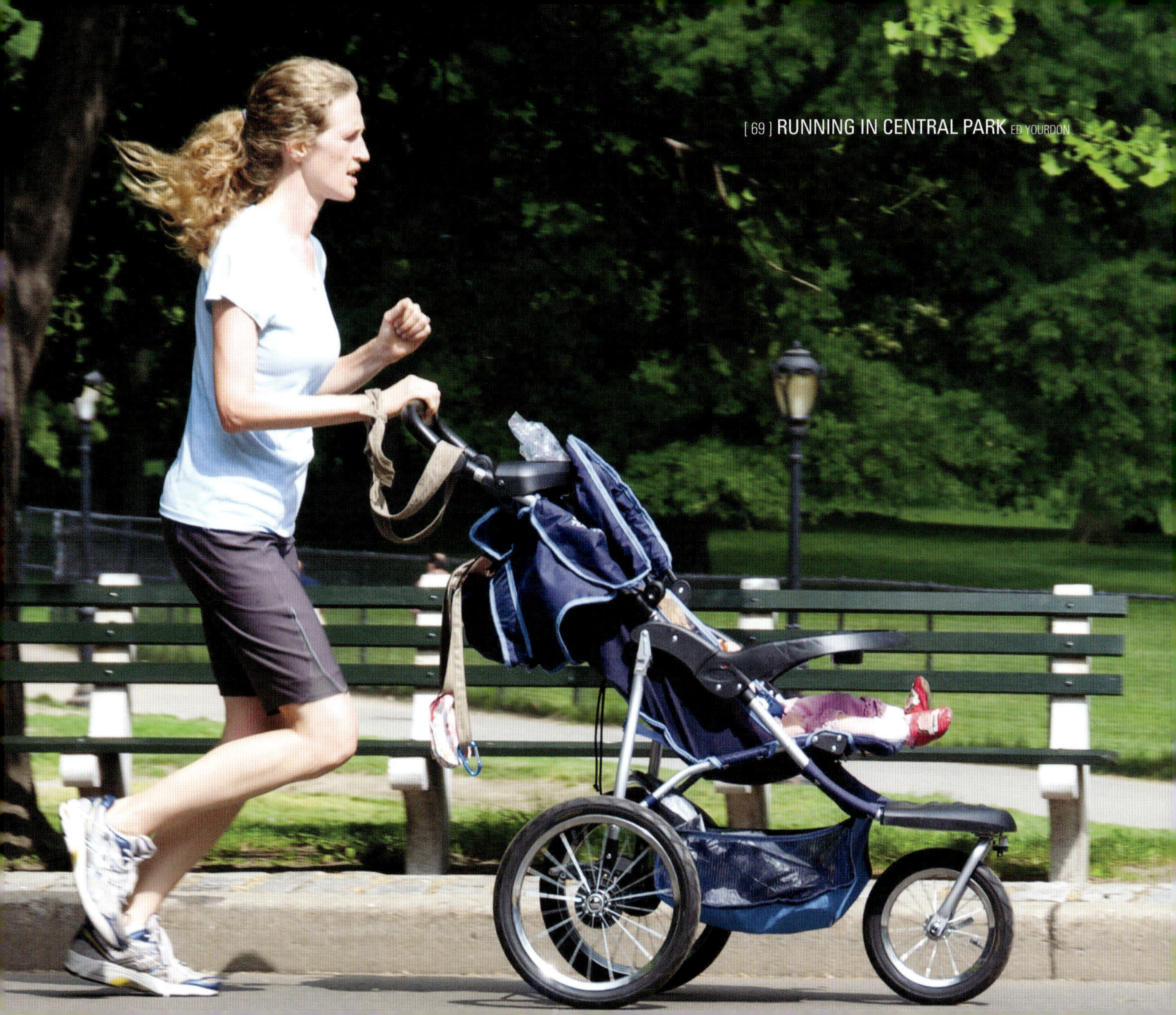

[69] RUNNING IN CENTRAL PARK ED YOURDON

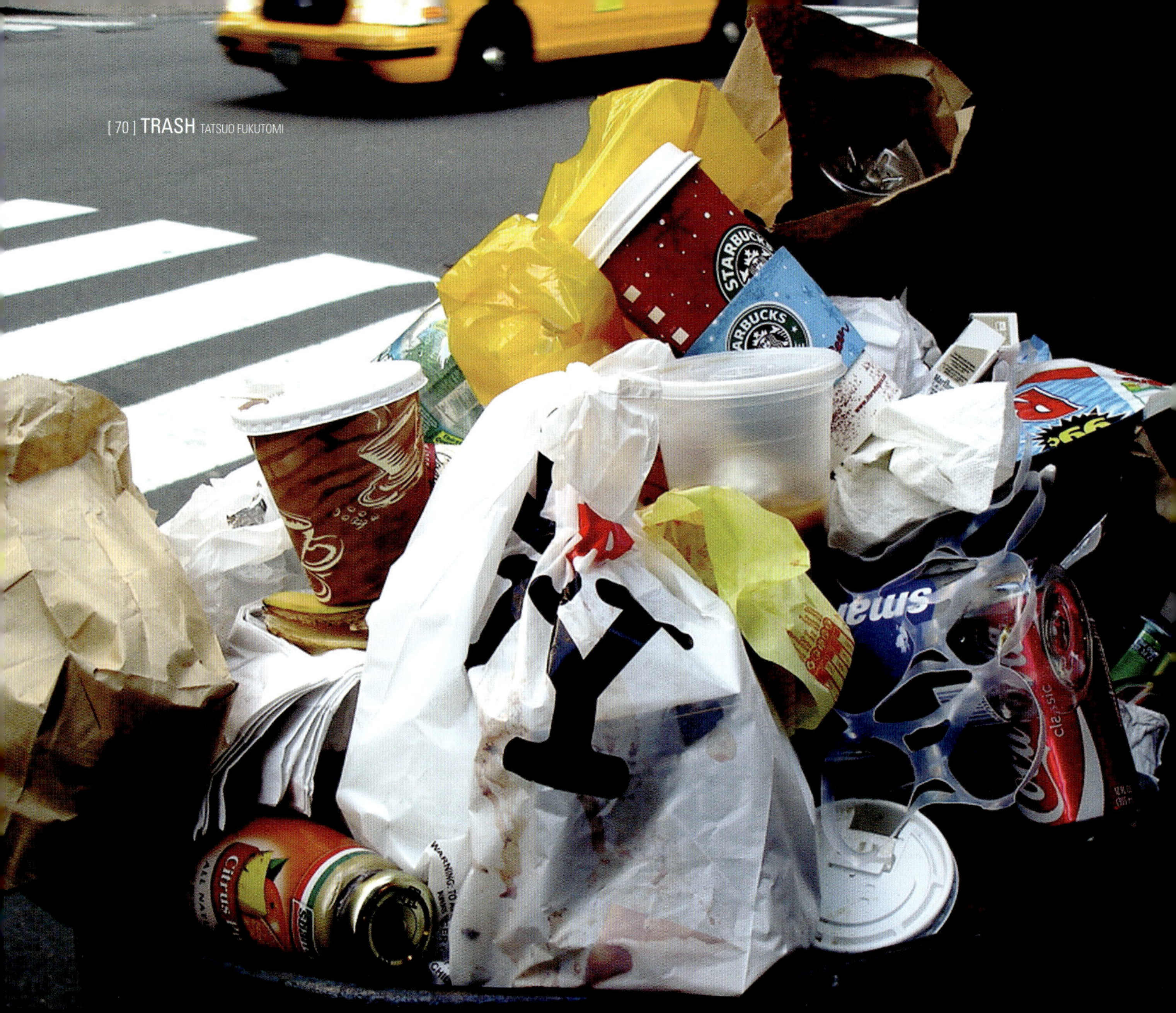
STARBUCKS
STARBUCKS
Citrus
classic

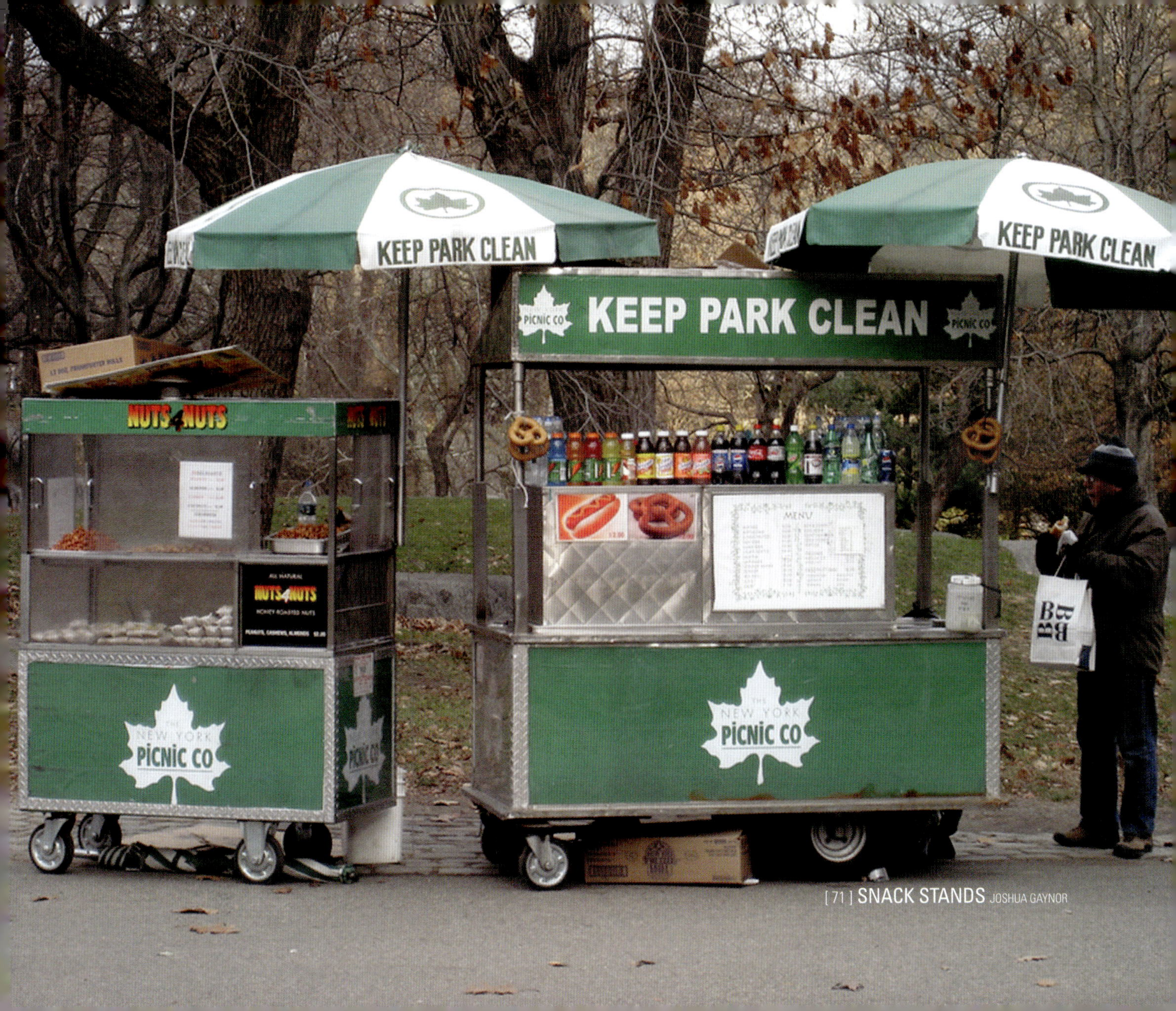

[71] SNACK STANDS JOSHUA GAYNOR

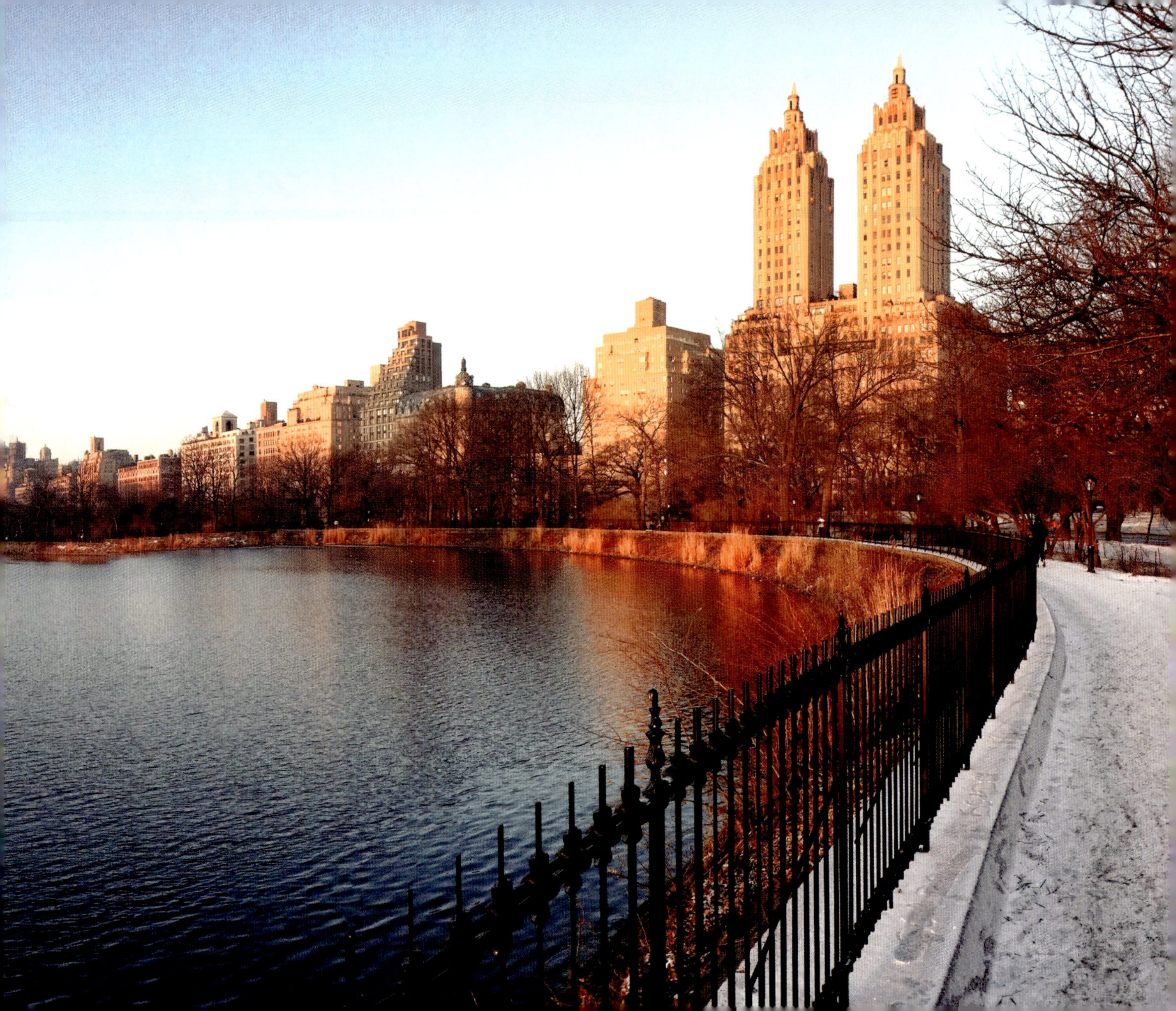

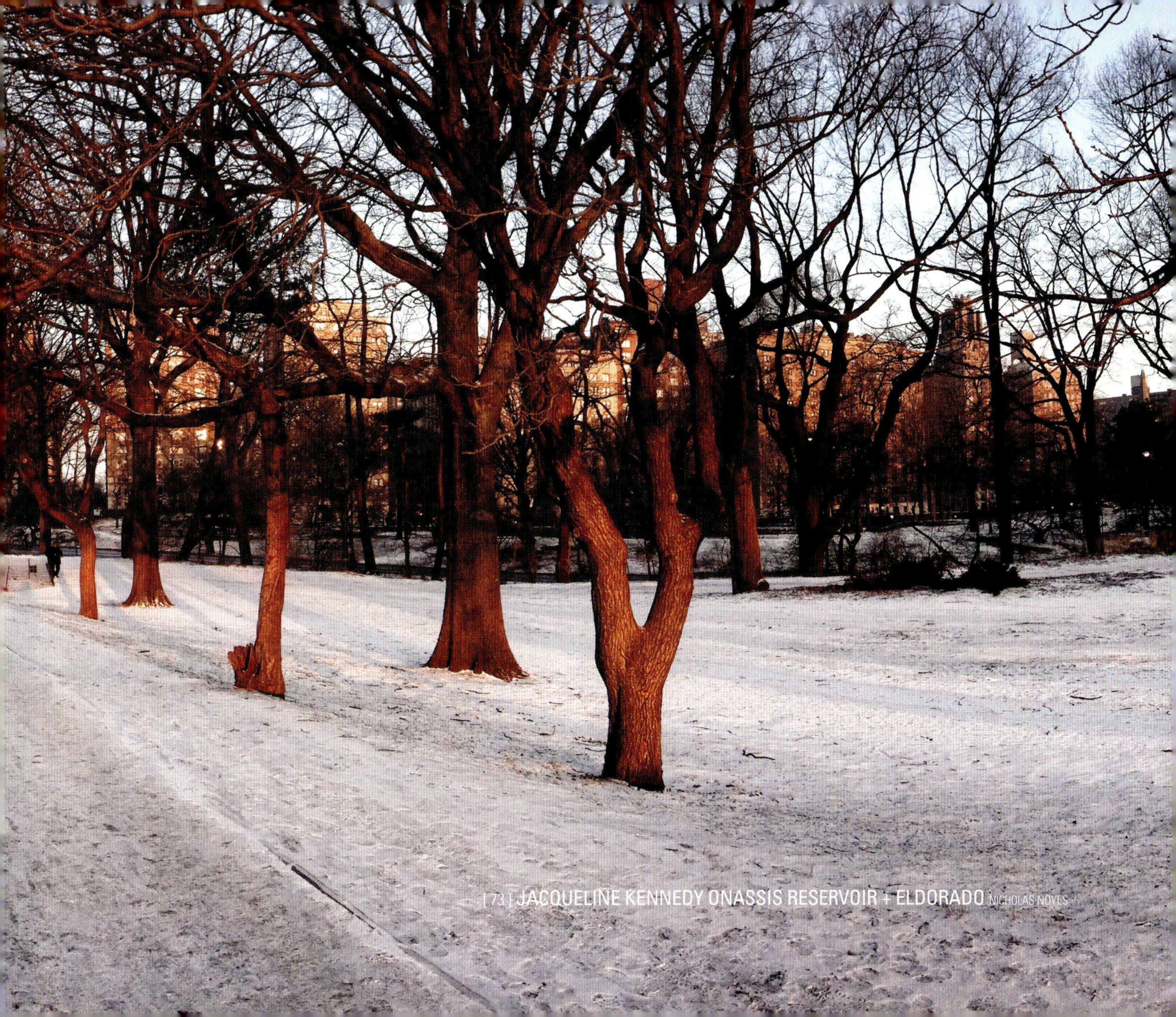

[73] JACQUELINE KENNEDY ONASSIS RESERVOIR + ELDORADO NICHOLAS NOYES

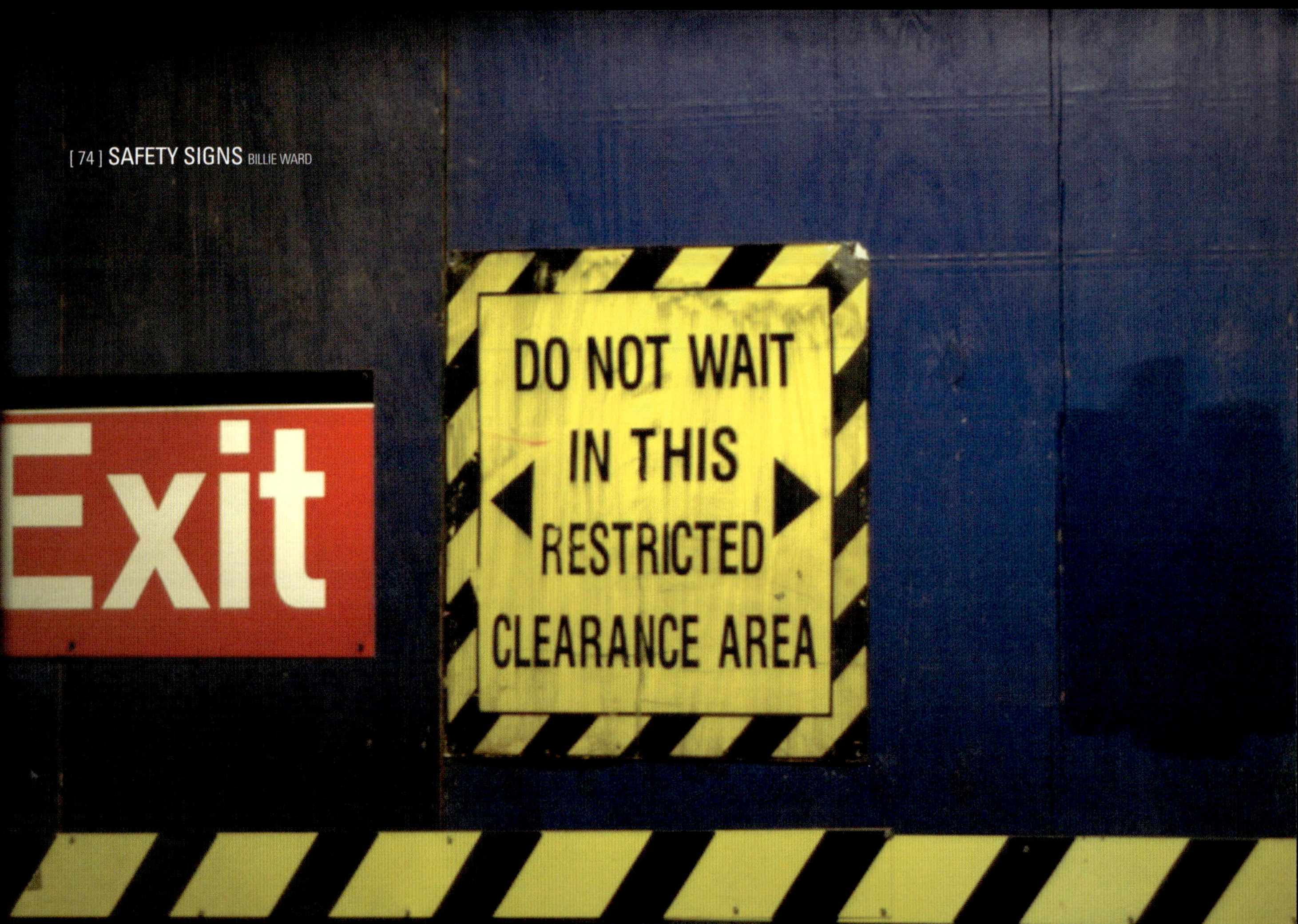
Exit
DO NOT WAIT
IN THIS
RESTRICTED
CLEARANCE AREA

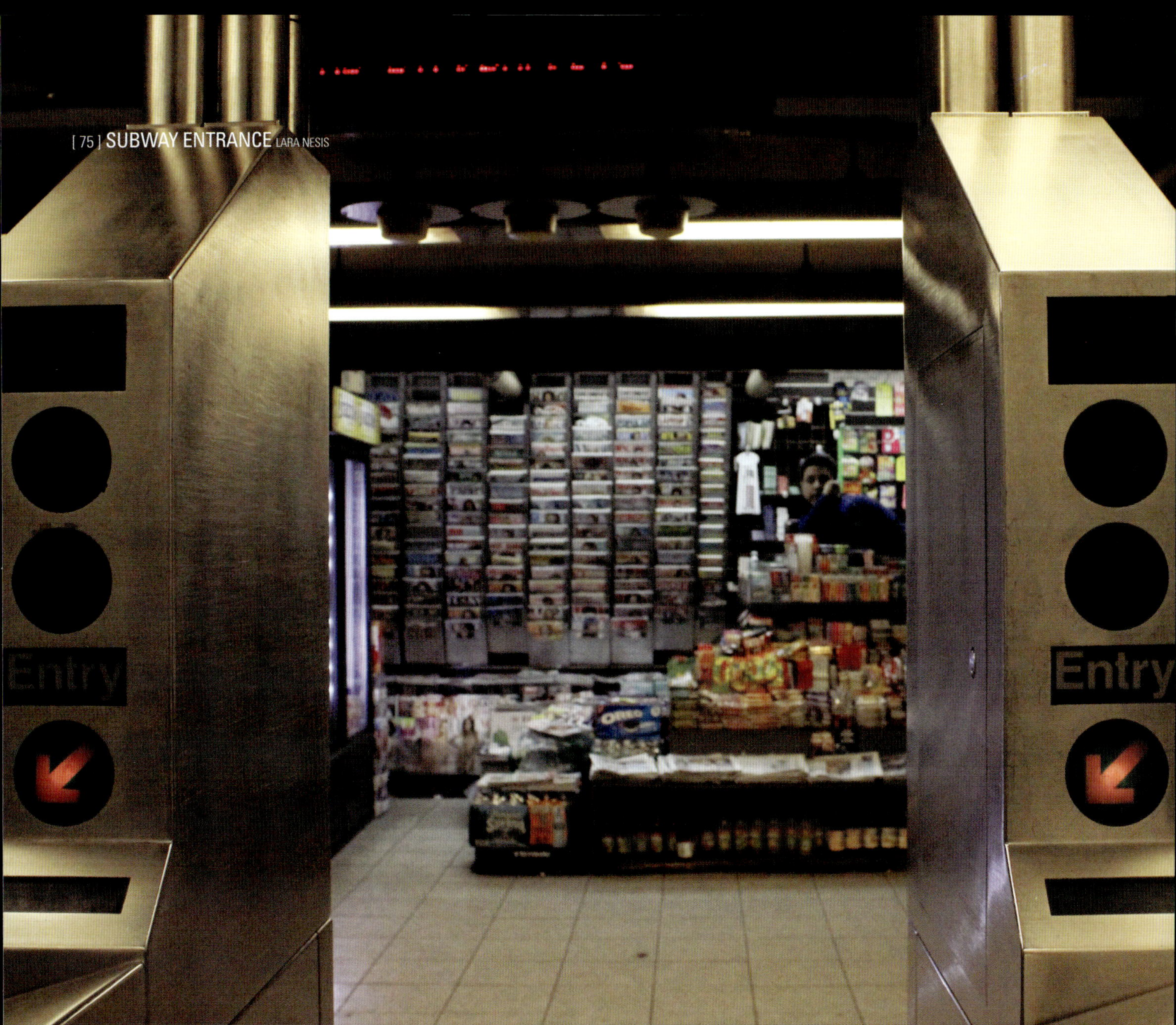

[75] SUBWAY ENTRANCE LARA NESIS

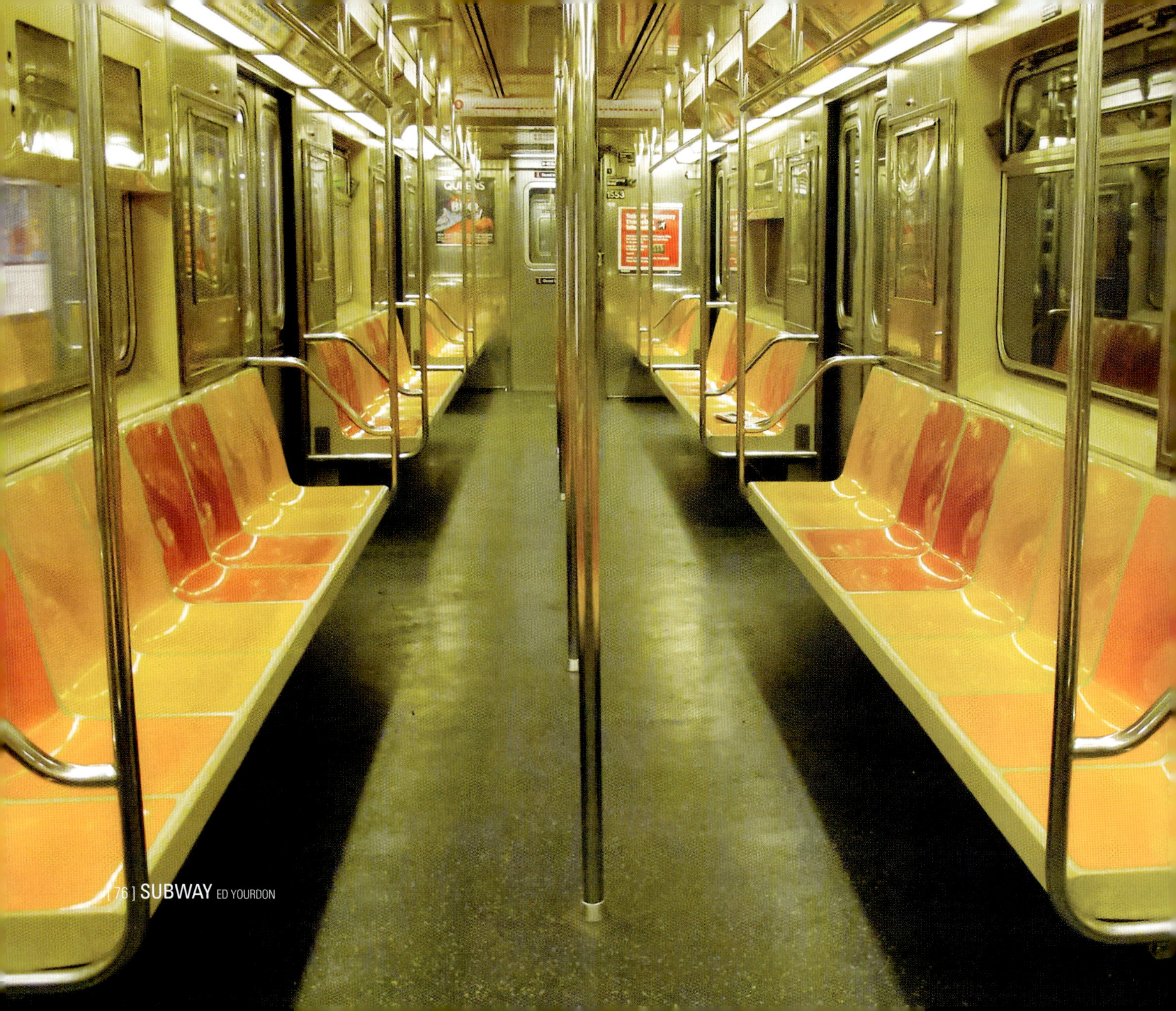

 SUBWAY ED YOURDON

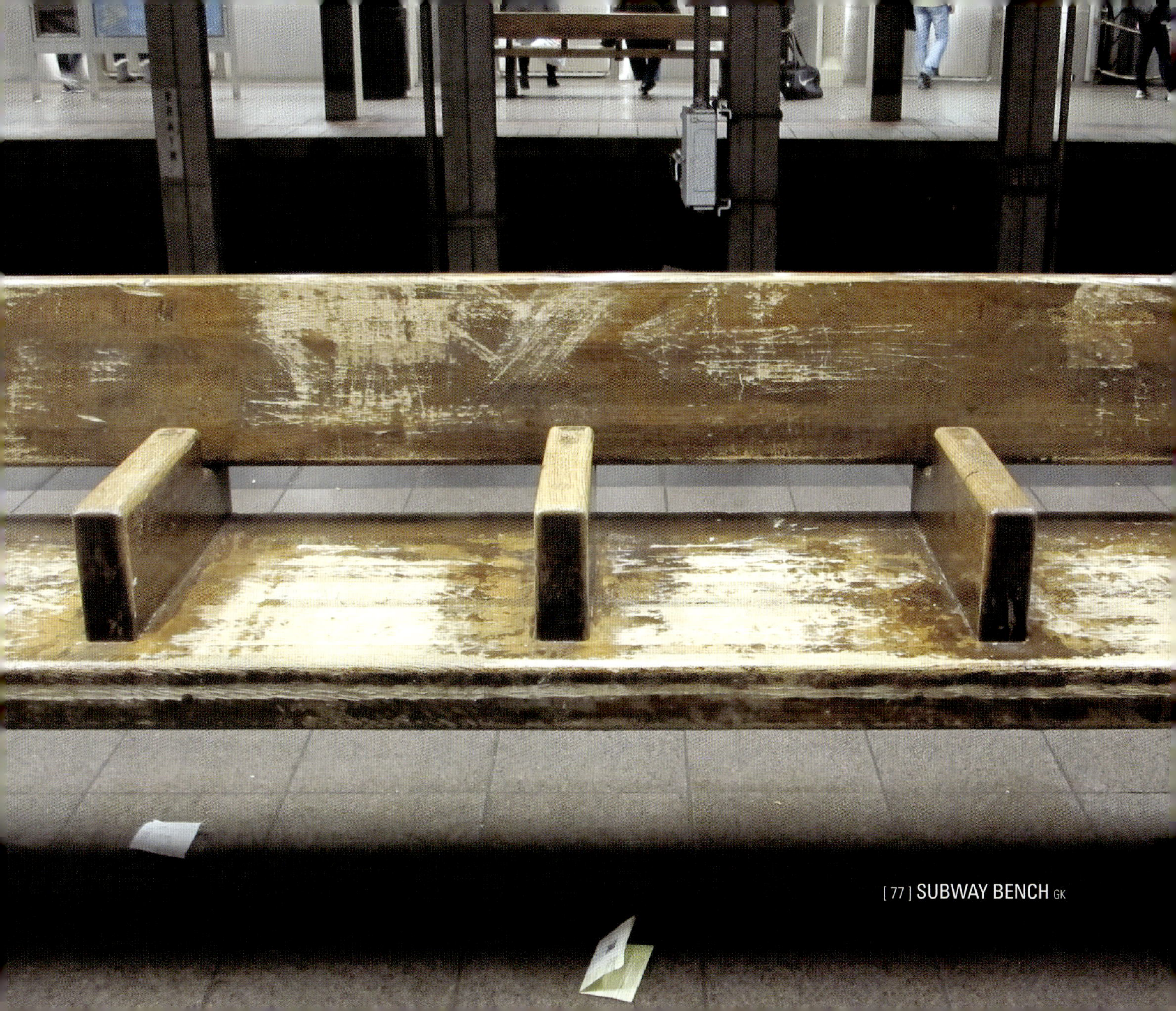

[77] SUBWAY BENCH GK

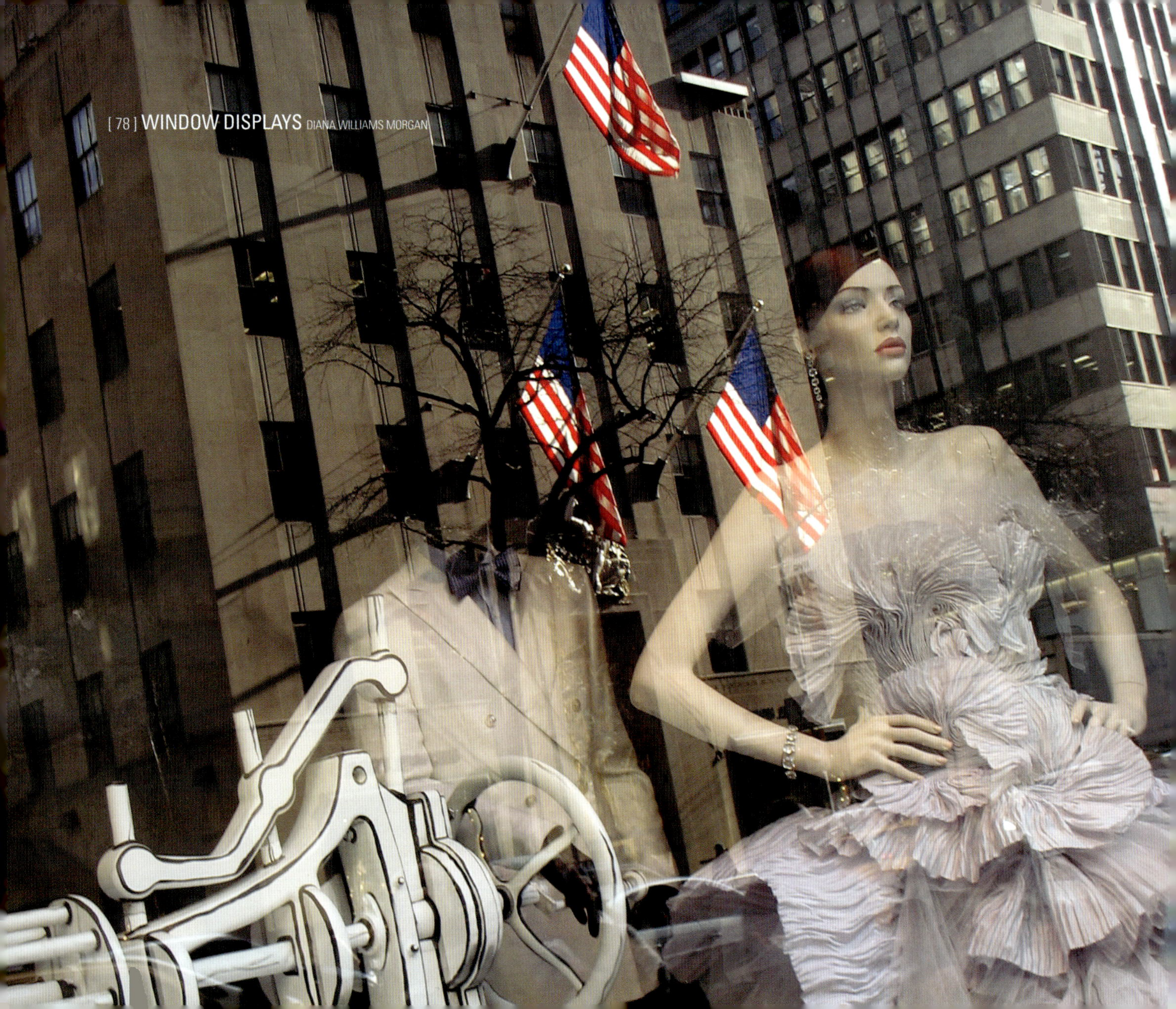

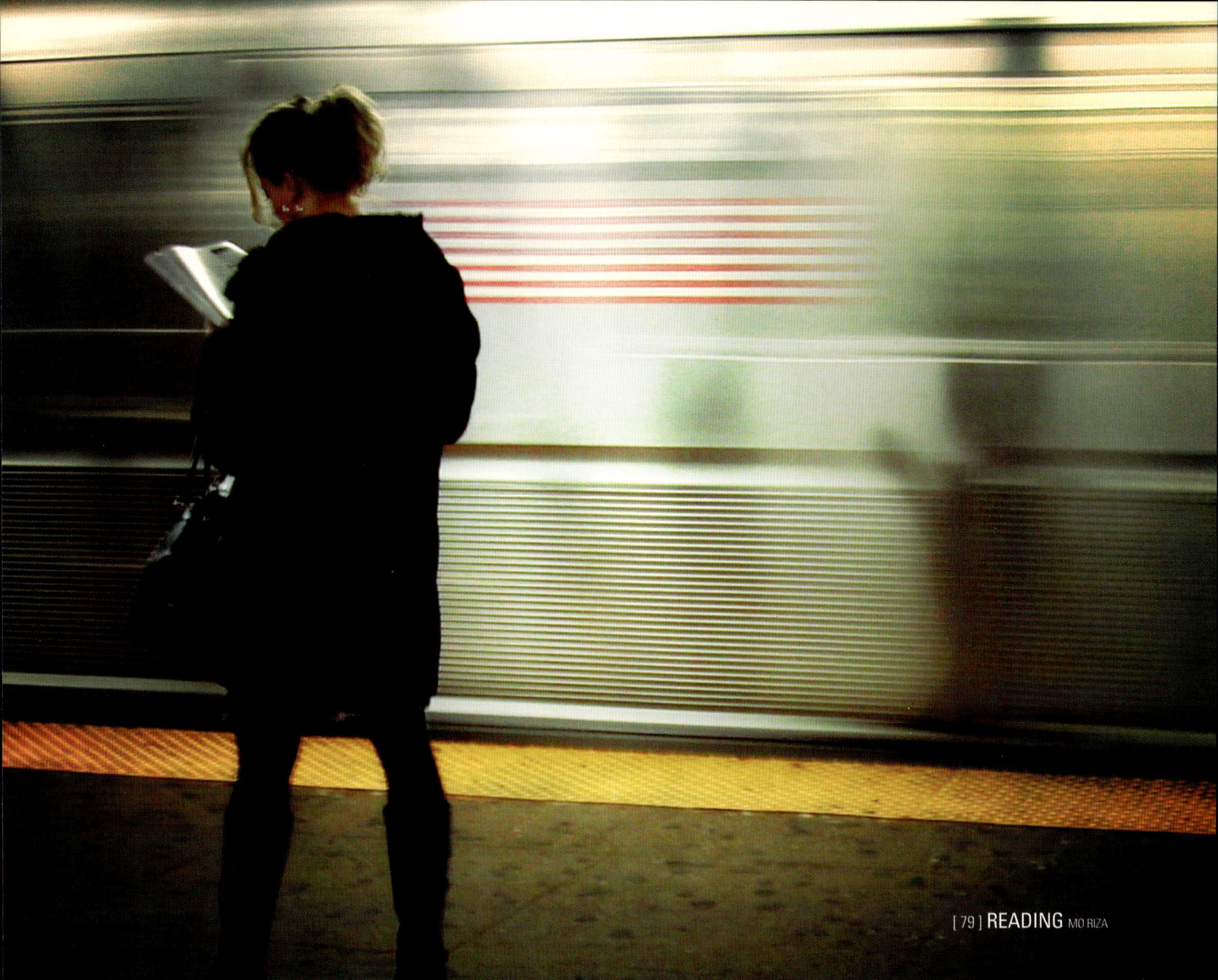

[79] **READING** MO RIZA

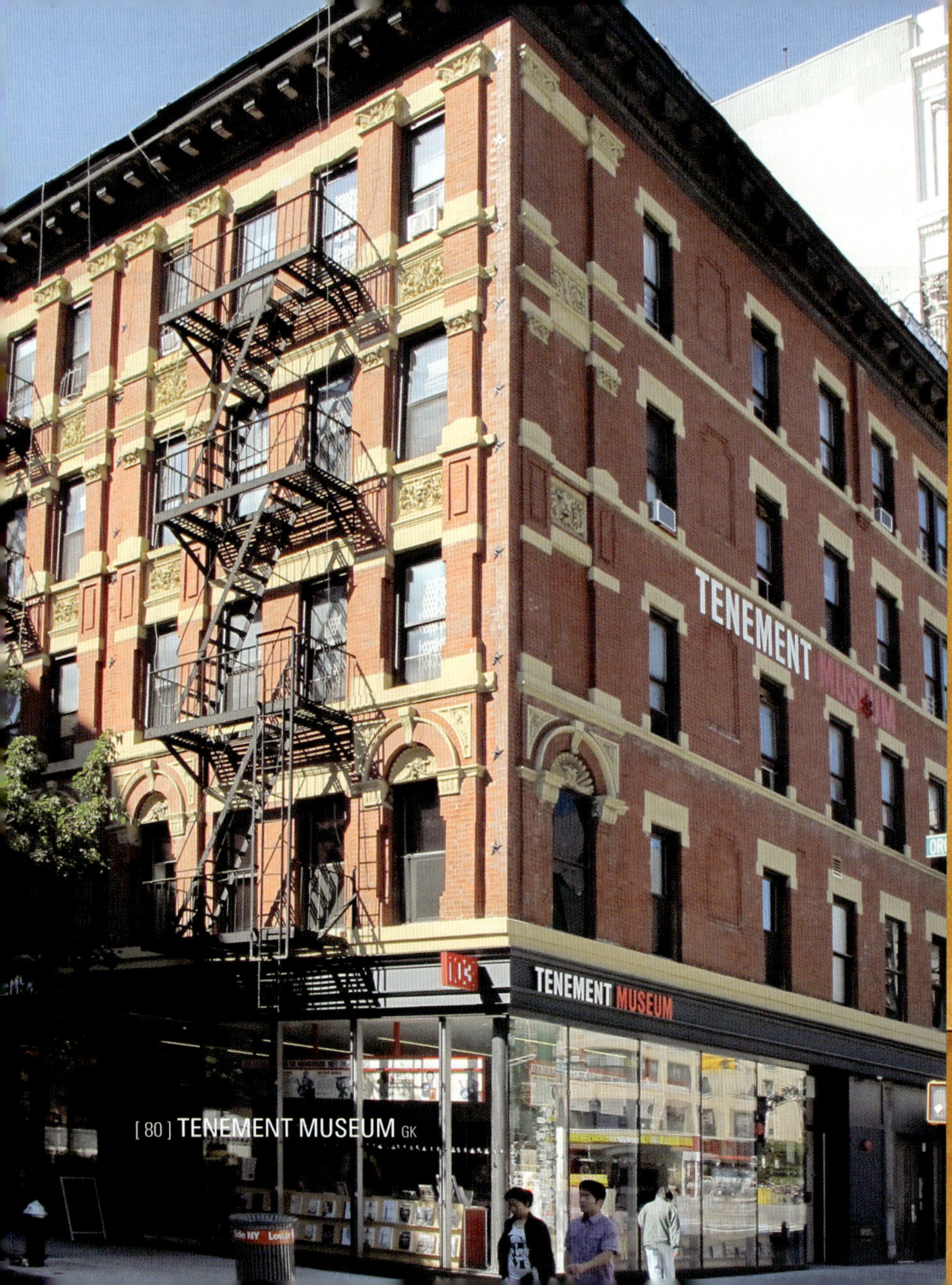

[80] TENEMENT MUSEUM GK

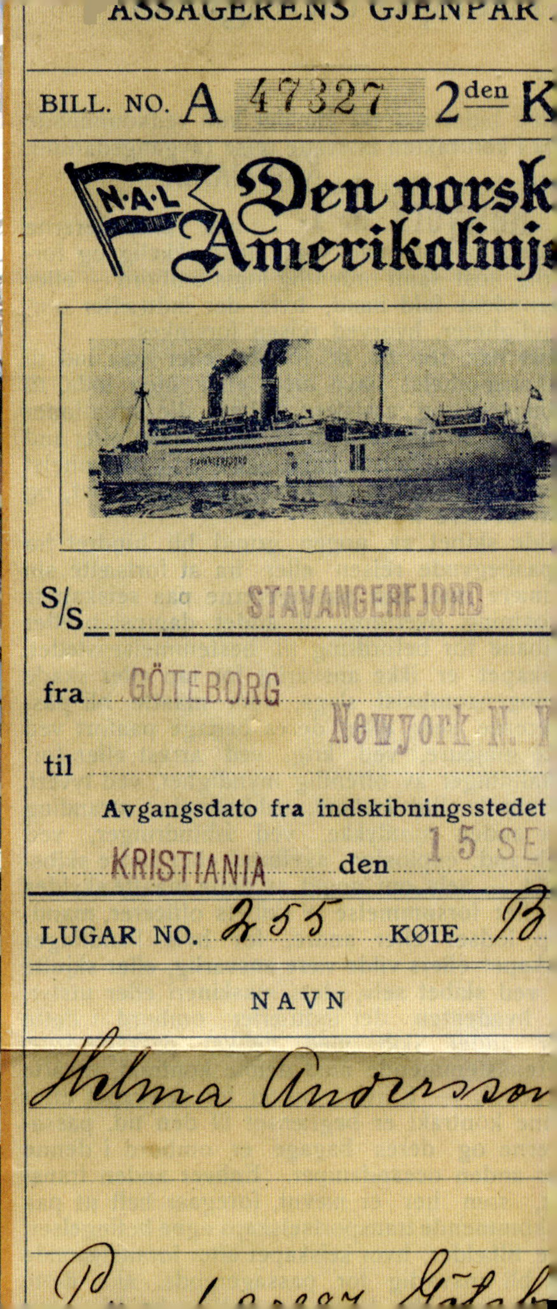

ASSAGERENS GJENPAR

BILL. NO. A 47327 2den K

N·A·L Den norsk Amerikalinje

S/S STAVANGERFJORD

fra GÖTEBORG

til Newyork N. Y

Avgangsdato fra indskibningsstedet

KRISTIANIA den 15 SE

LUGAR NO. 255 KØIE B

NAVN

Hilma Andersson

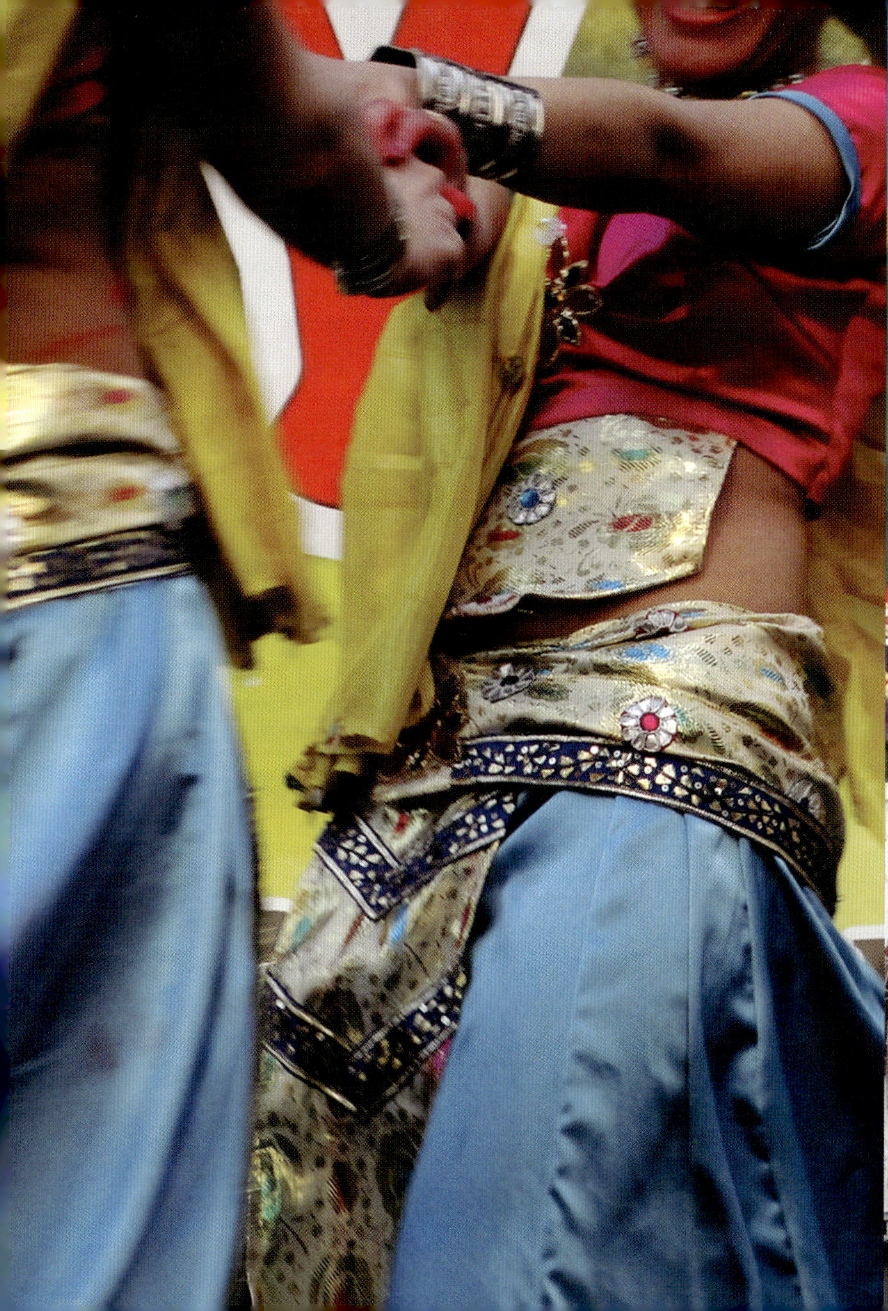

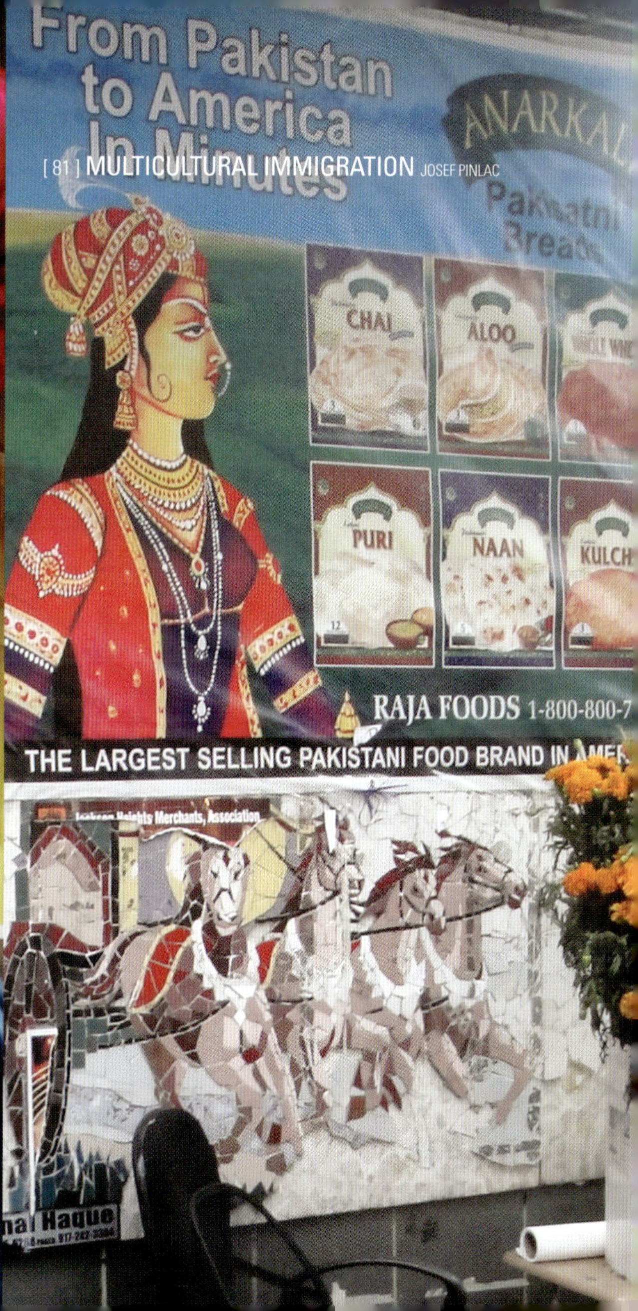
From Pakistan
to America
In Minutes
CHAI
ALOO
PURI
NAAN
RAJA FOODS

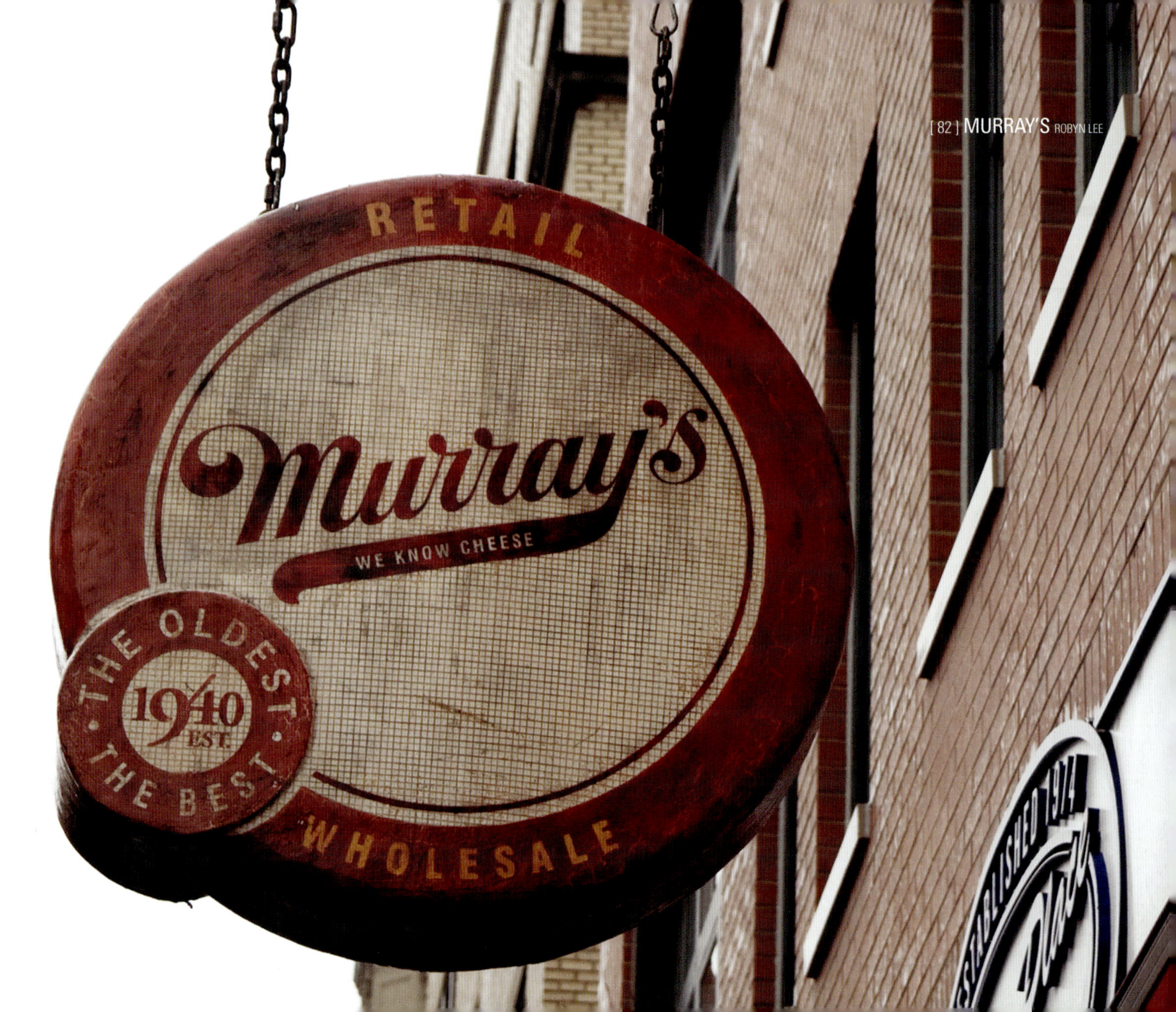

[82] MURRAY'S ROBYN LEE

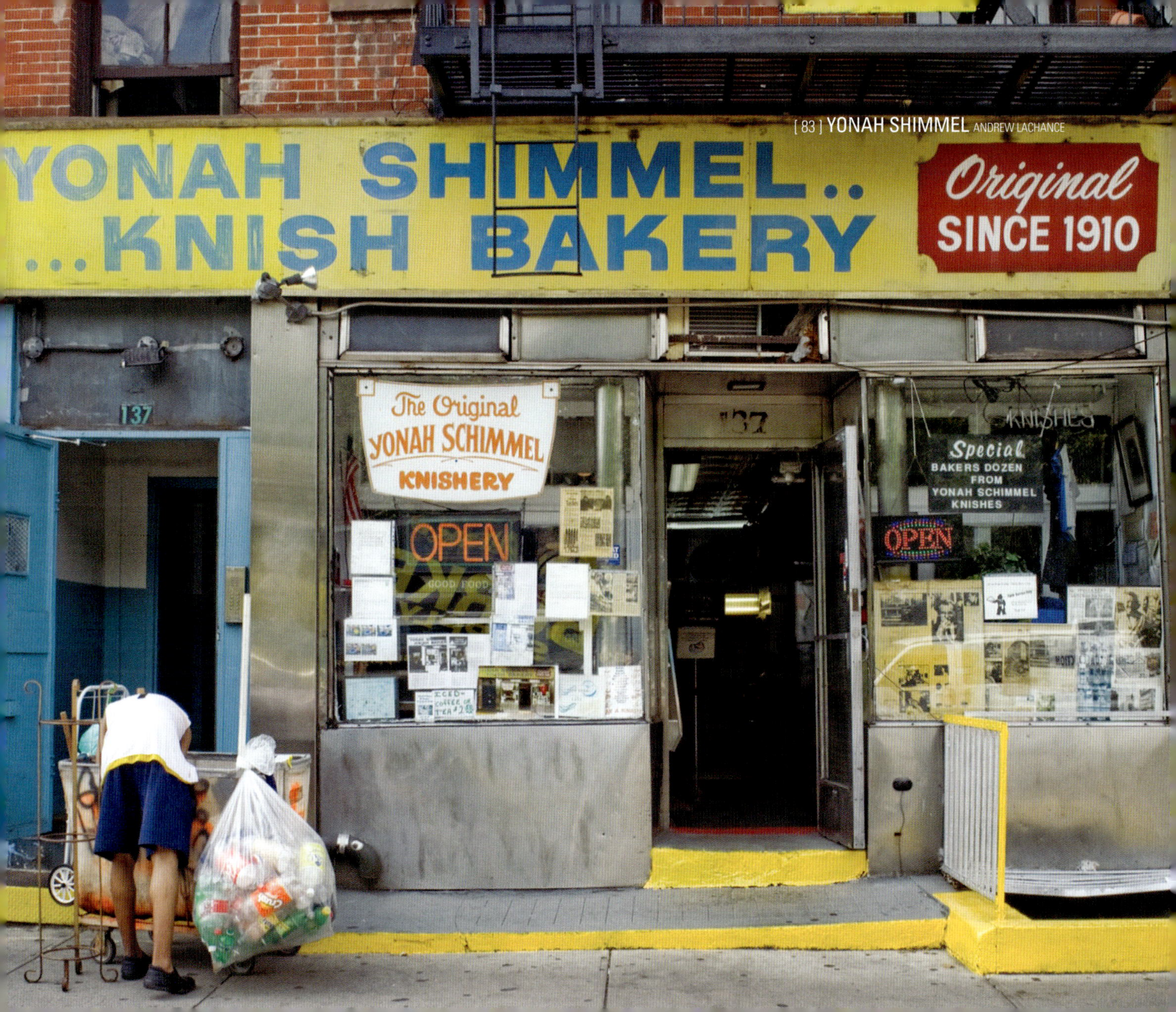

[83] YONAH SHIMMEL ANDREW LACHANCE

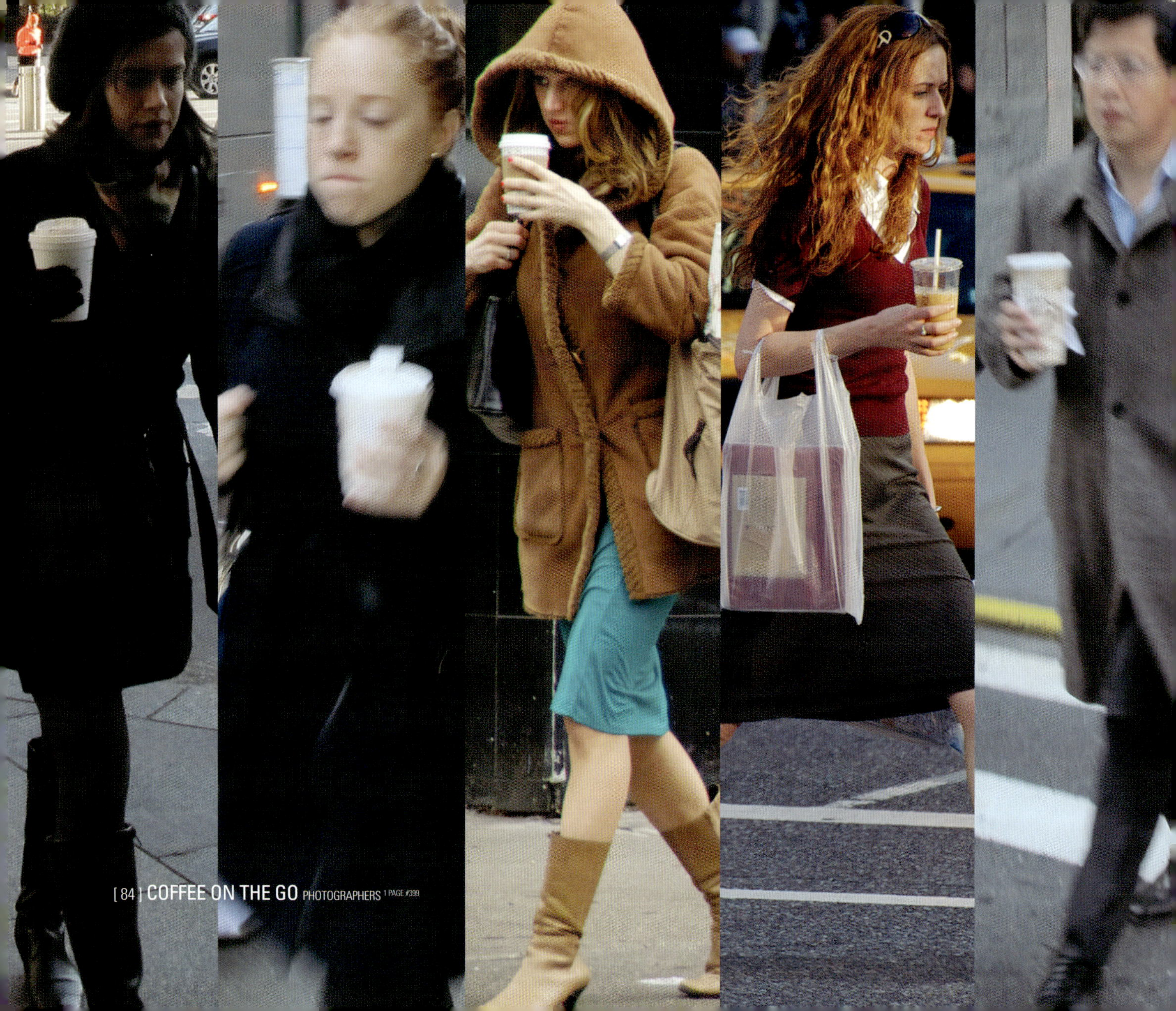

[84] COFFEE ON THE GO PHOTOGRAPHERS [1] PAGE #399

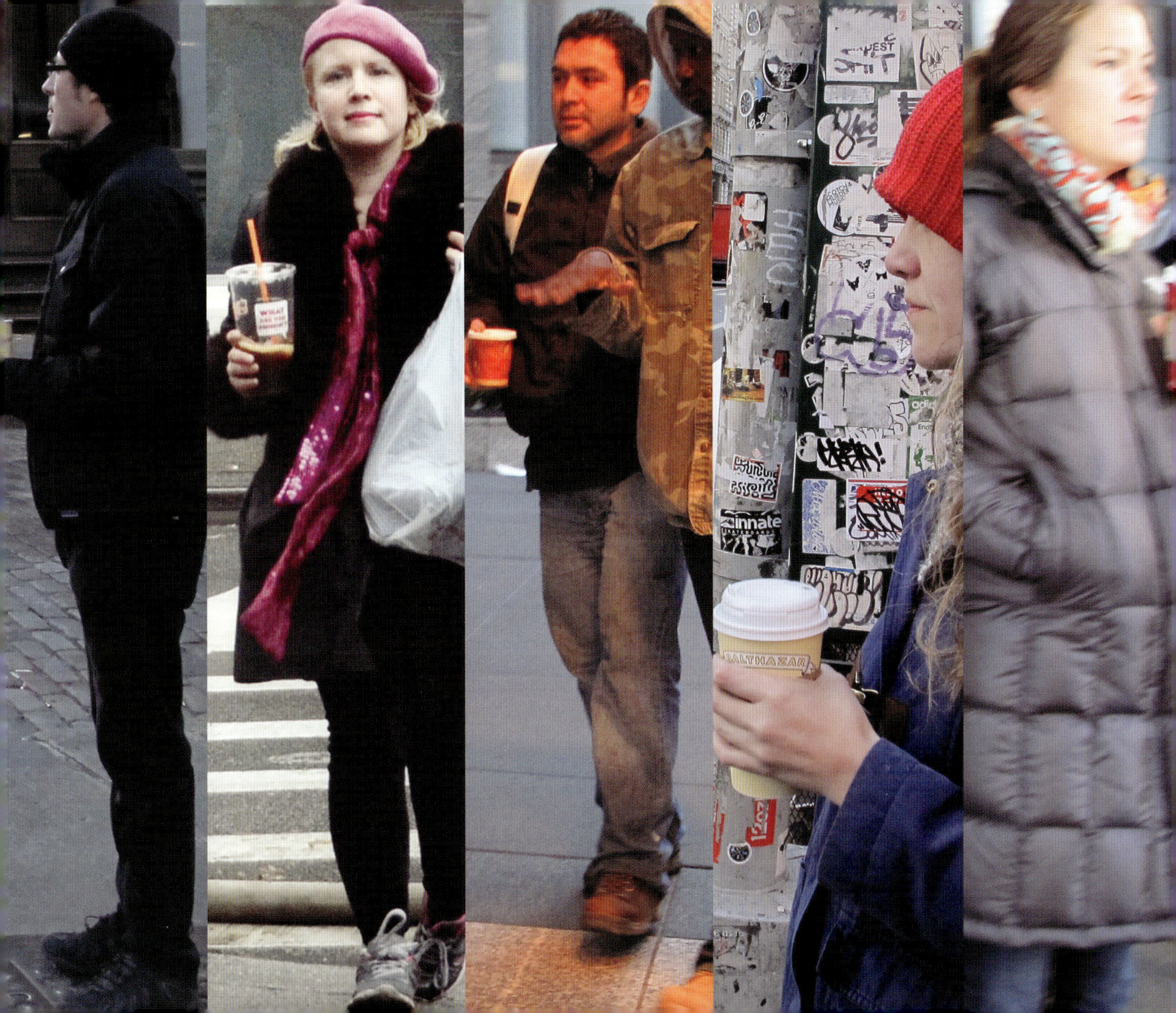
innate

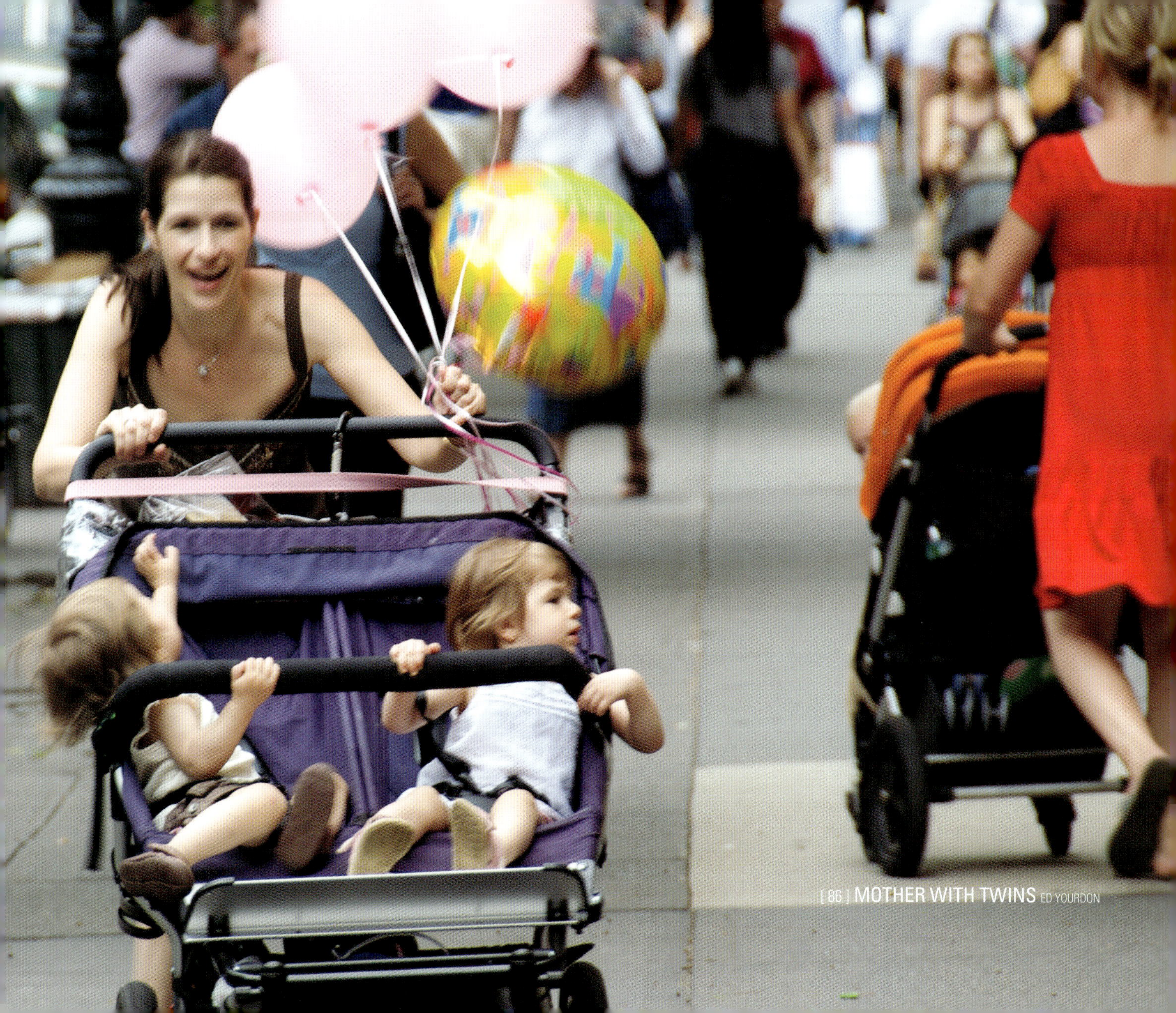

[86] MOTHER WITH TWINS ED YOURDON

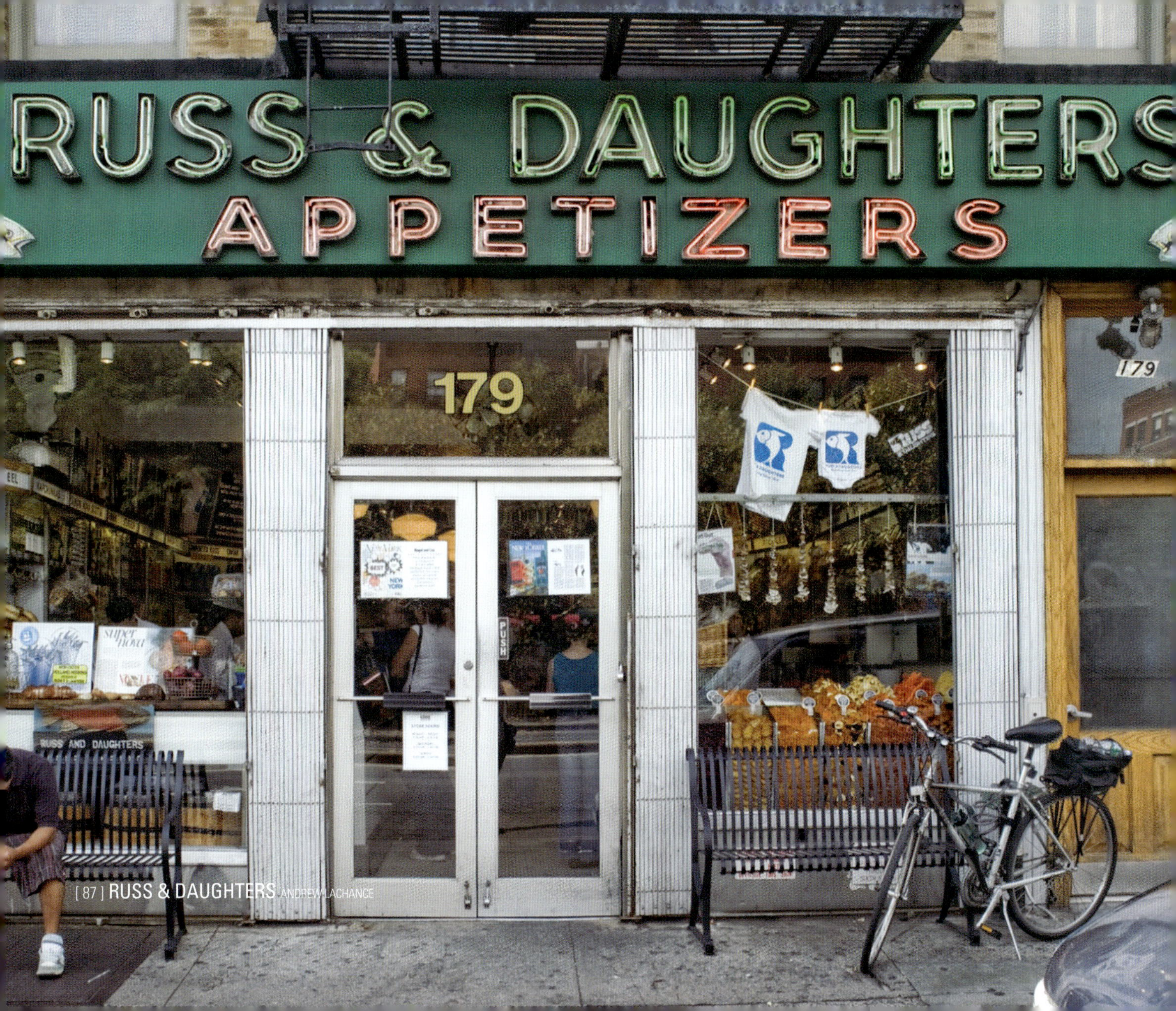

[87] RUSS & DAUGHTERS ANDREW LACHANCE

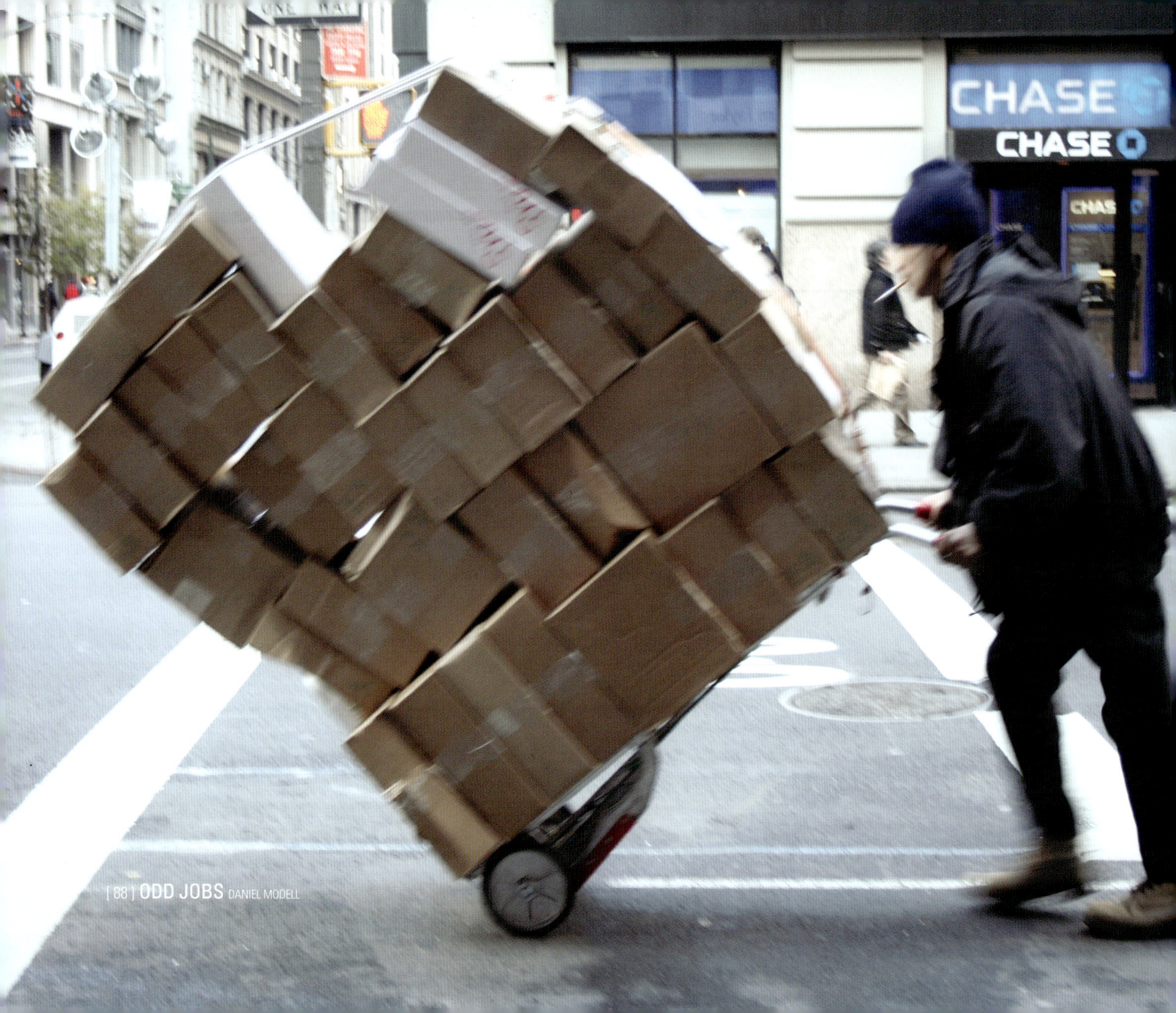
CHASE
CHASE

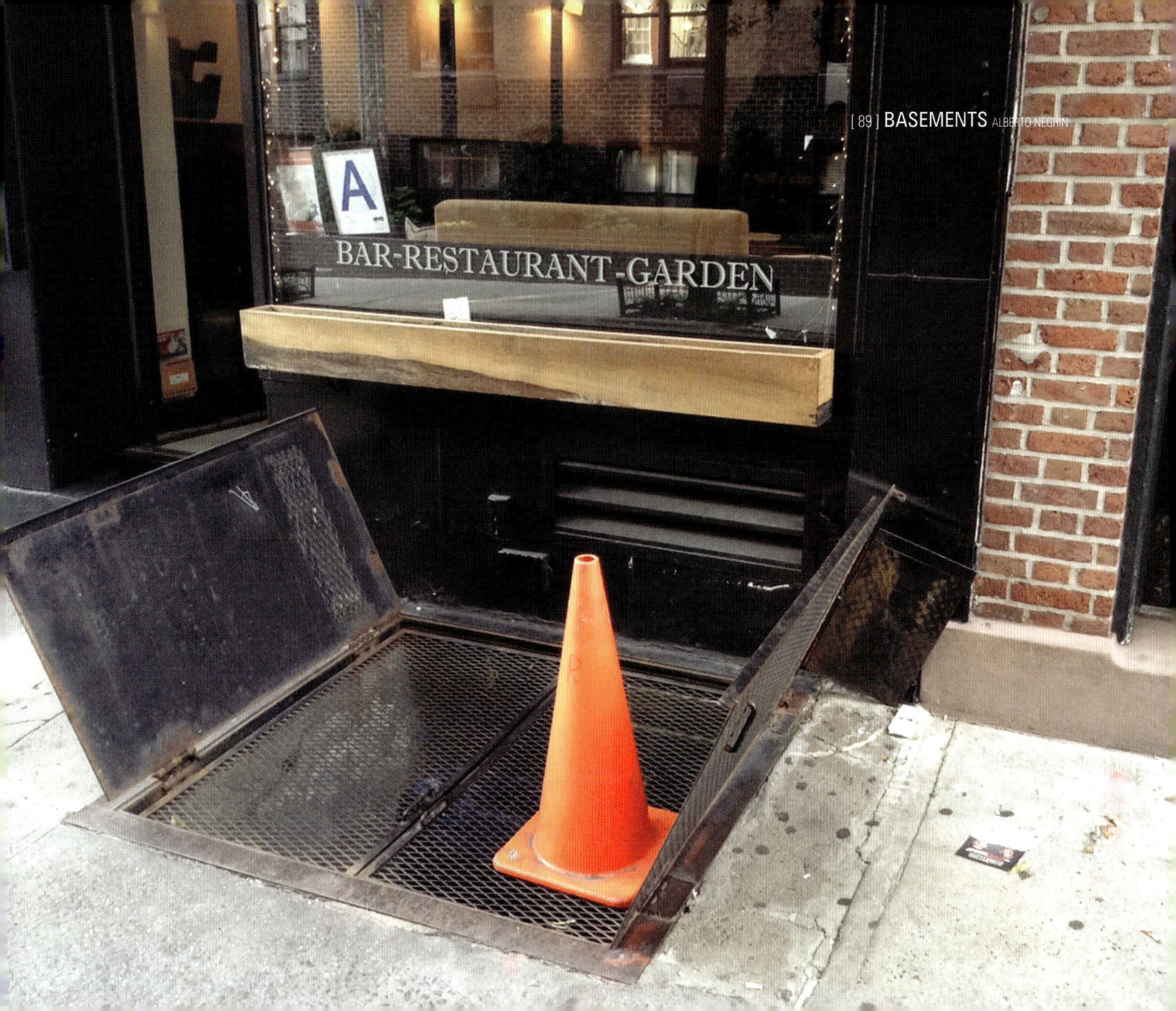
A
BAR-RESTAURANT-GARDEN

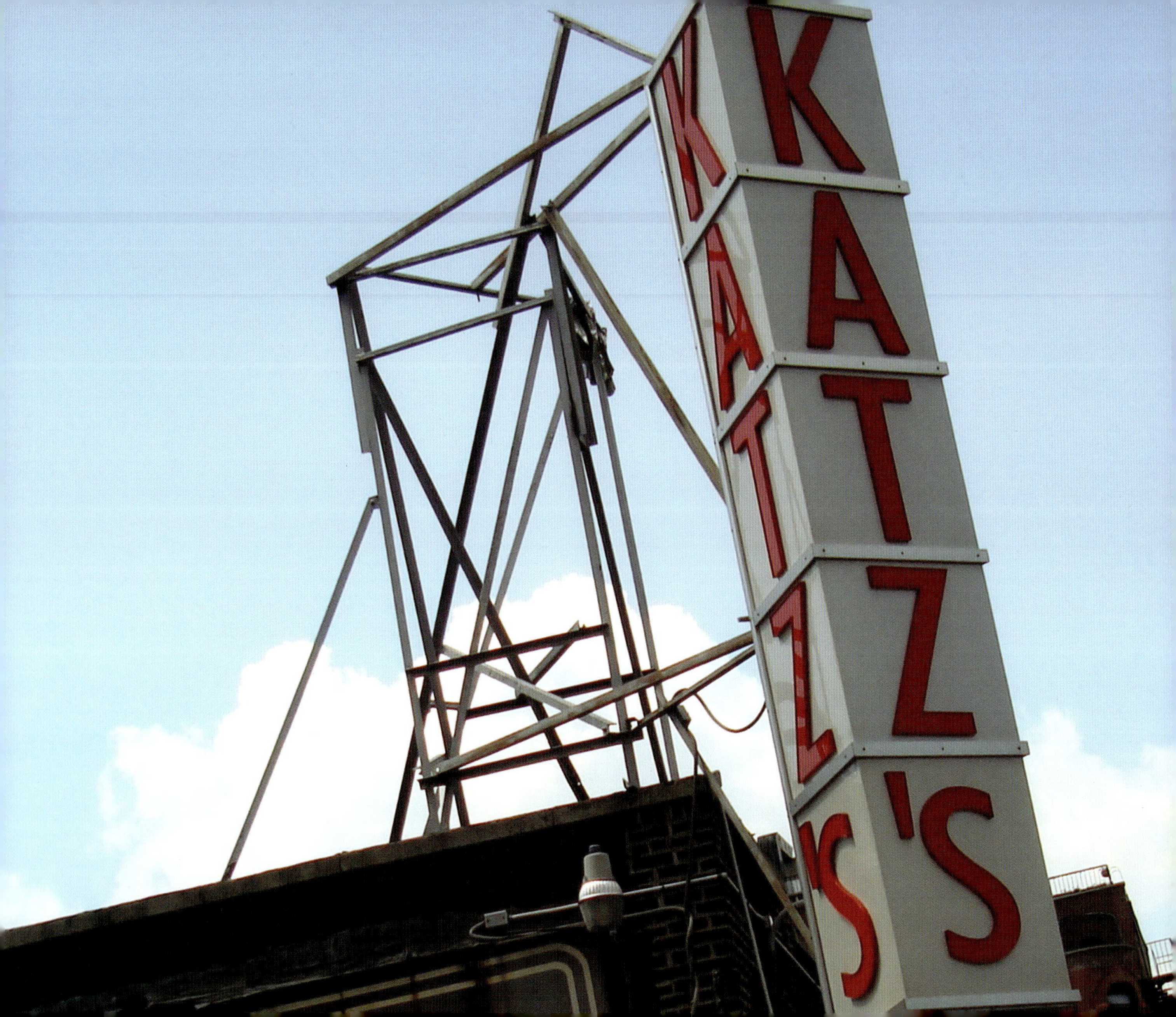
KATZ'S

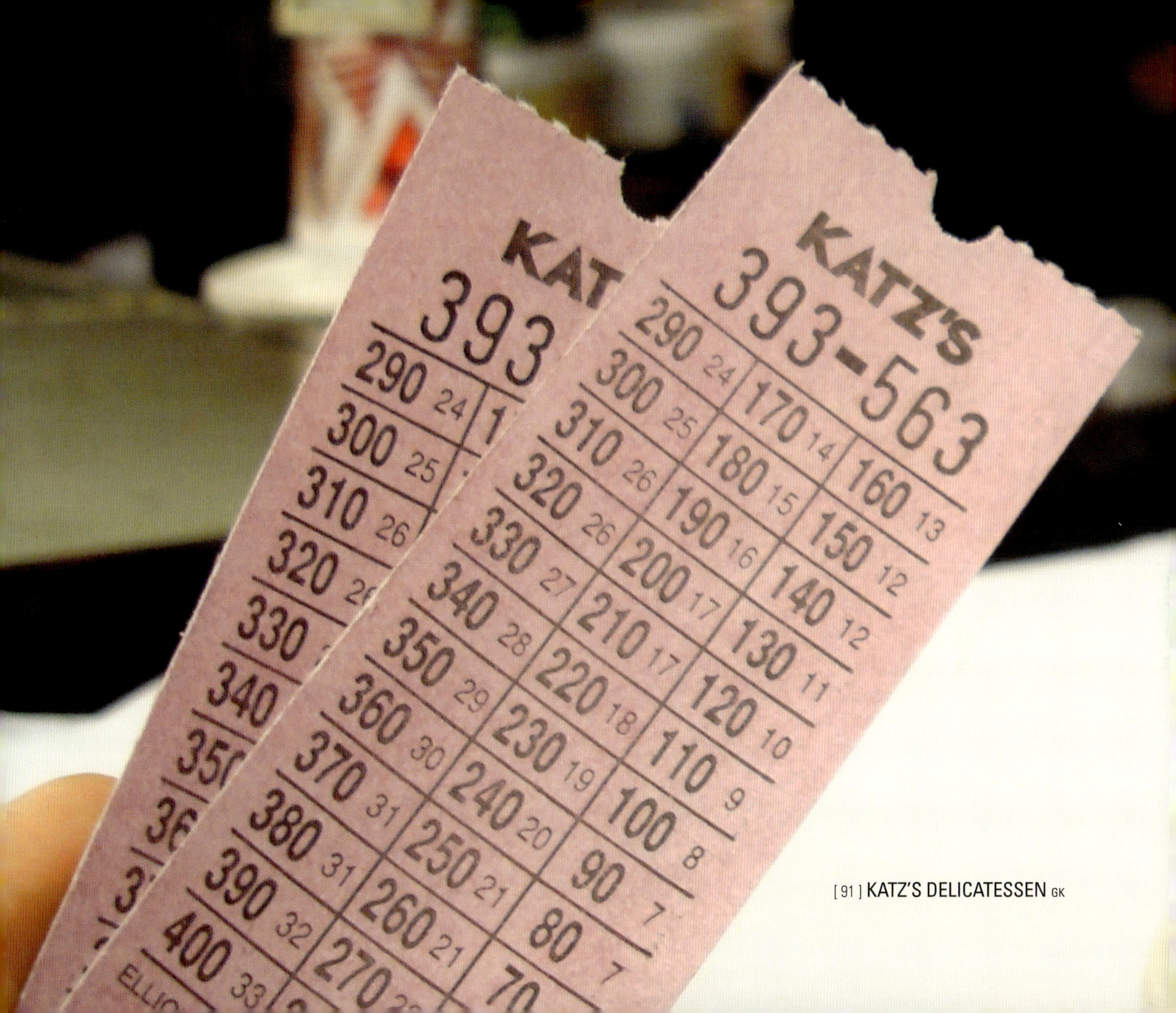

[91] KATZ'S DELICATESSEN GK

[92] WILLIAMSBURG BRIDGE GK

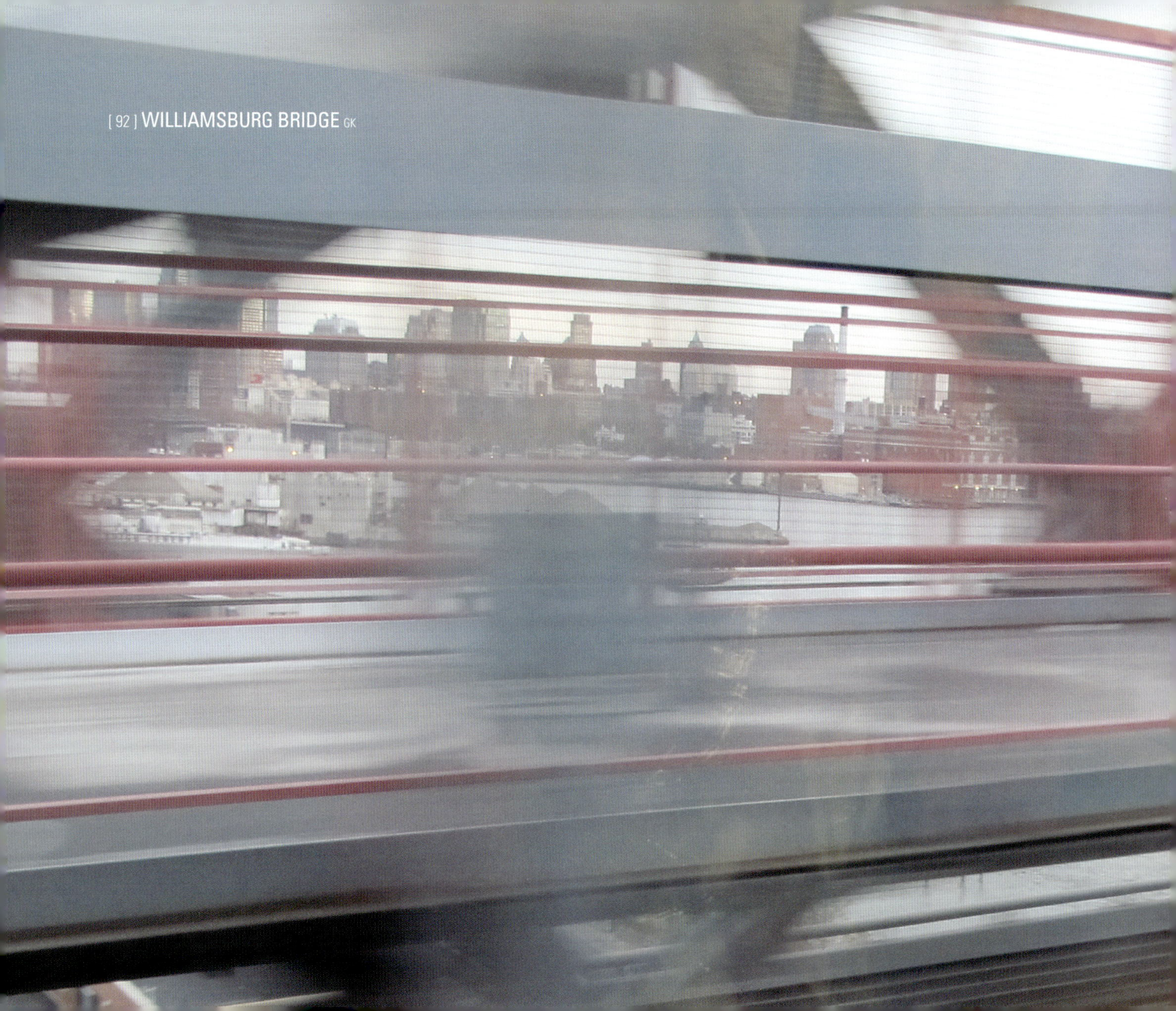

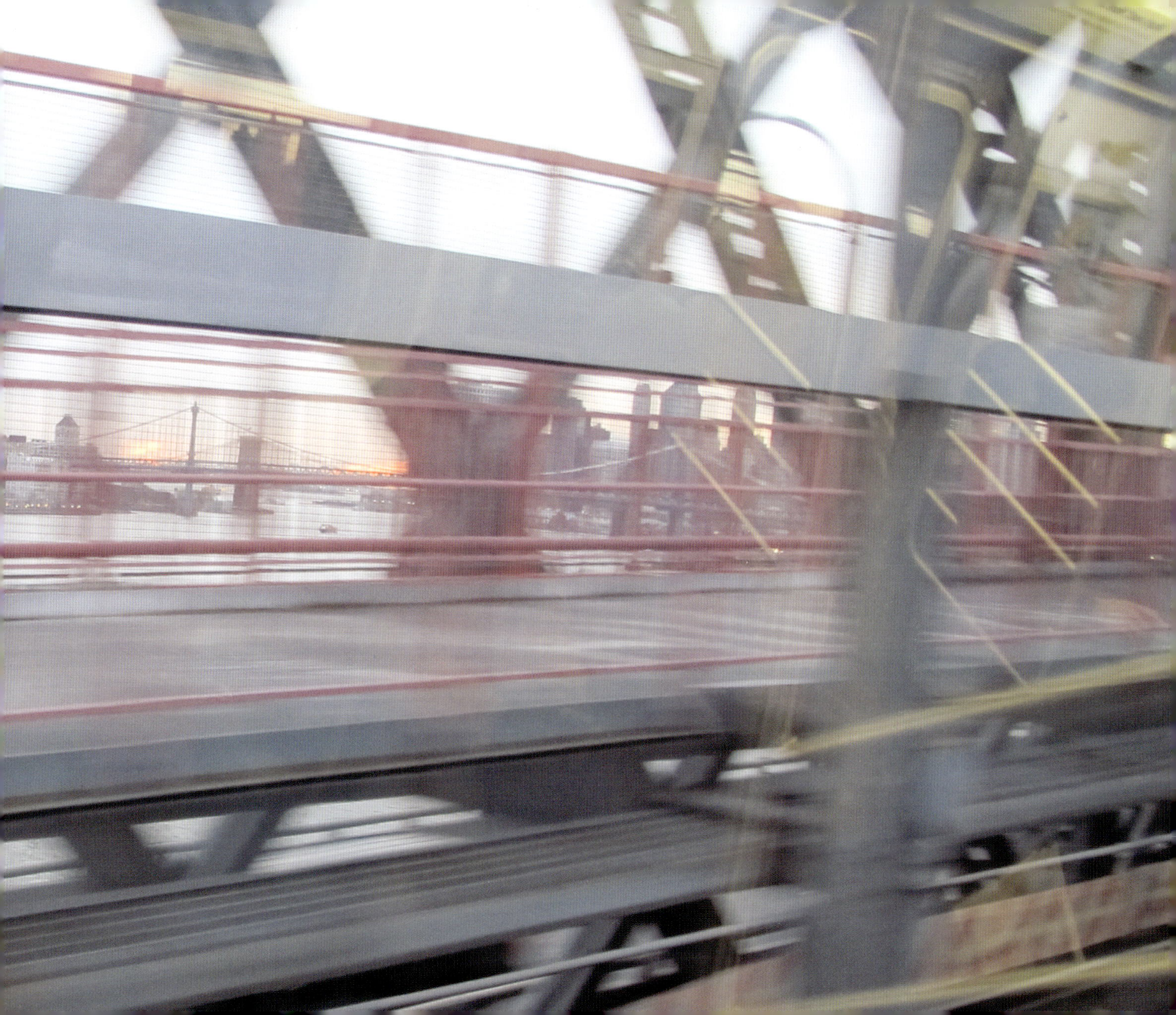

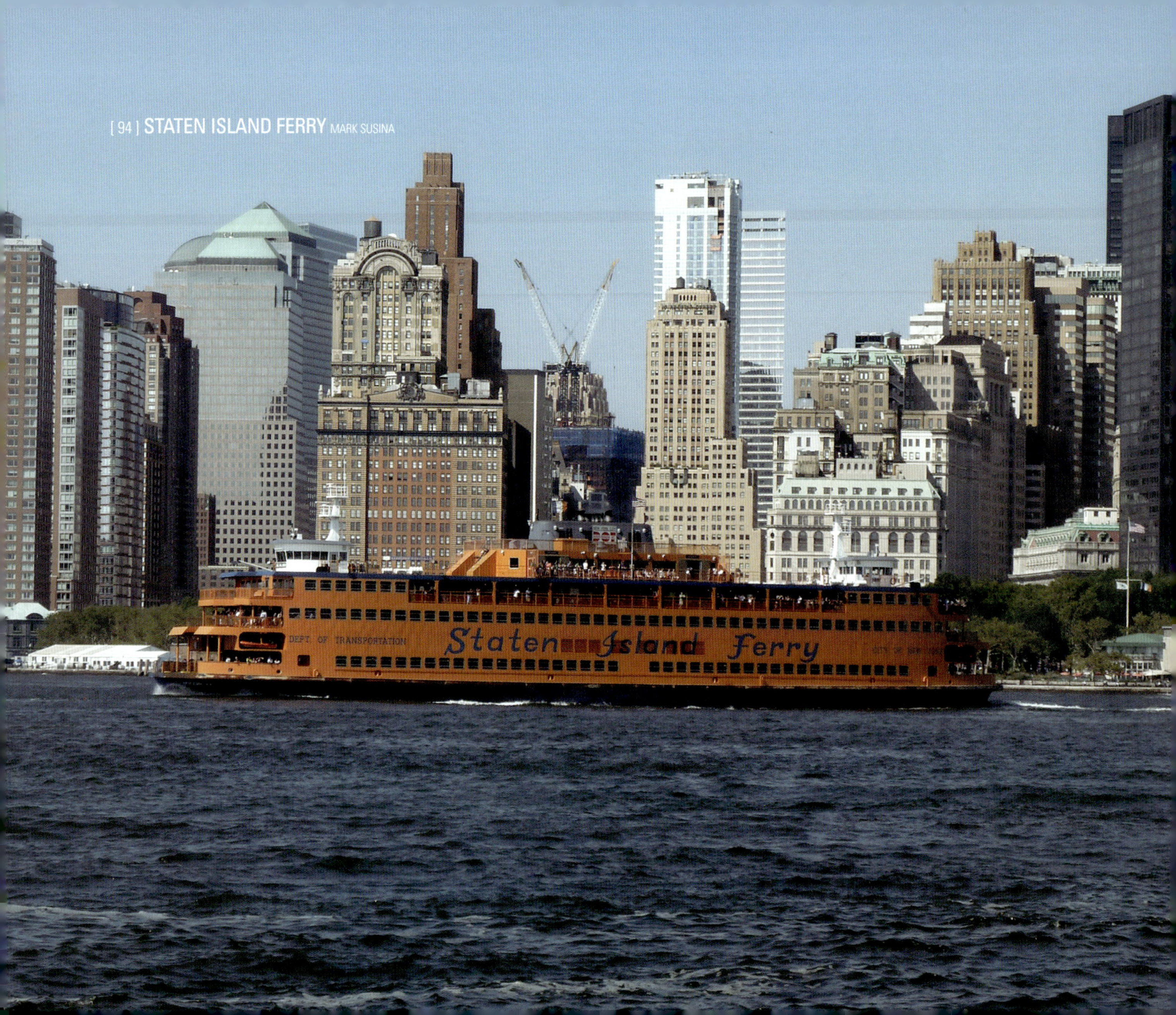

[94] STATEN ISLAND FERRY MARK SUSINA

[95] PHOTOGRAPHING MANHATTAN CLAY WILLIAMS

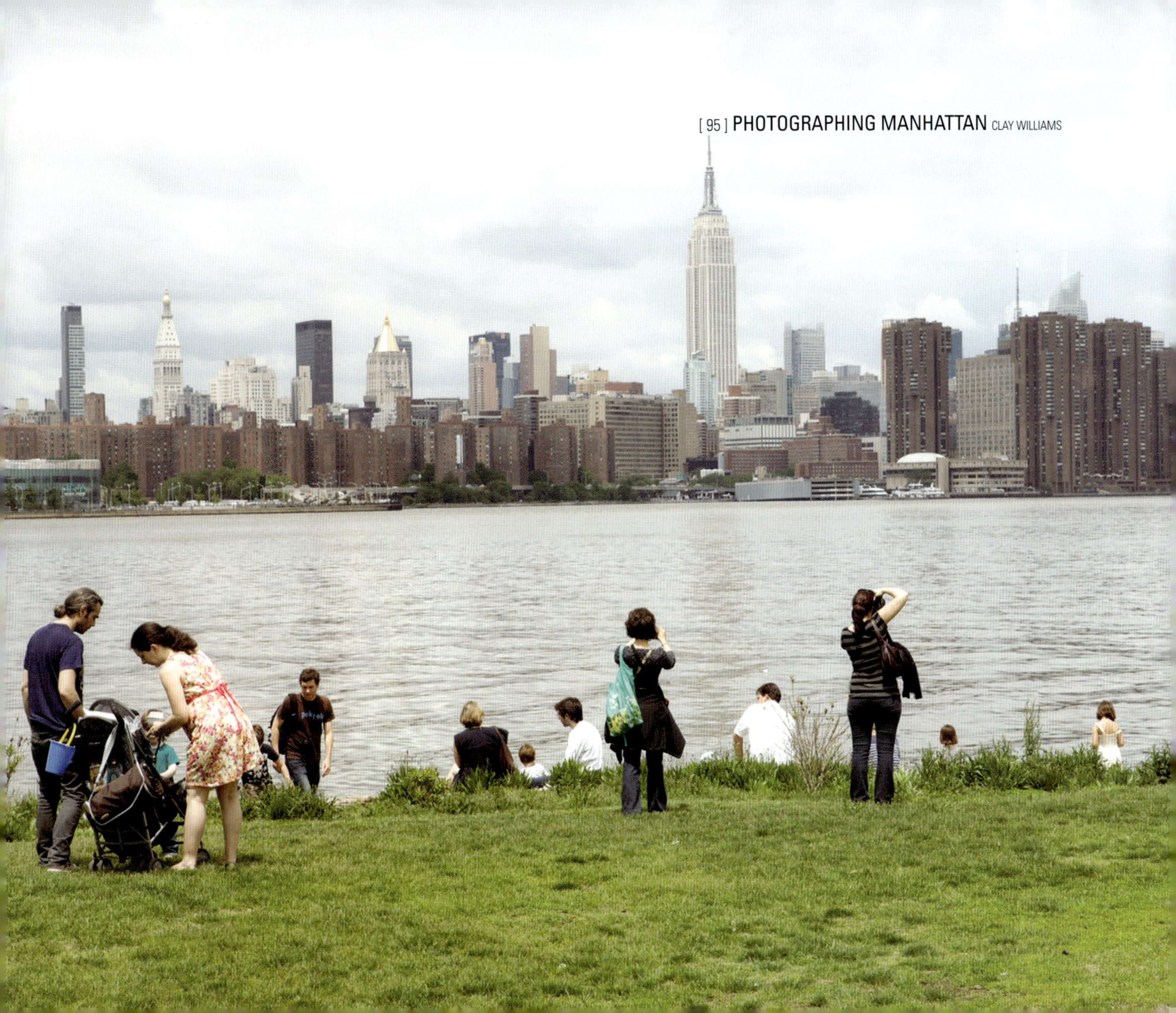

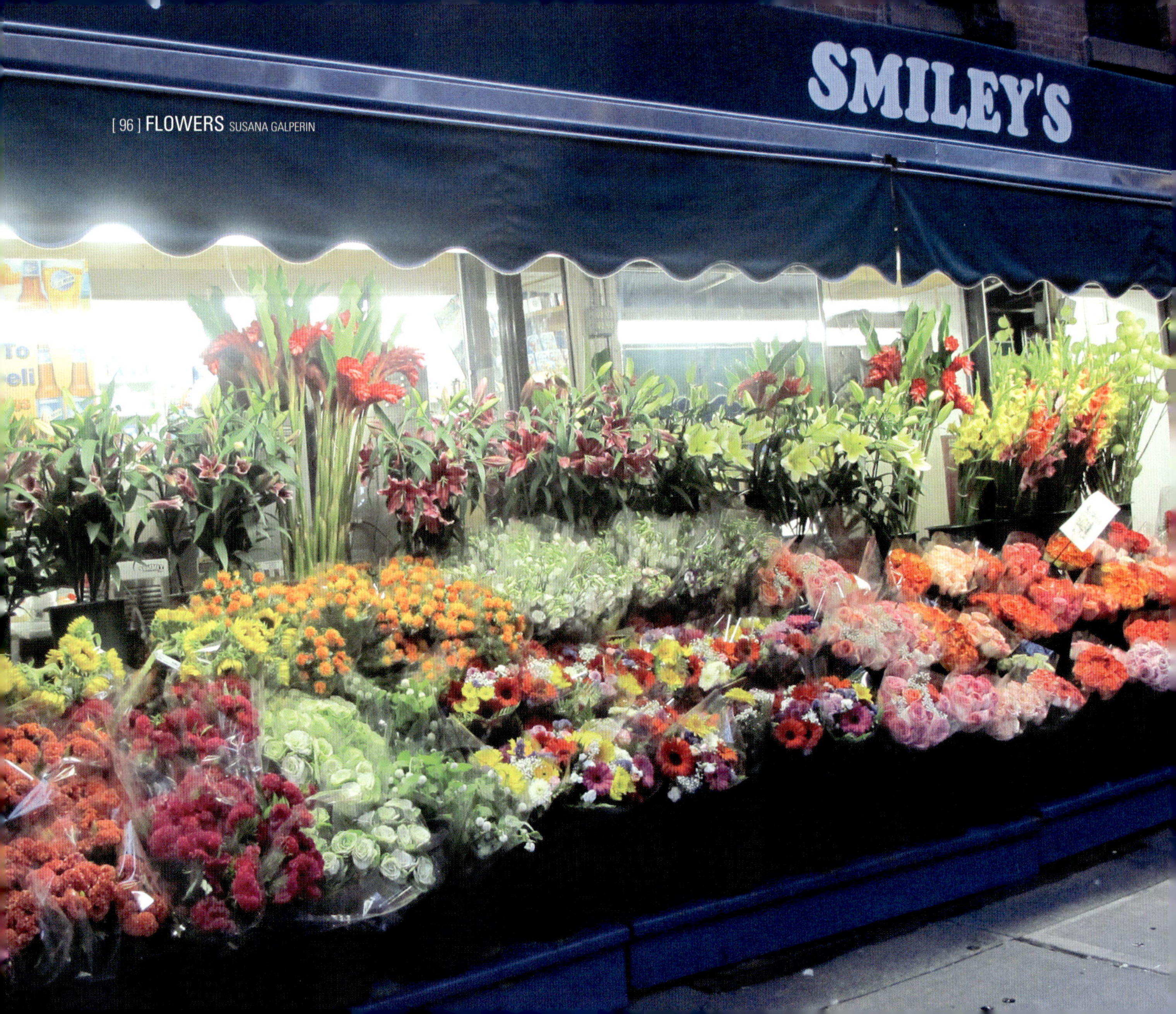
SMILEY'S

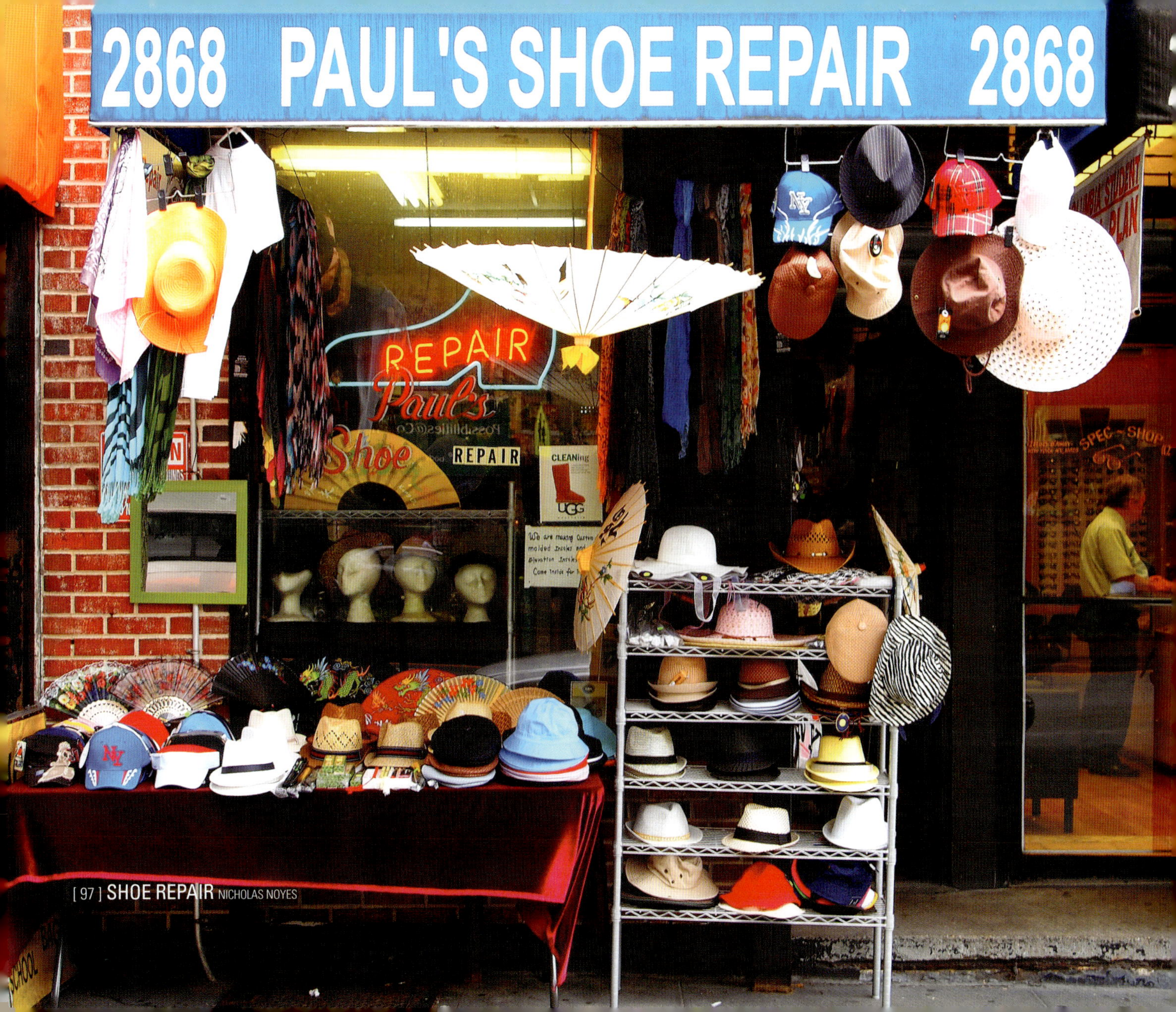

[97] SHOE REPAIR NICHOLAS NOYES

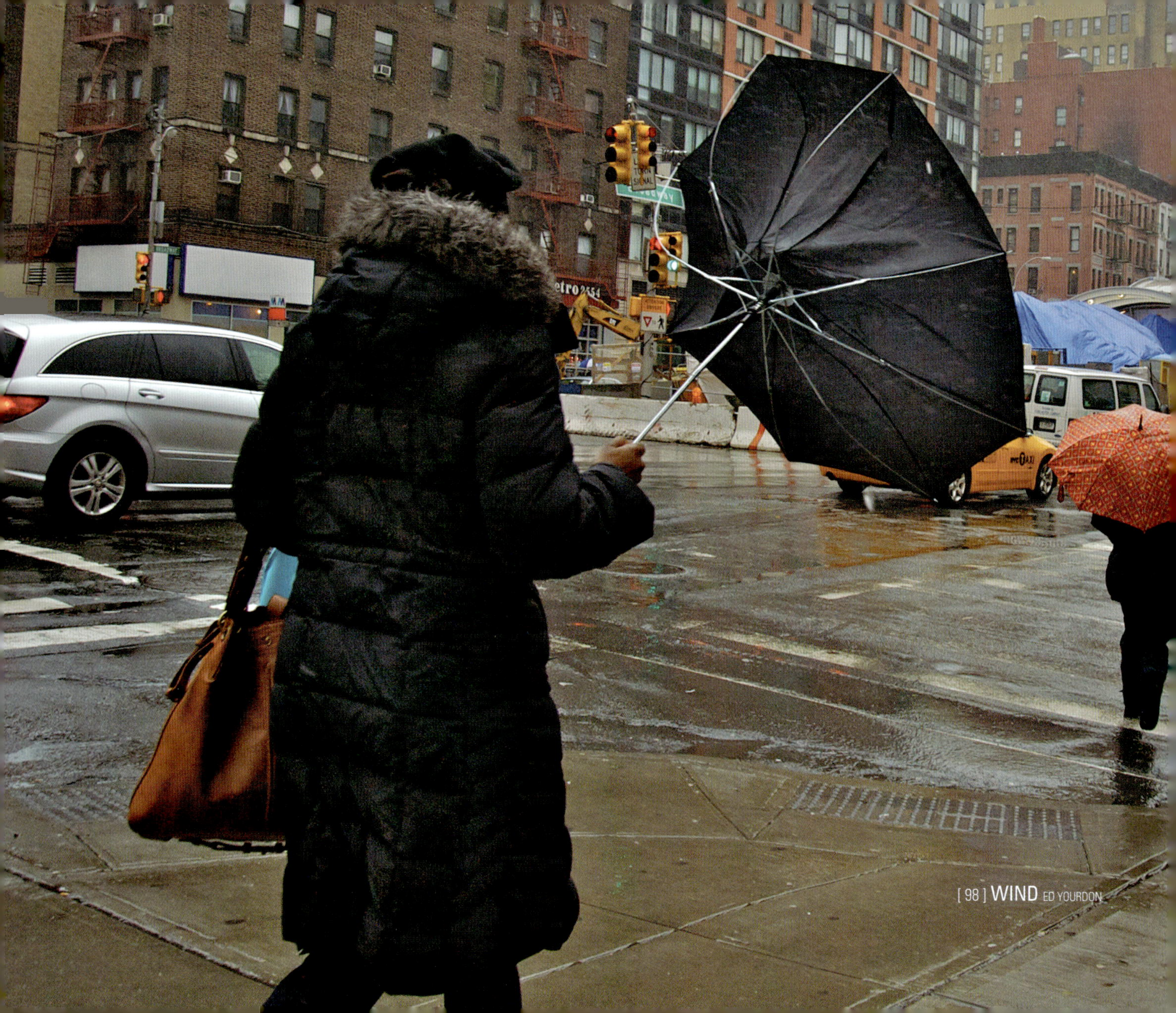

[98] WIND ED YOURDON

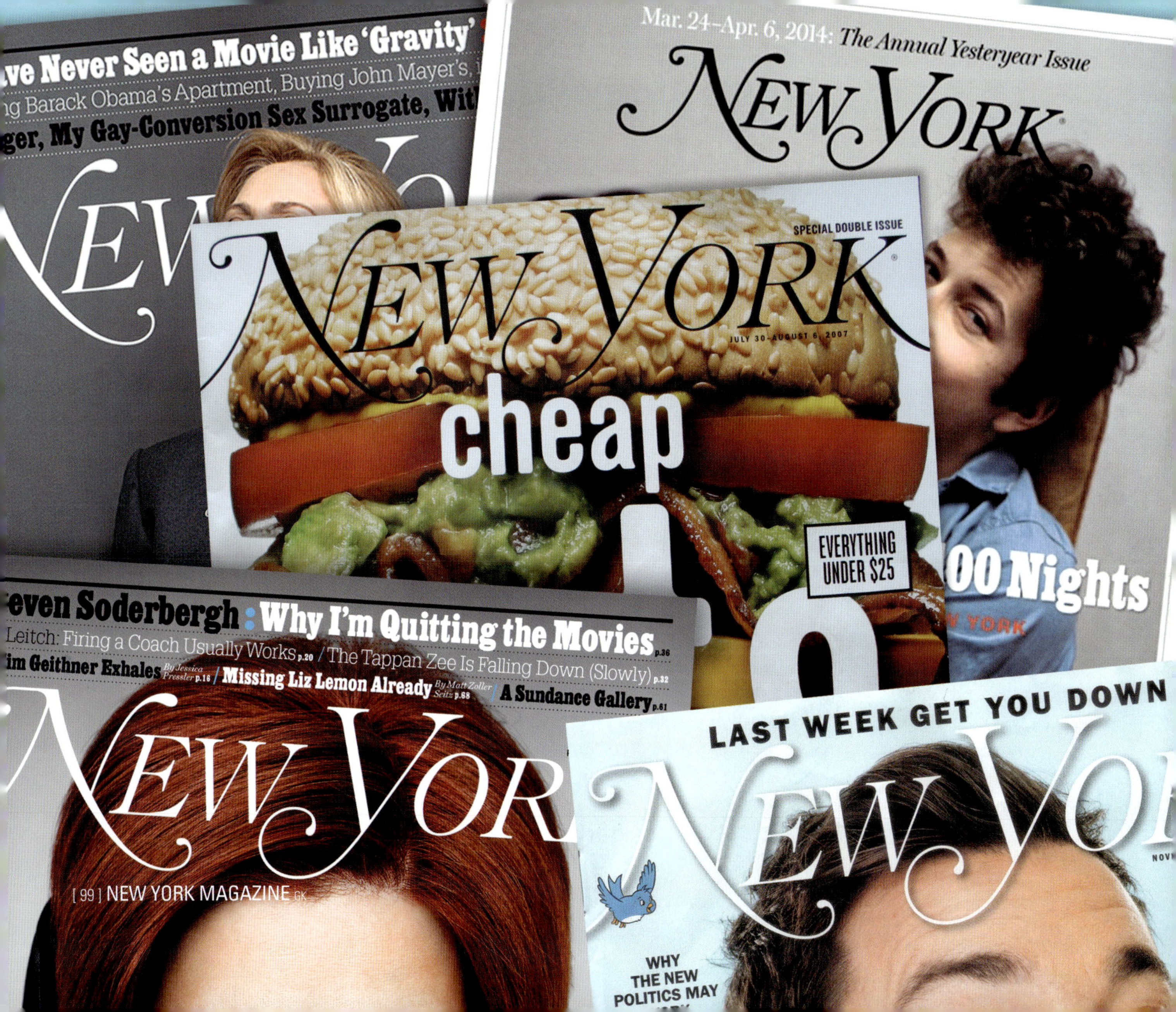
ve Never Seen a Movie Like 'Gravity'
g Barack Obama's Apartment, Buying John Mayer's,
ger, My Gay-Conversion Sex Surrogate, Wit
NEW YORK
Mar. 24–Apr. 6, 2014: The Annual Yesteryear Issue
NEW YORK
SPECIAL DOUBLE ISSUE
NEW YORK
JULY 30–AUGUST 6, 2007
cheap
EVERYTHING UNDER $25
00 Nights
even Soderbergh: Why I'm Quitting the Movies p.36
Leitch: Firing a Coach Usually Works p.20 / The Tappan Zee Is Falling Down (Slowly) p.32
im Geithner Exhales By Jessica Pressler p.18 / Missing Liz Lemon Already By Matt Zoller Seitz p.68 / A Sundance Gallery p.61
NEW YOR
[99] NEW YORK MAGAZINE
LAST WEEK GET YOU DOWN
NEW YO
WHY THE NEW POLITICS MAY

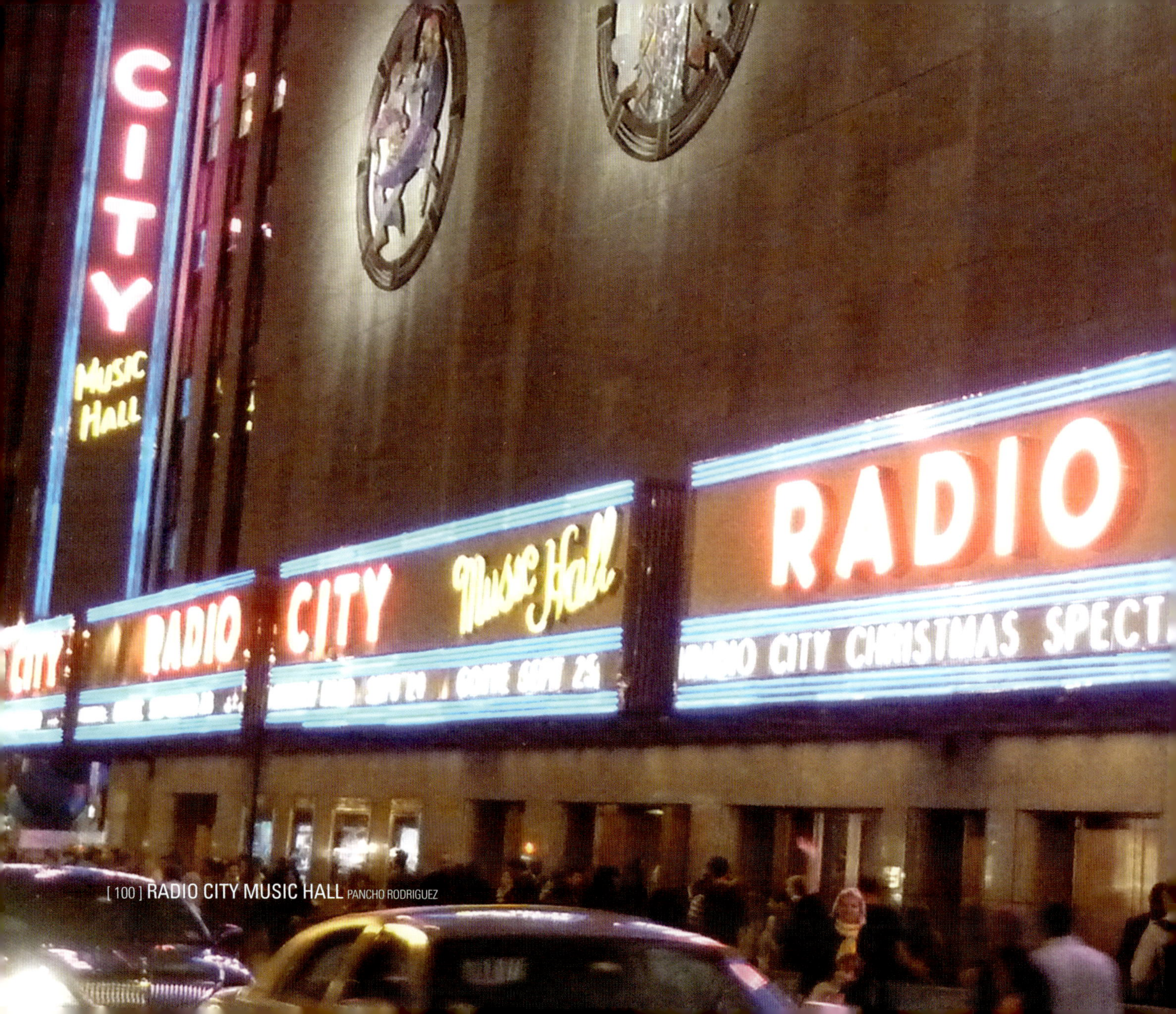

[100] RADIO CITY MUSIC HALL PANCHO RODRIGUEZ

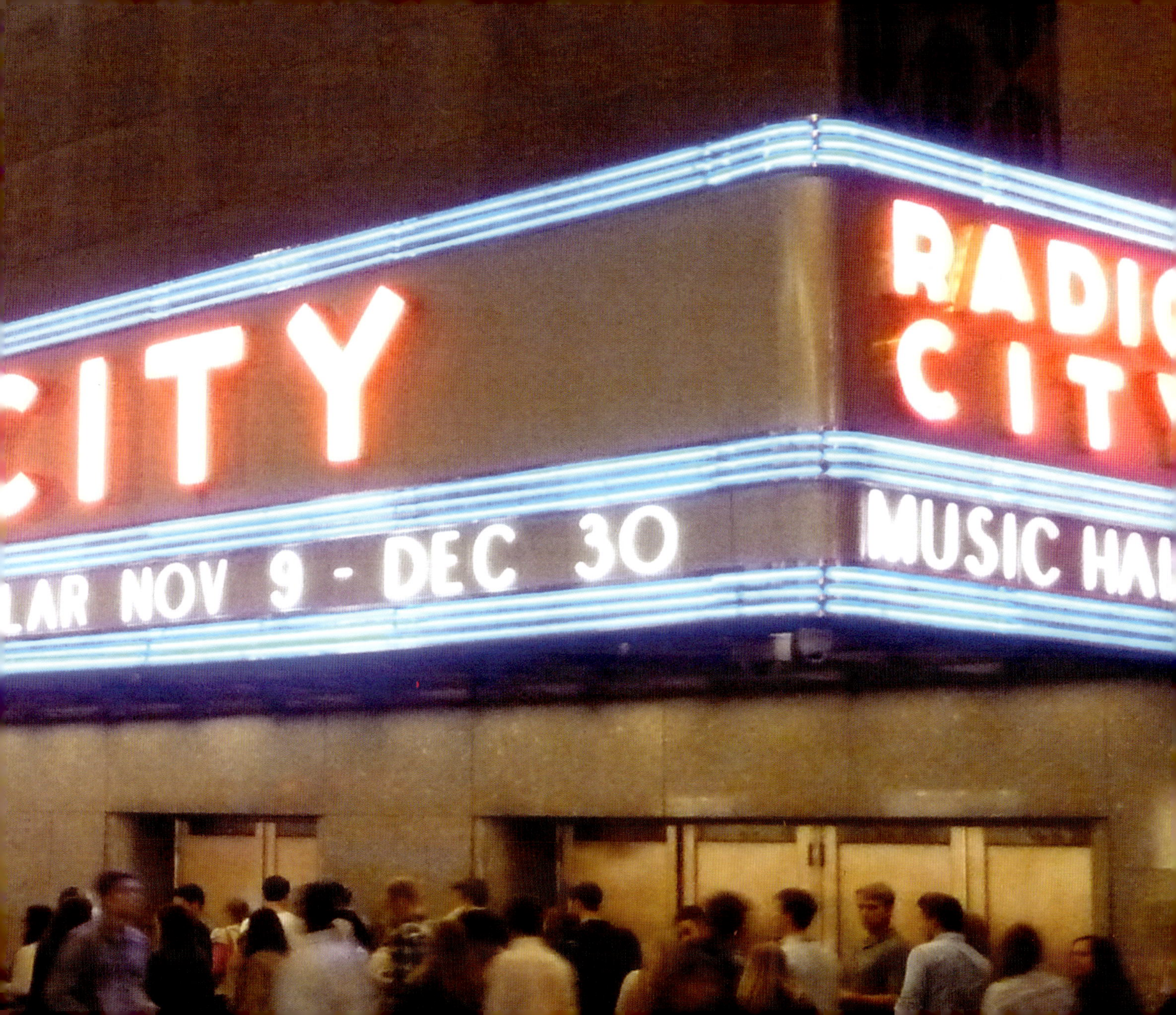
CITY
LAR NOV 9 - DEC 30
RADIO
CITY
MUSIC HAL

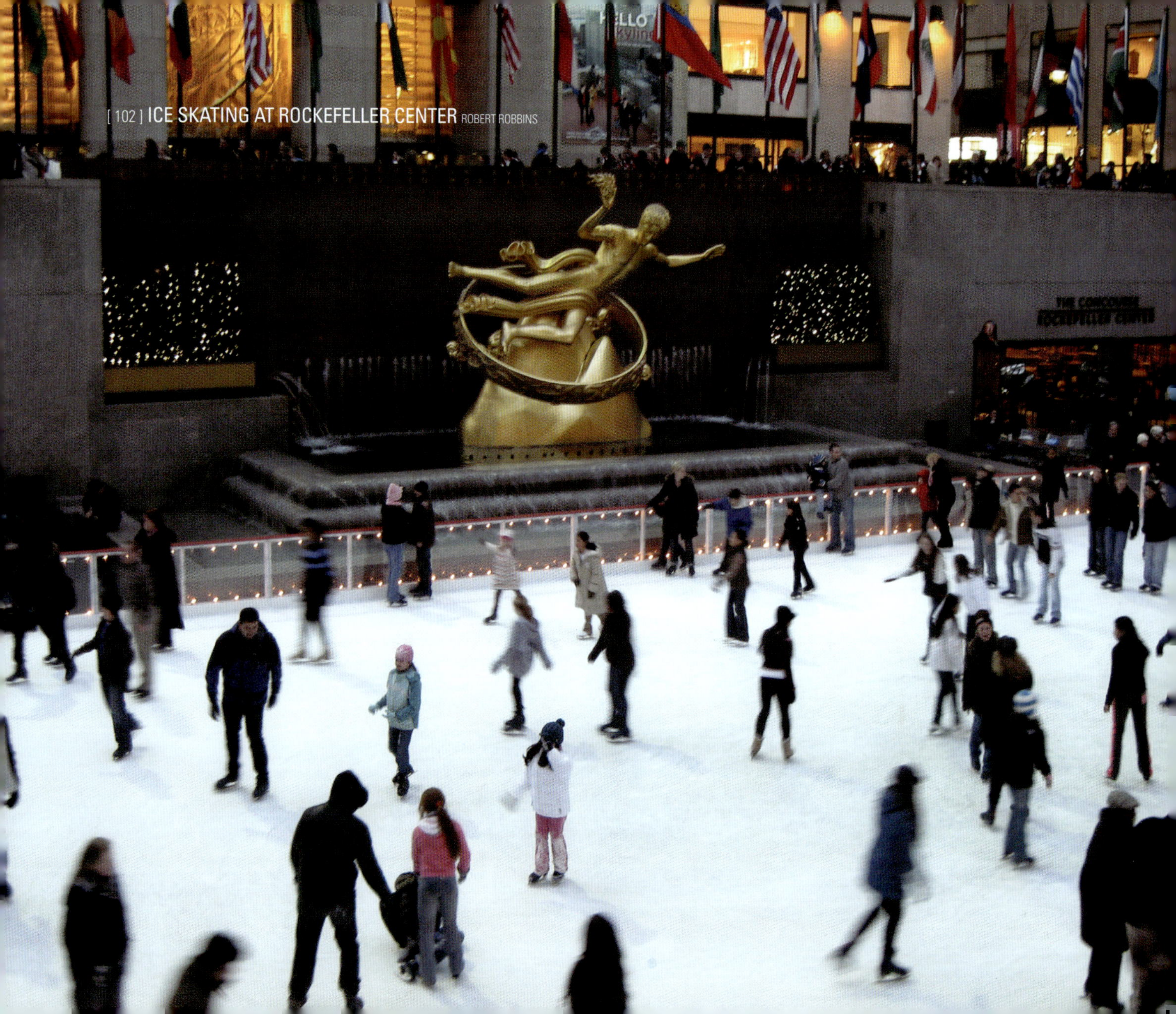

[102] ICE SKATING AT ROCKEFELLER CENTER ROBERT ROBBINS

[103] WOLLMAN RINK JOSEF PINLAC

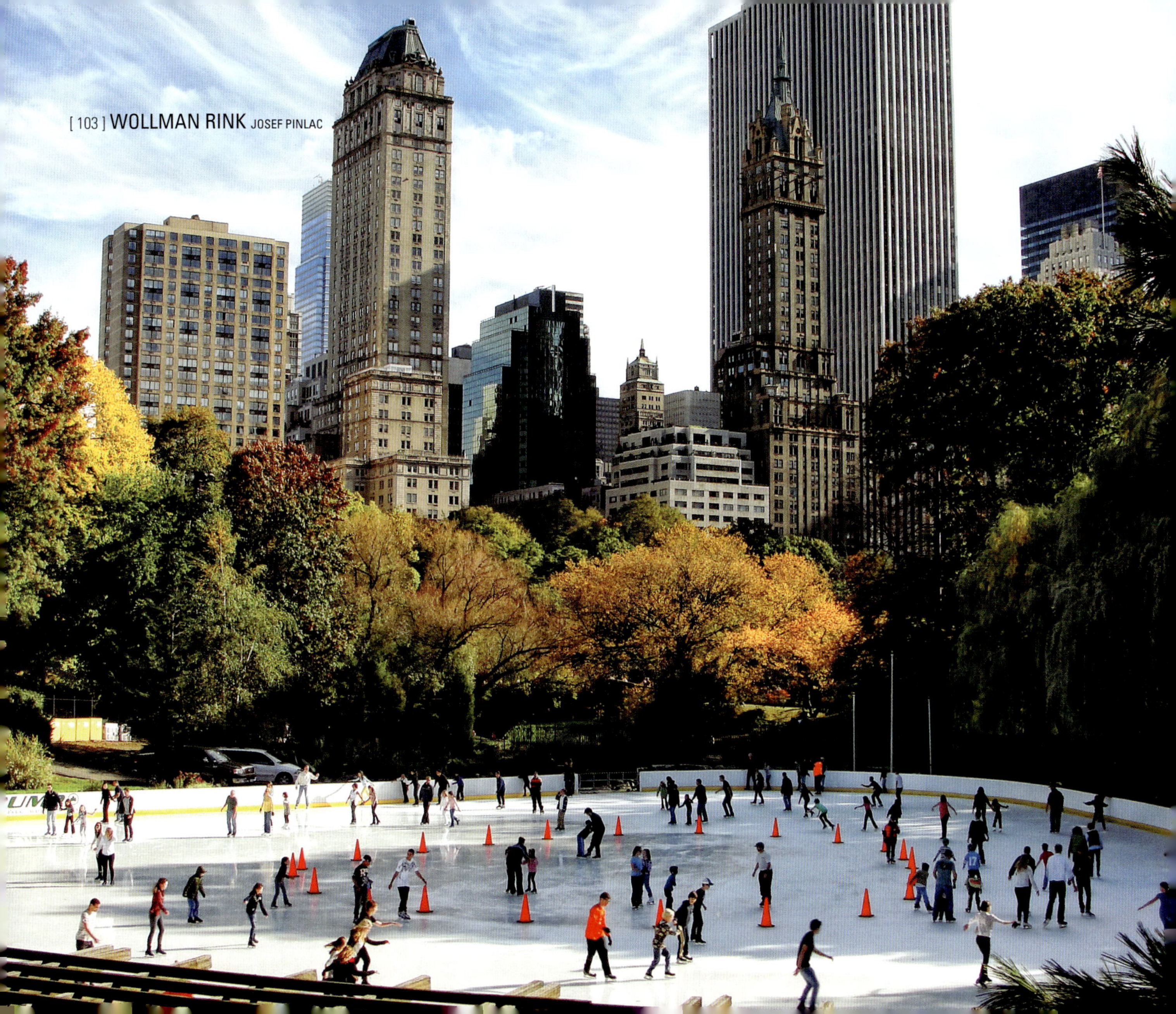

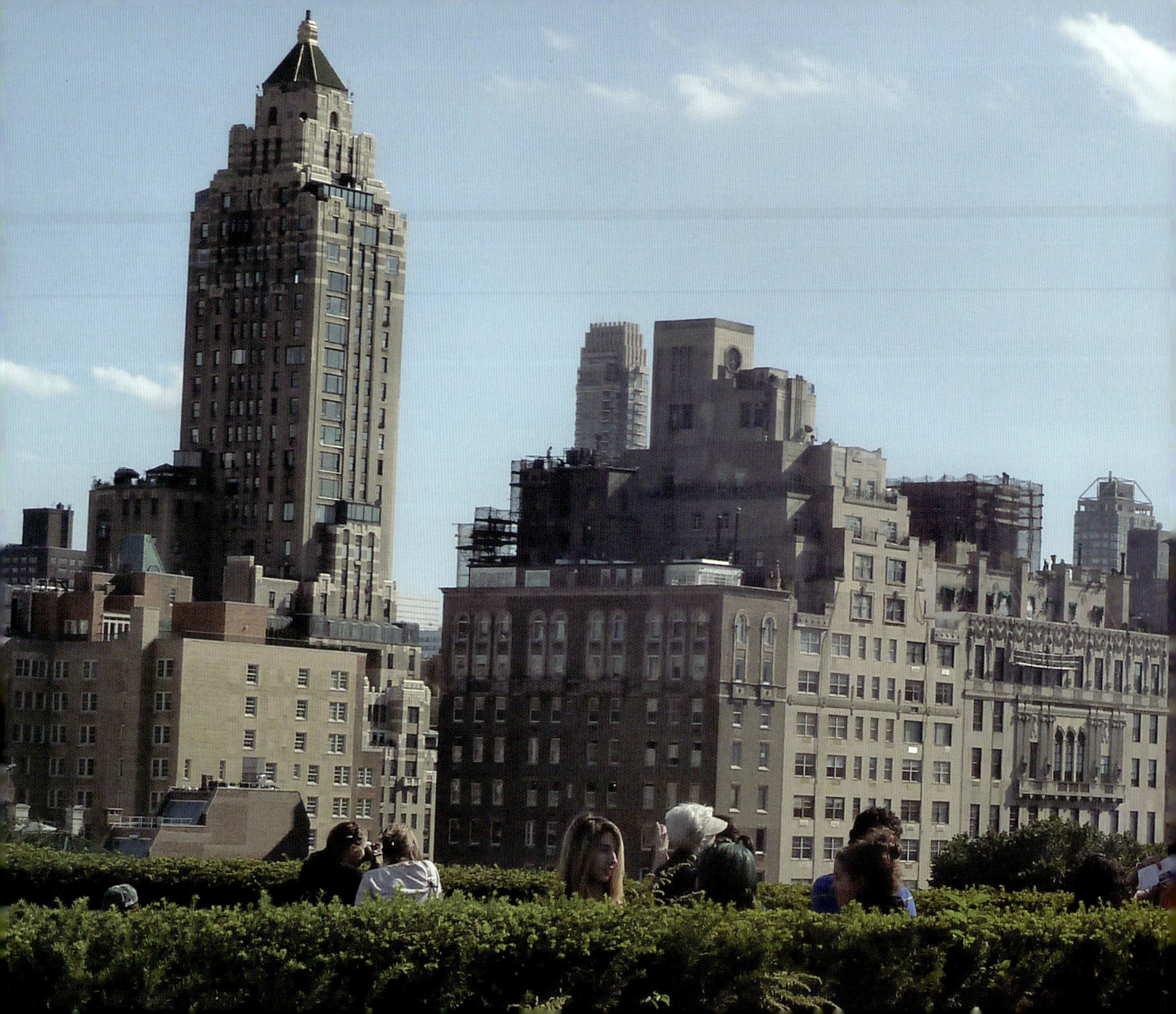

[105] THE ROOF TERRACE AT THE MET PANCHO RODRIGUEZ

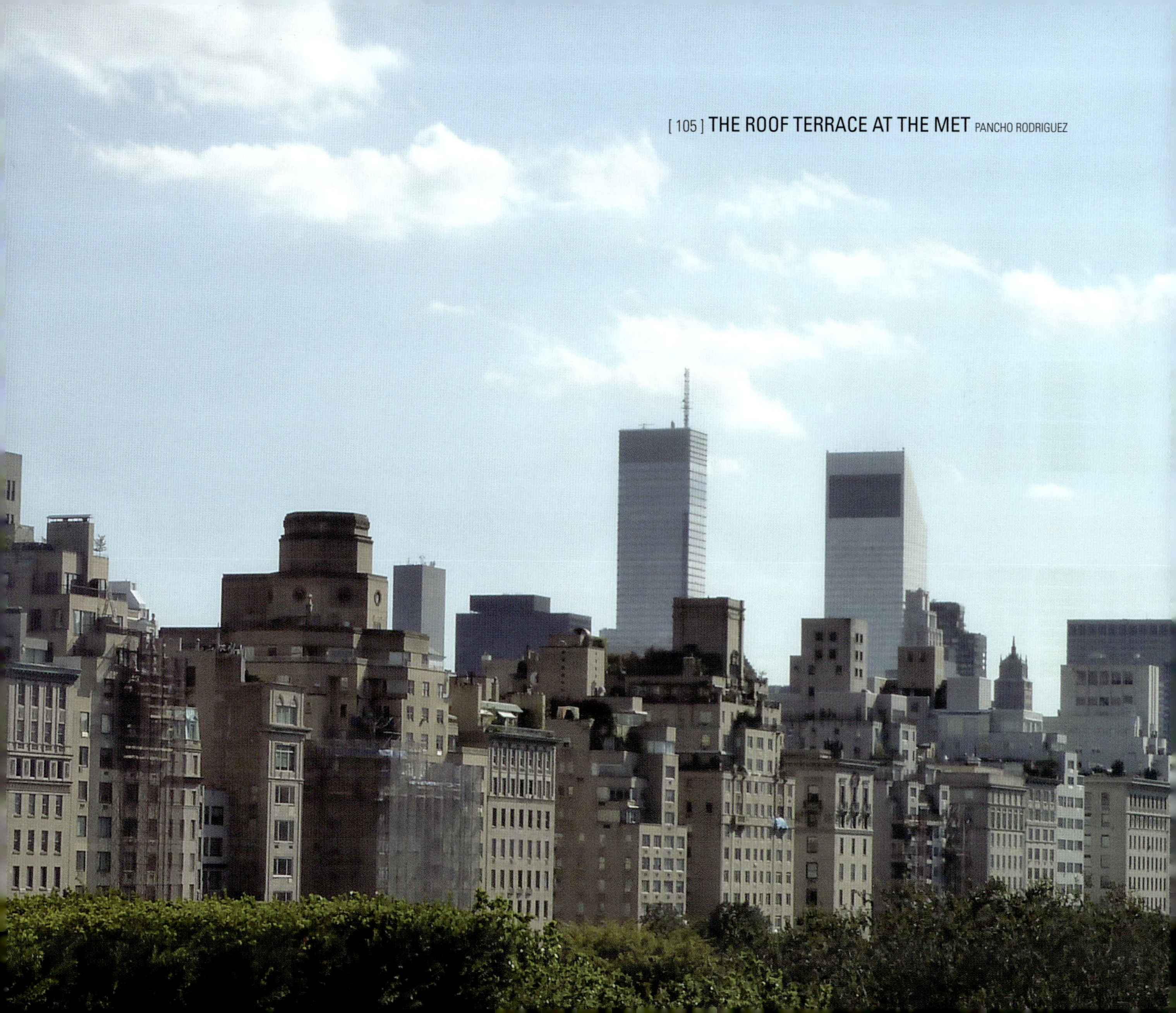

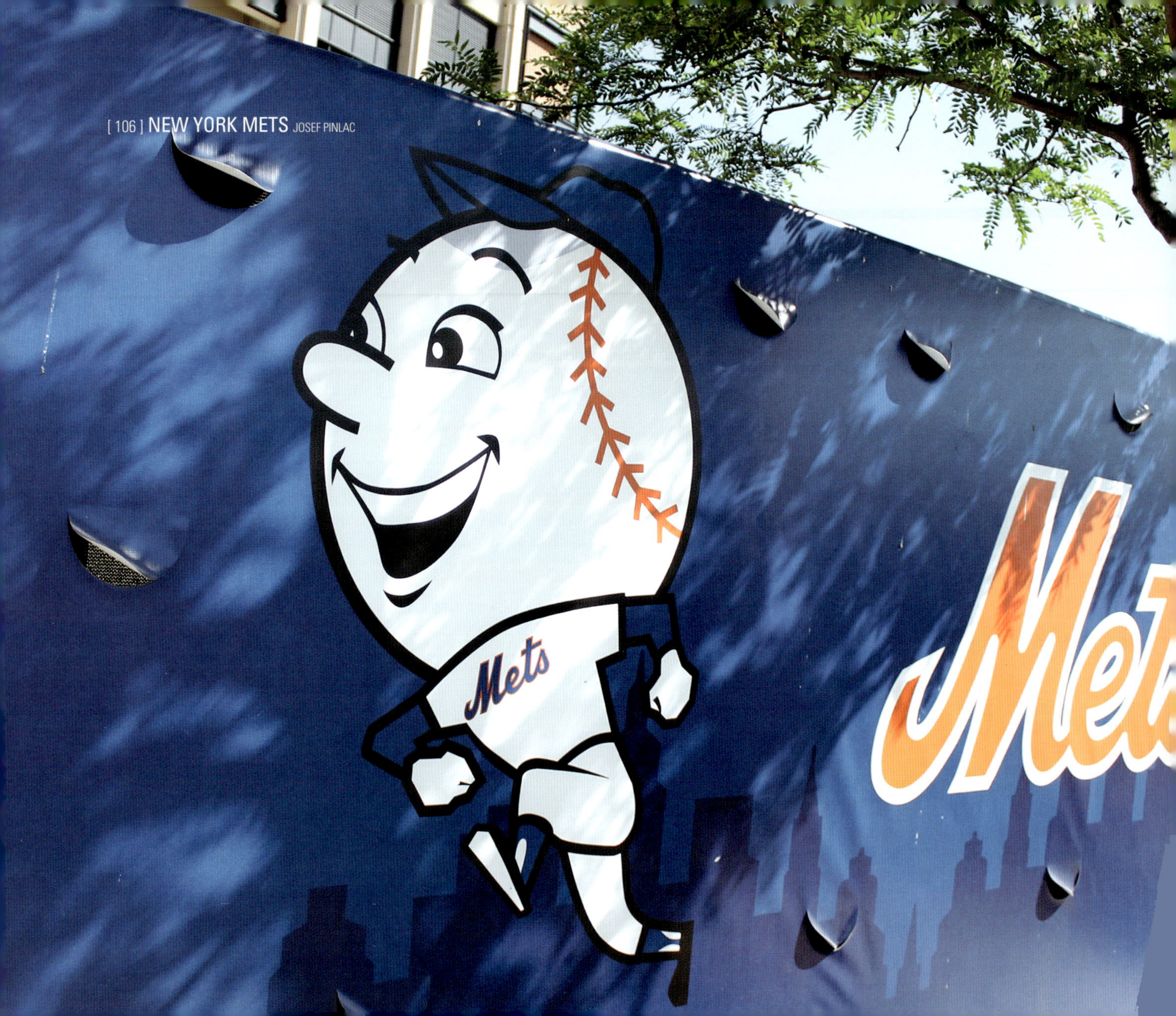
Mets
Met

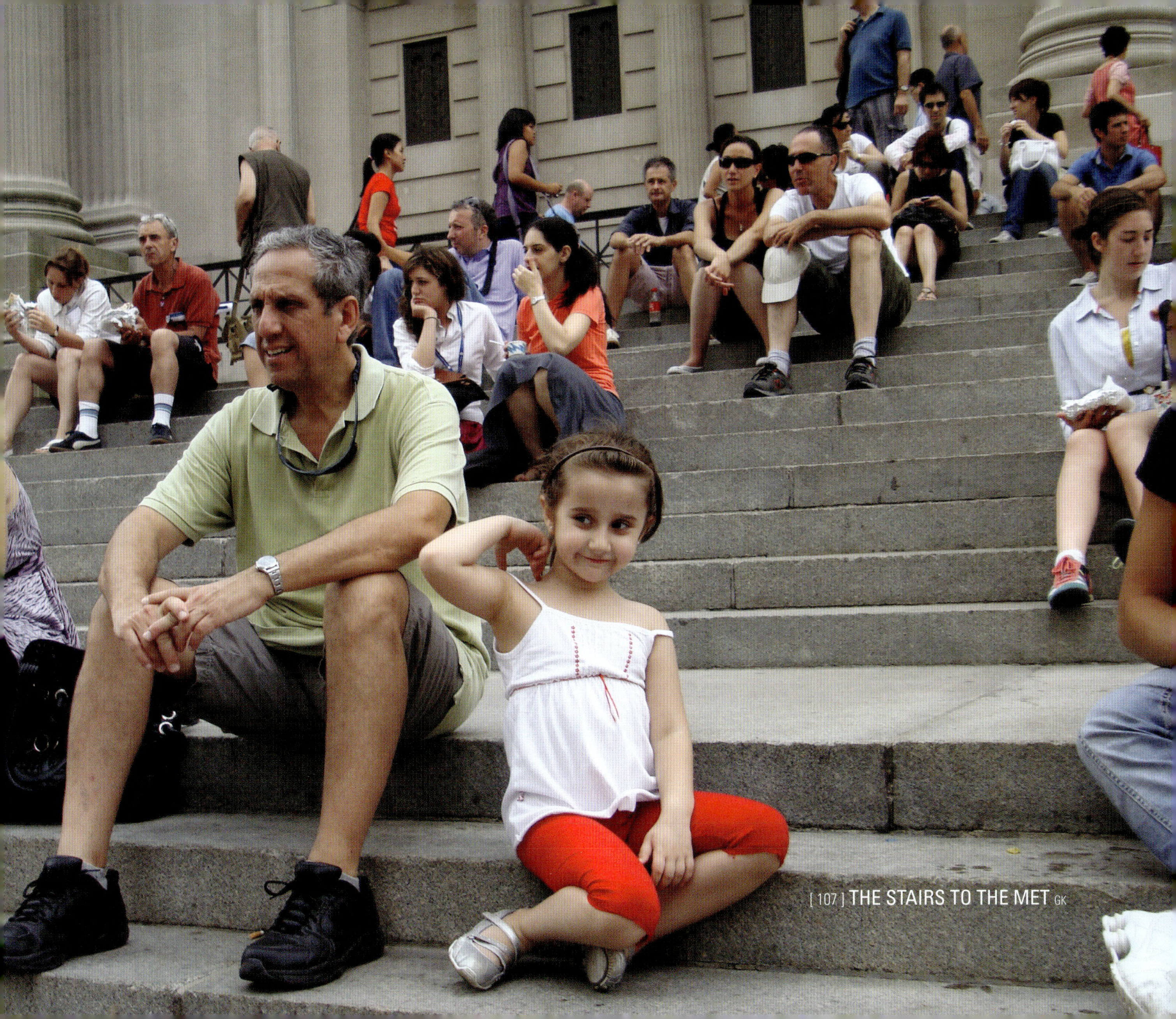

[107] THE STAIRS TO THE MET GK

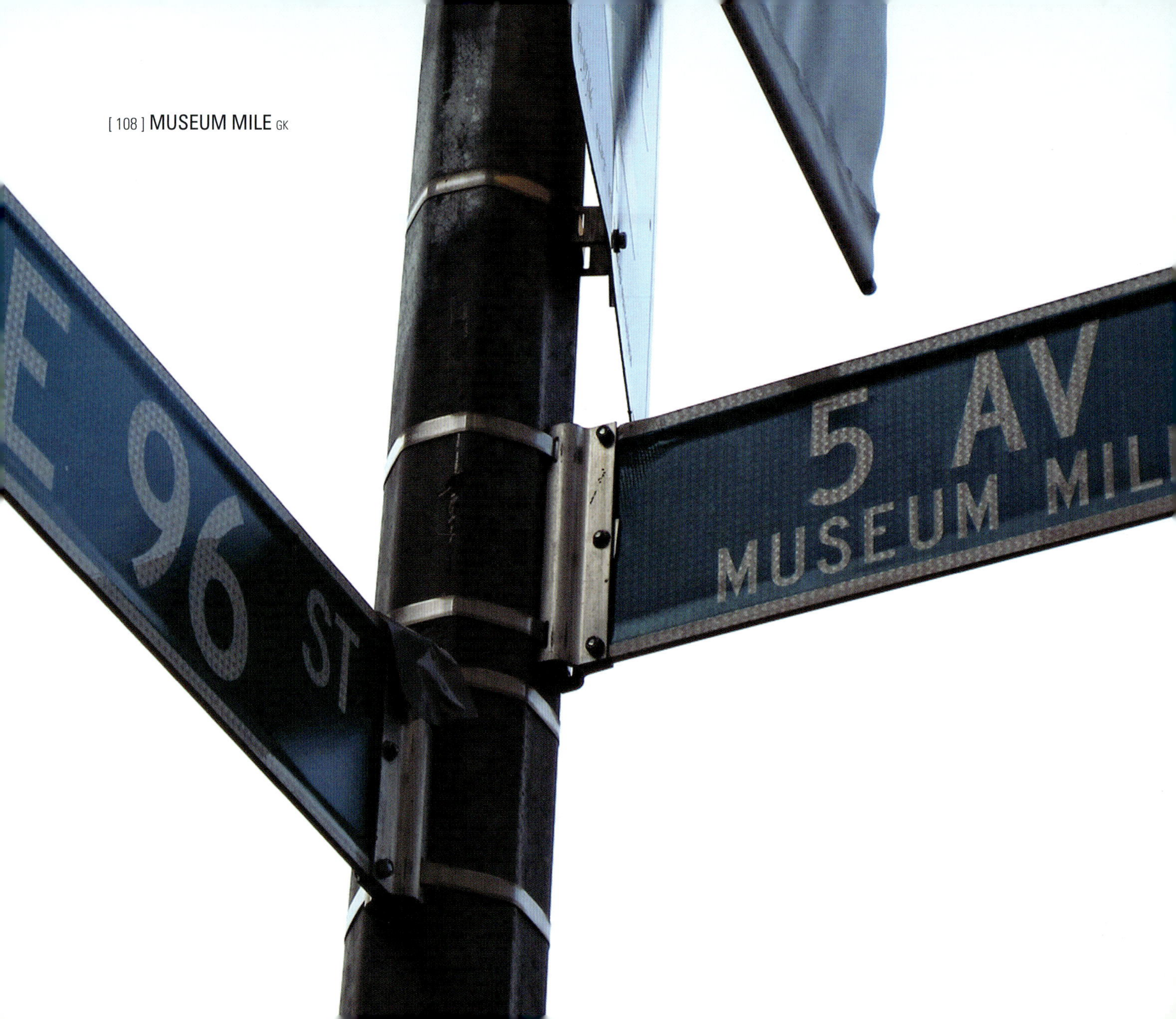
E 96 ST
5 AV
MUSEUM MIL

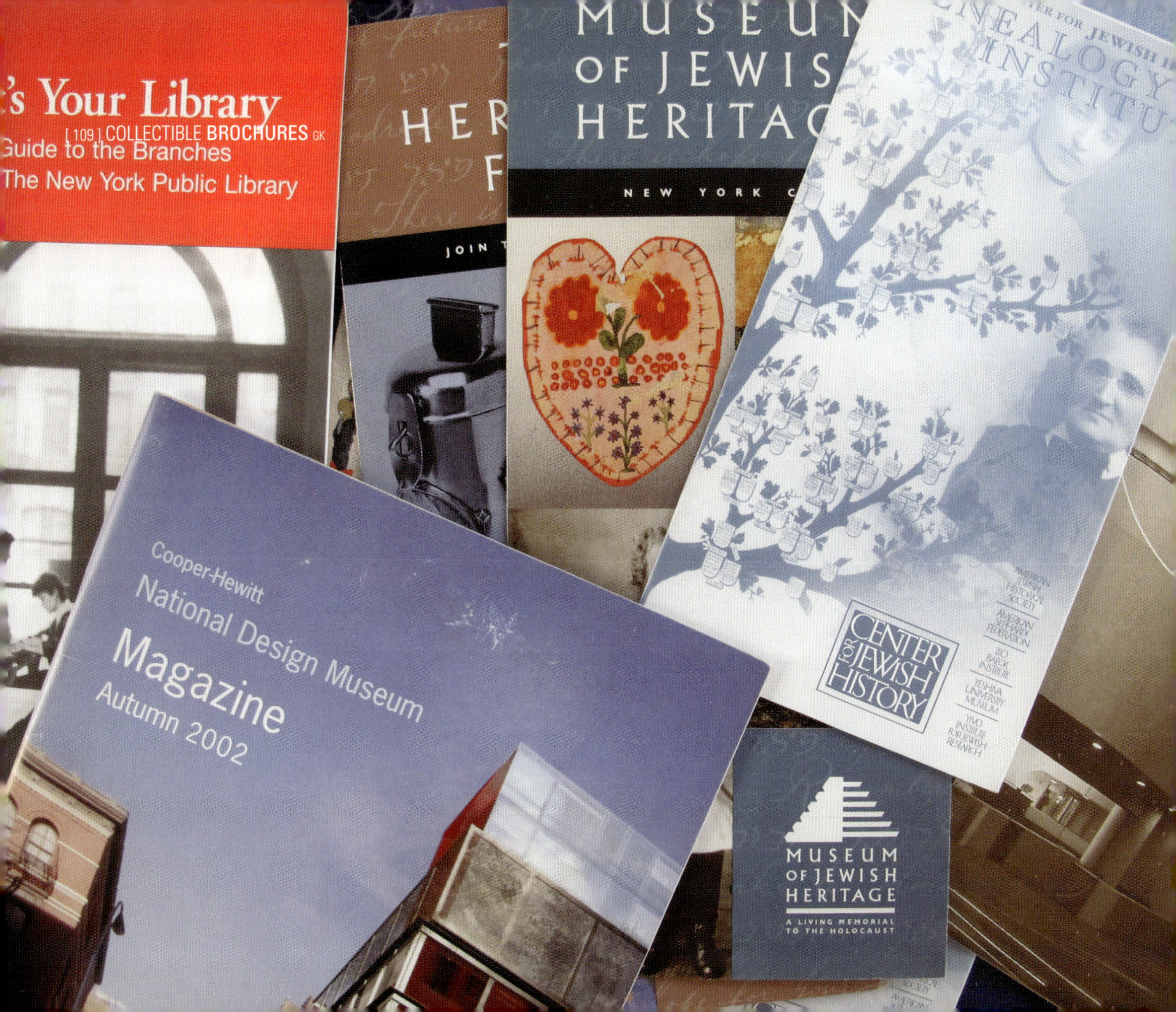

[109] COLLECTIBLE BROCHURES GK

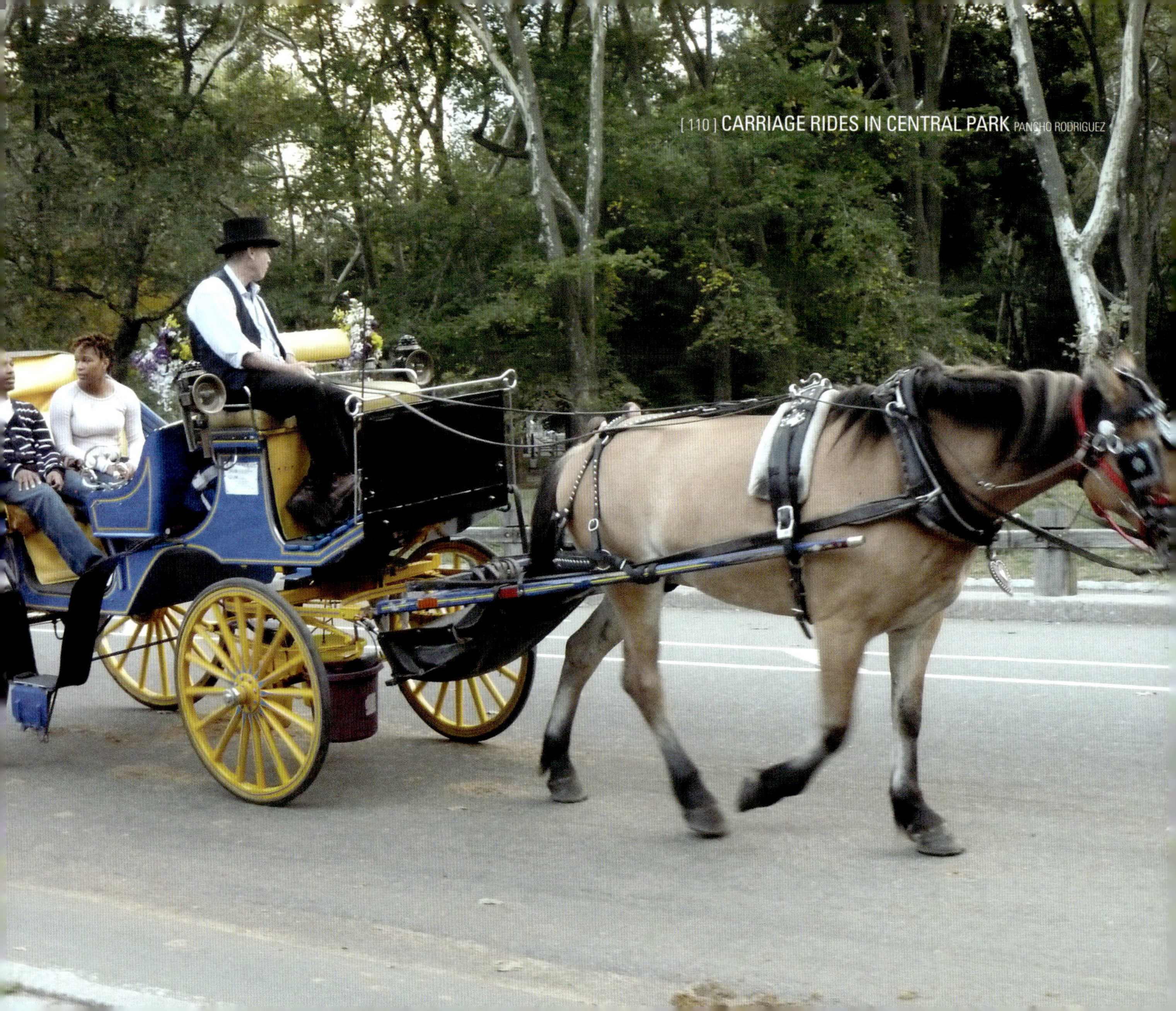

[110] CARRIAGE RIDES IN CENTRAL PARK PANCHO RODRIGUEZ

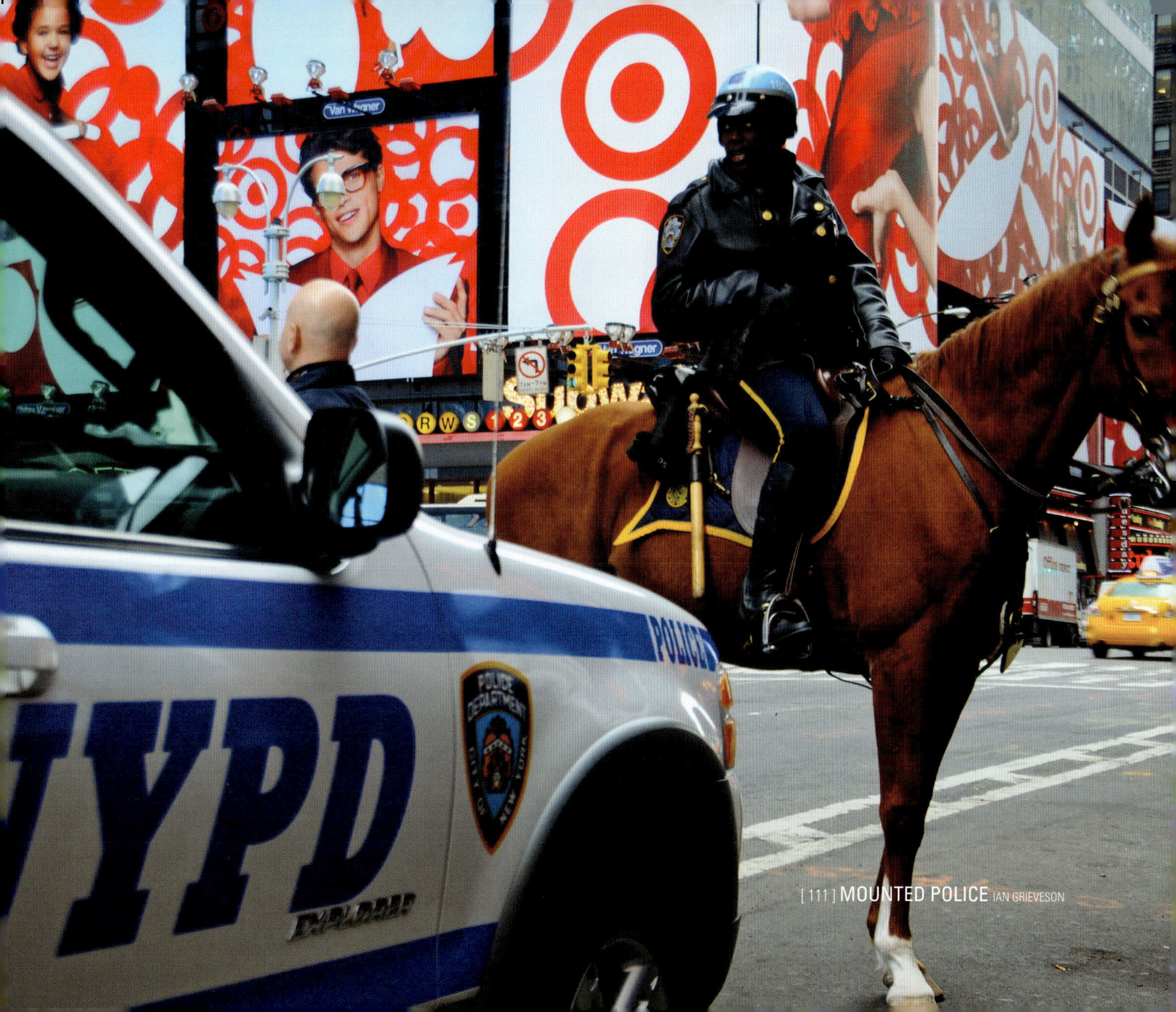

[111] MOUNTED POLICE IAN GRIEVESON

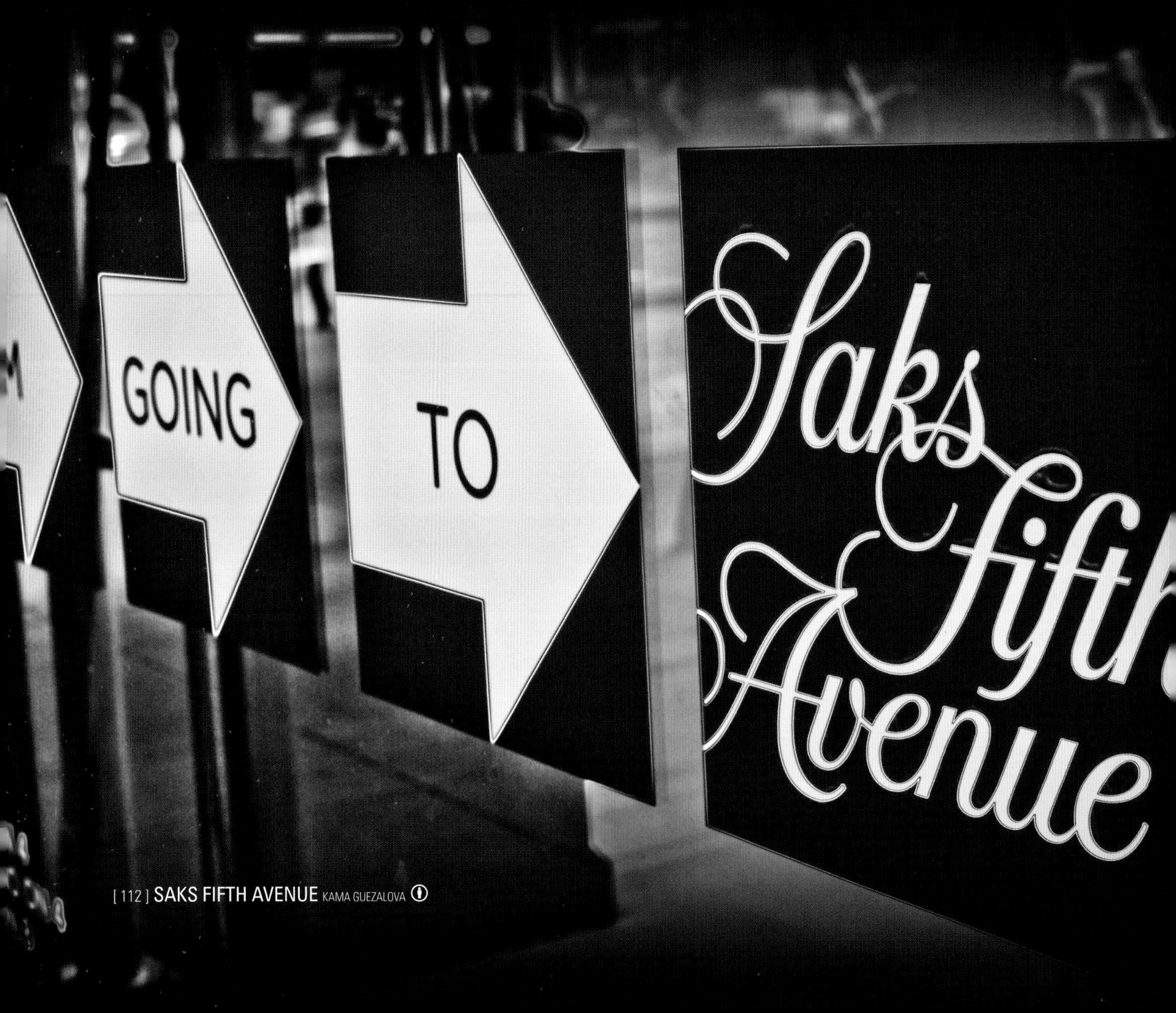

[112] SAKS FIFTH AVENUE KAMA GUEZALOVA

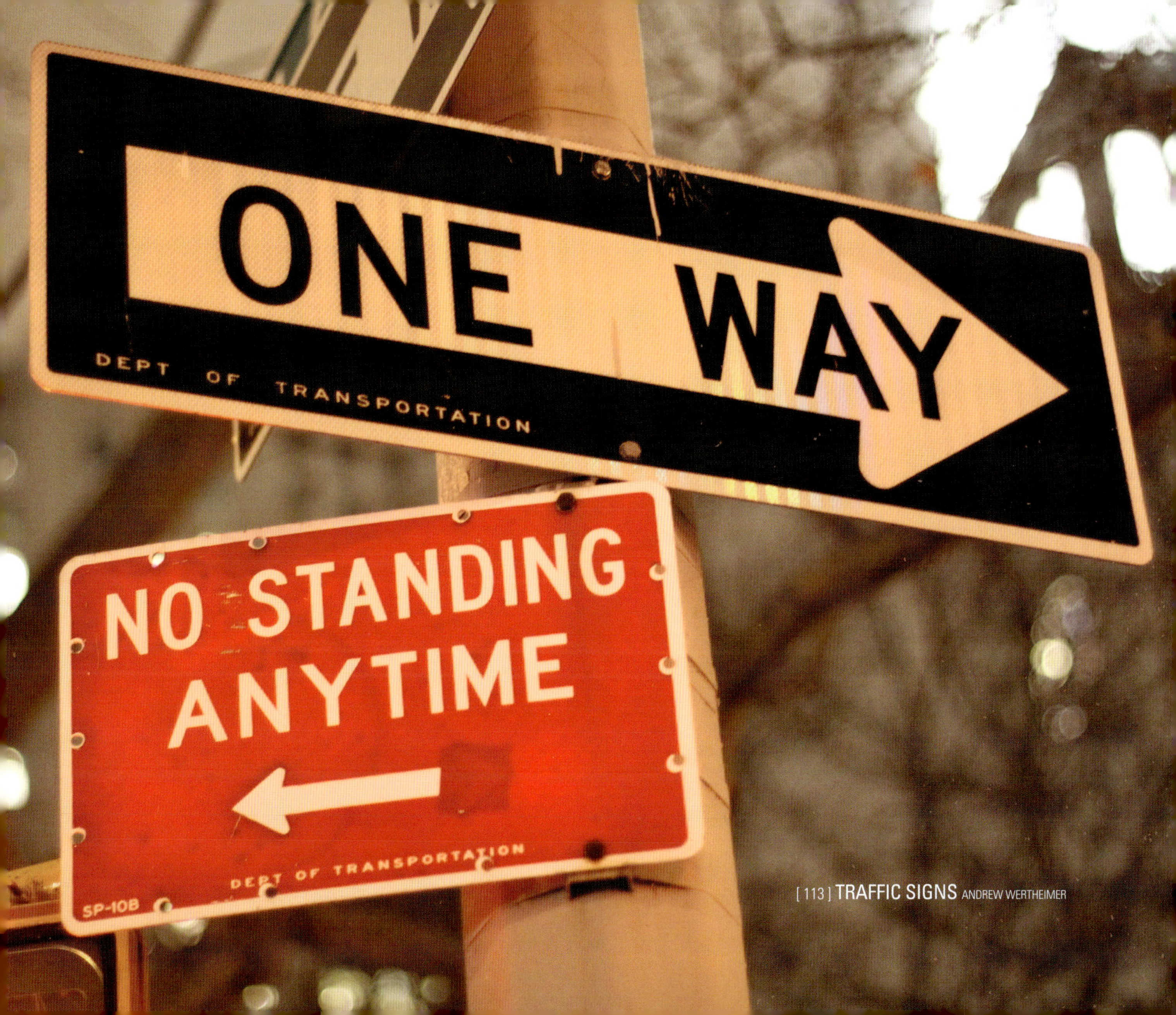

[113] TRAFFIC SIGNS ANDREW WERTHEIMER

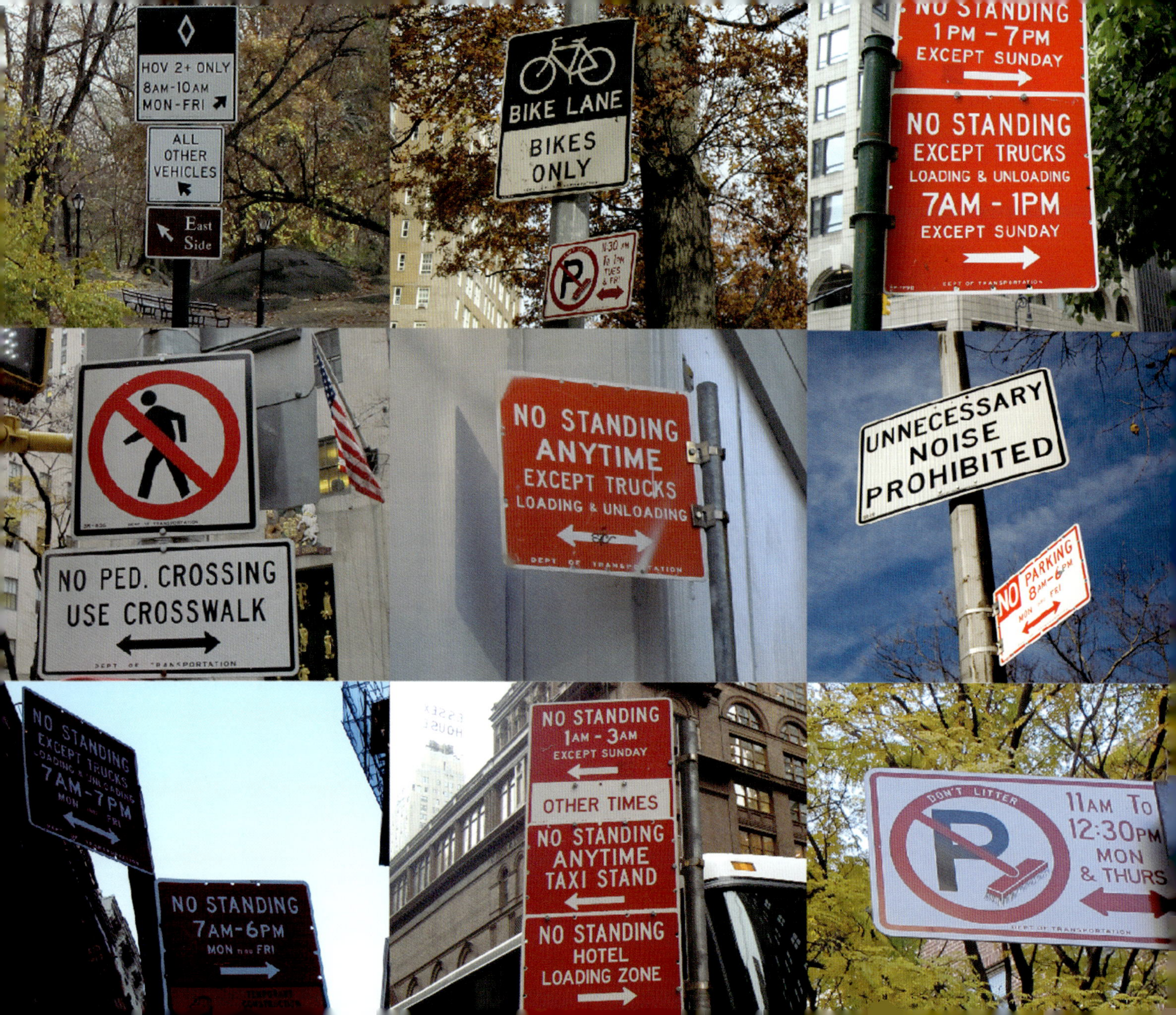

HOV 2+ ONLY
8AM-10AM
MON-FRI
ALL
OTHER
VEHICLES
East
Side
BIKE LANE
BIKES
ONLY
11:30 AM
To 1PM
TUES
& FRI
NO STANDING
1PM - 7PM
EXCEPT SUNDAY
NO STANDING
EXCEPT TRUCKS
LOADING & UNLOADING
7AM - 1PM
EXCEPT SUNDAY
DEPT OF TRANSPORTATION
NO PED. CROSSING
USE CROSSWALK
DEPT OF TRANSPORTATION
NO STANDING
ANYTIME
EXCEPT TRUCKS
LOADING & UNLOADING
DEPT OF TRANSPORTATION
UNNECESSARY
NOISE
PROHIBITED
NO PARKING
8AM-6PM
NO STANDING
EXCEPT TRUCKS
LOADING & UNLOADING
7AM-7PM
MON THRU FRI
NO STANDING
7AM-6PM
MON THRU FRI
NO STANDING
1AM - 3AM
EXCEPT SUNDAY
OTHER TIMES
NO STANDING
ANYTIME
TAXI STAND
NO STANDING
HOTEL
LOADING ZONE
DON'T LITTER
11AM To
12:30PM
MON
& THURS
DEPT OF TRANSPORTATION

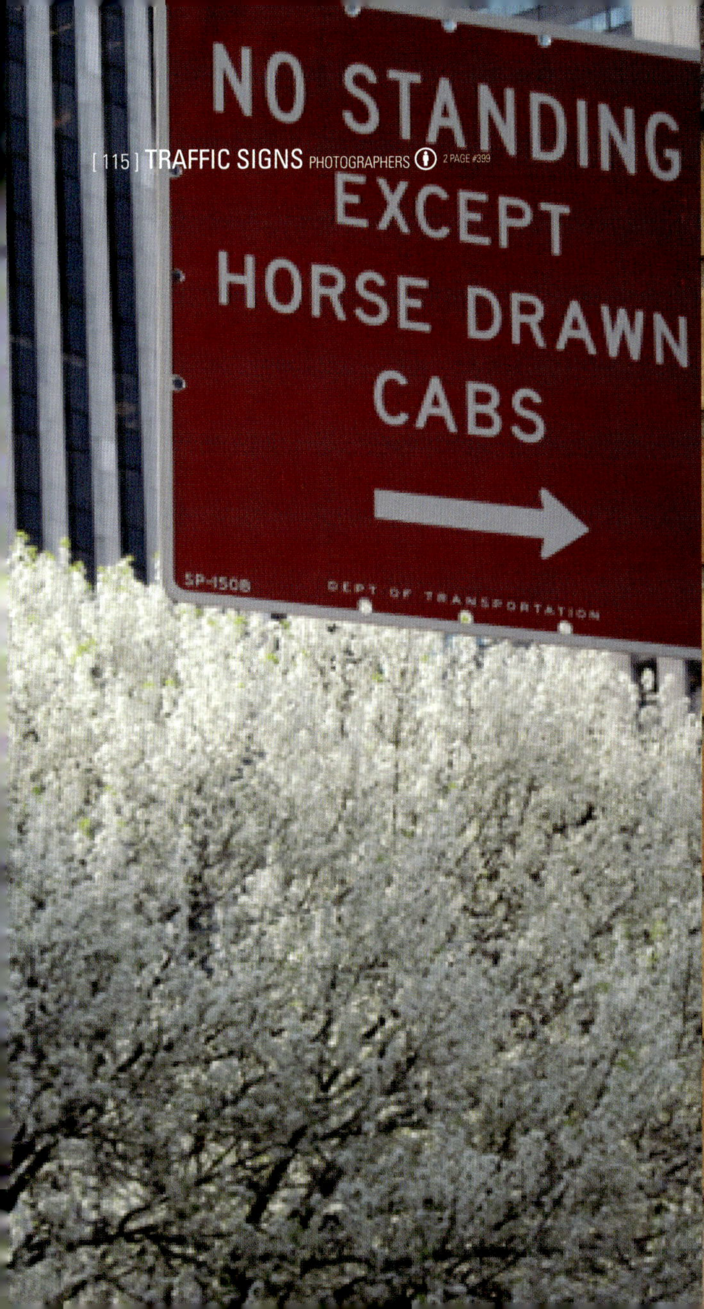
NO STANDING
EXCEPT
HORSE DRAWN
CABS
DEPT OF TRANSPORTATION

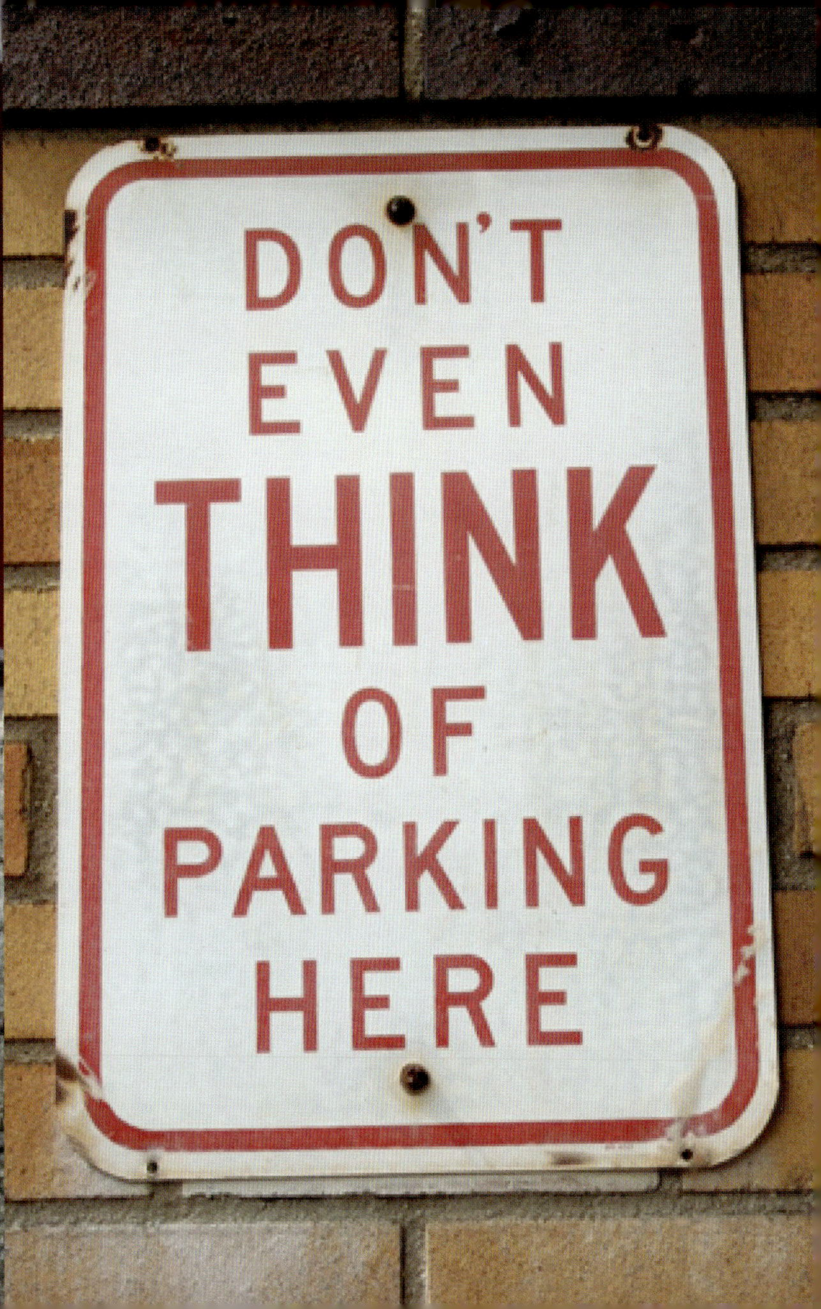
DON'T
EVEN
THINK
OF
PARKING
HERE

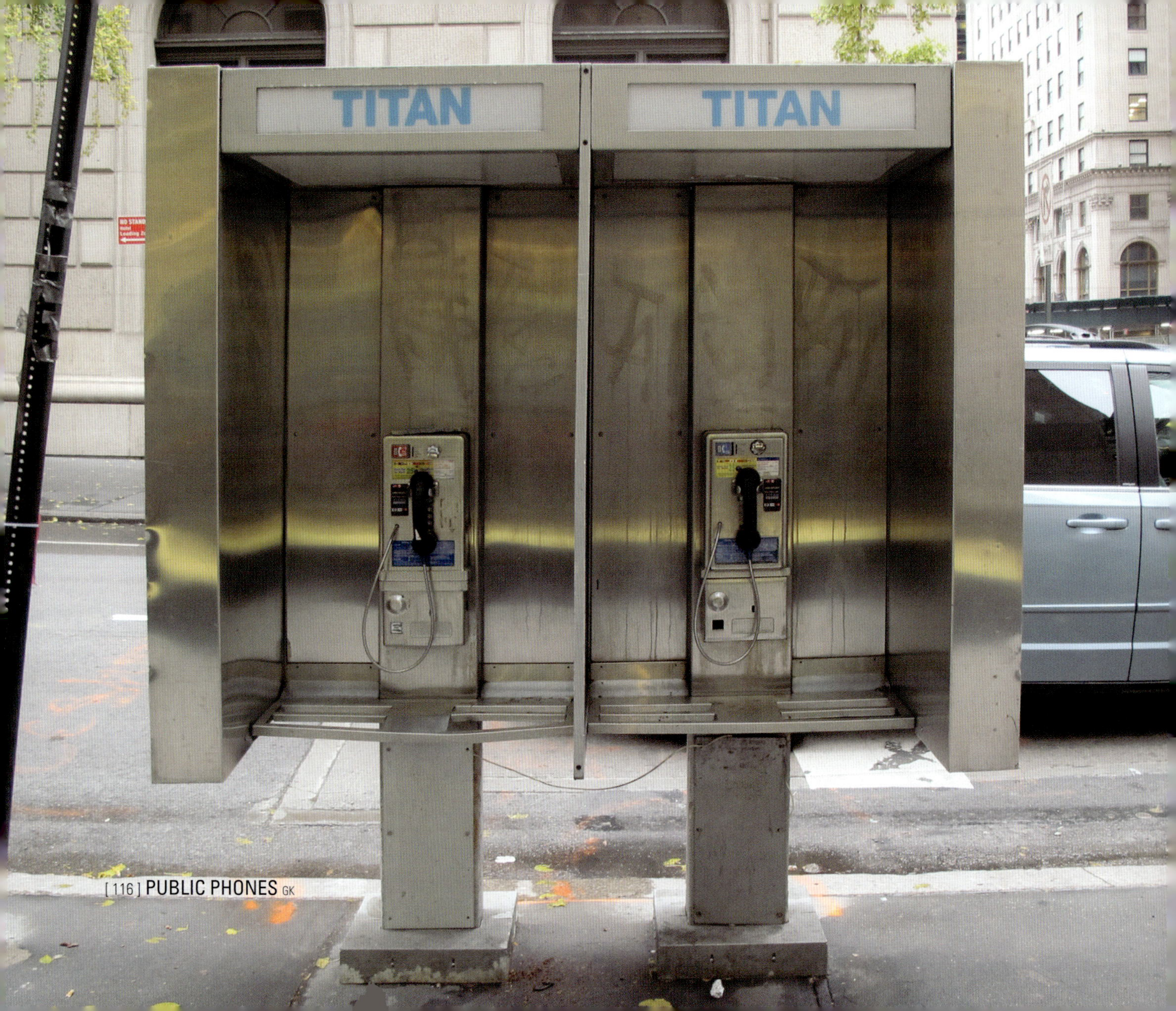

[116] PUBLIC PHONES GK

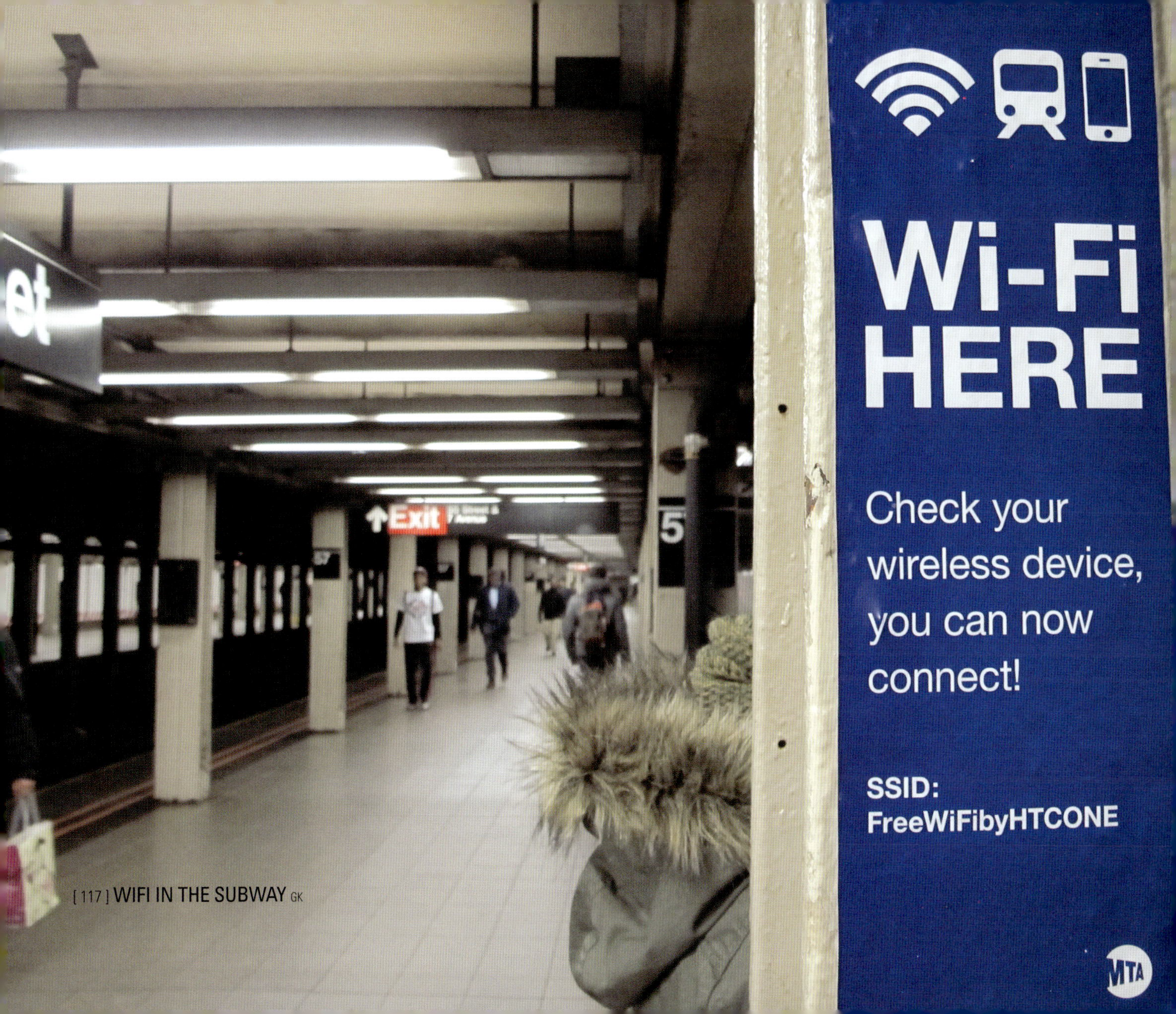

[117] WIFI IN THE SUBWAY GK

LANDMARKS OF NEW YORK
THE UNIVERSITY CLUB
THIS BUILDING, INSPIRED BY
PALACE ARCHITECTURE
OF THE ITALIAN RENAISSANCE,
WAS DESIGNED BY
MC KIM, MEAD & WHITE
AND WAS COMPLETED IN 1899.
PLAQUE ERECTED 1957 BY
THE NEW YORK COMMUNITY TRUST

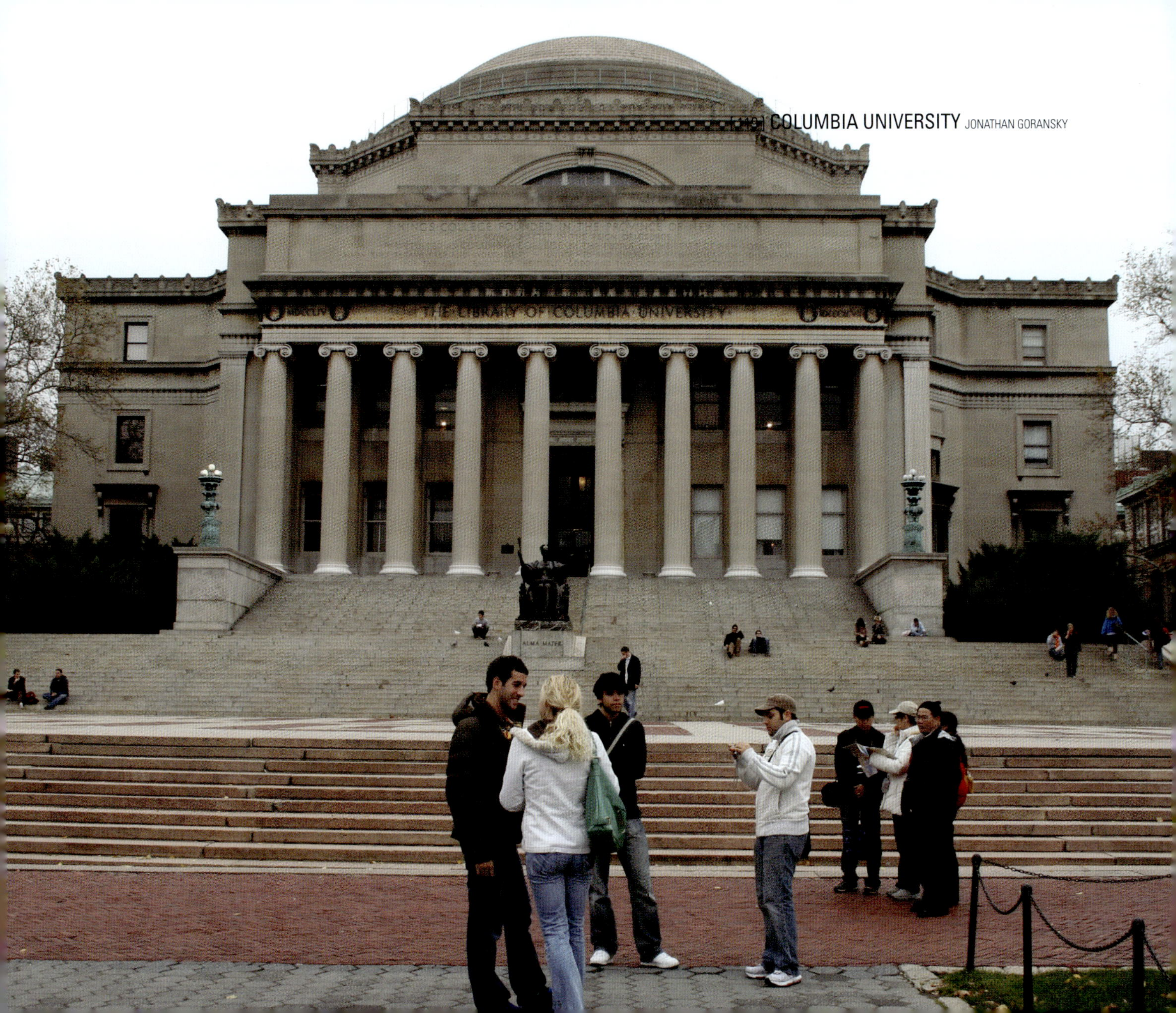

[119] COLUMBIA UNIVERSITY JONATHAN GORANSKY

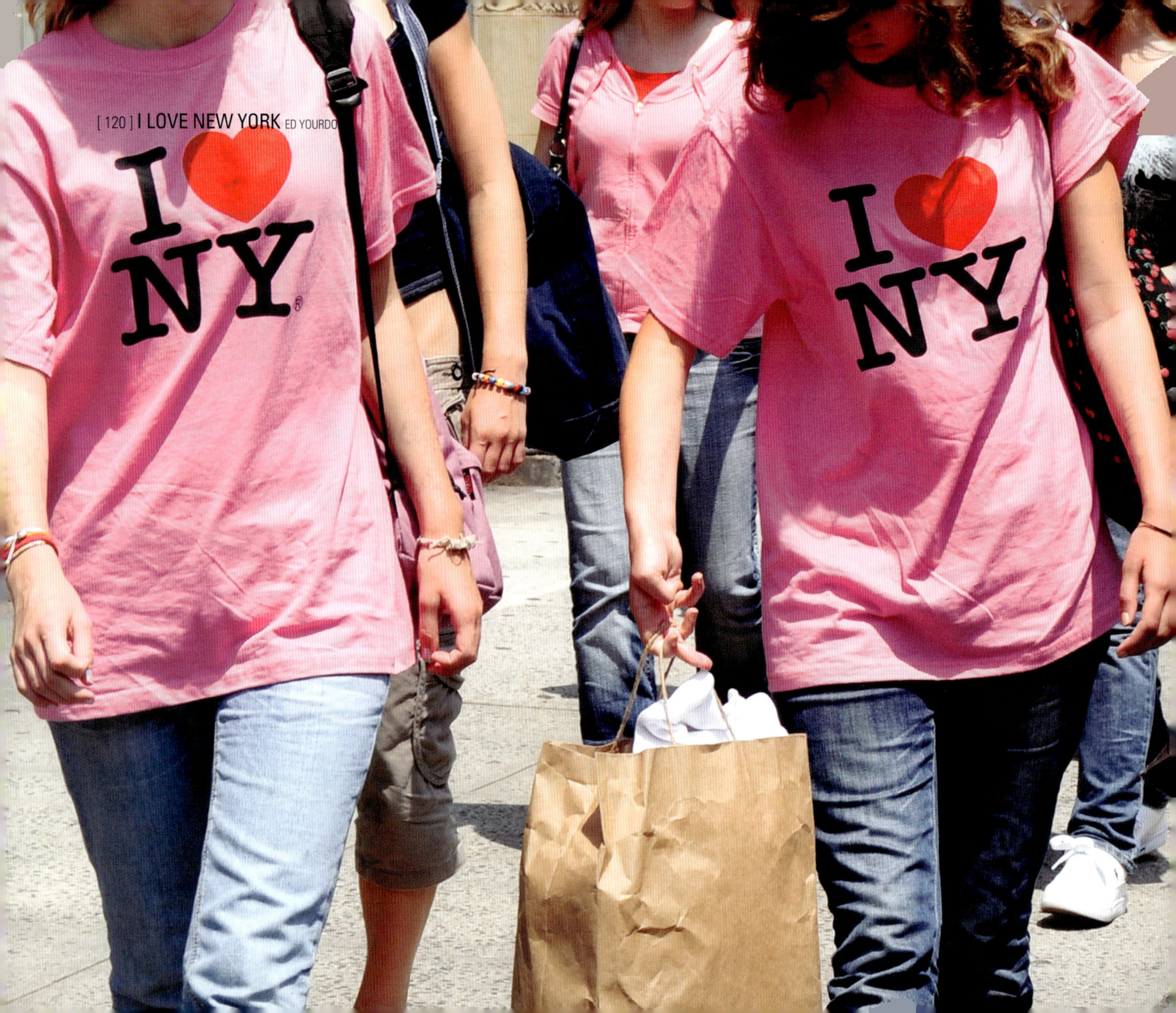
I NY
I NY

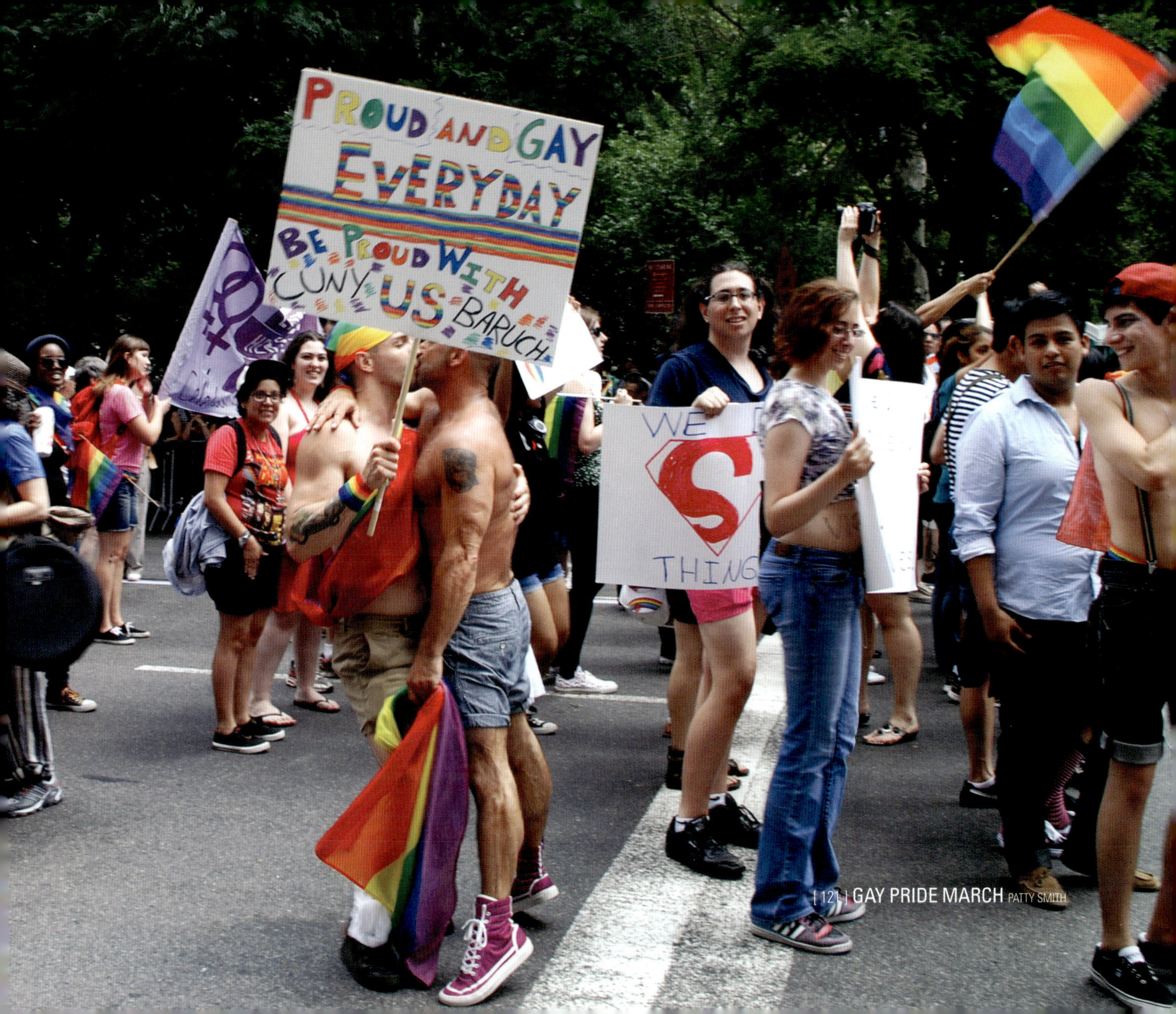

[121] GAY PRIDE MARCH PATTY SMITH

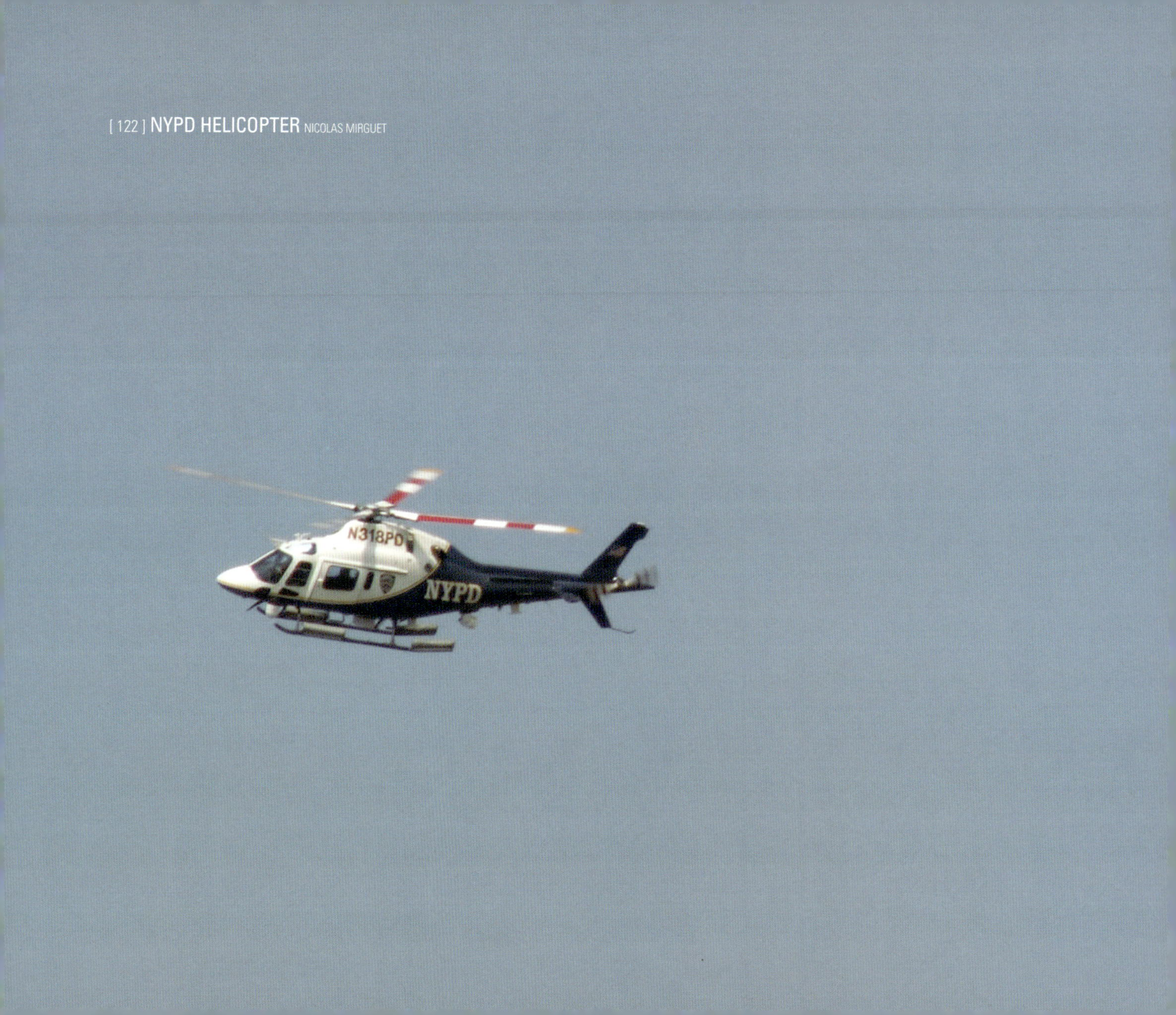

[122] NYPD HELICOPTER NICOLAS MIRGUET

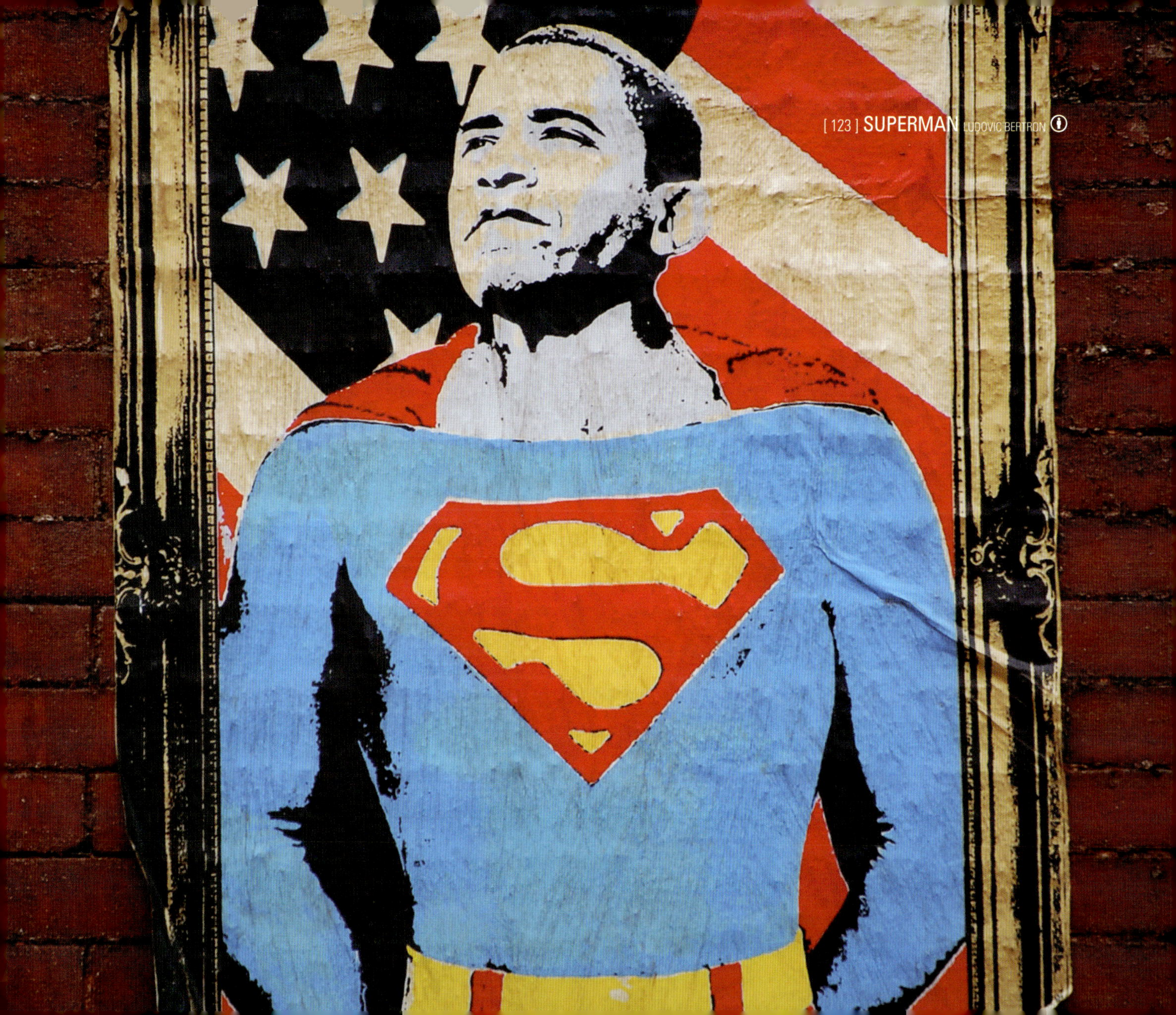

[123] SUPERMAN LUDOVIC BERTRON

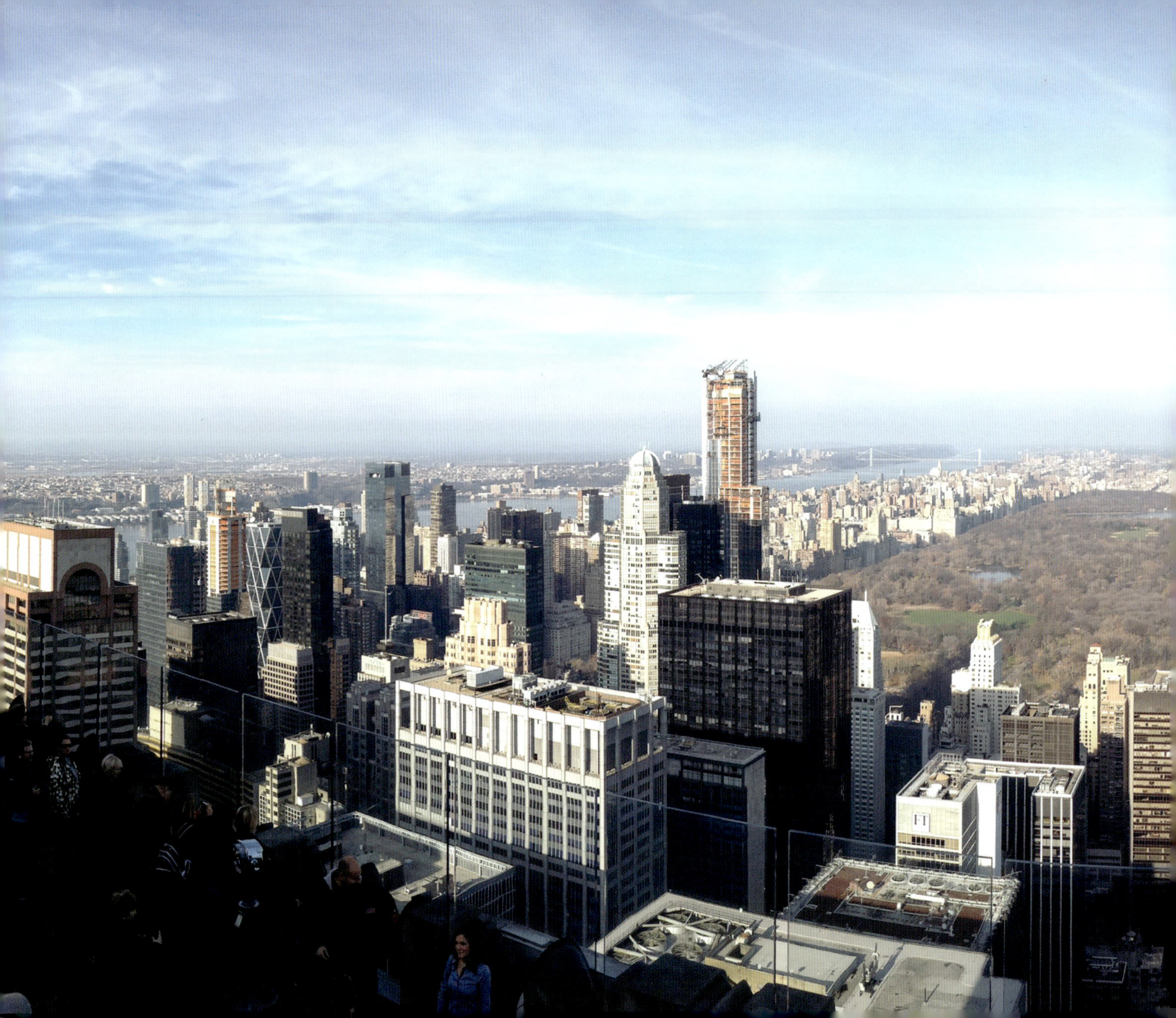

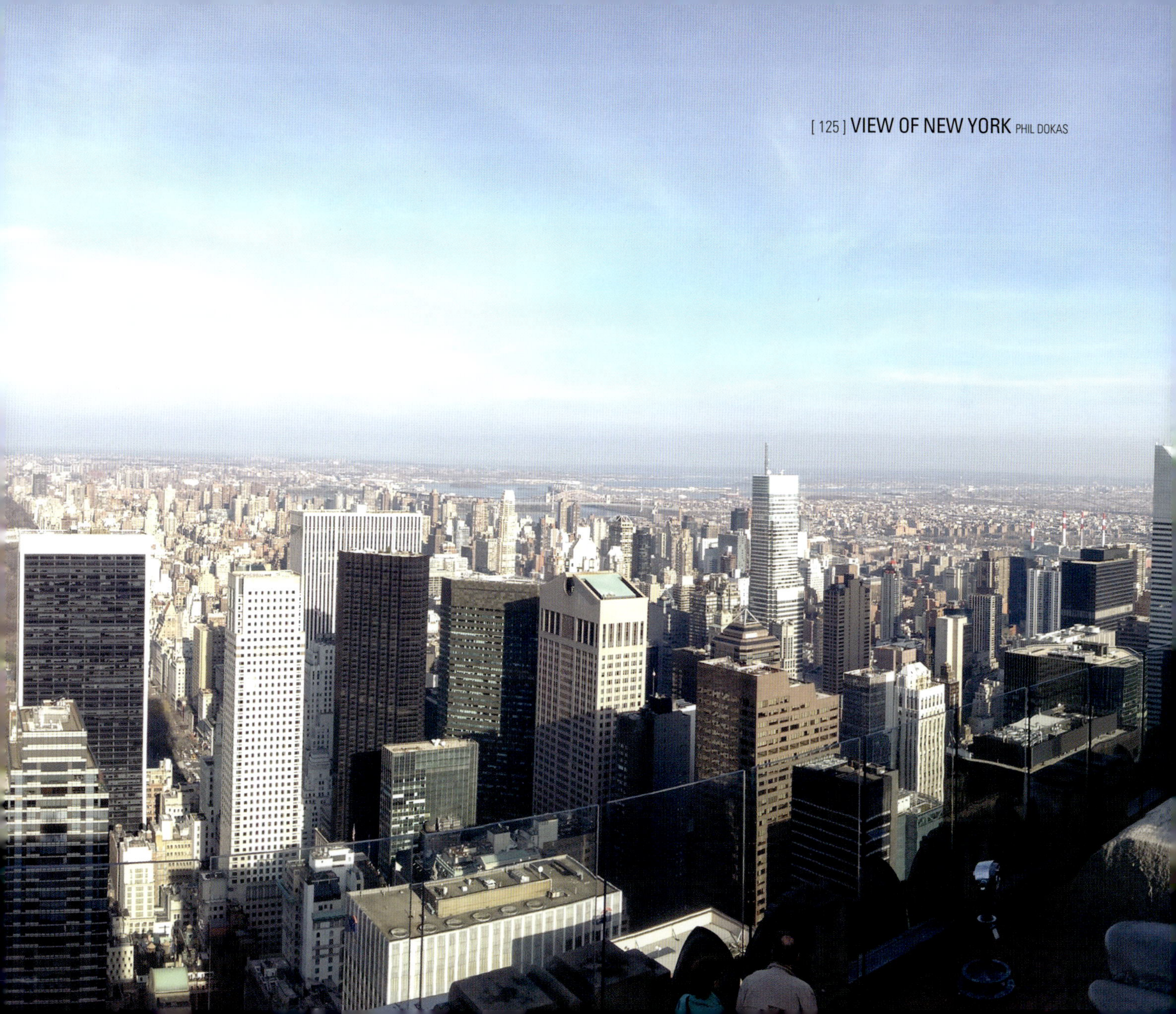

[125] VIEW OF NEW YORK PHIL DOKAS

[126] USS MAINE SHANE STROUD

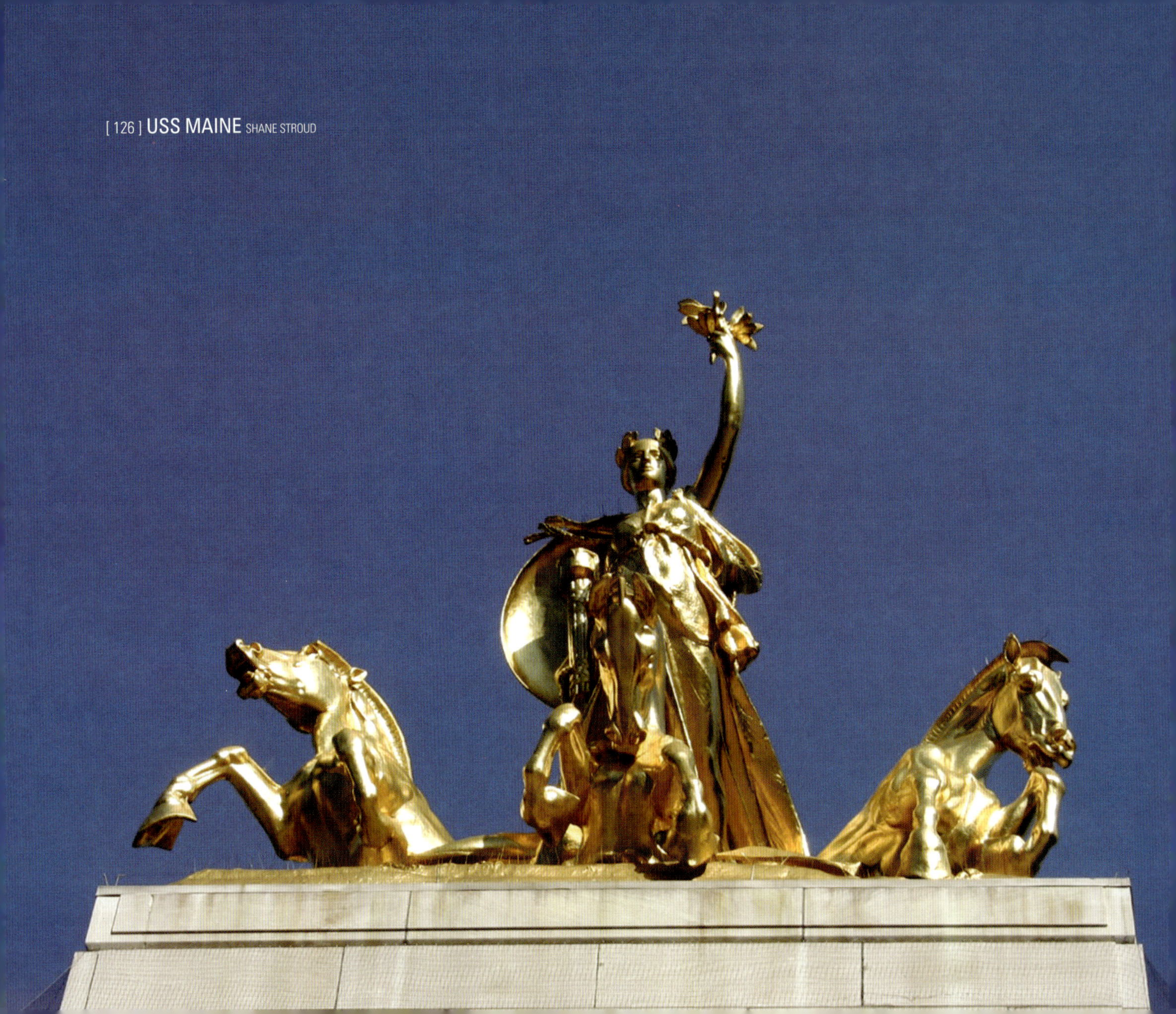

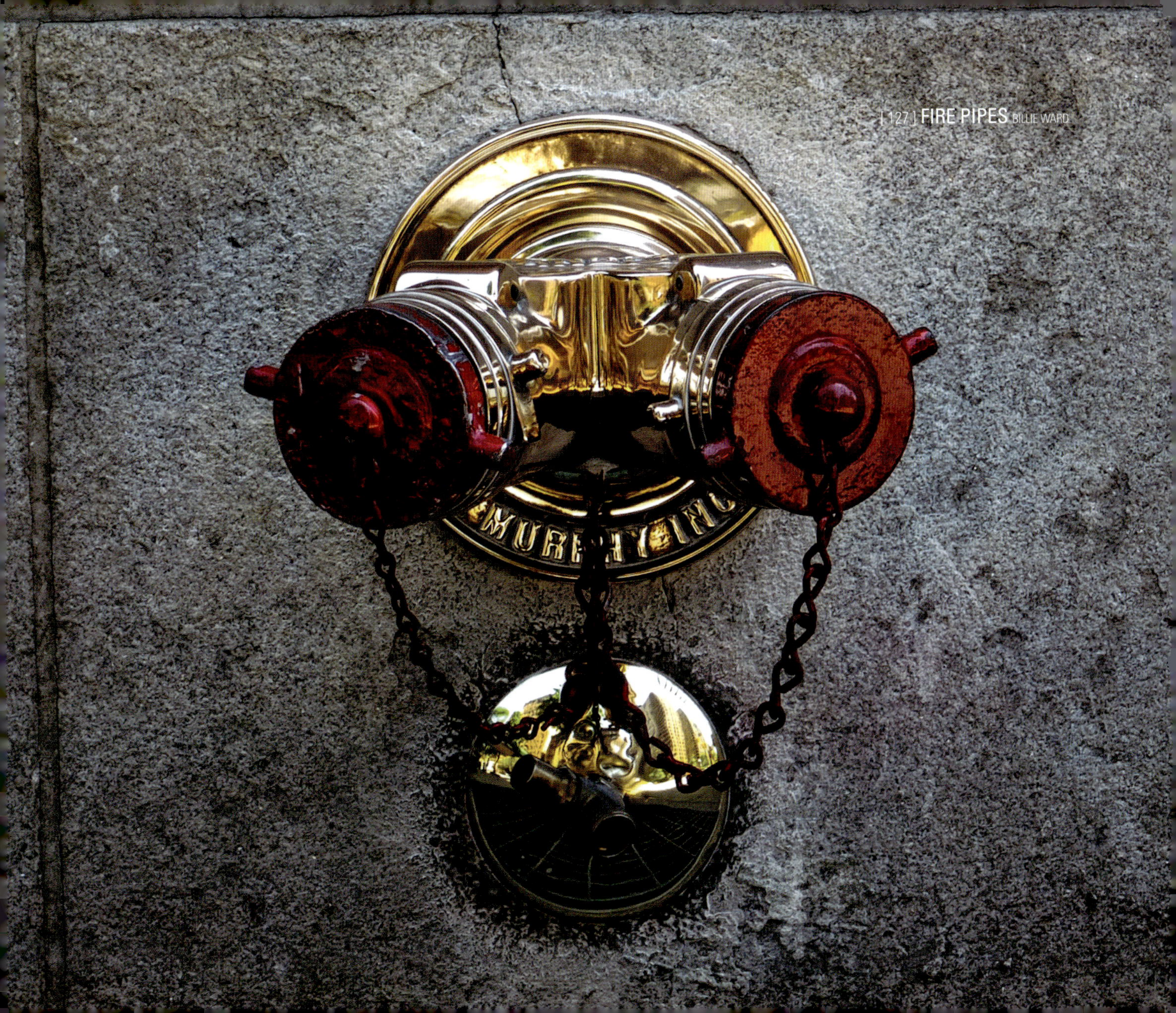

[127] FIRE PIPES BILLIE WARD

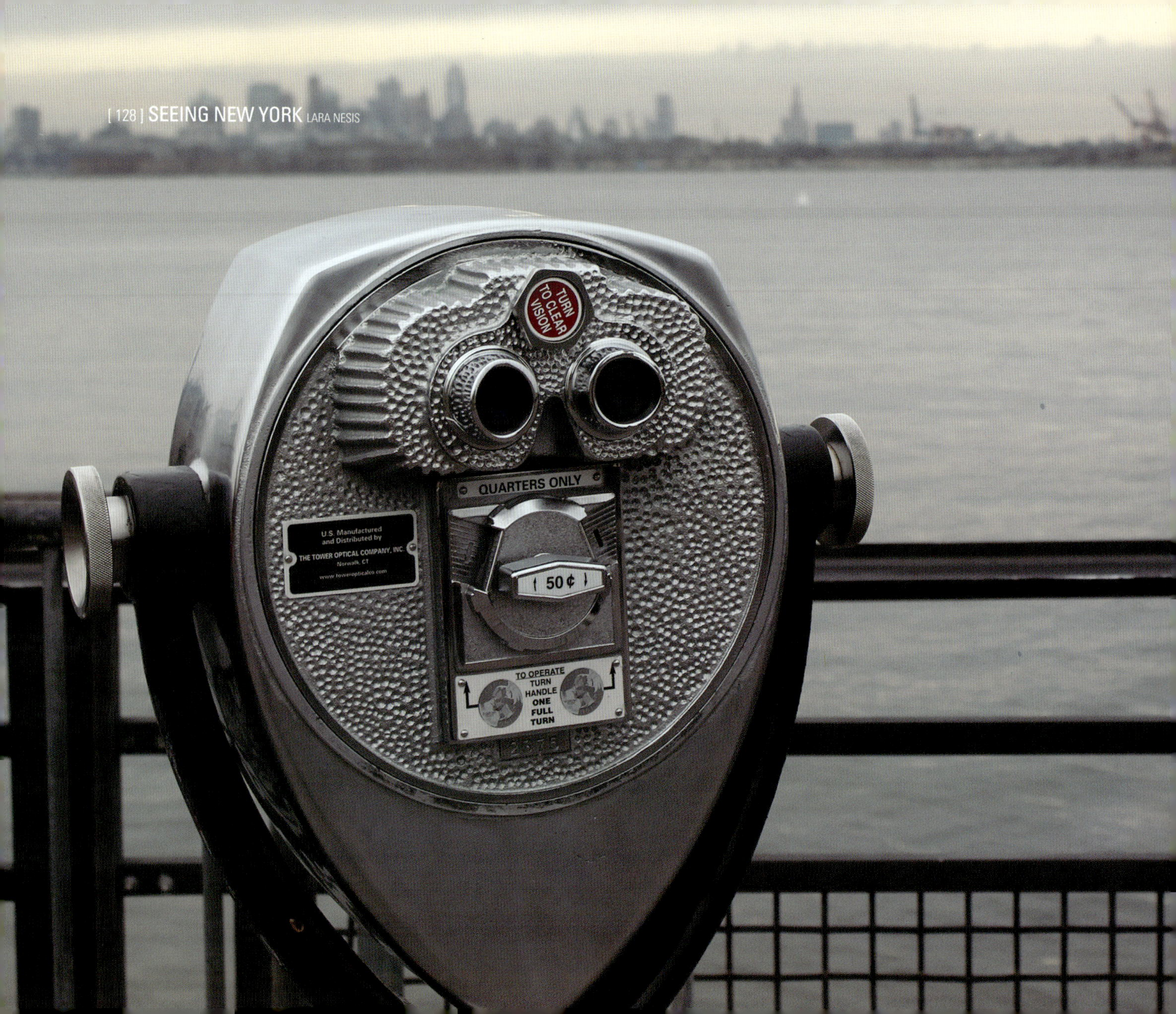
TURN TO CLEAR VISION
QUARTERS ONLY
U.S. Manufactured and Distributed by
THE TOWER OPTICAL COMPANY, INC.
Norwalk, CT
50¢
TO OPERATE
TURN HANDLE
ONE FULL TURN

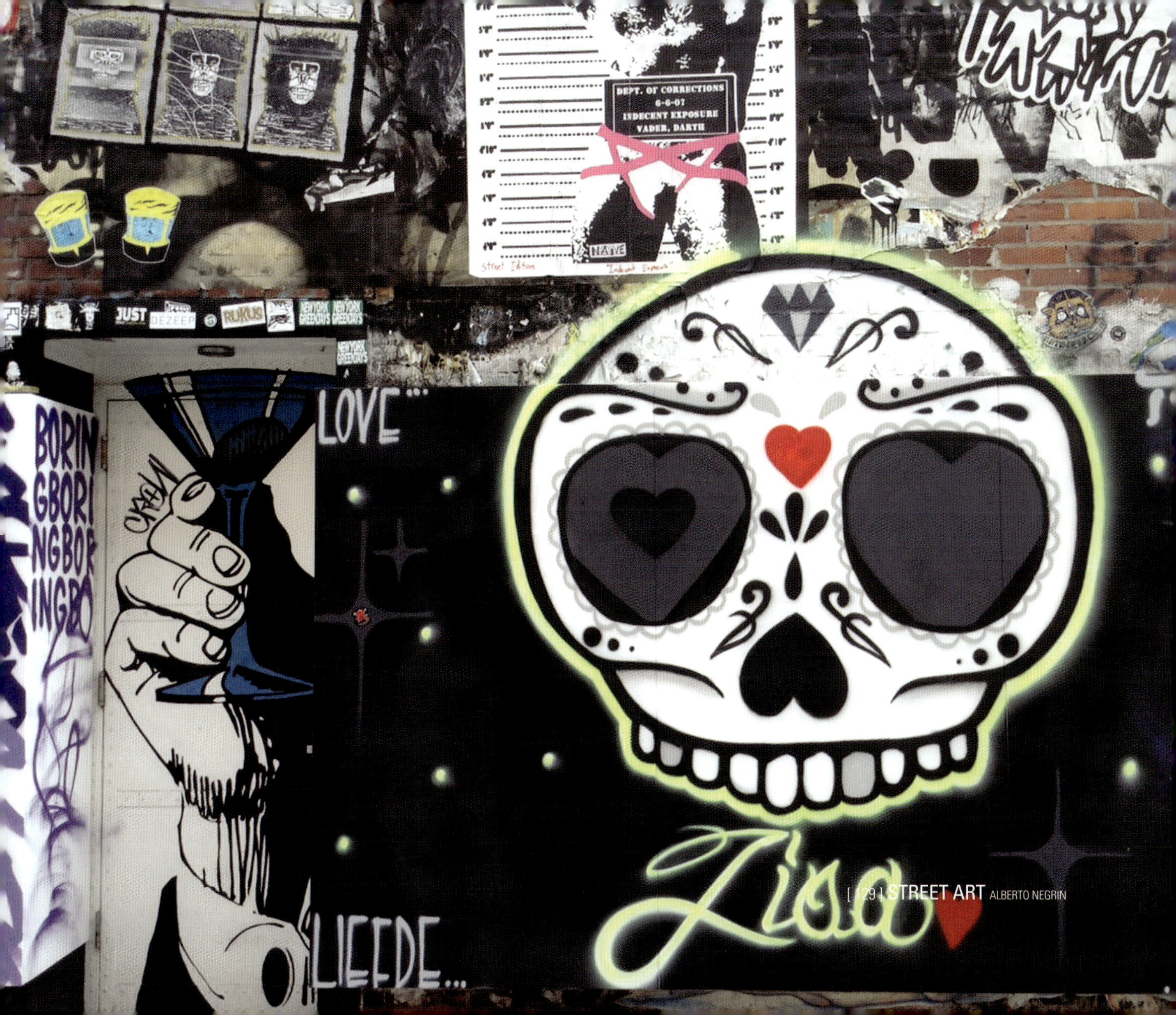
DEPT. OF CORRECTIONS
6-6-07
INDECENT EXPOSURE
VADER, DARTH
LOVE
LIEFDE...
Lisa

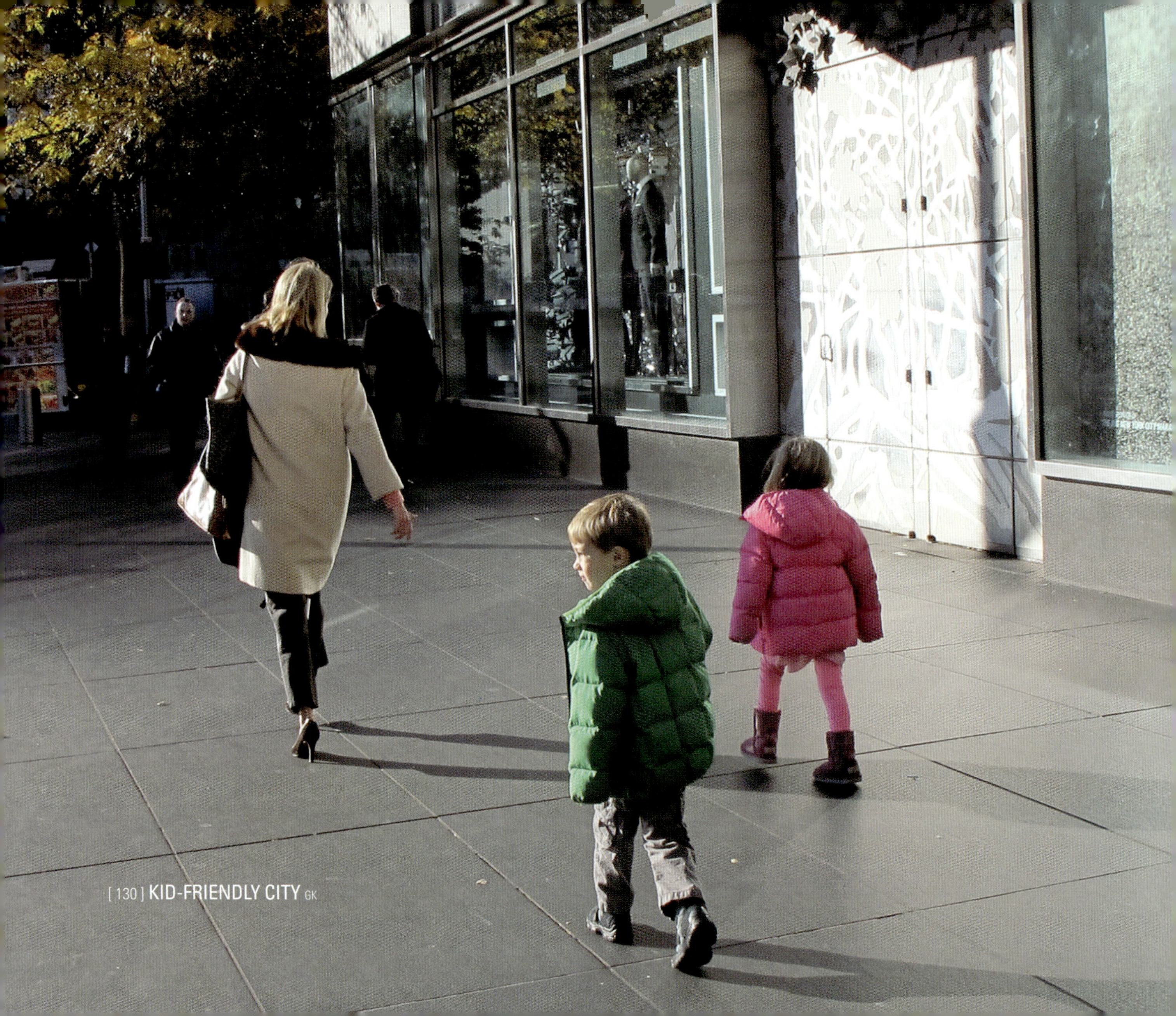

[130] **KID-FRIENDLY CITY** GK

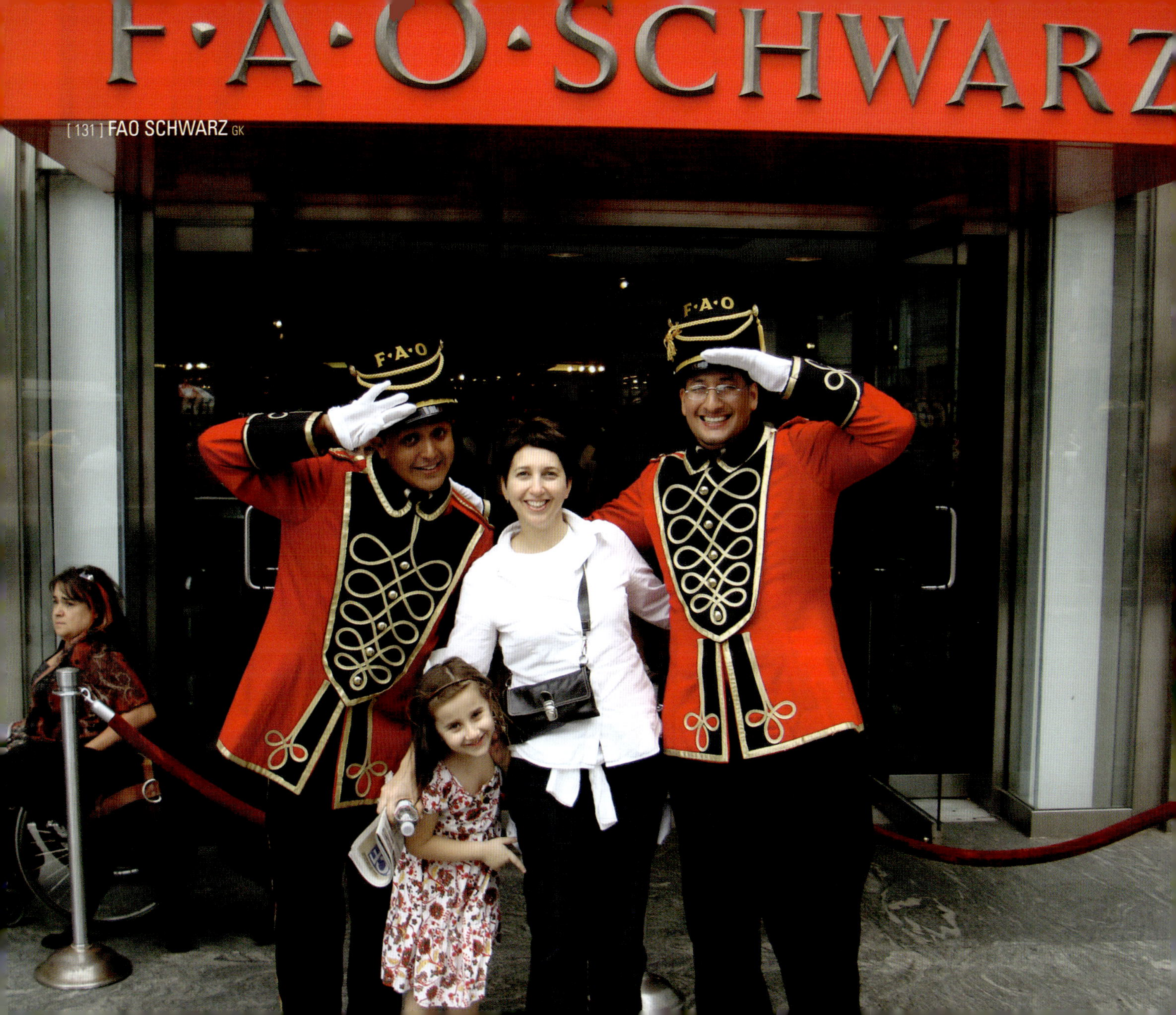

[131] FAO SCHWARZ GK

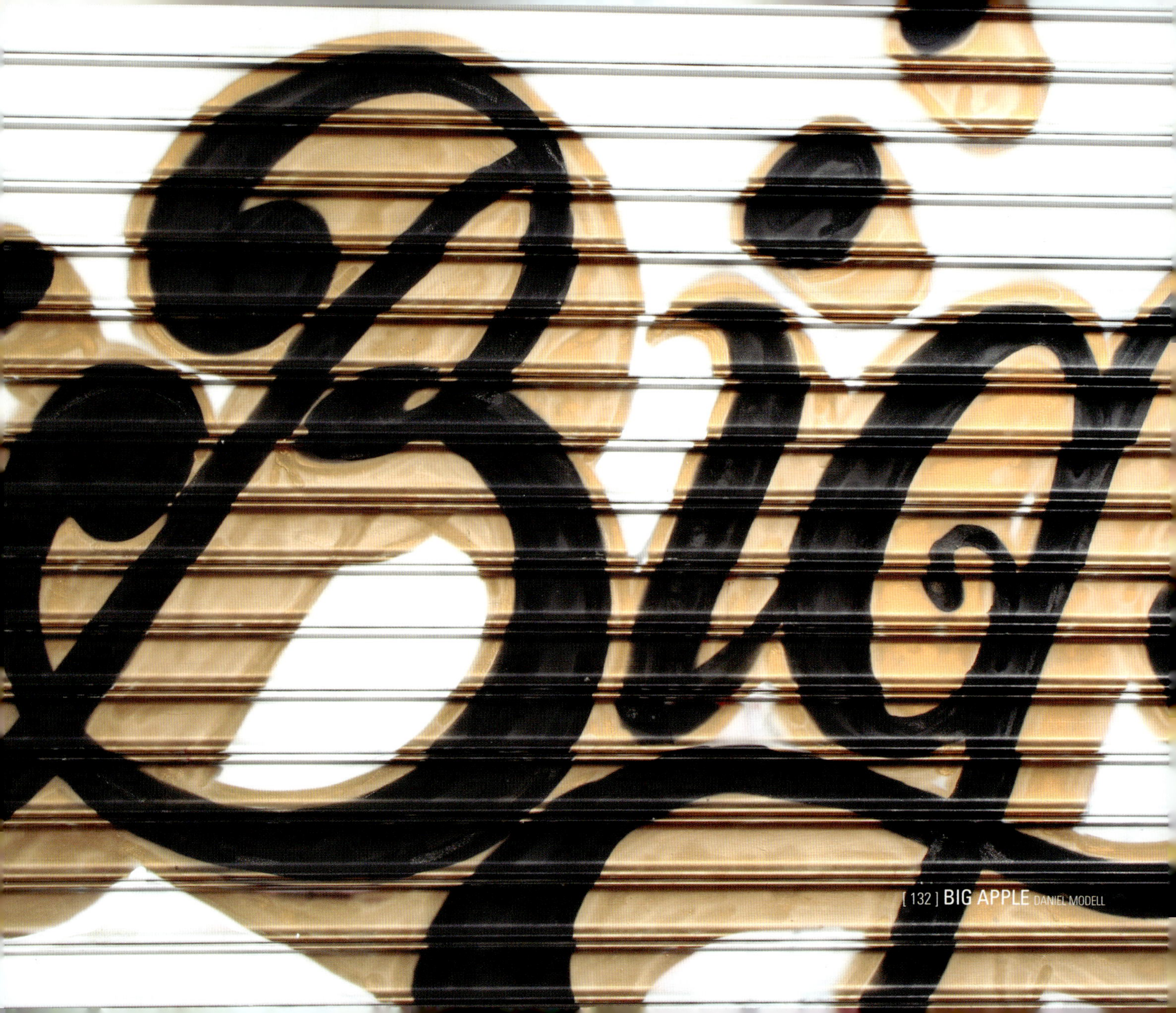

[132] BIG APPLE DANIEL MODELL

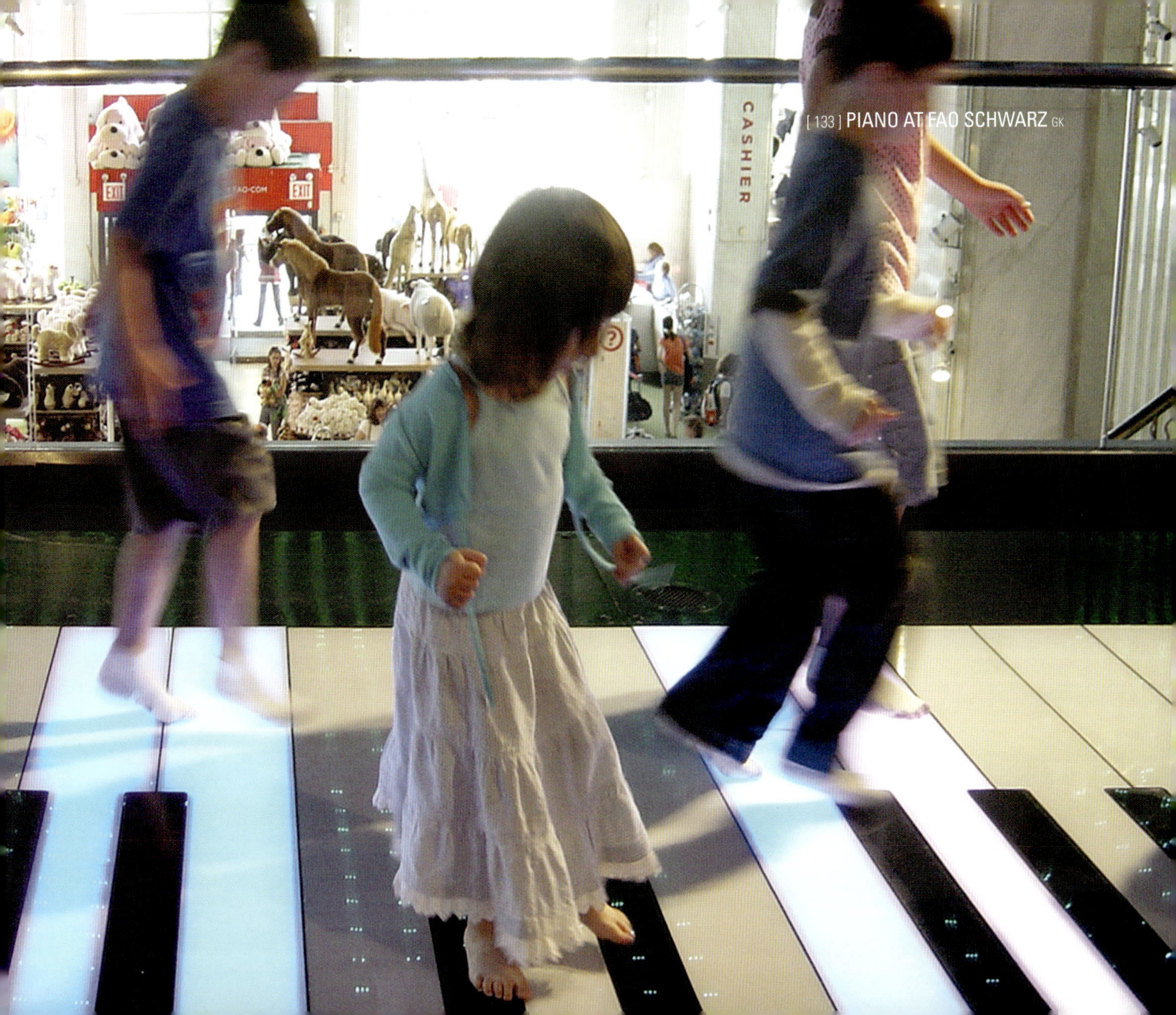

[133] PIANO AT FAO SCHWARZ GK

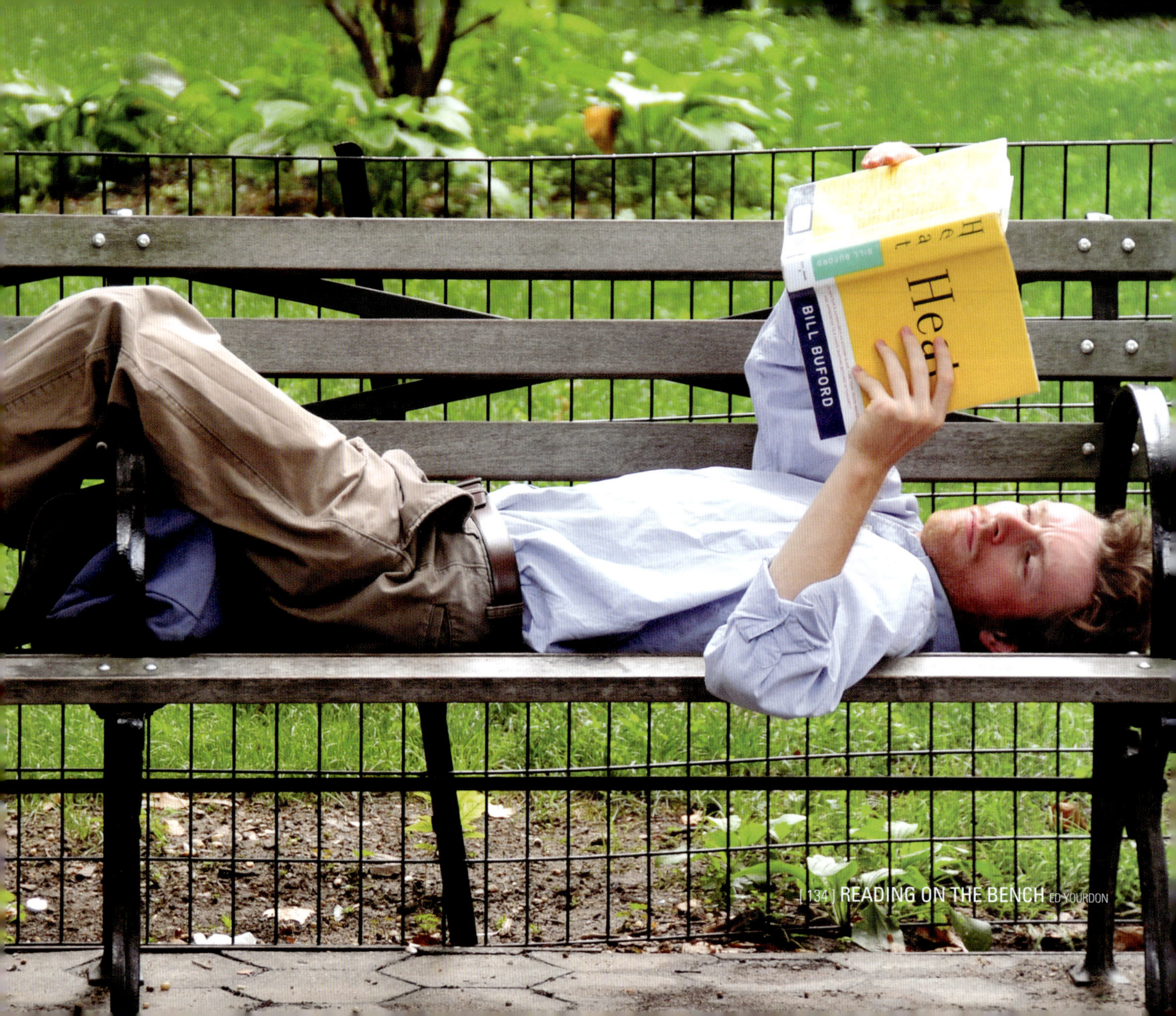

[134] READING ON THE BENCH ED YOURDON

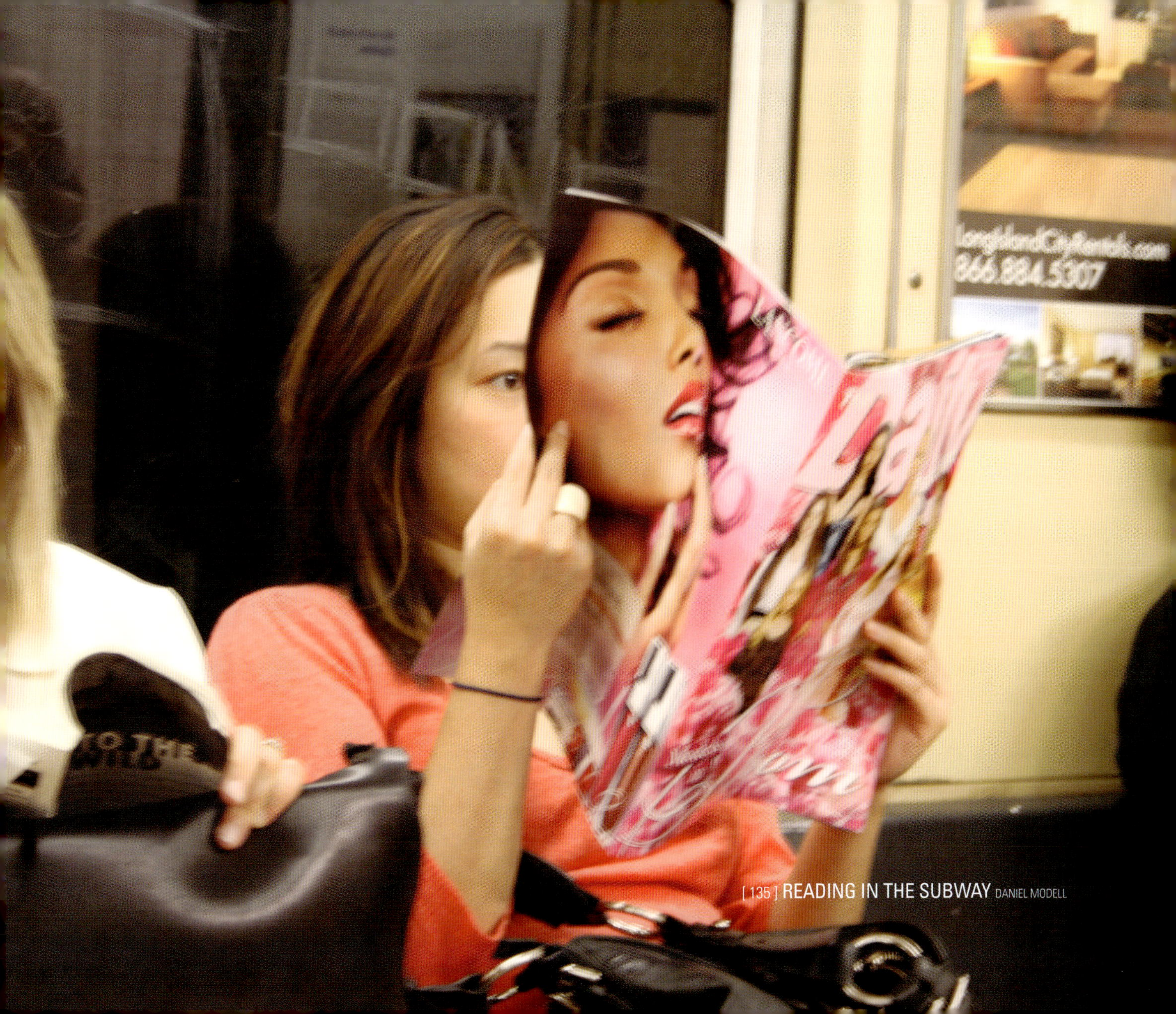

[135] READING IN THE SUBWAY DANIEL MODELL

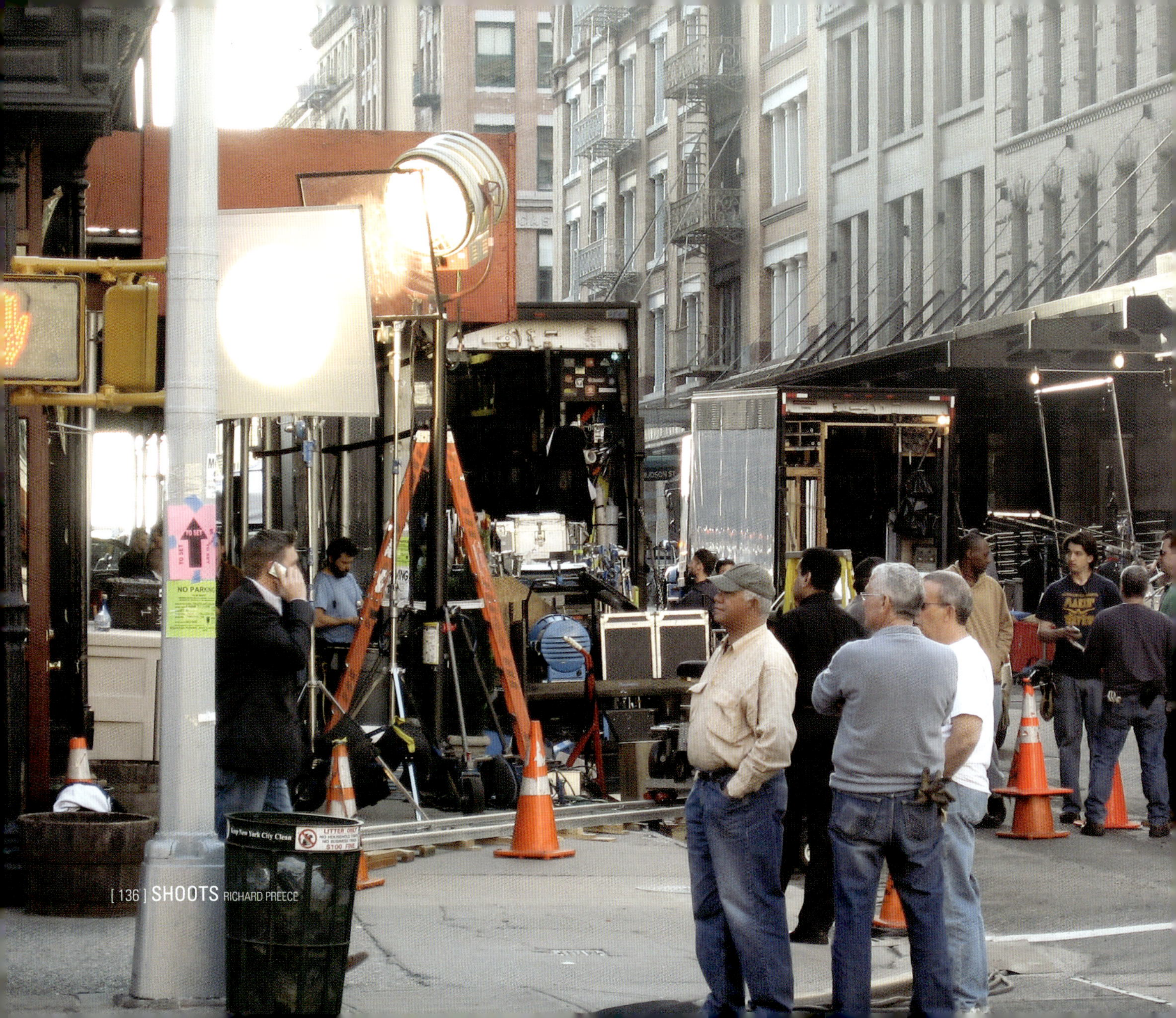
TO SET
NO PARKING
Keep New York City Clean
LITTER ONLY
$100 FINE

[137] NO PARKING PHOTOGRAPHERS' PAGE #399

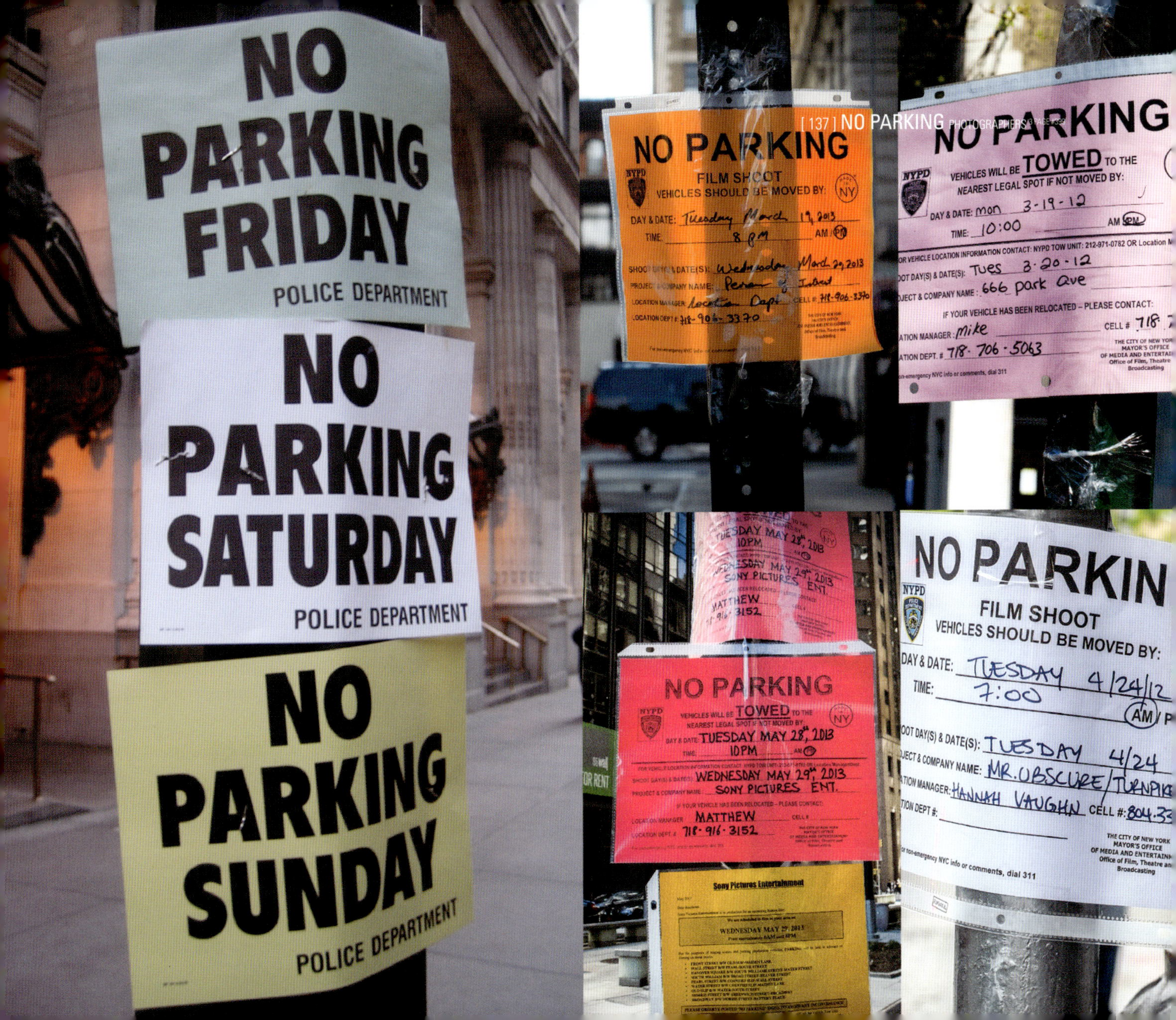

The New York Times Magazine

June 9, 2013 [138] THE NEW YORK TIMES MAGAZINE GK

THE DATE
The Gregorian calendar, the standard secular calendar for most of the world, was introduced by Pope Gregory XIII on Feb. 24, 1582.

THIS MAGAZINE
The first issue of The Times Magazine was published on Sept. 6, 1896. Like the Book Review and "All the News That's Fit to Print," it was introduced by Adolph Ochs soon after he took over the failing newspaper.

THE INNOVATIONS ISSUE

WHO MADE

THIS FONT
Known as LLCircular, it was designed in 2007 by the Swiss typographer Laurenz Brunr and was inspired by sans-serif typefaces like Futura (1927) and Avant Garde (1968).

Muller Martini created the first automatic wire saddle-stitching machine in 1954. The magazine still uses its equipment.

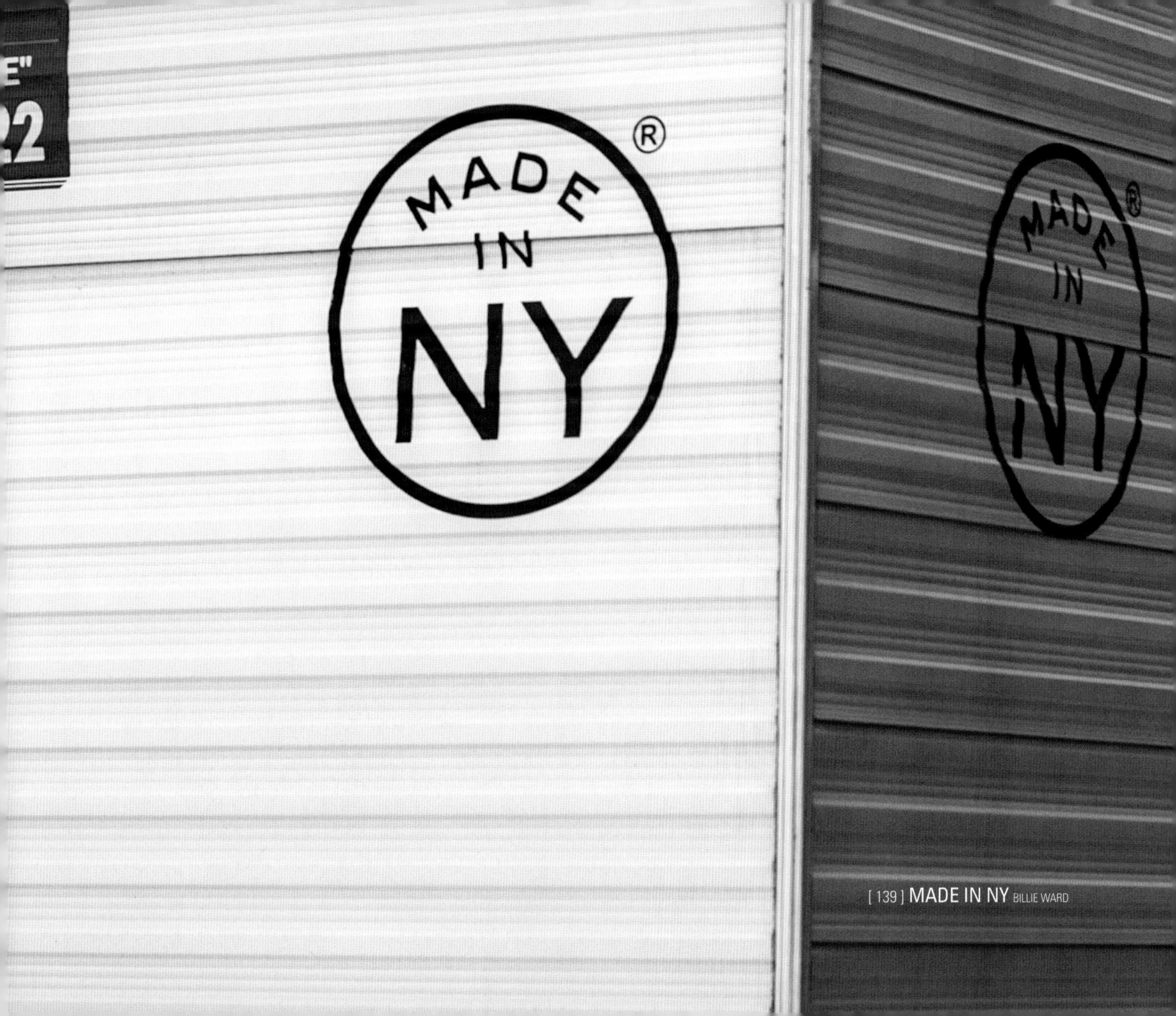

[139] MADE IN NY BILLIE WARD

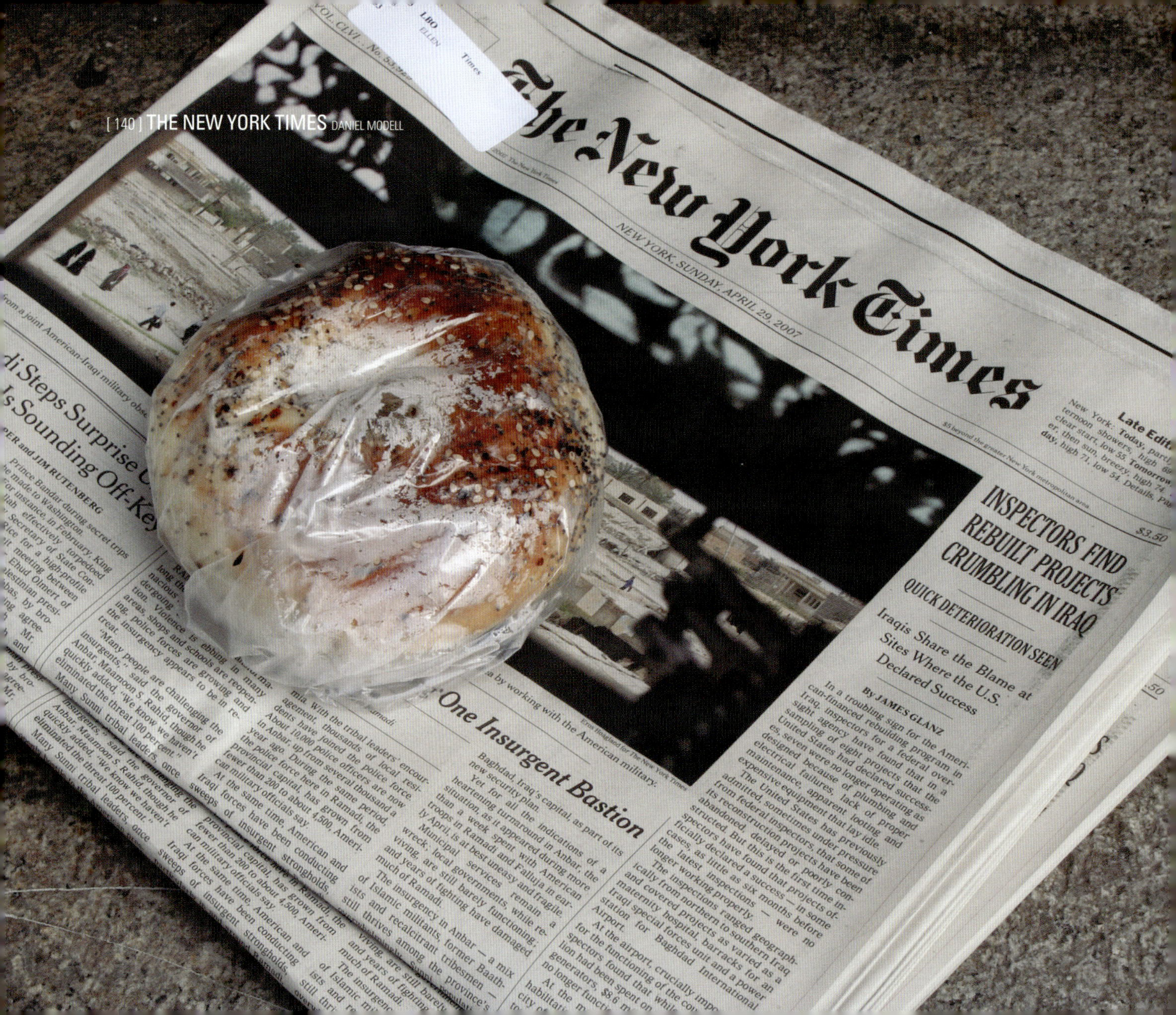
The New York Times
NEW YORK, SUNDAY, APRIL 29, 2007
Late Edition
$3.50
INSPECTORS FIND REBUILT PROJECTS CRUMBLING IN IRAQ
QUICK DETERIORATION SEEN
Iraqis Share the Blame at Sites Where the U.S. Declared Success
By JAMES GLANZ
One Insurgent Bastion

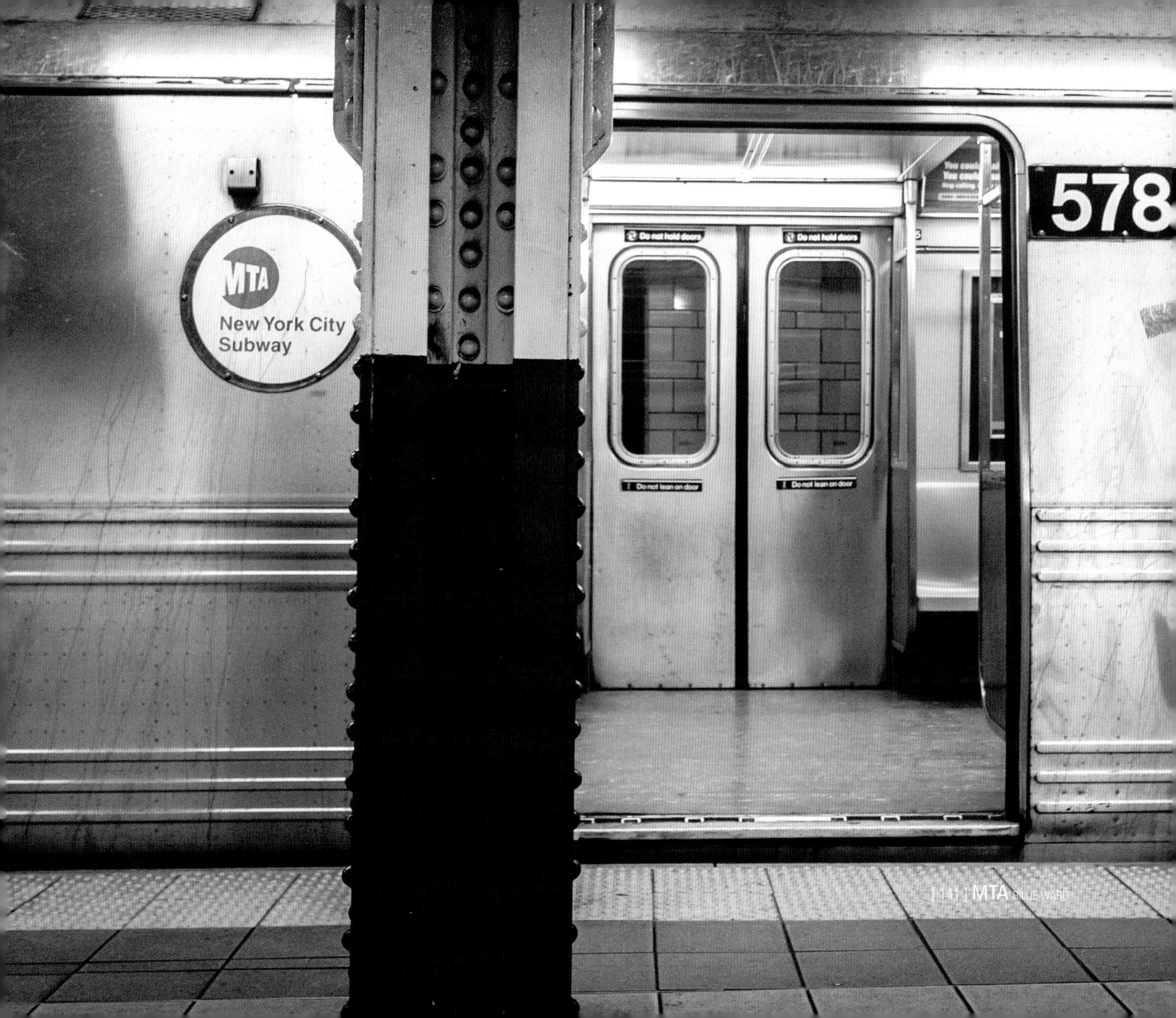

[141] MTA BILLIE WARD

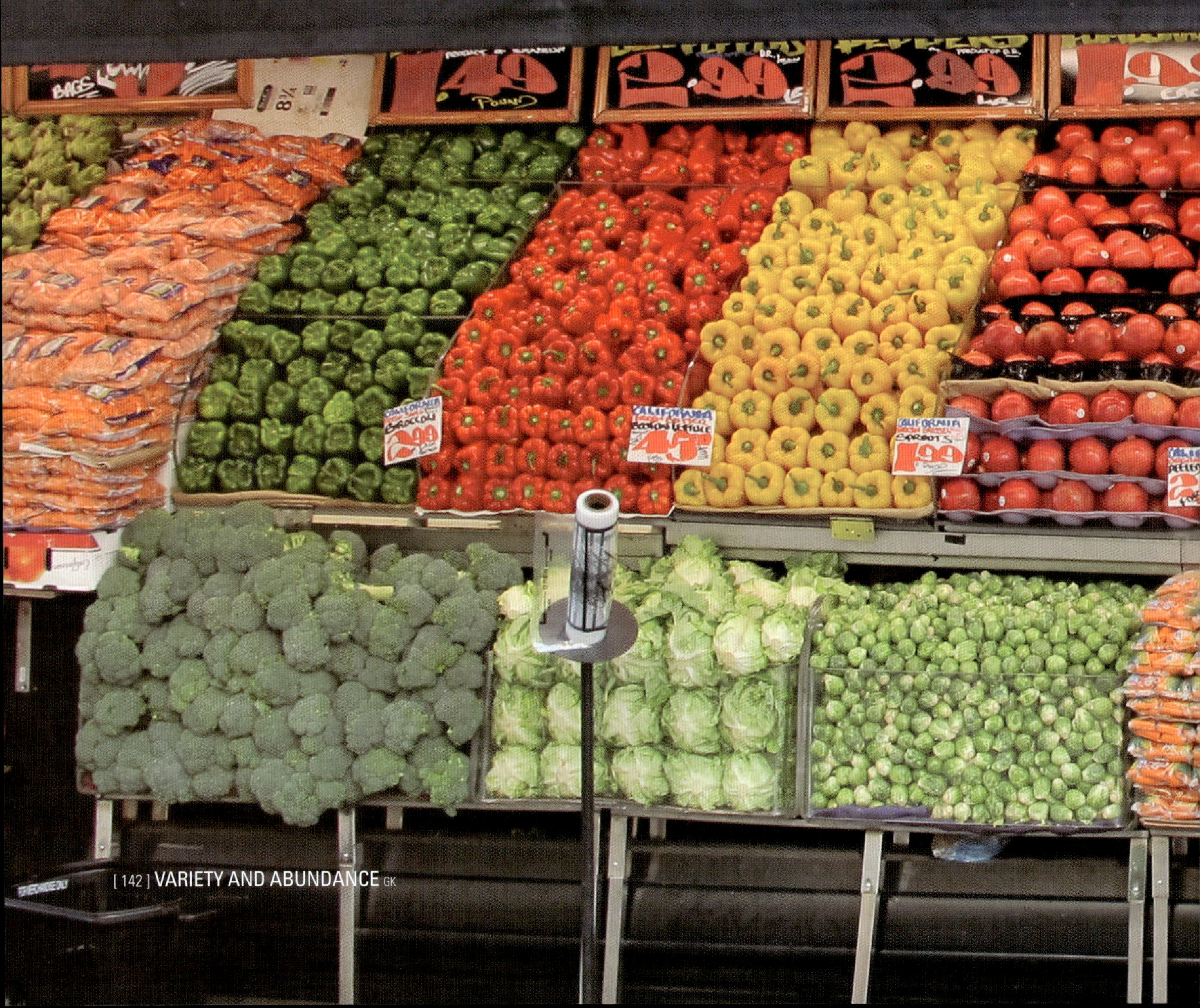

[142] VARIETY AND ABUNDANCE GK

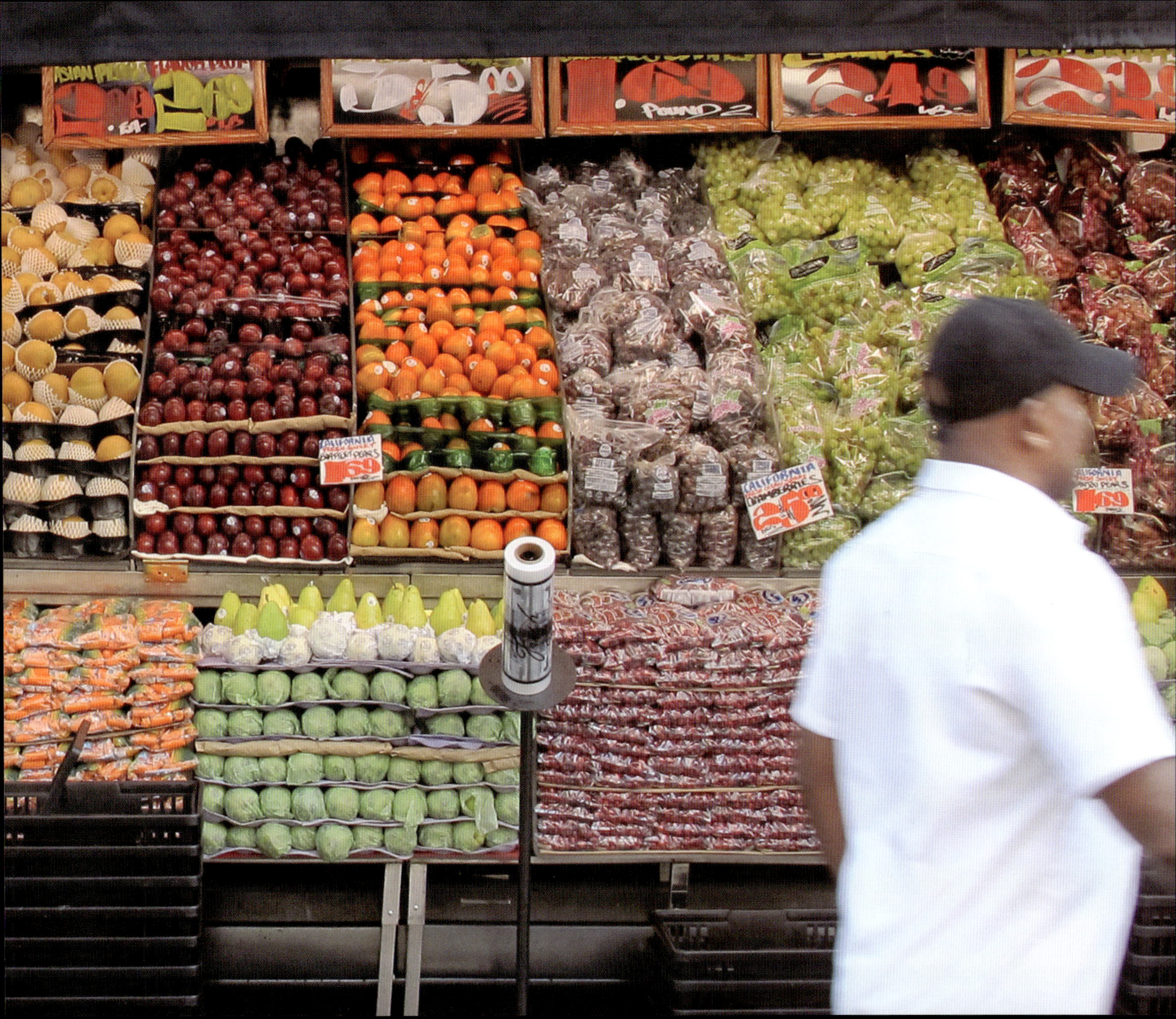
1.69
POUND 2
2.49
CALIFORNIA
BARTLETT PEARS
1.69
CALIFORNIA

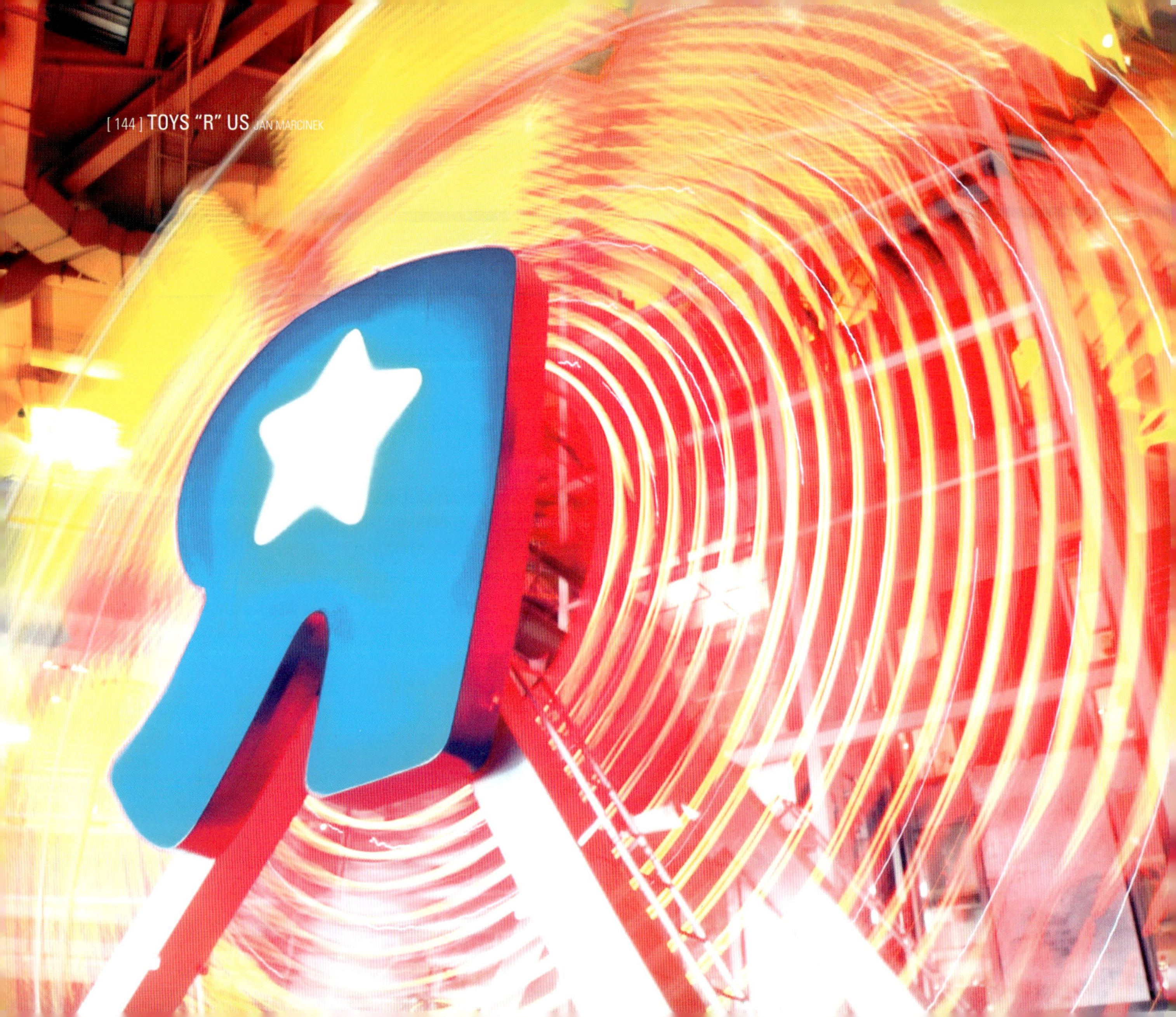

[144] TOYS "R" US JAN MARCINEK

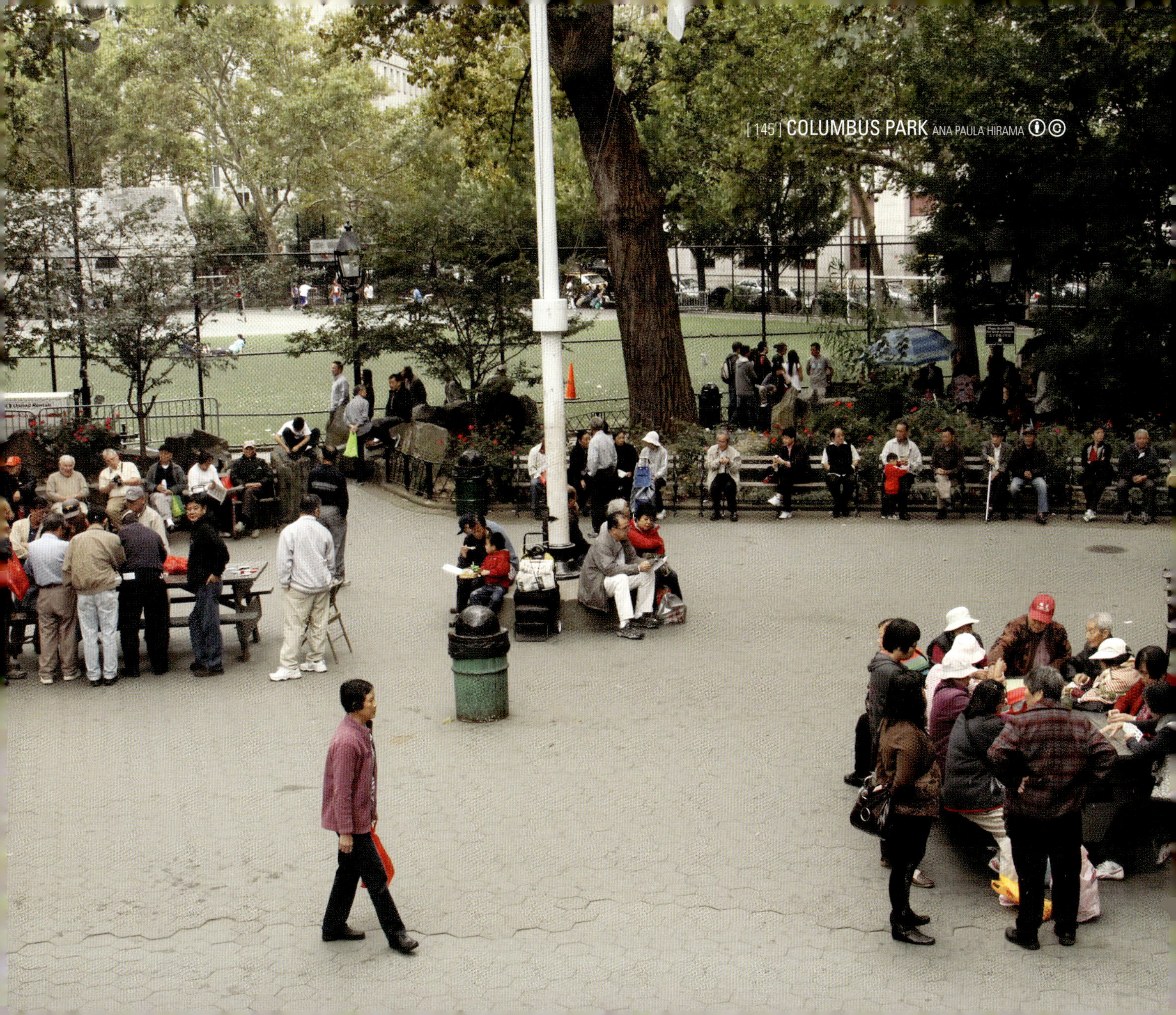

[145] COLUMBUS PARK ANA PAULA HIRAMA ⓘ©

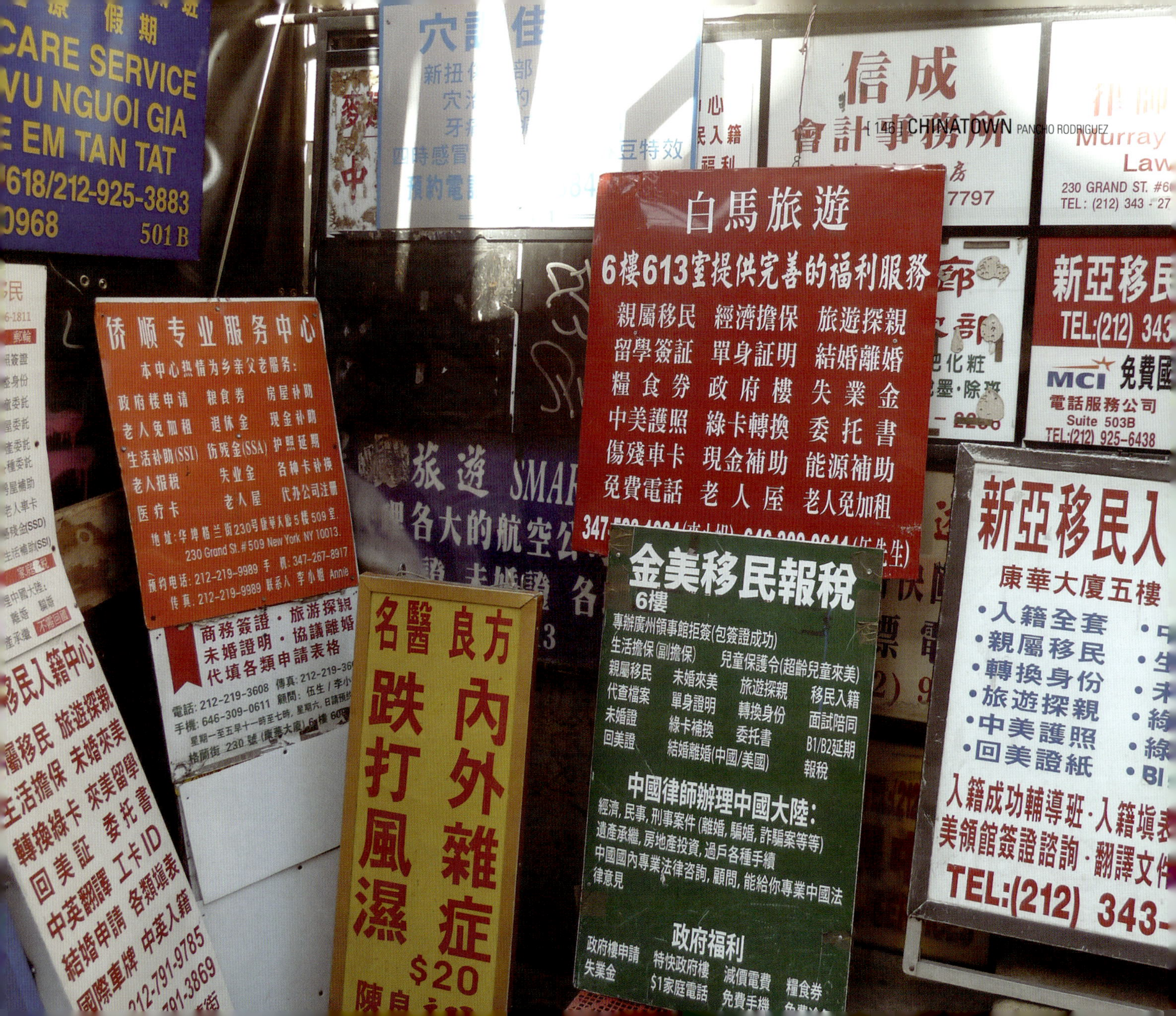

假期
CARE SERVICE
VU NGUOI GIA
E EM TAN TAT
618/212-925-3883
0968
501 B
信成
會計事務所
Murray
Law
230 GRAND ST.
TEL: (212) 343 - 27
7797
白馬旅遊
6樓613室提供完善的福利服務
親屬移民 經濟擔保 旅遊探親
留學簽証 單身証明 結婚離婚
糧食劵 政府樓 失業金
中美護照 綠卡轉換 委托書
傷殘車卡 現金補助 能源補助
免費電話 老人屋 老人免加租
新亞移民
TEL:(212) 343
MCI 免費國
電話服務公司
Suite 503B
TEL:(212) 925-6438
侨顺专业服务中心
本中心热情为乡亲父老服务:
政府楼申请 粮食券 房屋补助
老人免加租 退休金 现金补助
生活补助(SSI) 伤残金(SSA) 护照延期
老人报税 失业金 各种卡补换
医疗卡 老人屋 代办公司注册
230 Grand St. #509 New York NY 10013
预约电话: 212-219-9989
旅遊 SMA
商務簽證・旅遊探親
未婚證明・協議離婚
代填各類申請表格
電話: 212-219-3608
手機: 646-309-0611
金美移民報稅
6樓
專辦廣州領事館拒簽(包簽證成功)
生活擔保(副擔保) 兒童保護令(超齡兒童來美)
親屬移民 未婚來美 旅遊探親 移民入籍
代查檔案 單身證明 轉換身份 面試陪同
未婚證 綠卡補換 委托書 B1/B2延期
回美證 結婚離婚(中國/美國) 報稅
中國律師辦理中國大陸:
經濟,民事,刑事案件(離婚,騙婚,詐騙案等等)
遺產承繼,房地產投資,過戶各種手續
中國國內專業法律咨詢,顧問,能給你專業中國法律意見
政府福利
政府樓申請 特快政府樓 減價電費 糧食券
失業金 $1家庭電話 免費手機
名醫良方
跌打風濕
內外雜症
$20
新亞移民入
康華大廈五樓
•入籍全套
•親屬移民
•轉換身份
•旅遊探親
•中美護照
•回美證紙
入籍成功輔導班・入籍填表
美領館簽證諮詢・翻譯文件
TEL:(212) 343-
移民入籍中心
屬移民 旅遊探親
生活擔保 未婚來美
轉換綠卡 來美留學
回美証 委托書
中英翻譯 工卡ID
結婚申請 各類填表
國際重牌 中英入籍
212-791-9785
791-3869

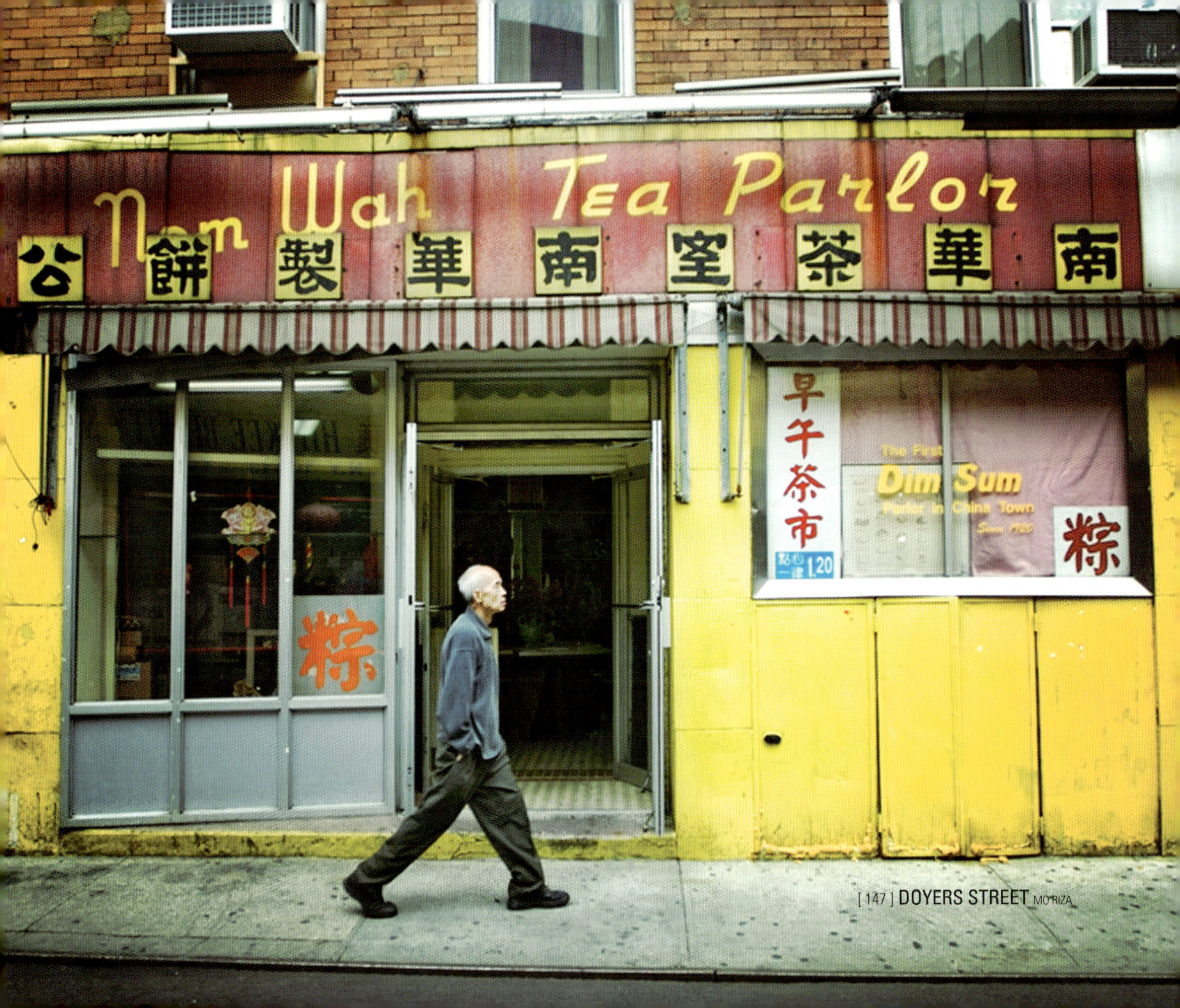

[147] DOYERS STREET MO RIZA

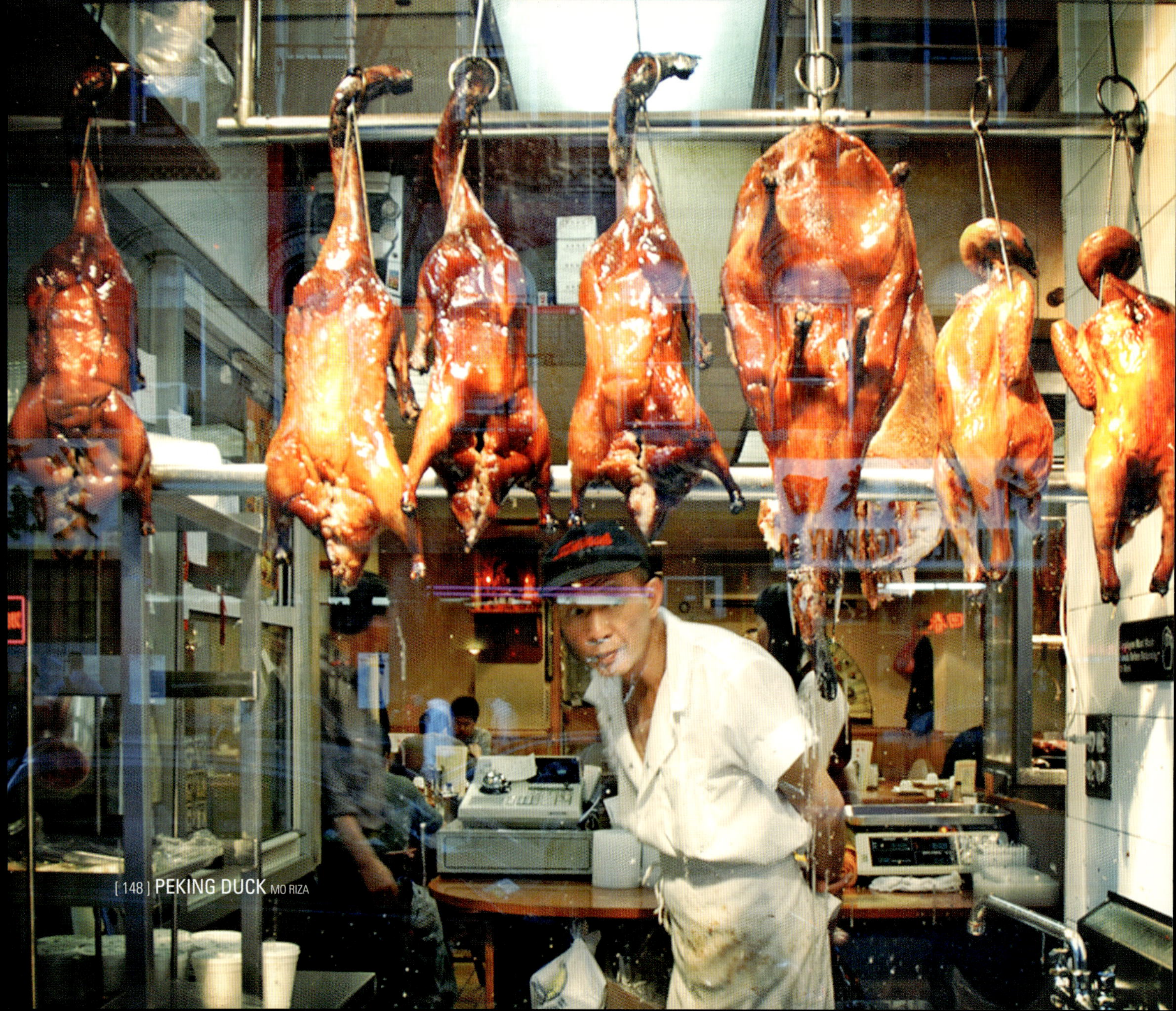

[148] PEKING DUCK MO RIZA

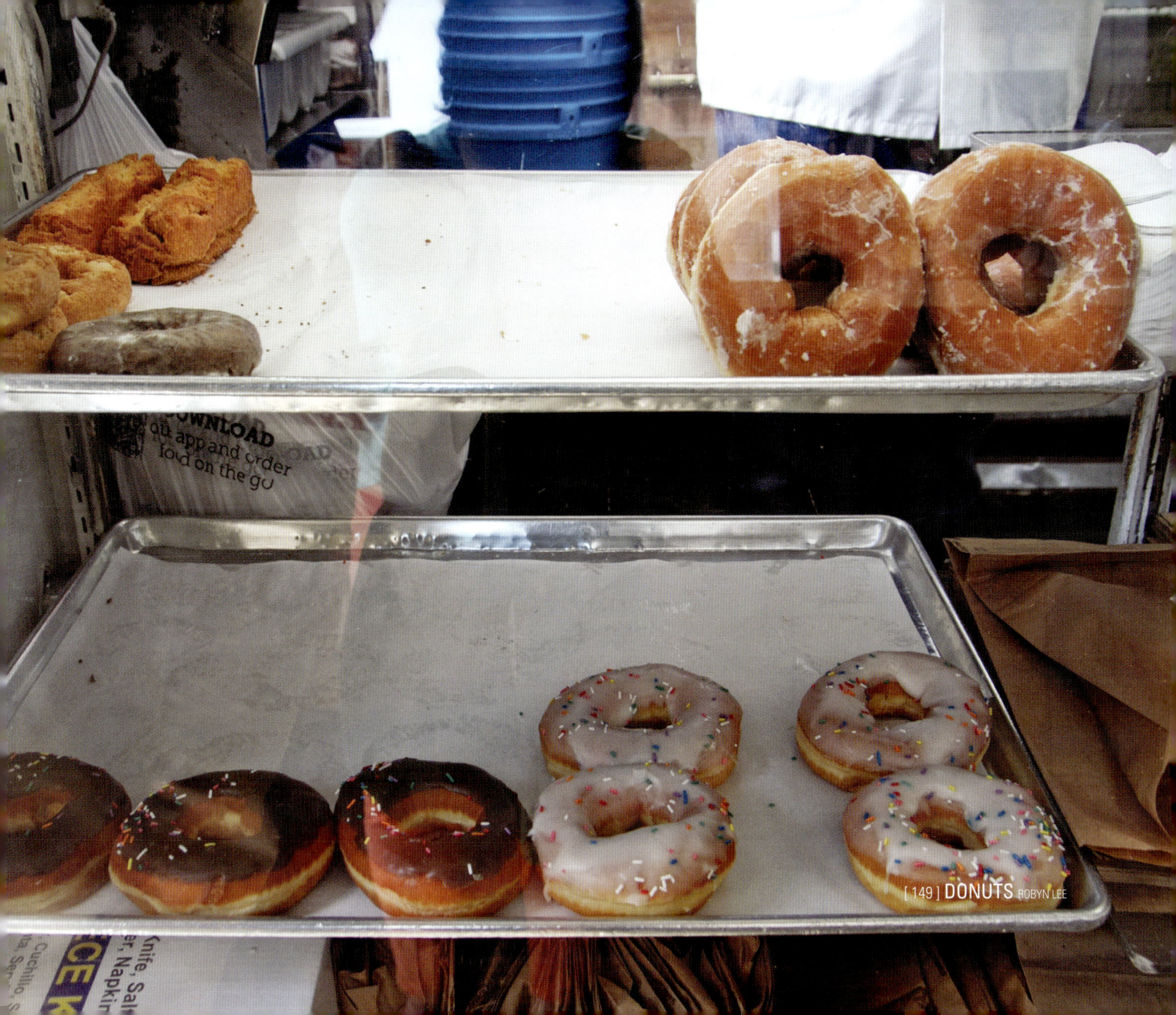

[149] DONUTS ROBYN LEE

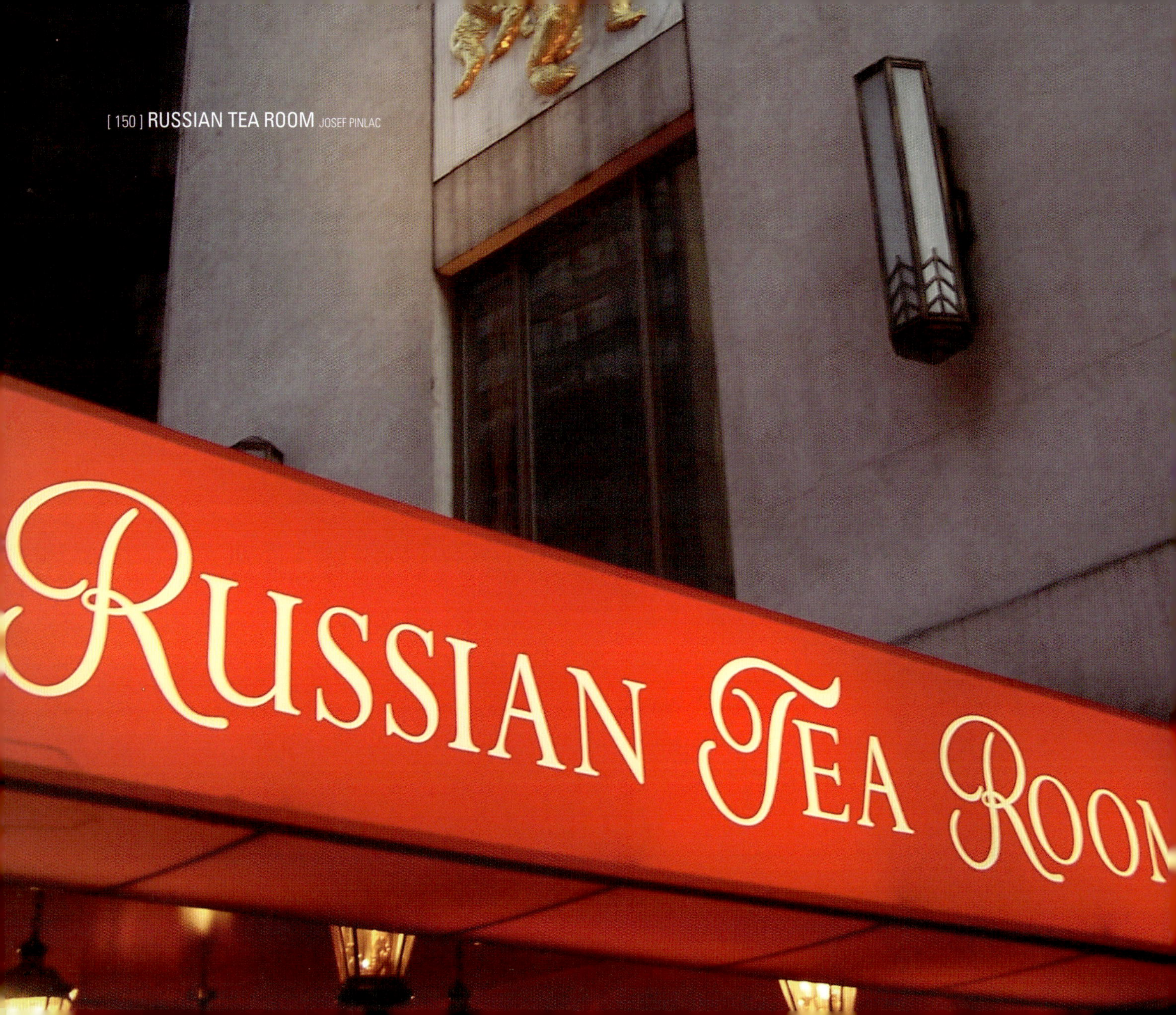

[150] RUSSIAN TEA ROOM JOSEF PINLAC

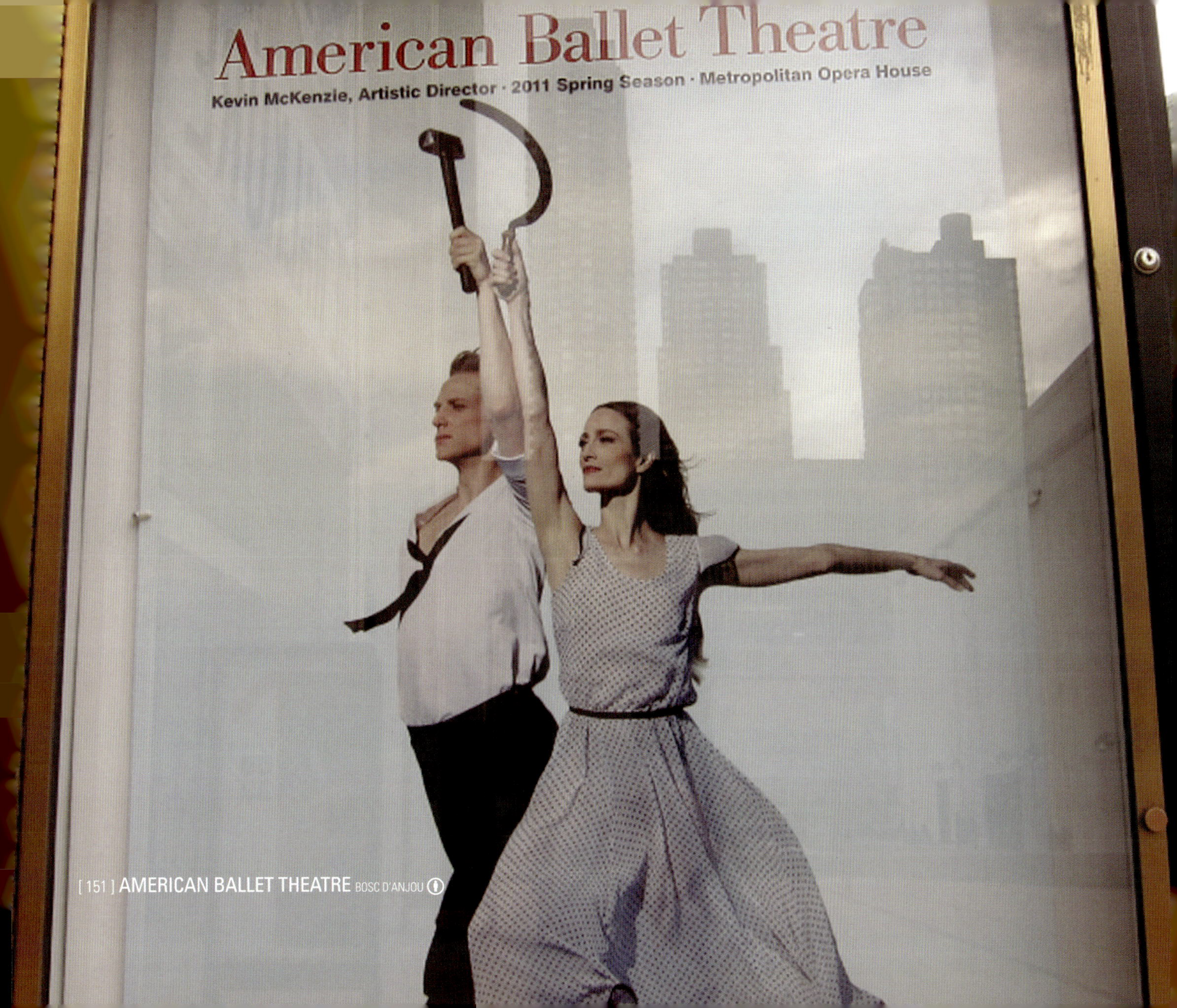

[151] AMERICAN BALLET THEATRE BOSC D'ANJOU

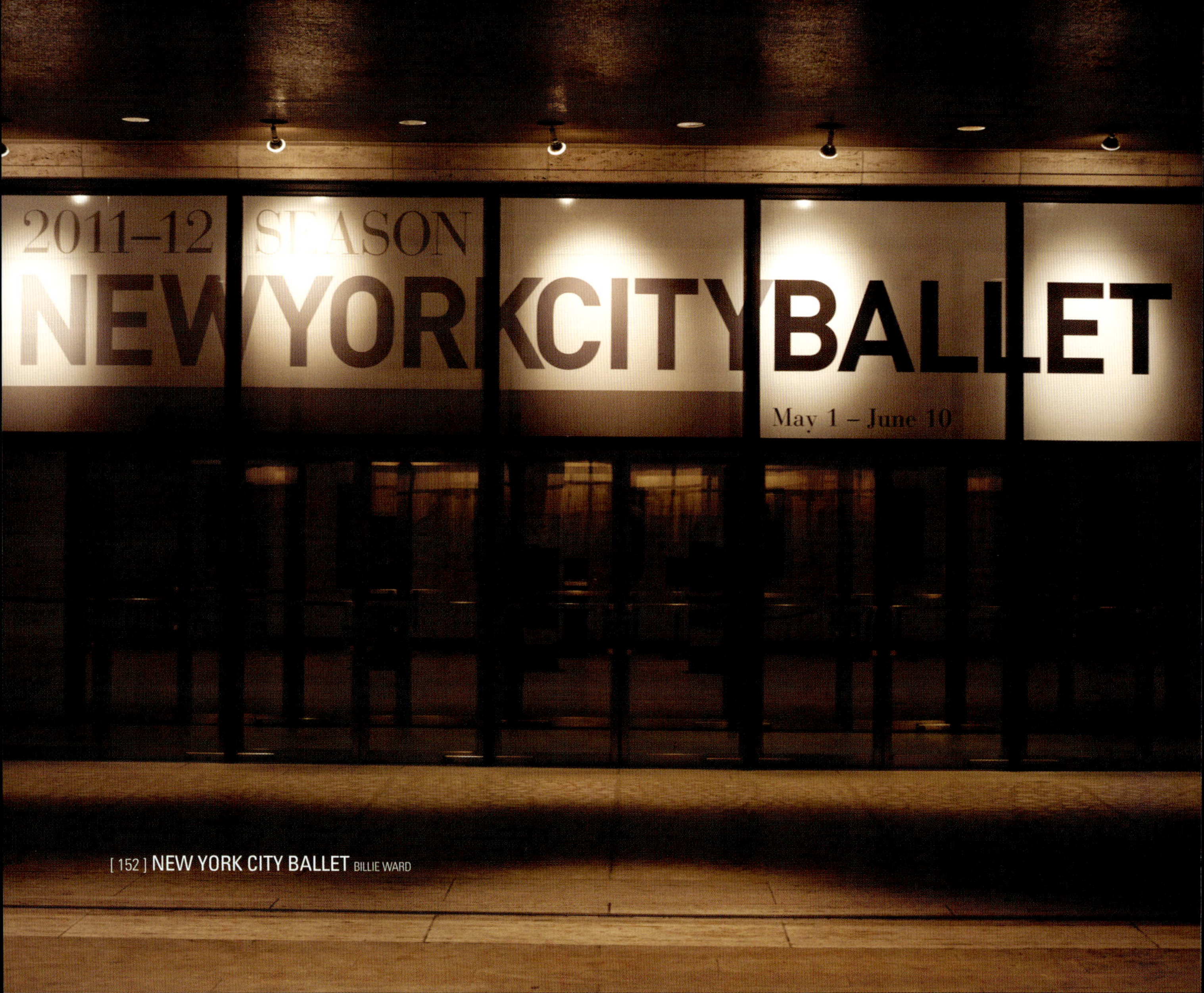

[152] NEW YORK CITY BALLET BILLIE WARD

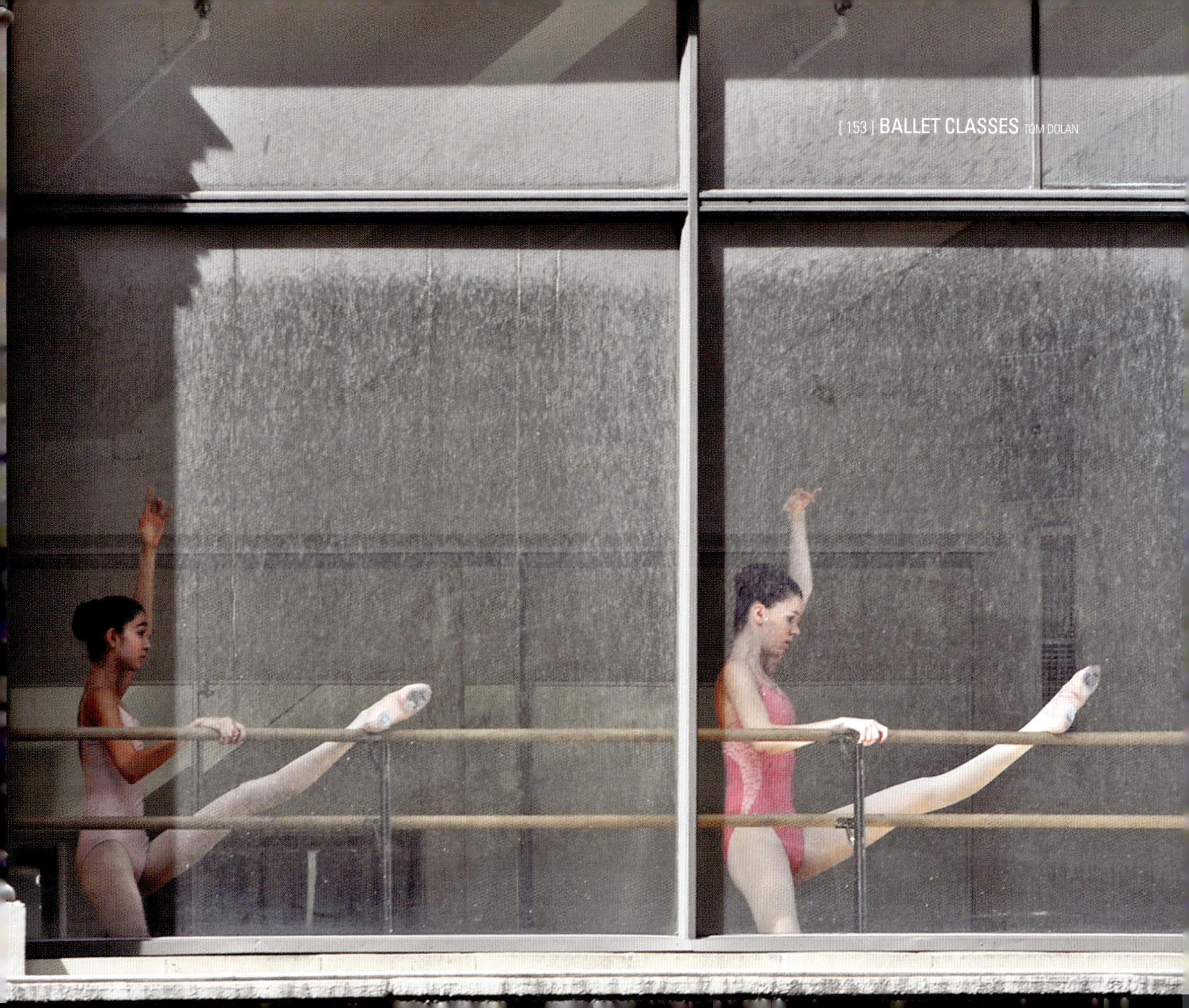

[153] BALLET CLASSES TOM DOLAN

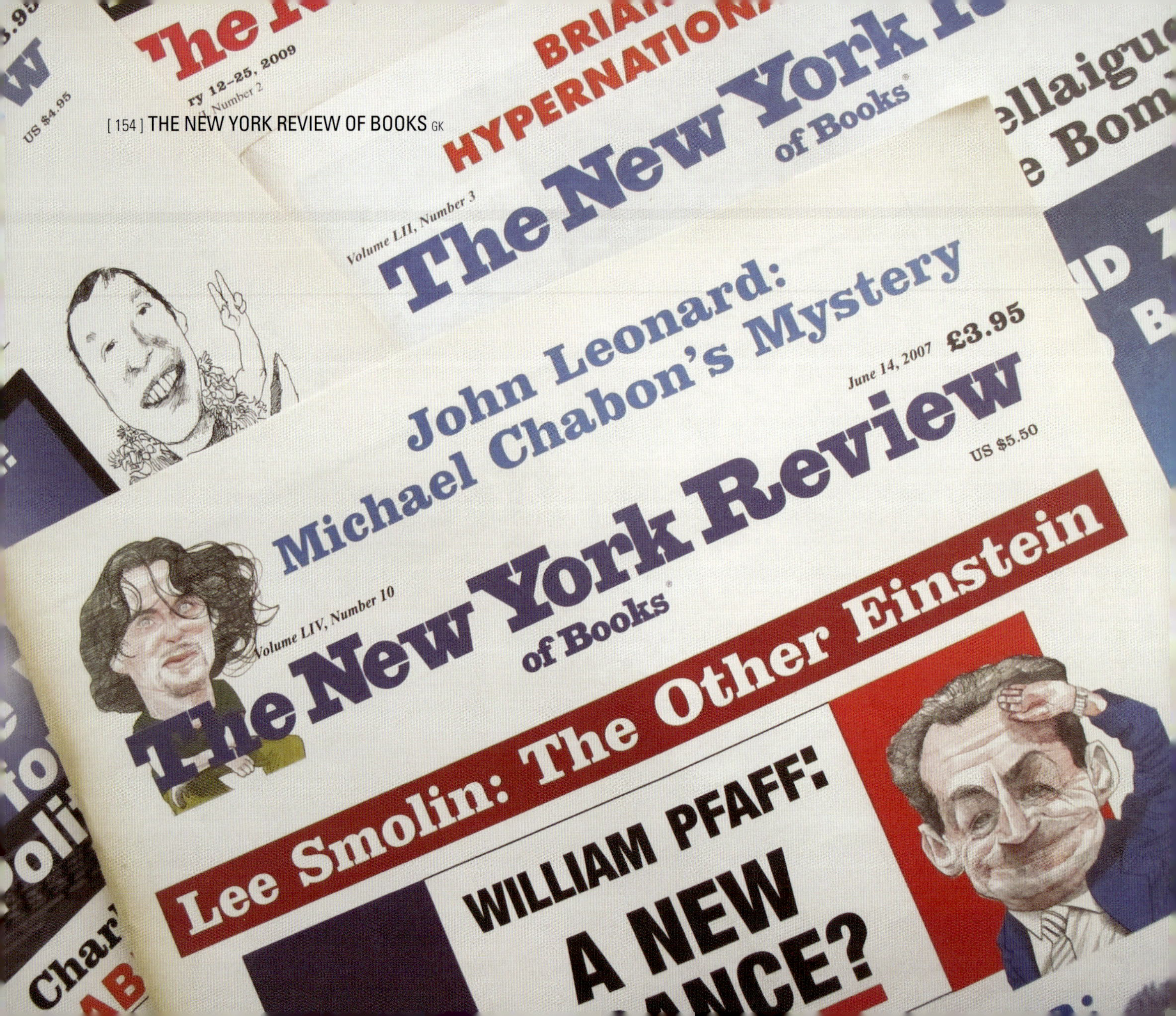
The New York Review of Books
Volume LIV, Number 10
June 14, 2007
£3.95
US $5.50
John Leonard:
Michael Chabon's Mystery
Lee Smolin: The Other Einstein
WILLIAM PFAFF:
A NEW
The New York
of Books
Volume LII, Number 3
HYPERNATIONA
BRIA
ry 12–25, 2009
Number 2
US $4.95

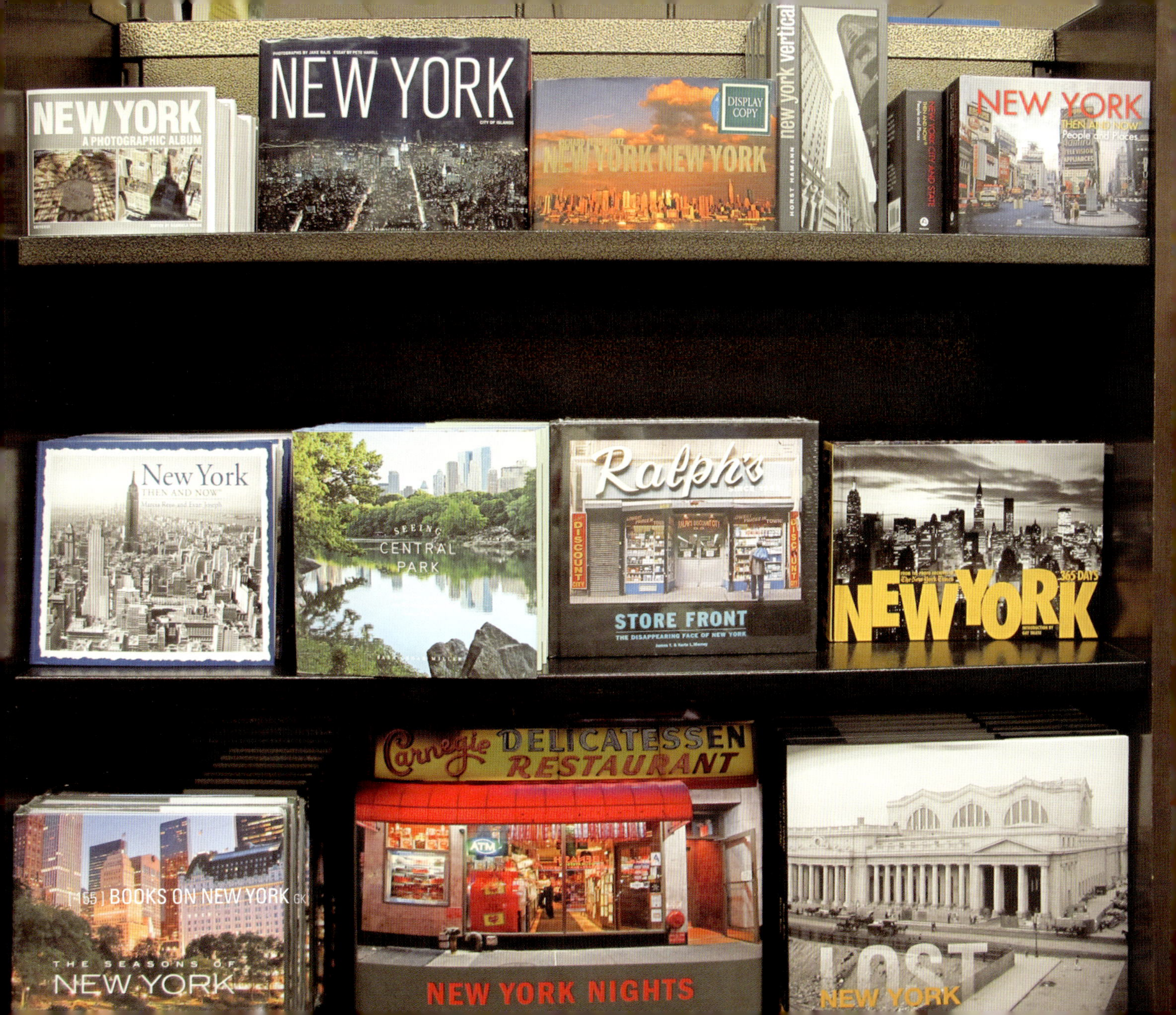

[155] BOOKS ON NEW YORK GK

Manhattan
Mini Storage.com
212-storage™
Hey...
you wanted
to live in
Manhattan.

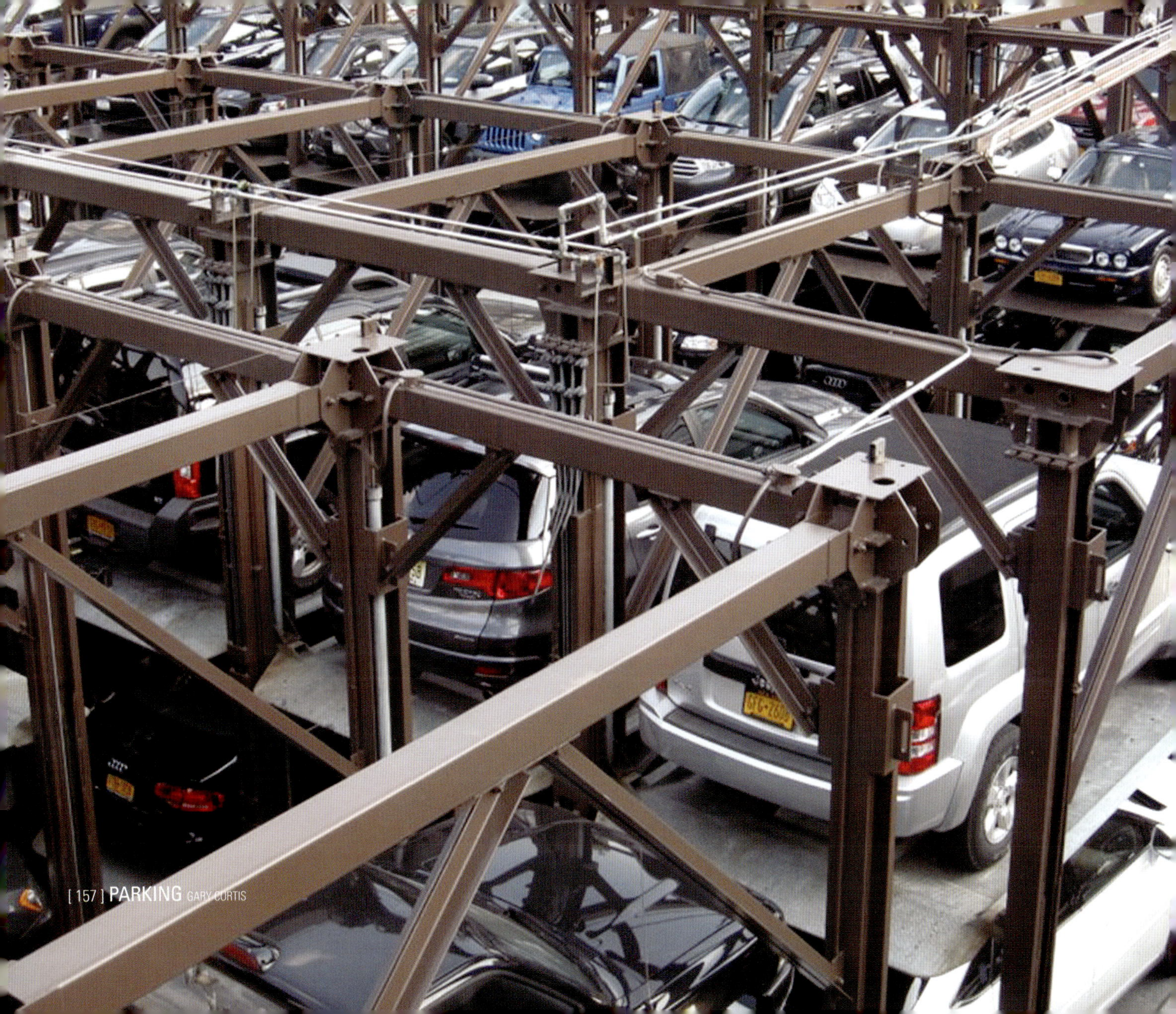

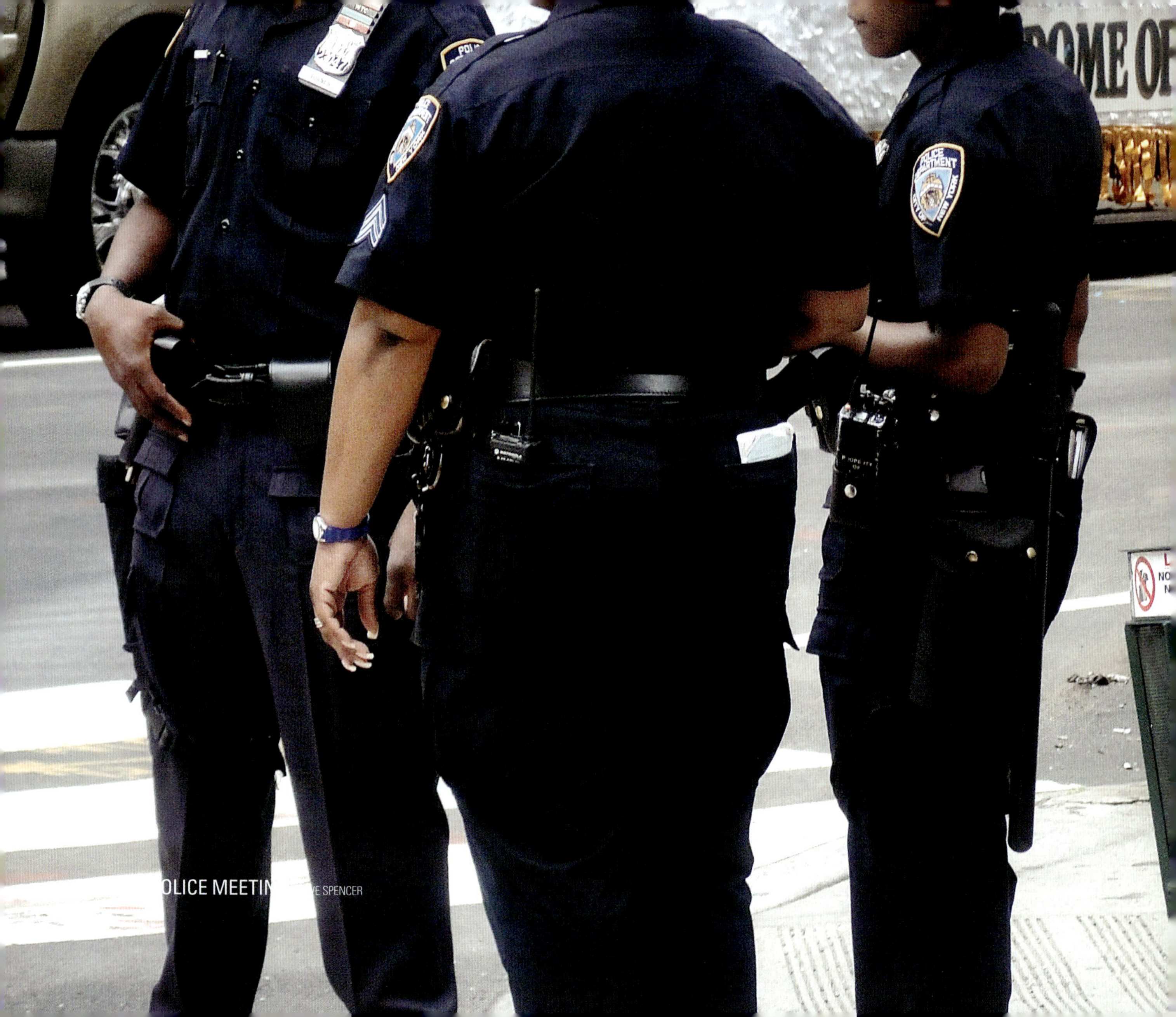

OLICE MEETIN VE SPENCER

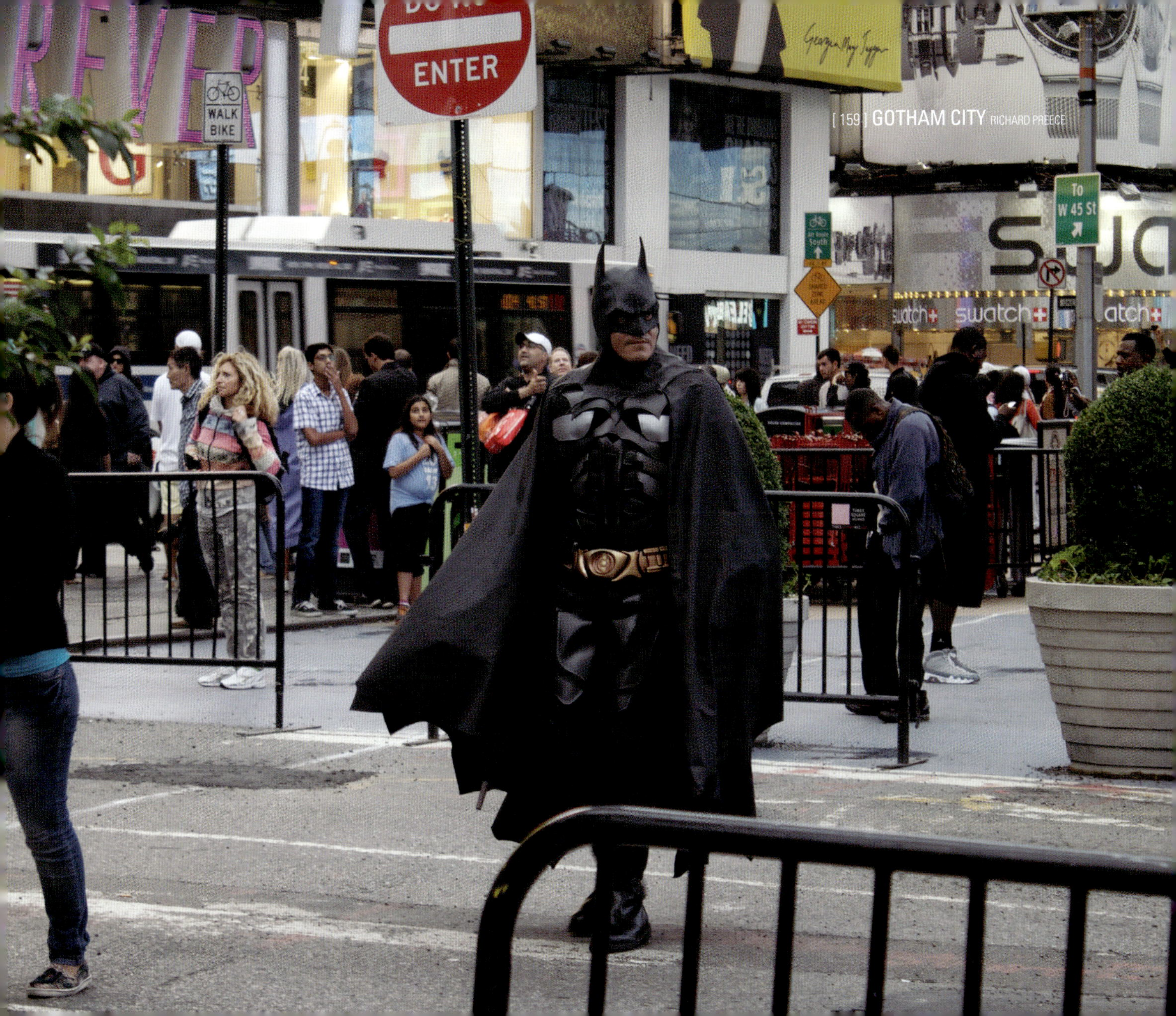

[159] GOTHAM CITY RICHARD PREECE

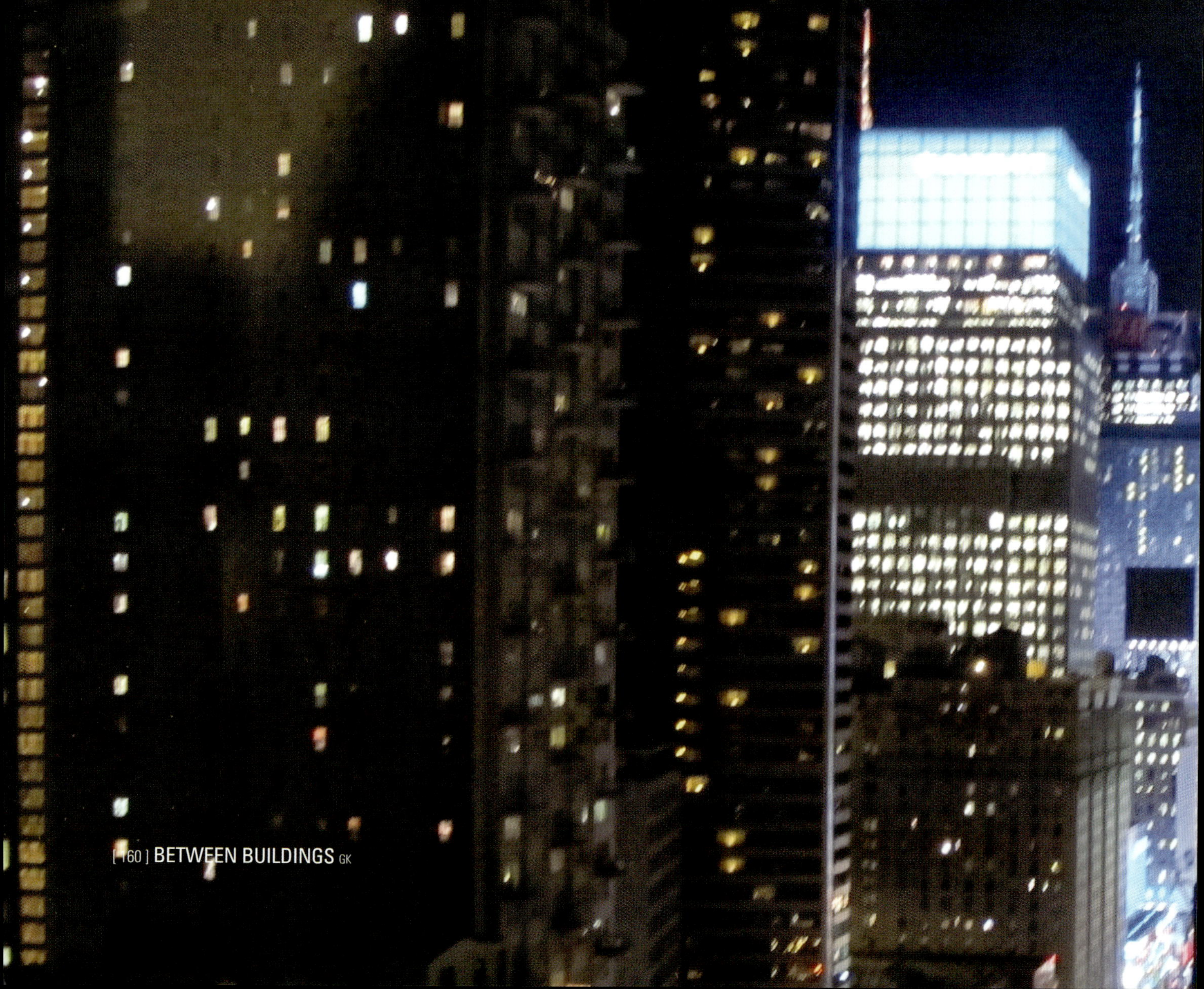

[160] BETWEEN BUILDINGS GK

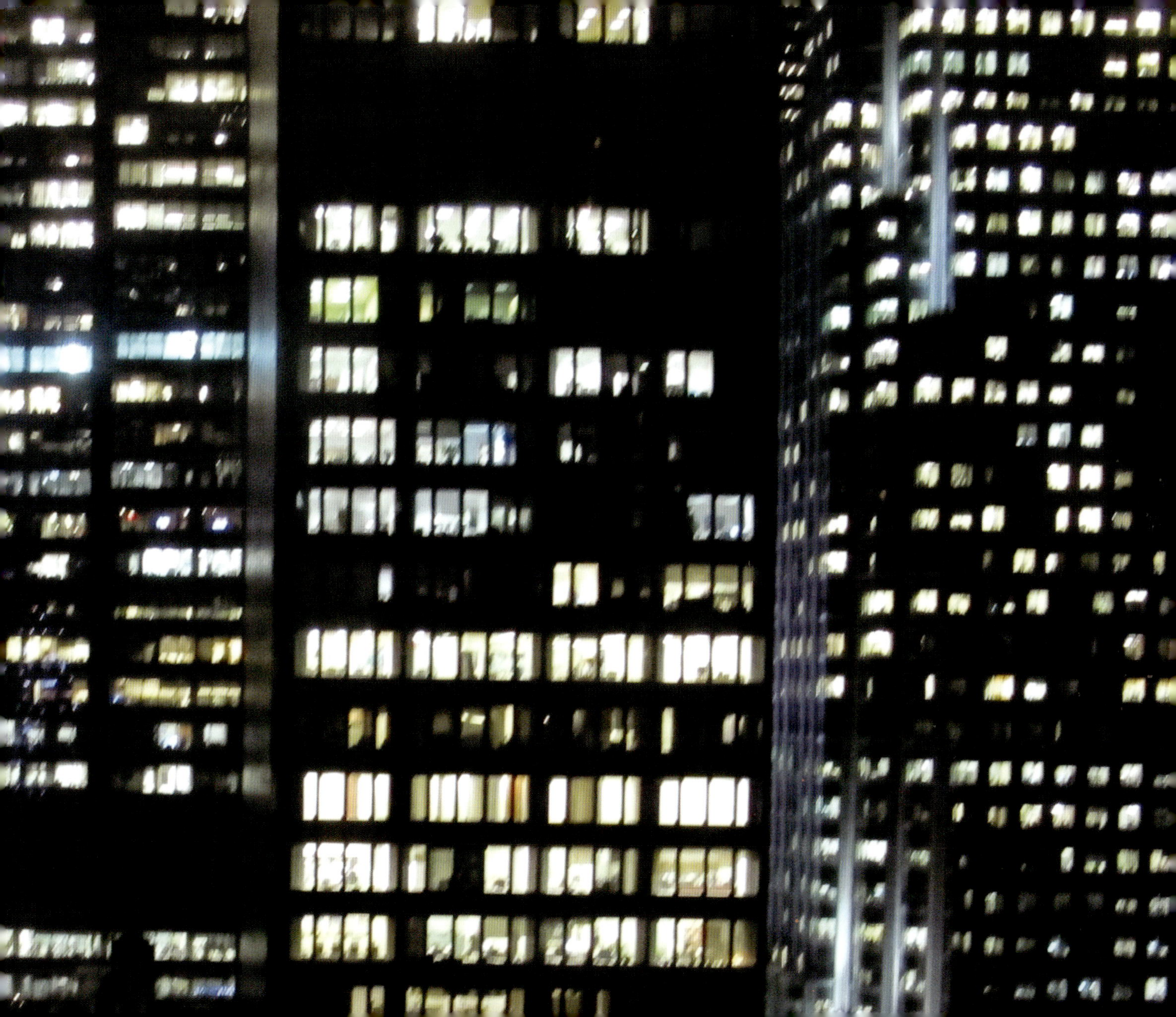

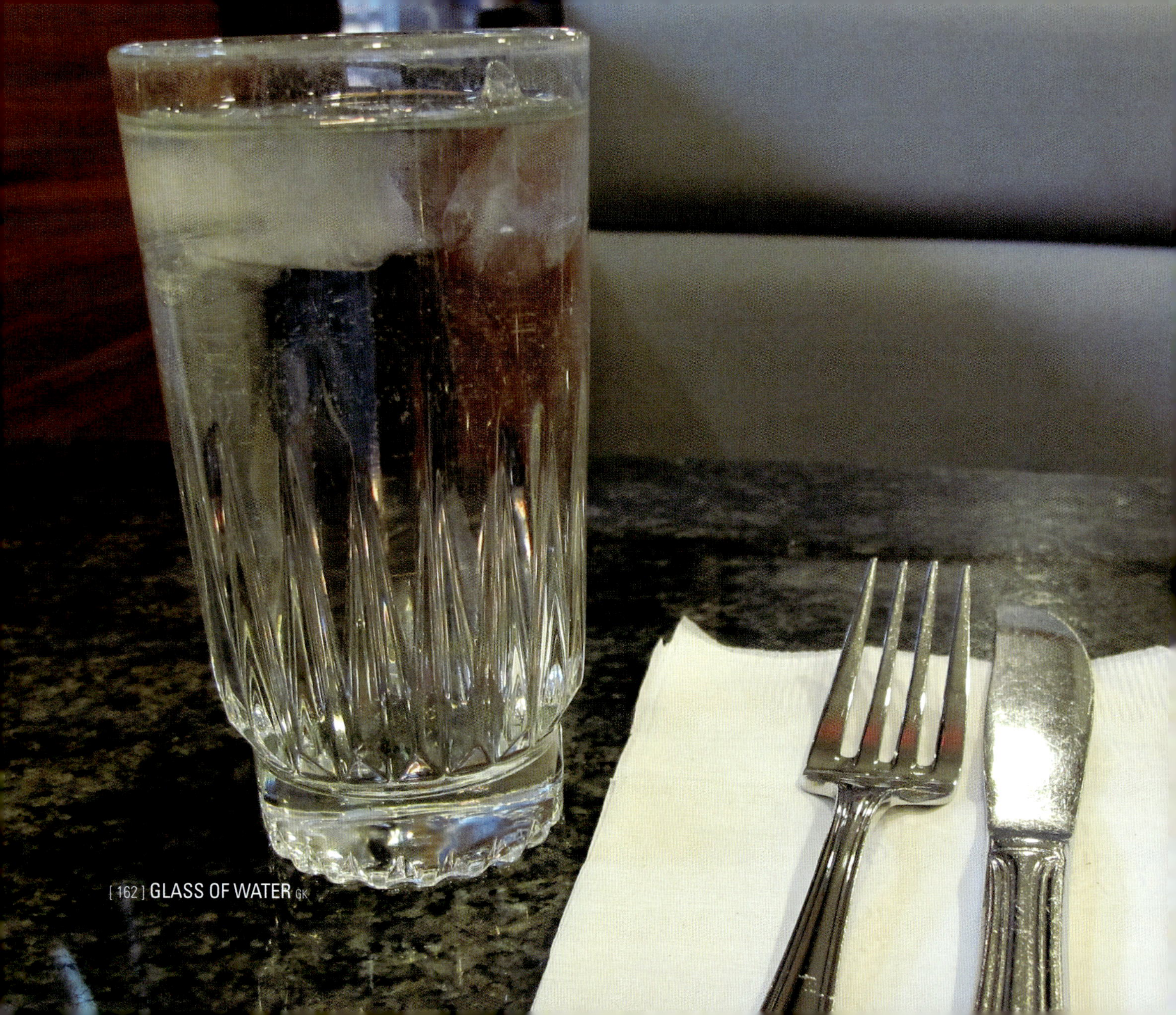

[162] GLASS OF WATER GK

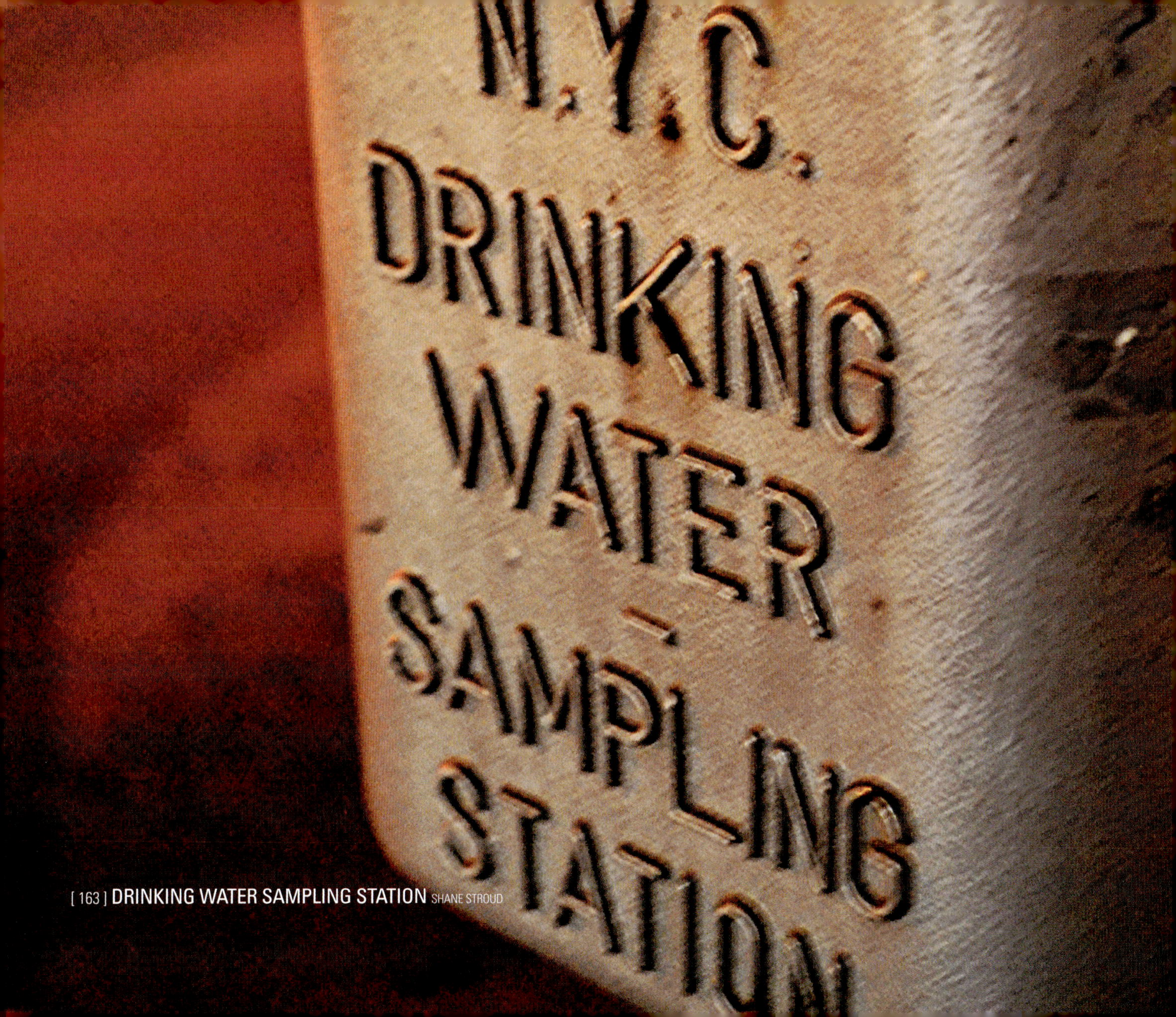

[163] DRINKING WATER SAMPLING STATION SHANE STROUD

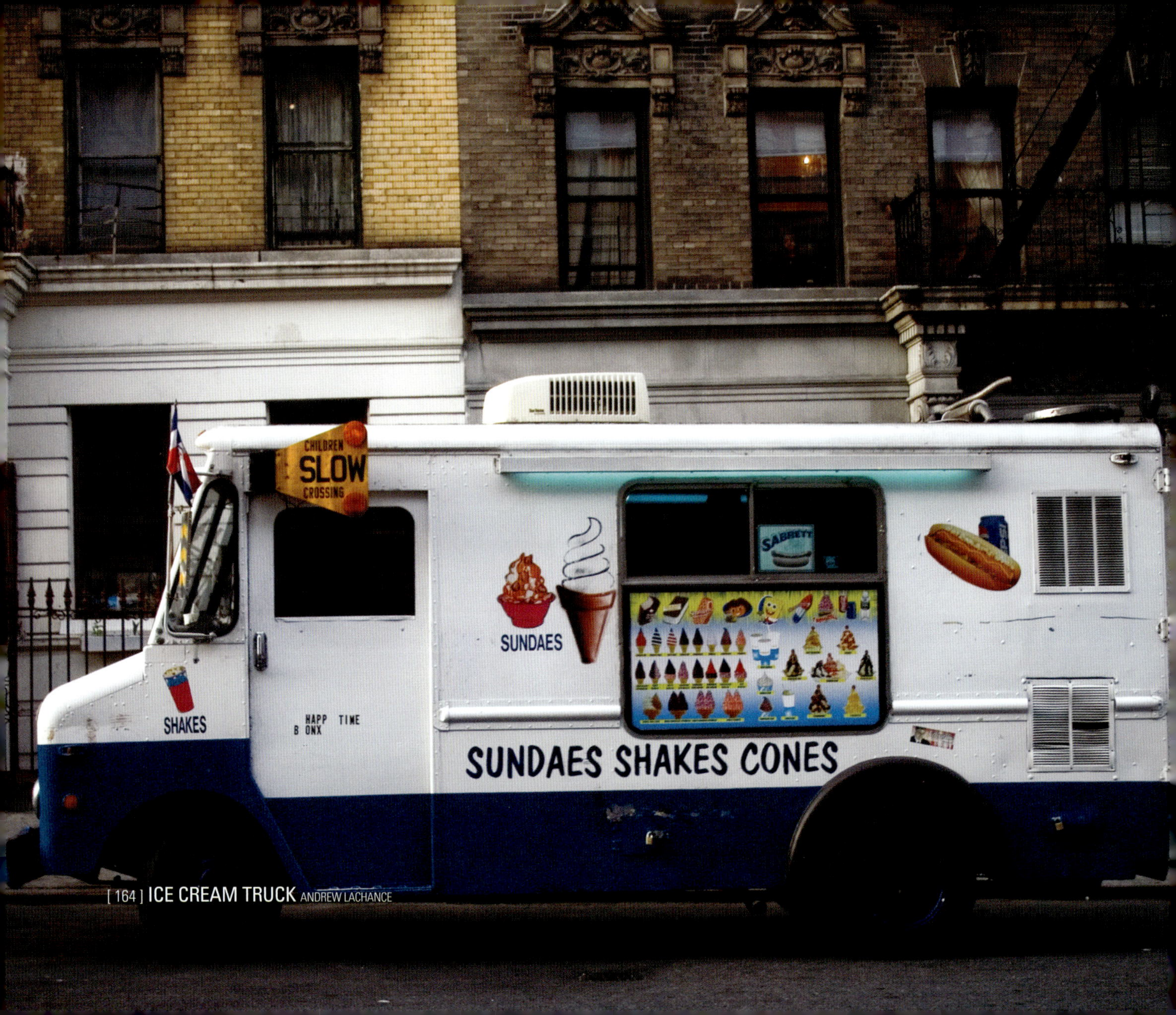

[164] **ICE CREAM TRUCK** ANDREW LACHANCE

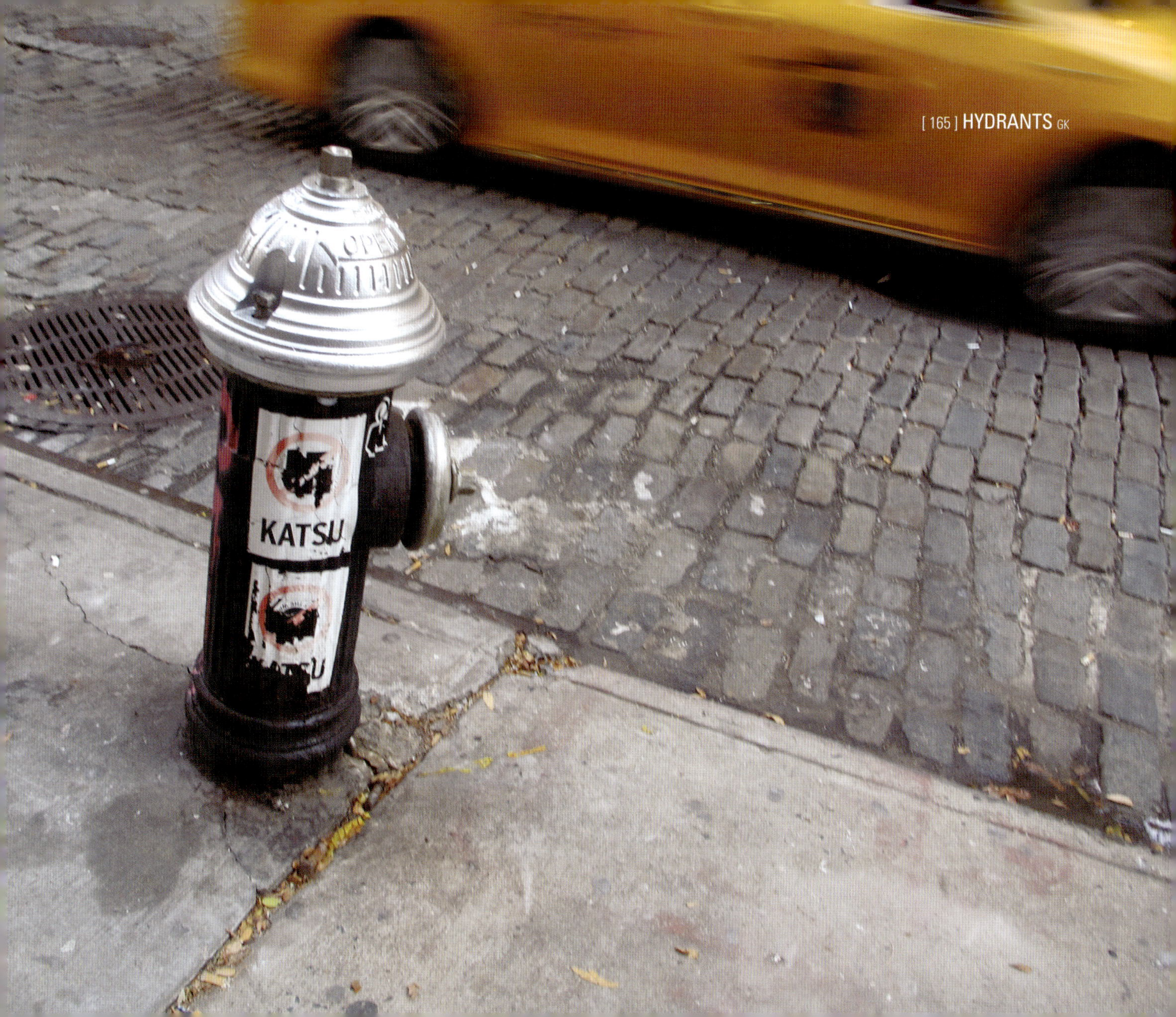

[165] HYDRANTS GK

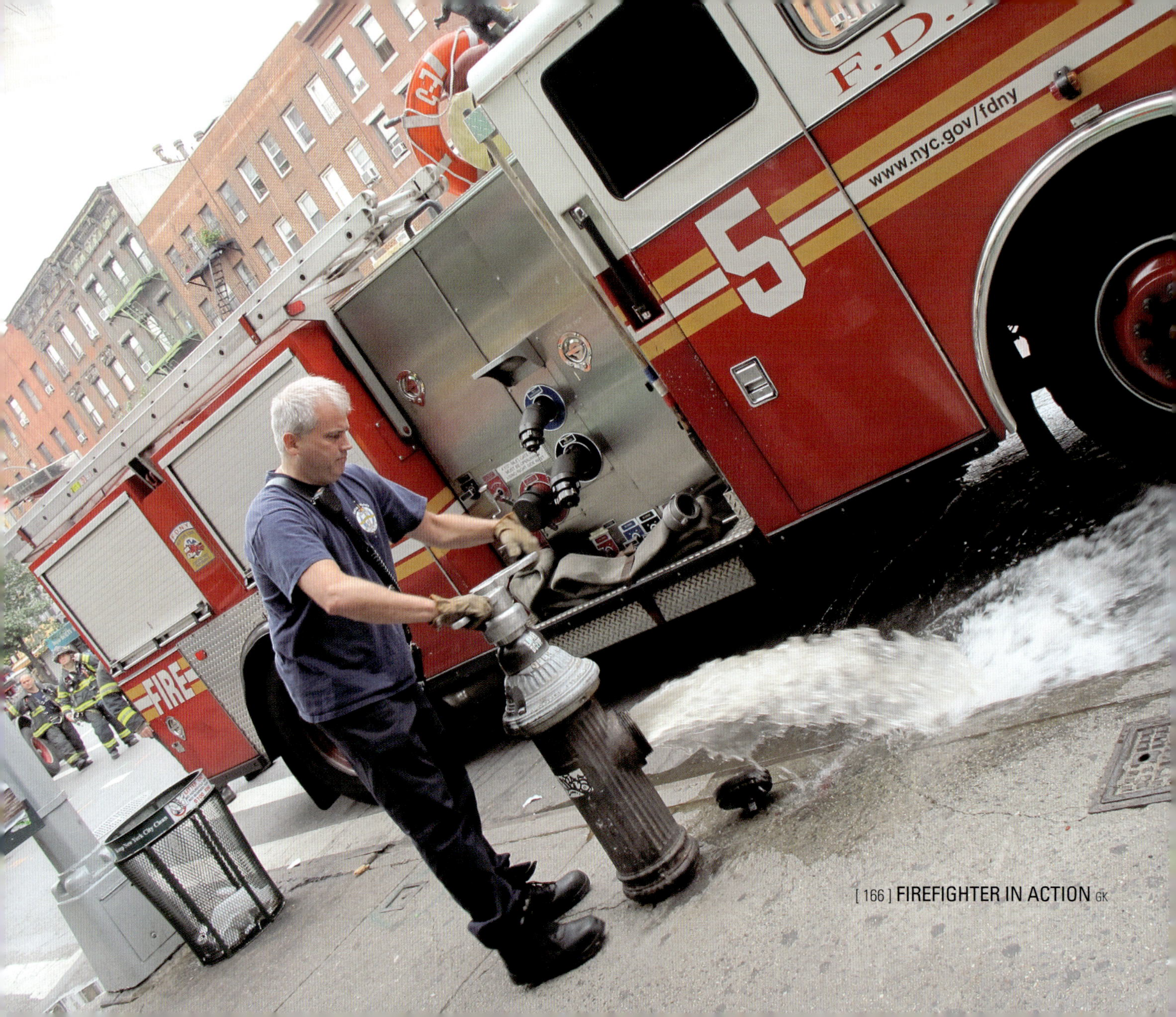

[166] **FIREFIGHTER IN ACTION** GK

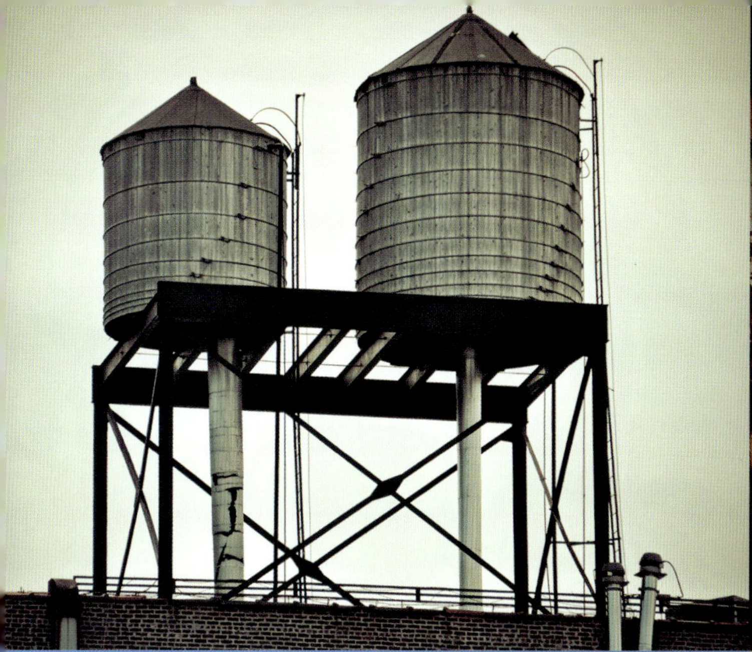

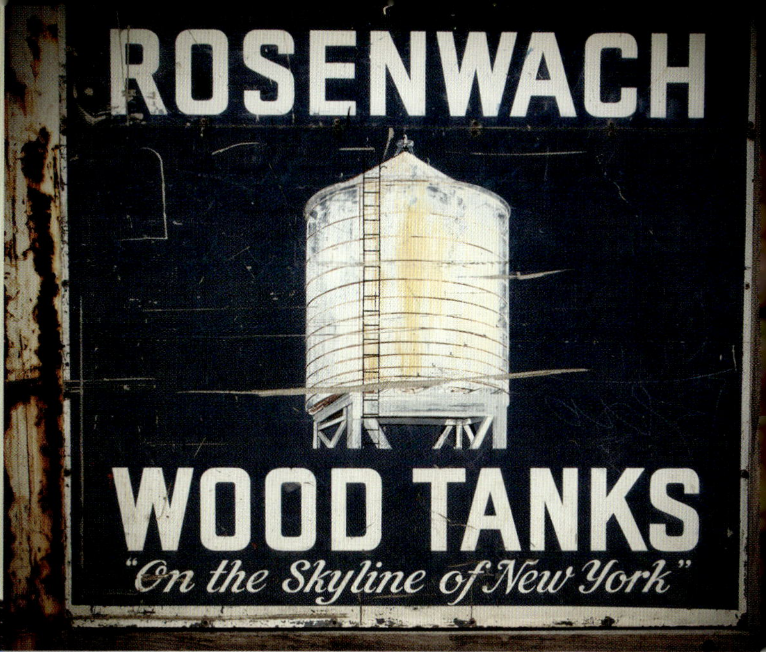

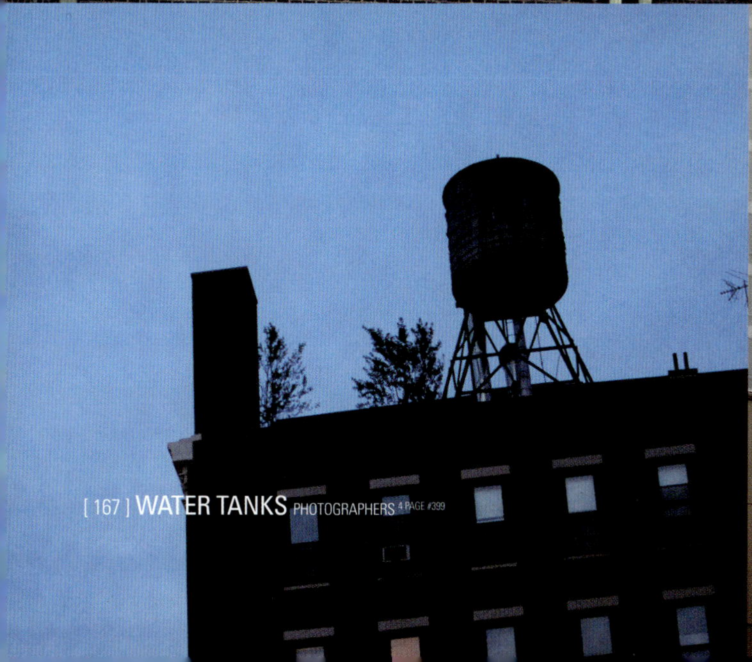

[167] WATER TANKS PHOTOGRAPHERS 4 PAGE #399

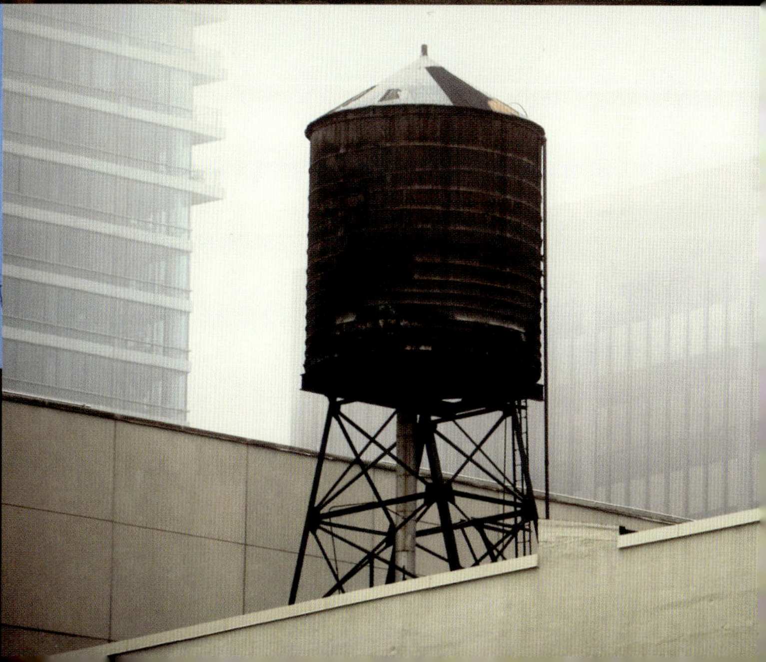

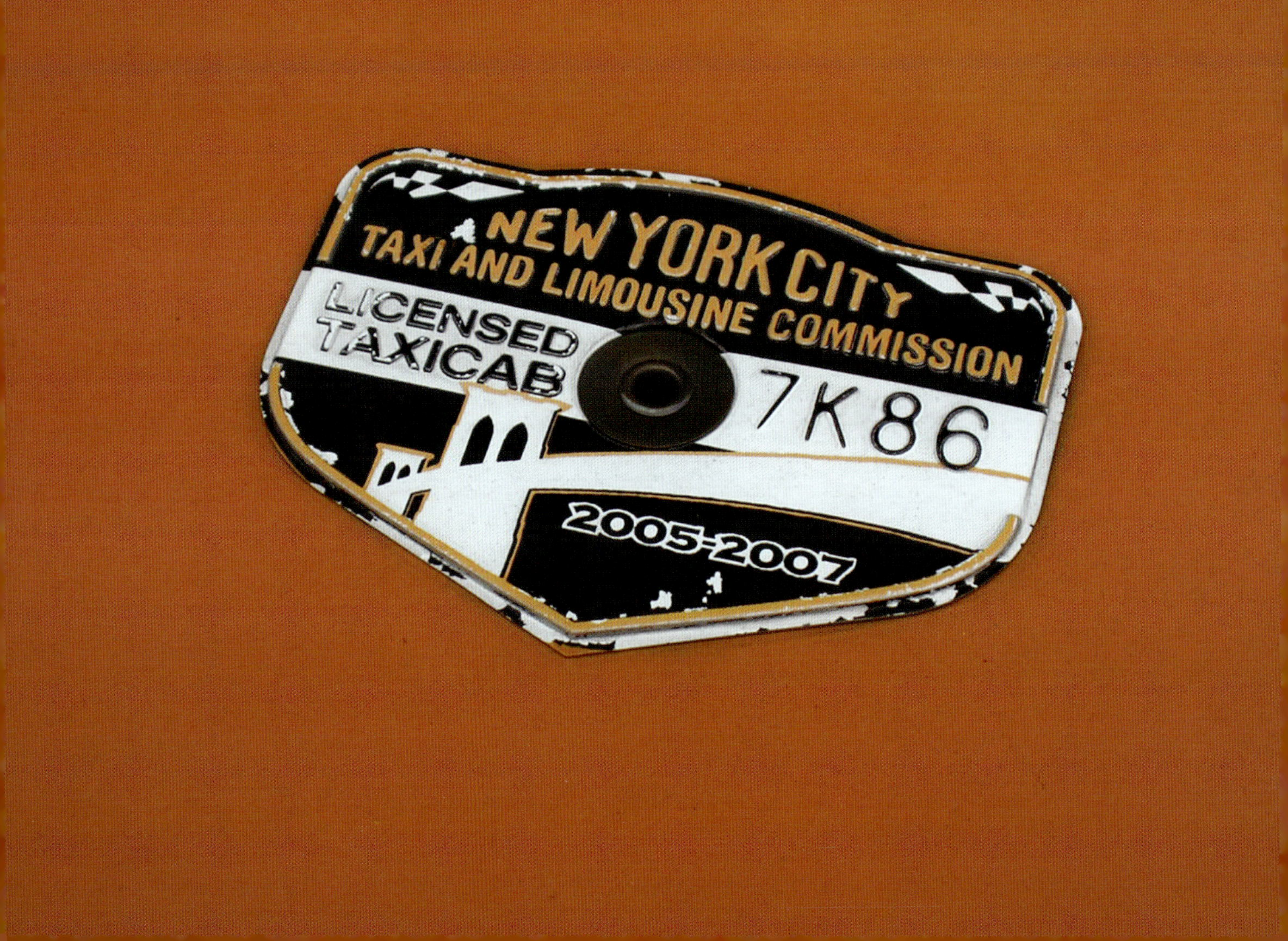
NEW YORK CITY
TAXI AND LIMOUSINE COMMISSION
LICENSED
TAXICAB
7K86
2005-2007

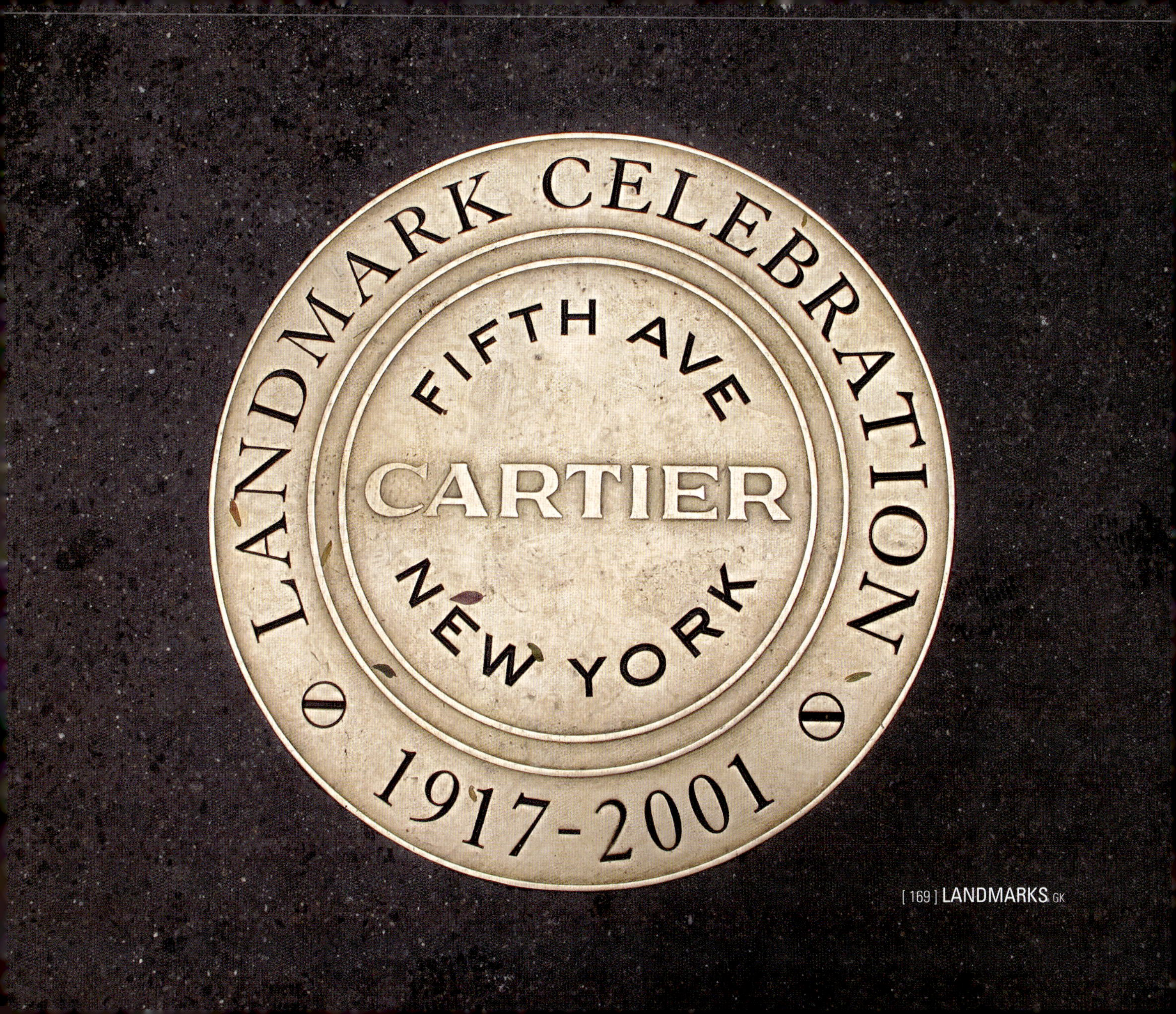
LANDMARK CELEBRATION
FIFTH AVE
CARTIER
NEW YORK
1917-2001

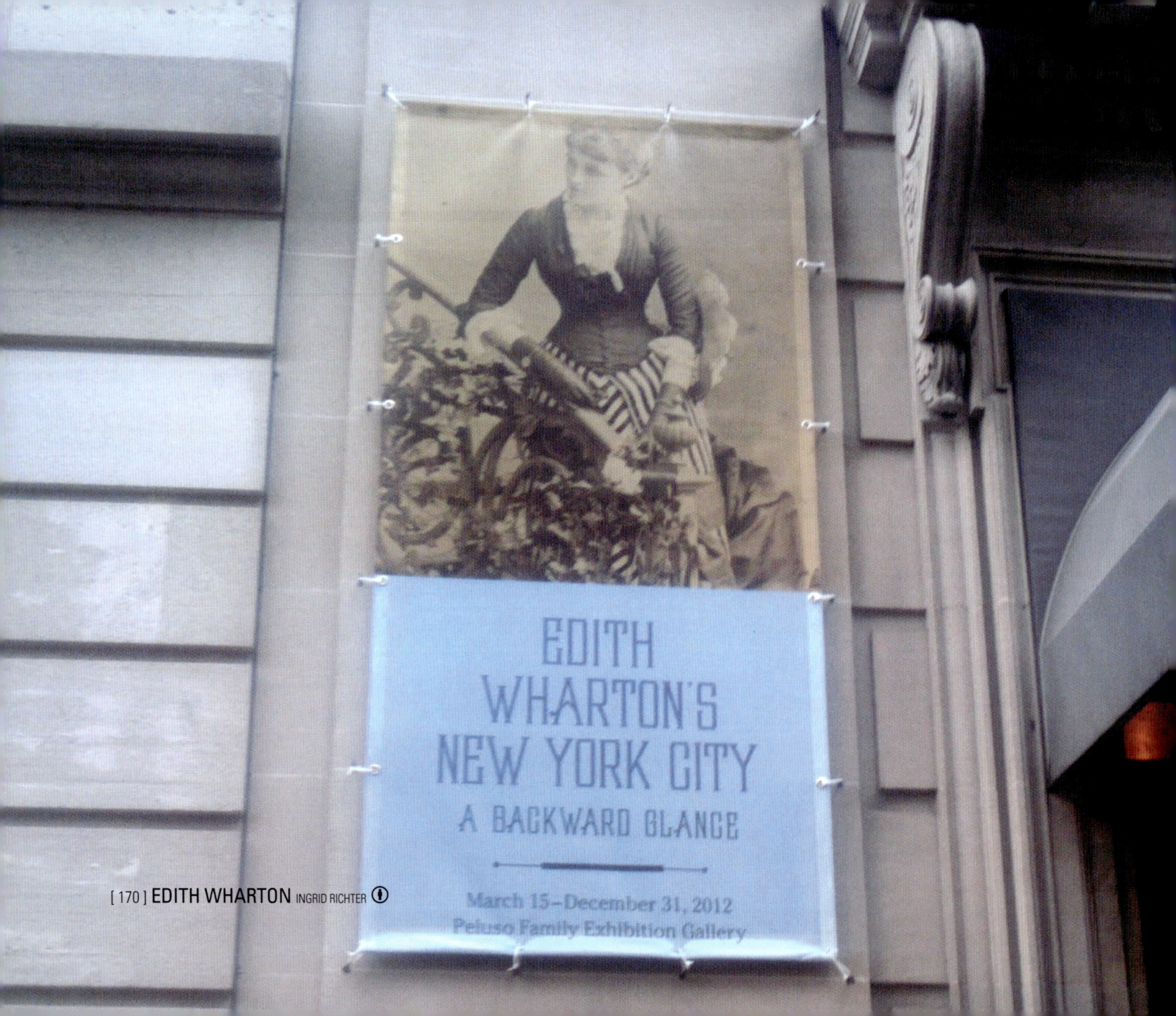

[170] EDITH WHARTON INGRID RICHTER

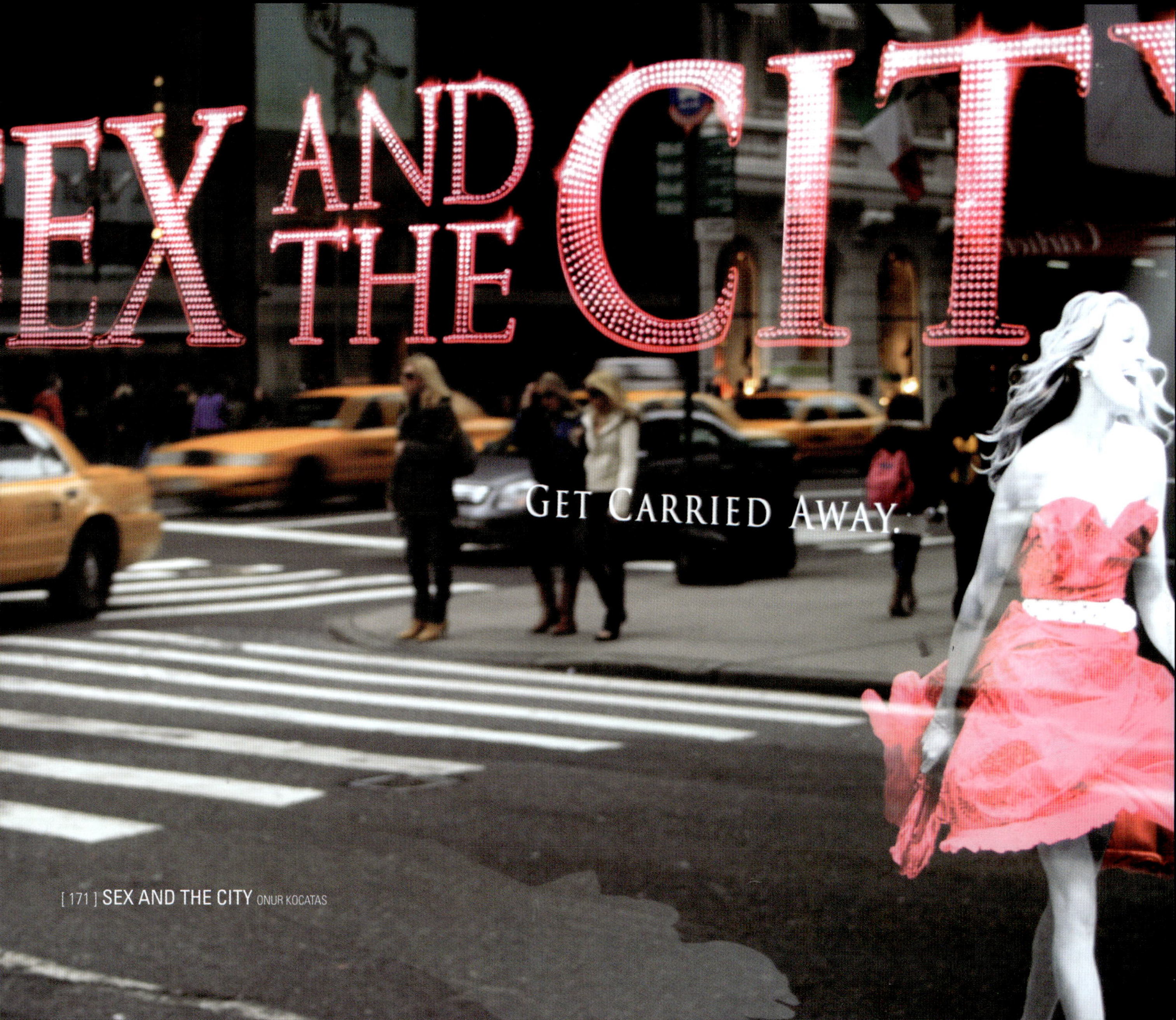

[171] SEX AND THE CITY ONUR KOCATAS

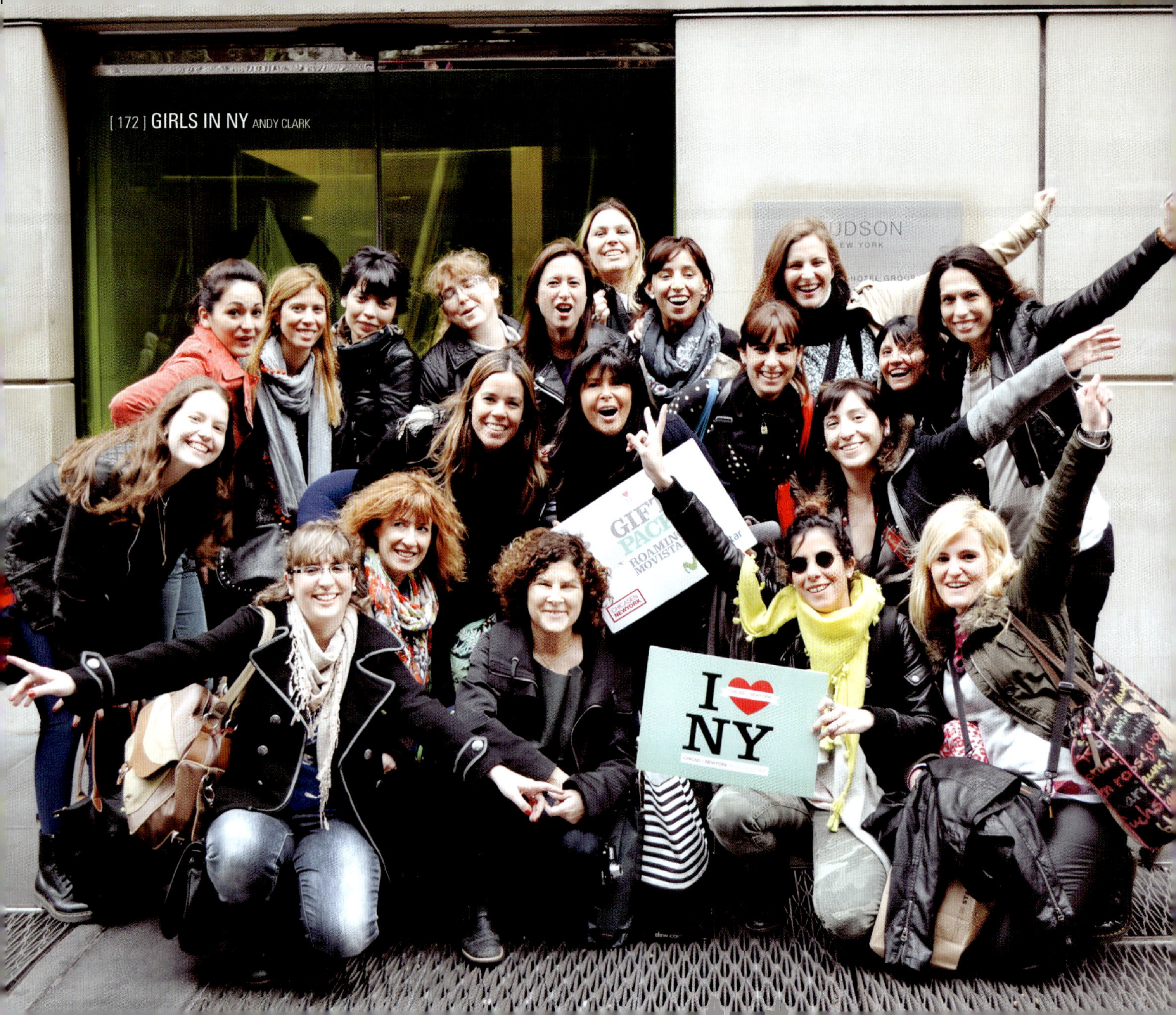

[172] GIRLS IN NY ANDY CLARK

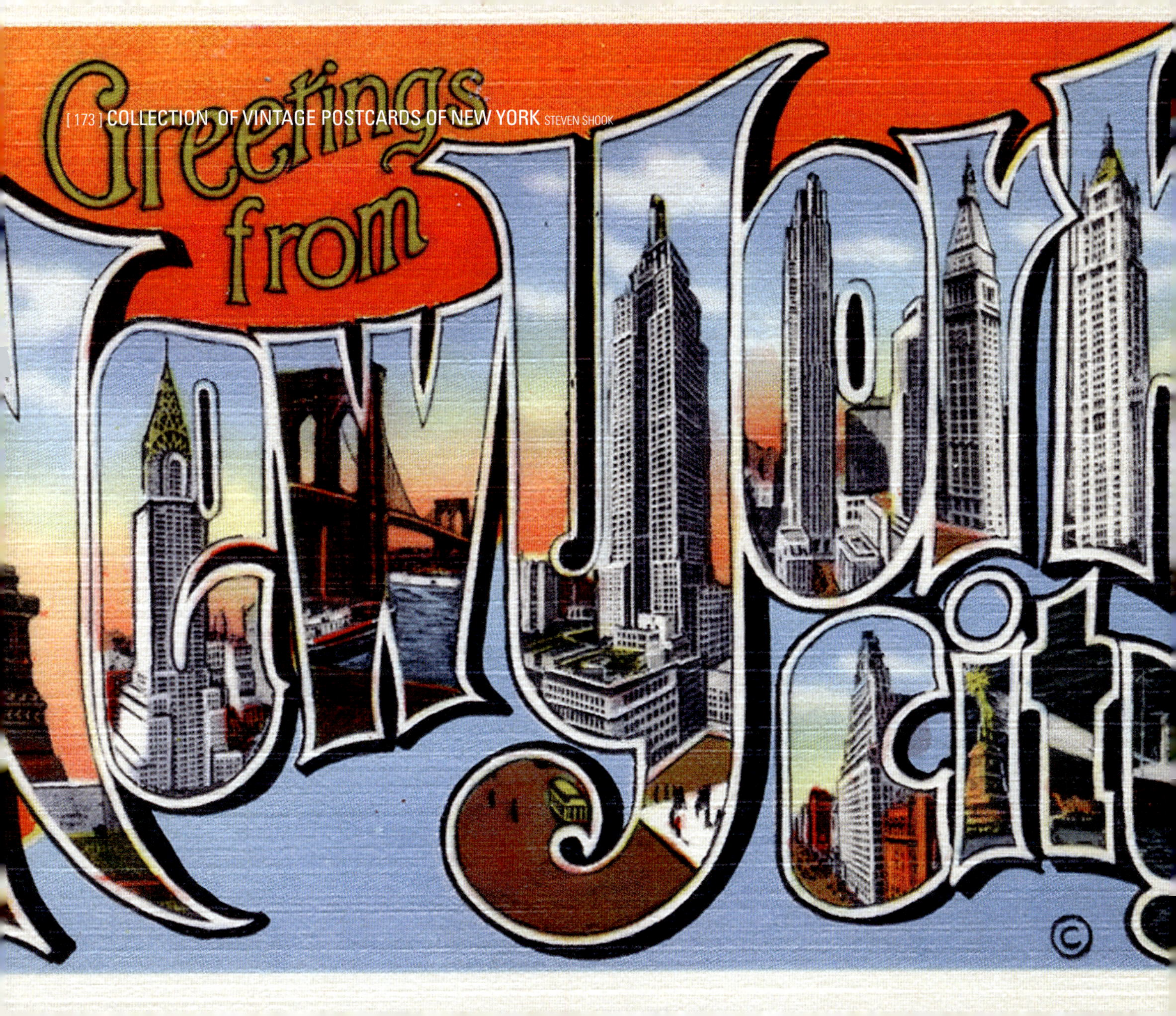

[173] COLLECTION OF VINTAGE POSTCARDS OF NEW YORK STEVEN SHOOK

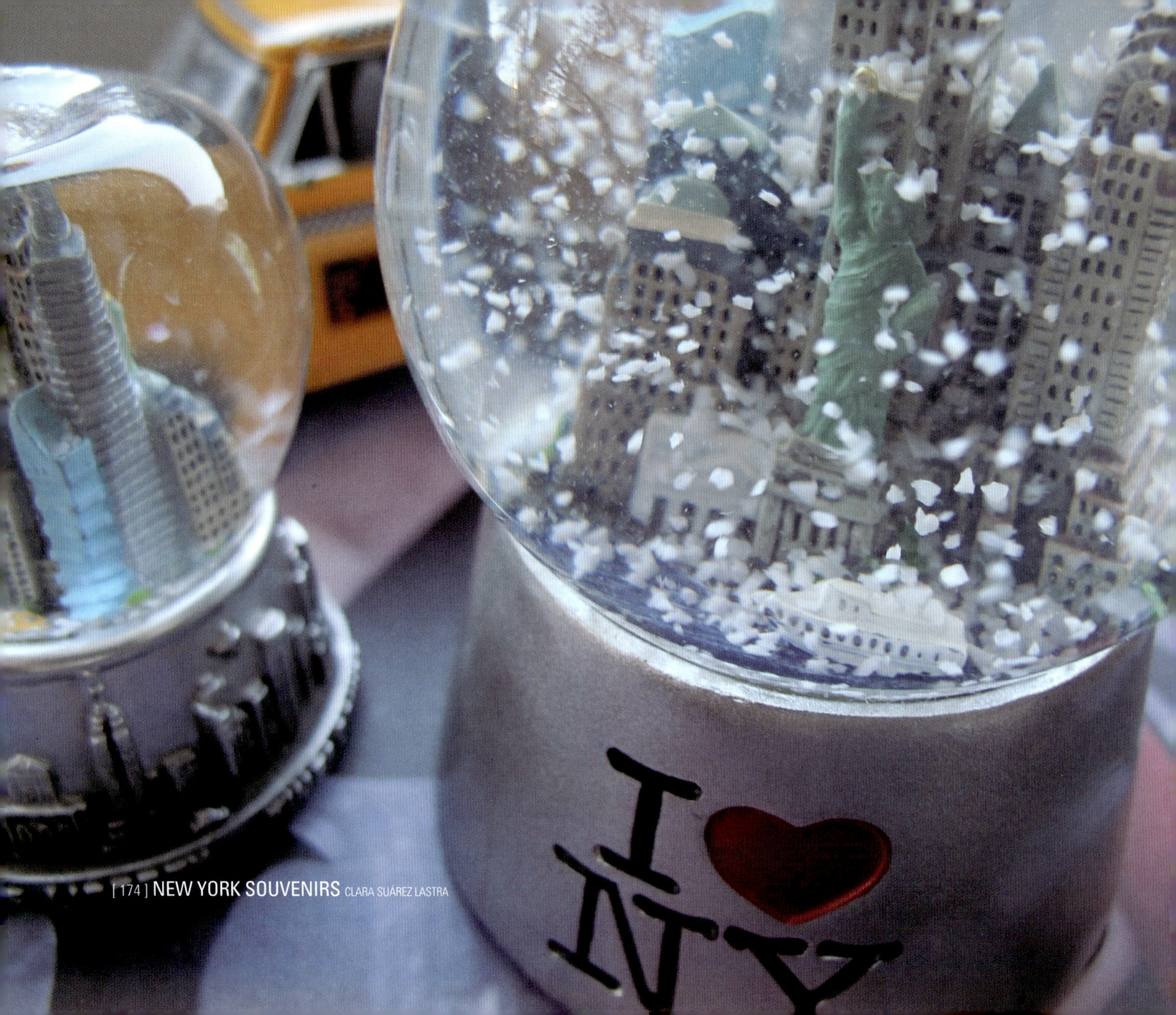

[174] NEW YORK SOUVENIRS CLARA SUÁREZ LASTRA

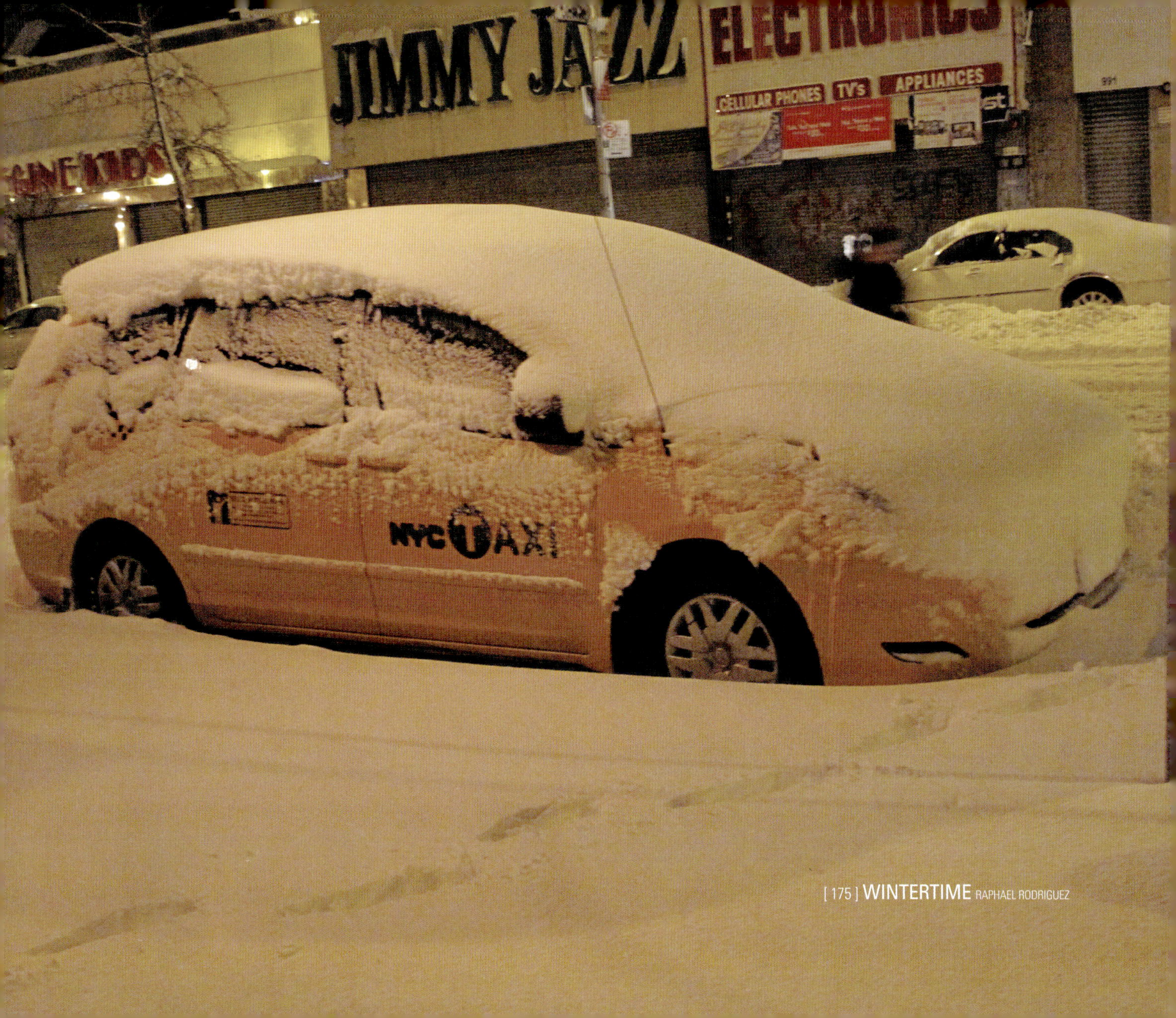

[175] WINTERTIME RAPHAEL RODRIGUEZ

[176] NEW YORK PIZZA ROBYN LEE

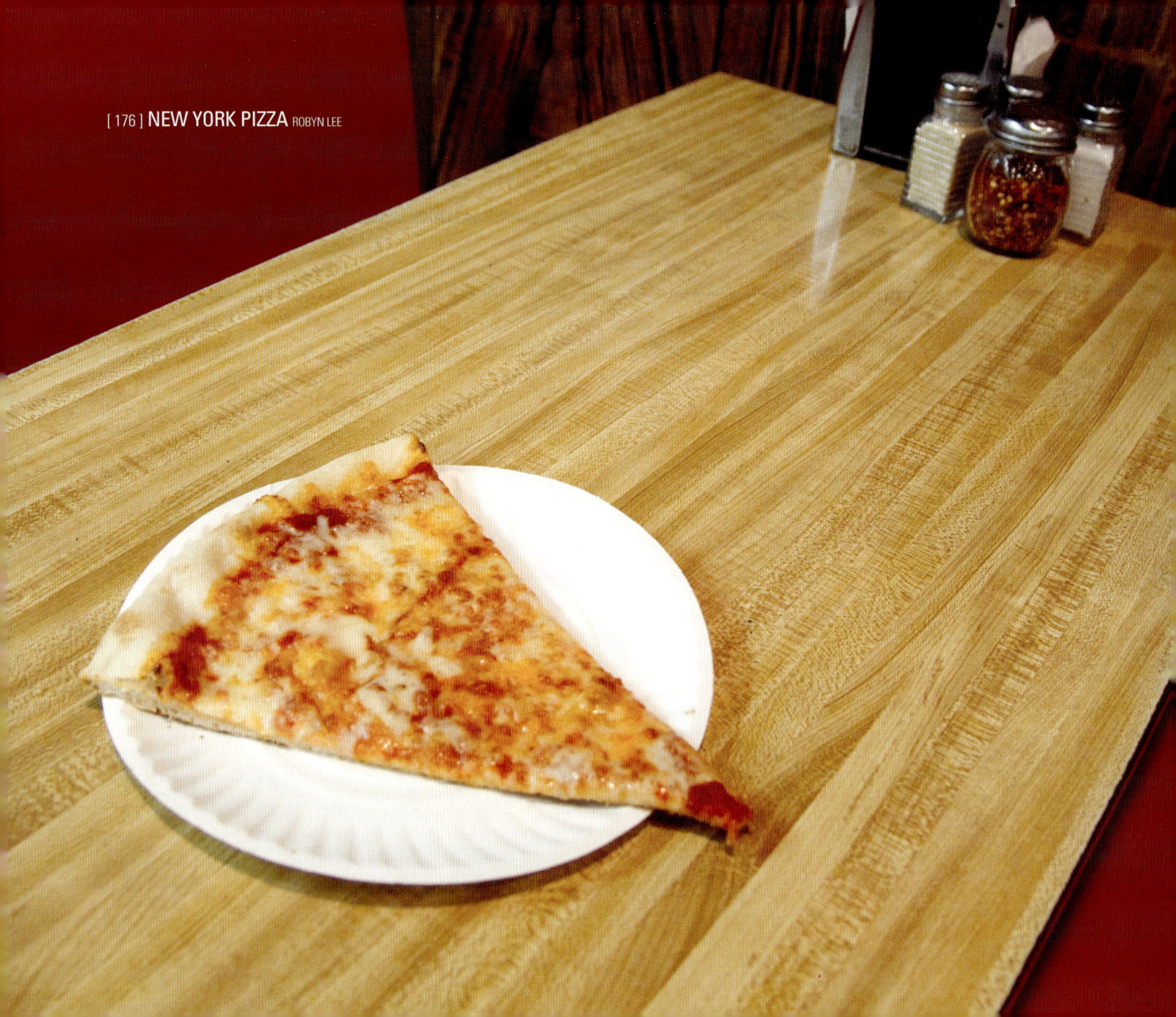

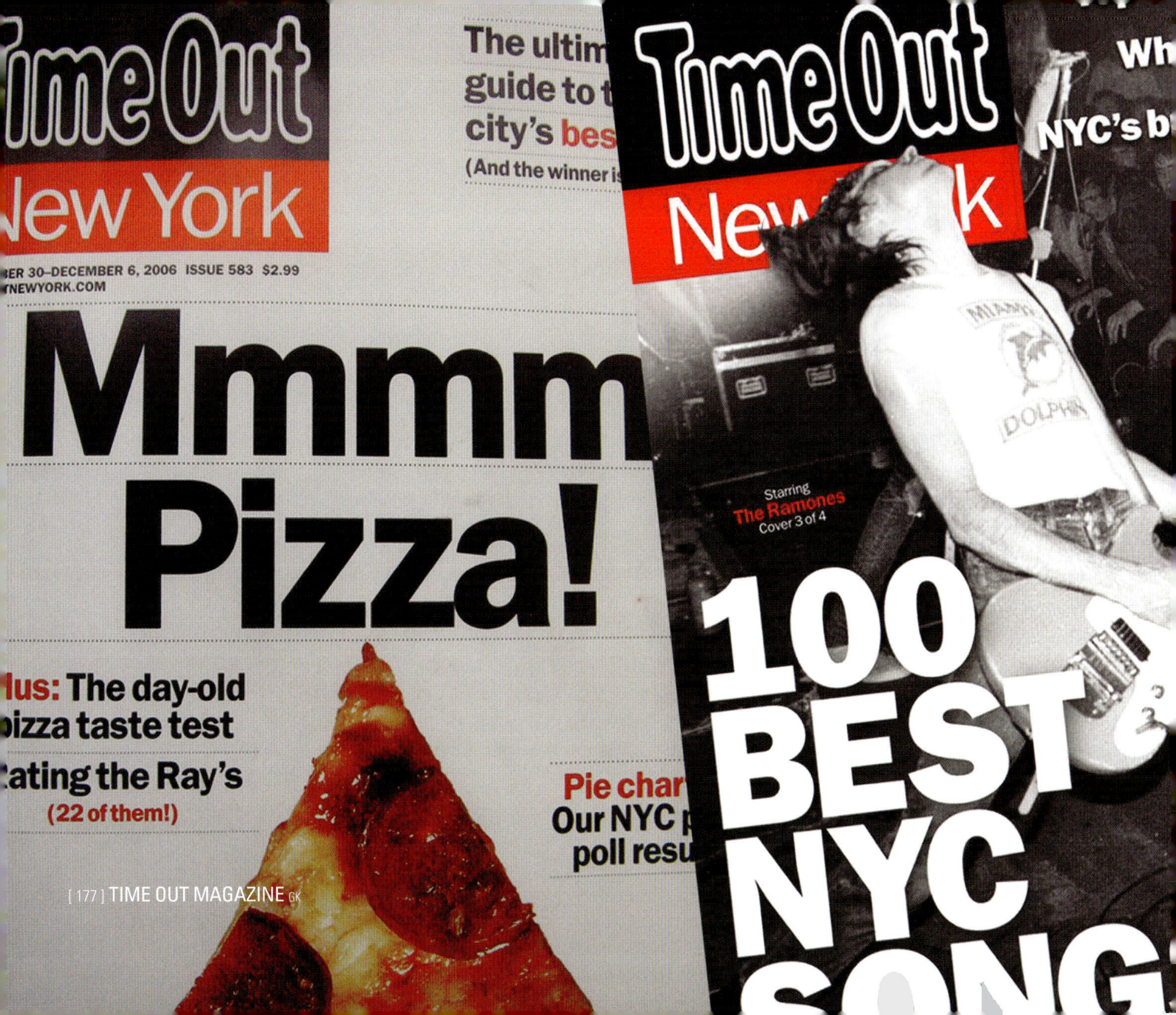

[177] TIME OUT MAGAZINE GK

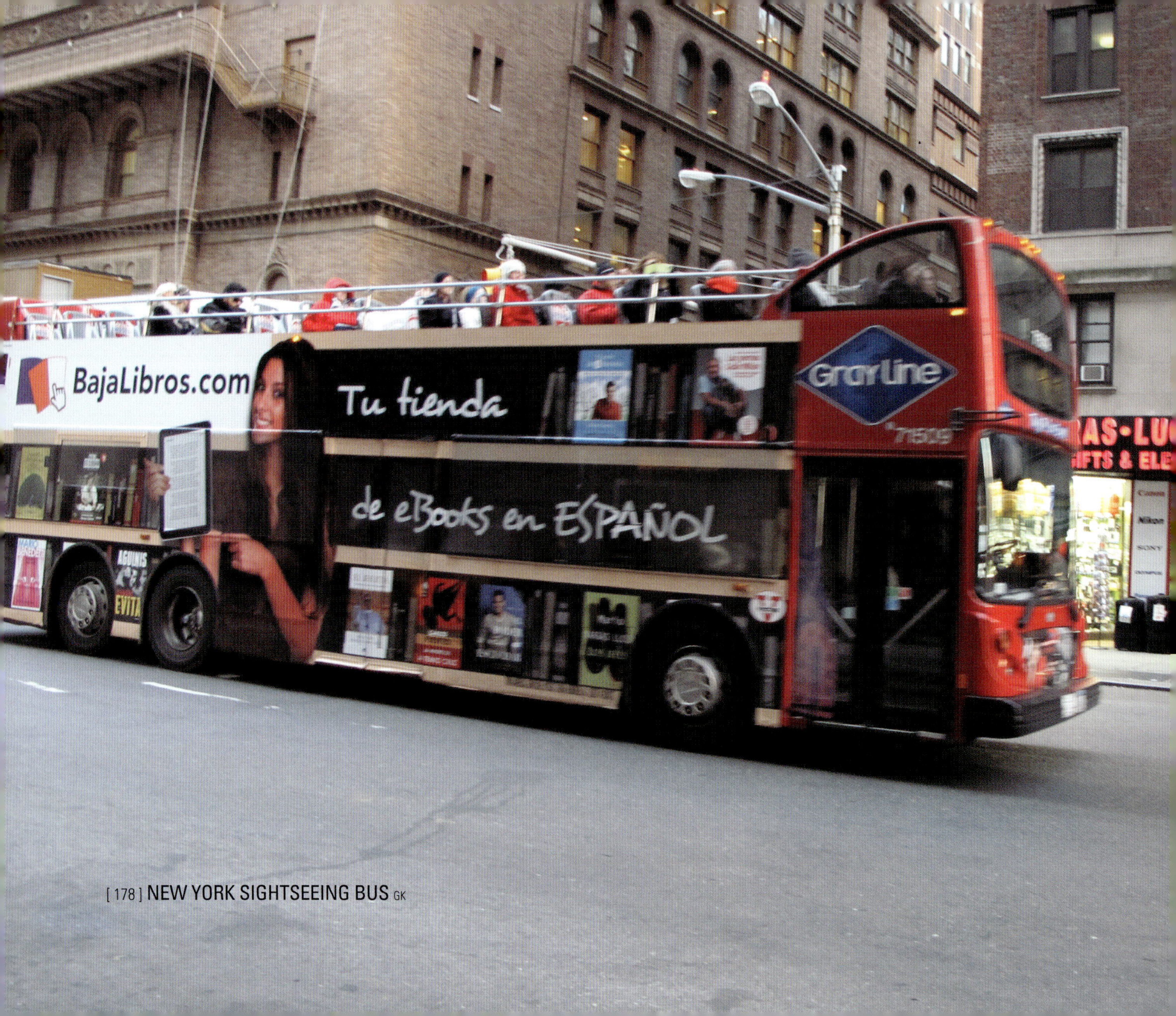

[178] NEW YORK SIGHTSEEING BUS GK

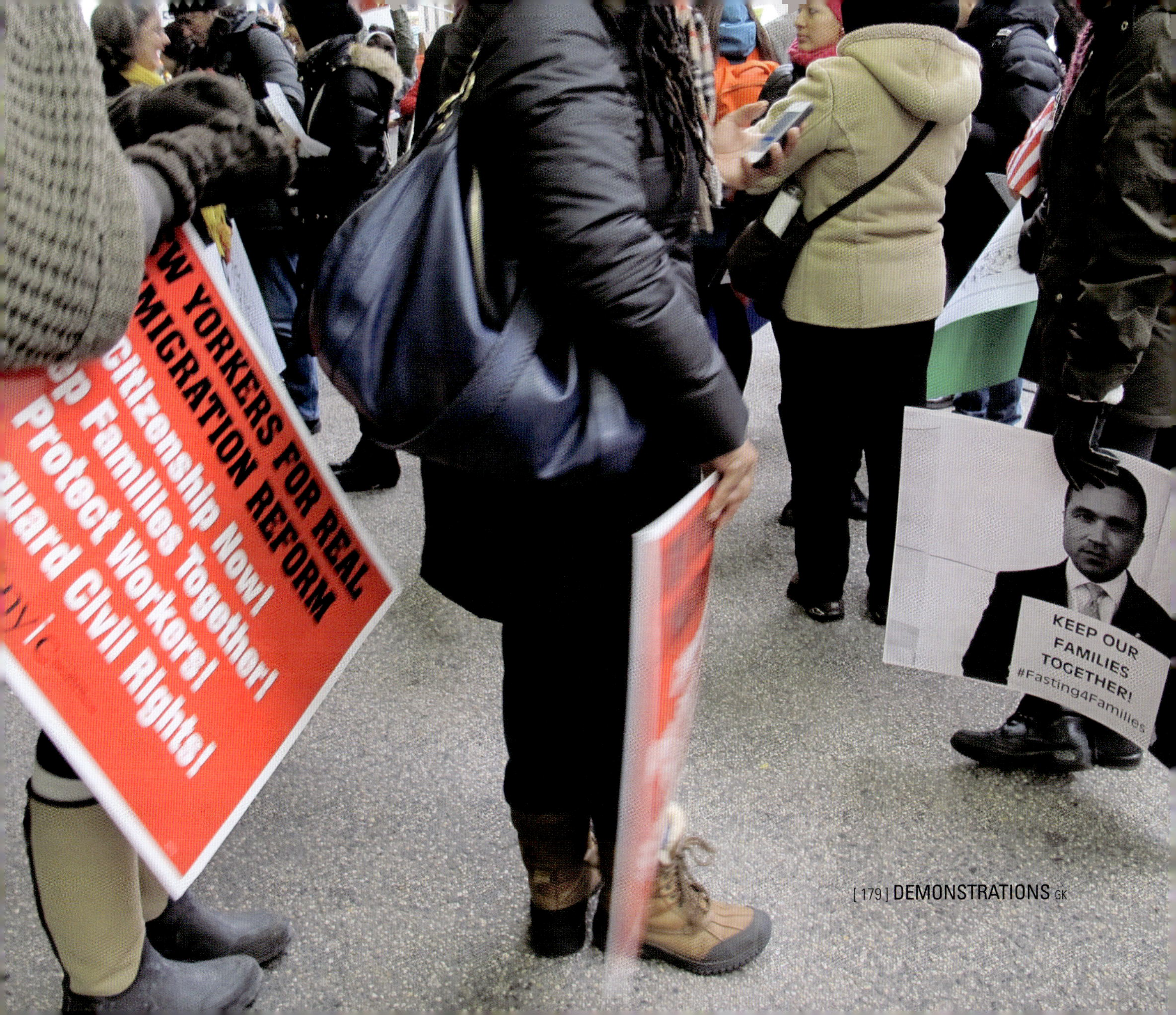
W YORKERS FOR REAL
MIGRATION REFORM
Citizenship Now!
p Families Together!
Protect Workers!
uard Civil Rights!
KEEP OUR
FAMILIES
TOGETHER!
#Fasting4Families

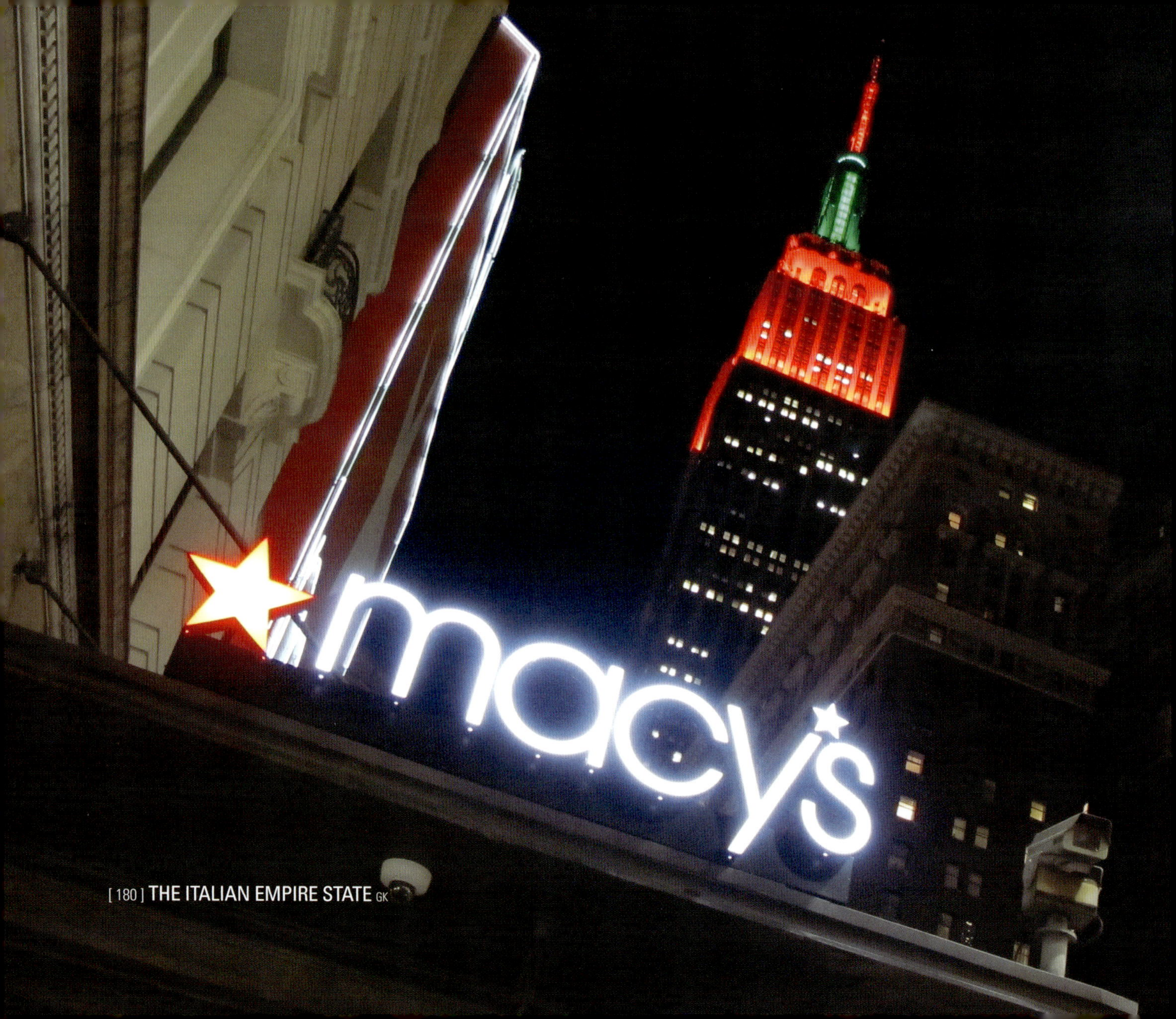

[180] THE ITALIAN EMPIRE STATE GK

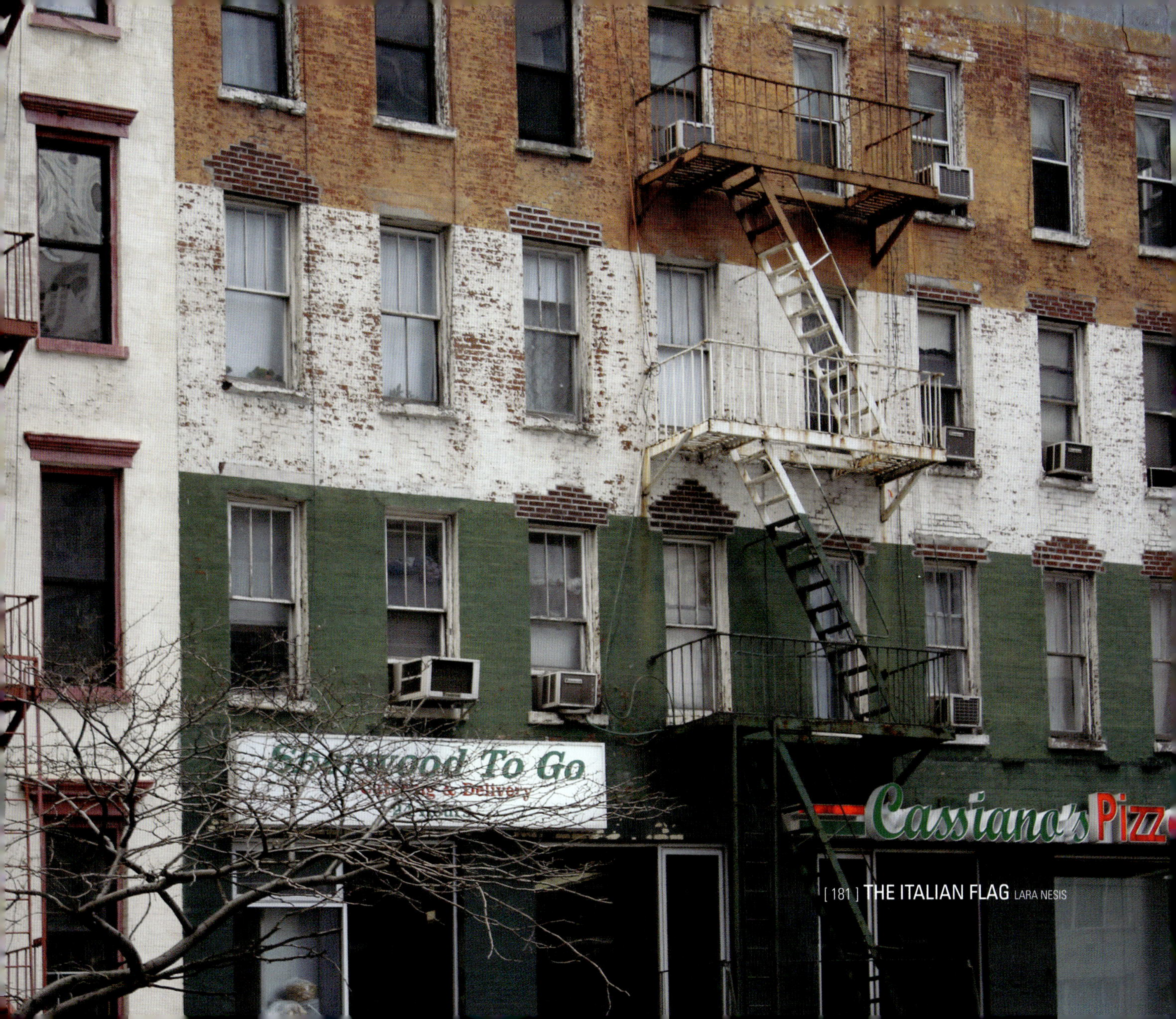

[181] THE ITALIAN FLAG LARA NESIS

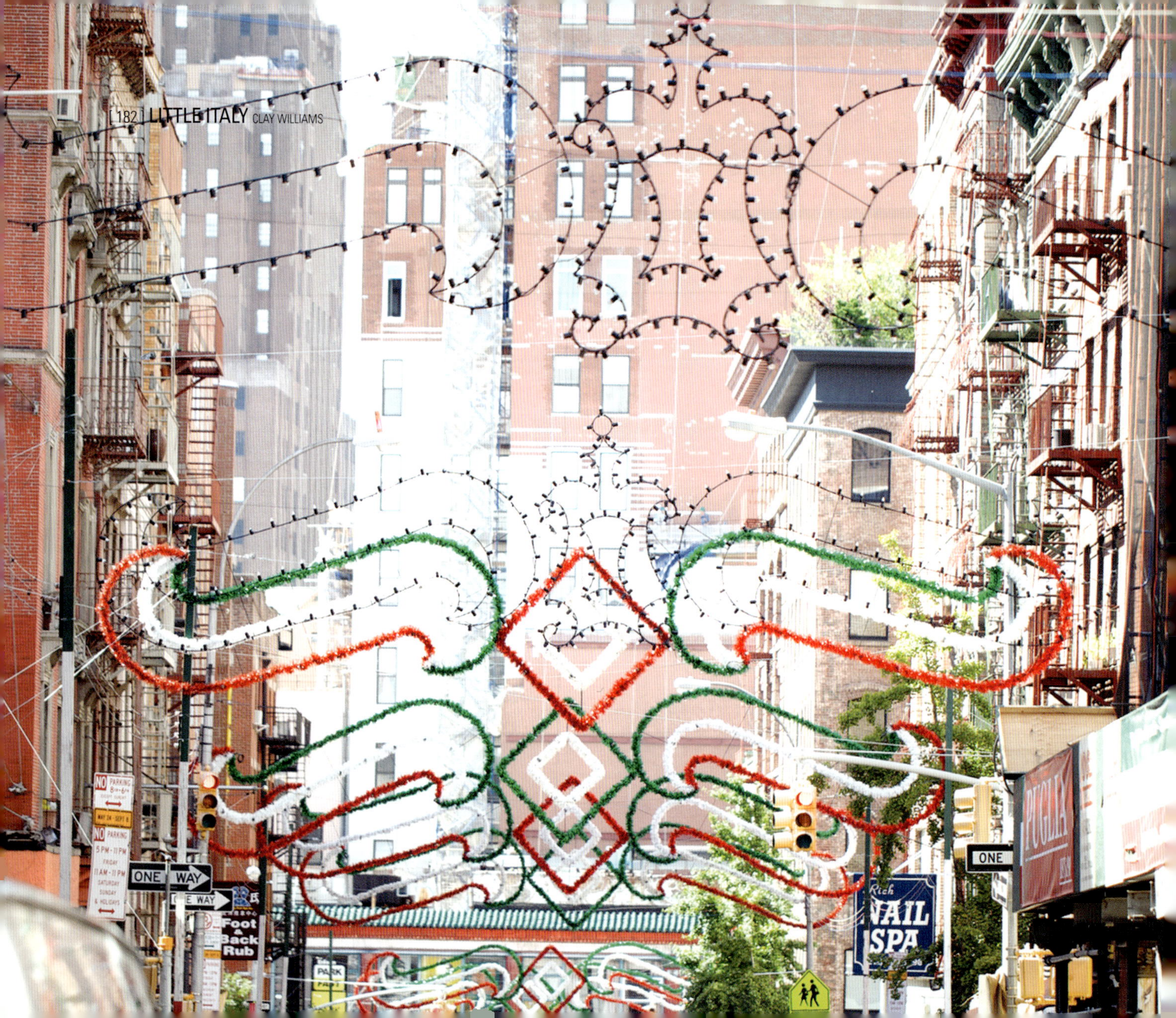
ONE WAY
ONE WAY
Foot & Back Rub
Rich NAIL SPA
ONE
PUGLIA

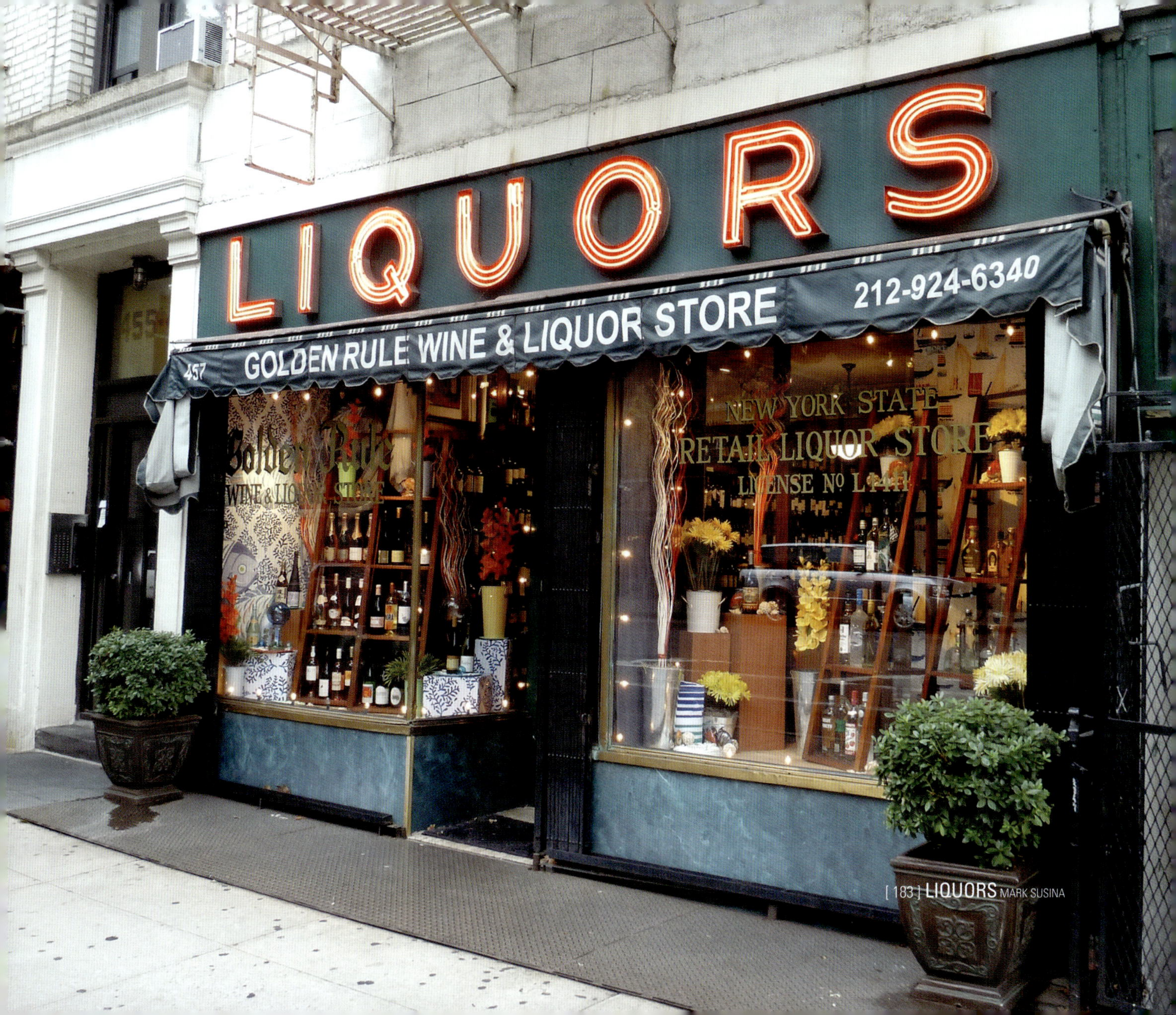

[183] **LIQUORS** MARK SUSINA

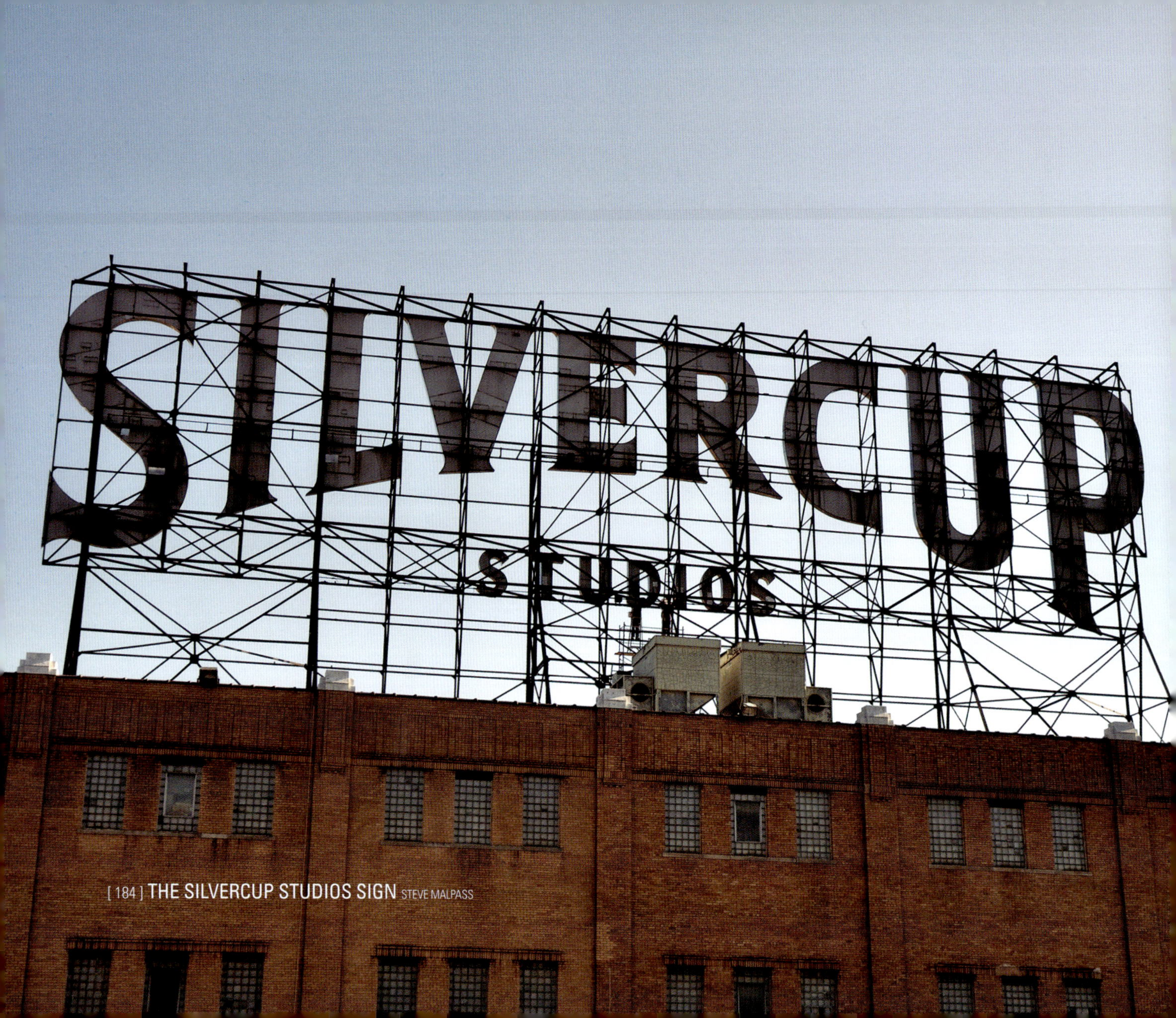

[184] THE SILVERCUP STUDIOS SIGN STEVE MALPASS

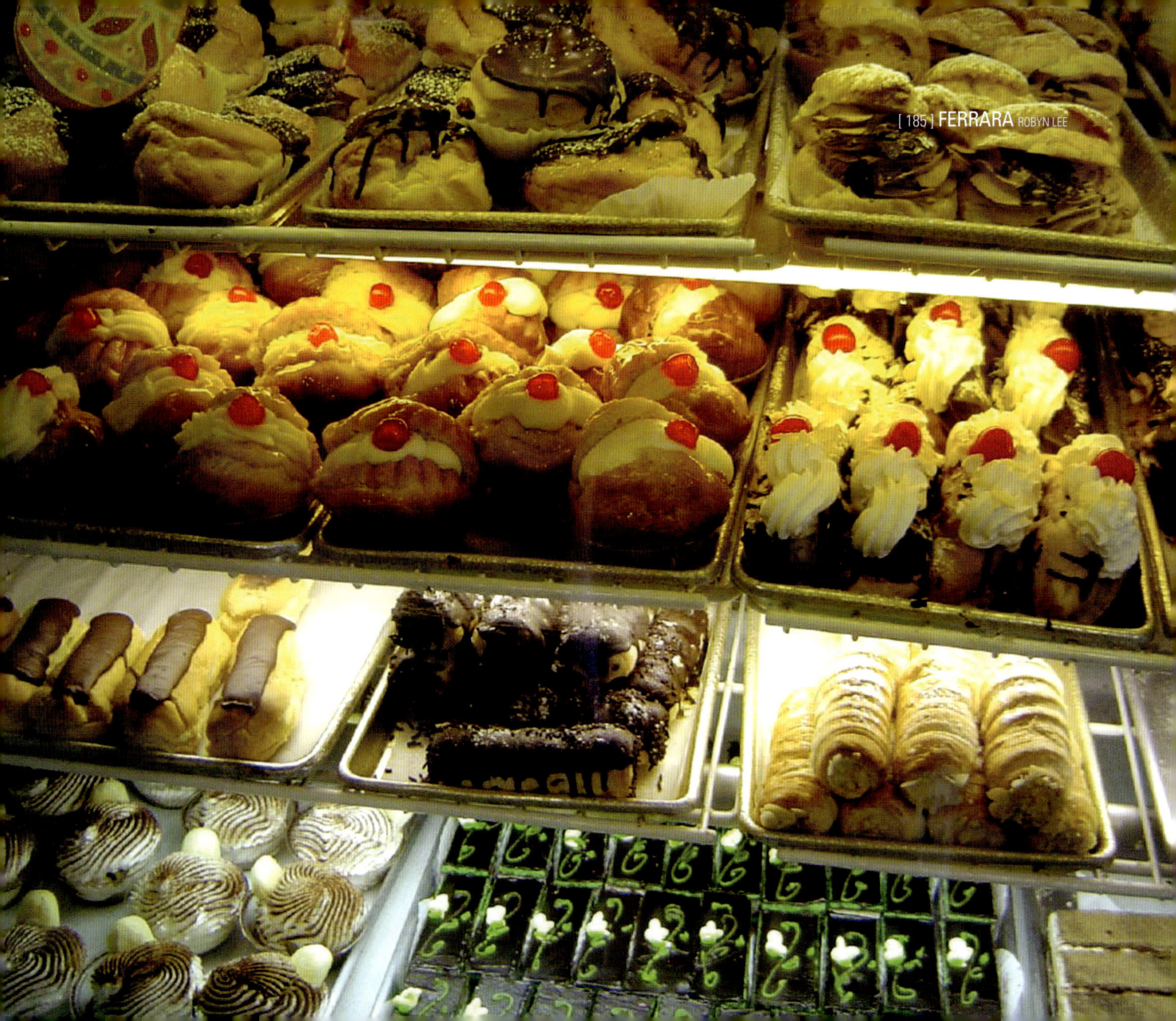

[185] FERRARA ROBYN LEE

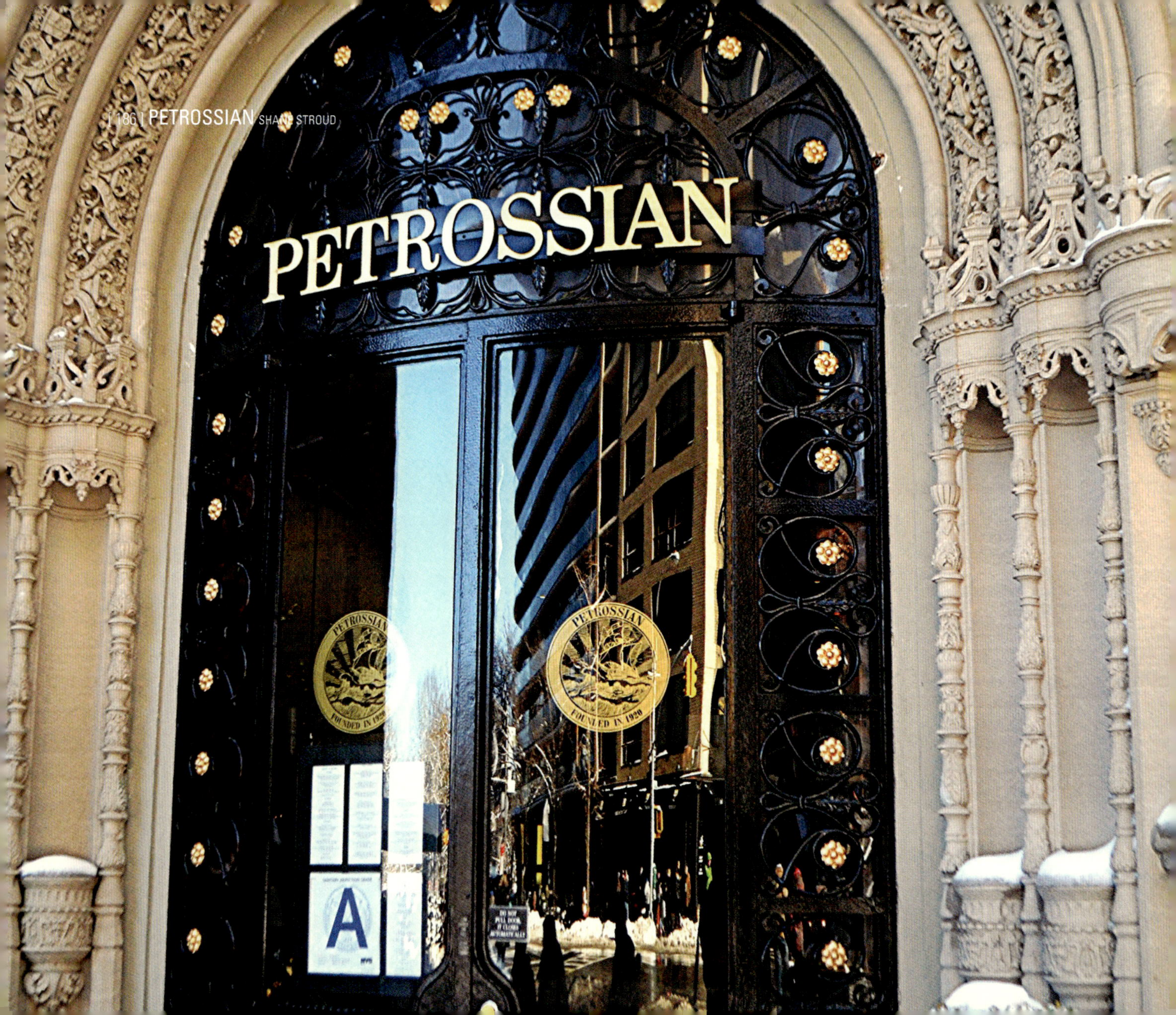
PETROSSIAN
PETROSSIAN
FOUNDED IN 1920
A

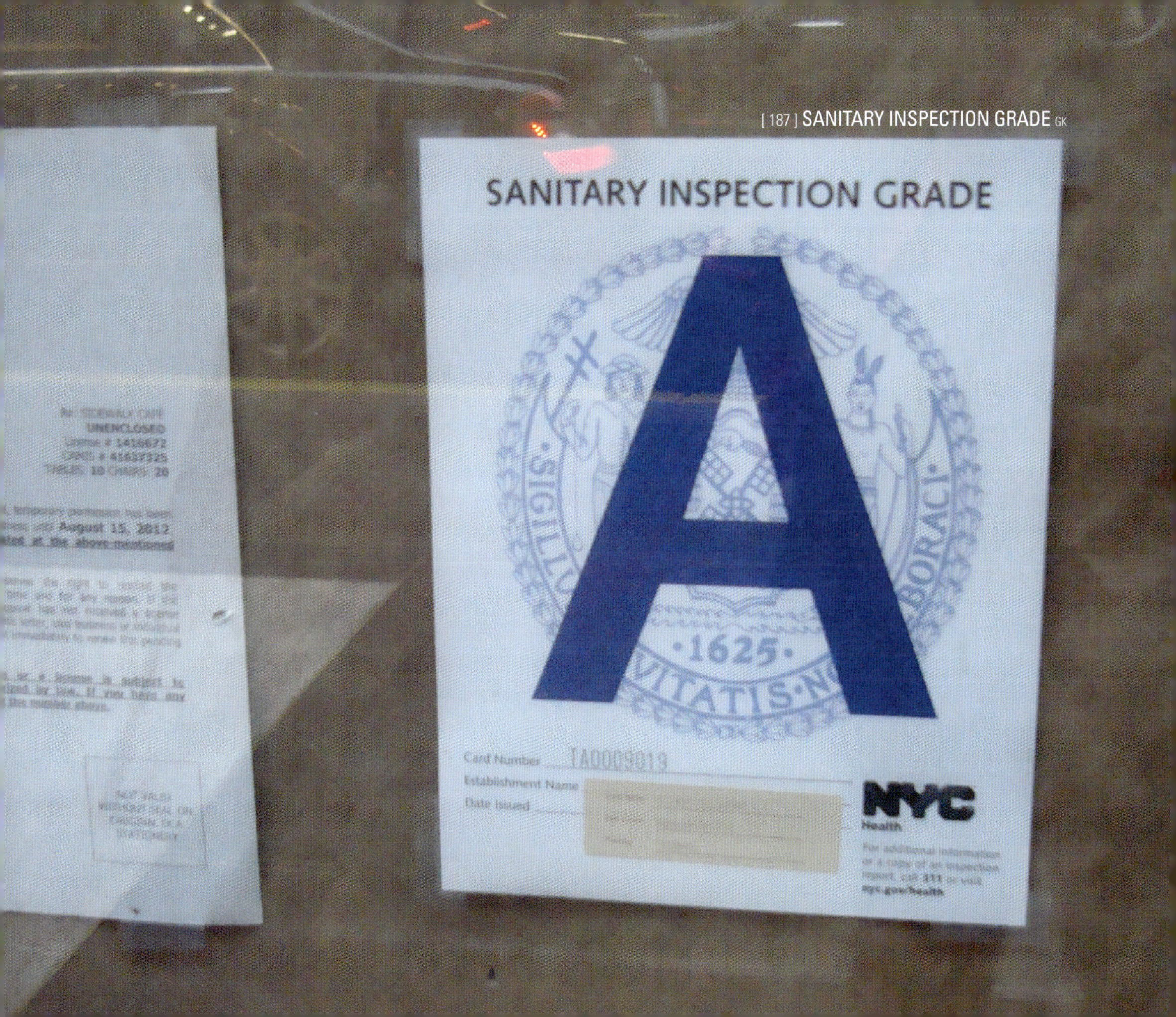
SANITARY INSPECTION GRADE
A
1625
Card Number
Establishment Name
Date Issued
NYC
Health
UNENCLOSED
August 15, 2012

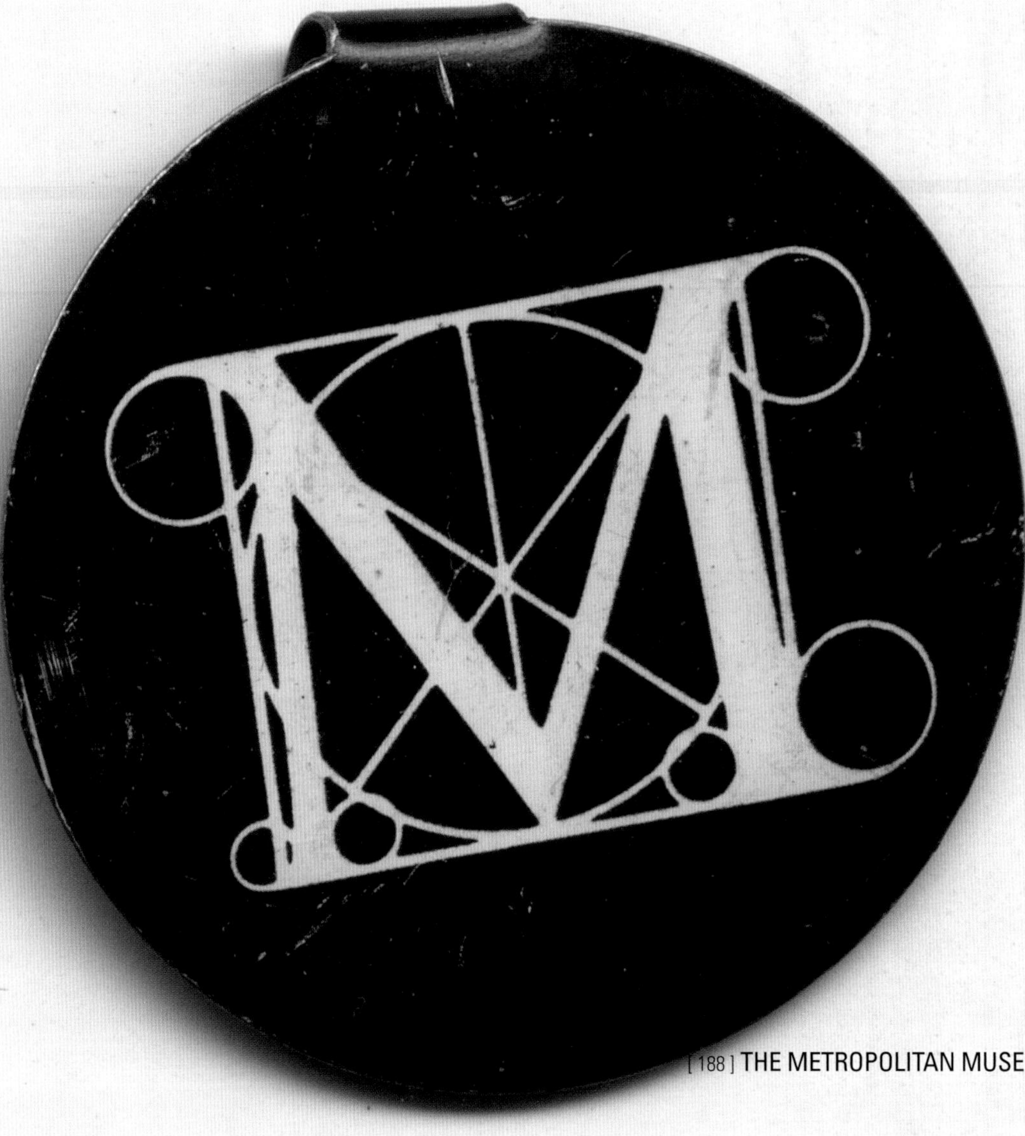

[188] THE METROPOLITAN MUSEUM OF ART GK

[189] MAGNOLIA BAKERY GK

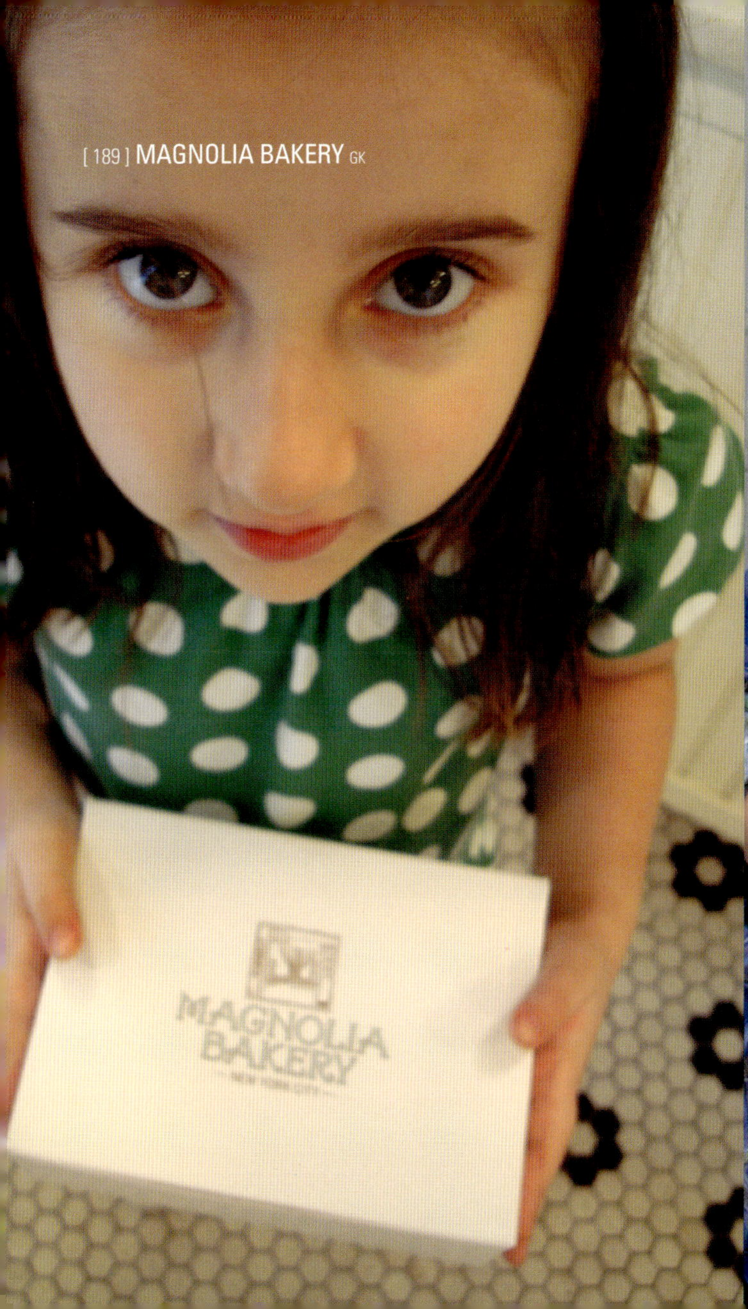

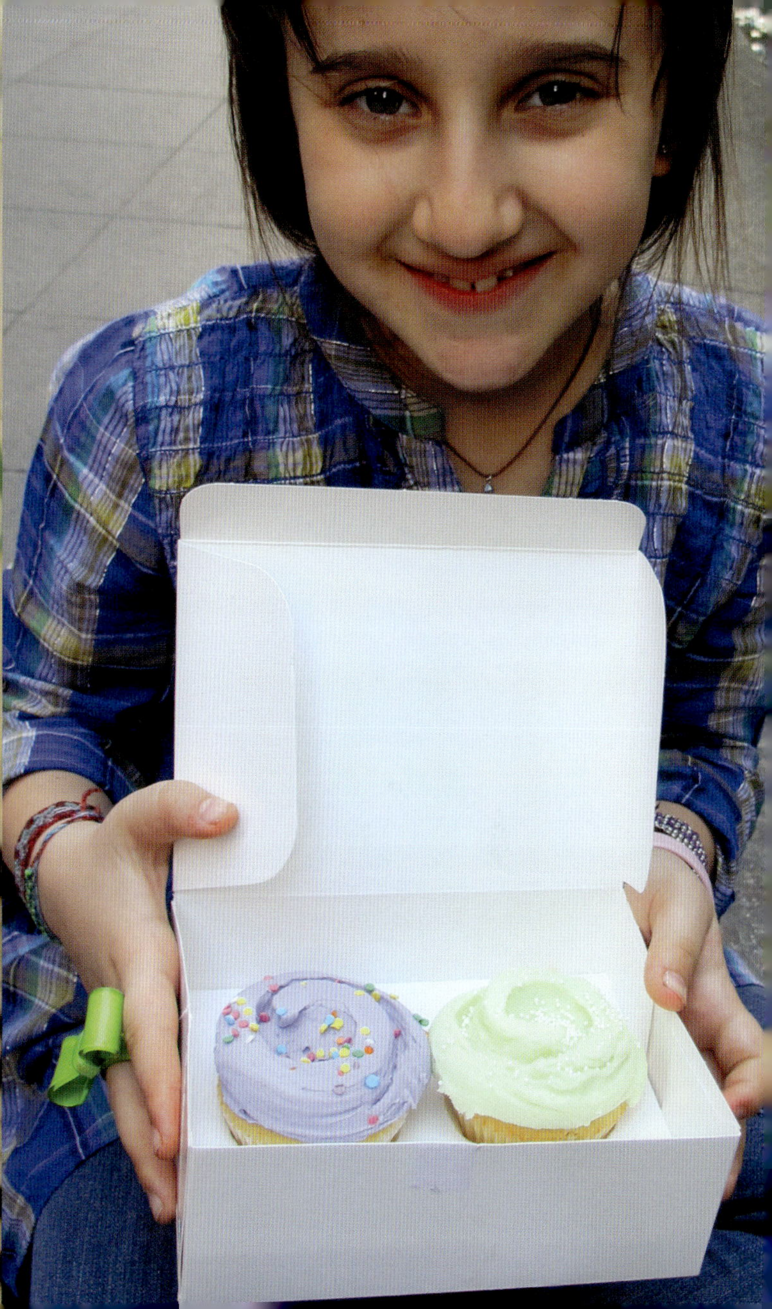

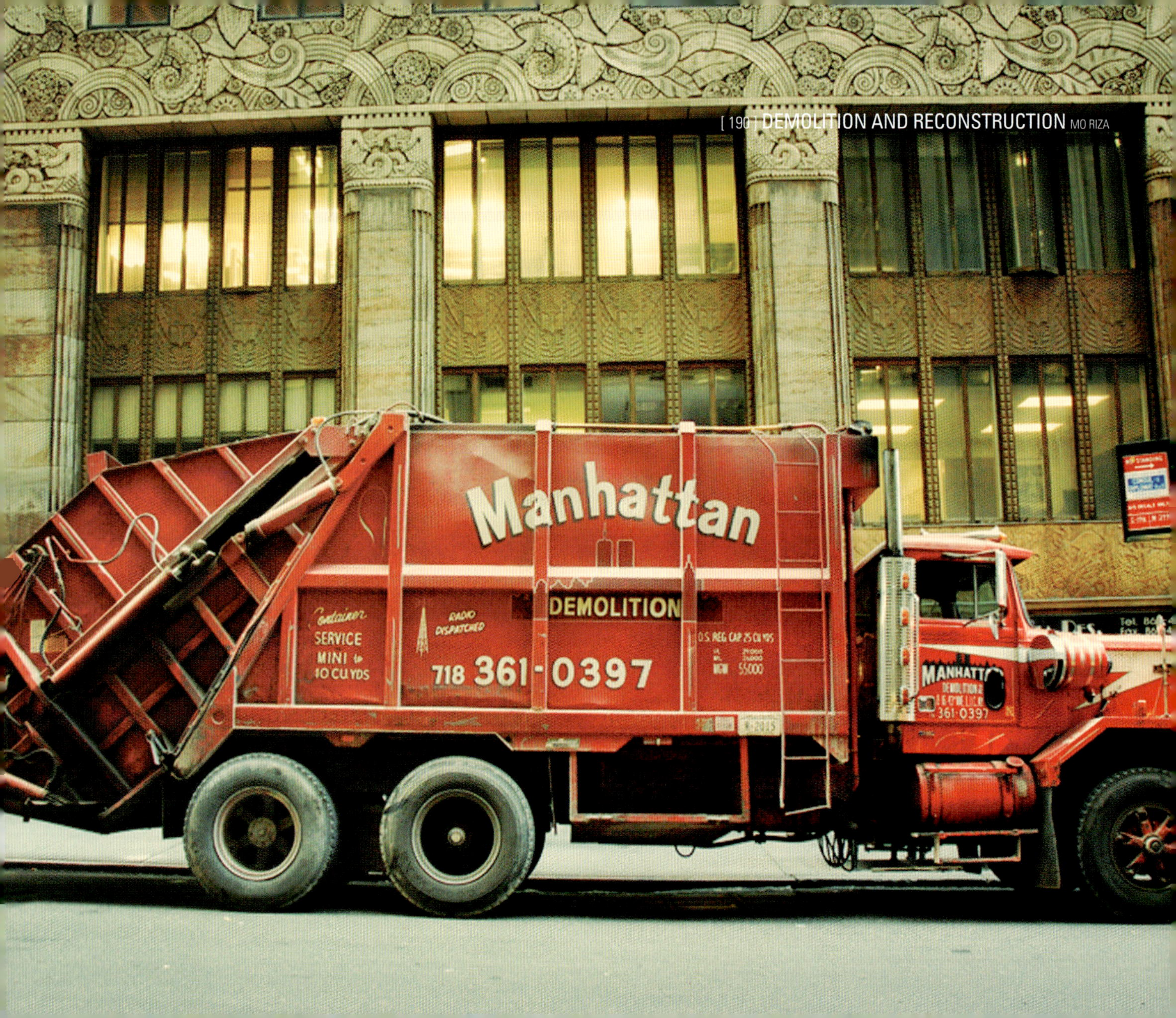
Manhattan
DEMOLITION
Container SERVICE MINI to 10 CU YDS
RADIO DISPATCHED
718 361-0397
O.S. REG CAP 25 CU YDS
MANHATTAN
361-0397

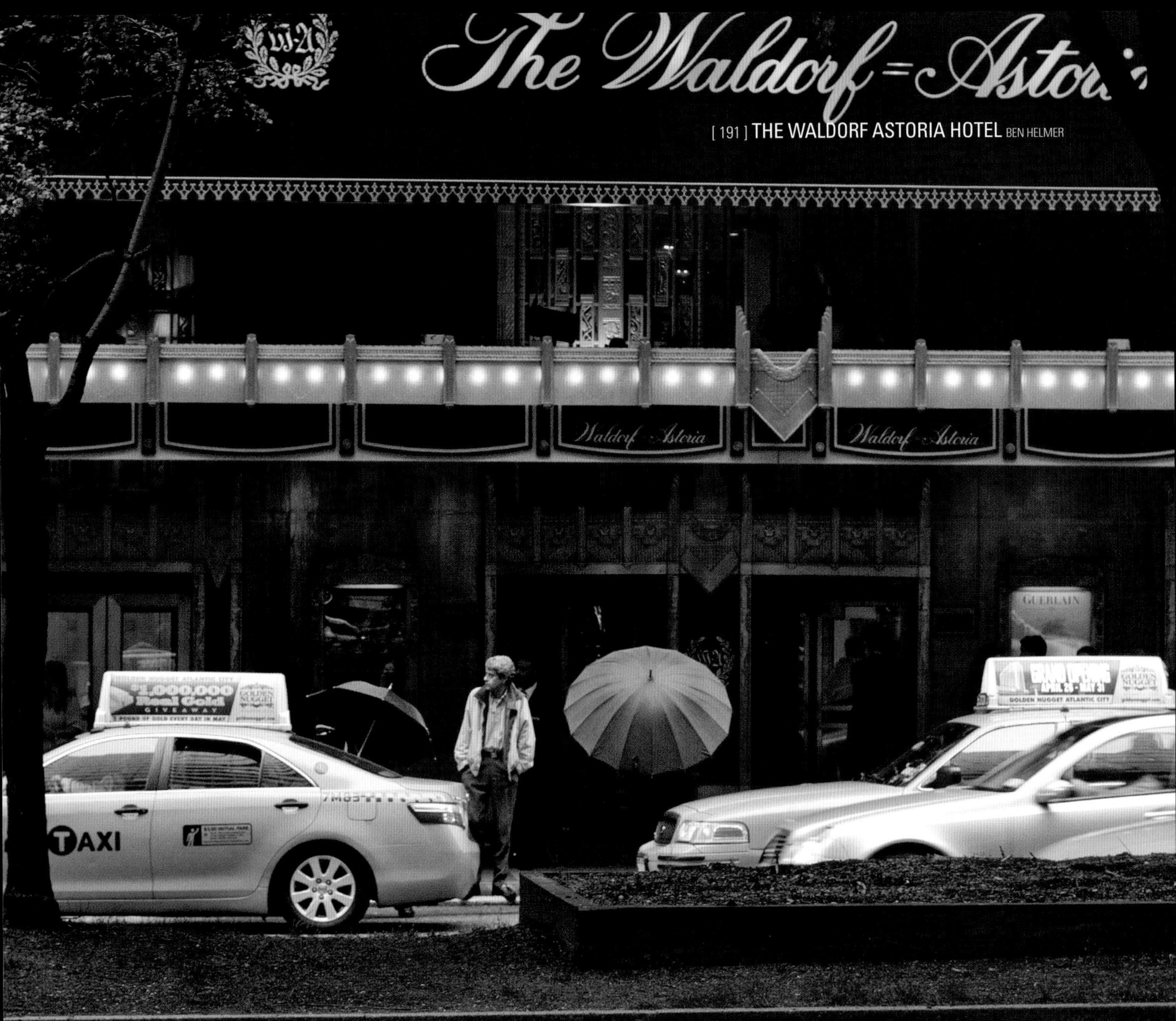

[191] THE WALDORF ASTORIA HOTEL BEN HELMER

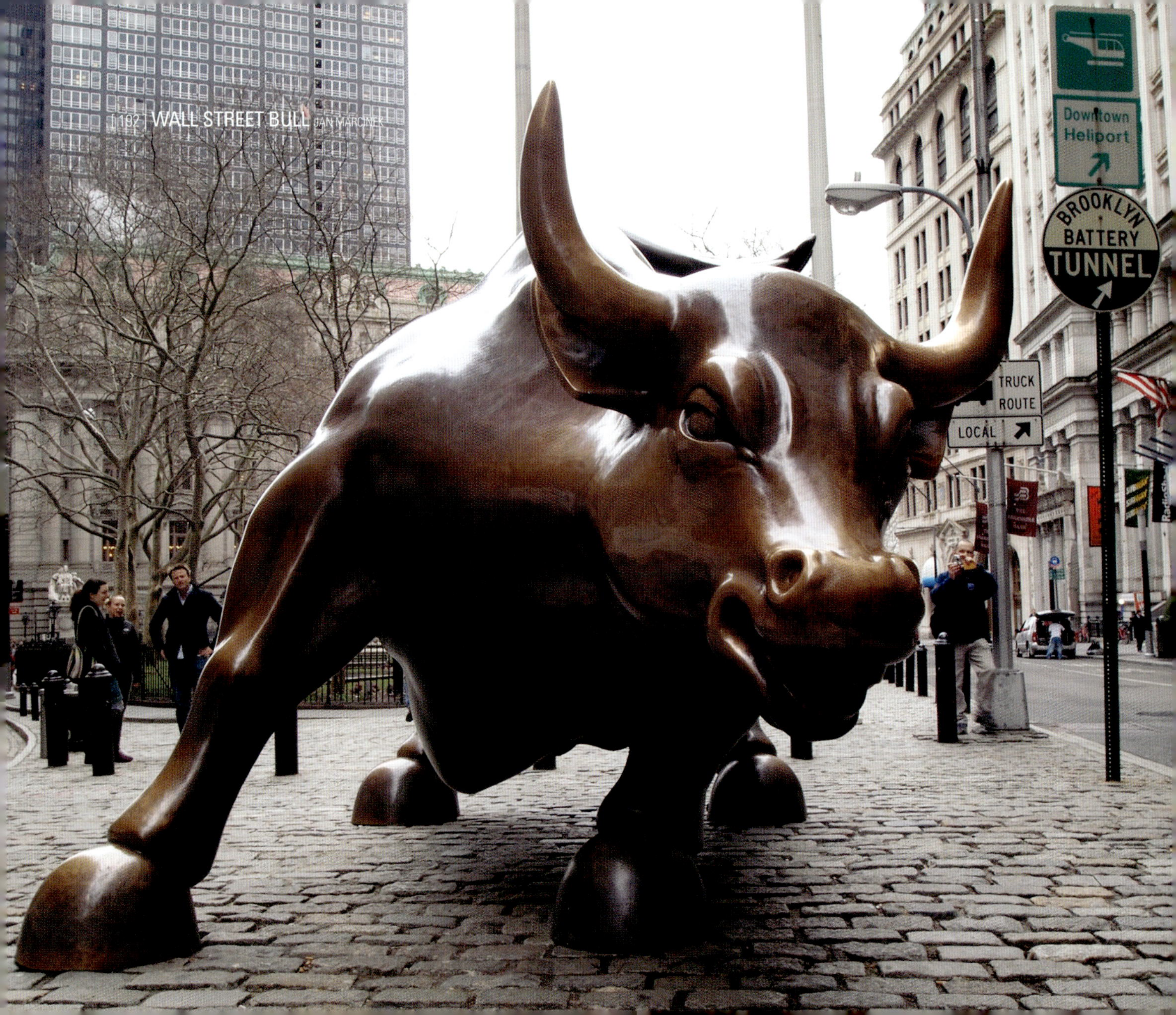

[192] WALL STREET BULL JAN MARCINEK

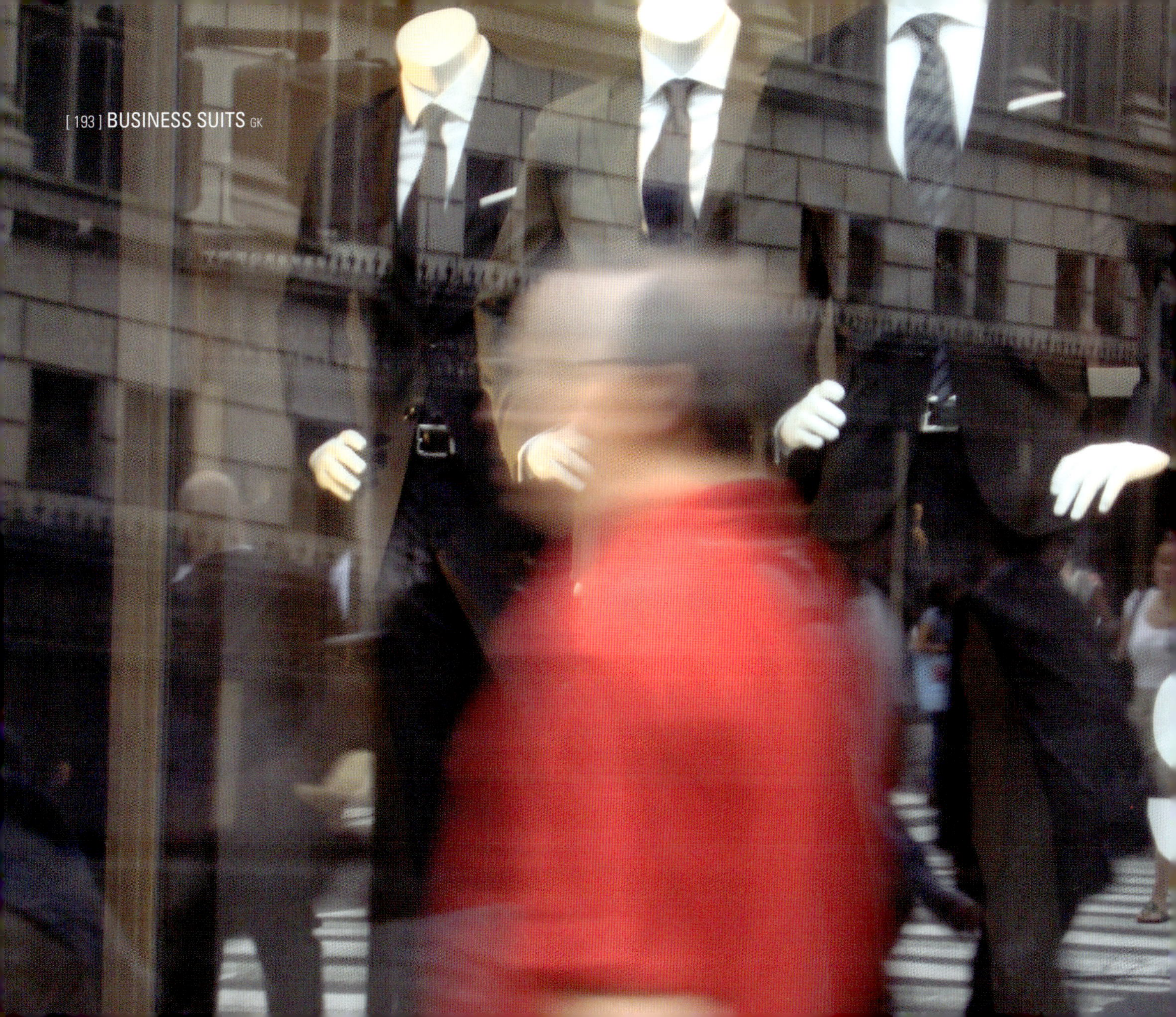

[193] BUSINESS SUITS GK

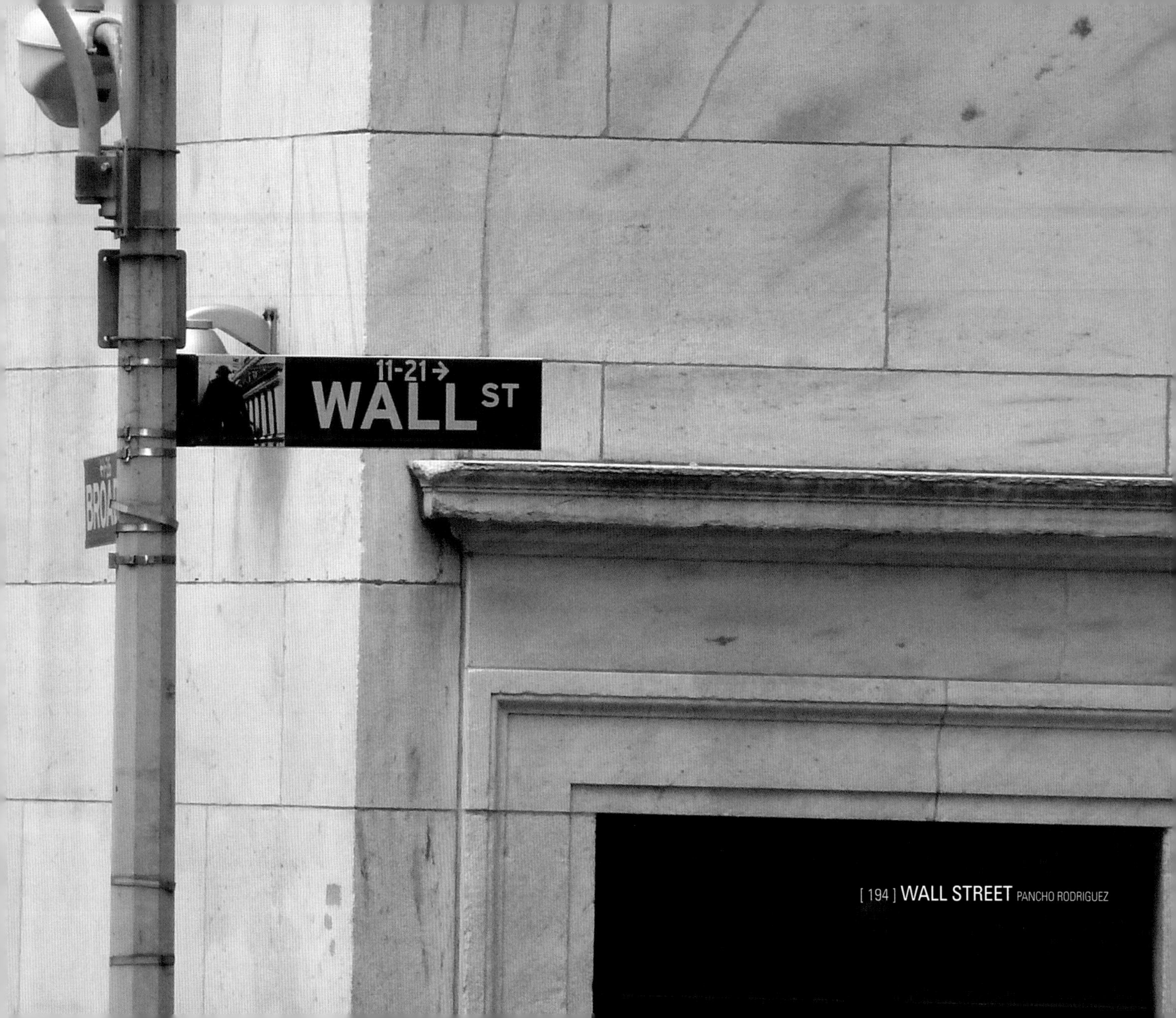

[194] WALL STREET PANCHO RODRIGUEZ

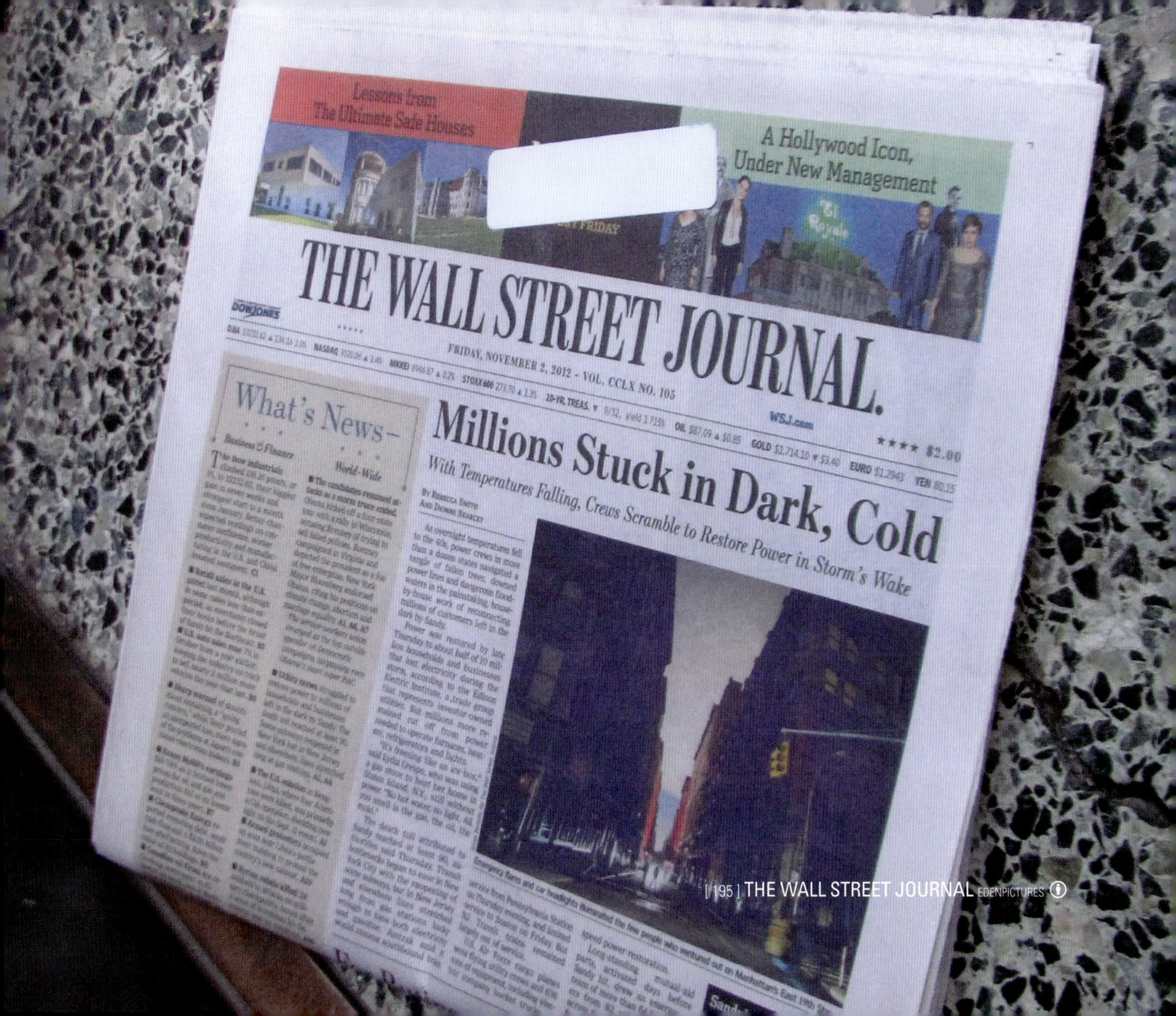

[195] THE WALL STREET JOURNAL EDENPICTURES

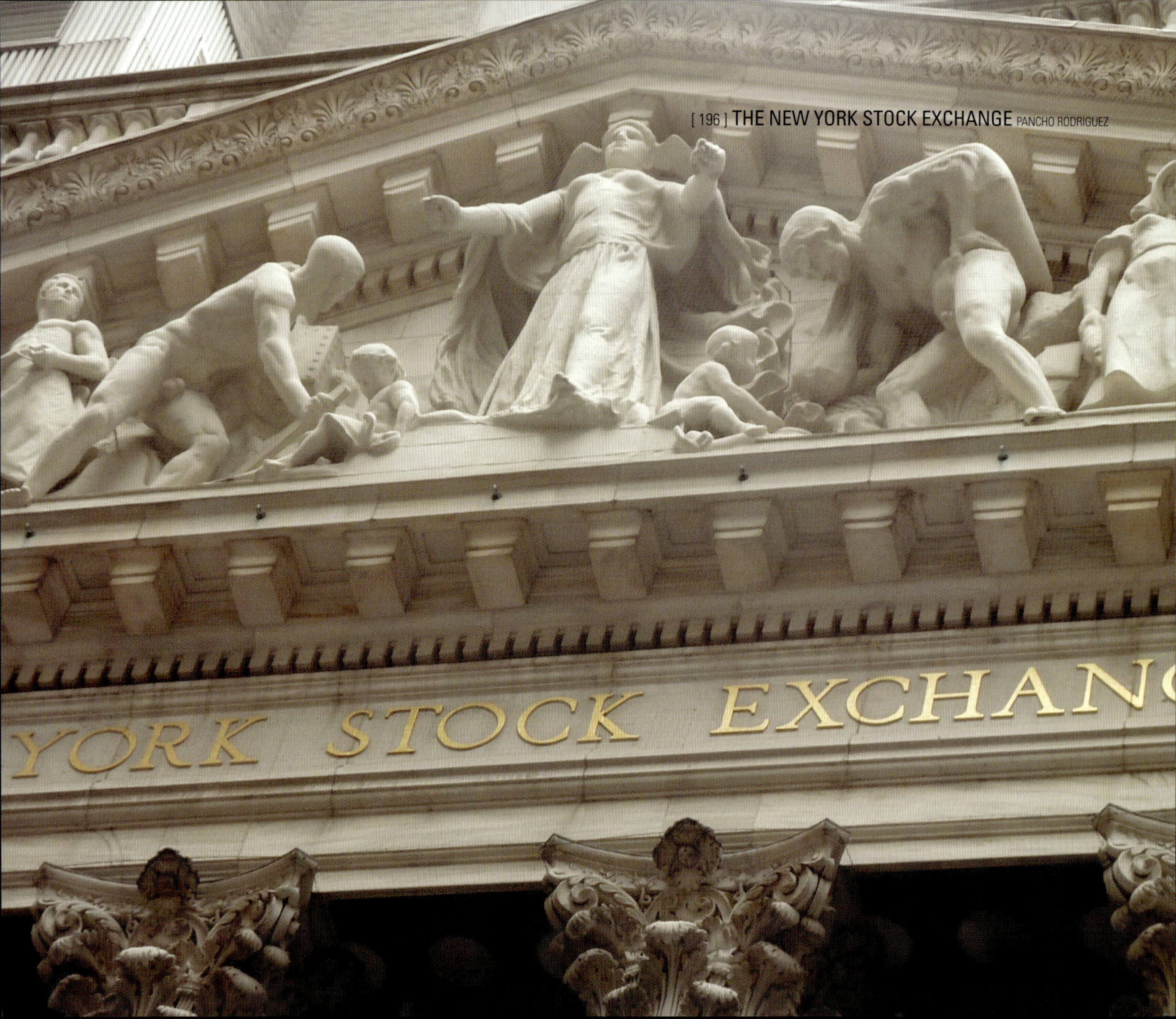
YORK STOCK EXCHAN

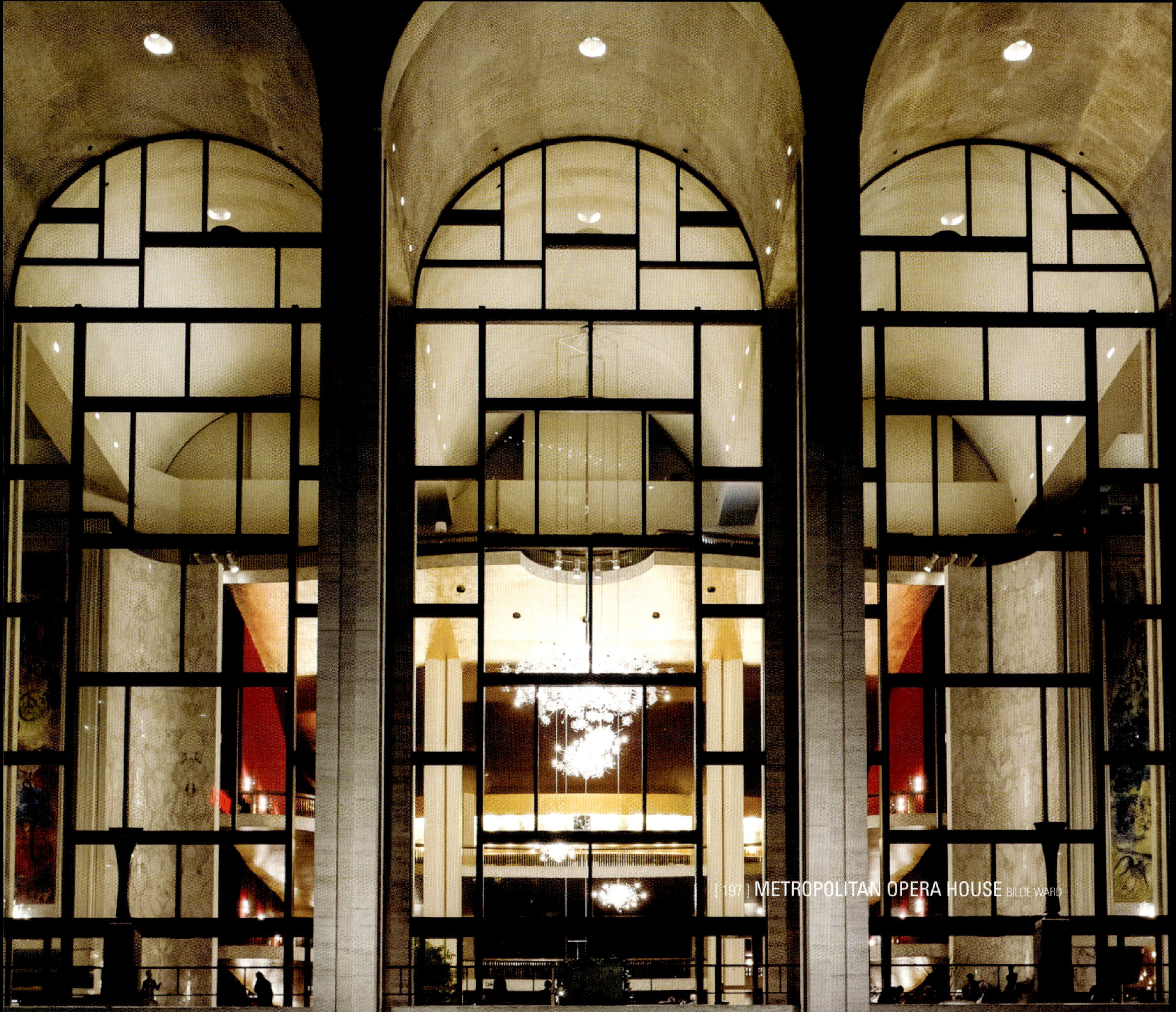

[197] METROPOLITAN OPERA HOUSE BILLIE WARD

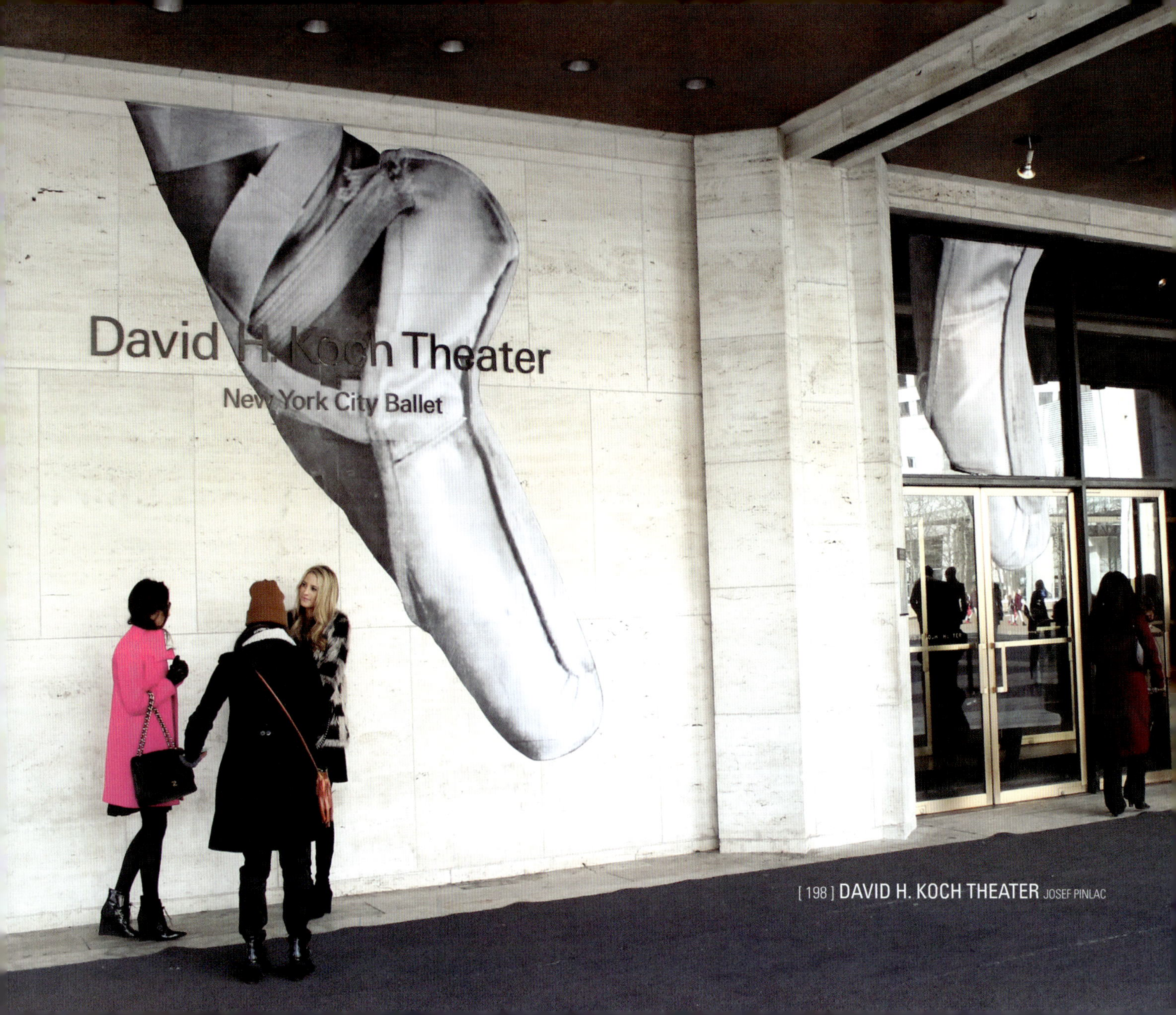

[198] DAVID H. KOCH THEATER JOSEF PINLAC

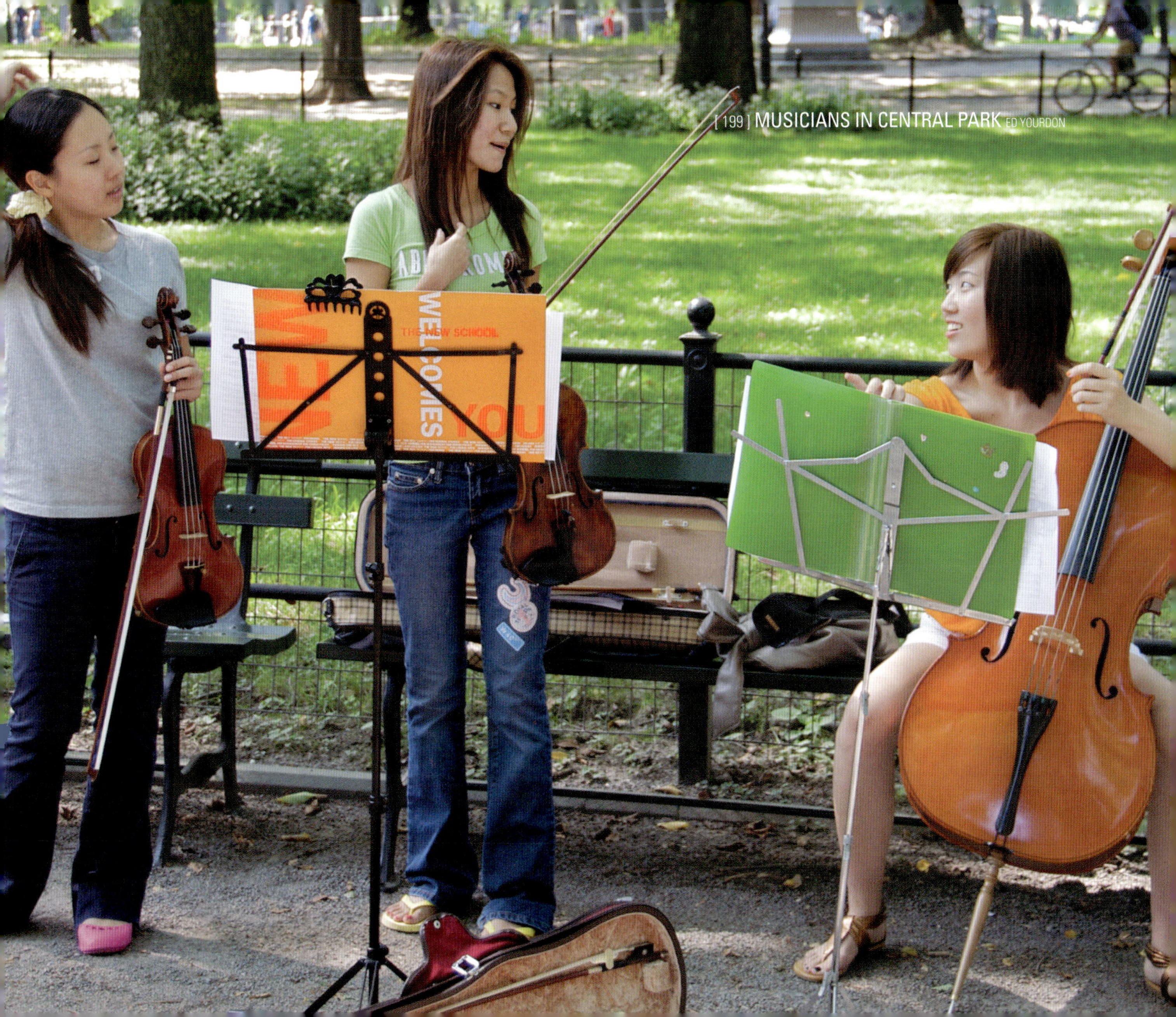

[199] MUSICIANS IN CENTRAL PARK ED YOURDON

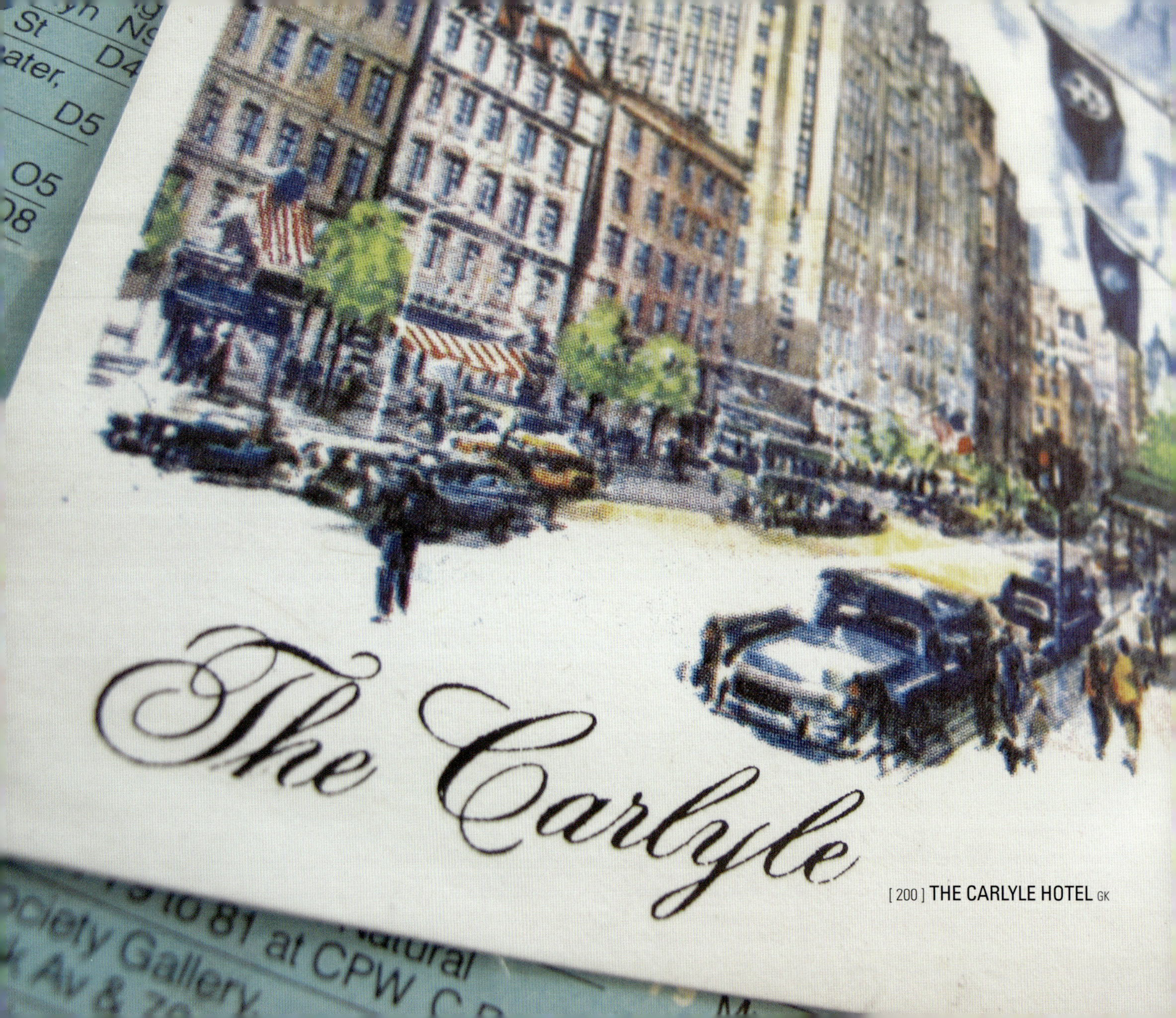

[200] THE CARLYLE HOTEL GK

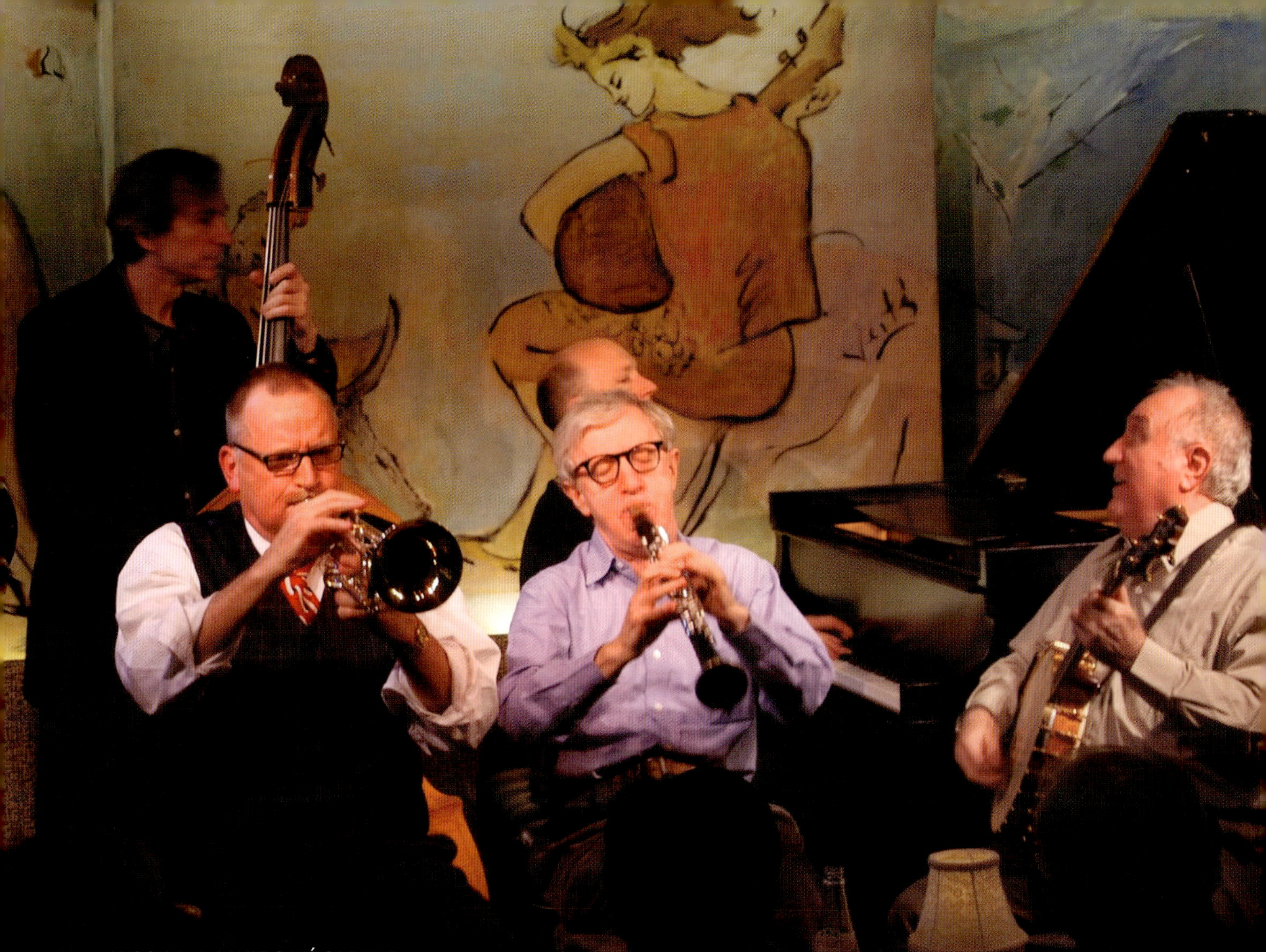

[201] WOODY ALLEN AT CAFÉ CARLYLE JAN MARCINEK

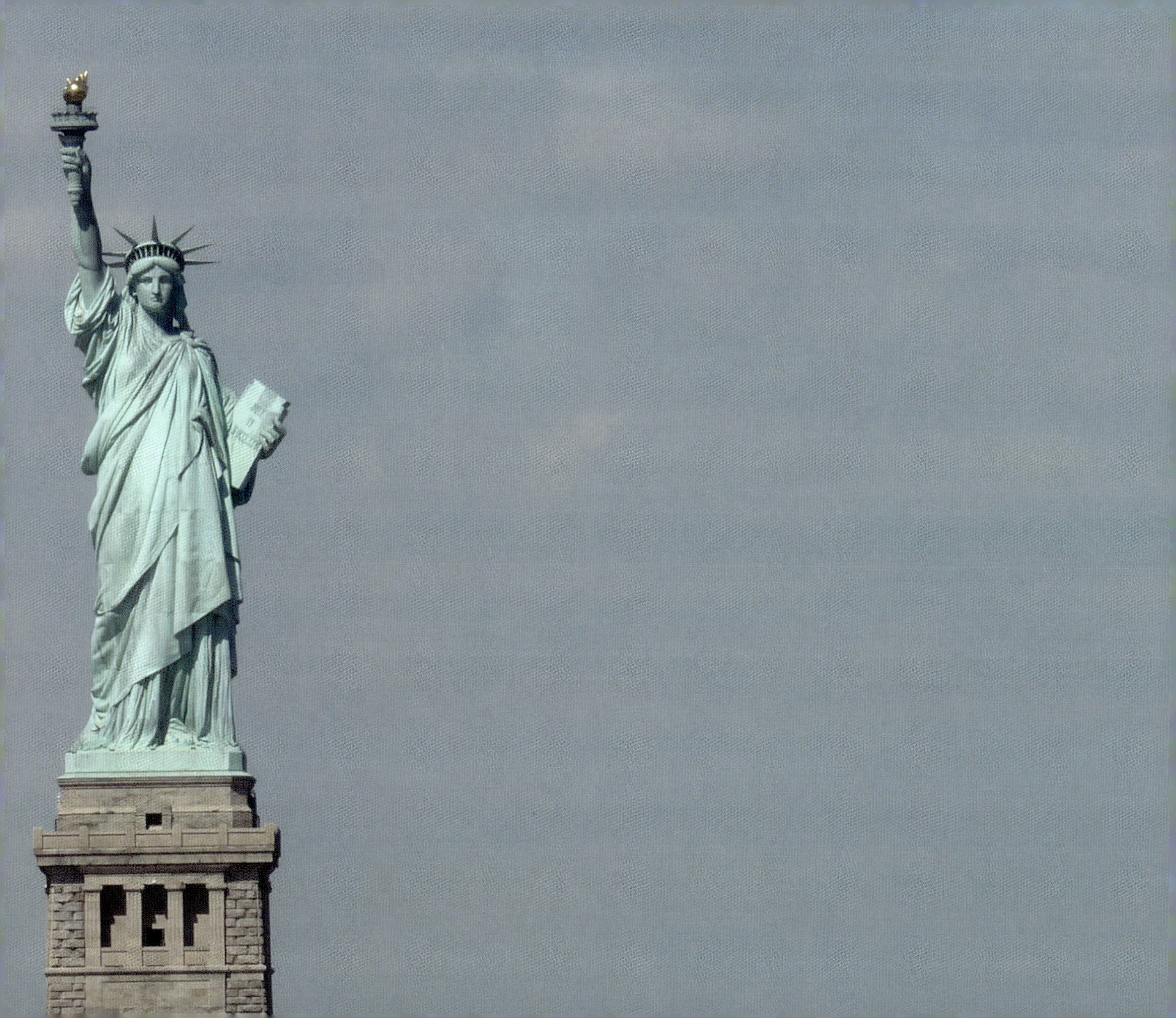

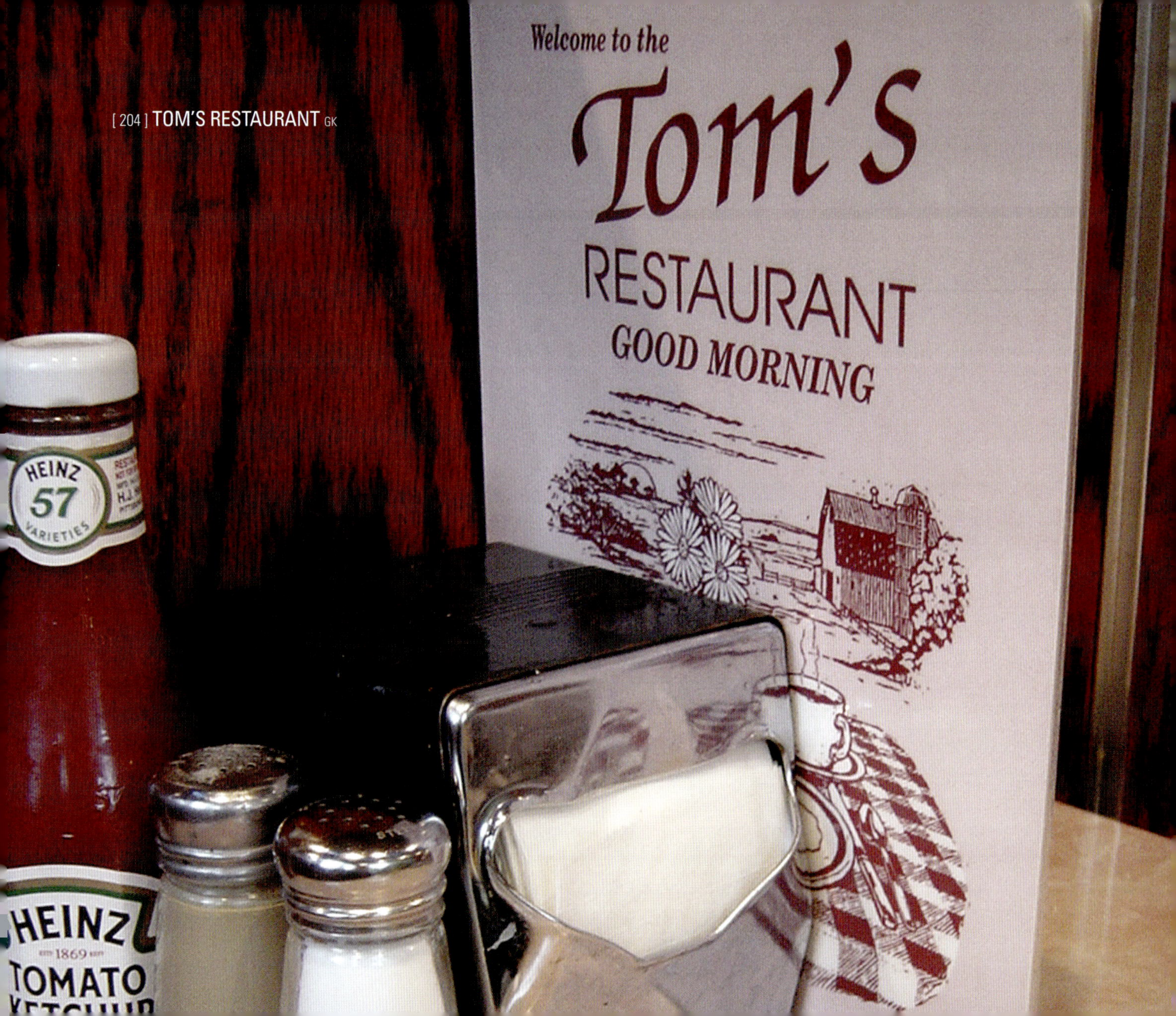

[204] TOM'S RESTAURANT GK

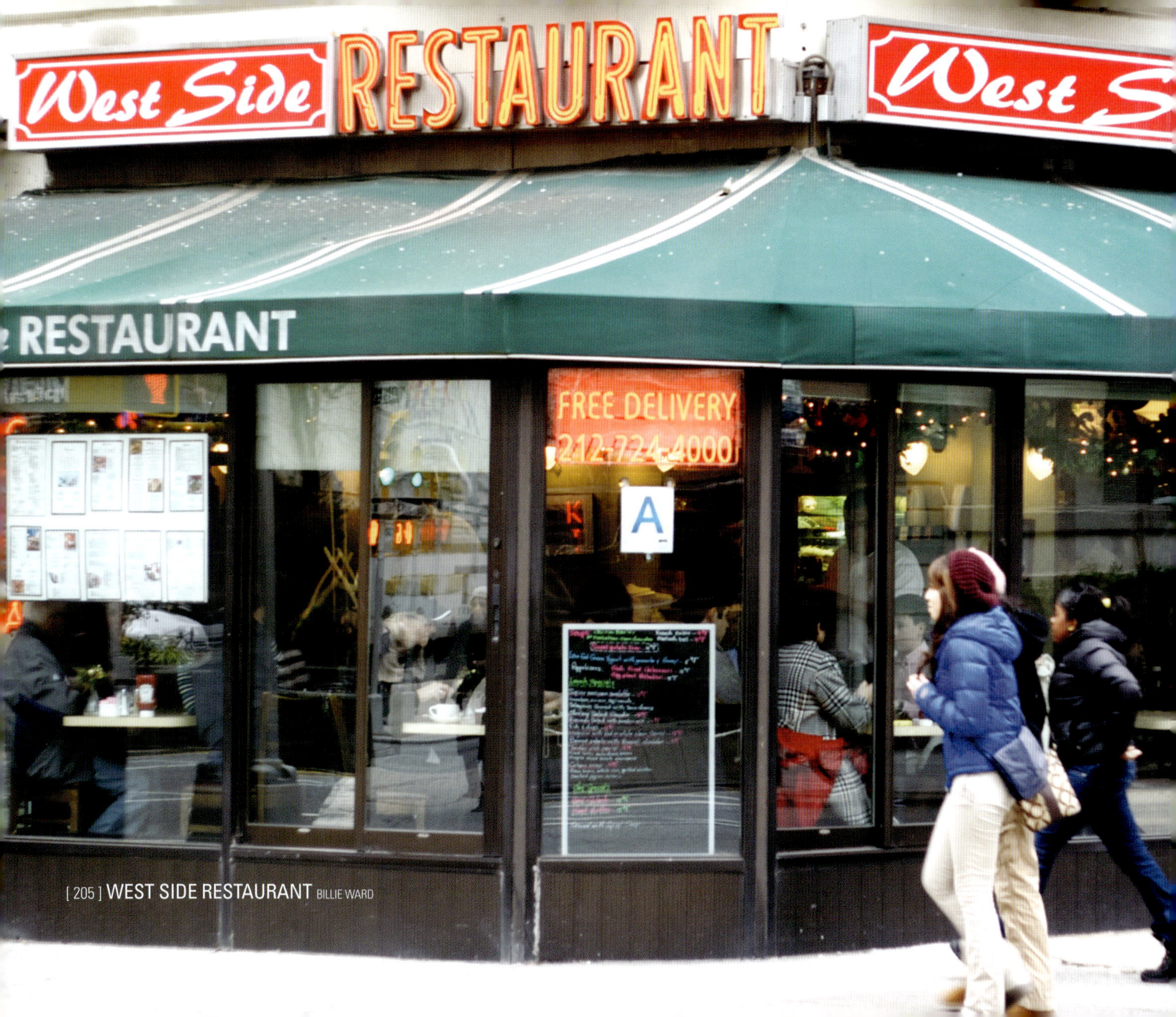

[205] WEST SIDE RESTAURANT BILLIE WARD

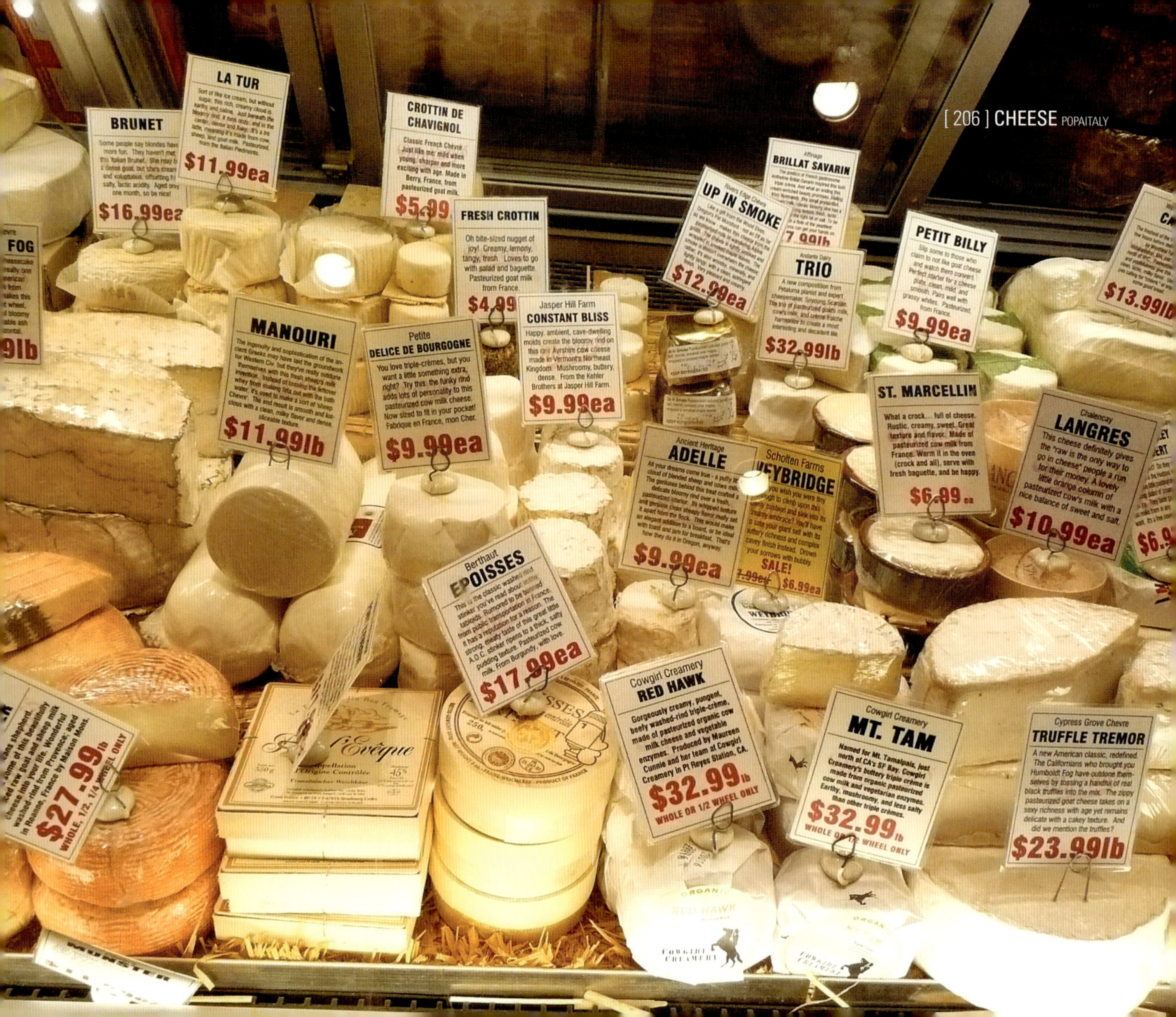
BRUNET
$16.99ea
LA TUR
$11.99ea
CROTTIN DE CHAVIGNOL
$5.99
FRESH CROTTIN
$4.99
UP IN SMOKE
$12.99ea
BRILLAT SAVARIN
TRIO
$32.99lb
PETIT BILLY
$9.99ea
$13.99lb
MANOURI
$11.99lb
Petite
DELICE DE BOURGOGNE
$9.99ea
Jasper Hill Farm
CONSTANT BLISS
$9.99ea
ST. MARCELLIN
$6.99 ea
Chalencay
LANGRES
$10.99ea
Ancient Heritage
ADELLE
$9.99ea
Scholten Farms
WEYBRIDGE
SALE!
$6.99ea
Berthaut
EPOISSES
$17.99ea
$27.99lb
WHOLE, 1/2, 1/4 WHEEL ONLY
Cowgirl Creamery
RED HAWK
$32.99lb
WHOLE OR 1/2 WHEEL ONLY
Cowgirl Creamery
MT. TAM
$32.99lb
Cypress Grove Chevre
TRUFFLE TREMOR
$23.99lb
MUNSTER

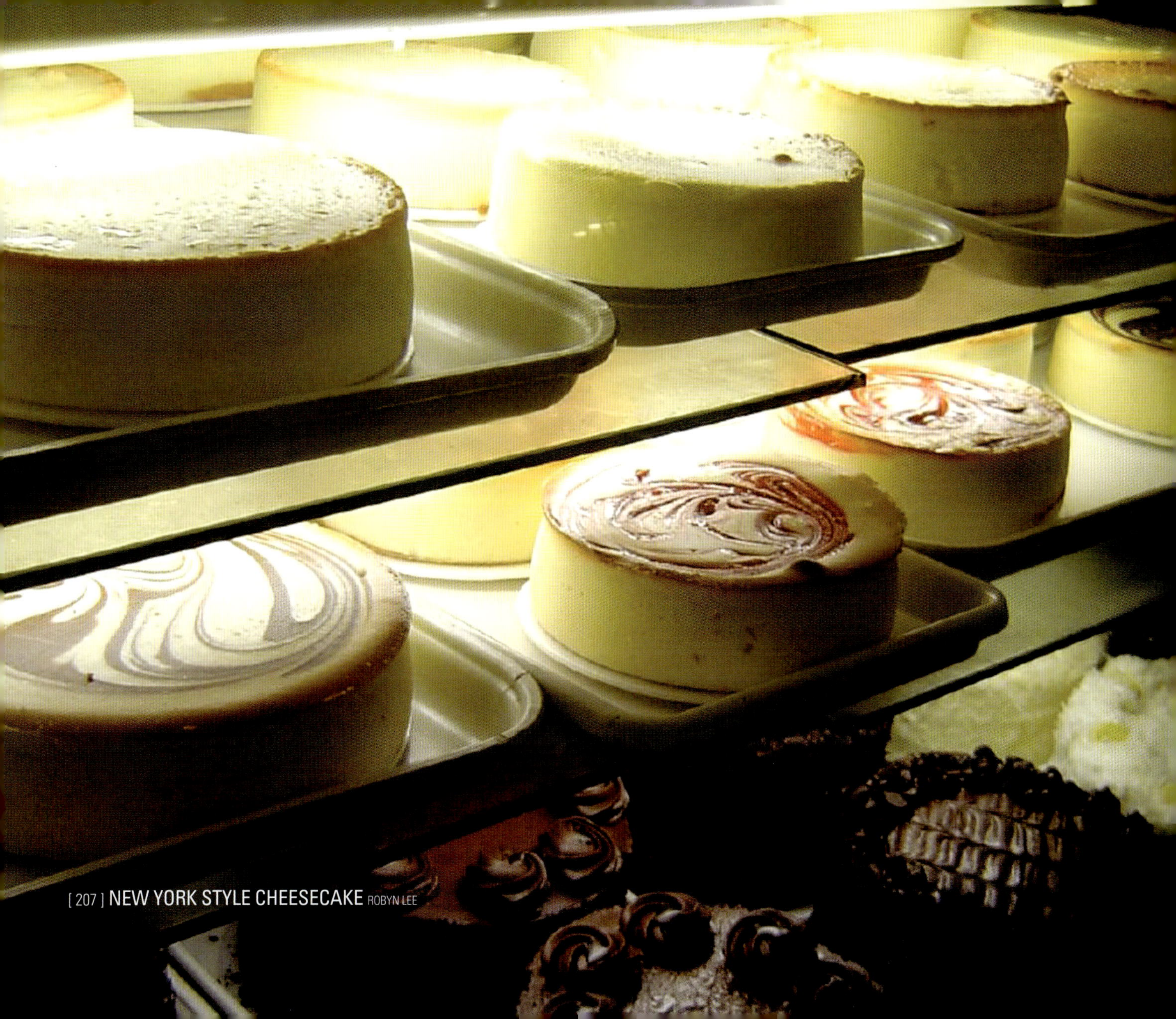

[207] NEW YORK STYLE CHEESECAKE ROBYN LEE

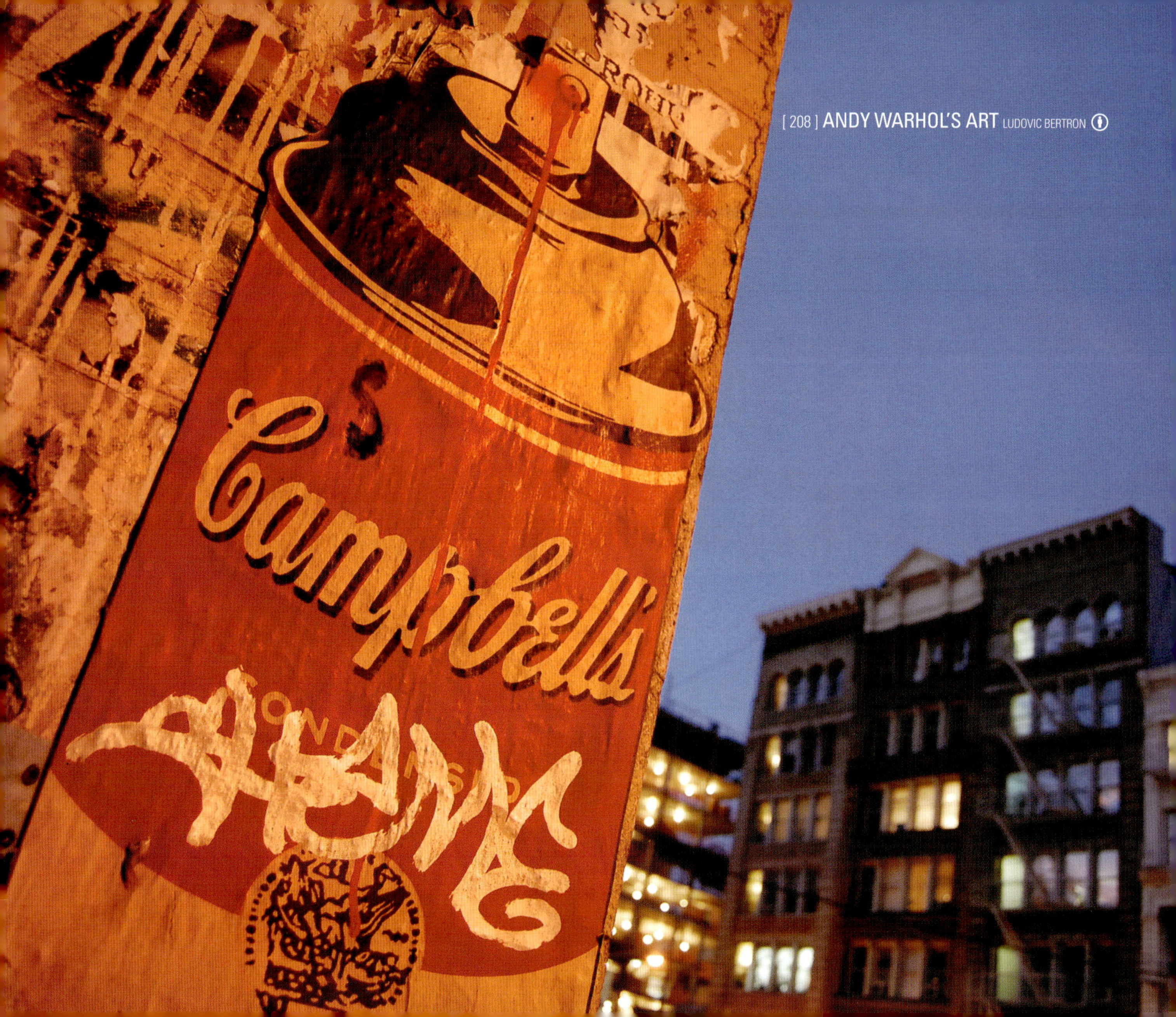

[208] ANDY WARHOL'S ART LUDOVIC BERTRON

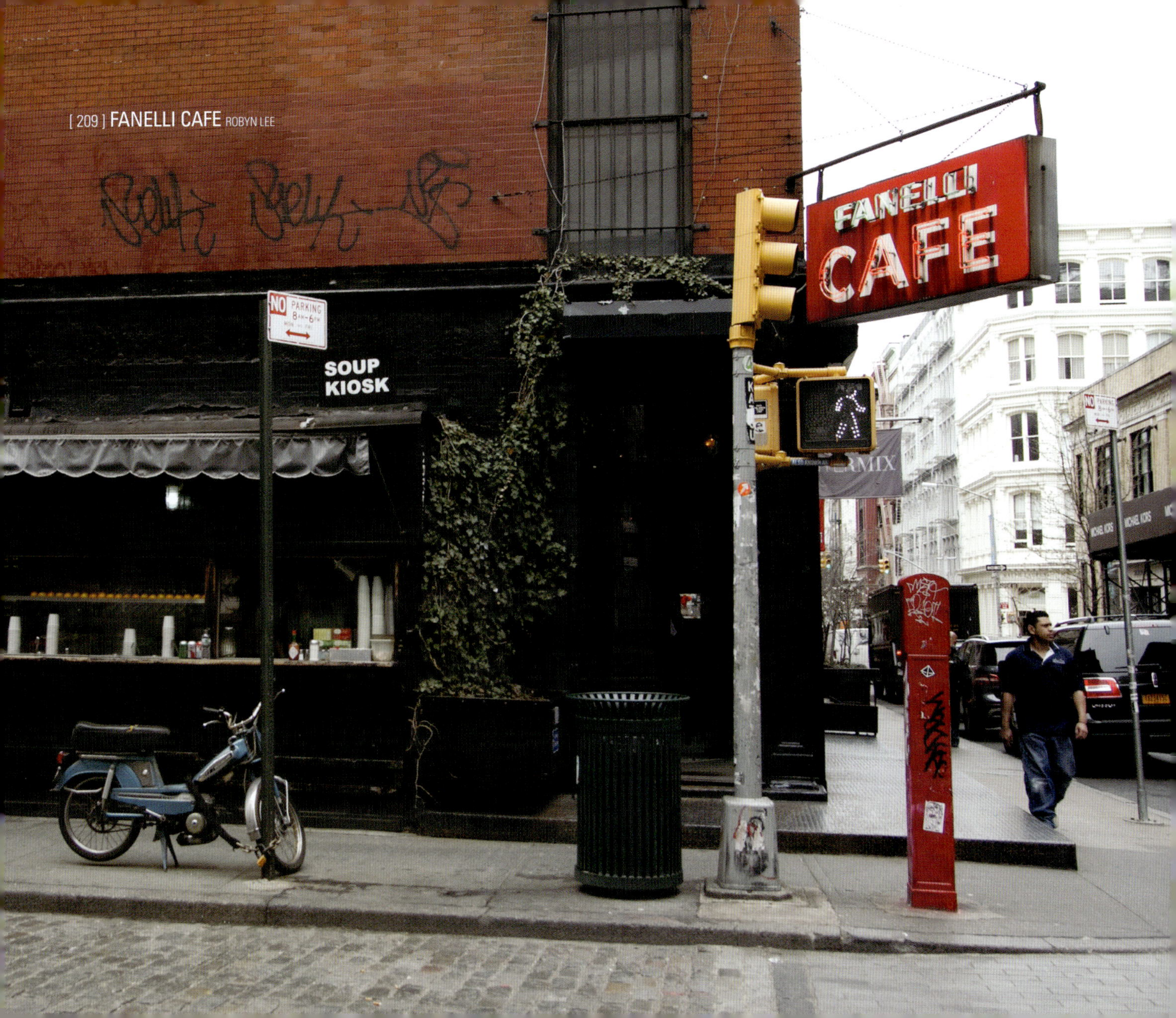

[209] FANELLI CAFE ROBYN LEE

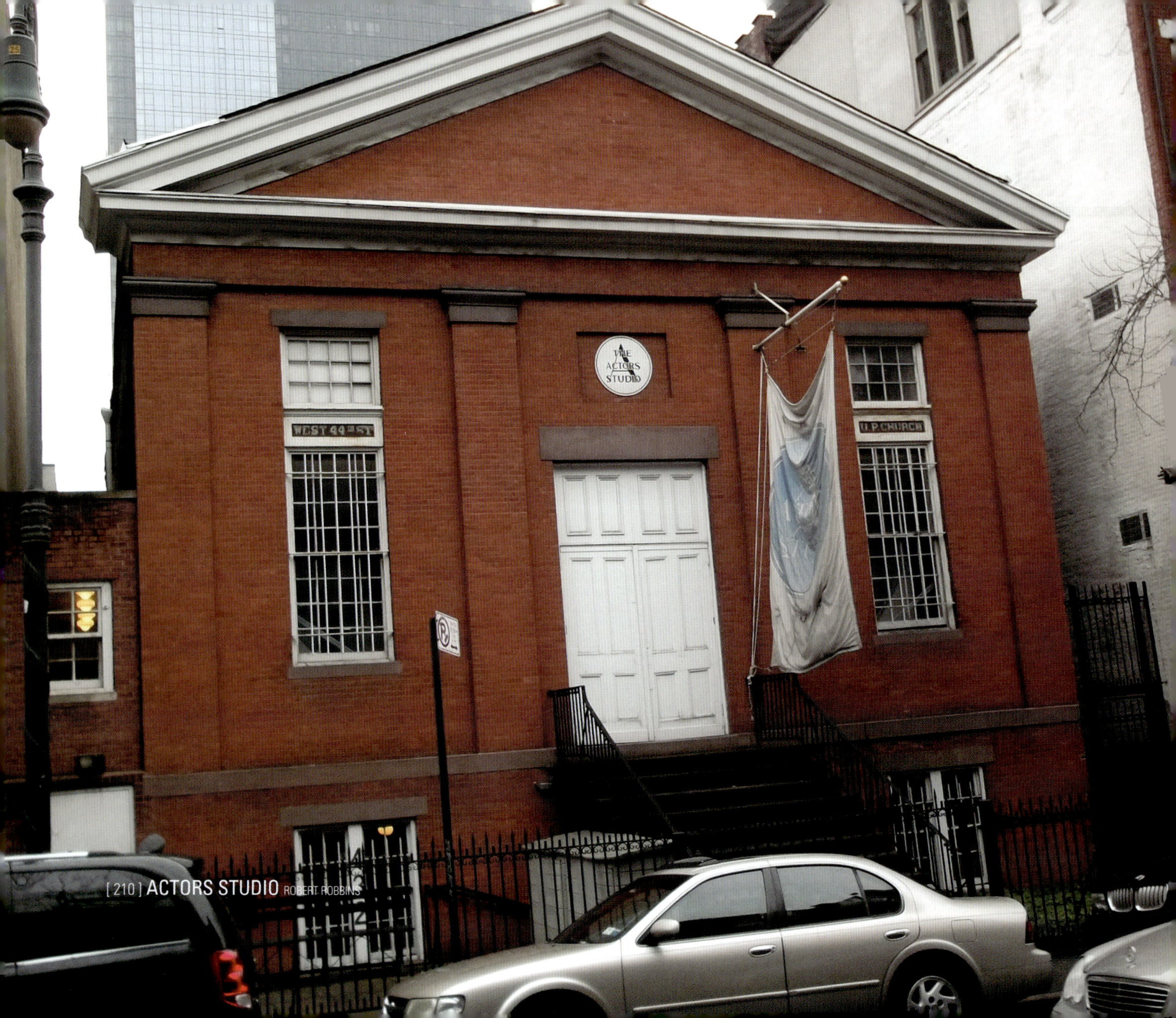

[210] ACTORS STUDIO ROBERT ROBBINS

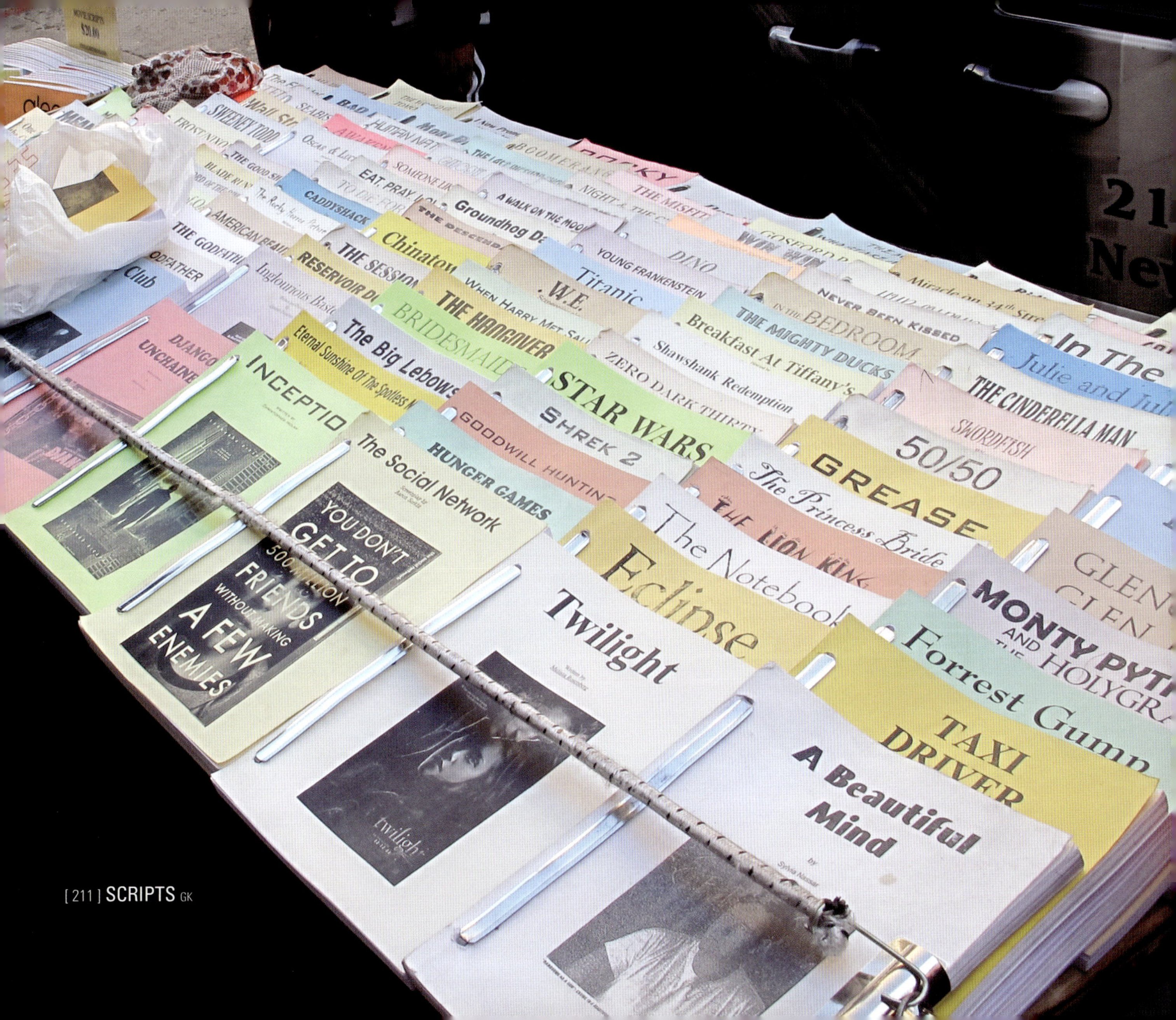

[211] SCRIPTS GK

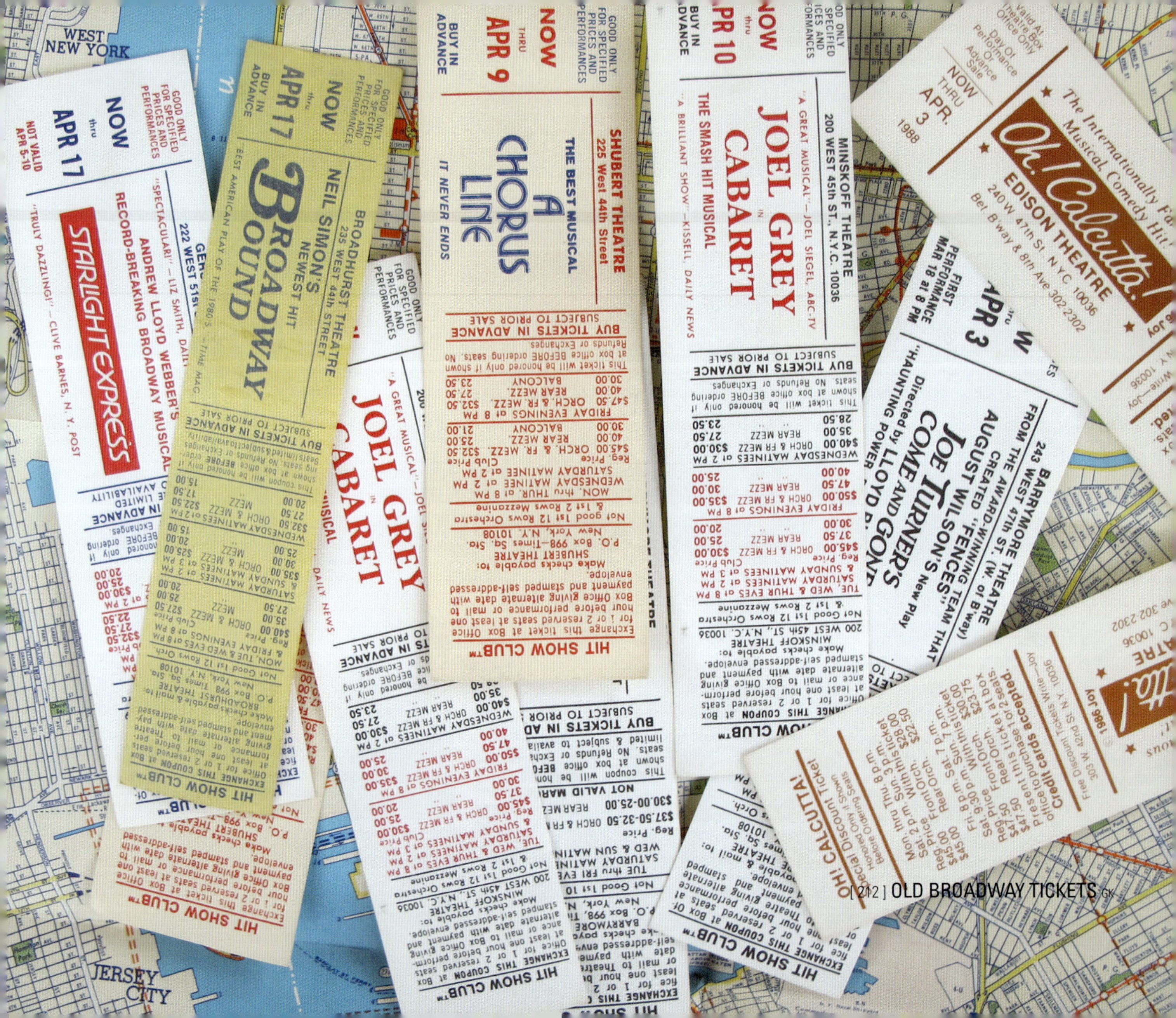

[212] OLD BROADWAY TICKETS GK

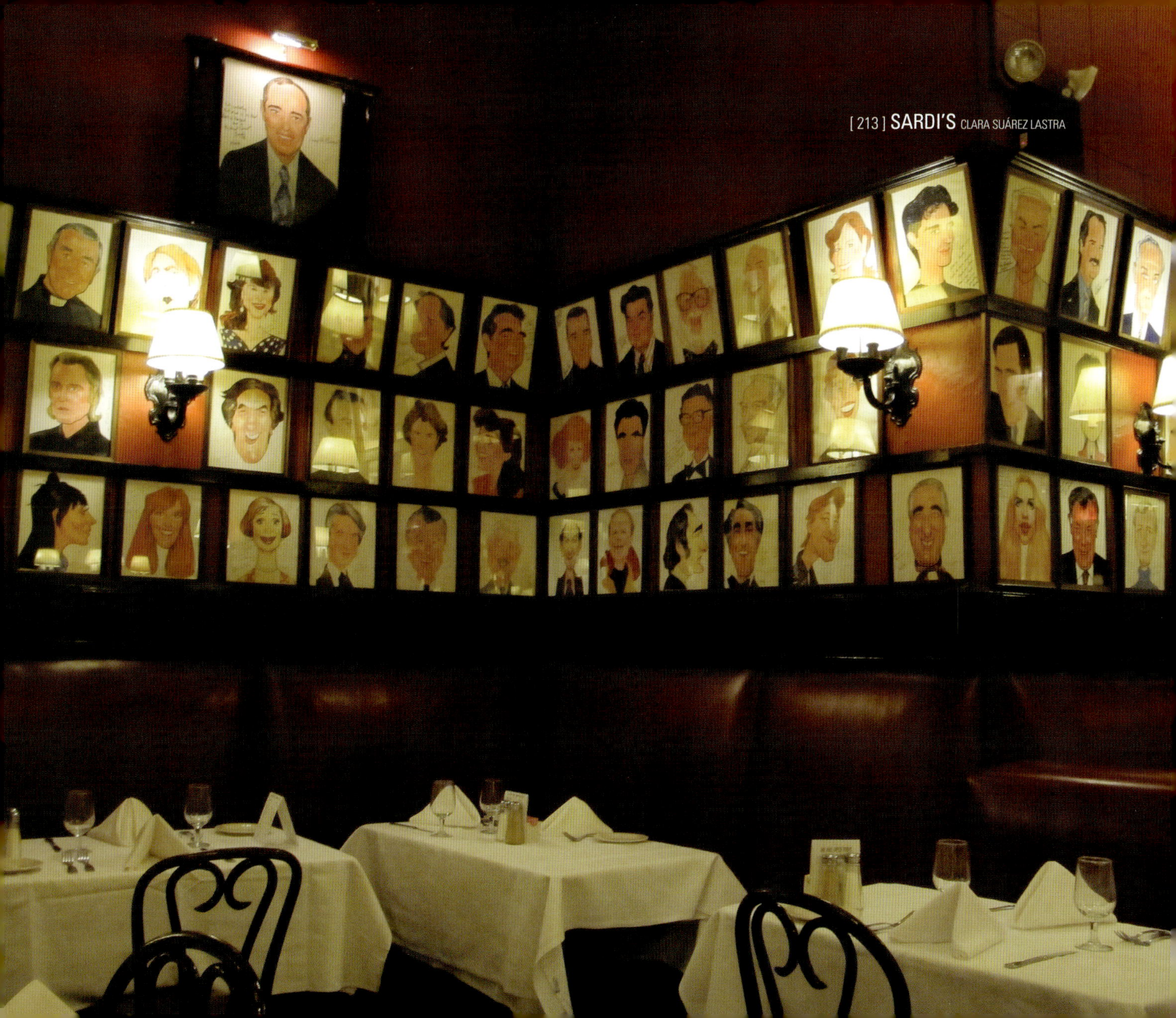

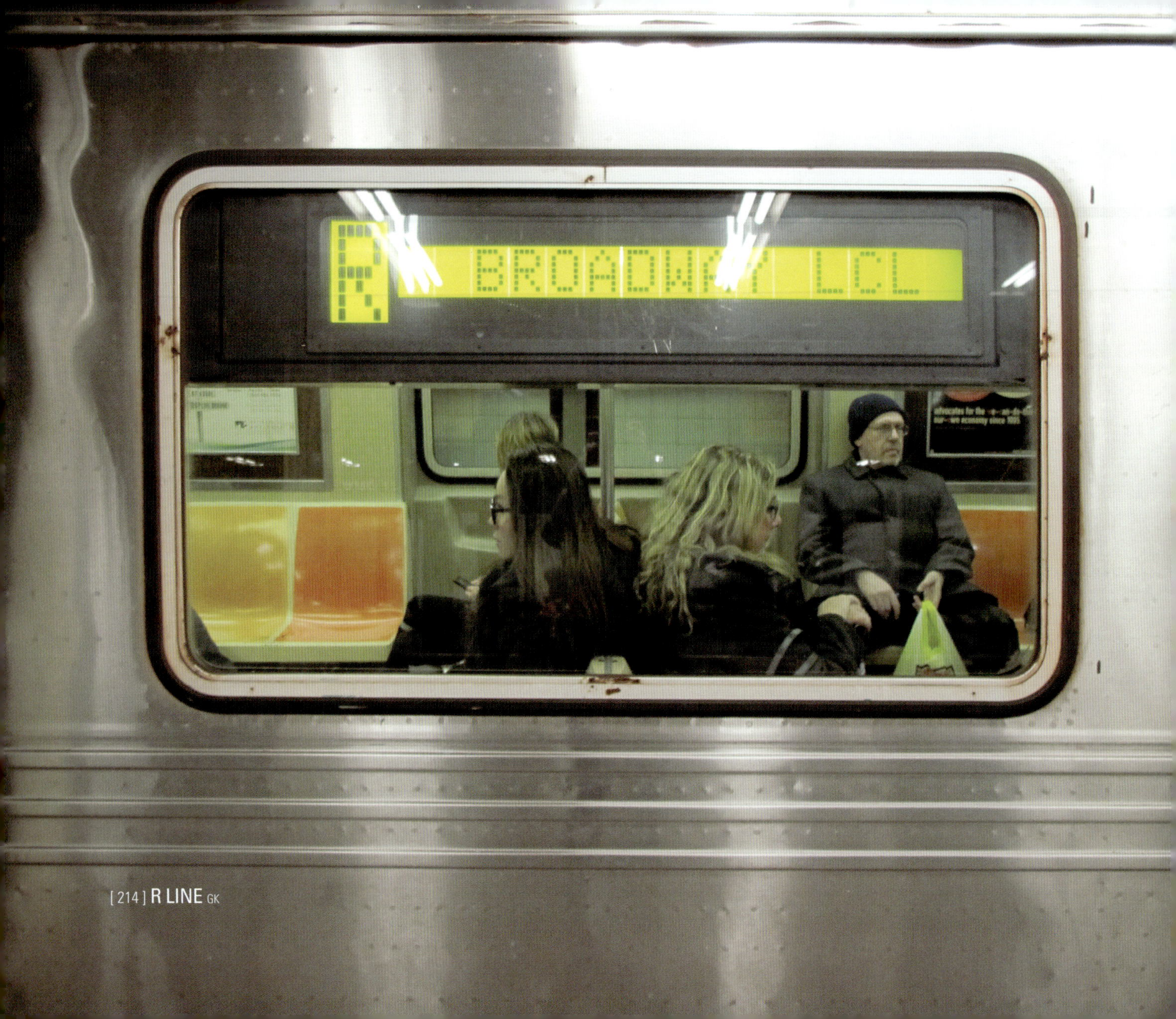

[214] R LINE GK

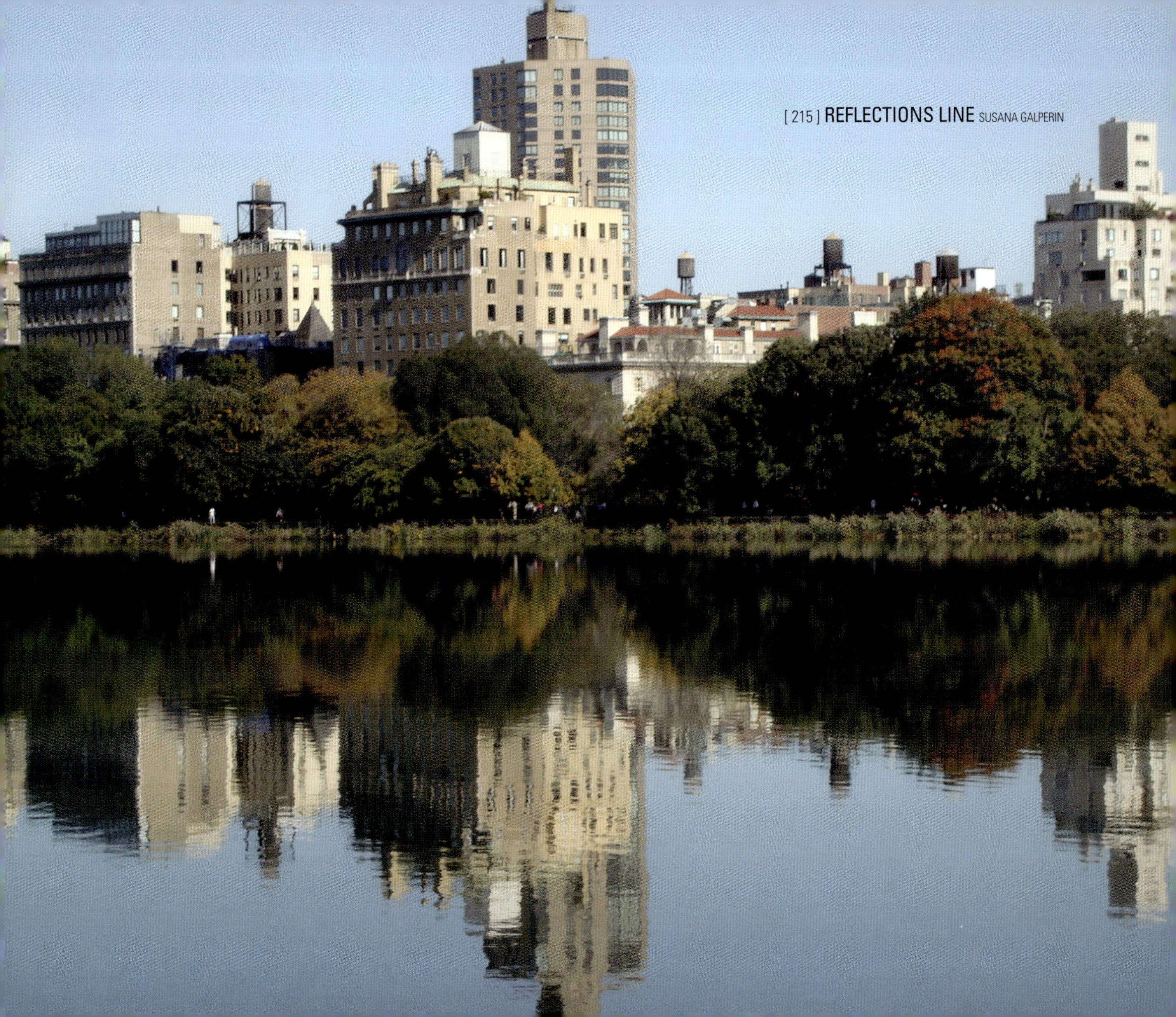

[215] REFLECTIONS LINE SUSANA GALPERIN

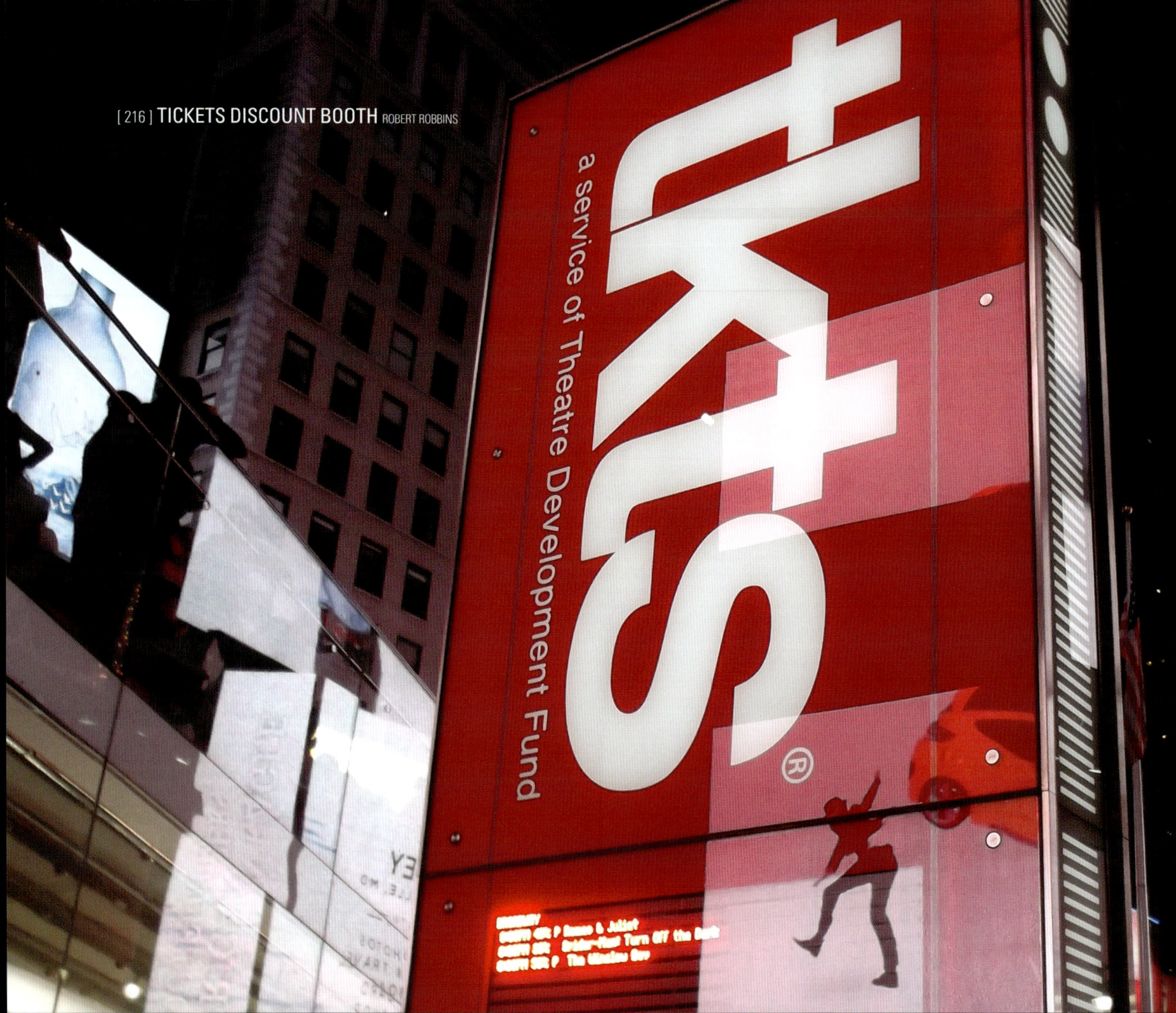

[216] **TICKETS DISCOUNT BOOTH** ROBERT ROBBINS

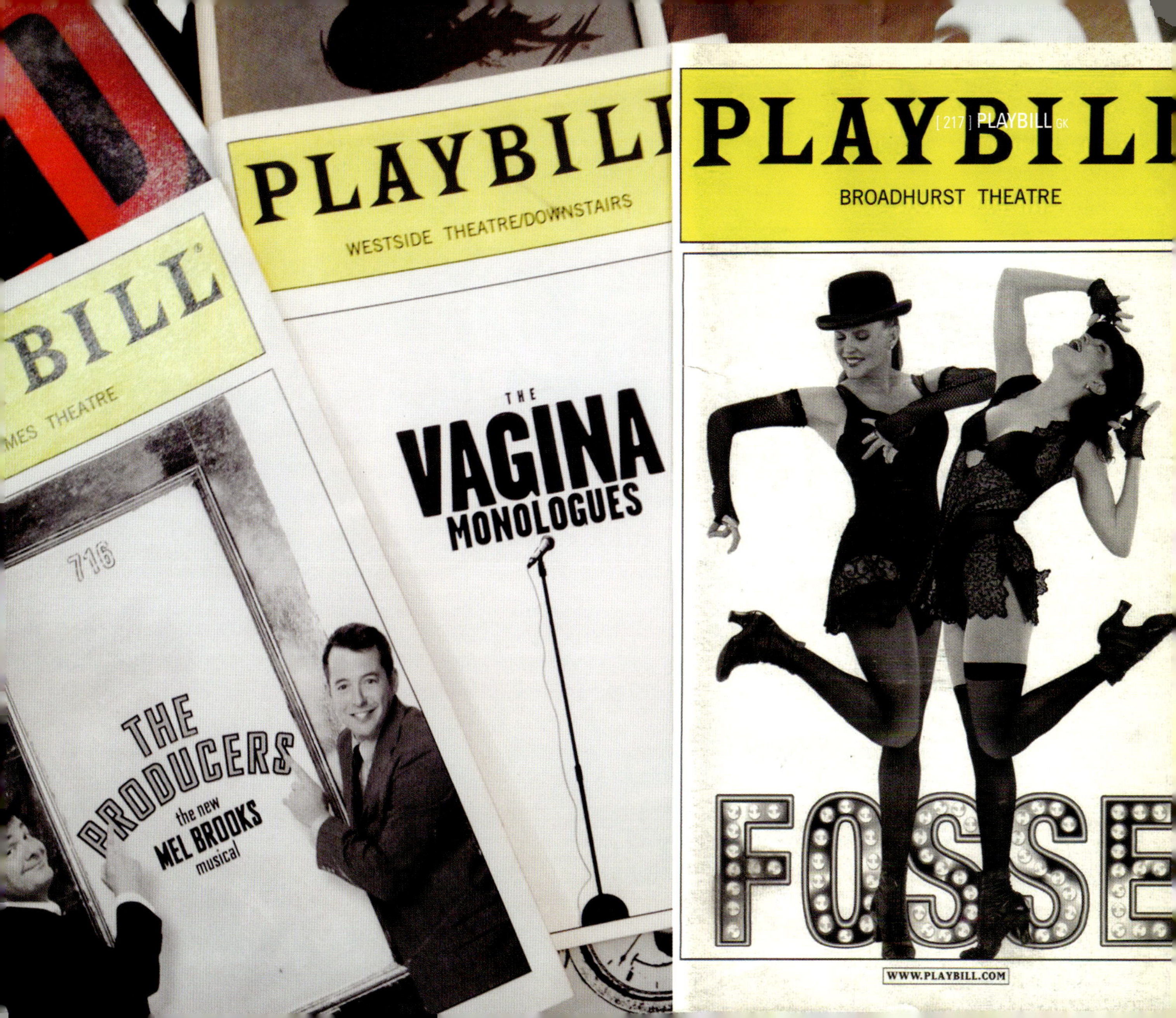
BILL
MES THEATRE
716
THE PRODUCERS
the new MEL BROOKS musical
PLAYBILL
WESTSIDE THEATRE/DOWNSTAIRS
THE VAGINA MONOLOGUES
PLAYBILL
BROADHURST THEATRE
FOSSE
WWW.PLAYBILL.COM

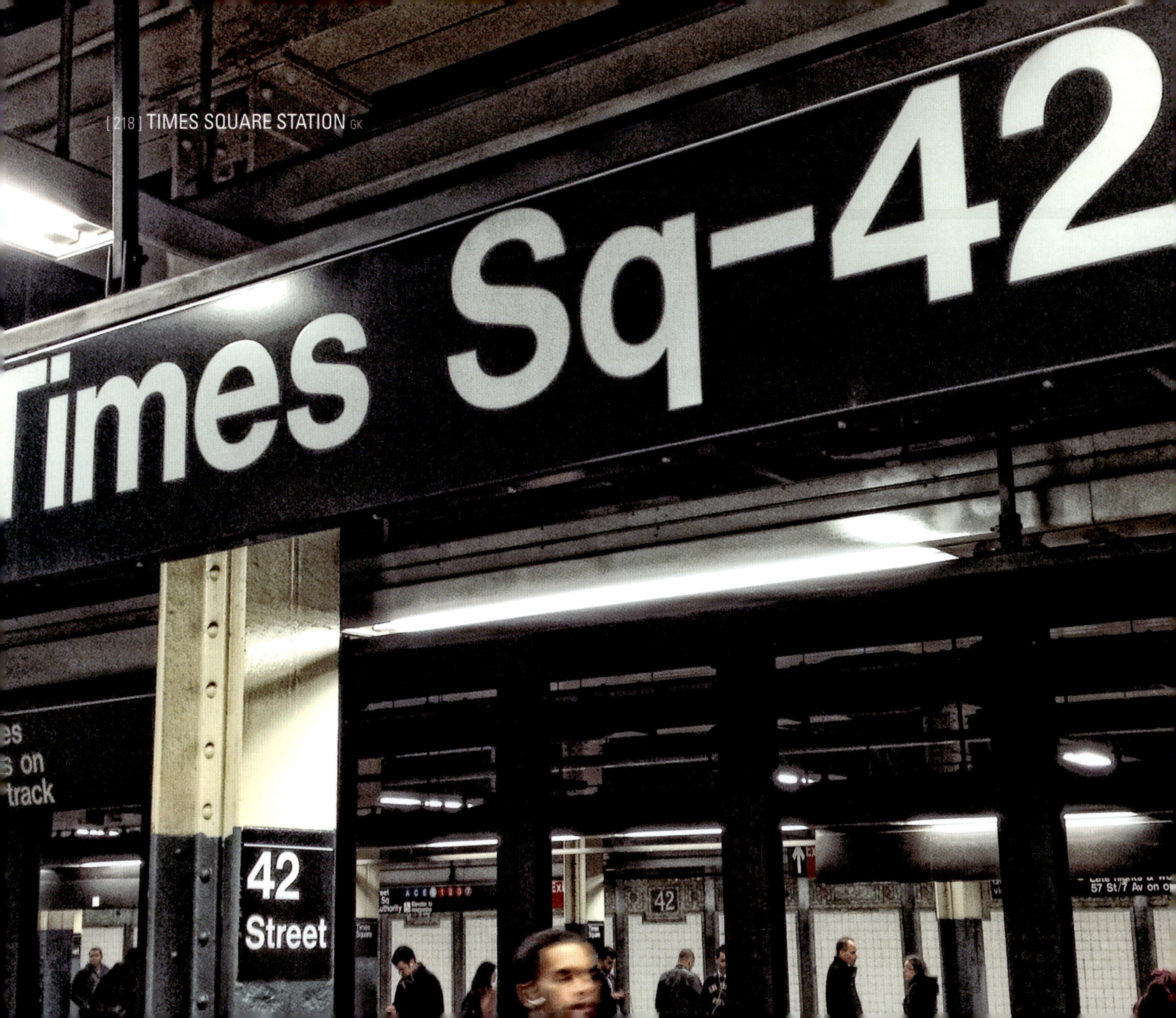

[218] TIMES SQUARE STATION GK

[219] SCREEN IN TIMES SQUARE MARINA KOGAN

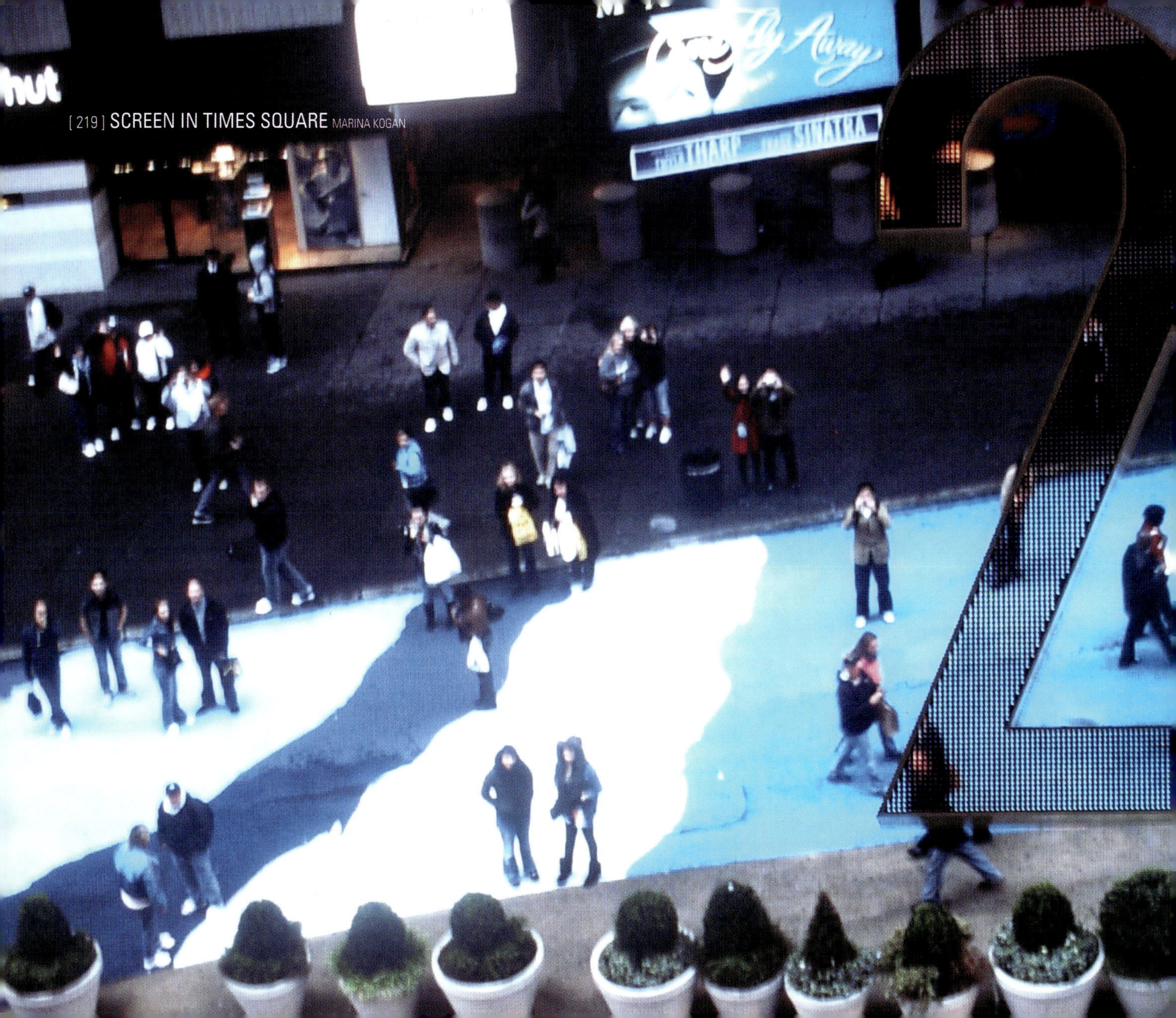

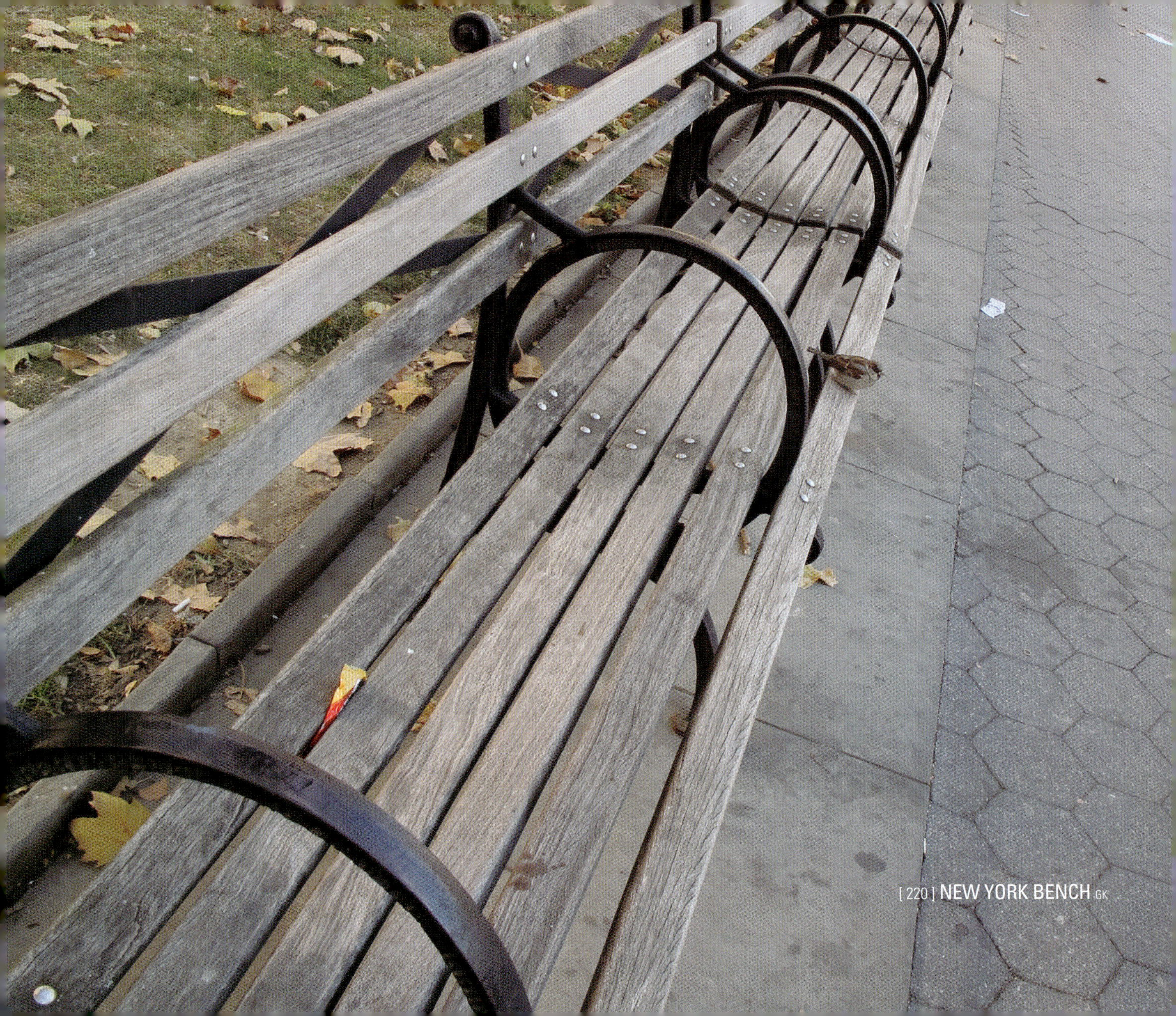

[220] NEW YORK BENCH GK

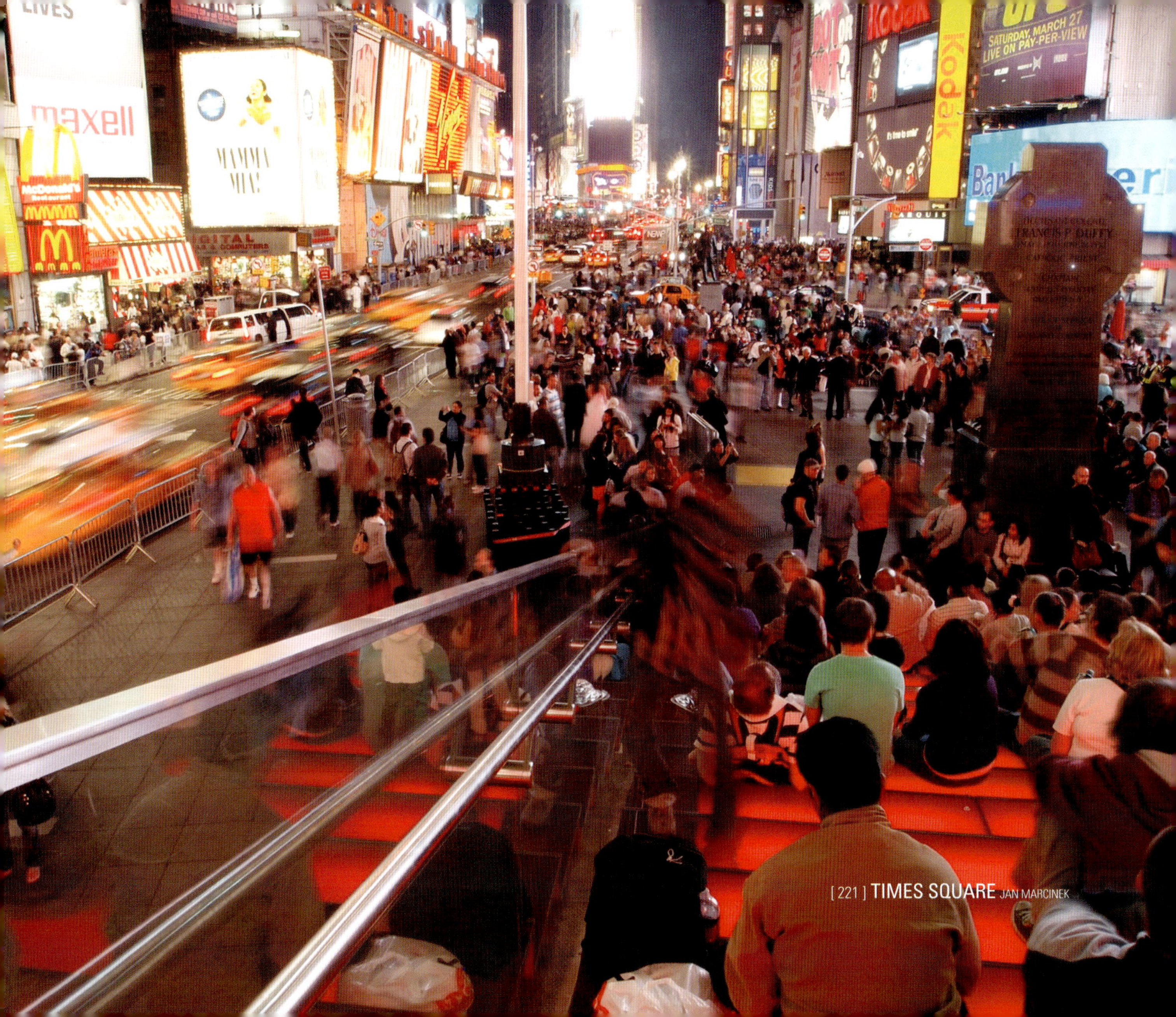

[221] TIMES SQUARE JAN MARCINEK

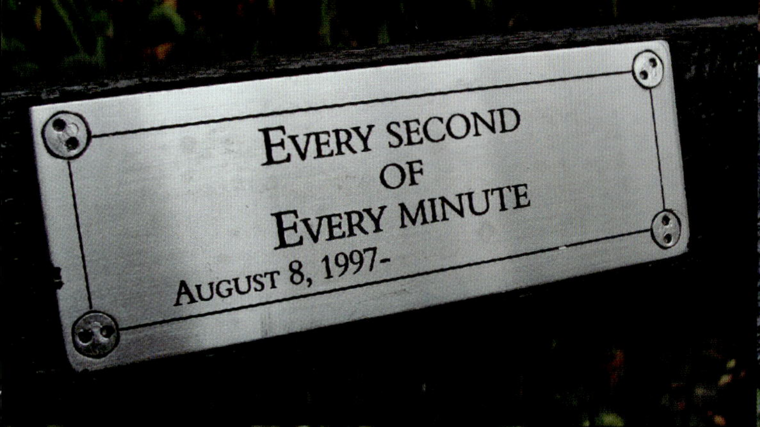
Every second
of
Every minute
August 8, 1997-

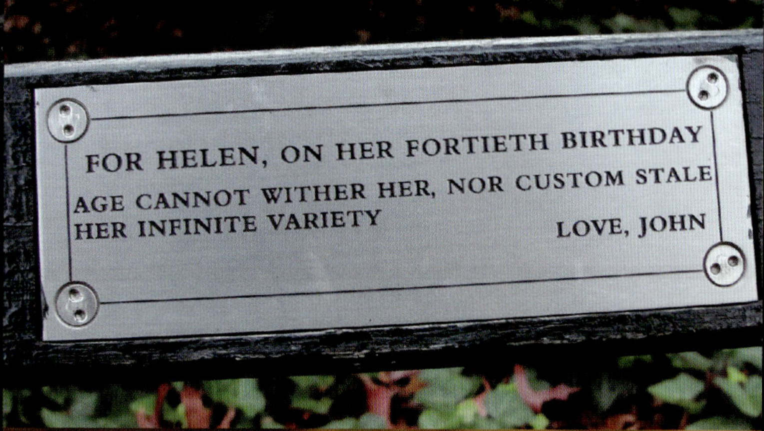
For Helen, on her fortieth birthday
Age cannot wither her, nor custom stale
Her infinite variety
Love, John

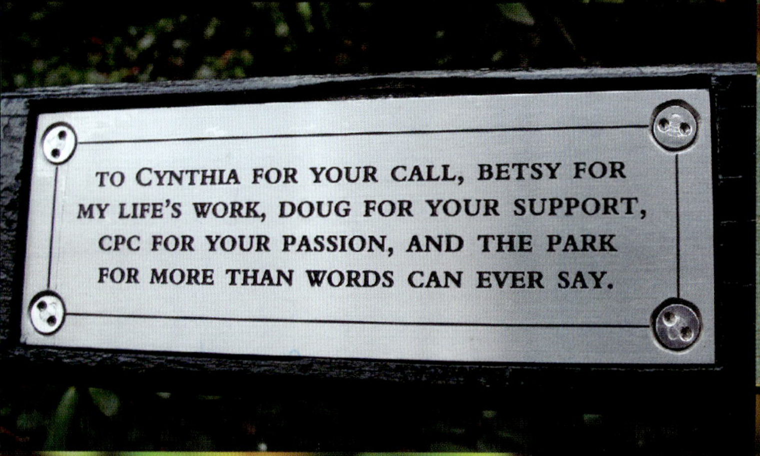
To Cynthia for your call, Betsy for
my life's work, Doug for your support,
CPC for your passion, and the park
for more than words can ever say.

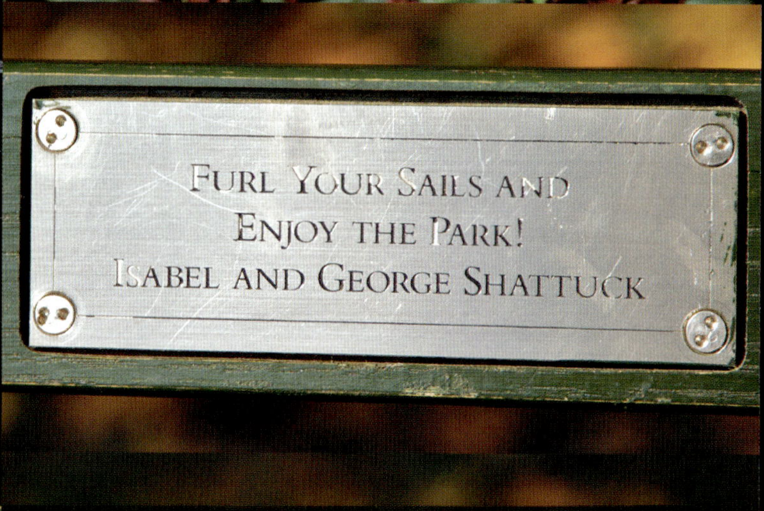
Furl Your Sails and
Enjoy the Park!
Isabel and George Shattuck

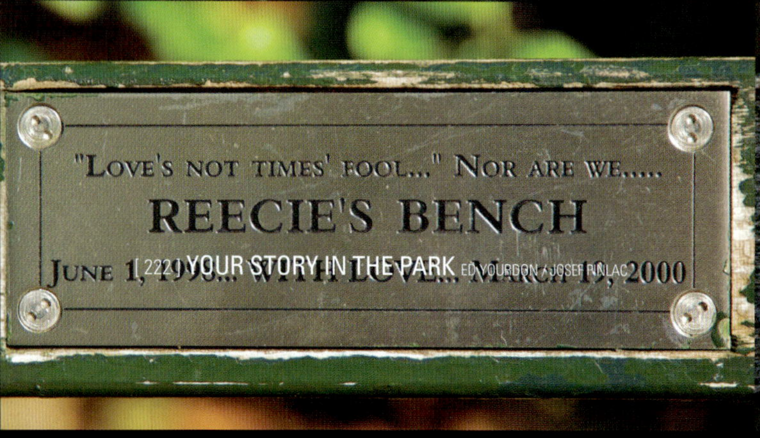
"Love's not times' fool..." Nor are we.....
REECIE'S BENCH

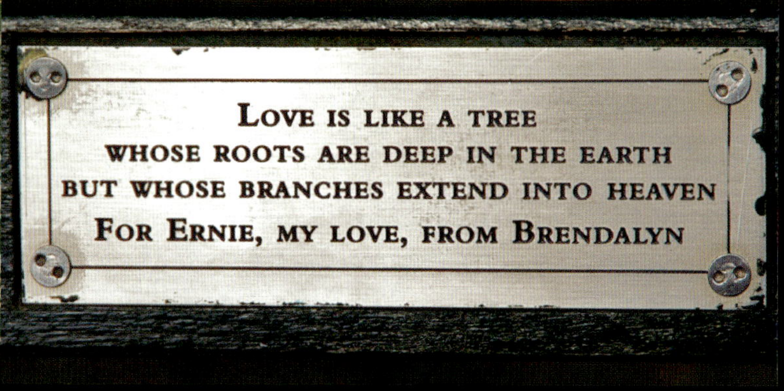
Love is like a tree
whose roots are deep in the earth
but whose branches extend into heaven
For Ernie, my love, from Brendalyn

[223] ESSEX HOUSE STEVE MALPASS

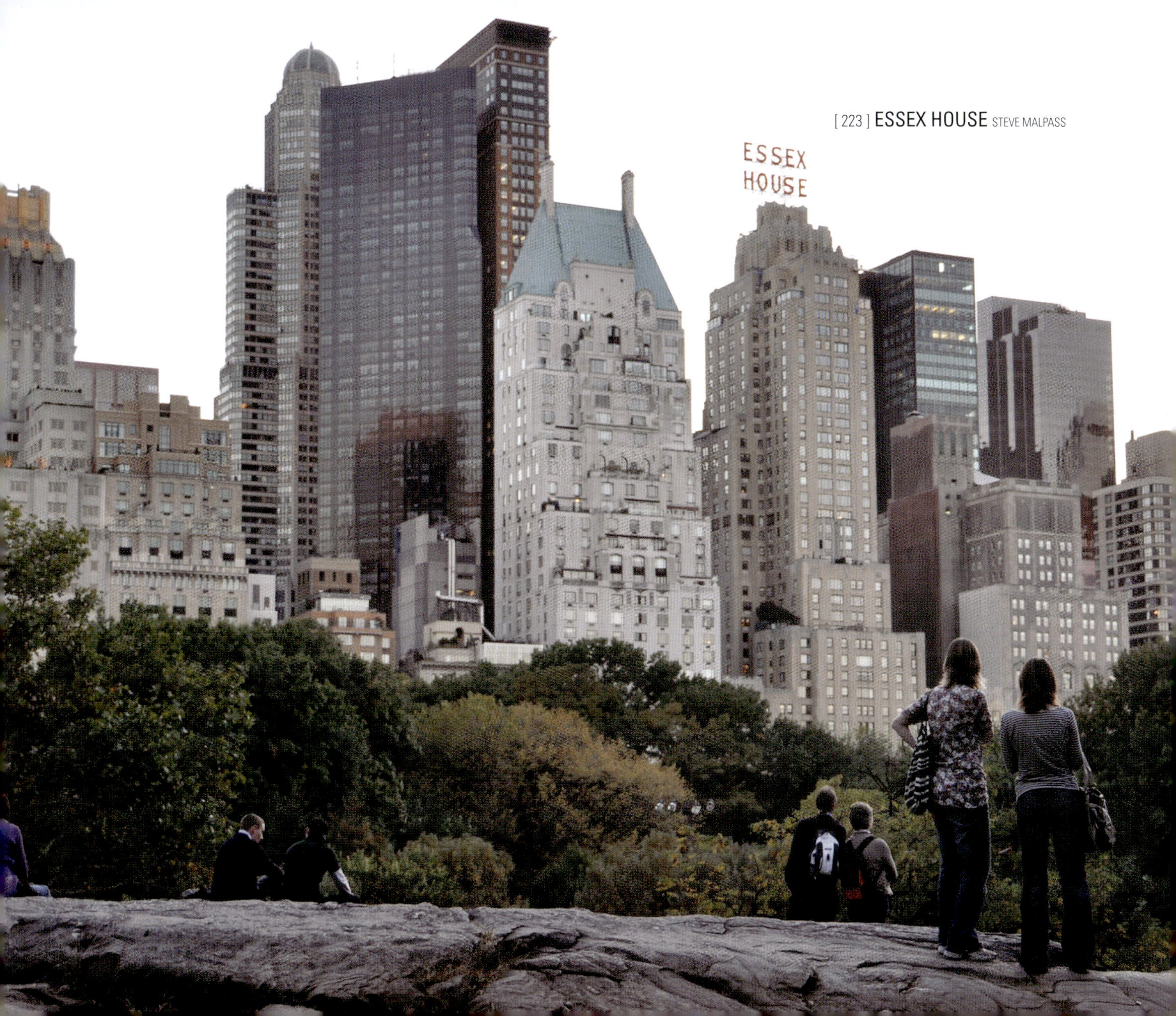

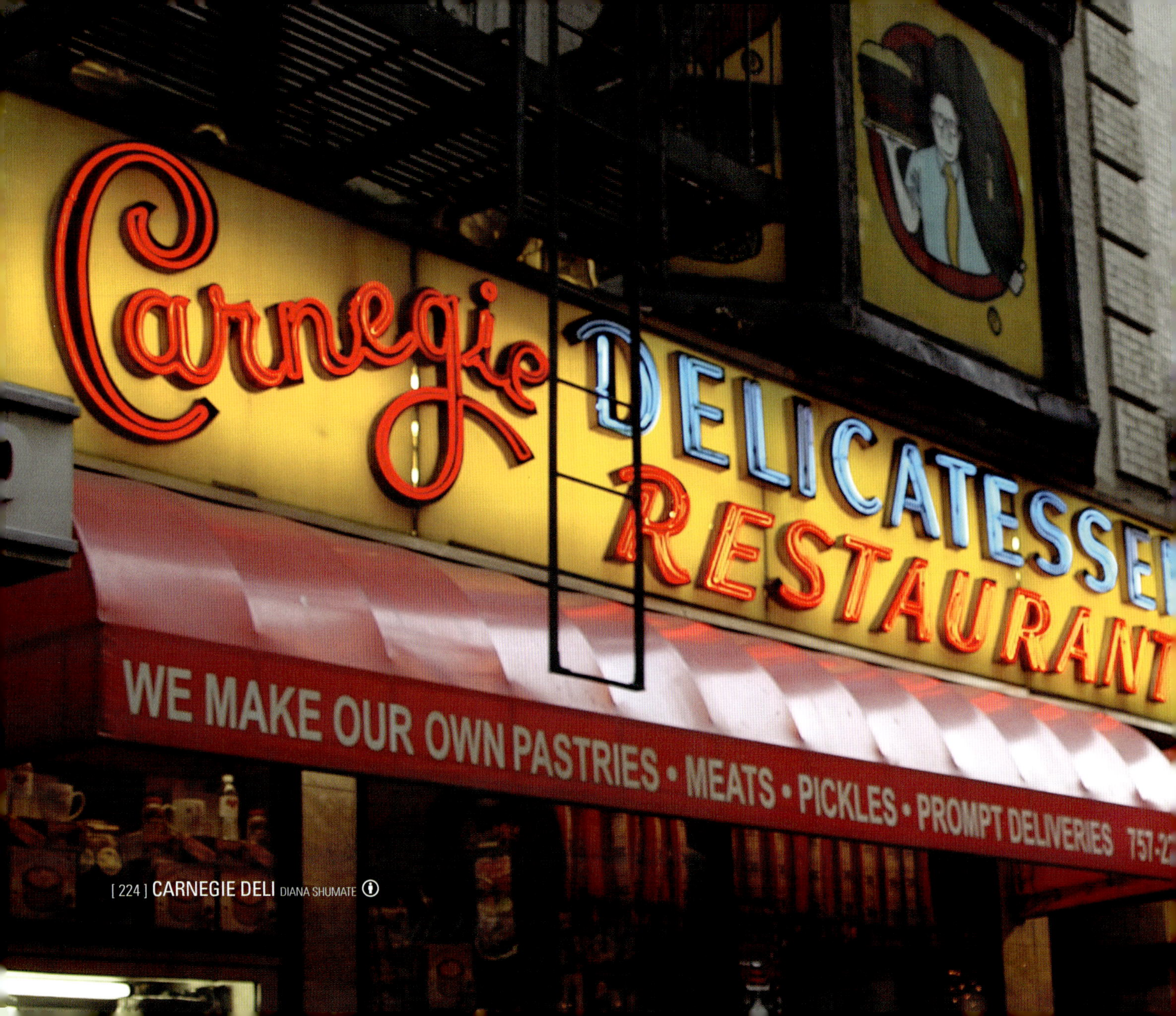

[224] CARNEGIE DELI DIANA SHUMATE

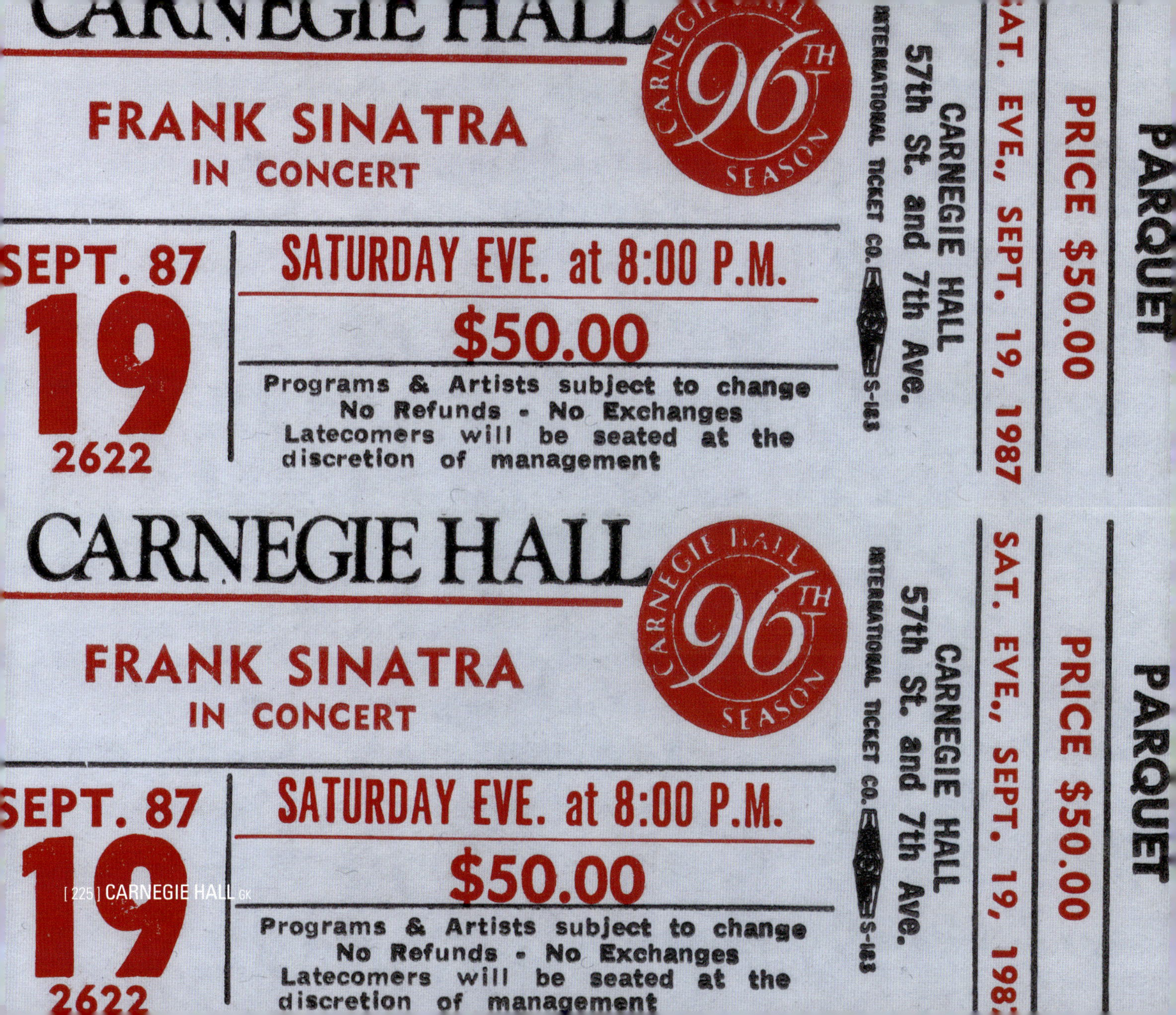
CARNEGIE HALL
CARNEGIE HALL 96TH SEASON
FRANK SINATRA
IN CONCERT
SEPT. 87
19
2622
SATURDAY EVE. at 8:00 P.M.
$50.00
Programs & Artists subject to change
No Refunds - No Exchanges
Latecomers will be seated at the
discretion of management
CARNEGIE HALL
57th St. and 7th Ave.
INTERNATIONAL TICKET CO.
S-183
SAT. EVE., SEPT. 19, 1987
PRICE $50.00
PARQUET

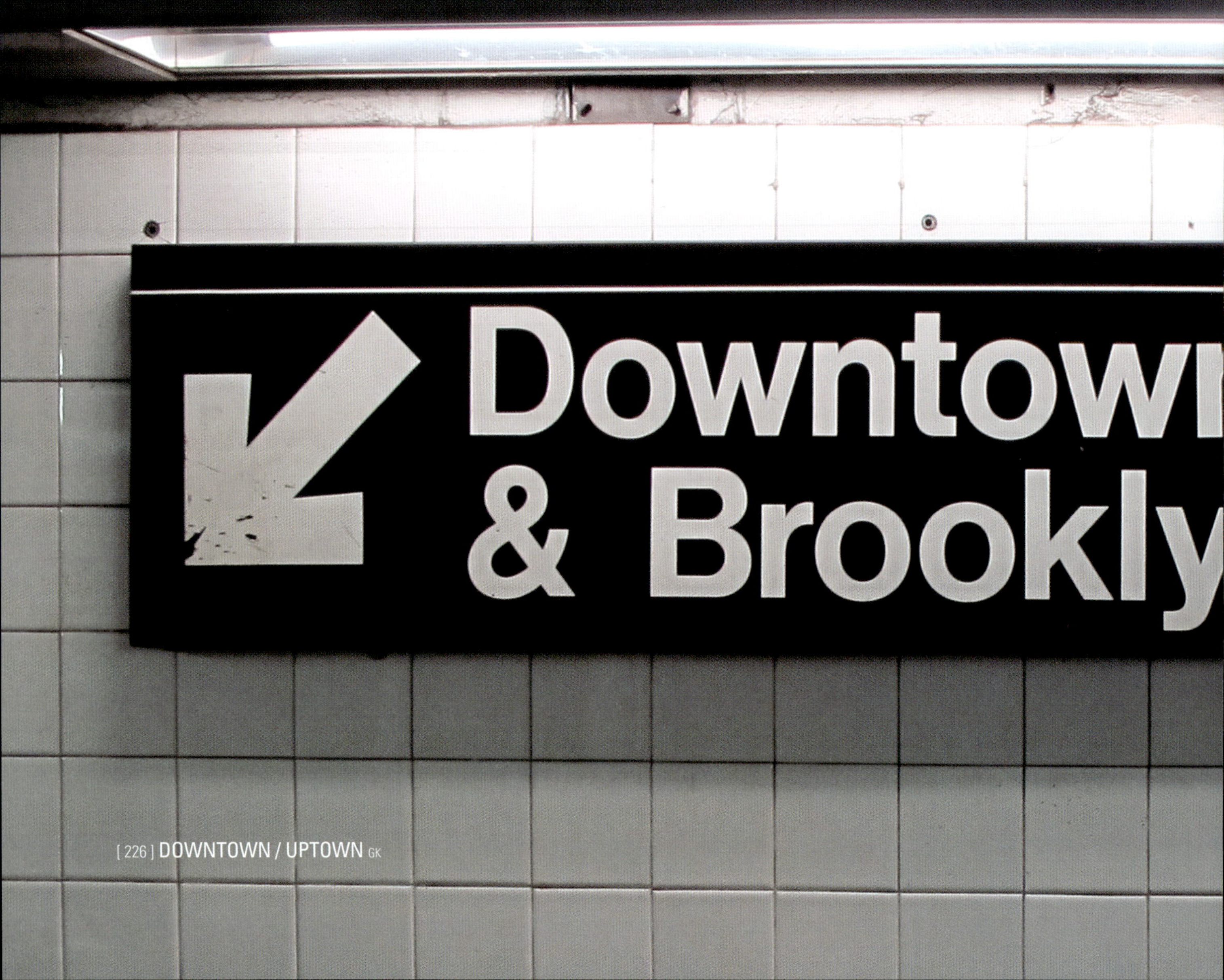

[226] DOWNTOWN / UPTOWN GK

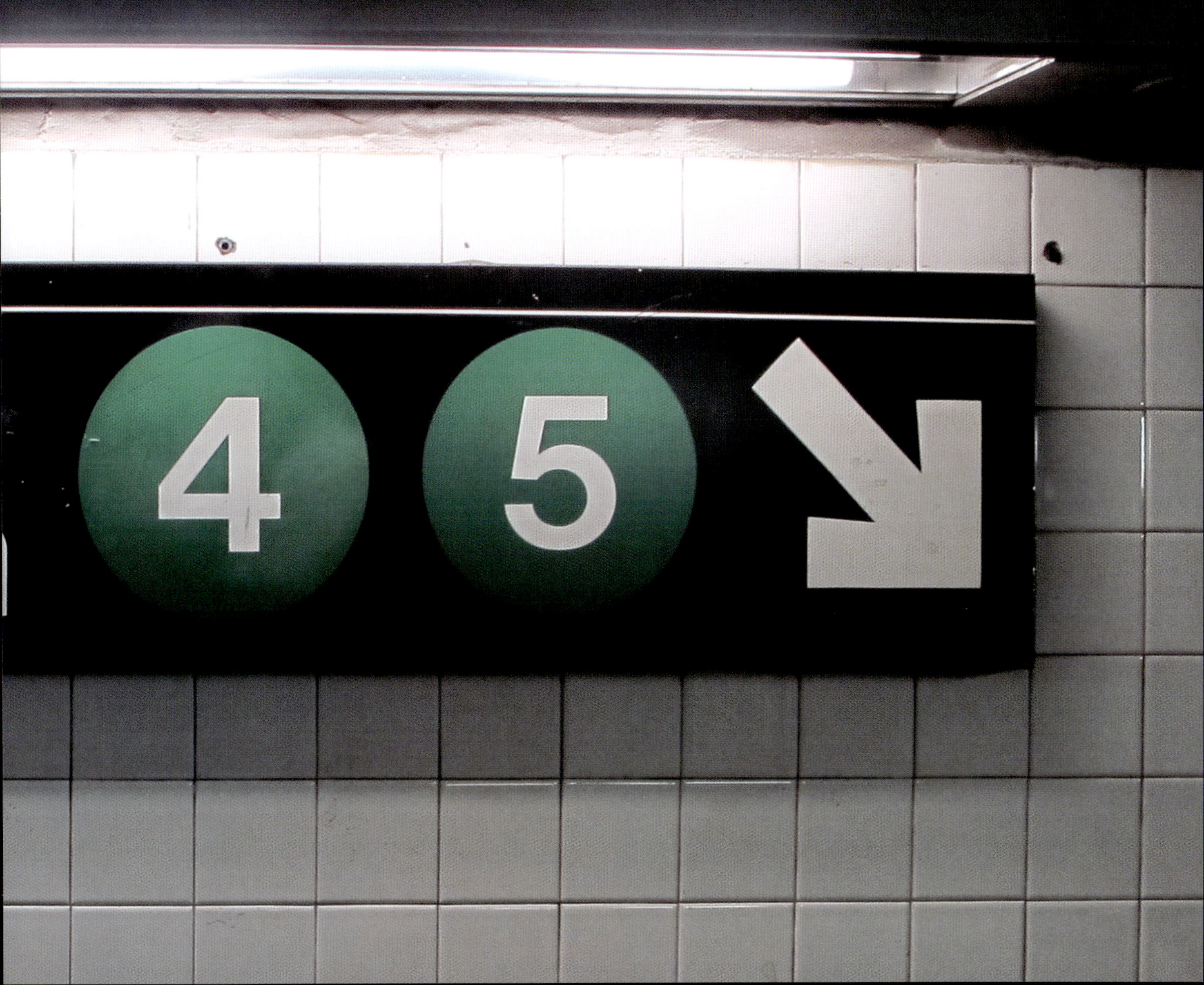

4
5

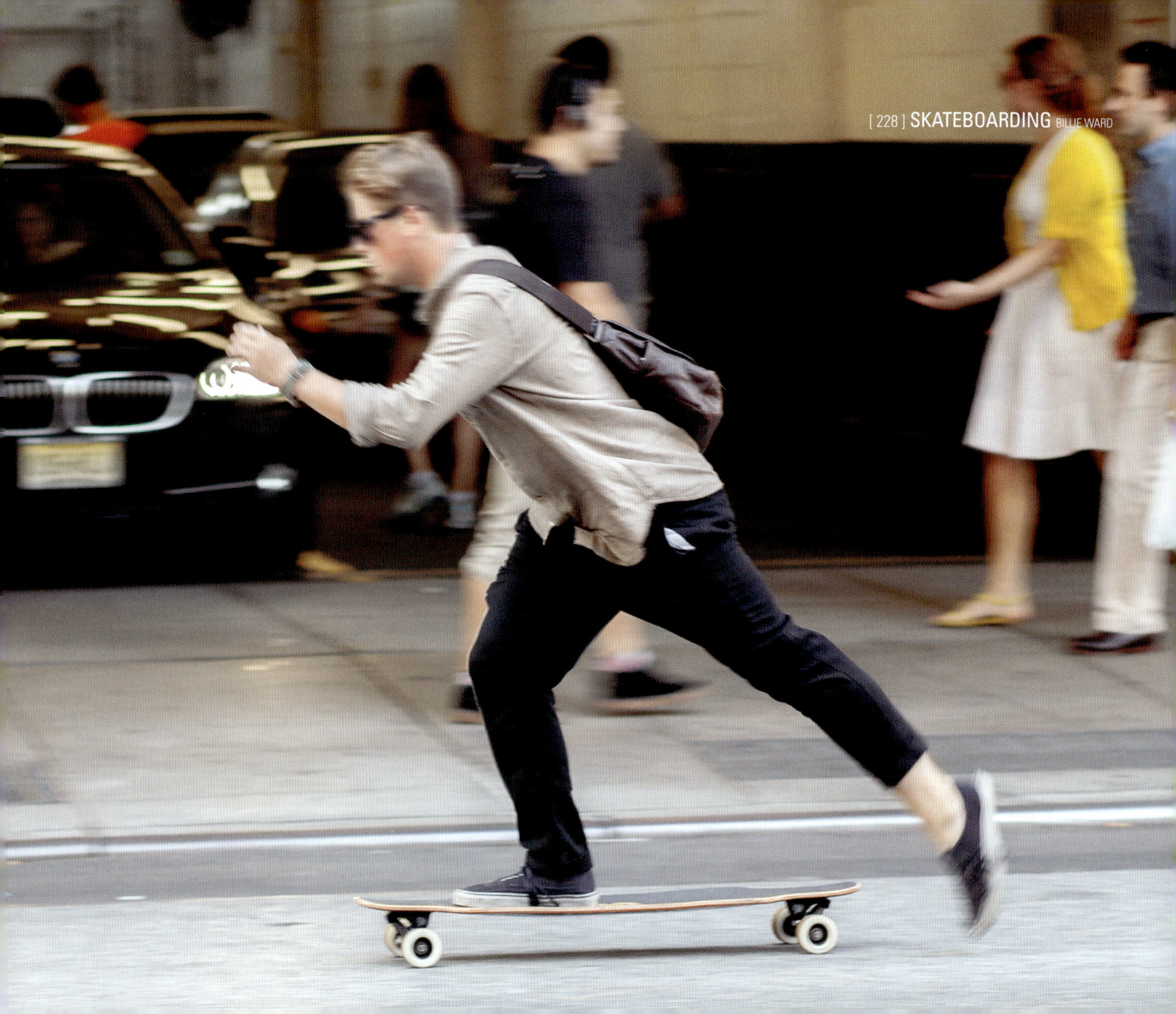

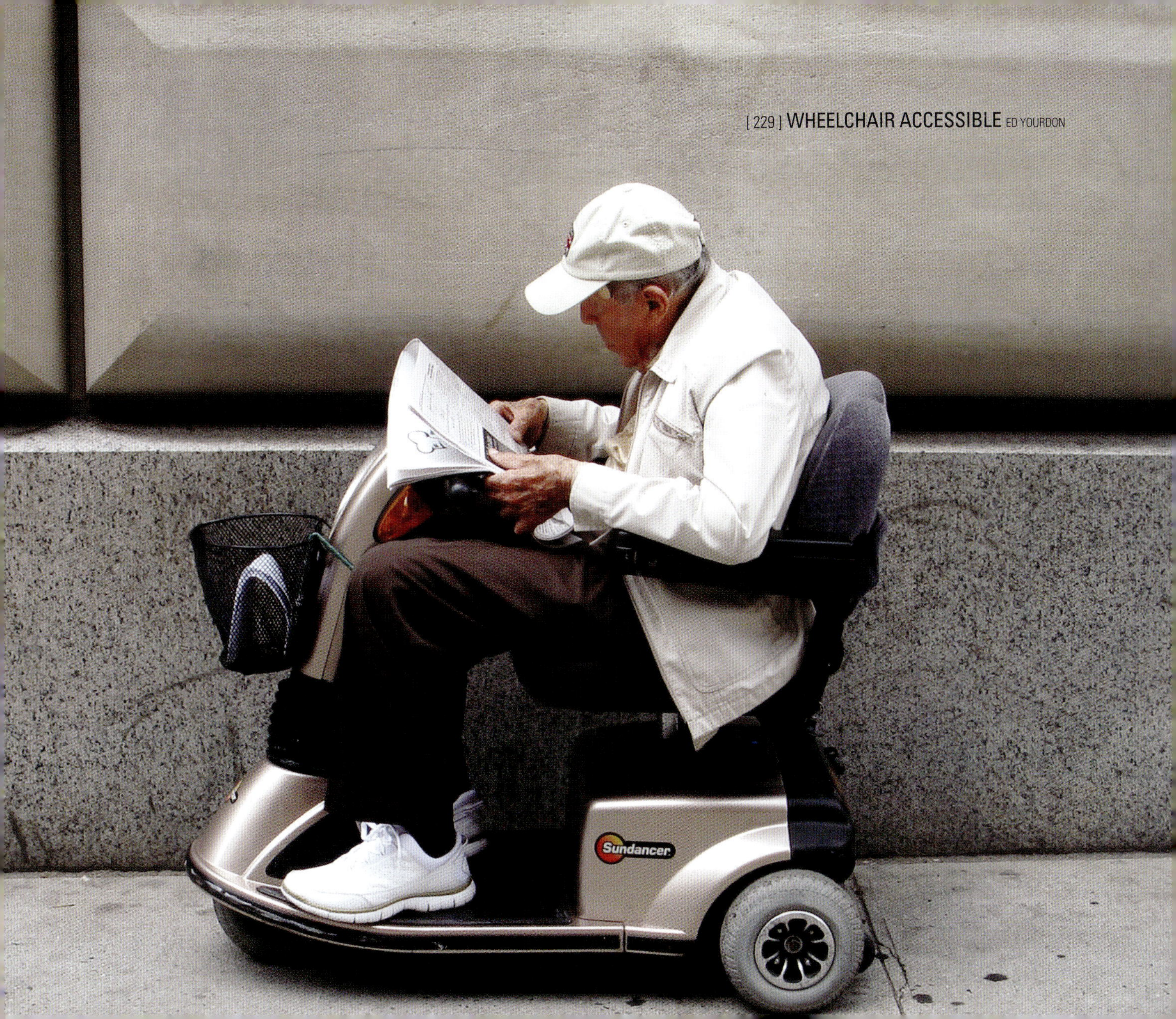

[229] WHEELCHAIR ACCESSIBLE ED YOURDON

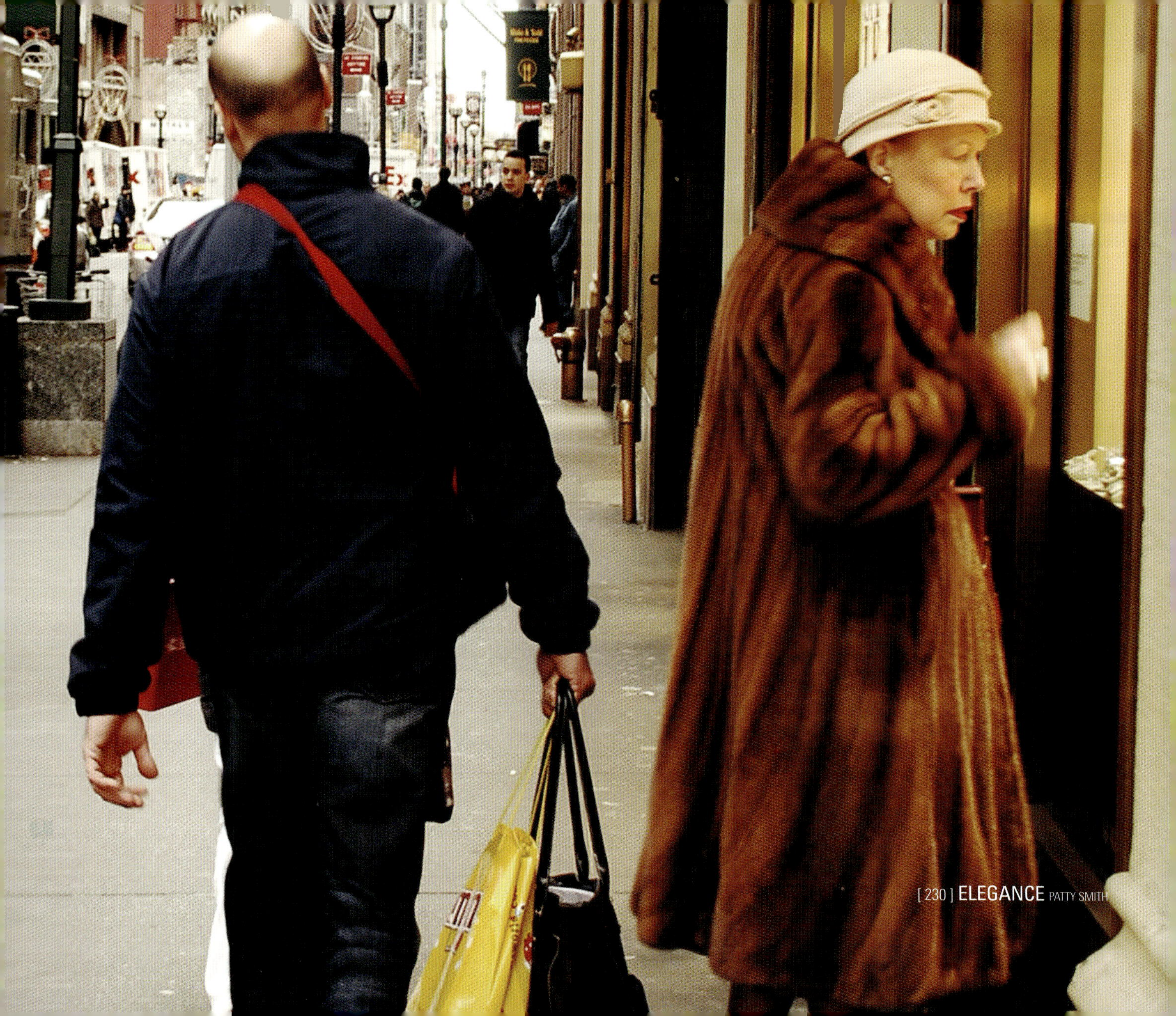

[230] ELEGANCE PATTY SMITH

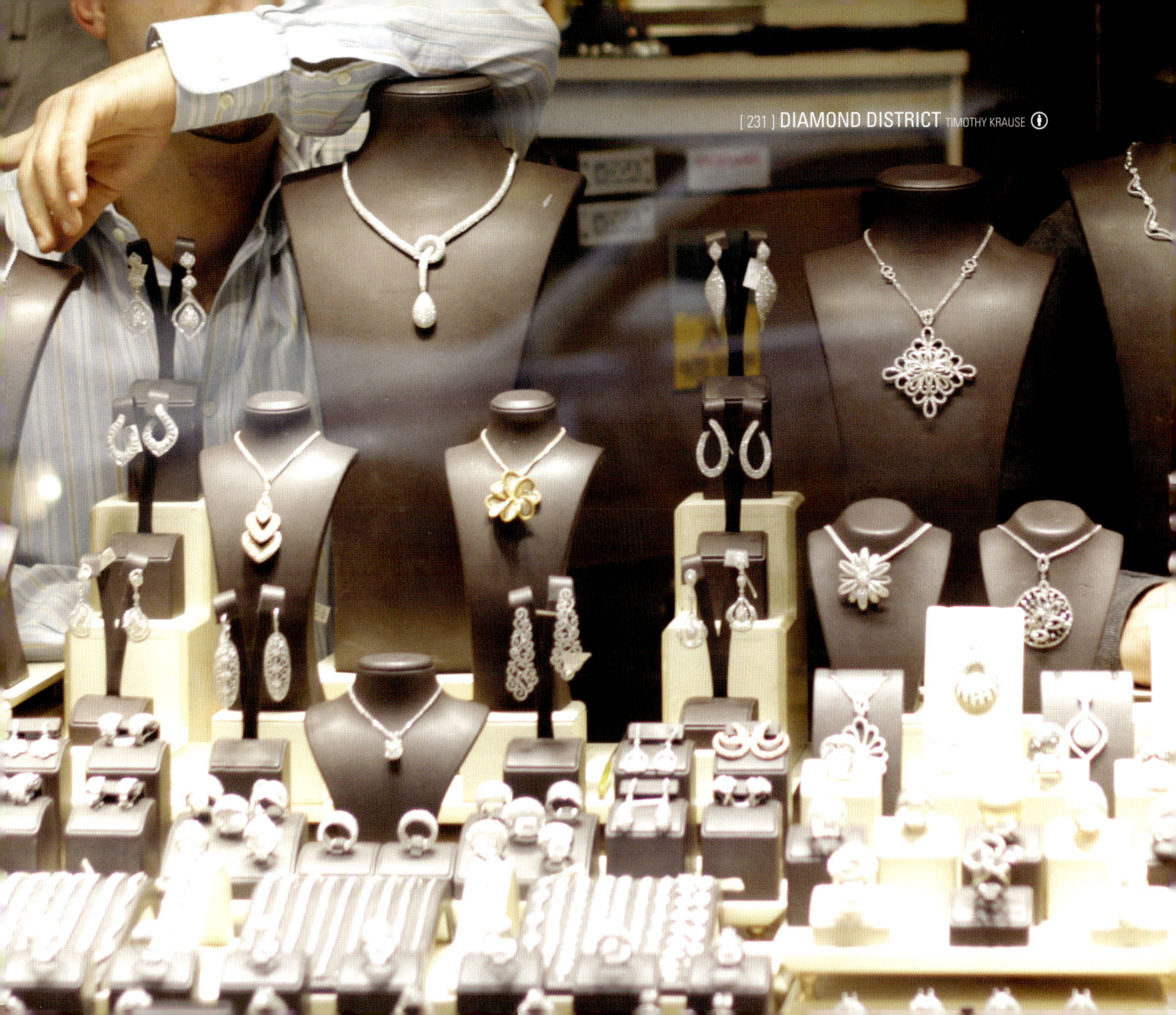

[231] DIAMOND DISTRICT TIMOTHY KRAUSE

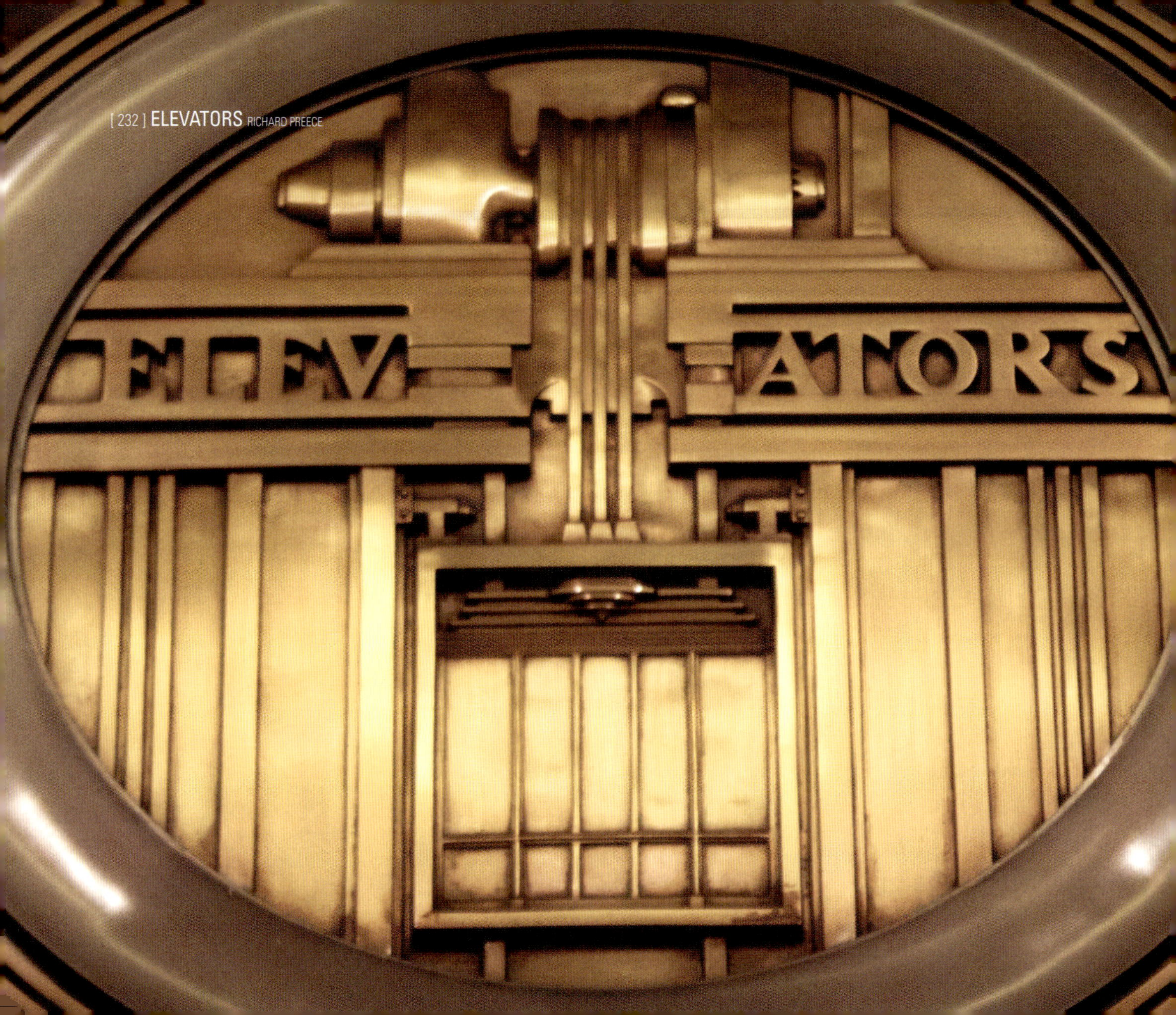
ELEV
ATORS

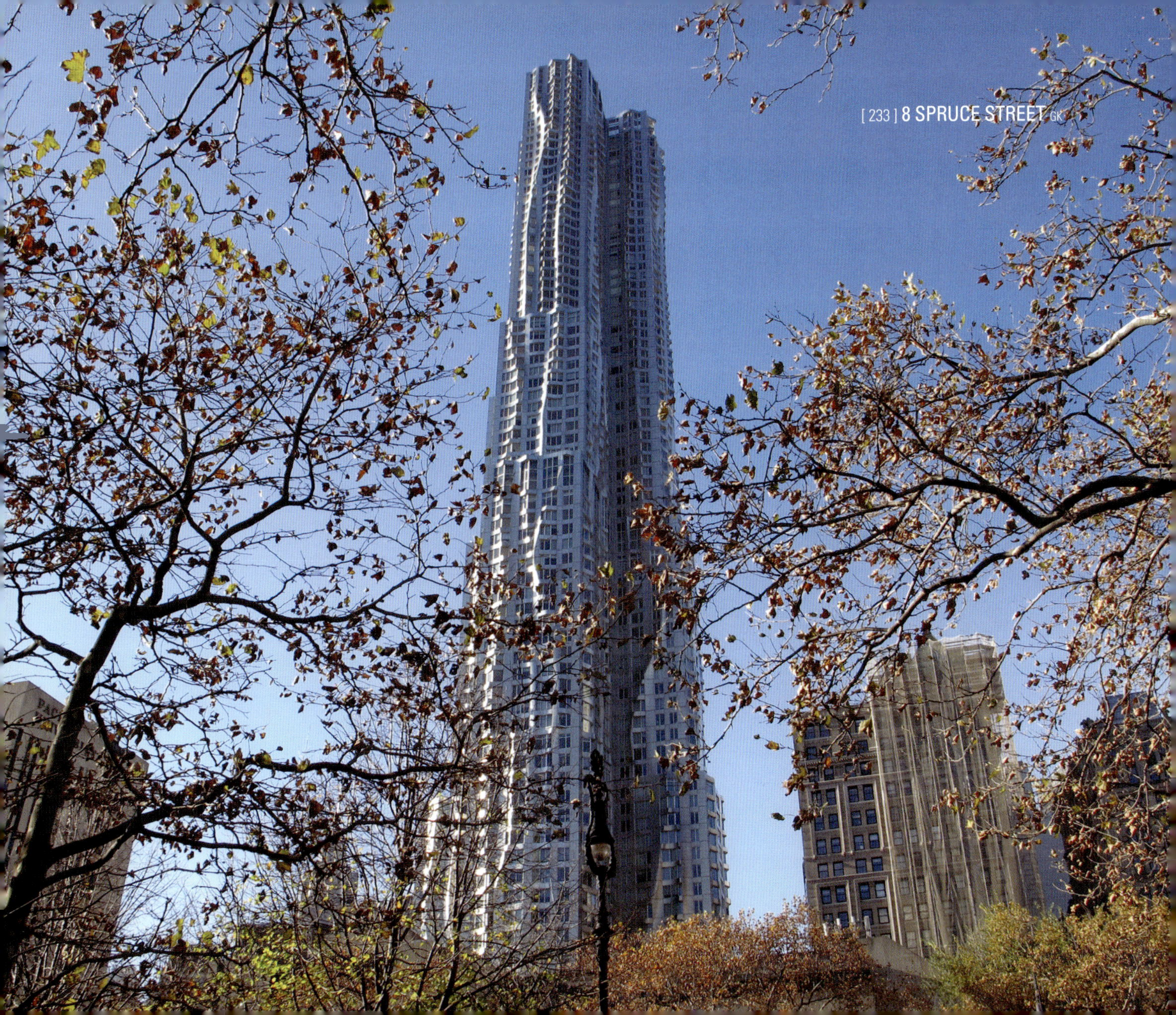

[233] 8 SPRUCE STREET GK

[234] FLATIRON GK

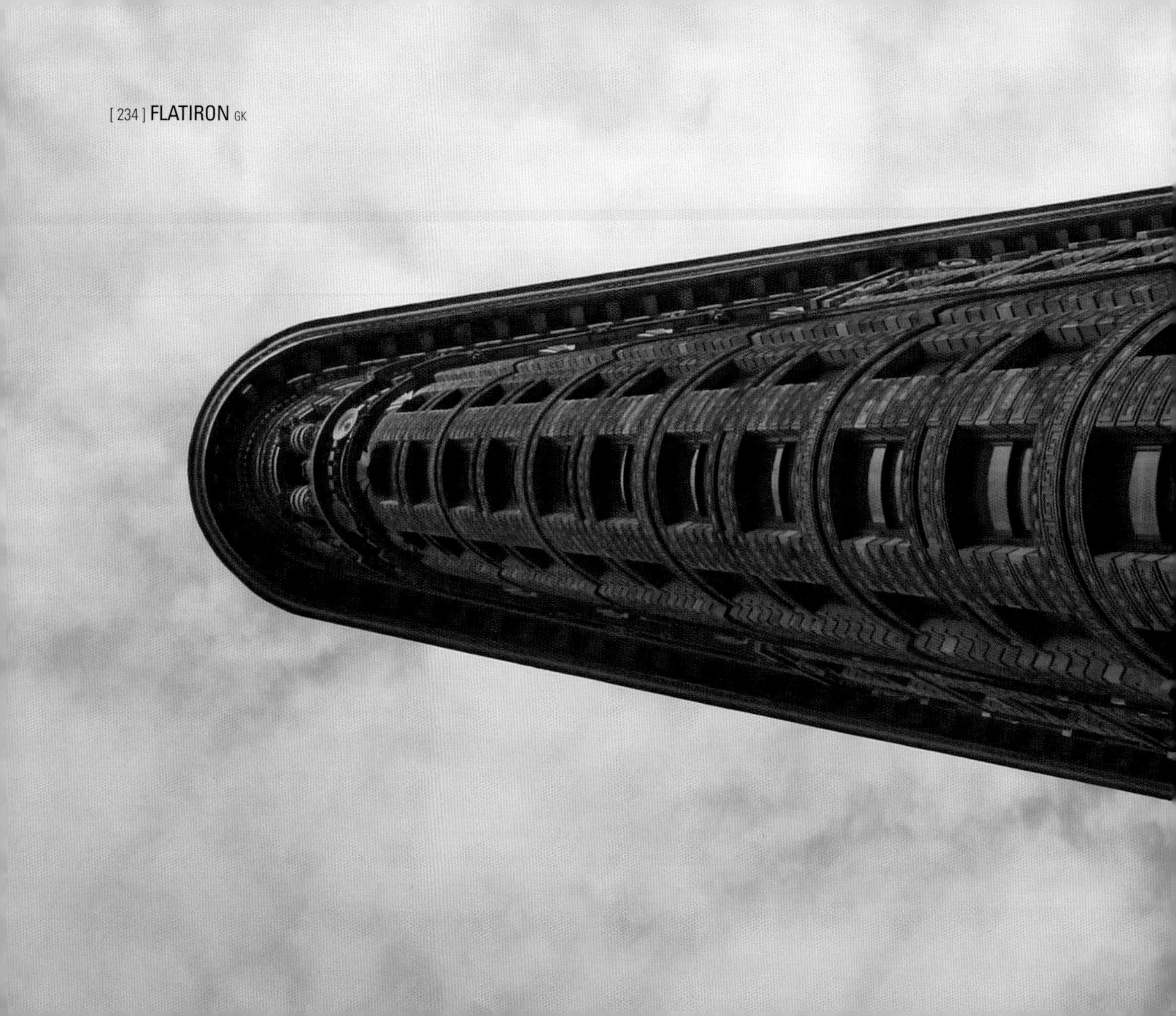

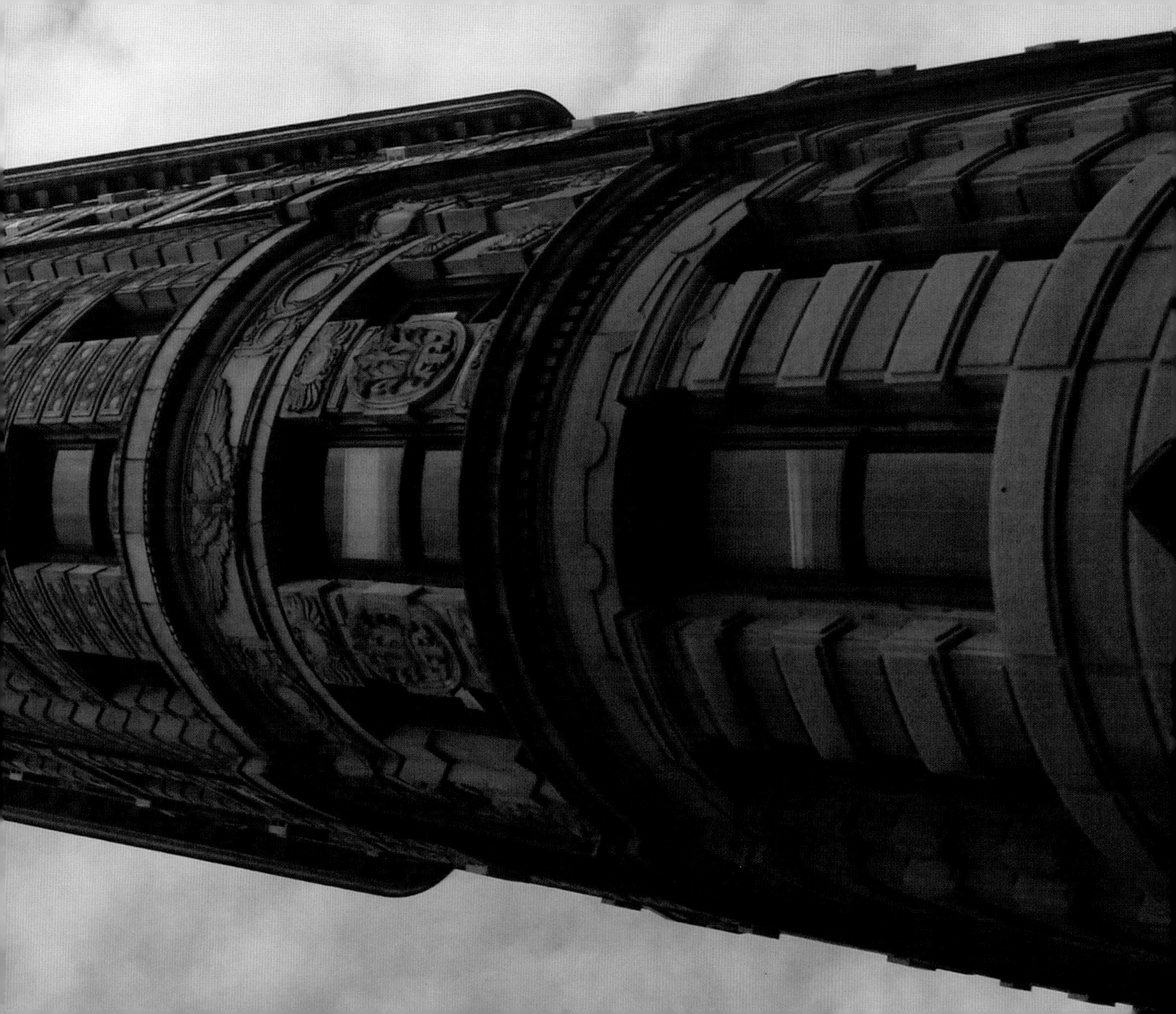

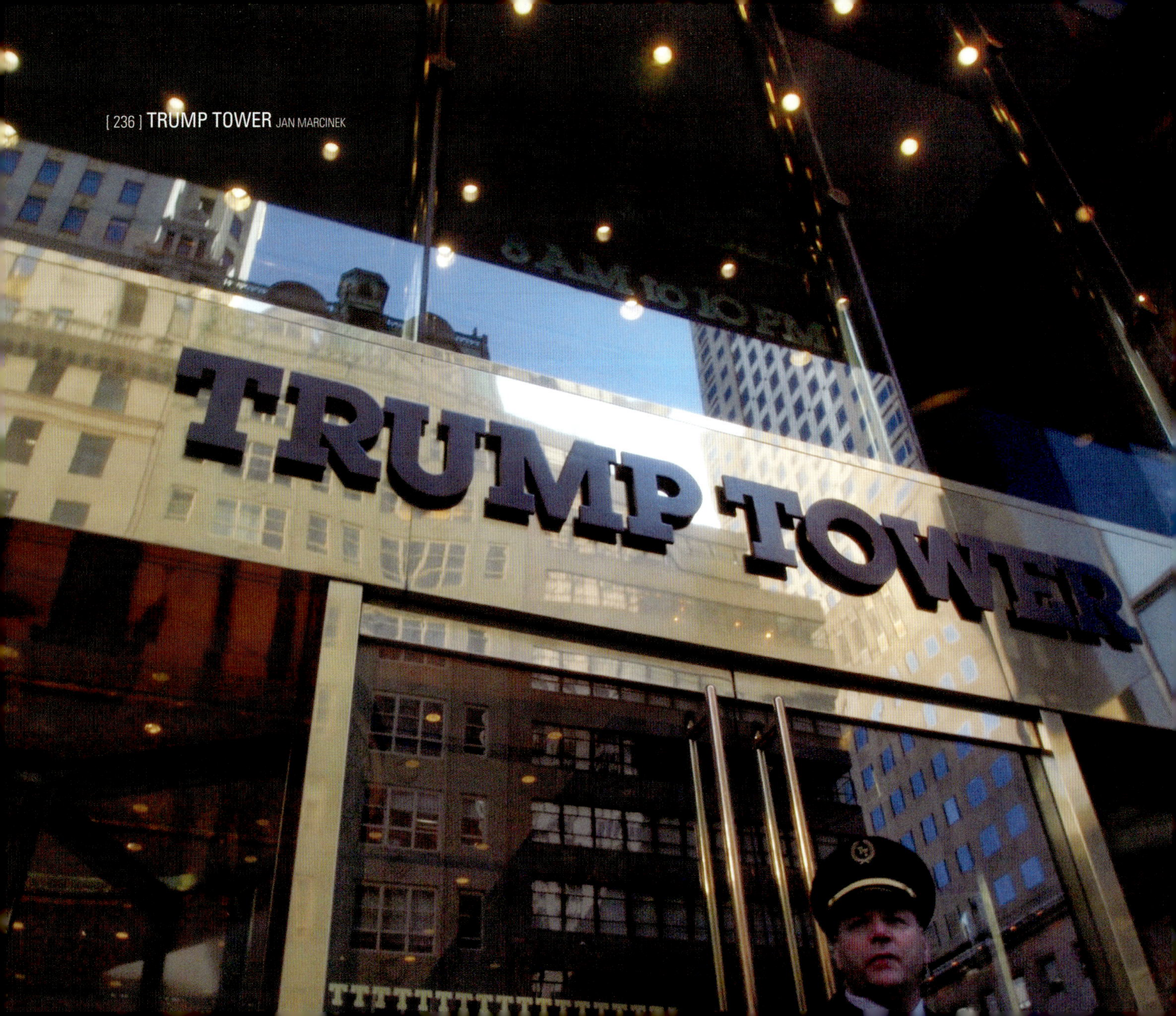

[236] TRUMP TOWER JAN MARCINEK

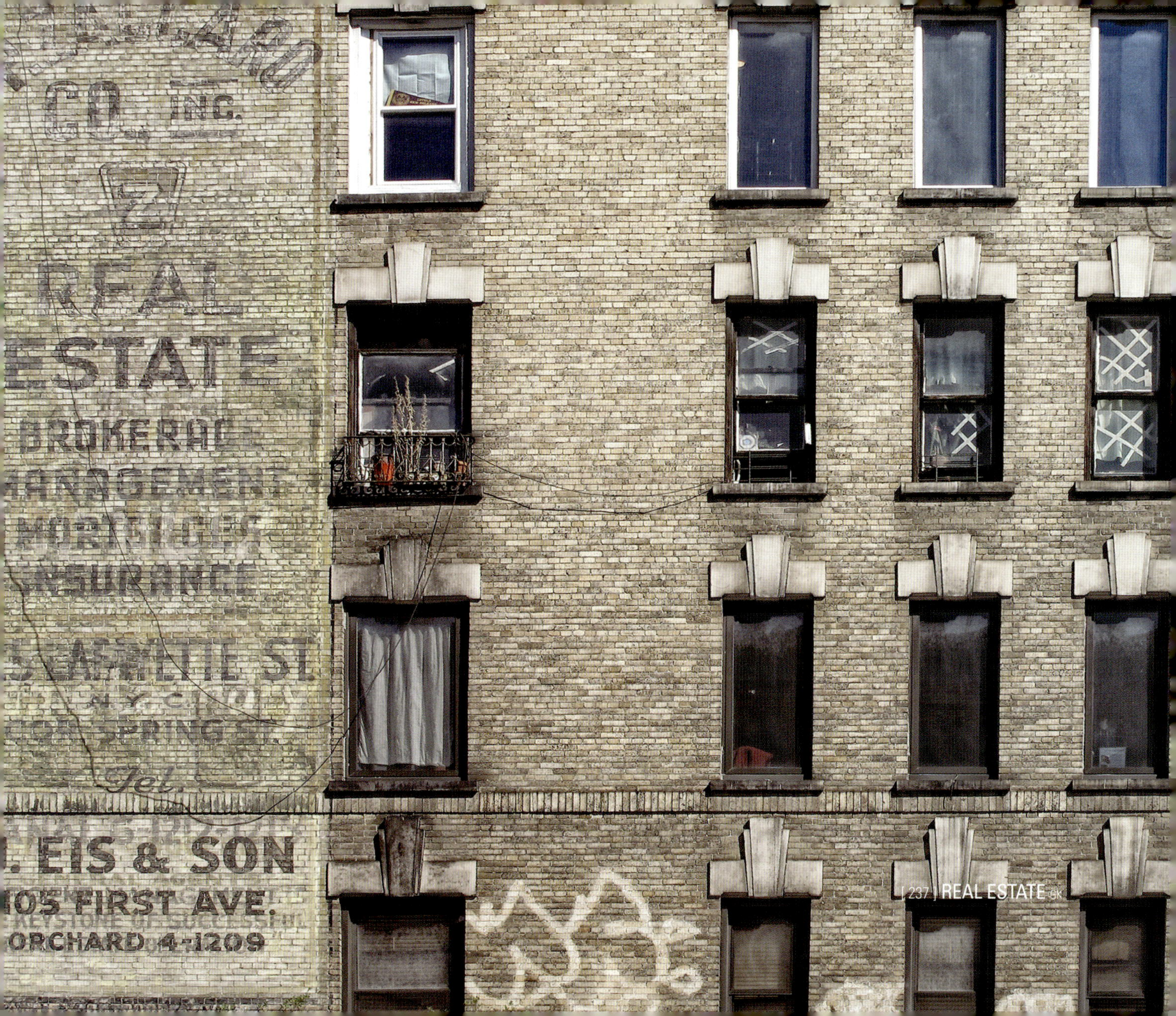

[237] REAL ESTATE BK

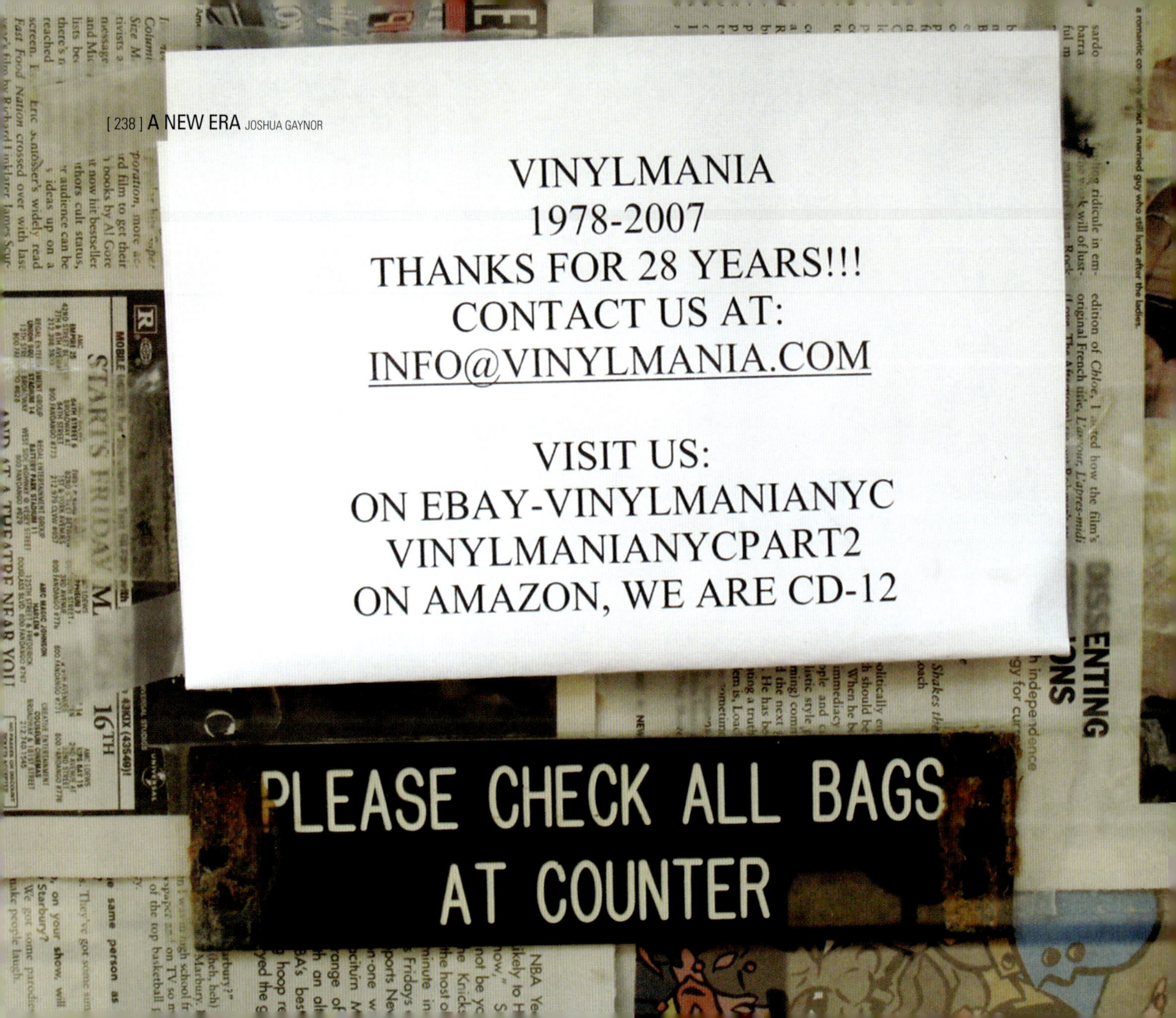
VINYLMANIA
1978-2007
THANKS FOR 28 YEARS!!!
CONTACT US AT:
INFO@VINYLMANIA.COM
VISIT US:
ON EBAY-VINYLMANIANYC
VINYLMANIANYCPART2
ON AMAZON, WE ARE CD-12
PLEASE CHECK ALL BAGS
AT COUNTER

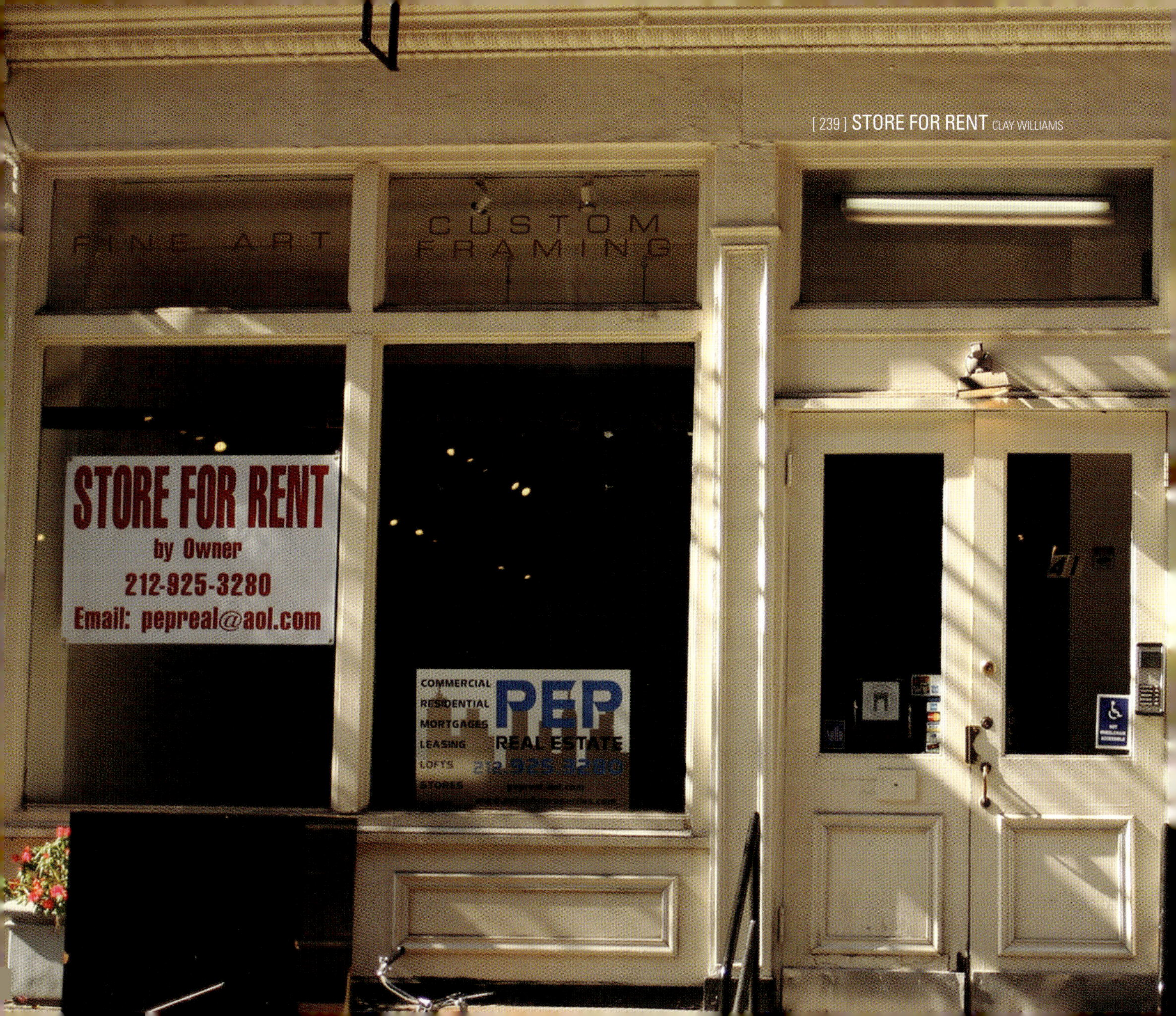

[239] STORE FOR RENT CLAY WILLIAMS

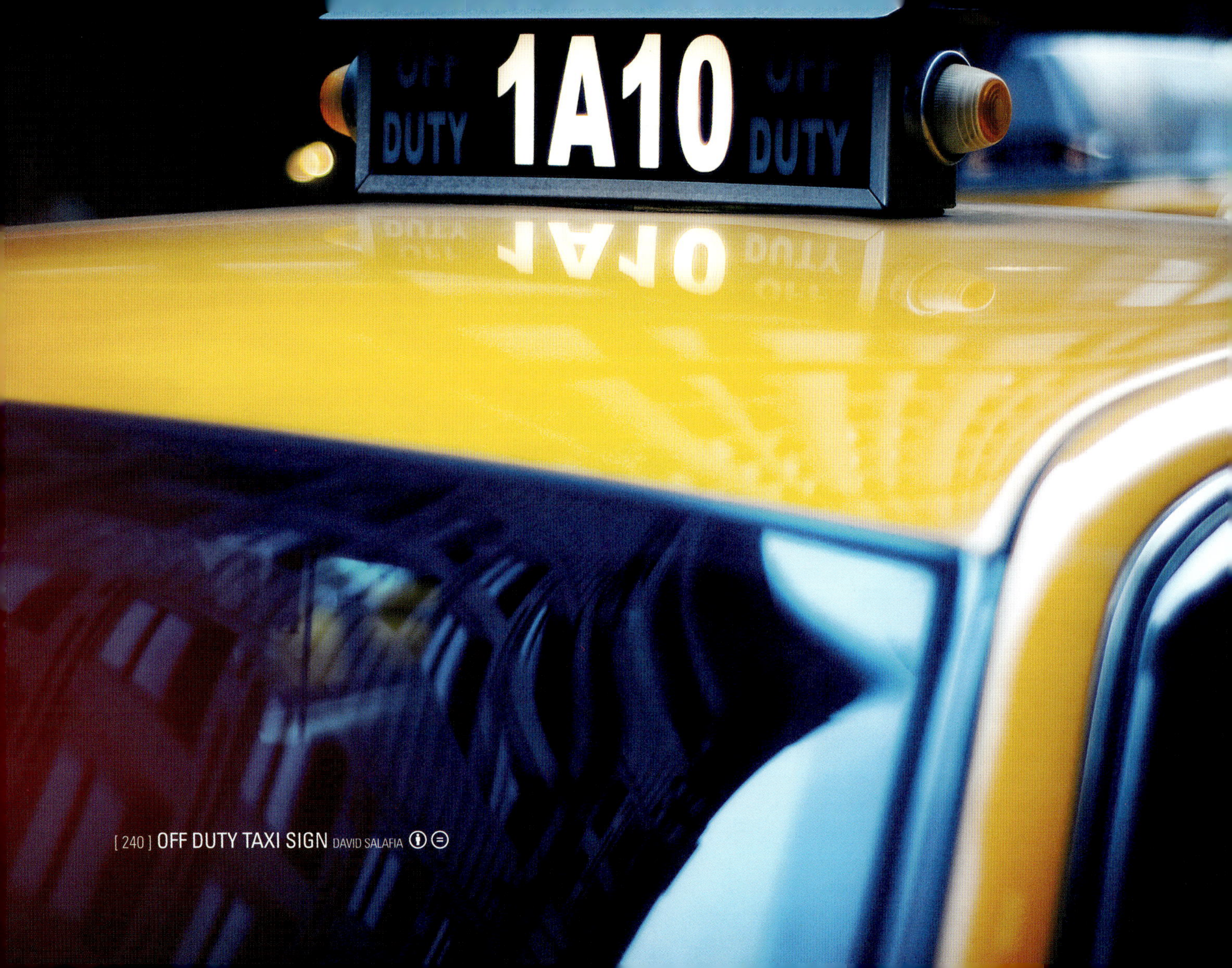

[240] OFF DUTY TAXI SIGN DAVID SALAFIA

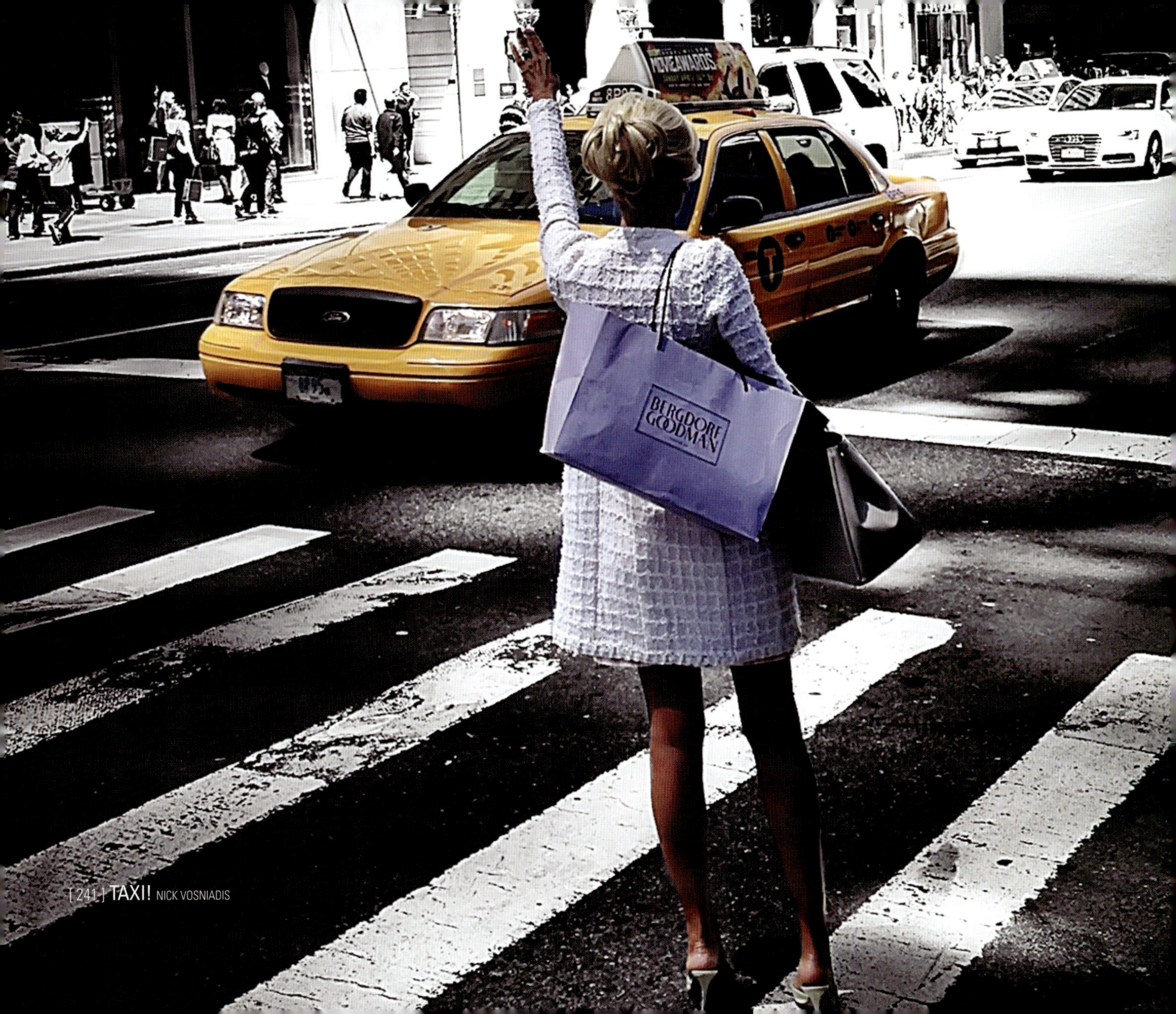

[241] TAXI! NICK VOSNIADIS

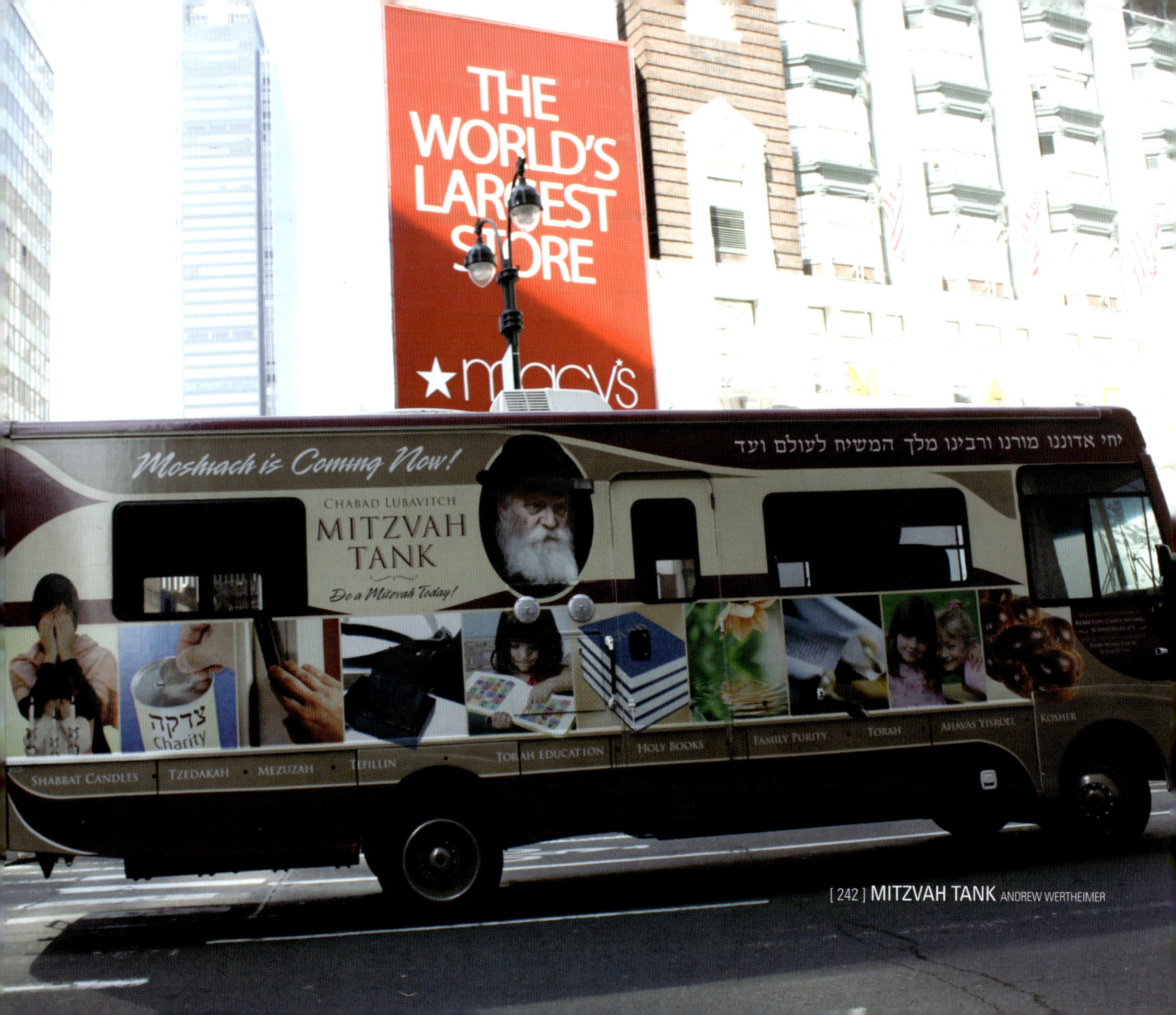

[242] **MITZVAH TANK** ANDREW WERTHEIMER

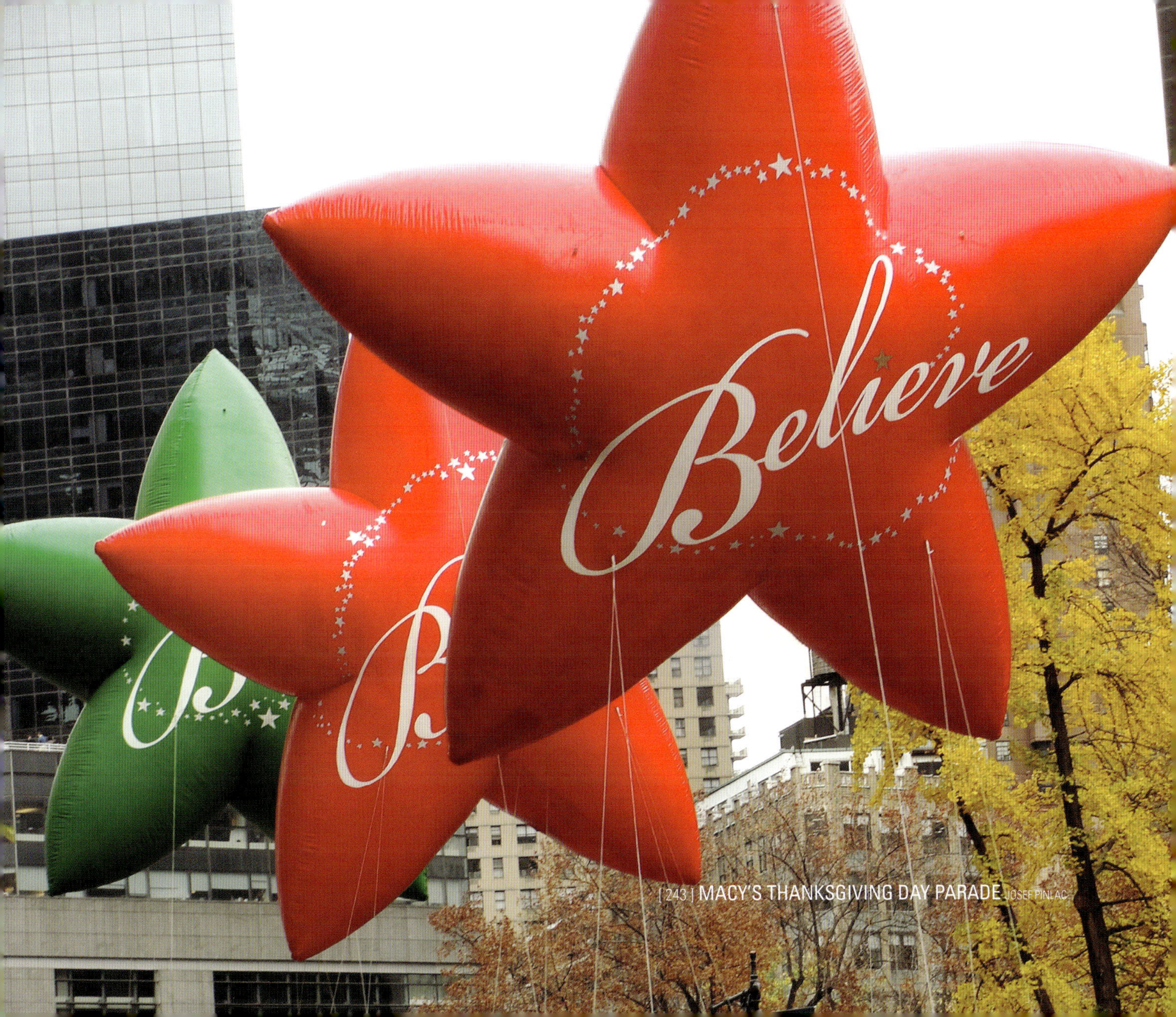

[243] MACY'S THANKSGIVING DAY PARADE JOSEF PINLAC

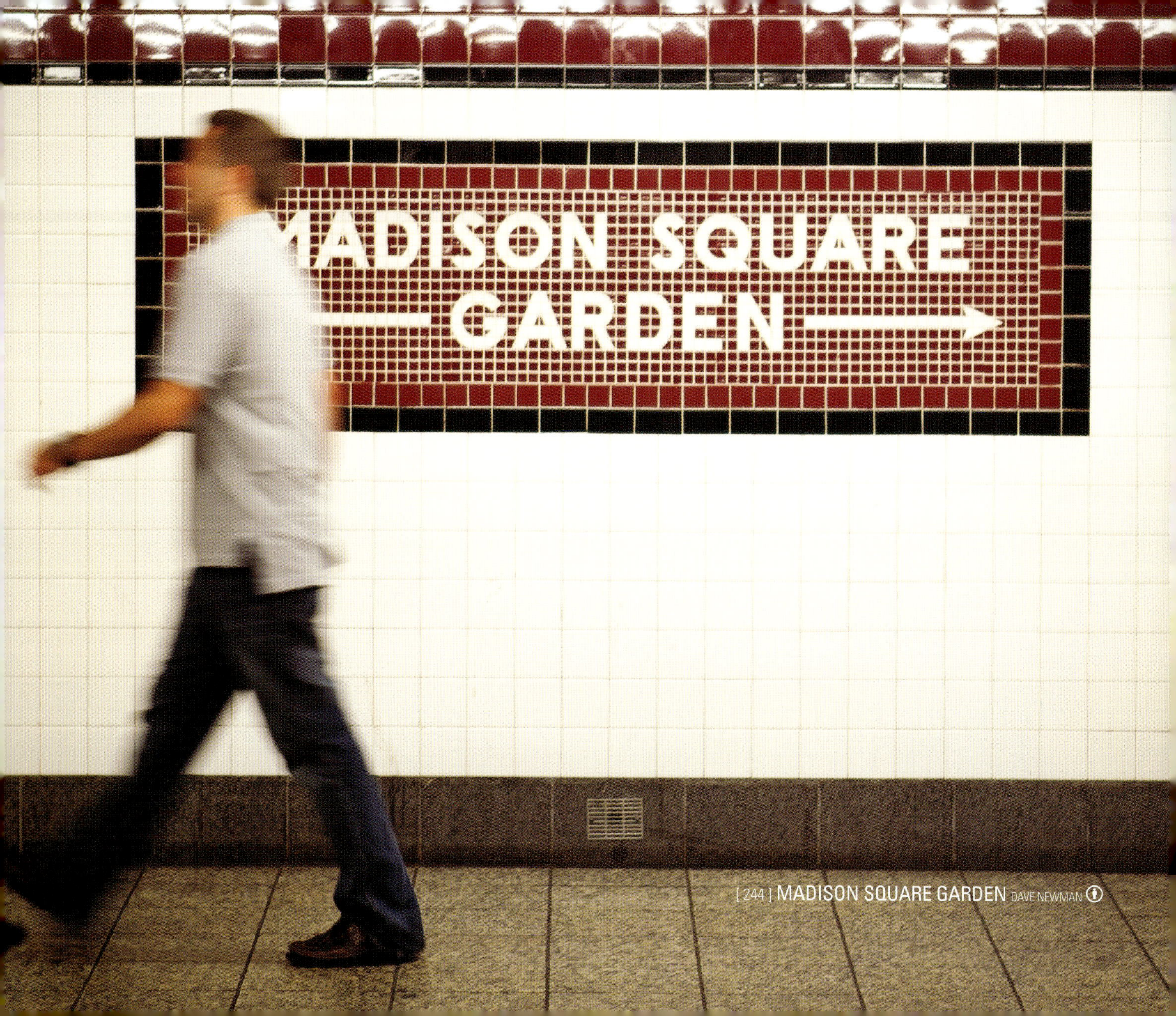

[244] MADISON SQUARE GARDEN DAVE NEWMAN

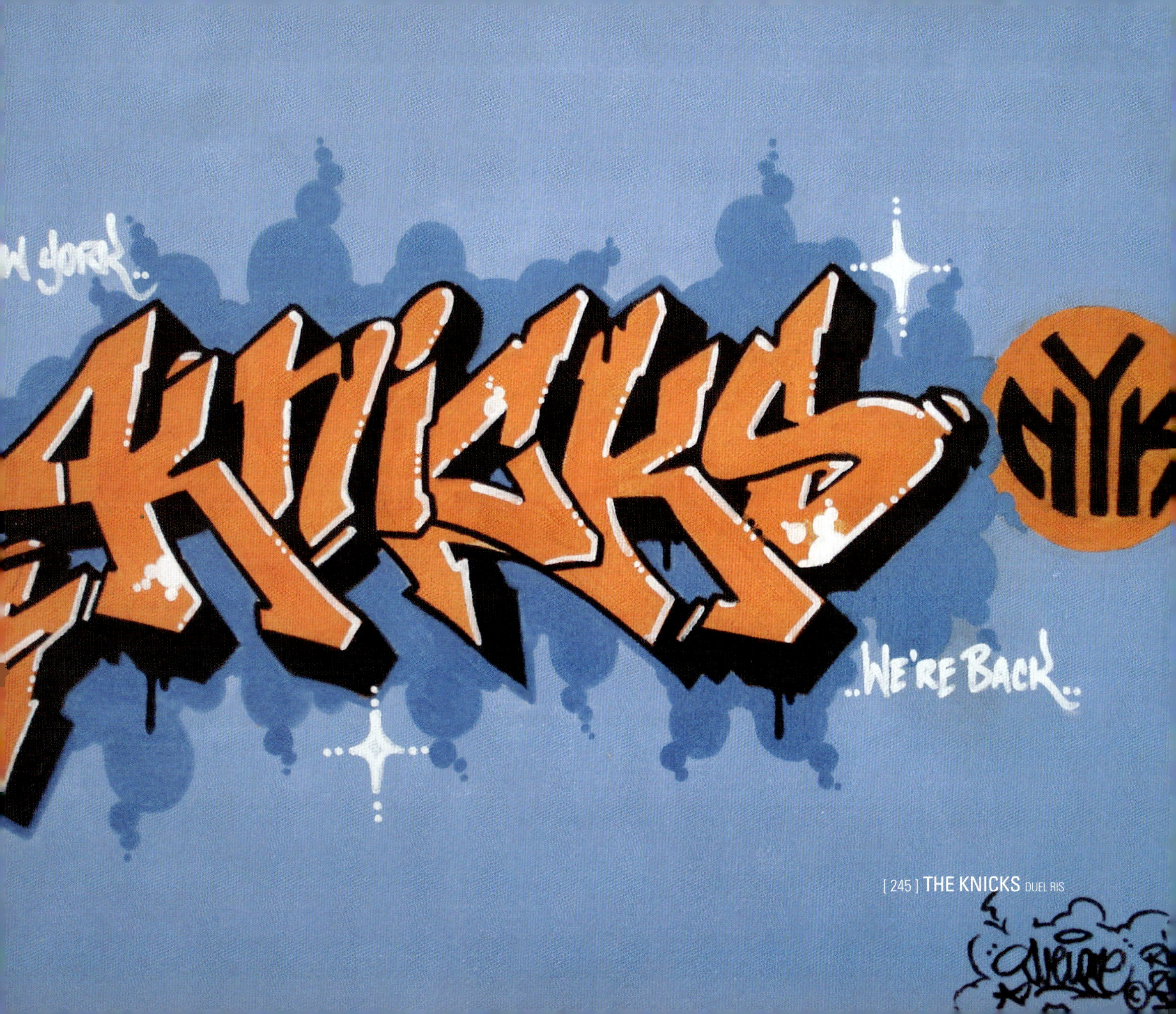

[245] **THE KNICKS** DUEL RIS

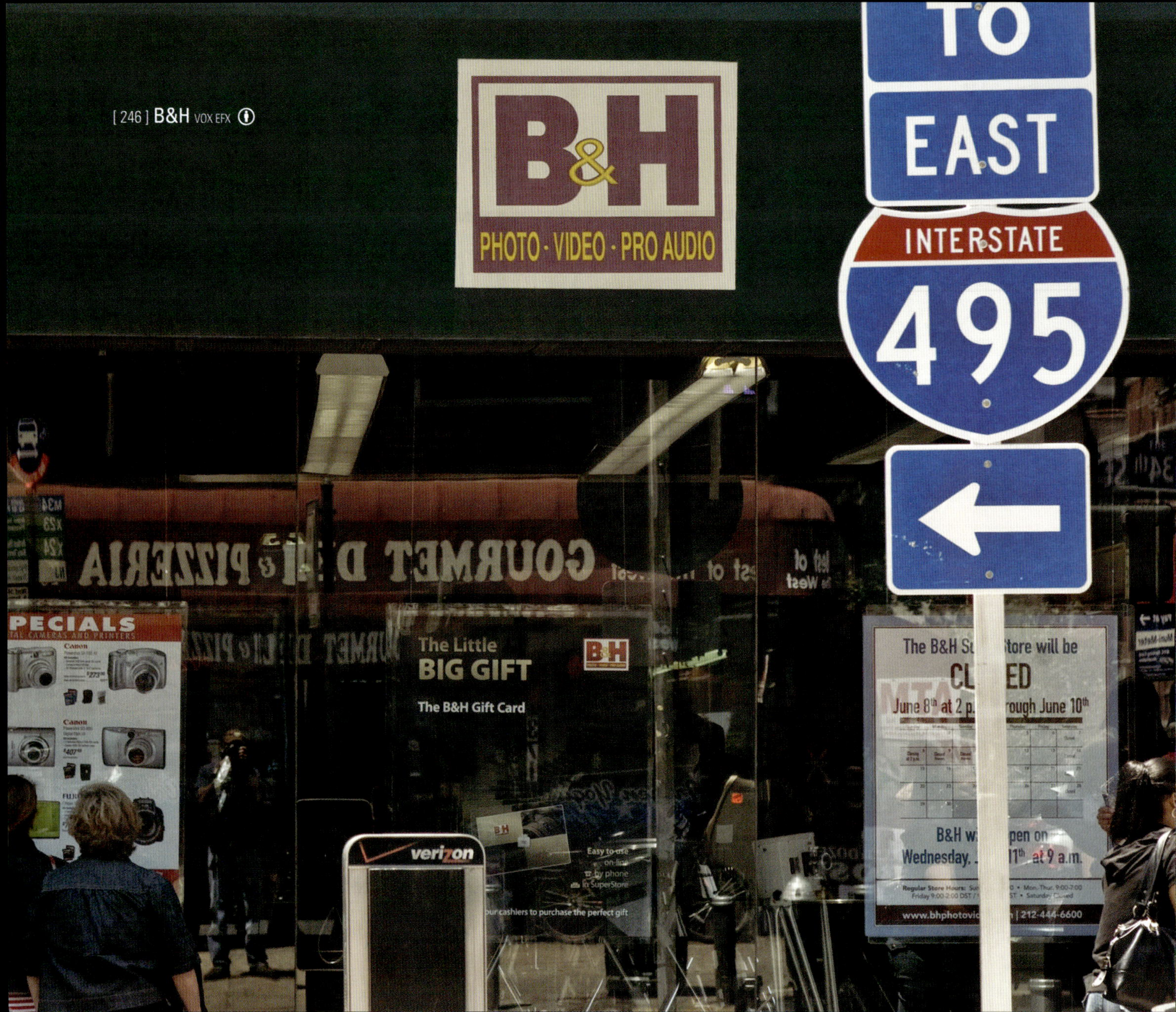
B&H
PHOTO · VIDEO · PRO AUDIO
TO
EAST
INTERSTATE
495
GOURMET DELI & PIZZERIA
The Little
BIG GIFT
The B&H Gift Card
verizon

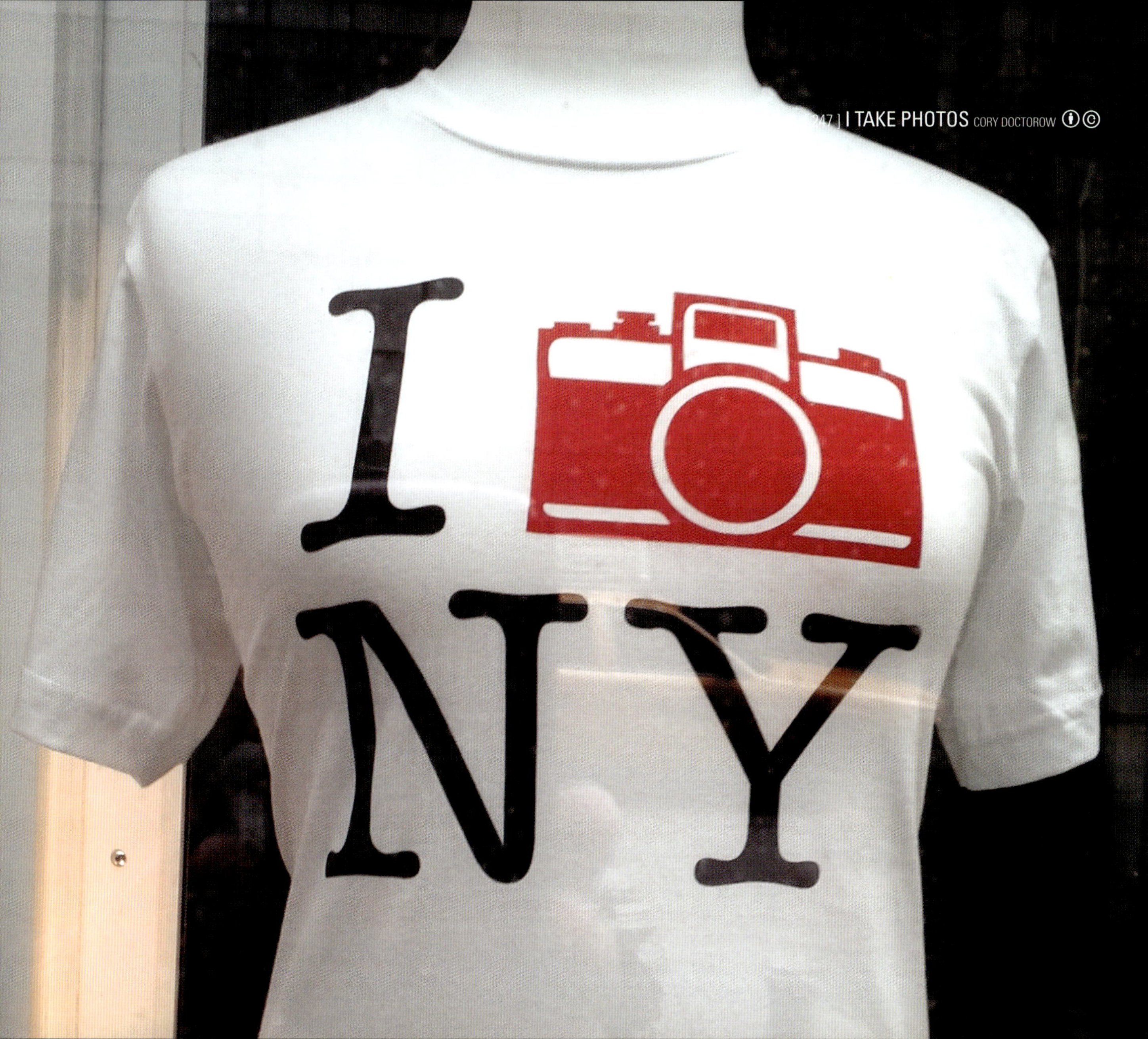

[247] I TAKE PHOTOS CORY DOCTOROW

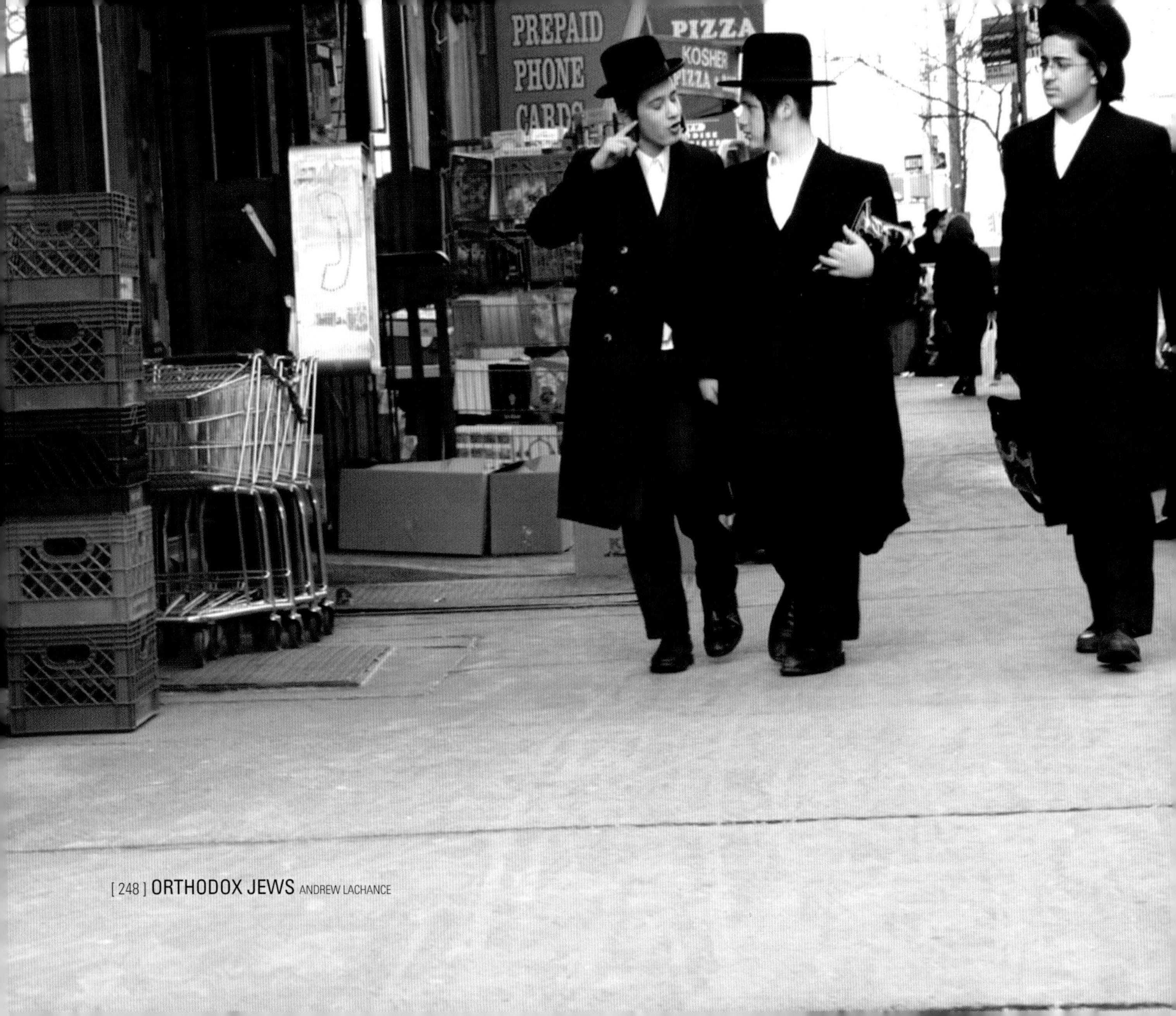

[248] **ORTHODOX JEWS** ANDREW LACHANCE

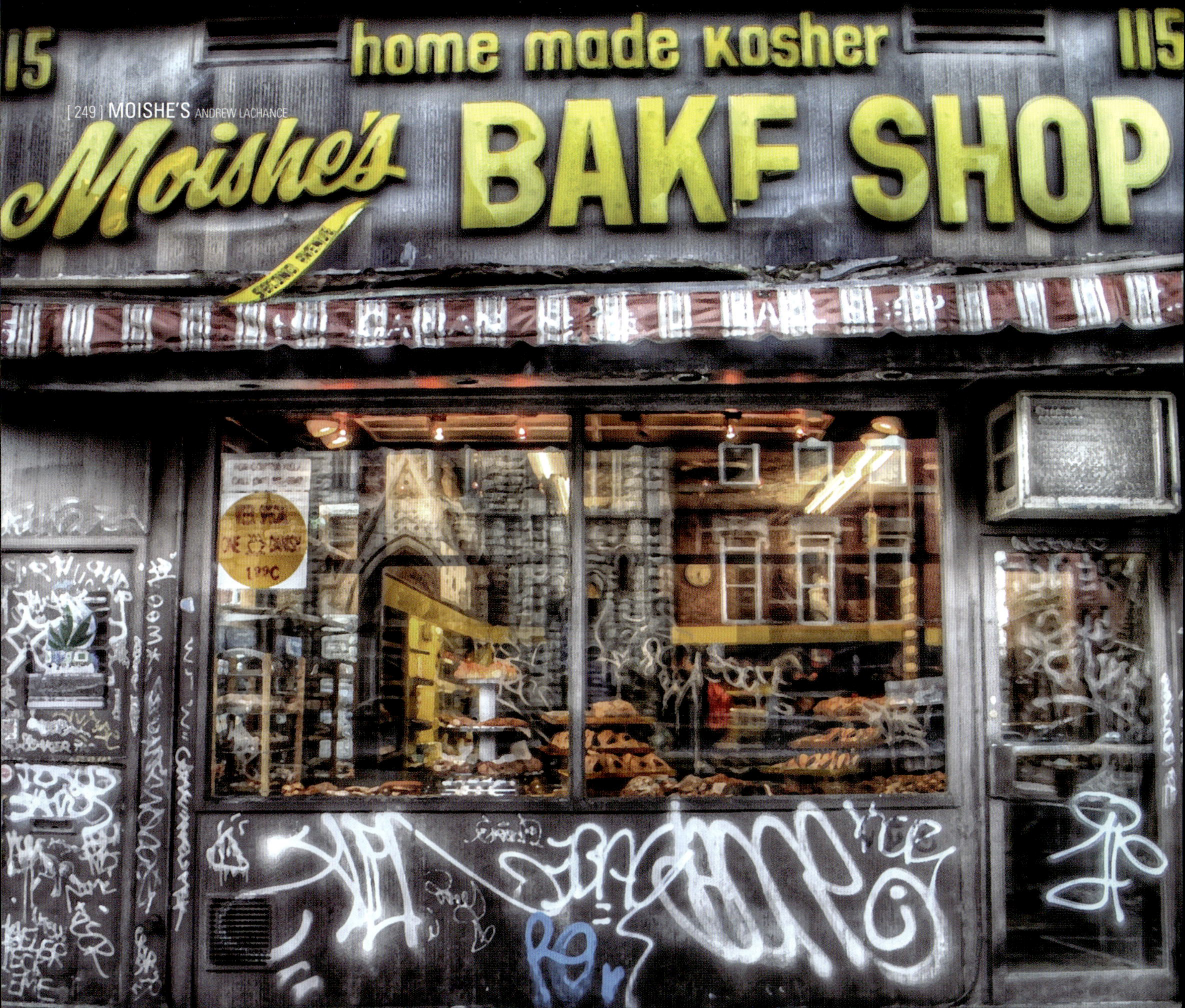

[249] MOISHE'S ANDREW LACHANCE

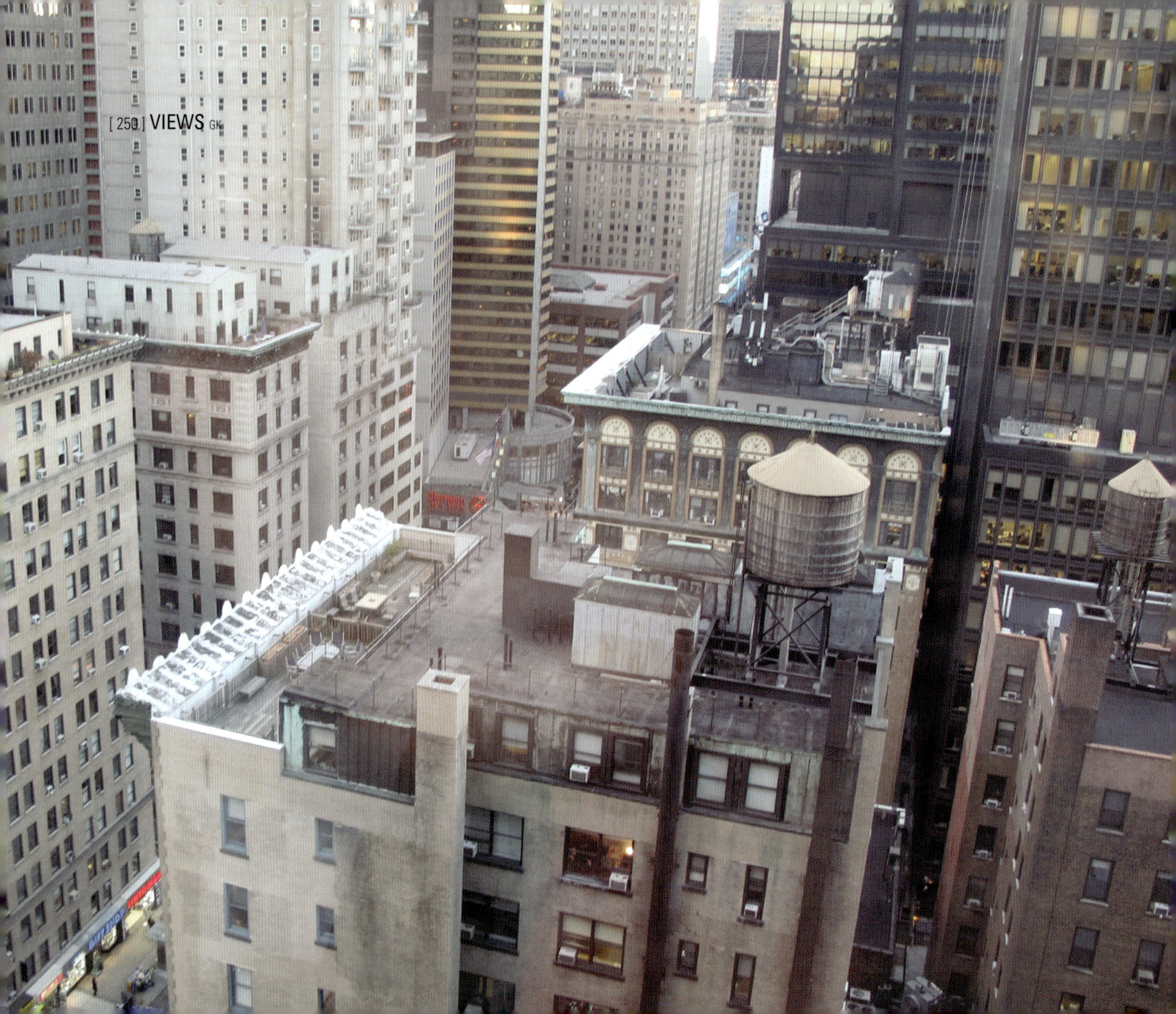

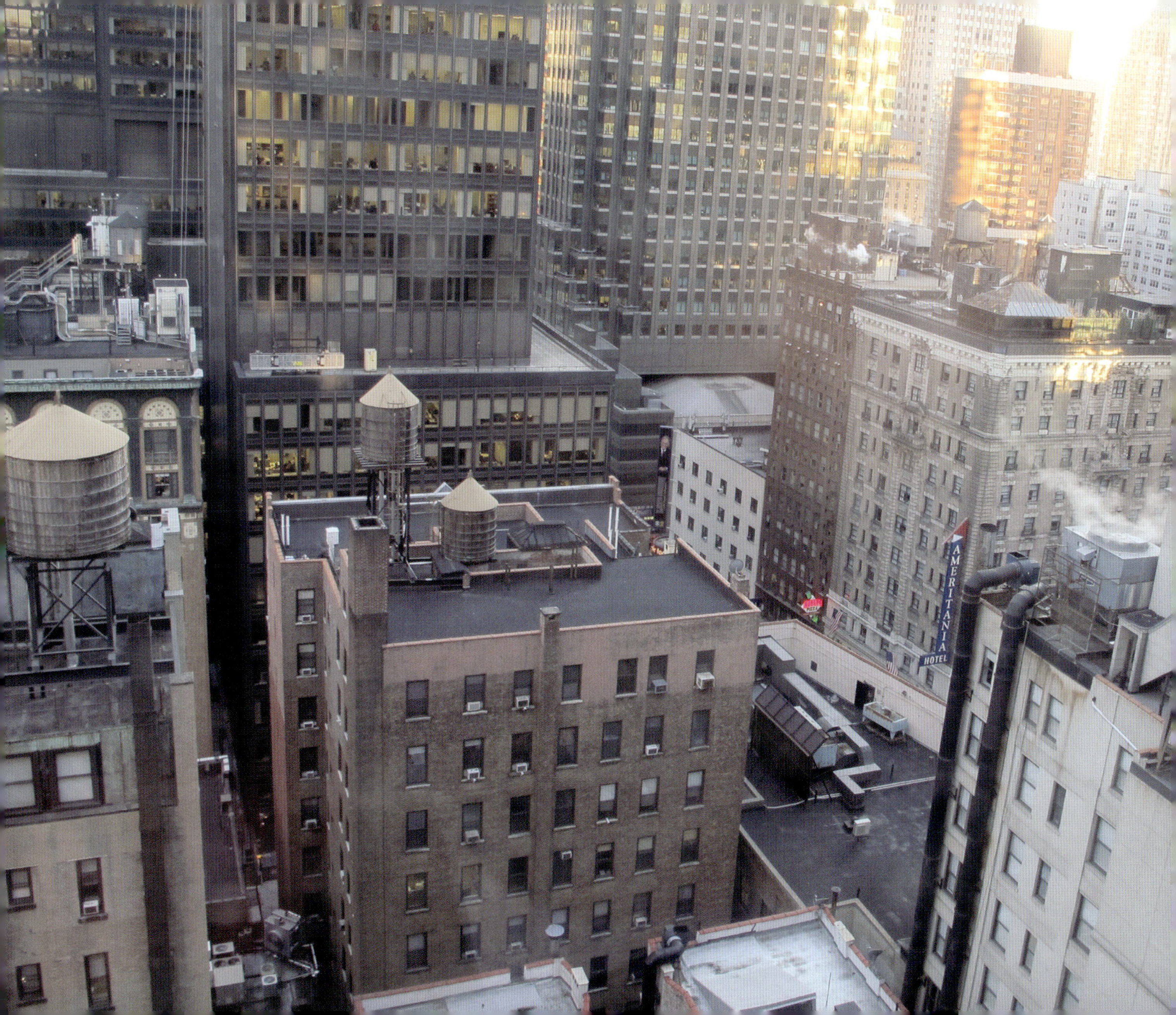
AMERITANIA
HOTEL

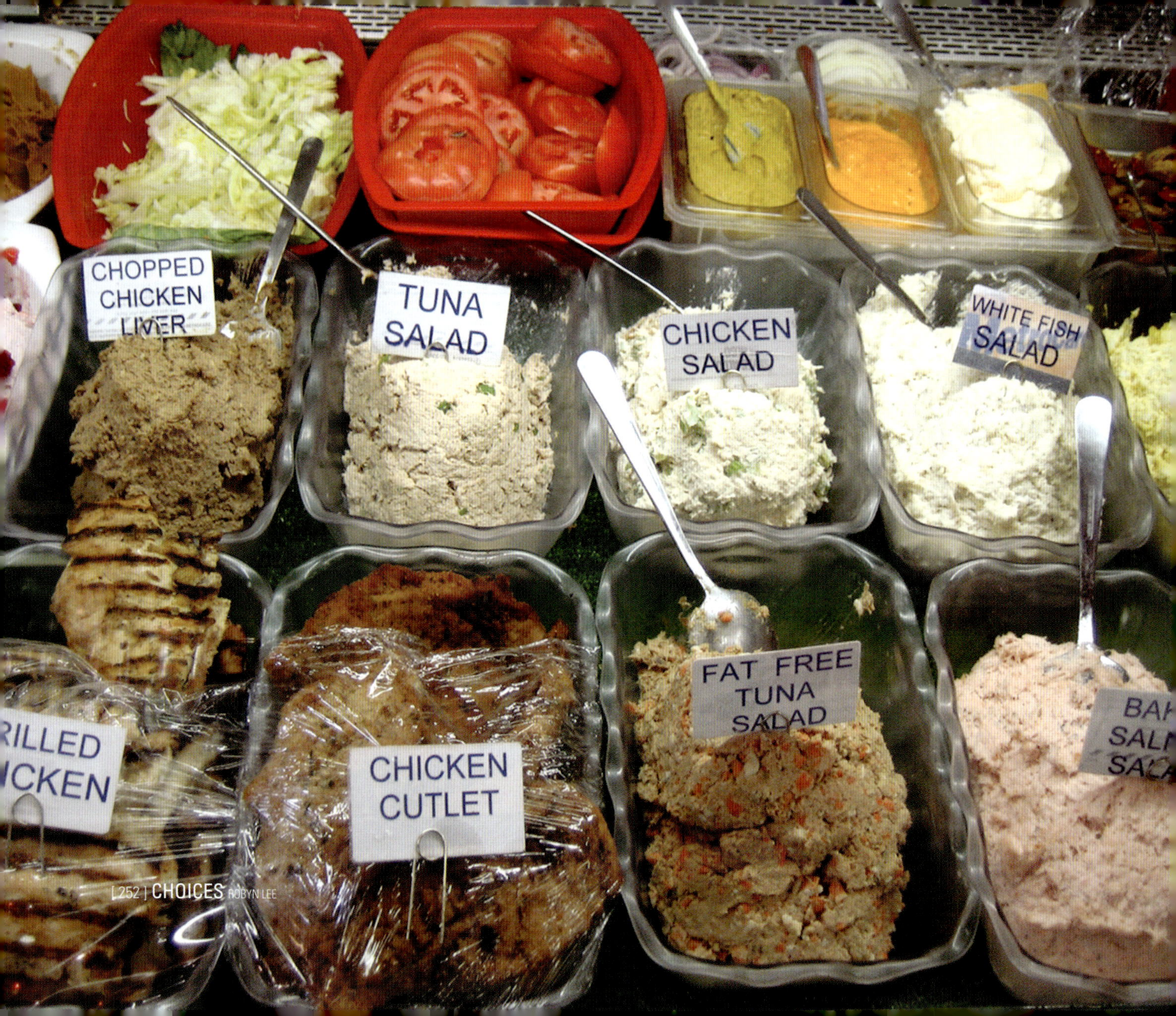

[252] CHOICES ROBYN LEE

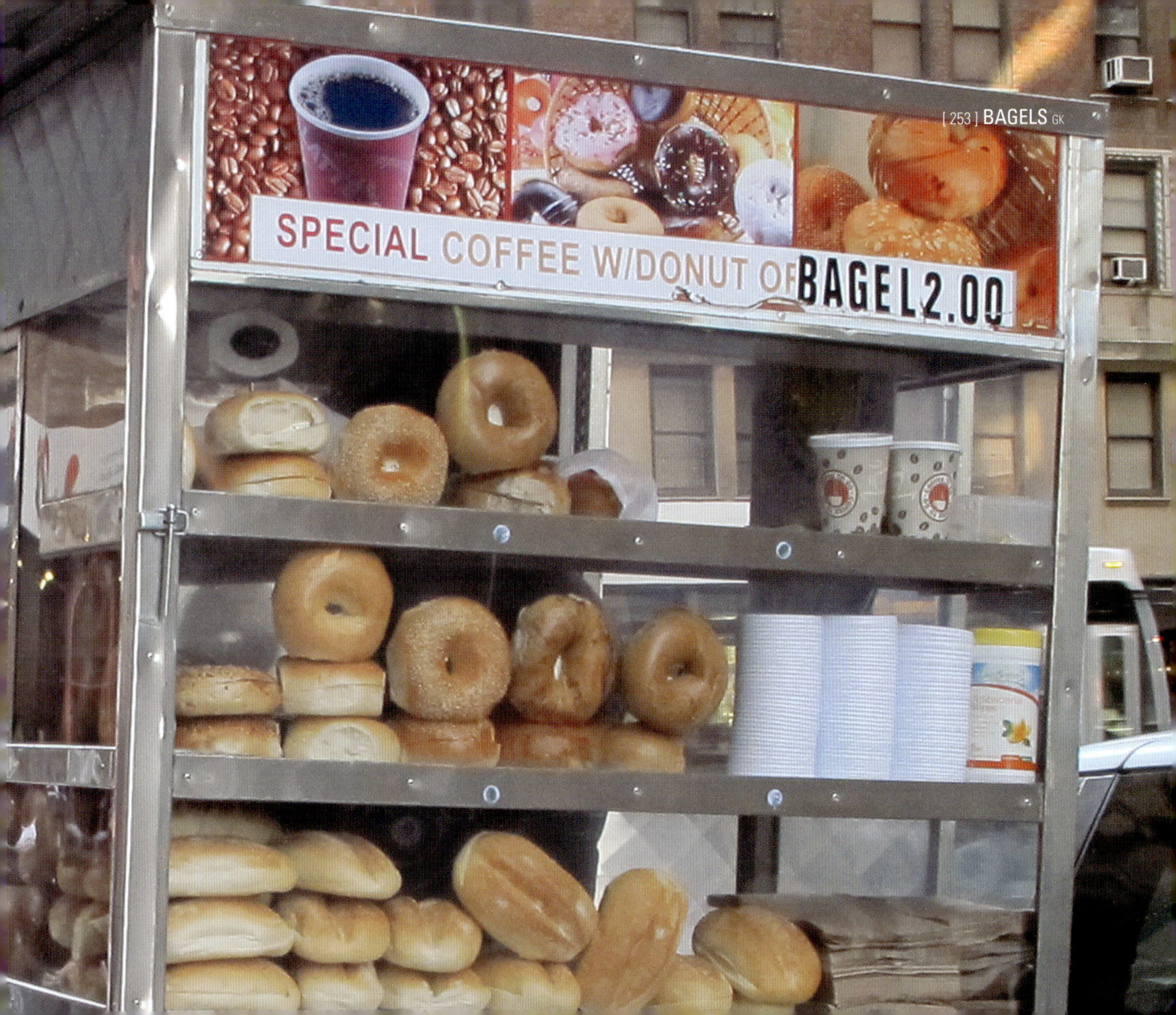
SPECIAL COFFEE W/DONUT OF BAGEL 2.00

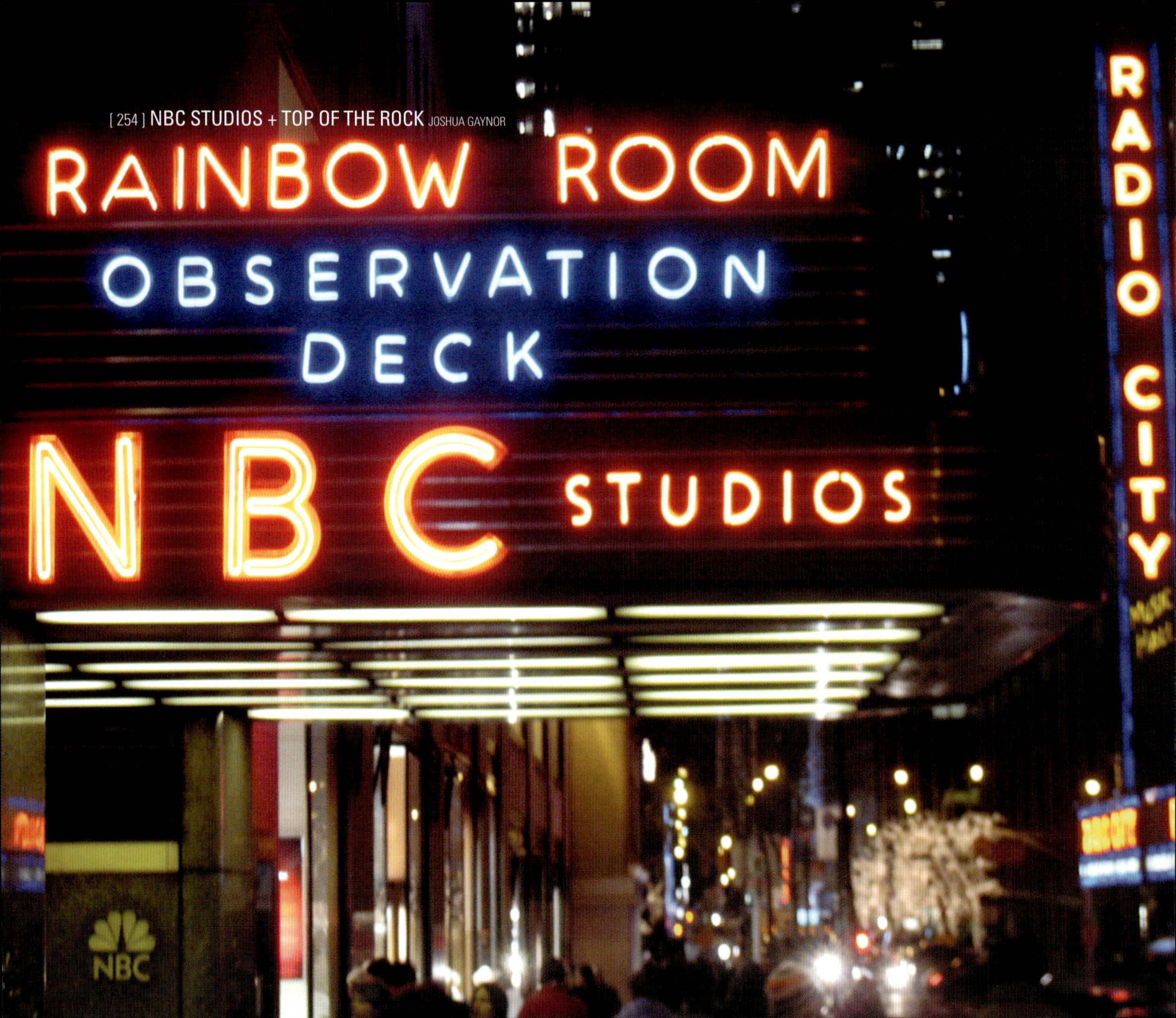

[254] NBC STUDIOS + TOP OF THE ROCK JOSHUA GAYNOR

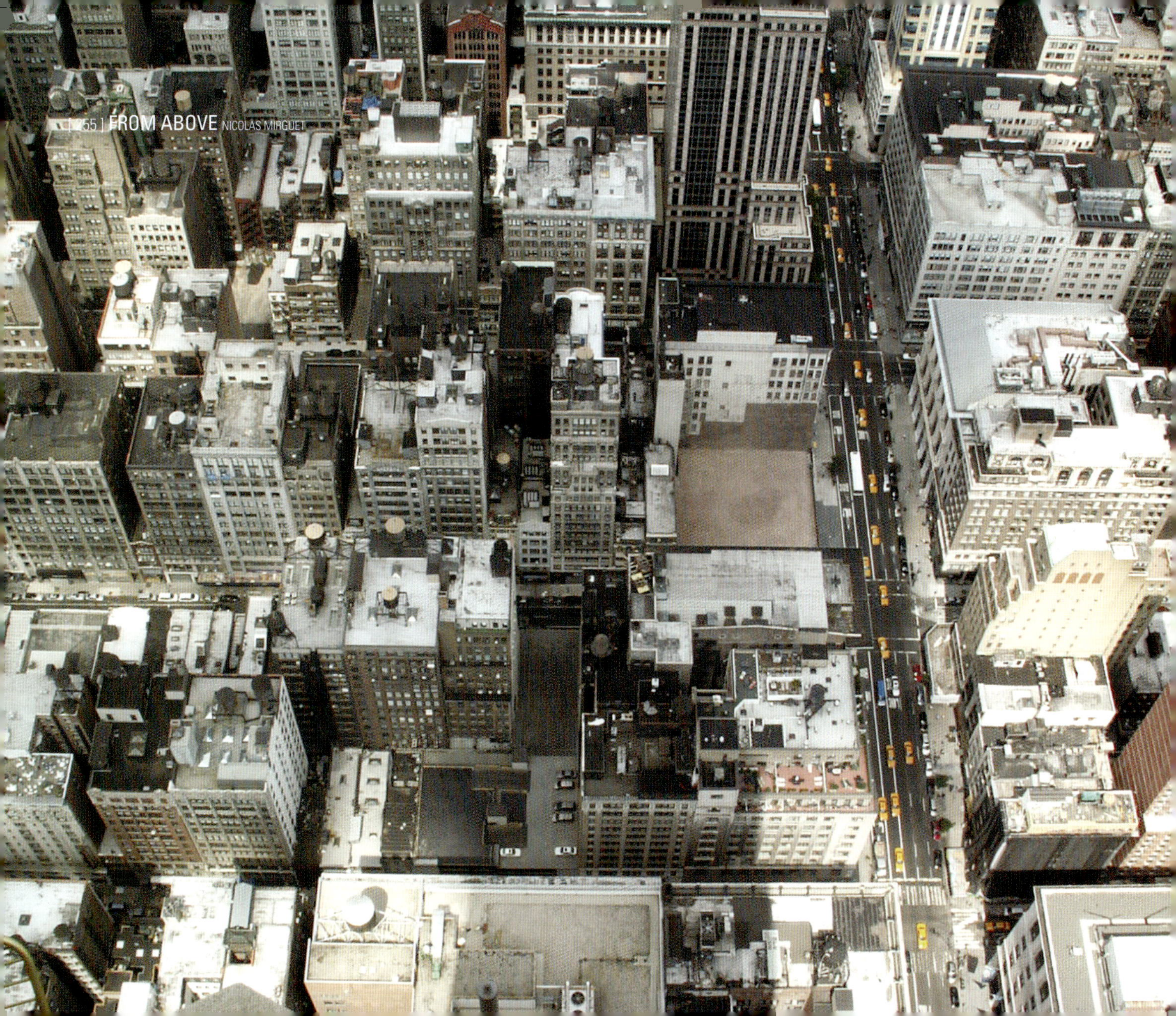

[256] APOLLO THEATER GWENAËL PIASER

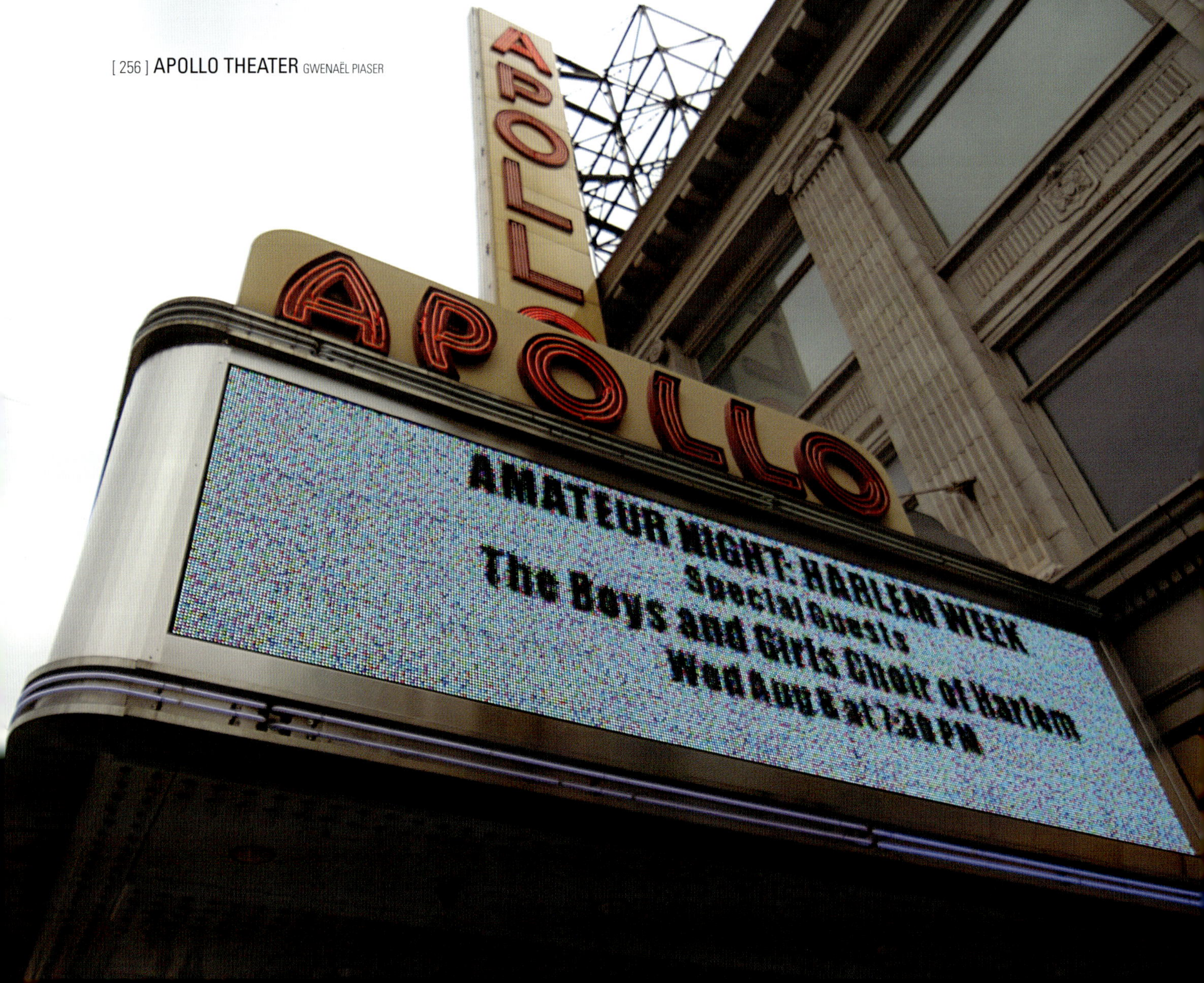

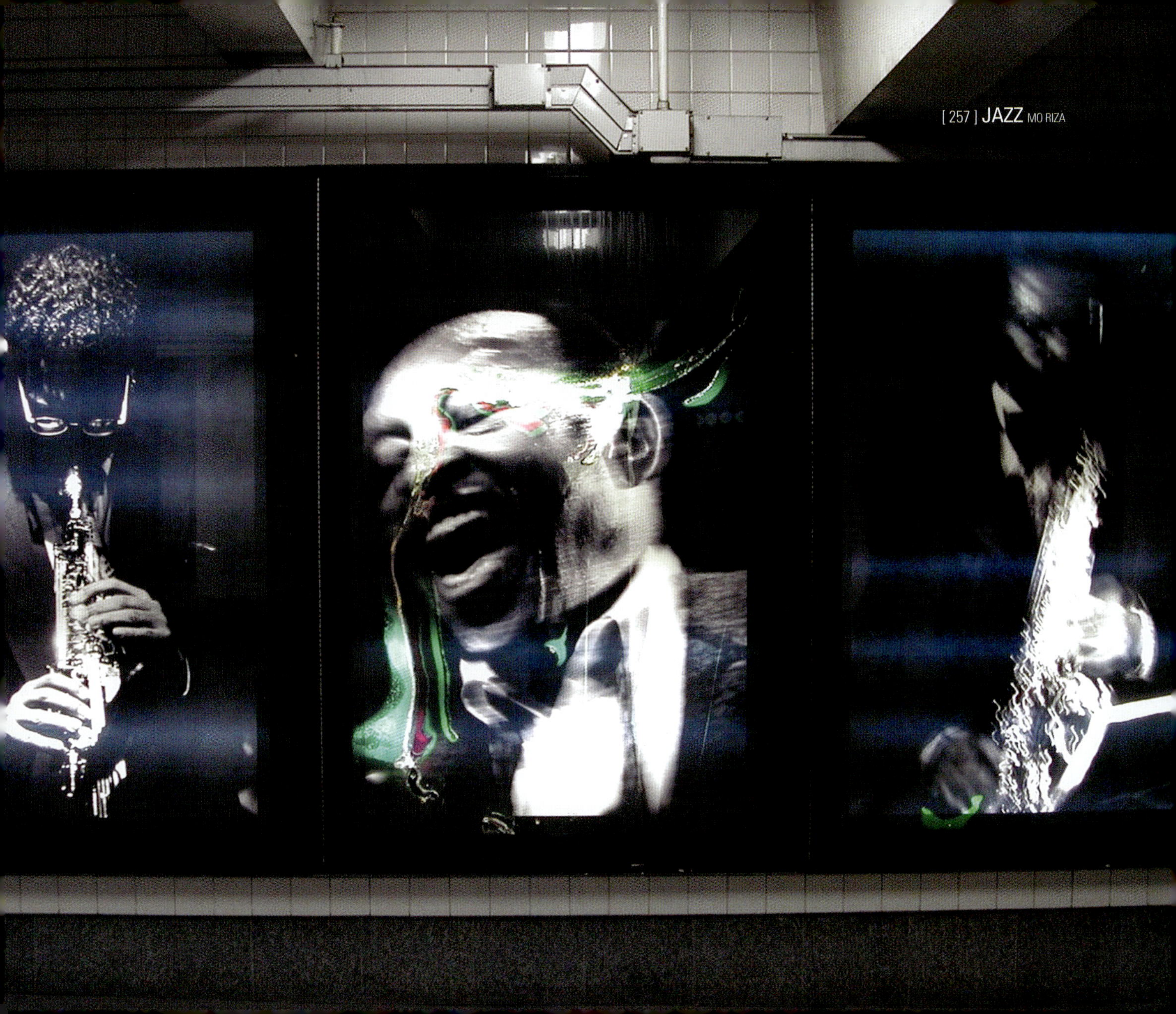

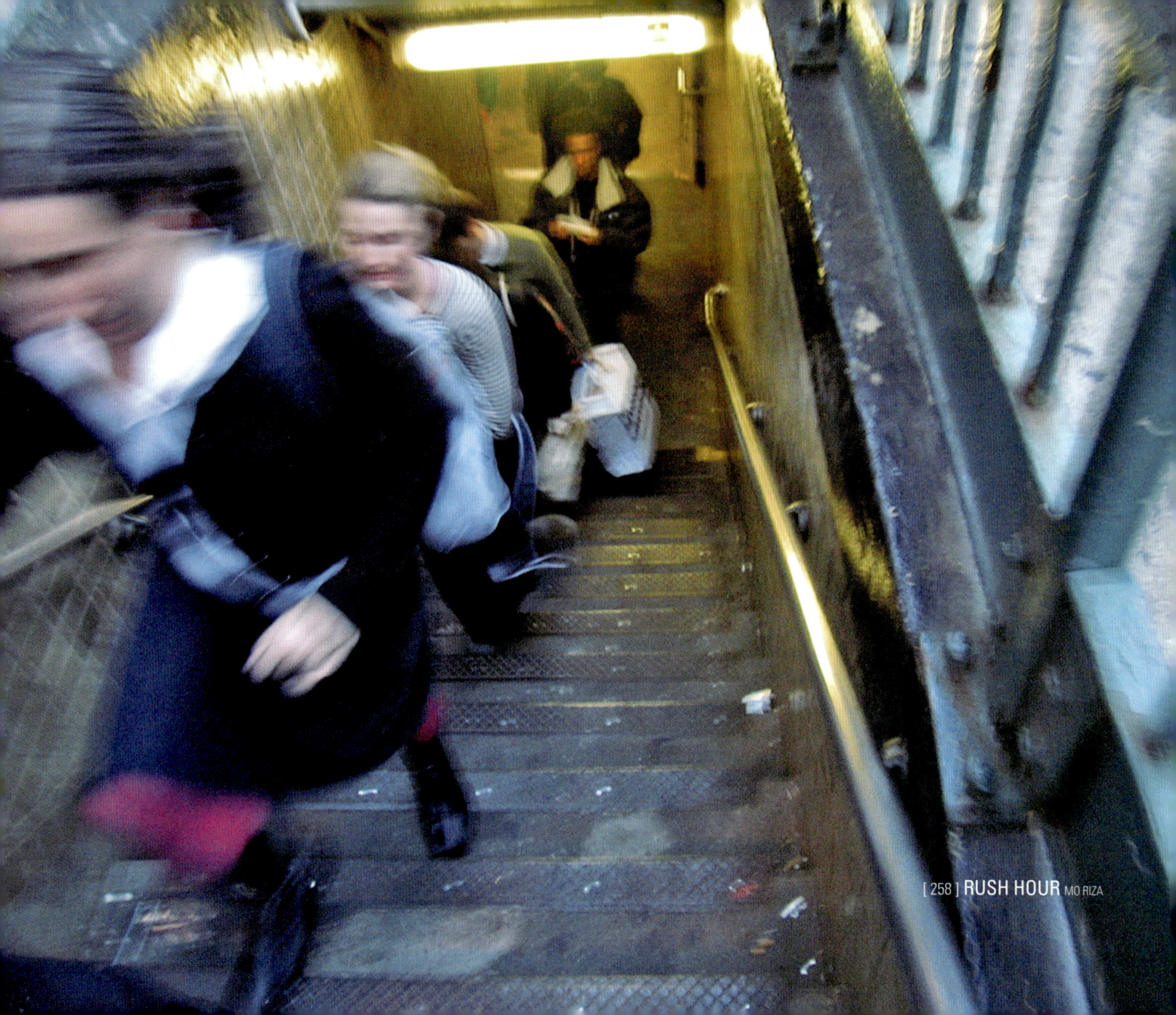

[258] RUSH HOUR MO RIZA

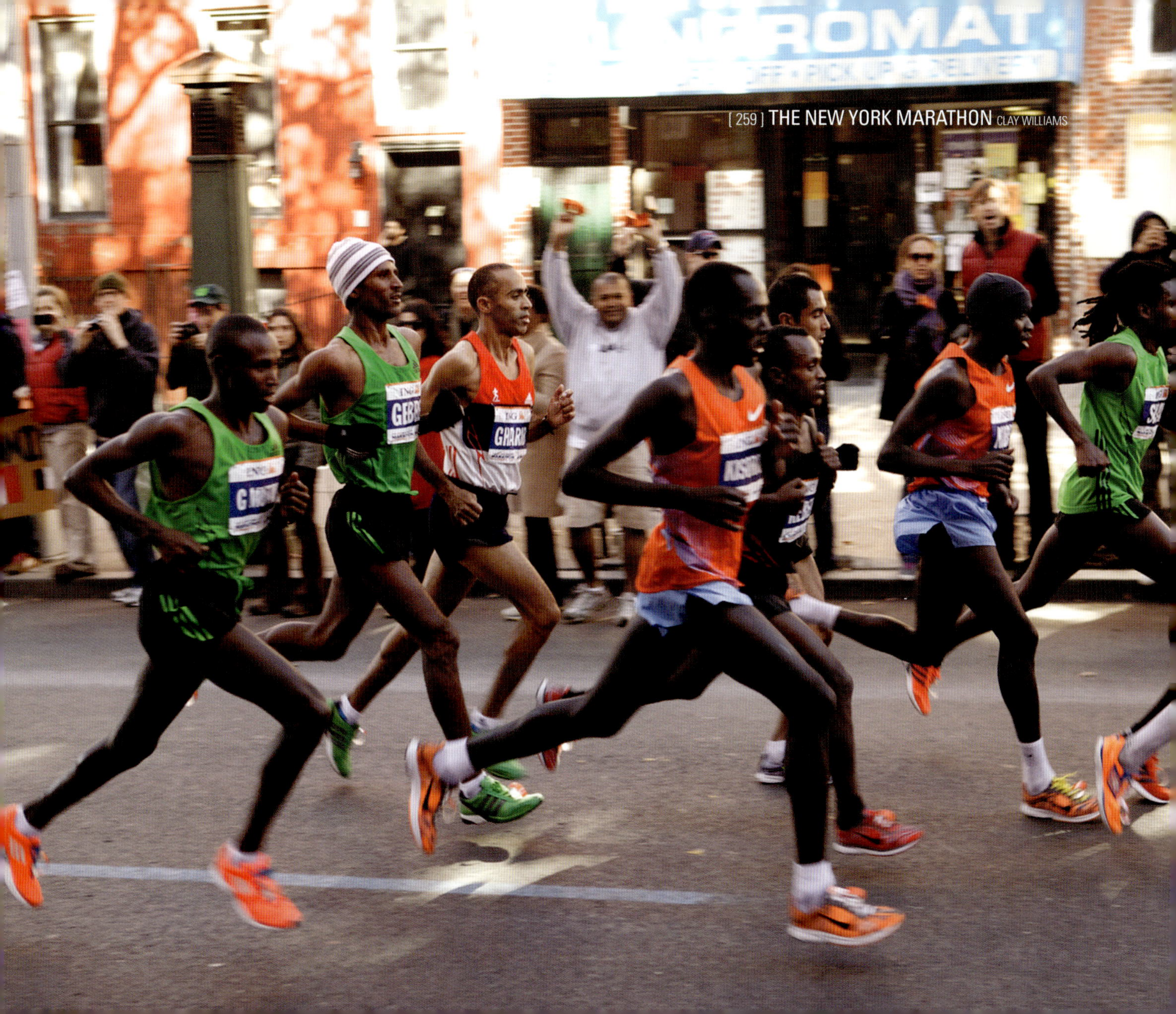

[259] THE NEW YORK MARATHON CLAY WILLIAMS

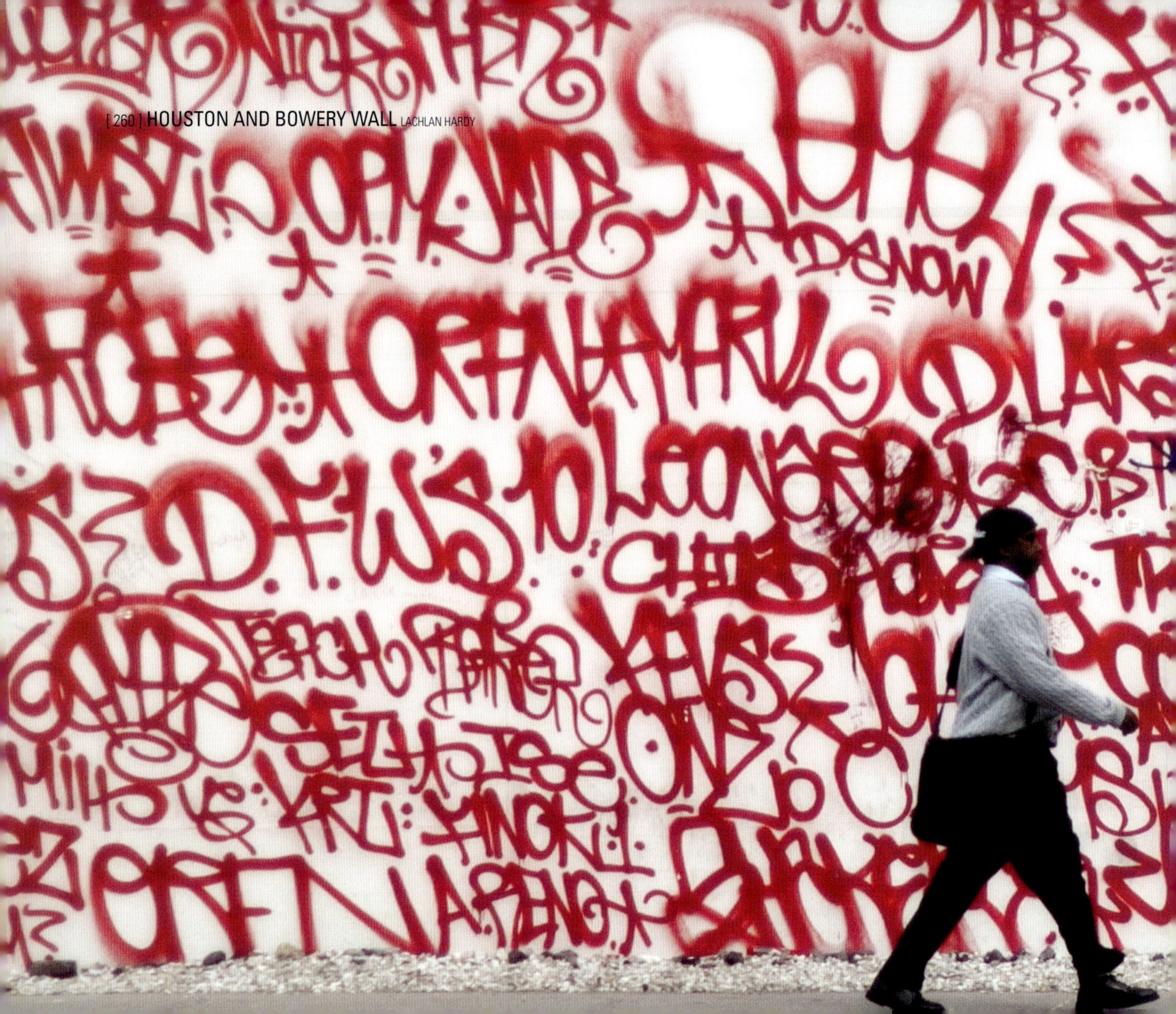

[260] **HOUSTON AND BOWERY WALL** LACHLAN HARDY

CHAMA
C.B.T.
MATT. B
HARD
THE WIZ
C.B.T.

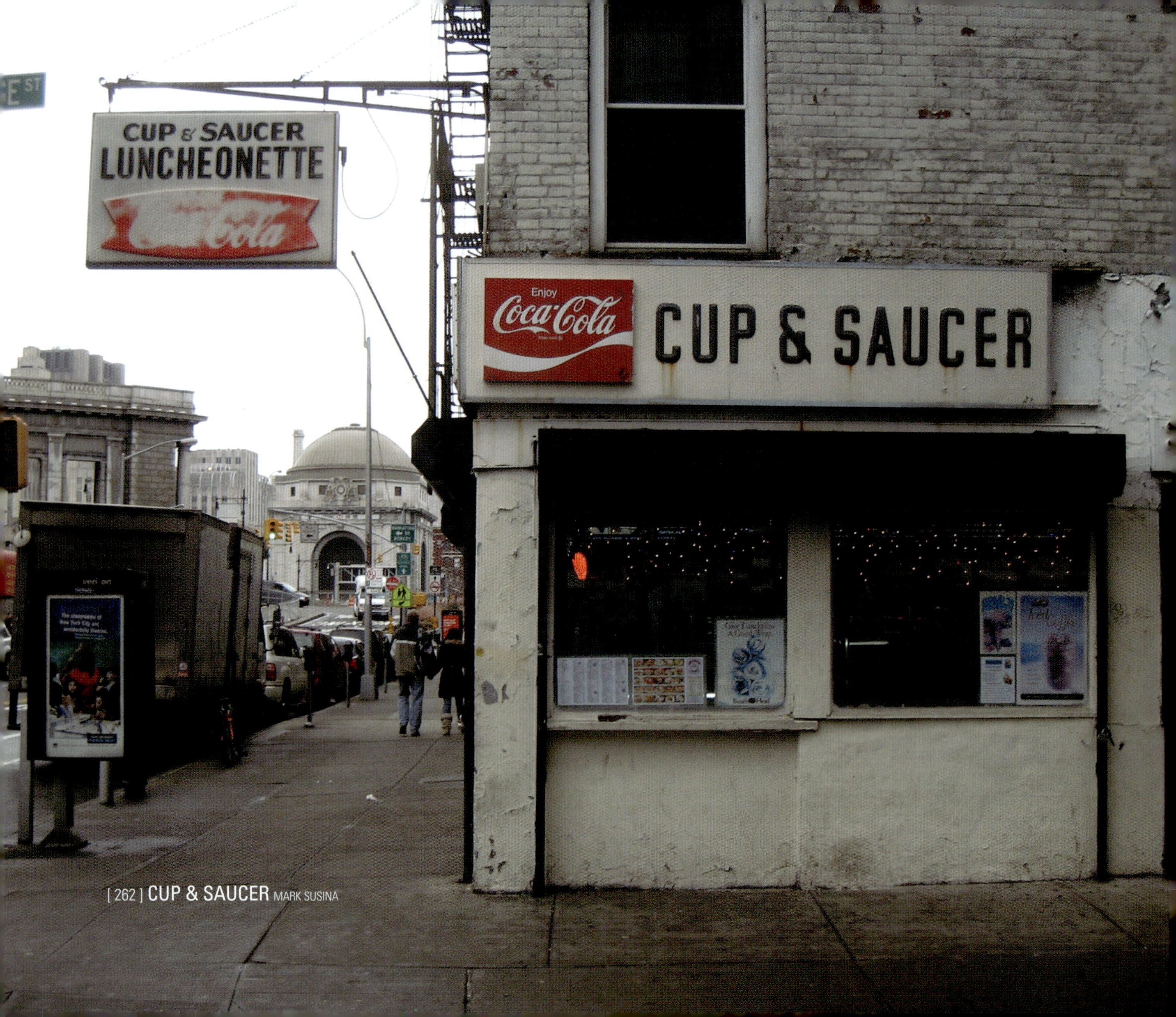

[262] CUP & SAUCER MARK SUSINA

[263] WHITNEY MUSEUM NICHOLAS NOYES + LORI L. STALTERI

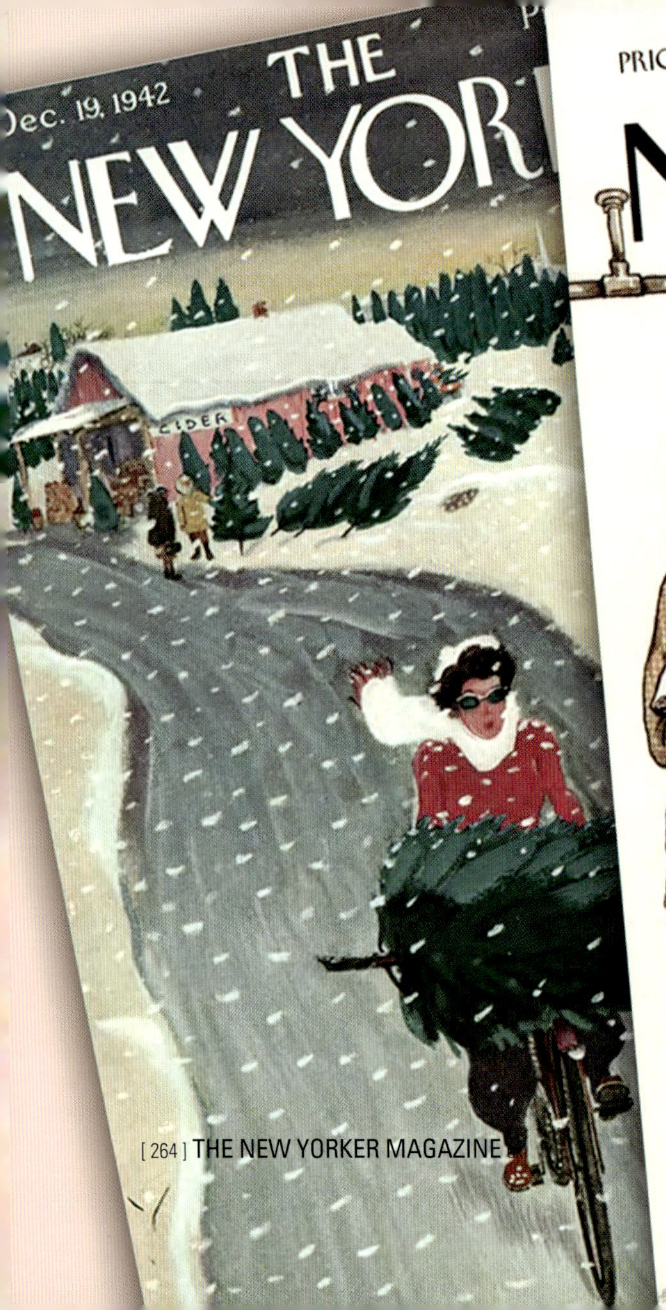
Dec. 19, 1942
THE
CIDER

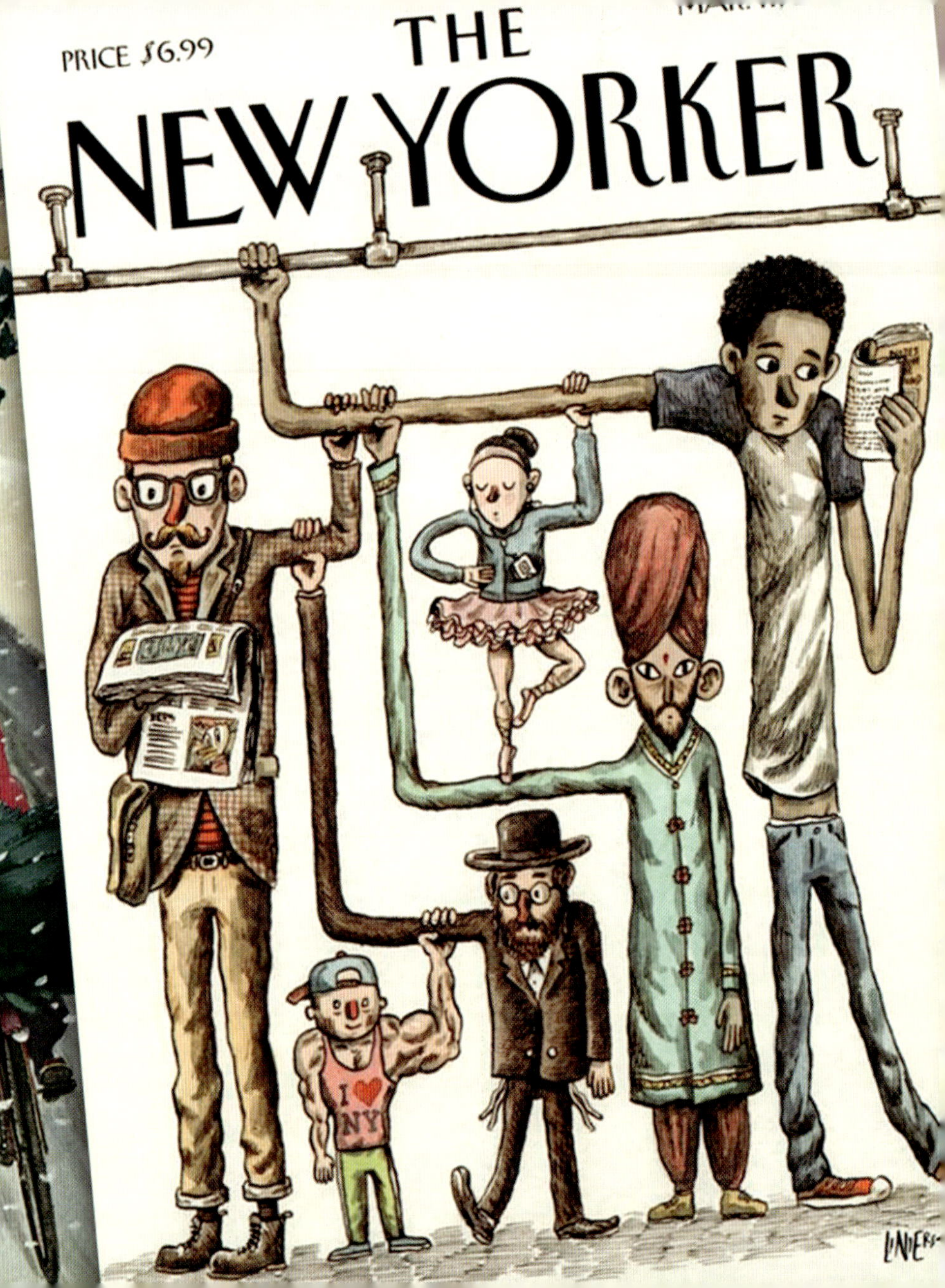
PRICE $6.99
THE
NEW YORKER
I ♥ NY
LINIERS

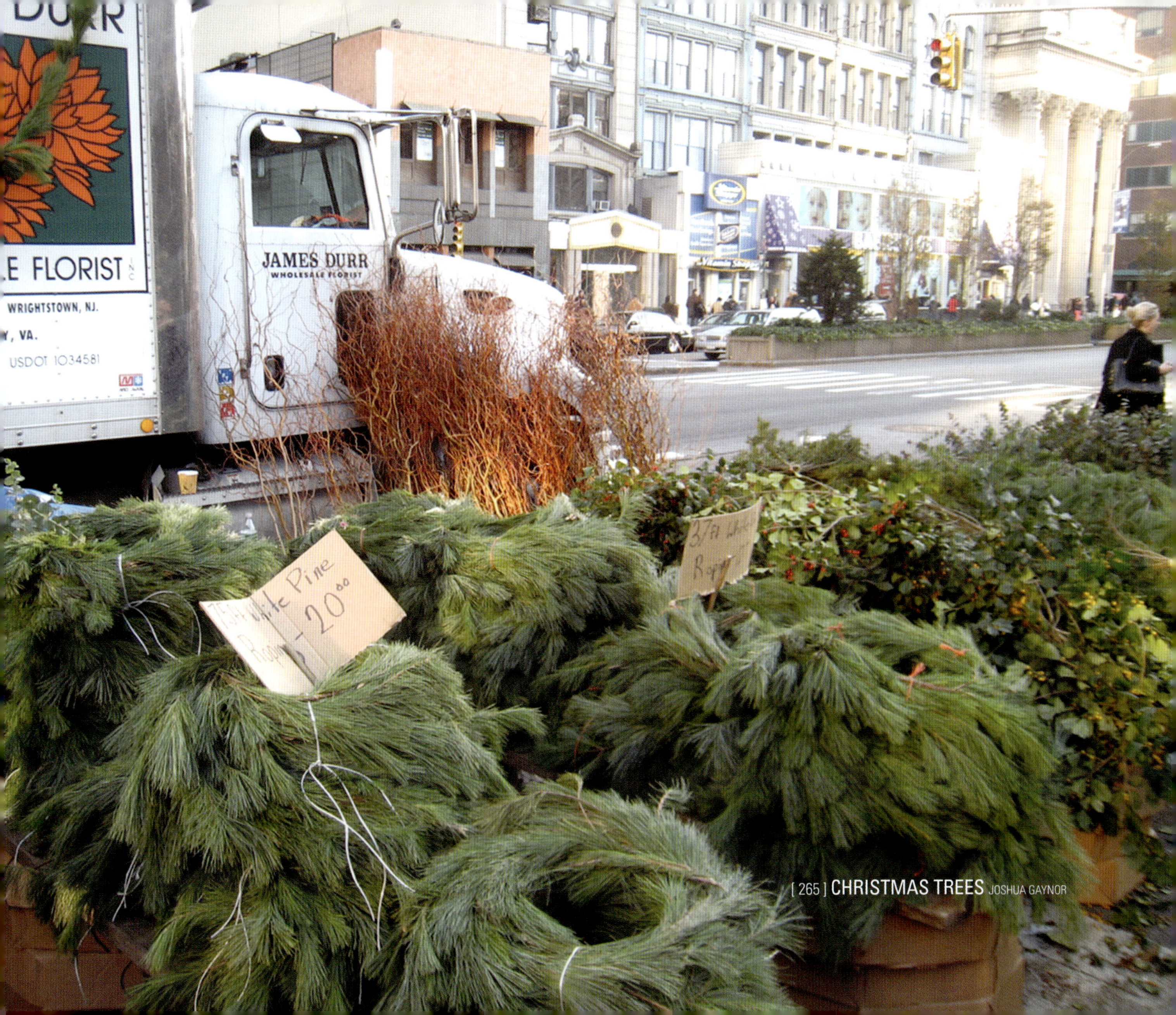

[265] CHRISTMAS TREES JOSHUA GAYNOR

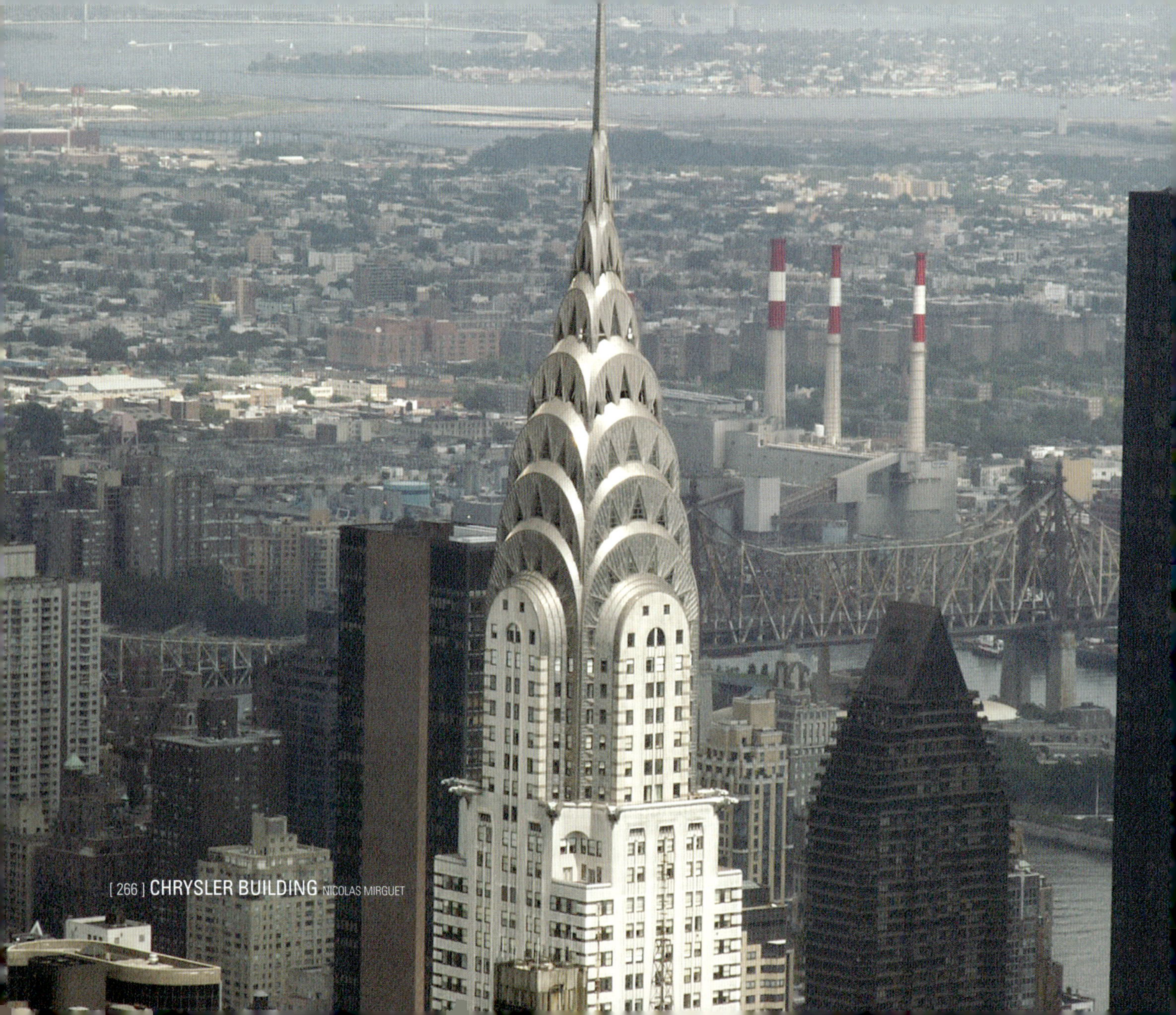

[266] CHRYSLER BUILDING NICOLAS MIRGUET

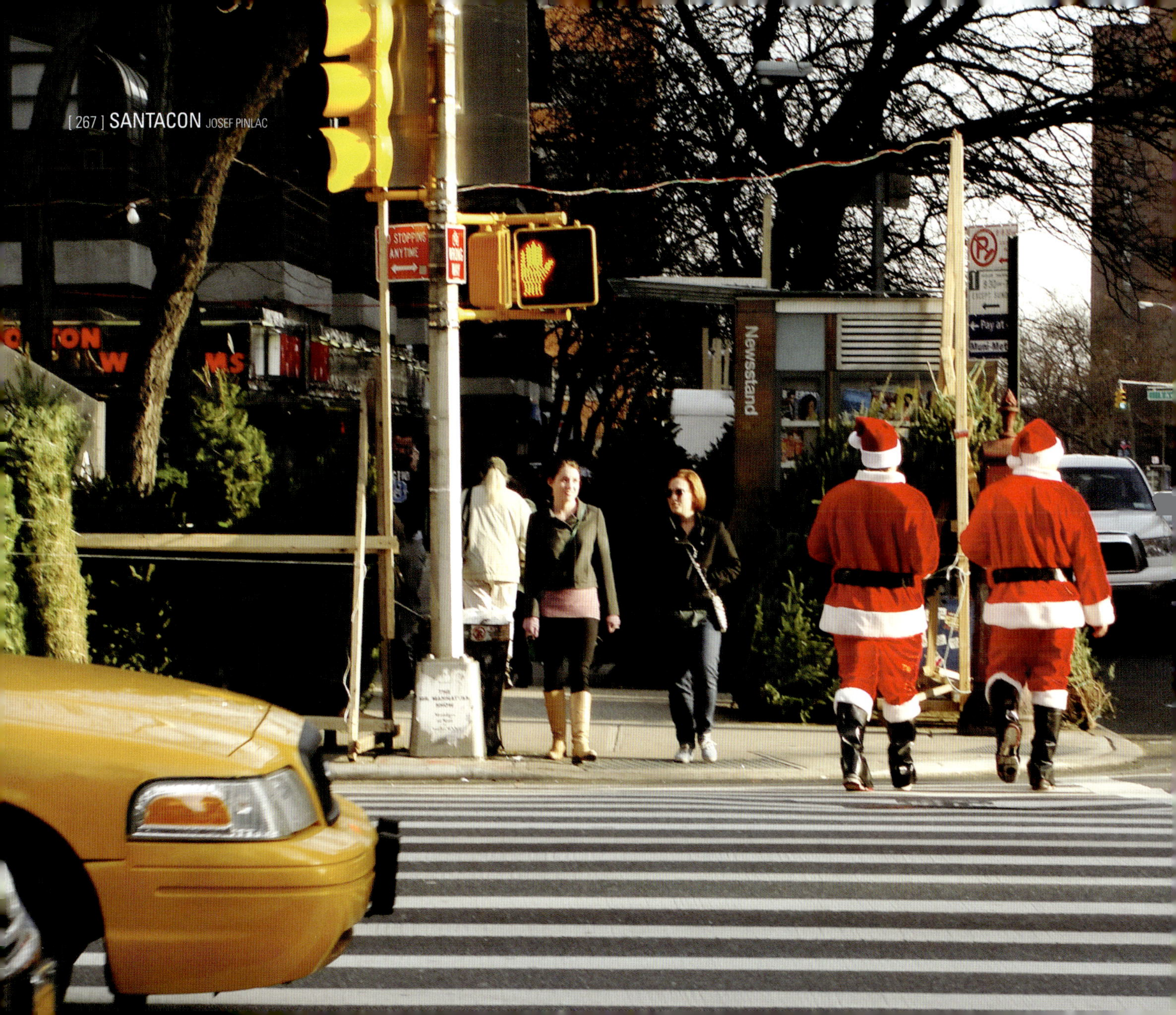

[267] SANTACON JOSEF PINLAC

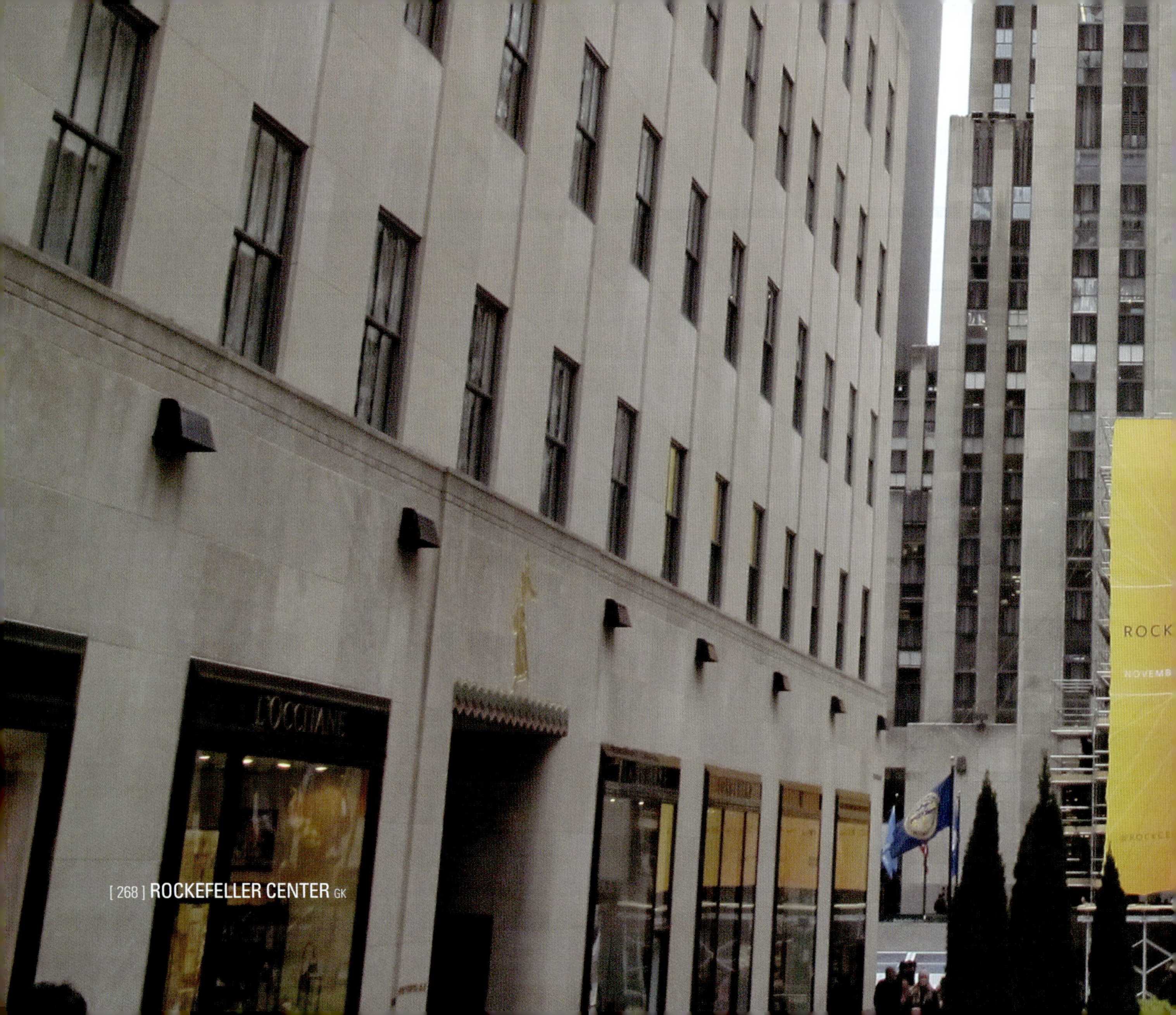

[268] ROCKEFELLER CENTER GK

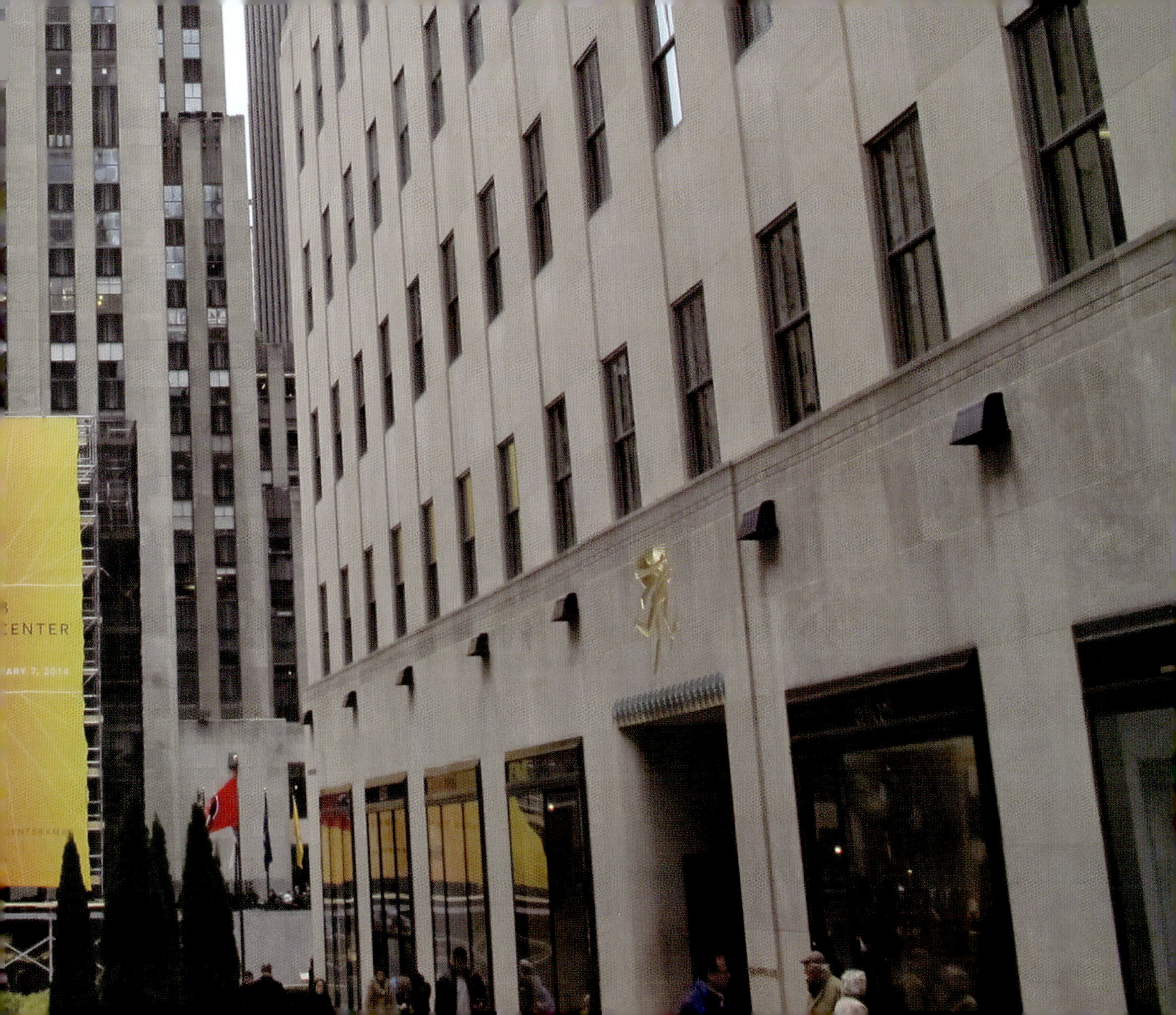

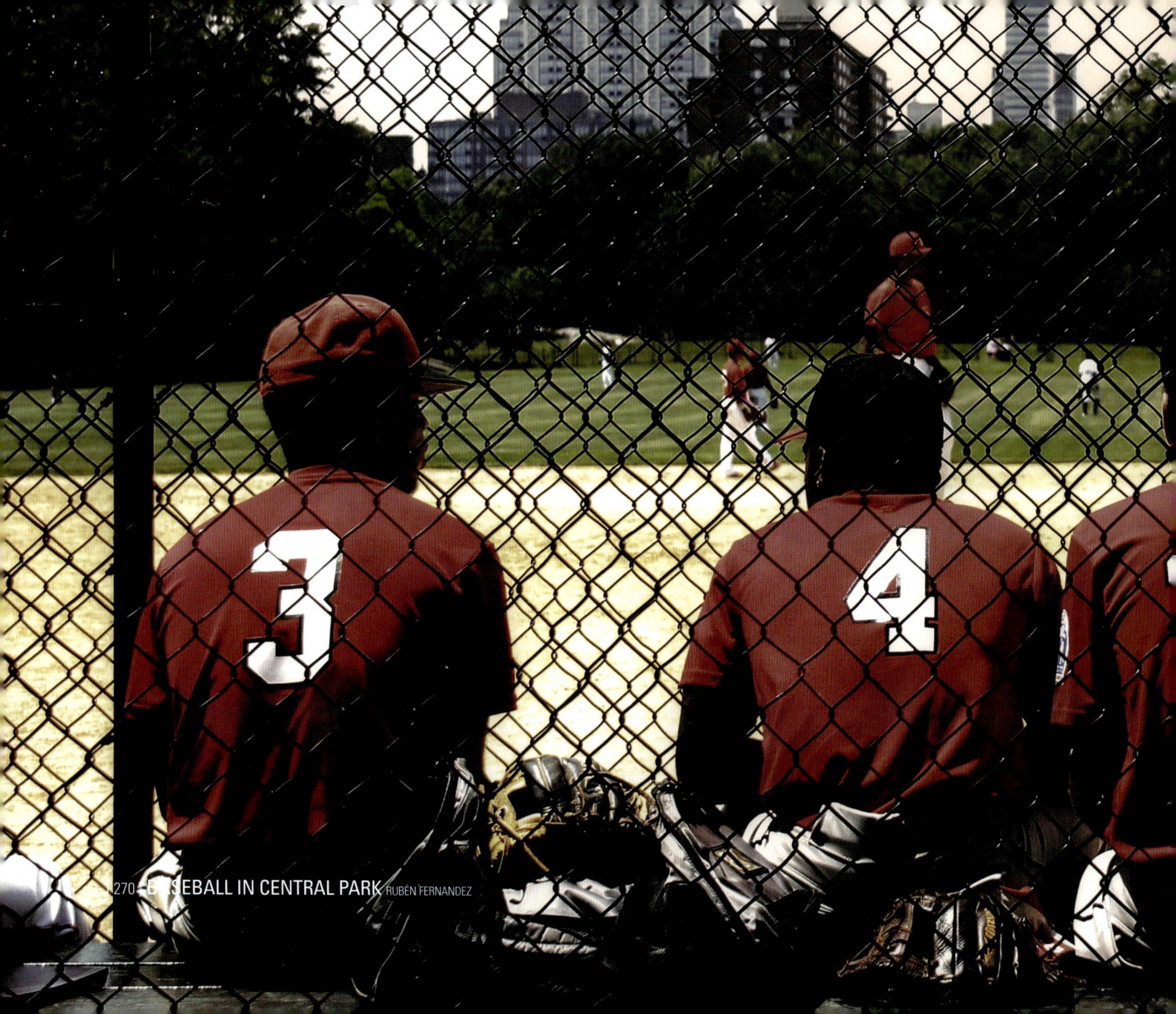

270 BASEBALL IN CENTRAL PARK RUBÉN FERNANDEZ

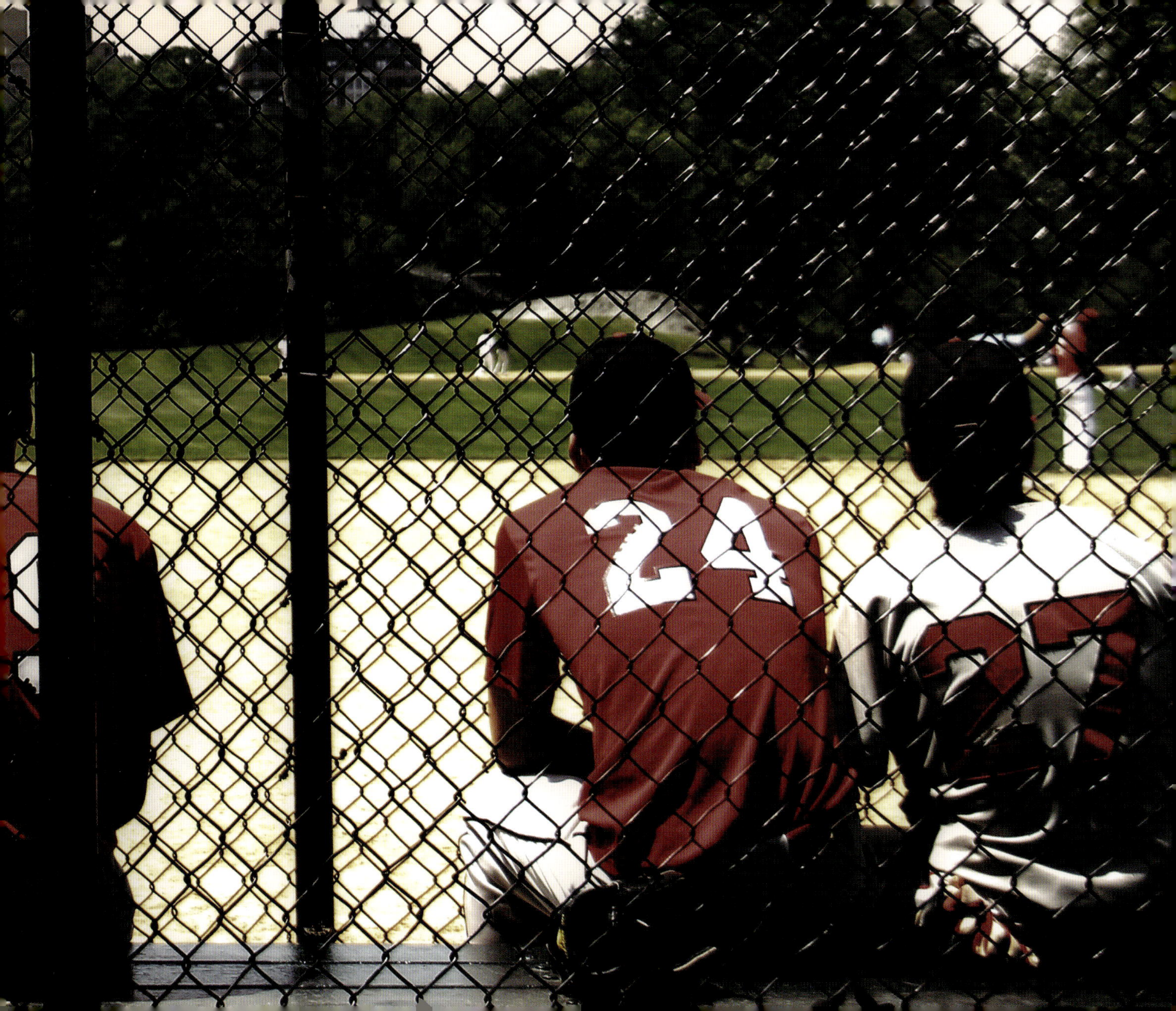
24

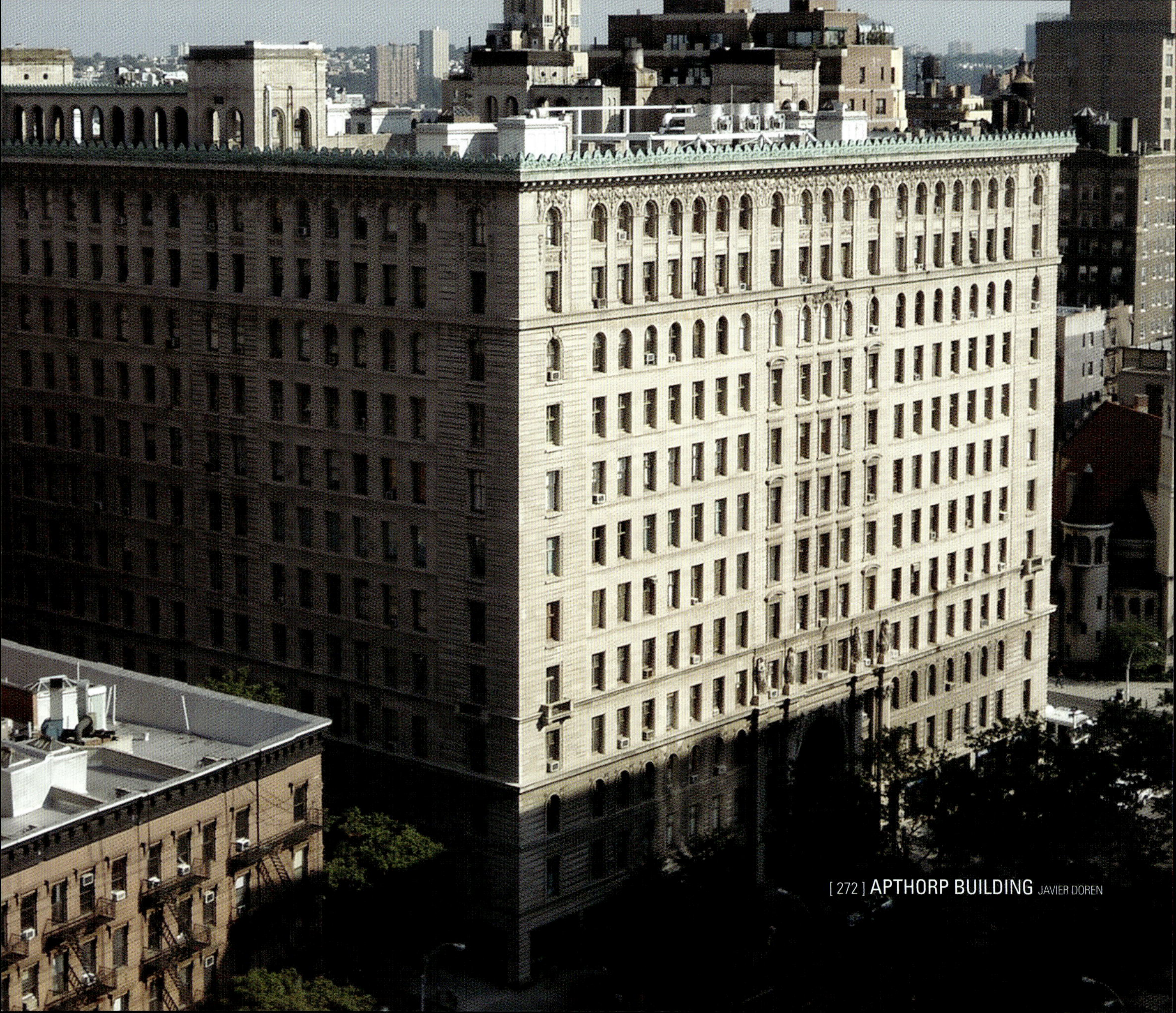

[272] APTHORP BUILDING JAVIER DOREN

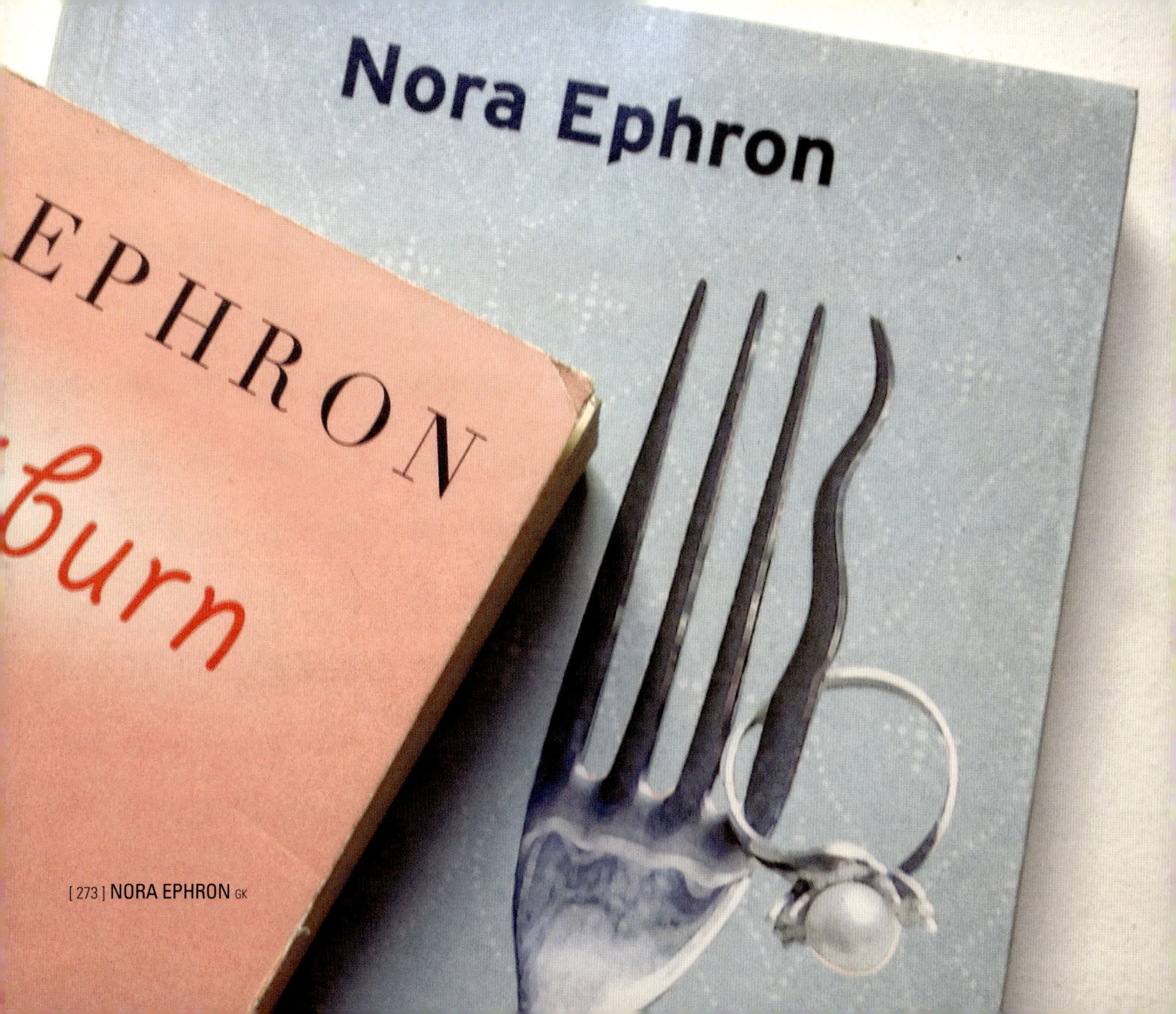

[273] NORA EPHRON GK

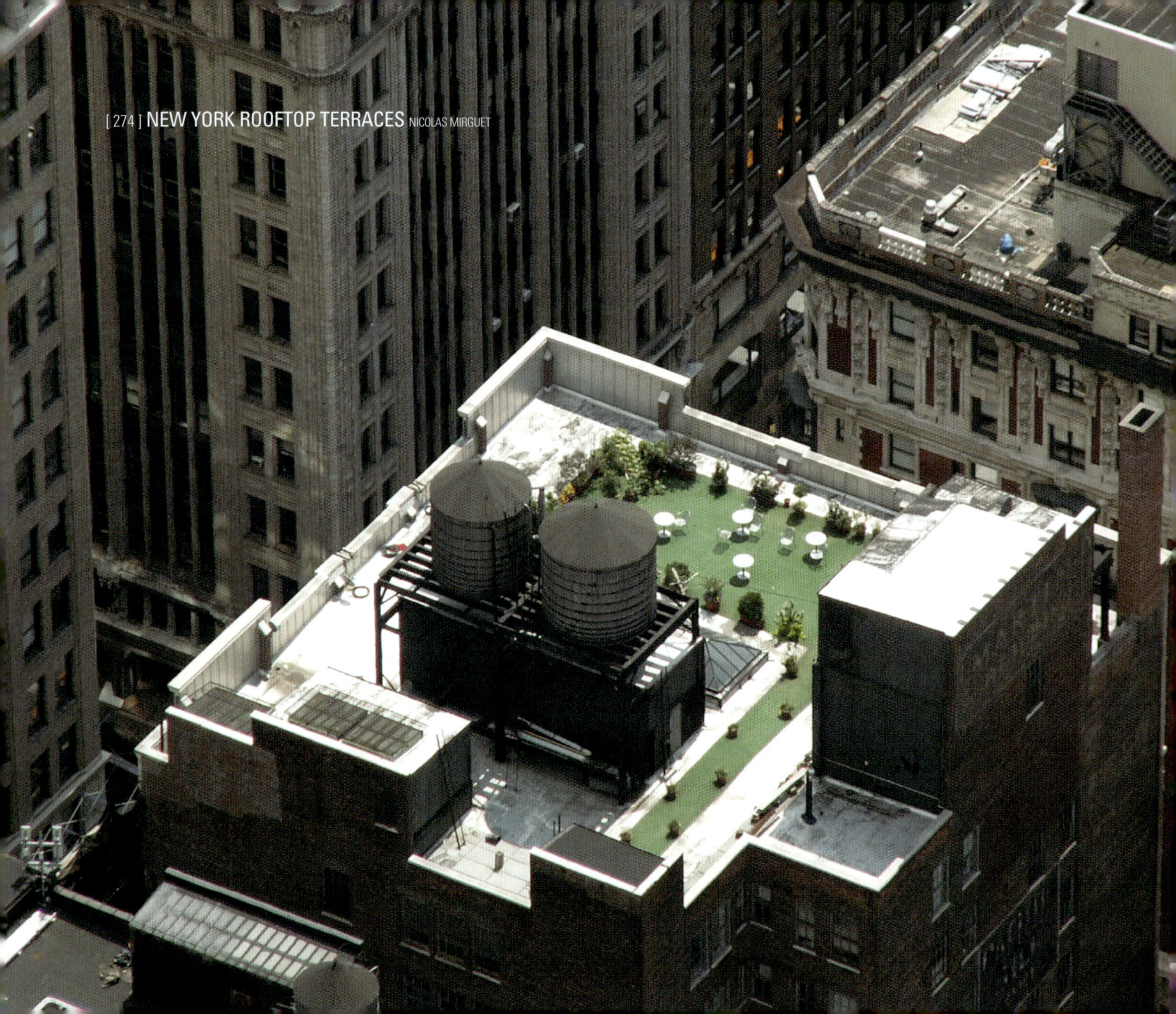

[275] HIGHLINE ANDREW LACHANCE

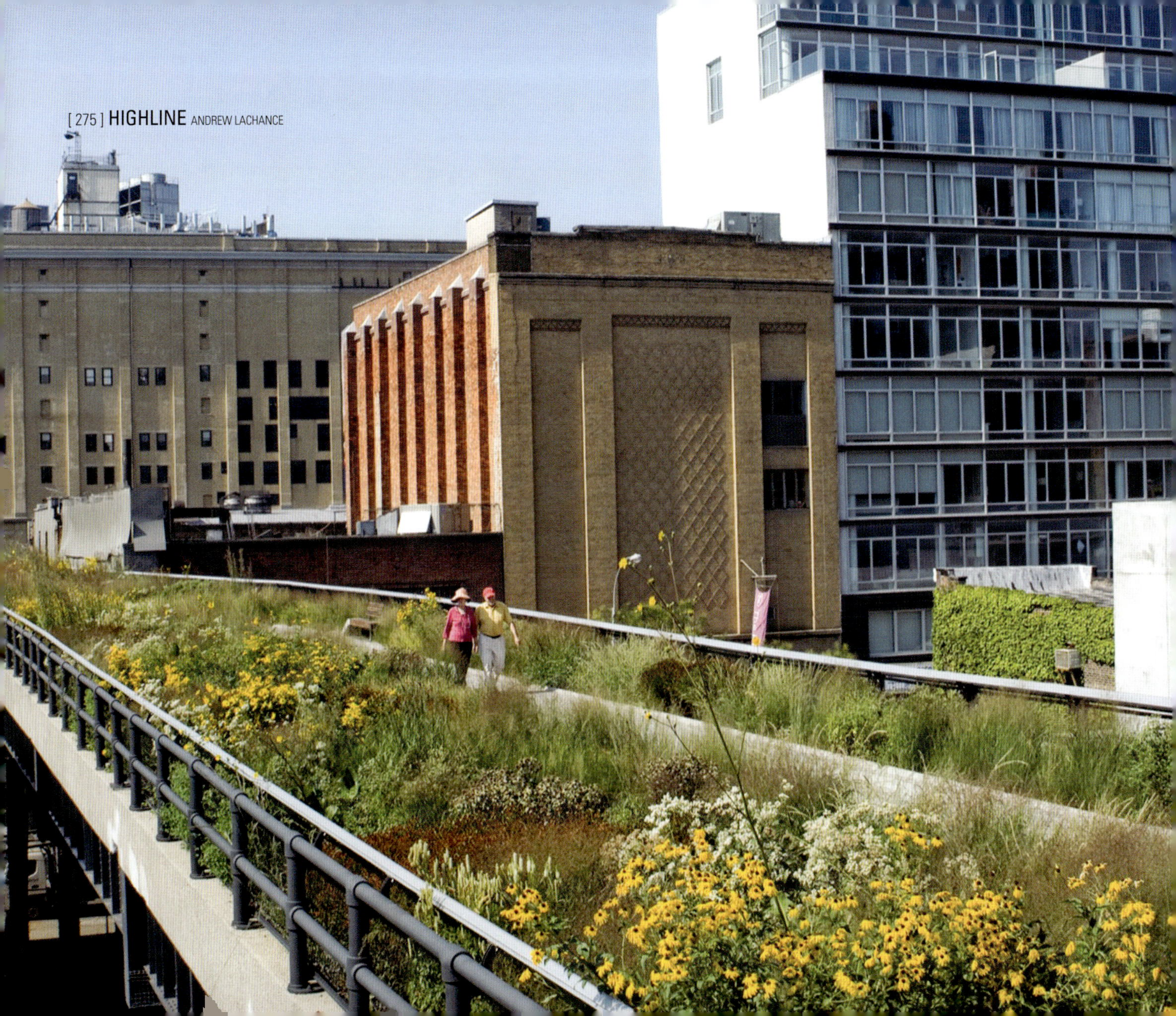

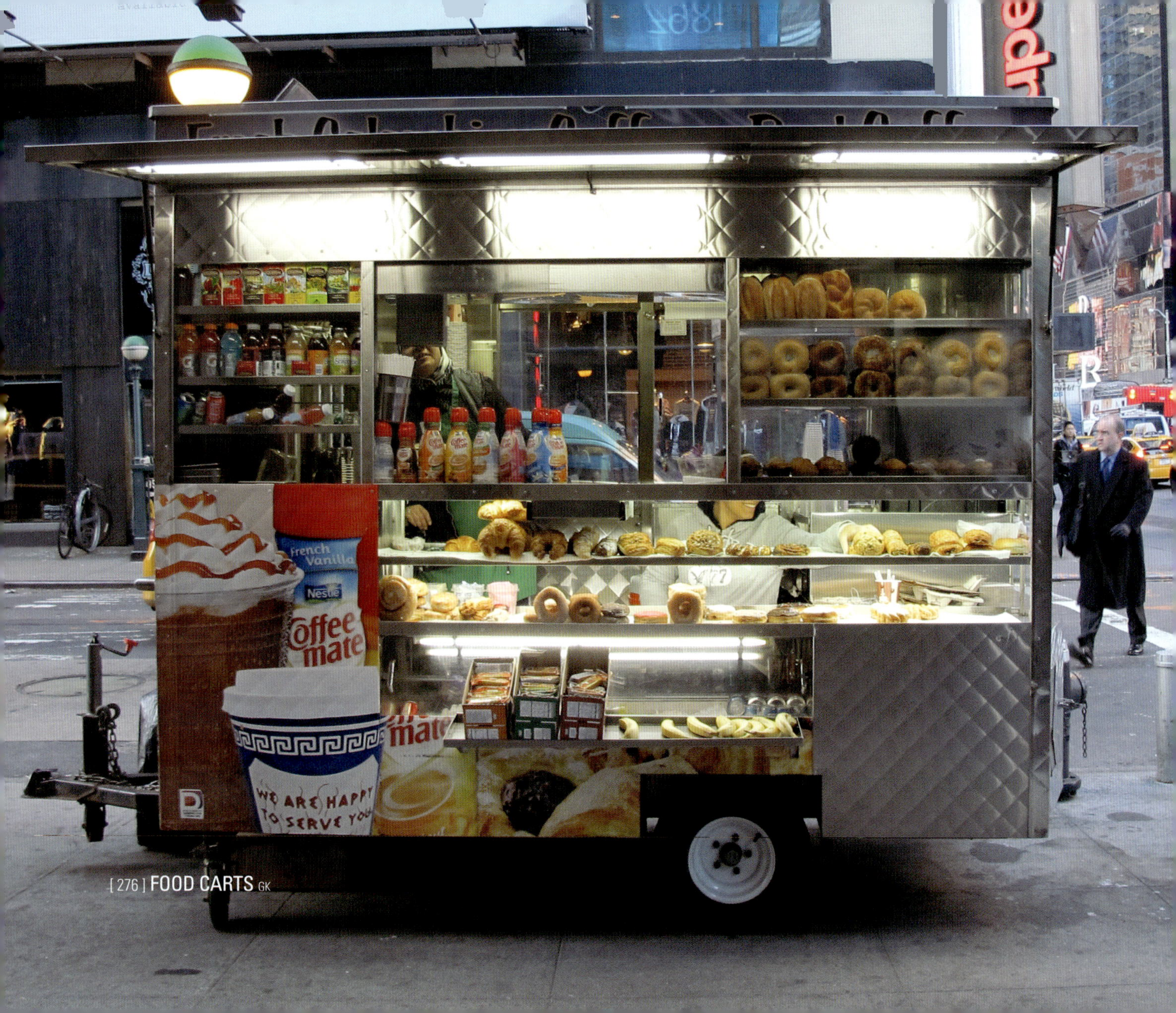

[276] FOOD CARTS GK

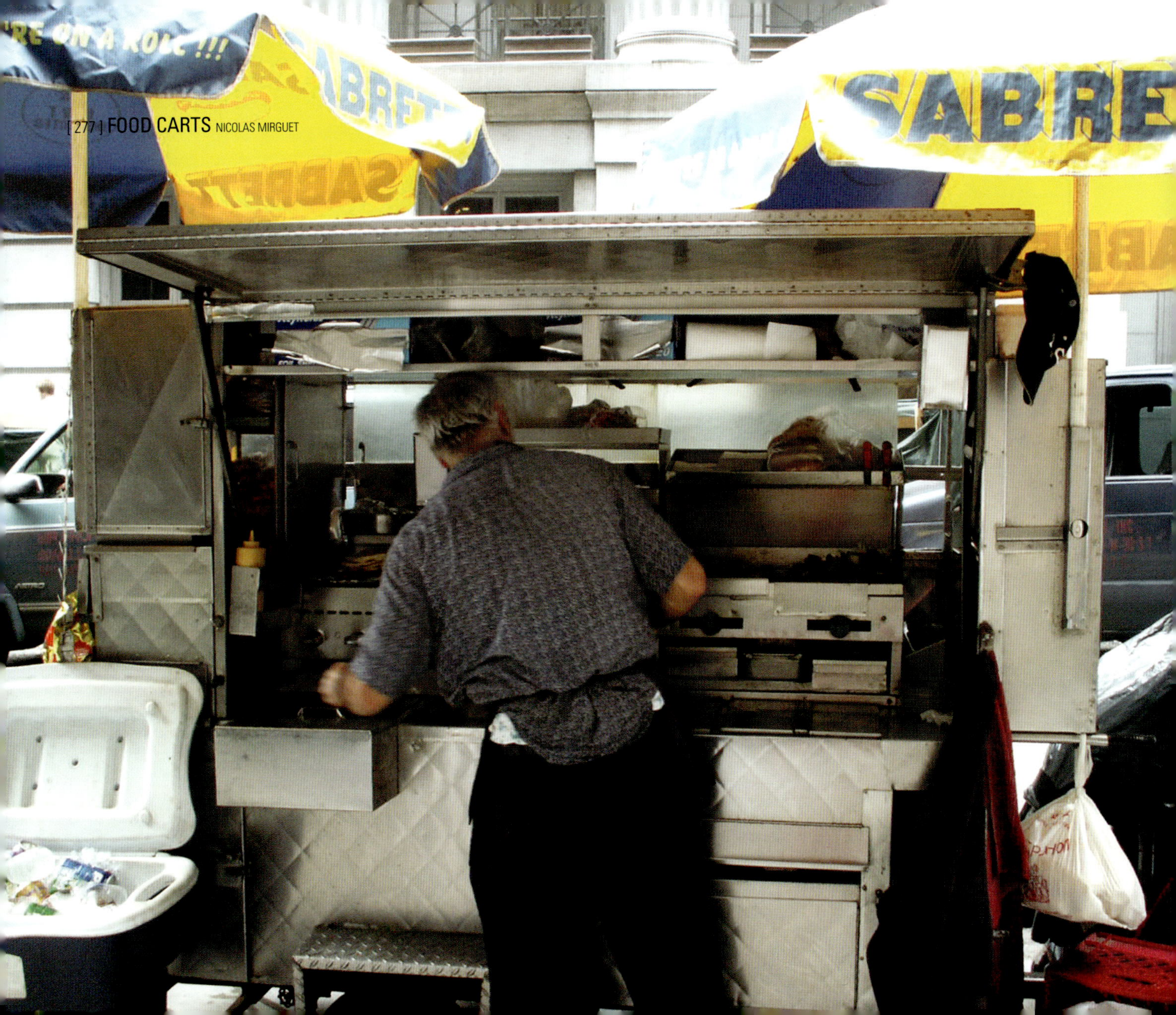
SABRE

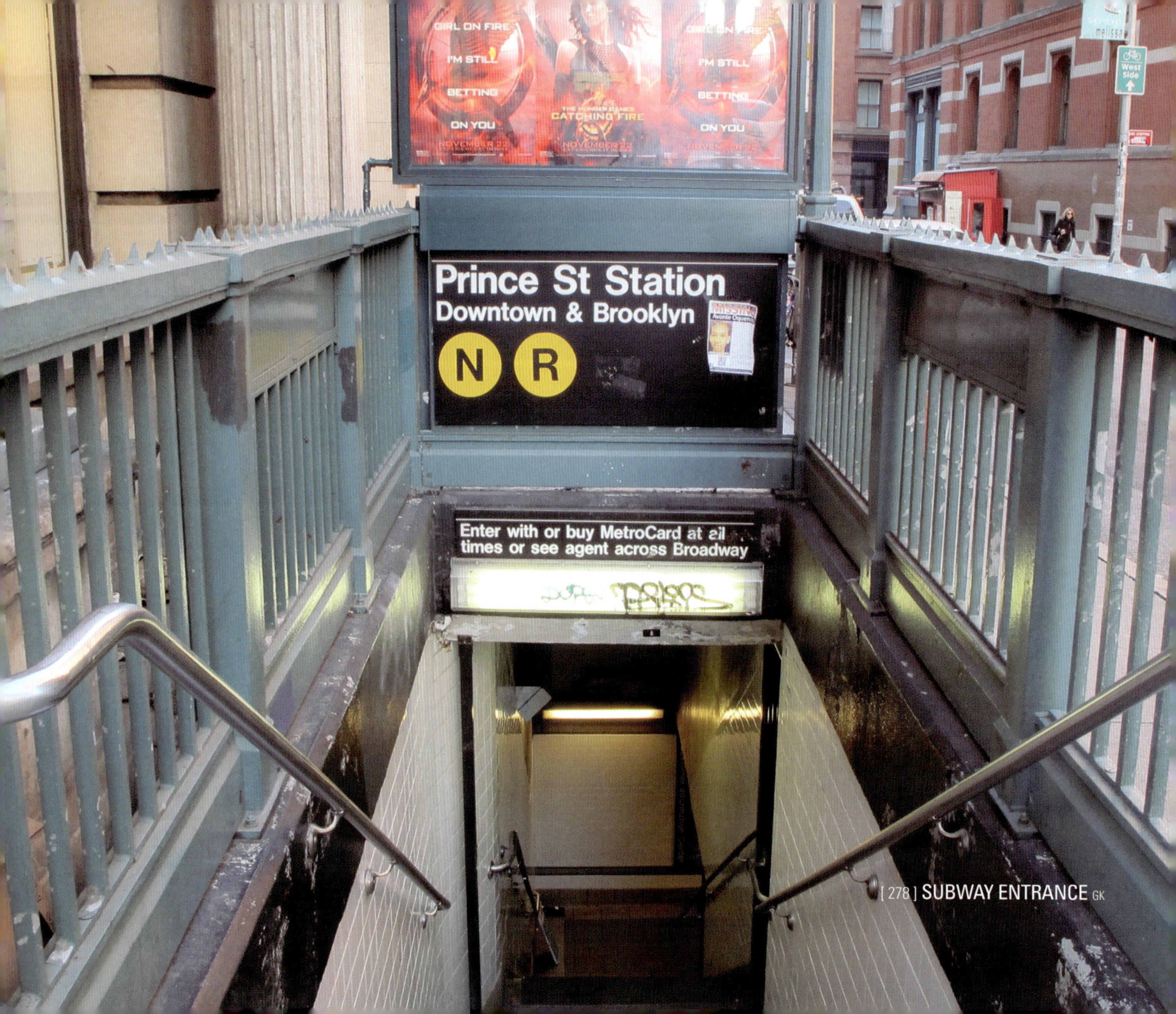

[278] SUBWAY ENTRANCE GK

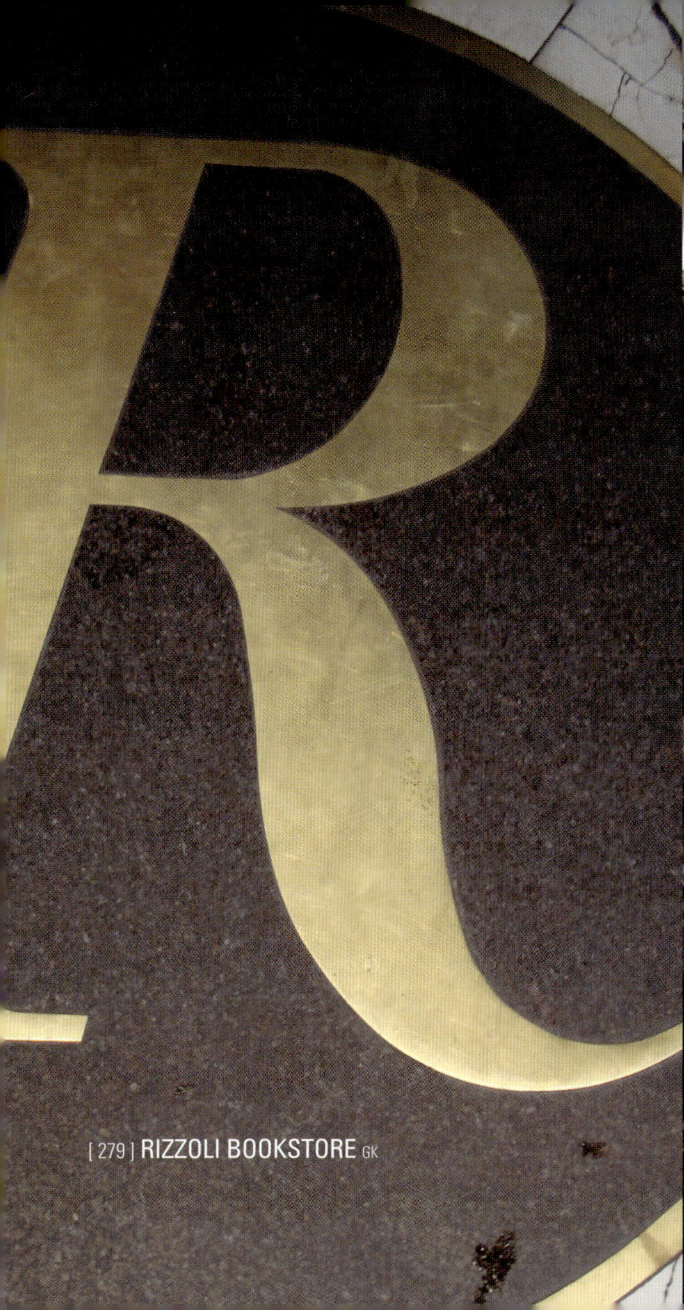

[279] RIZZOLI BOOKSTORE GK

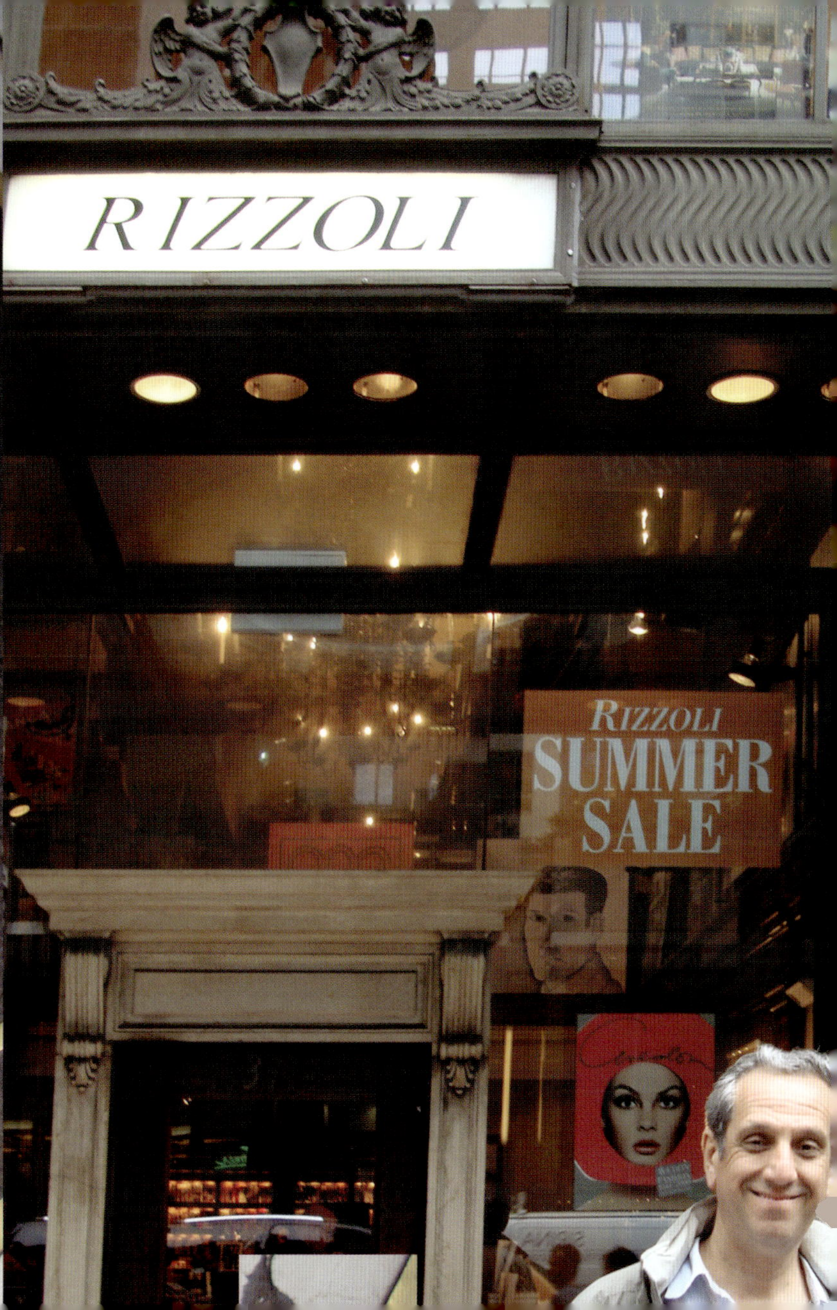

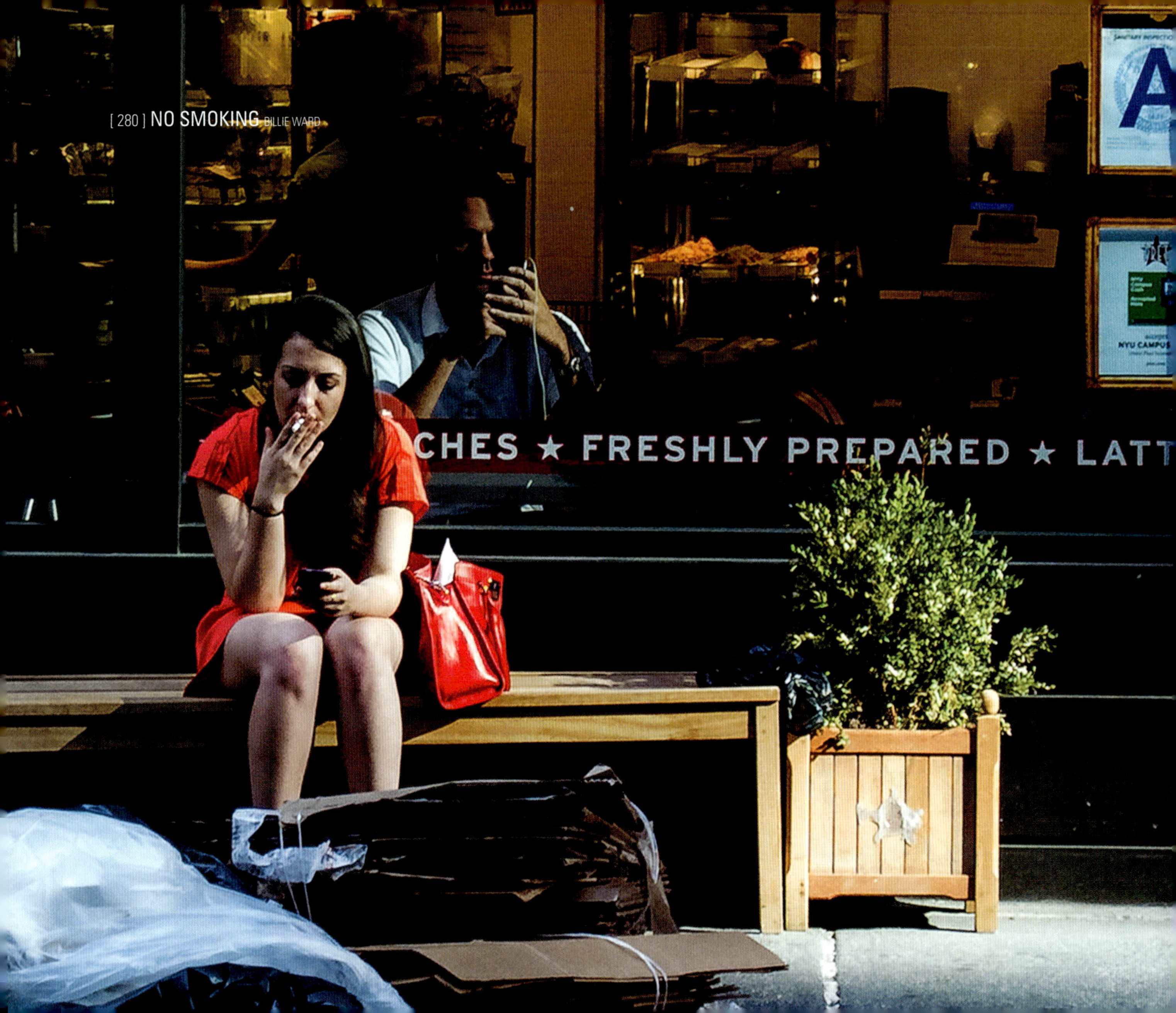

[280] NO SMOKING BILLIE WARD

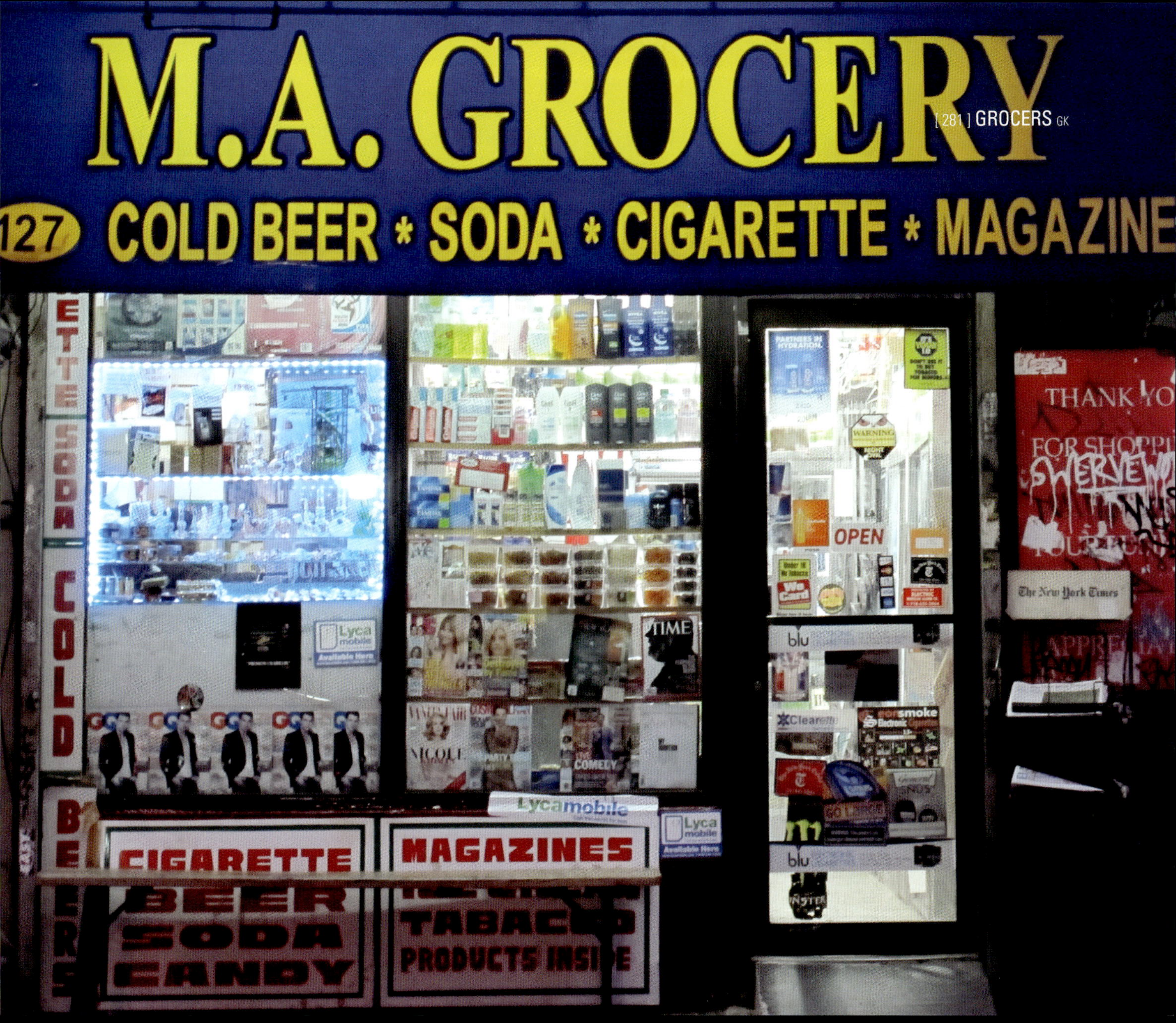
M.A. GROCERY
127
COLD BEER * SODA * CIGARETTE * MAGAZINE
OPEN
TIME
Lycamobile
CIGARETTE
MAGAZINES
BEER
SODA
CANDY
The New York Times

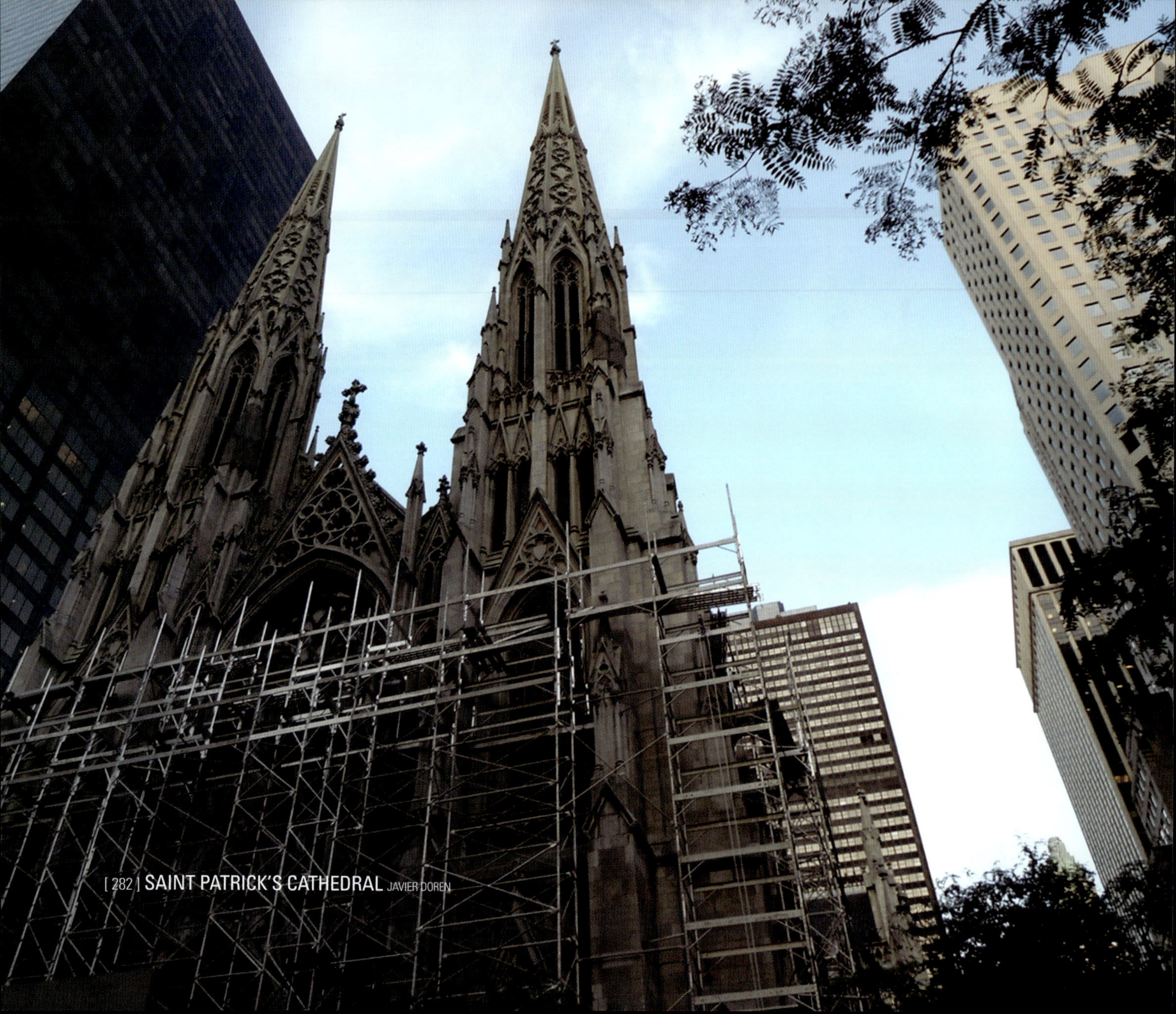

[282] SAINT PATRICK'S CATHEDRAL JAVIER DOREN

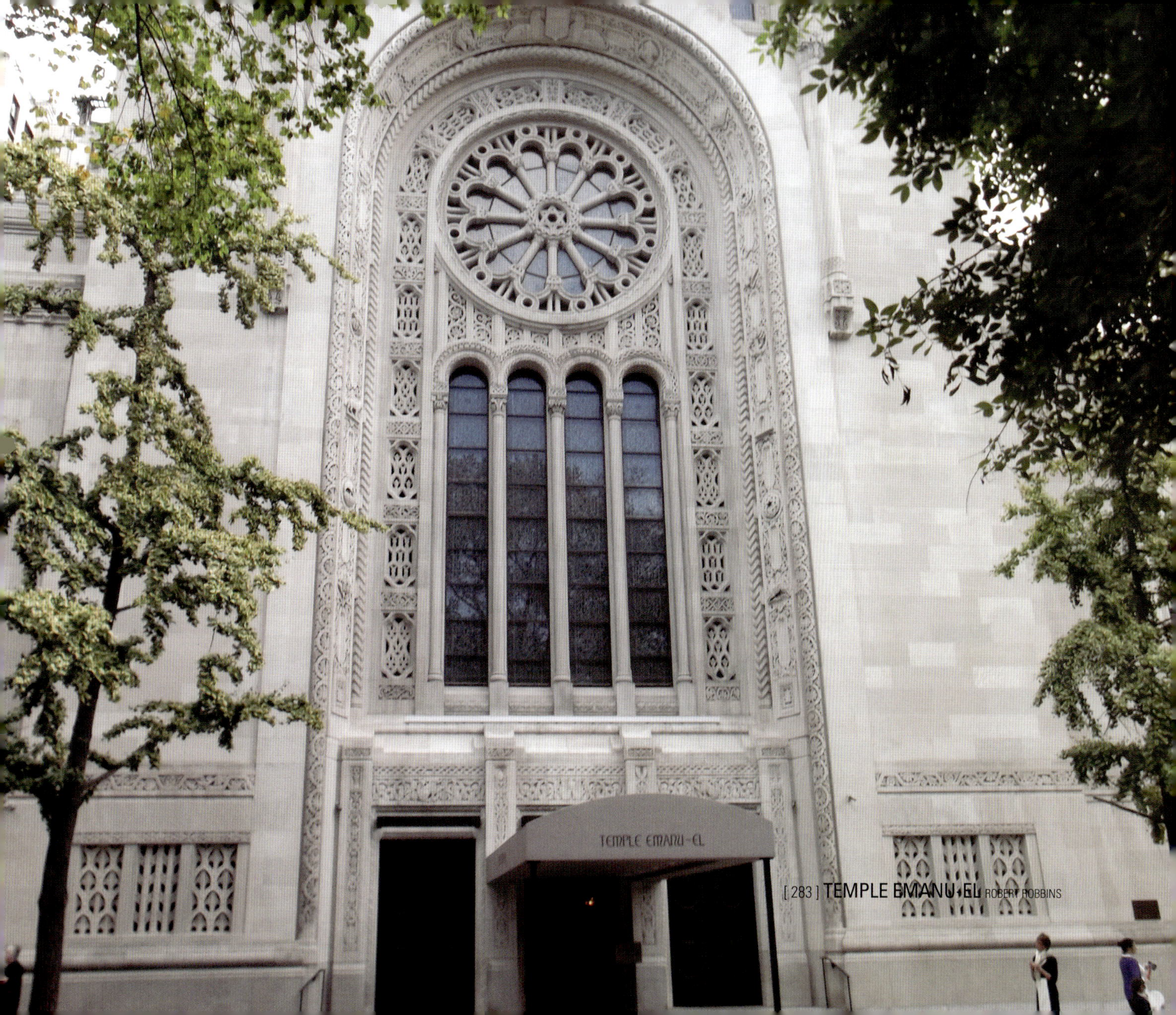

[283] TEMPLE EMANU-EL ROBERT ROBBINS

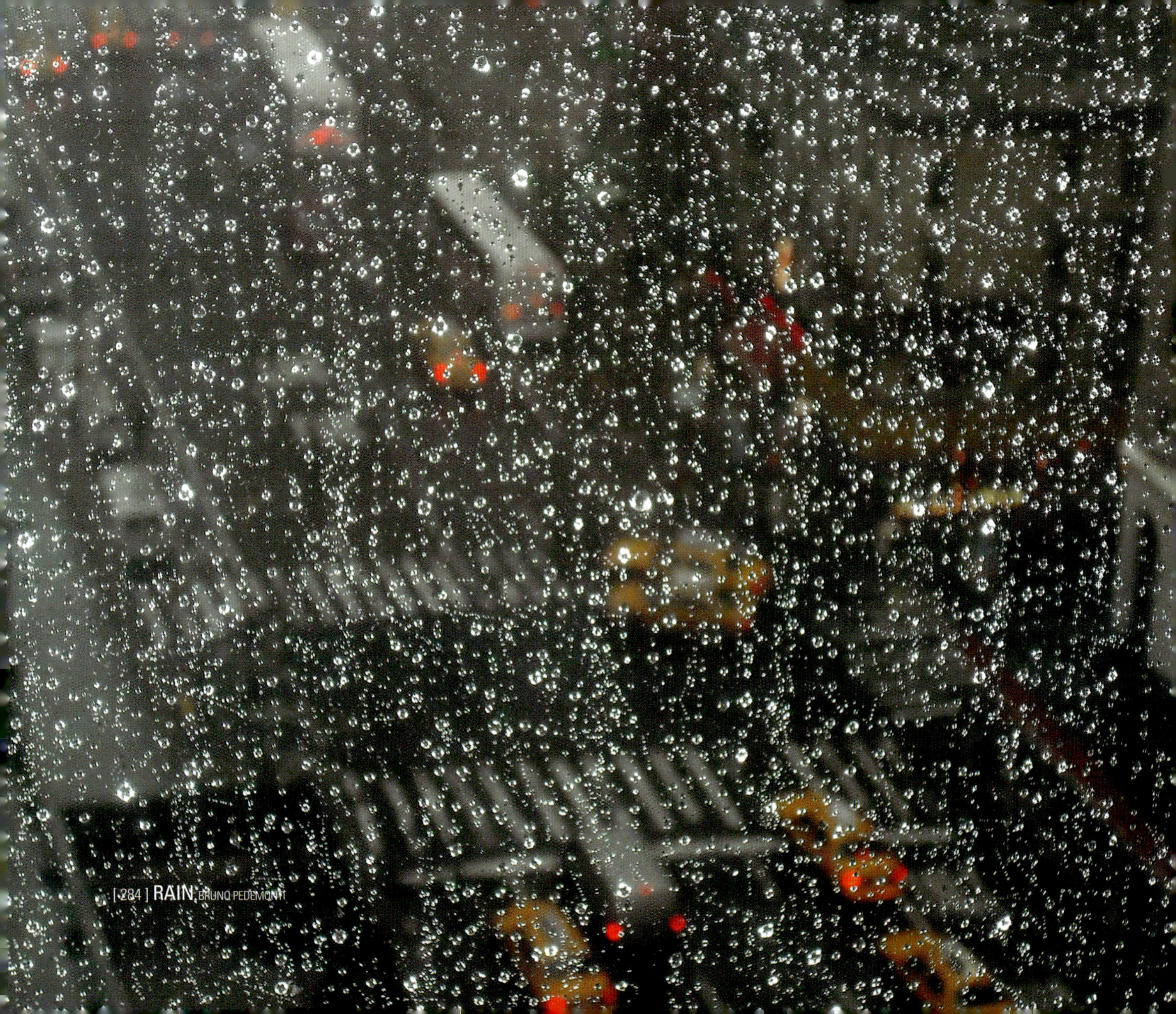

[284] RAIN, BRUNO PEDEMONTI

[285] MACY'S MO RIZA

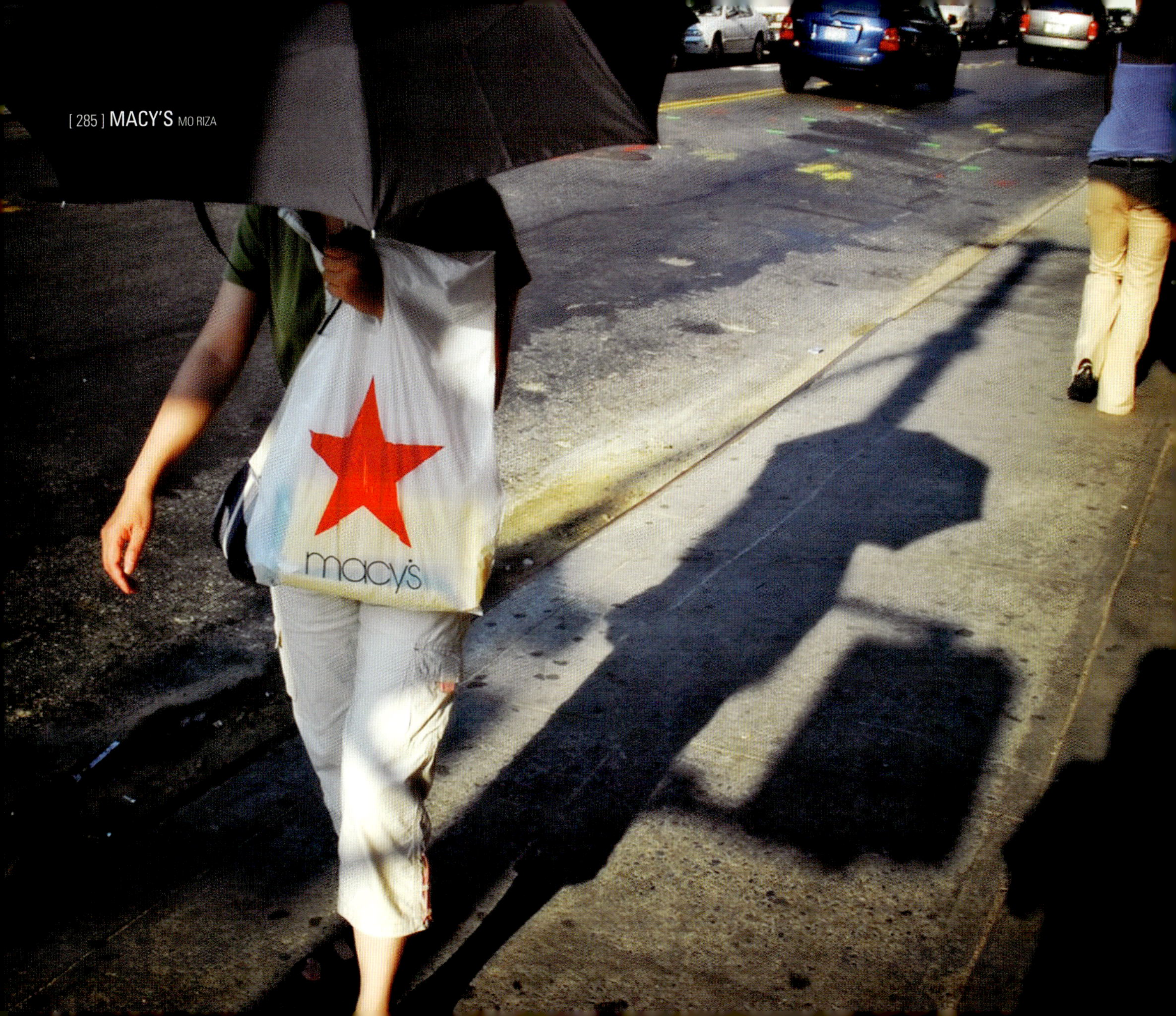

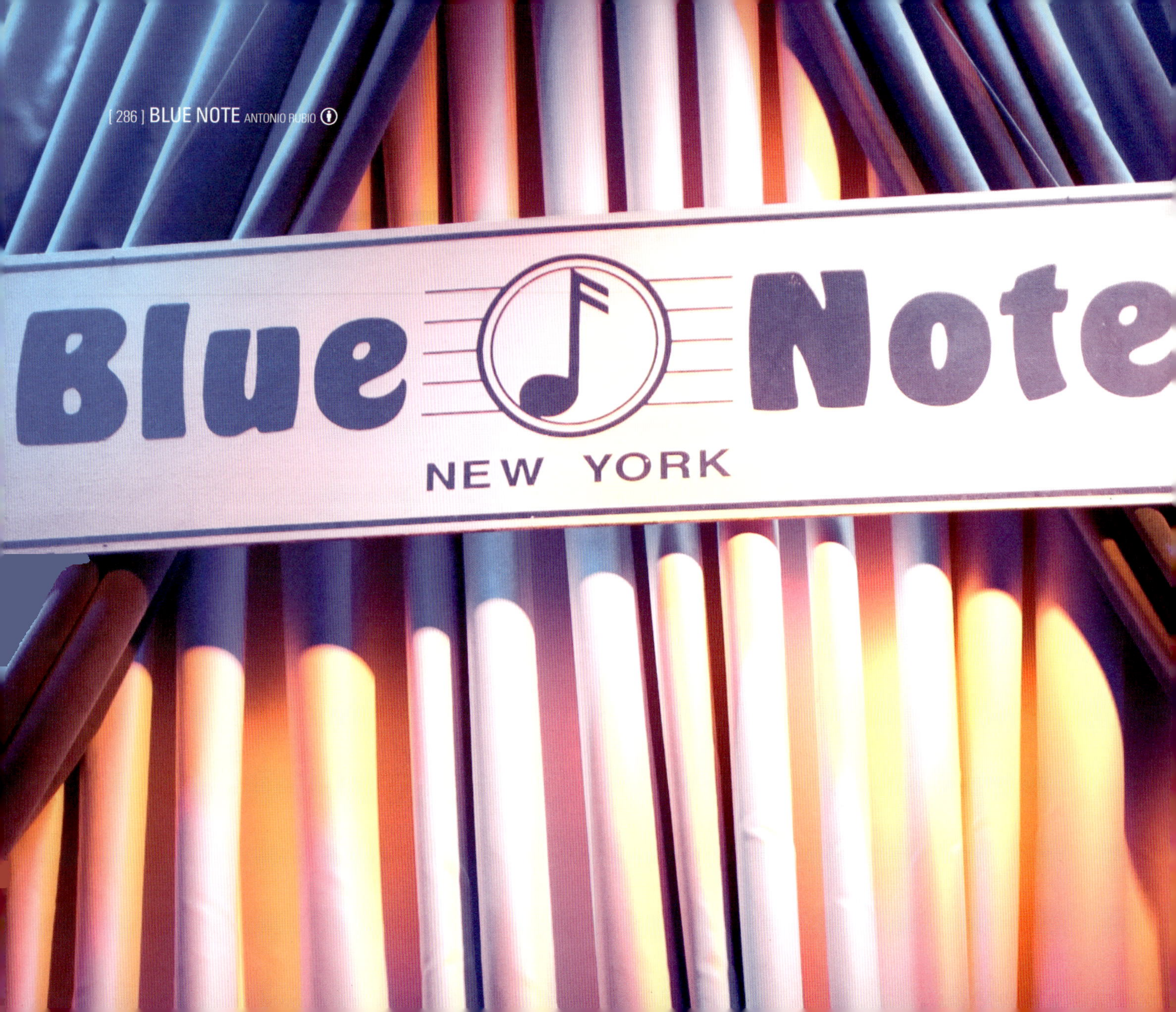
Blue Note
NEW YORK

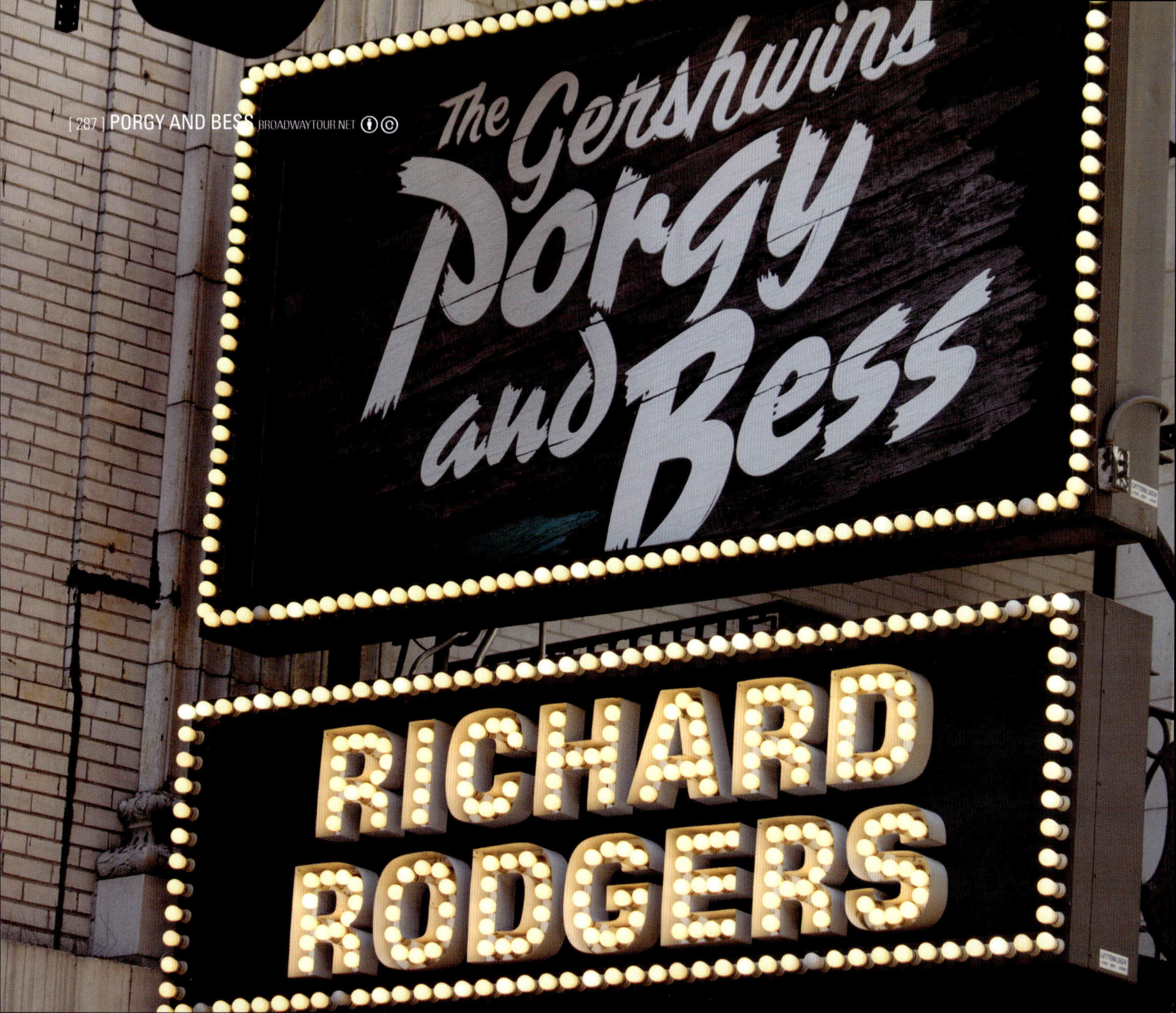

[287] PORGY AND BESS BROADWAYTOUR.NET

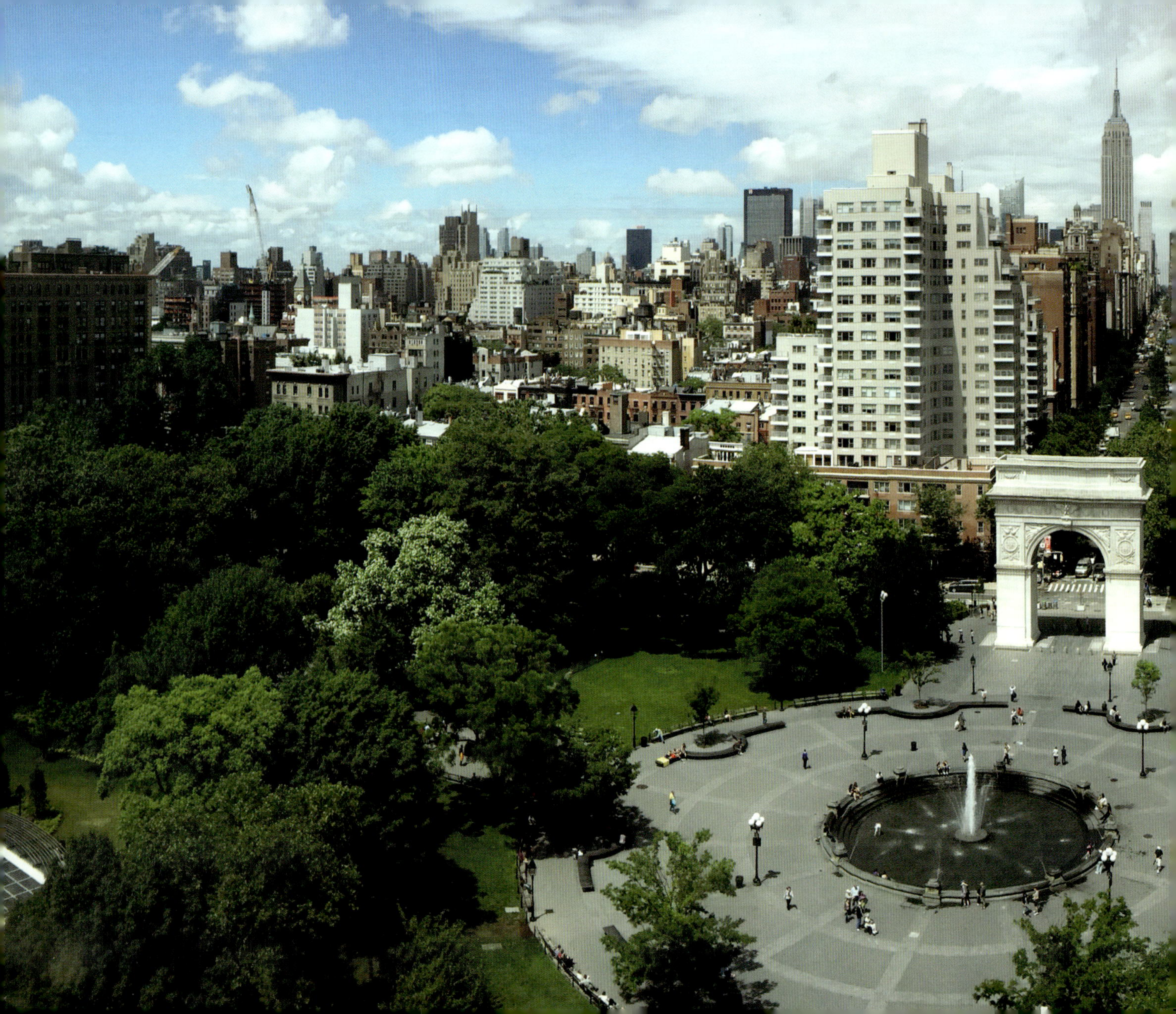

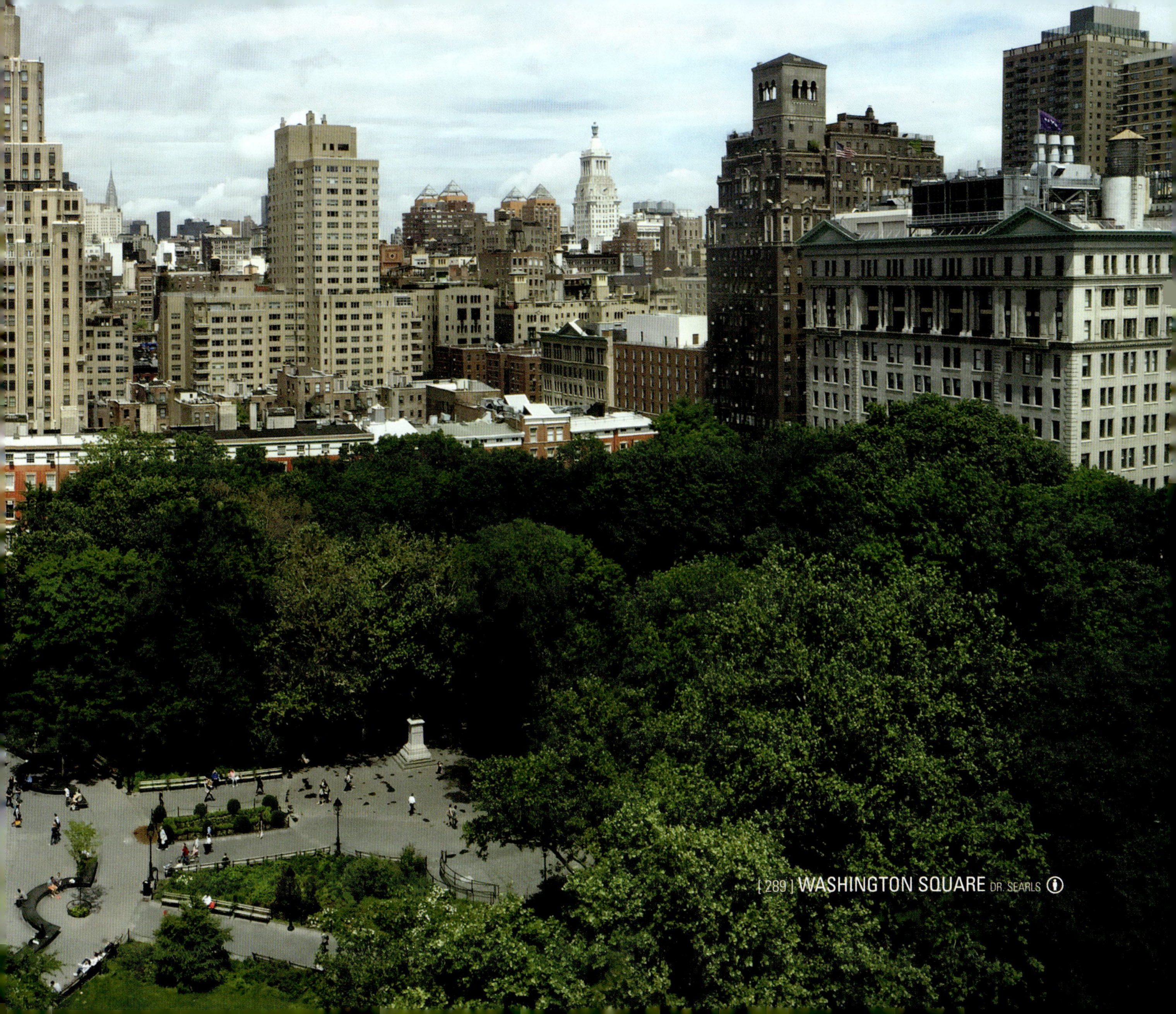

[289] WASHINGTON SQUARE DR. SEARLS ⓘ

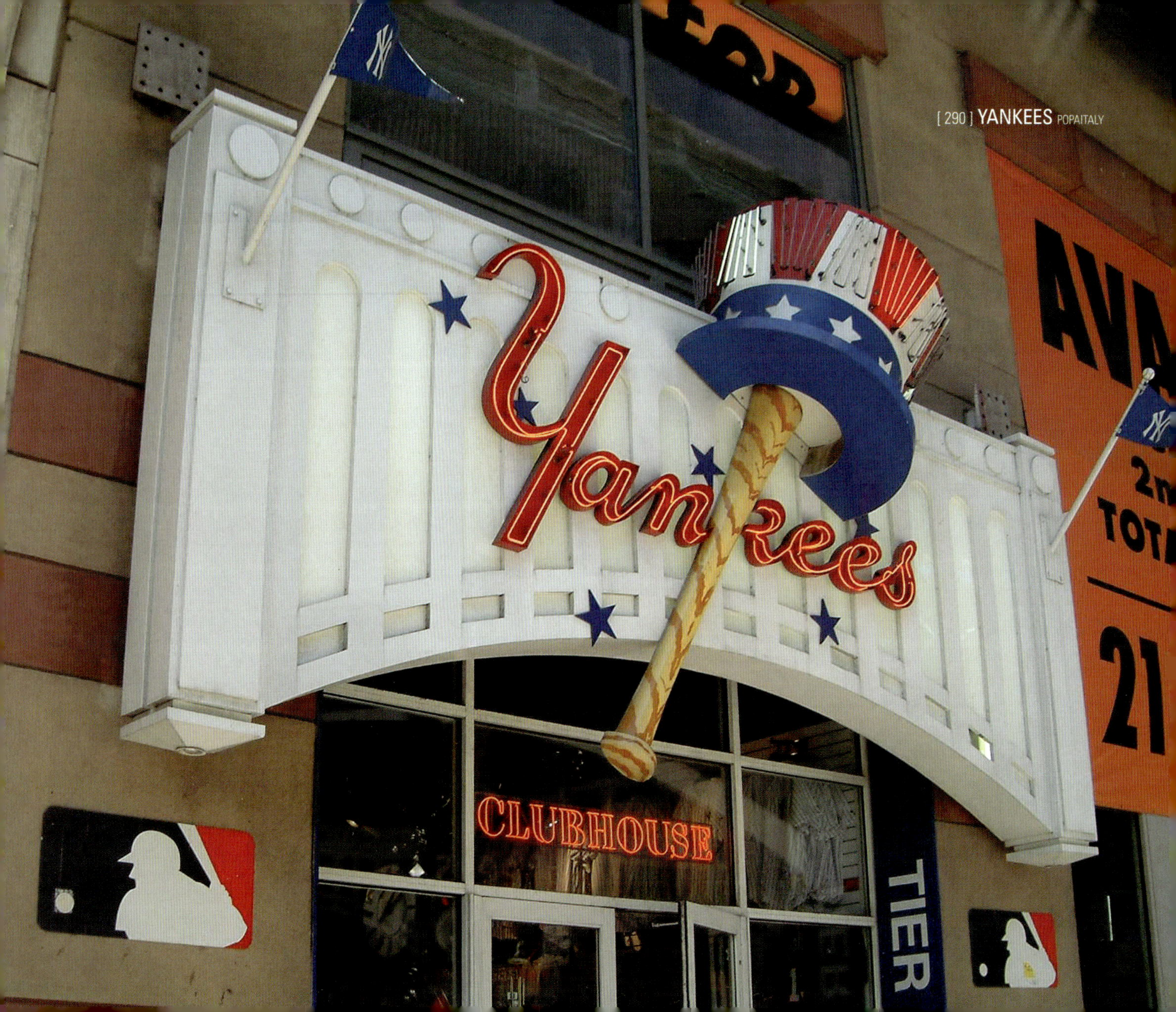
Yankees
CLUBHOUSE
TIER

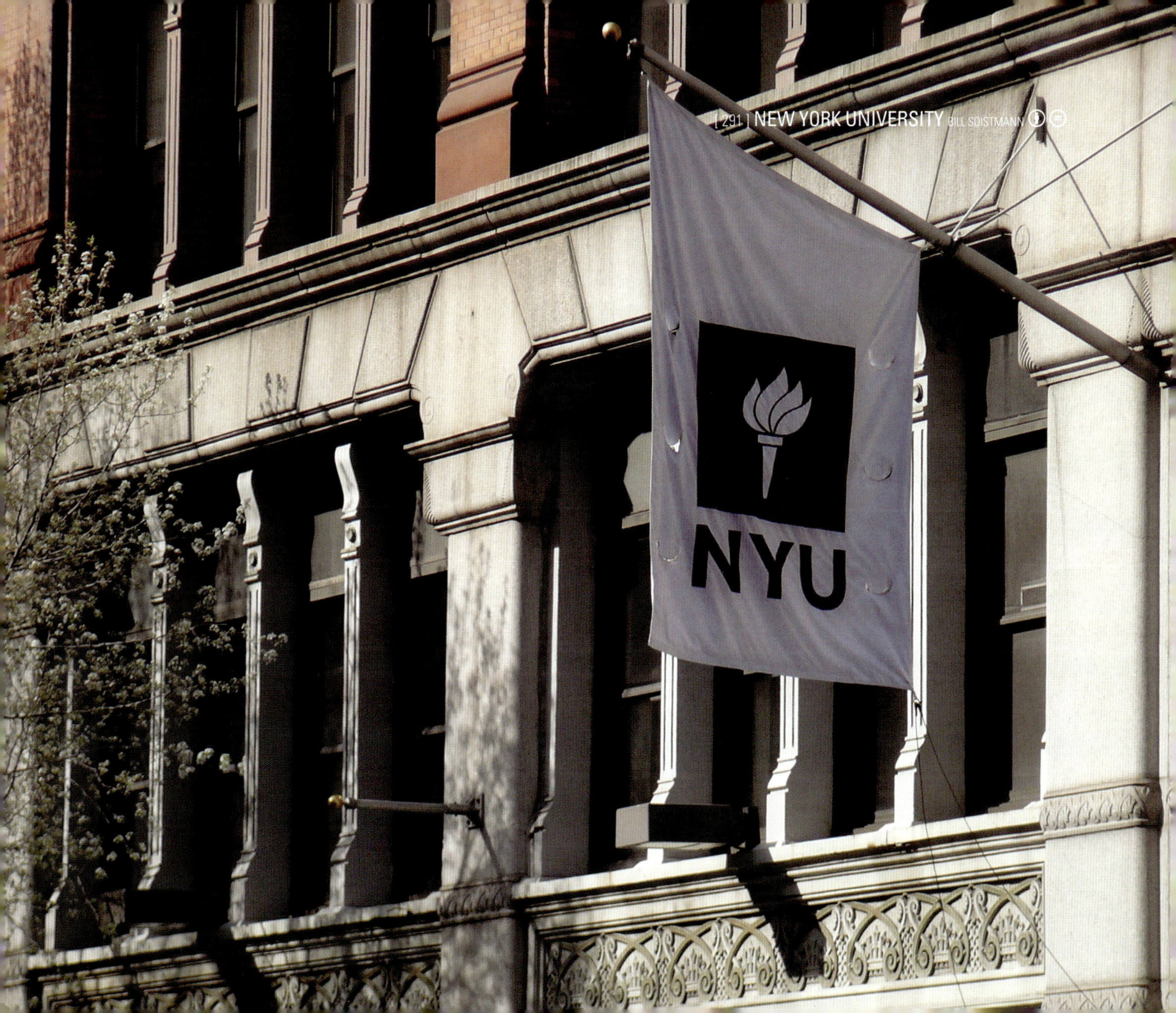

[291] NEW YORK UNIVERSITY BILL SOISTMANN

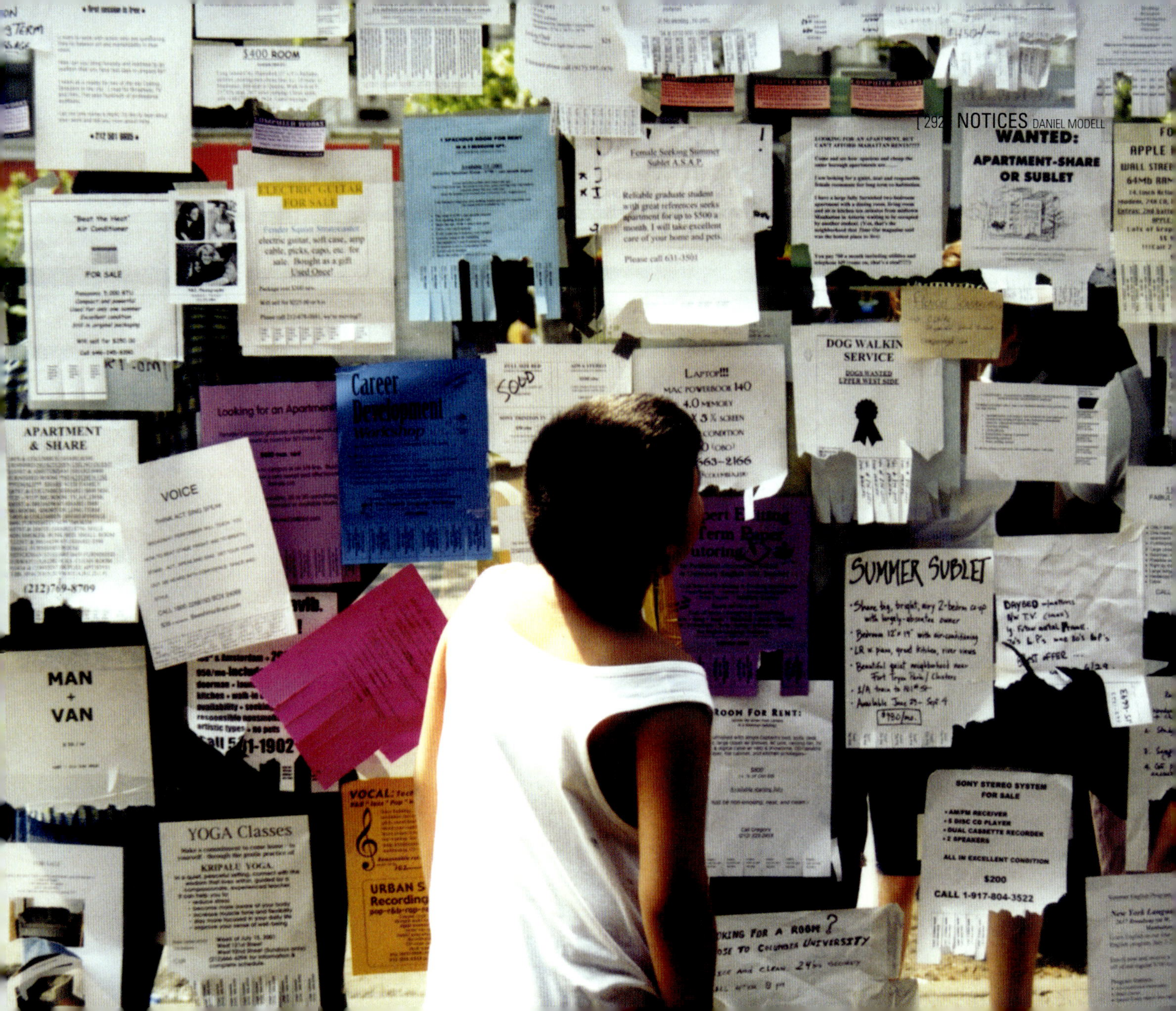
$400 ROOM
ELECTRIC GUITAR FOR SALE
Female Seeking Summer Sublet A.S.A.P.
Reliable graduate student with great references seeks apartment for up to $500 a month. I will take excellent care of your home and pets.
Please call 631-3501
WANTED:
APARTMENT-SHARE OR SUBLET
"Beat the Heat" Air Conditioner
FOR SALE
Career Development Workshop
Looking for an Apartment
SOLD
LAPTOP!!!
MAC POWERBOOK 140
DOG WALKING SERVICE
APARTMENT & SHARE
(212)769-8709
VOICE
SUMMER SUBLET
MAN + VAN
ROOM FOR RENT:
SONY STEREO SYSTEM FOR SALE
$200
CALL 1-917-804-3522
YOGA Classes
KRIPALE YOGA
VOCAL
URBAN S
Recording
LOOKING FOR A ROOM?
CLOSE TO COLUMBIA UNIVERSITY

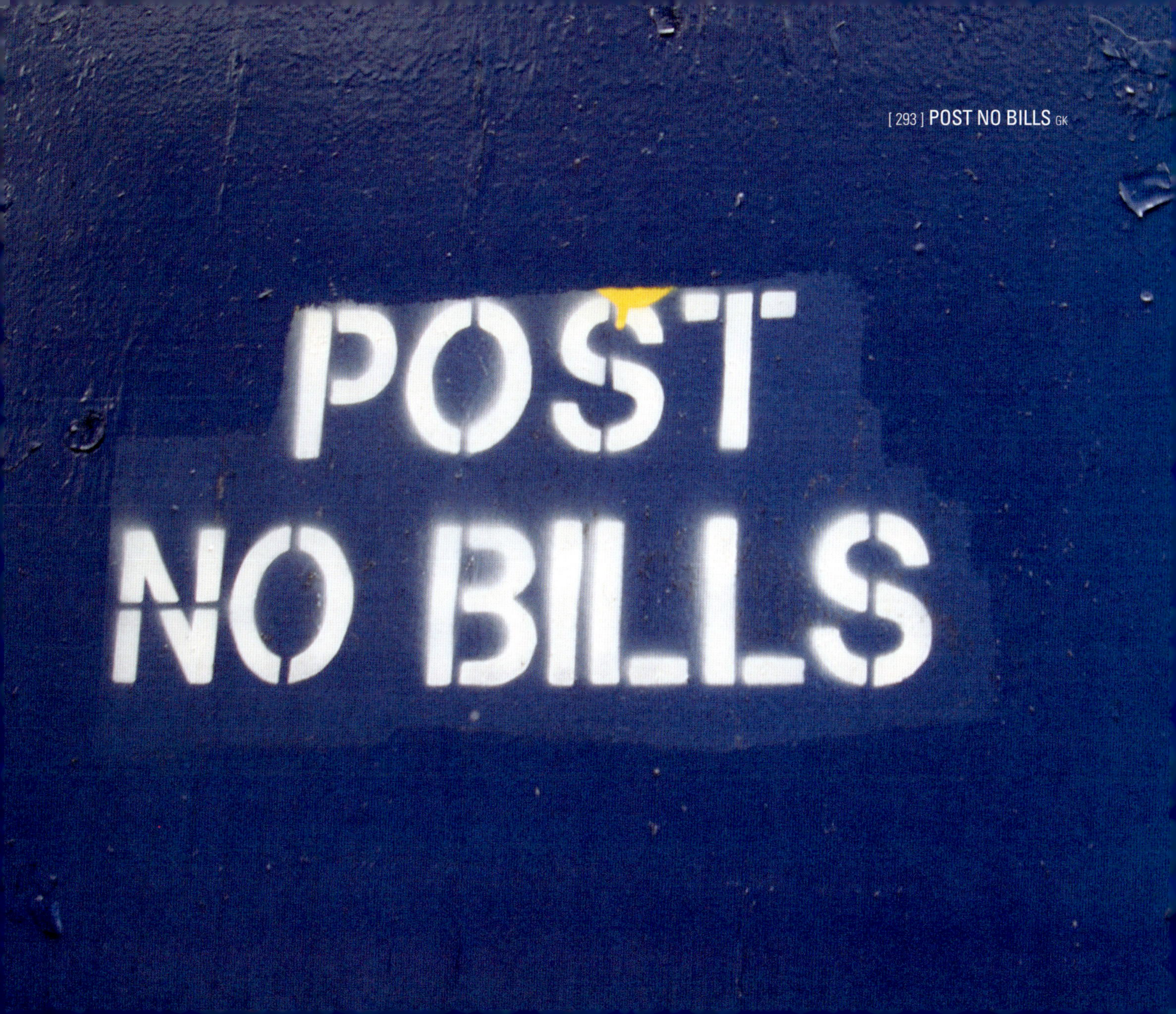

[293] POST NO BILLS GK

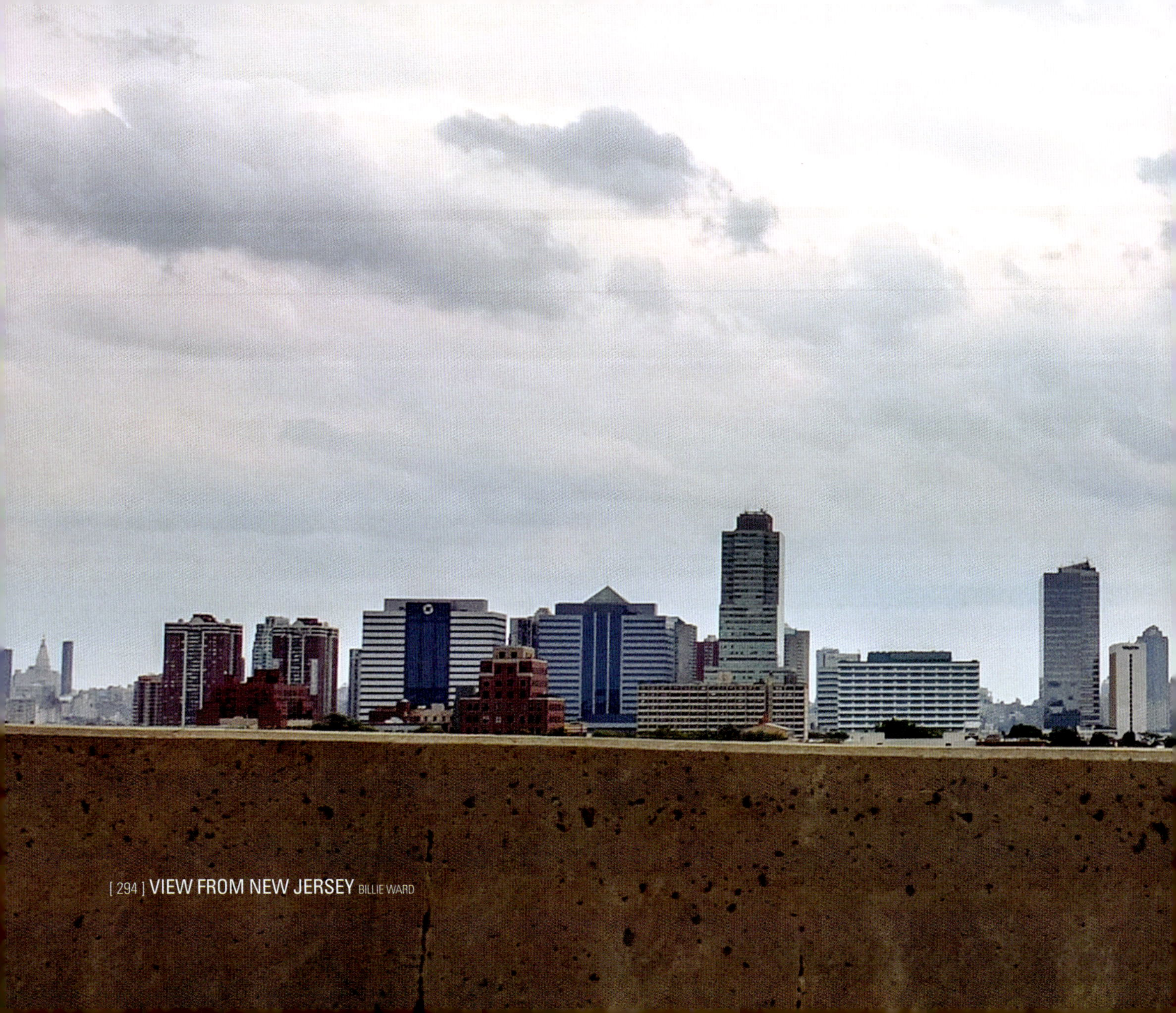

[294] VIEW FROM NEW JERSEY BILLIE WARD

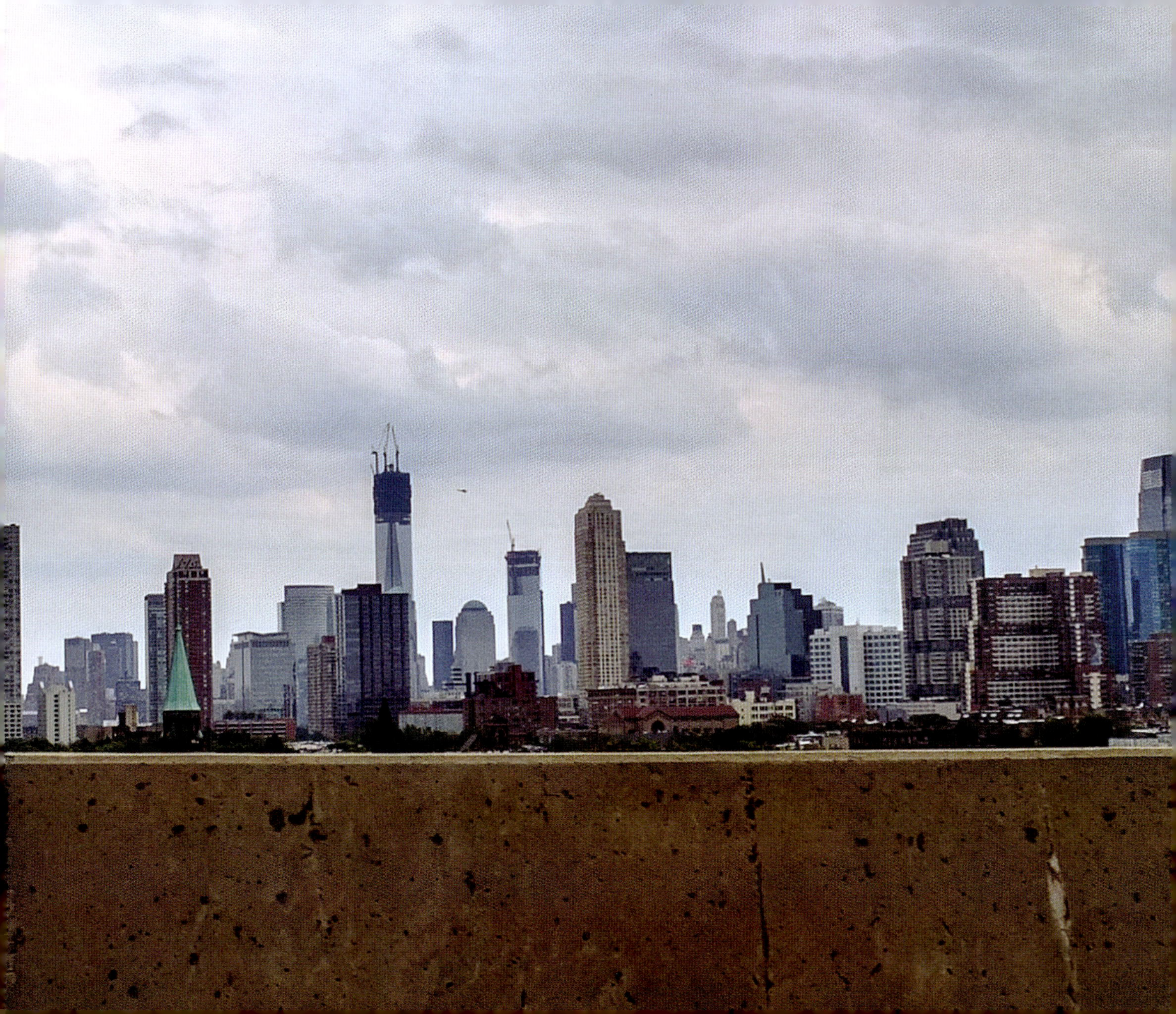

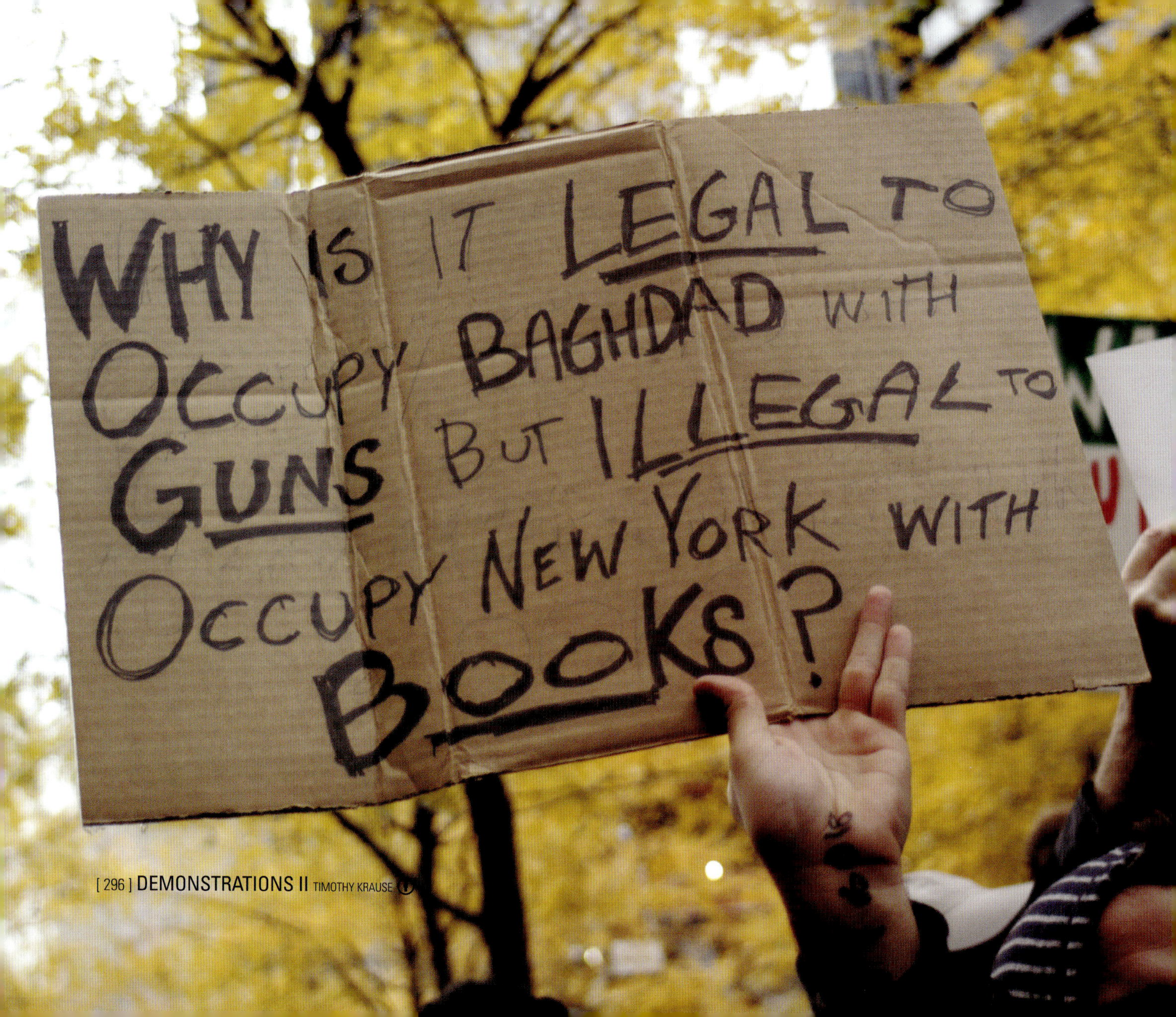
WHY IS IT LEGAL TO
OCCUPY BAGHDAD WITH
GUNS BUT ILLEGAL TO
OCCUPY NEW YORK WITH
BOOKS?

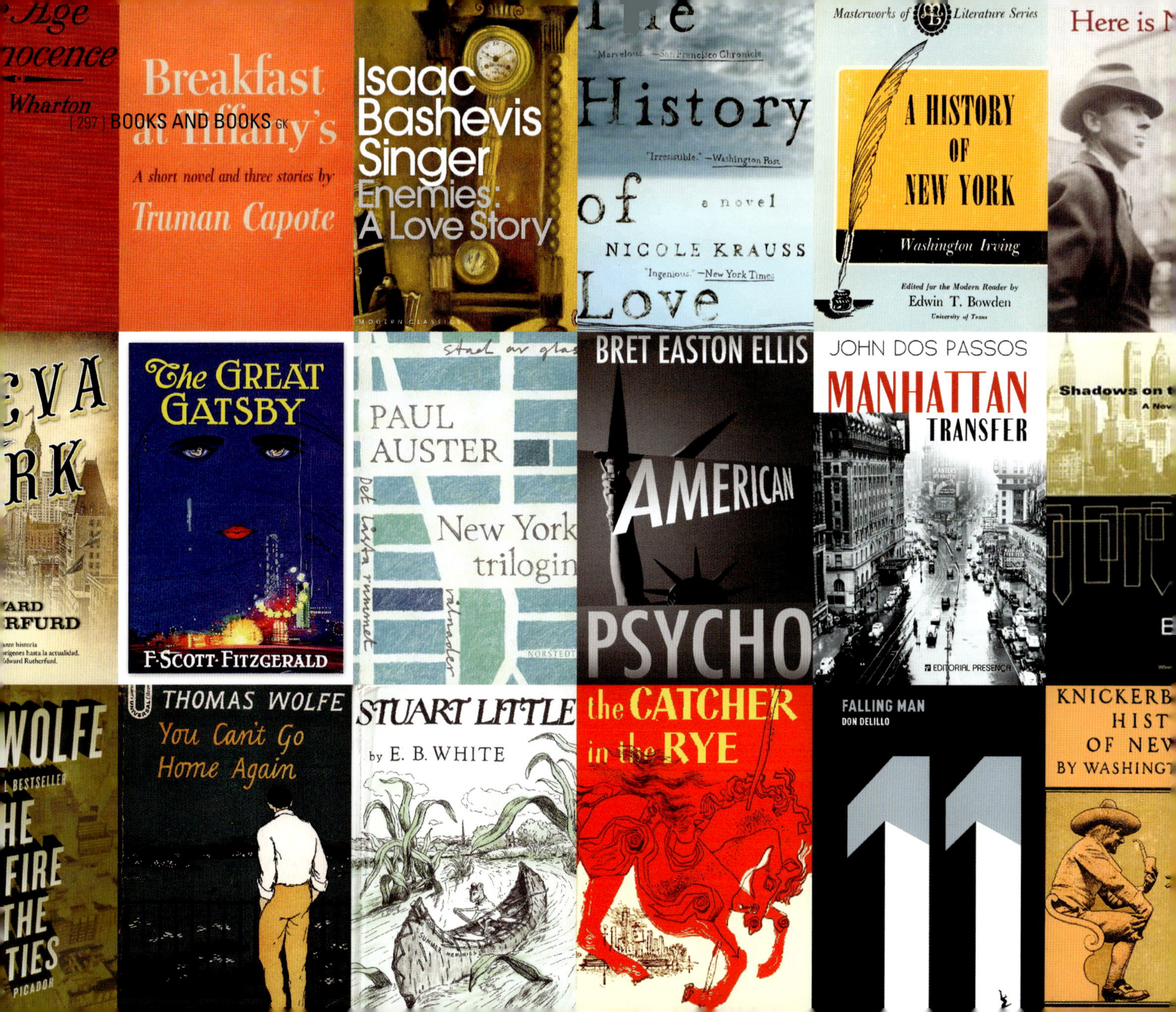
Wharton
Breakfast at Tiffany's
A short novel and three stories by
Truman Capote
Isaac Bashevis Singer
Enemies: A Love Story
The History of Love
"Marvelous." —San Francisco Chronicle
"Irresistible." —Washington Post
a novel
NICOLE KRAUSS
"Ingenious." —New York Times
Masterworks of Literature Series
A HISTORY OF NEW YORK
Washington Irving
Edited for the Modern Reader by
Edwin T. Bowden
University of Texas
Here is
The GREAT GATSBY
F·SCOTT·FITZGERALD
PAUL AUSTER
New York trilogin
NORSTEDTS
BRET EASTON ELLIS
AMERICAN PSYCHO
JOHN DOS PASSOS
MANHATTAN TRANSFER
EDITORIAL PRESENÇA
Shadows on t
WOLFE
THOMAS WOLFE
You Can't Go Home Again
STUART LITTLE
by E. B. WHITE
the CATCHER in the RYE
FALLING MAN
DON DELILLO
KNICKERB
HIST
OF NEW
BY WASHINGT

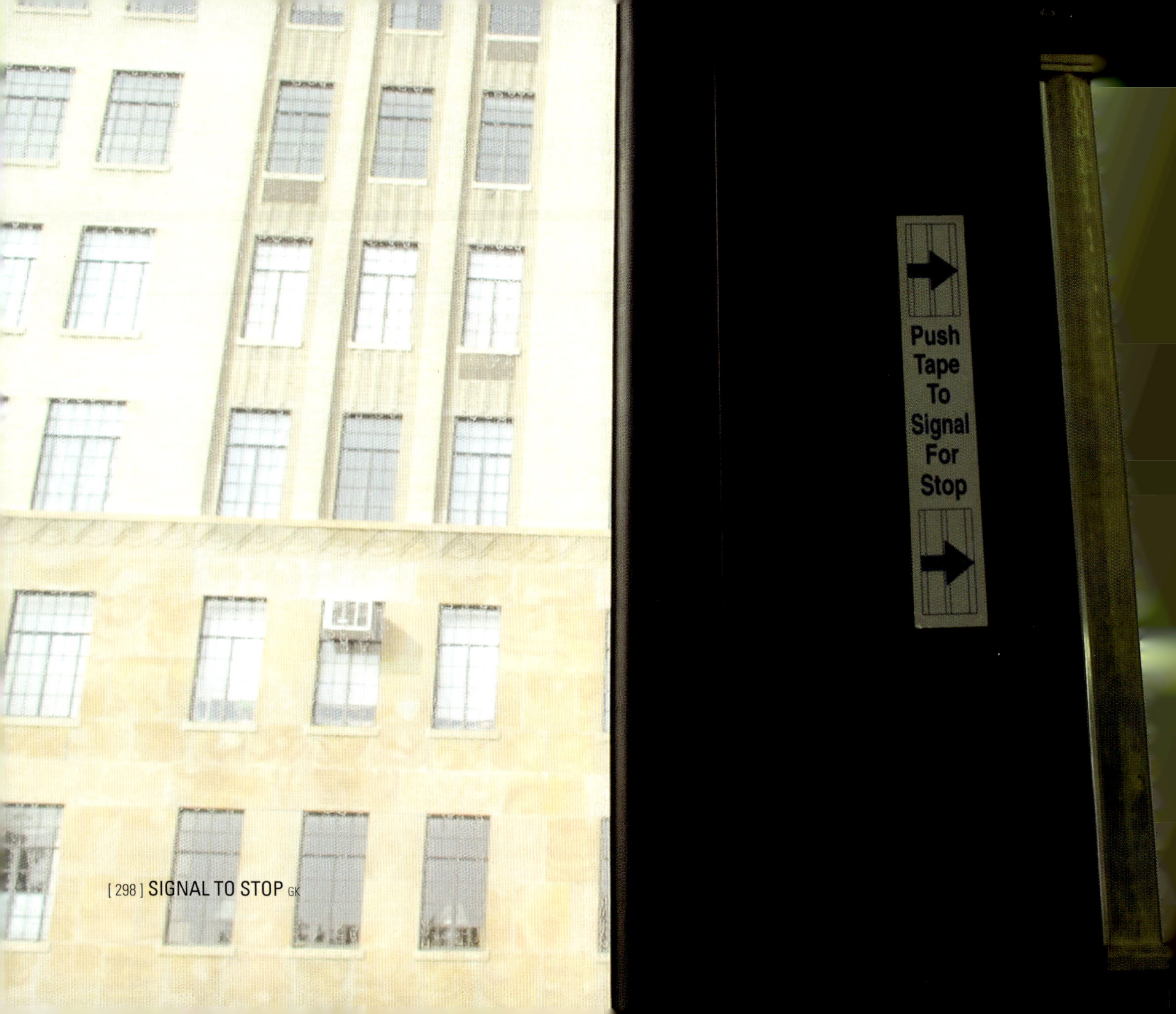

[298] SIGNAL TO STOP GK

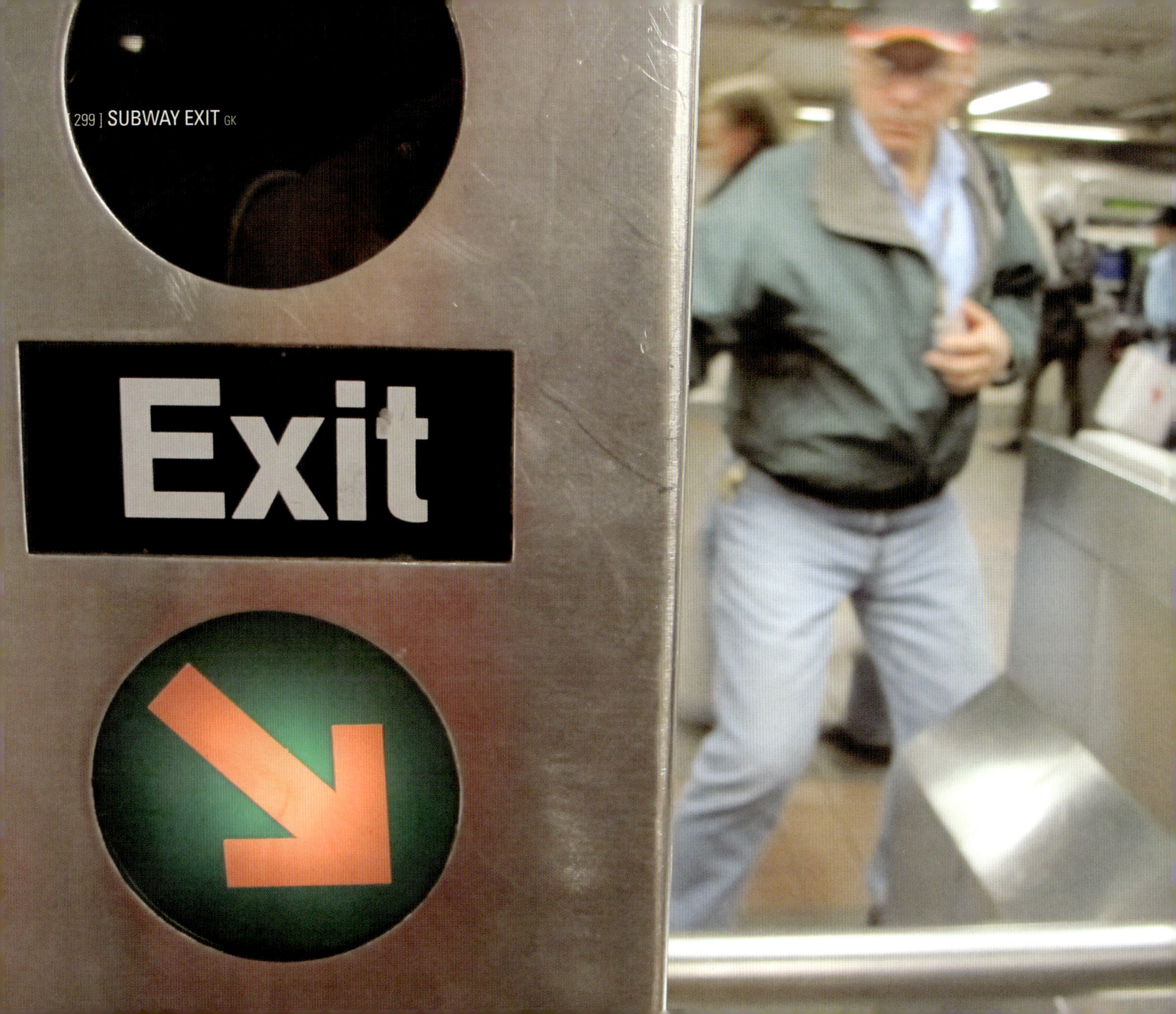

[299] SUBWAY EXIT GK

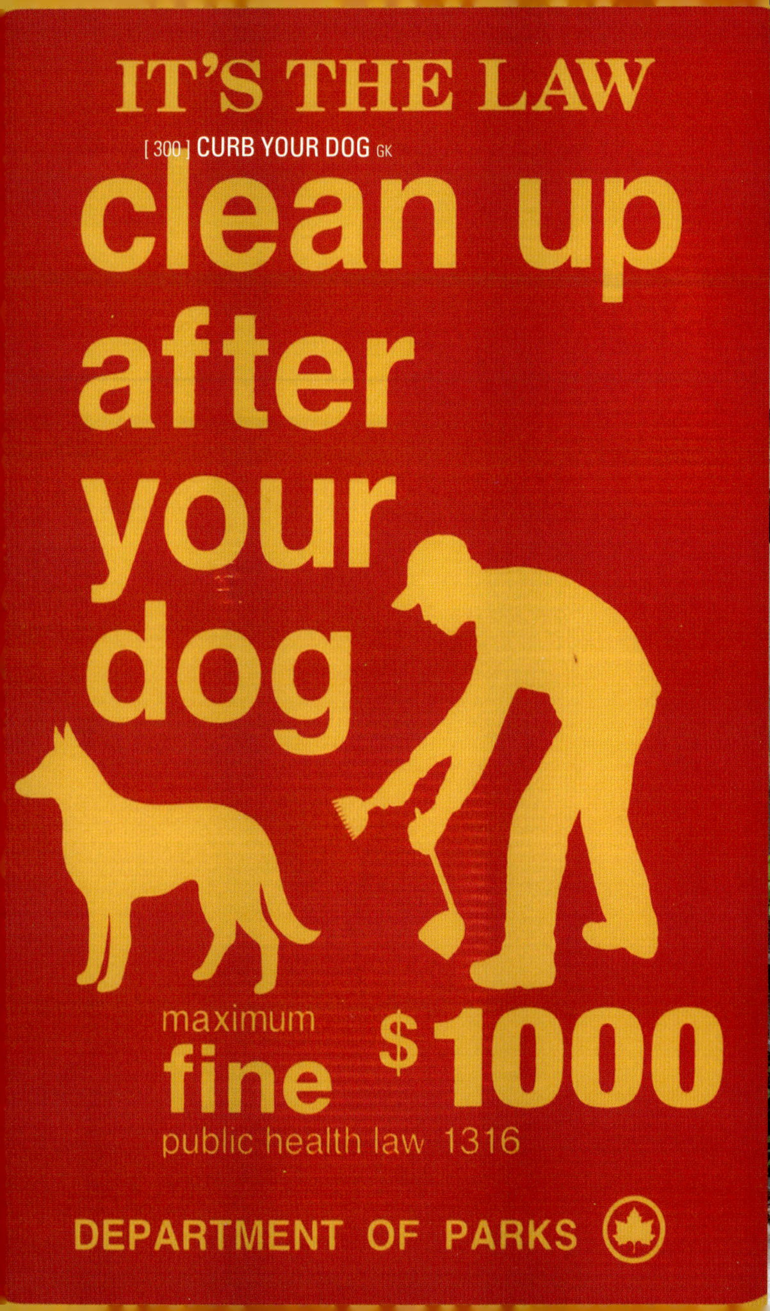

[300] CURB YOUR DOG GK

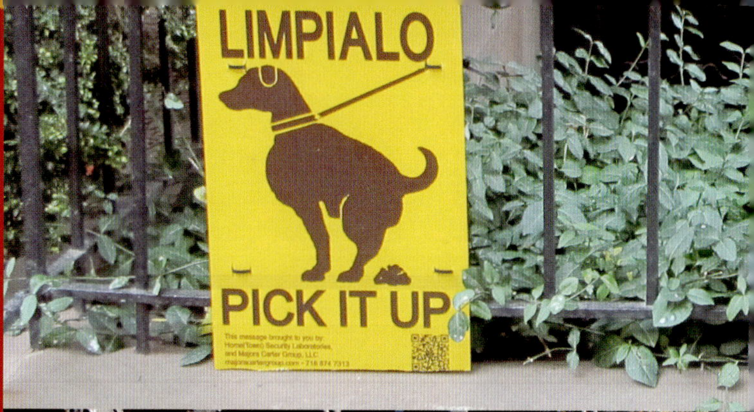

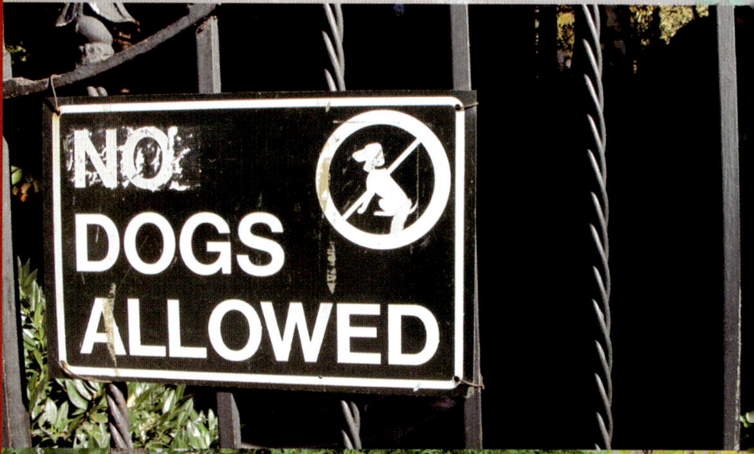

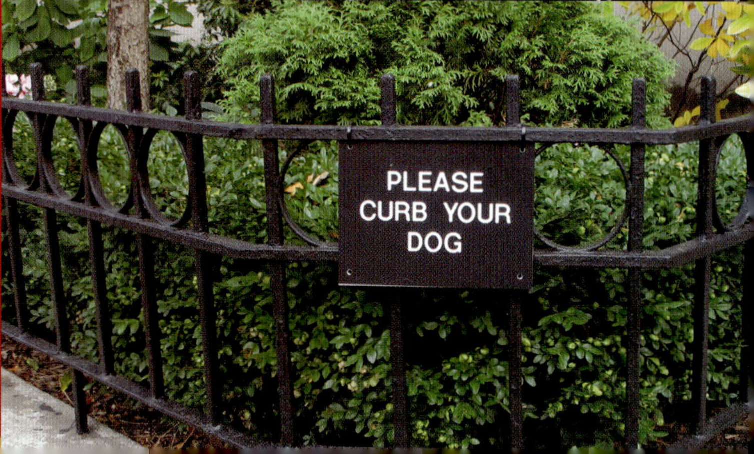

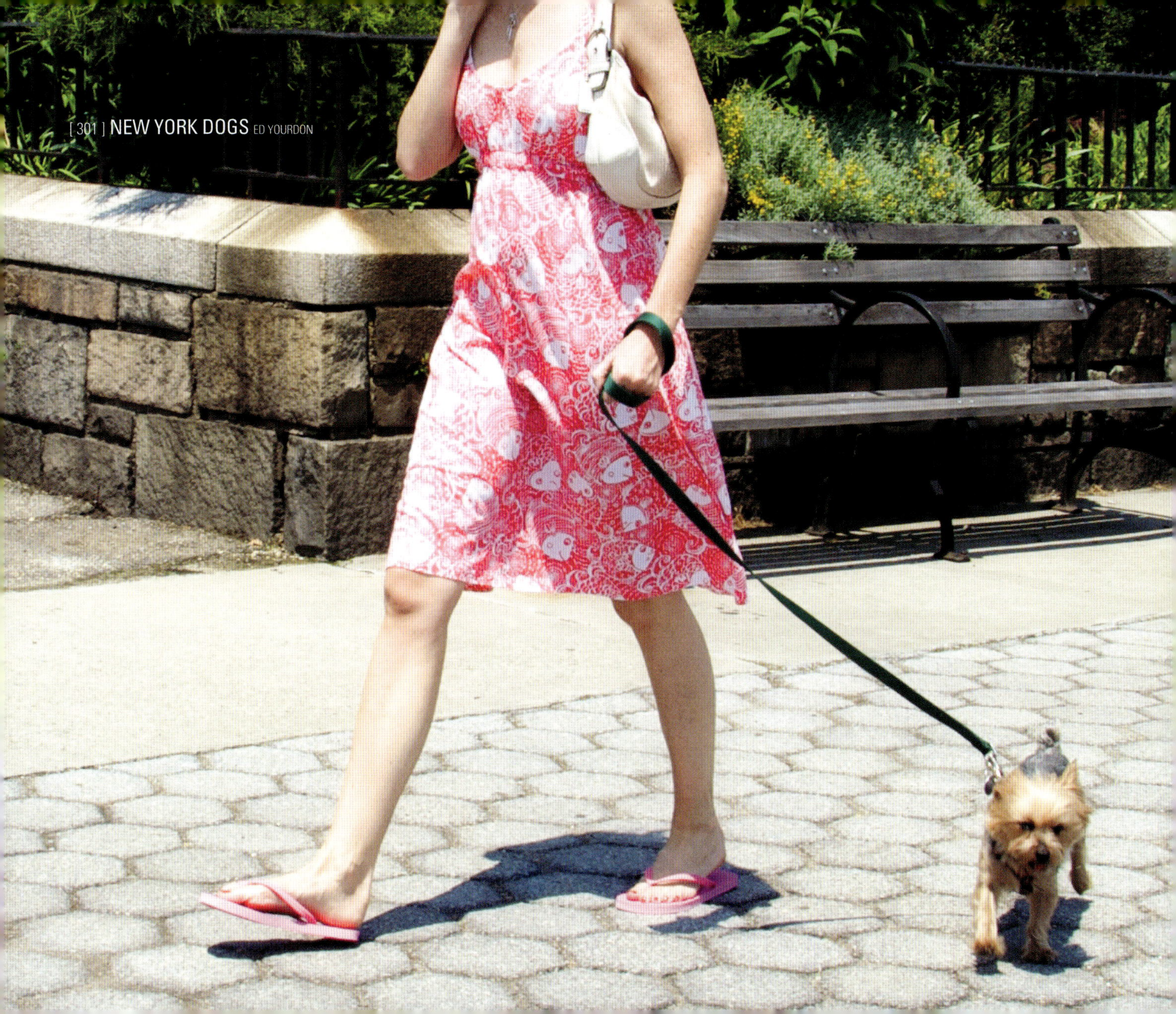

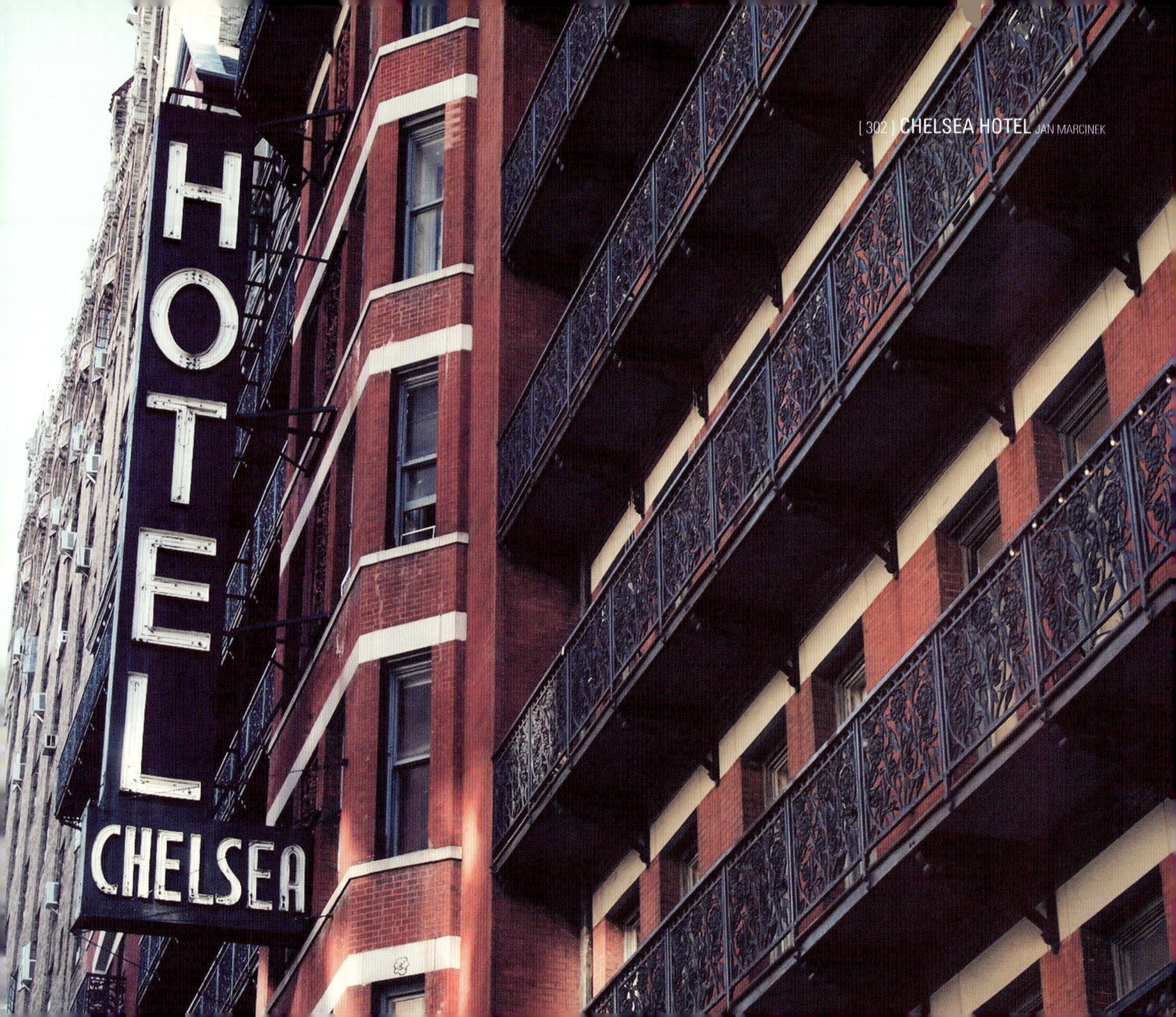

[302] CHELSEA HOTEL JAN MARCINEK

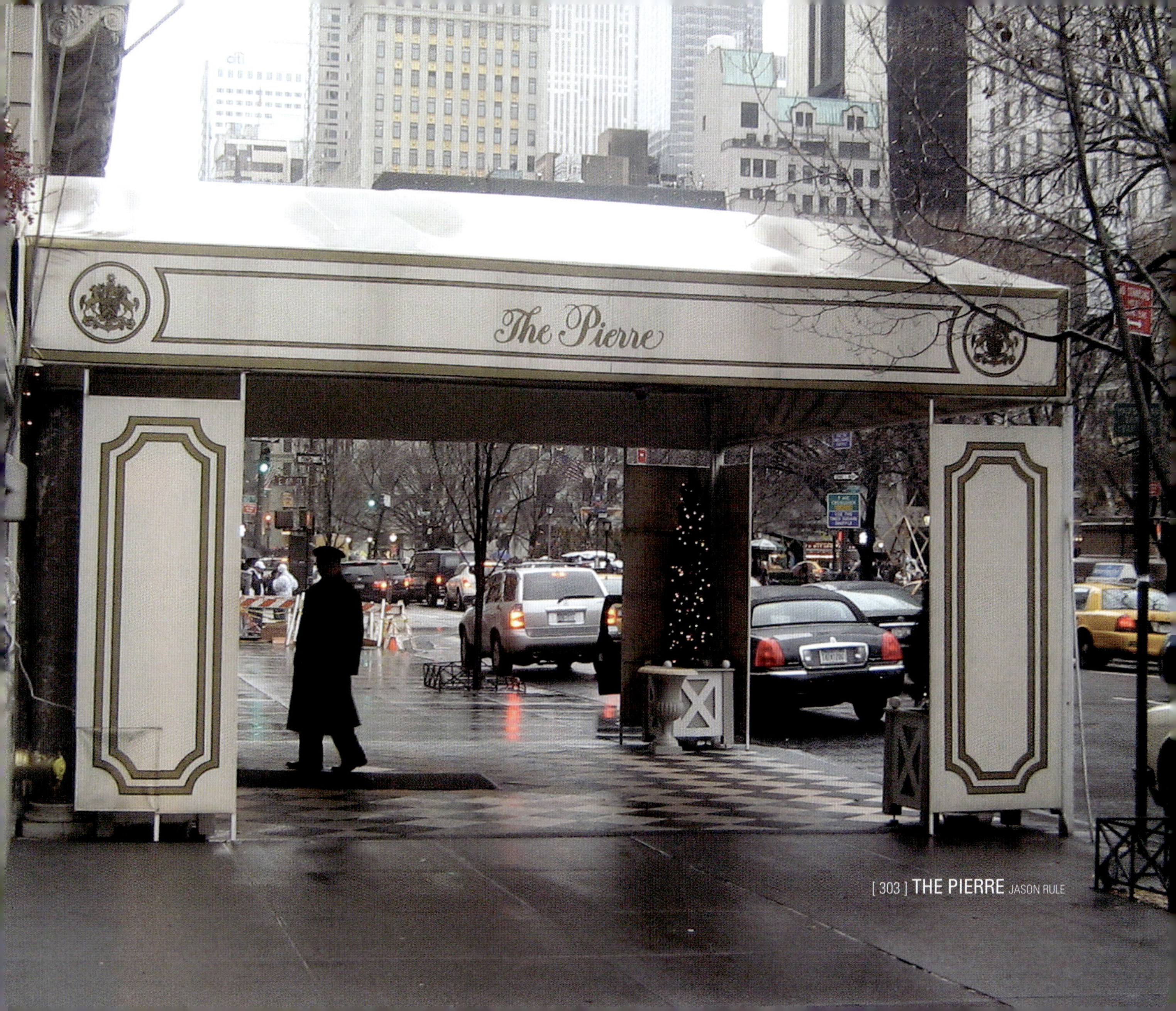

[303] **THE PIERRE** JASON RULE

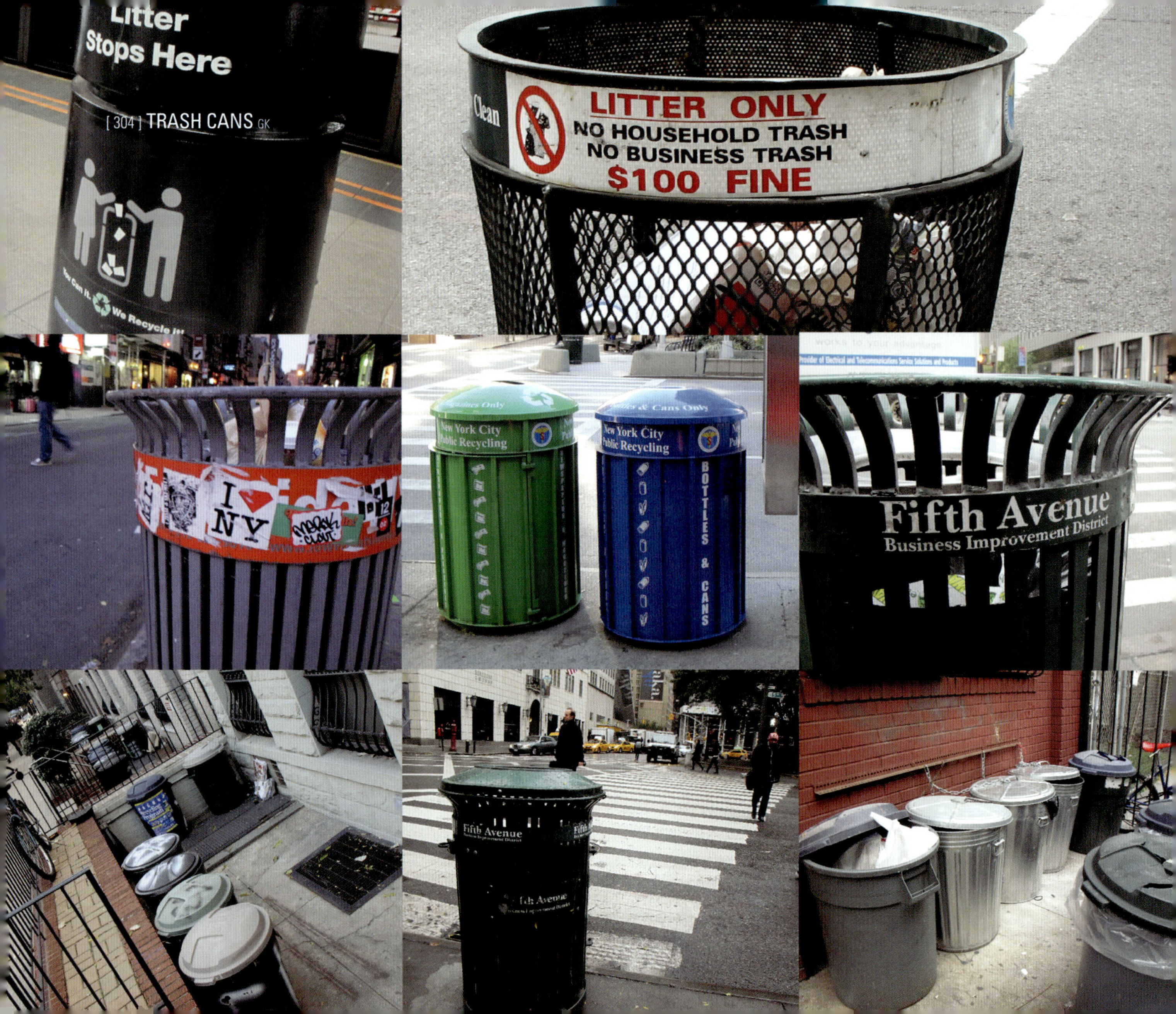

[304] TRASH CANS GK

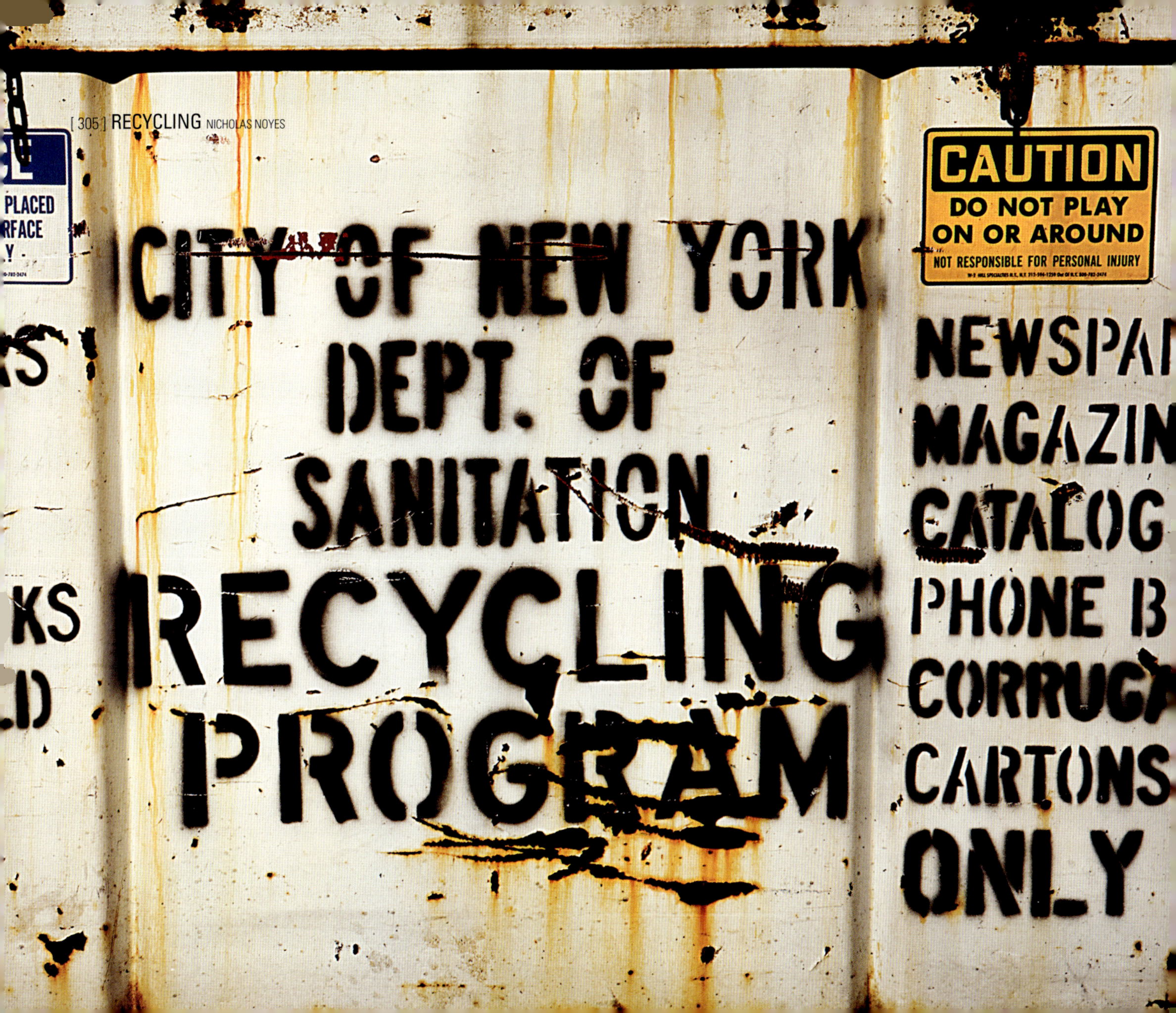
CITY OF NEW YORK
DEPT. OF
SANITATION
RECYCLING
PROGRAM
CAUTION
DO NOT PLAY
ON OR AROUND
NOT RESPONSIBLE FOR PERSONAL INJURY
CATALOG
CARTONS
ONLY

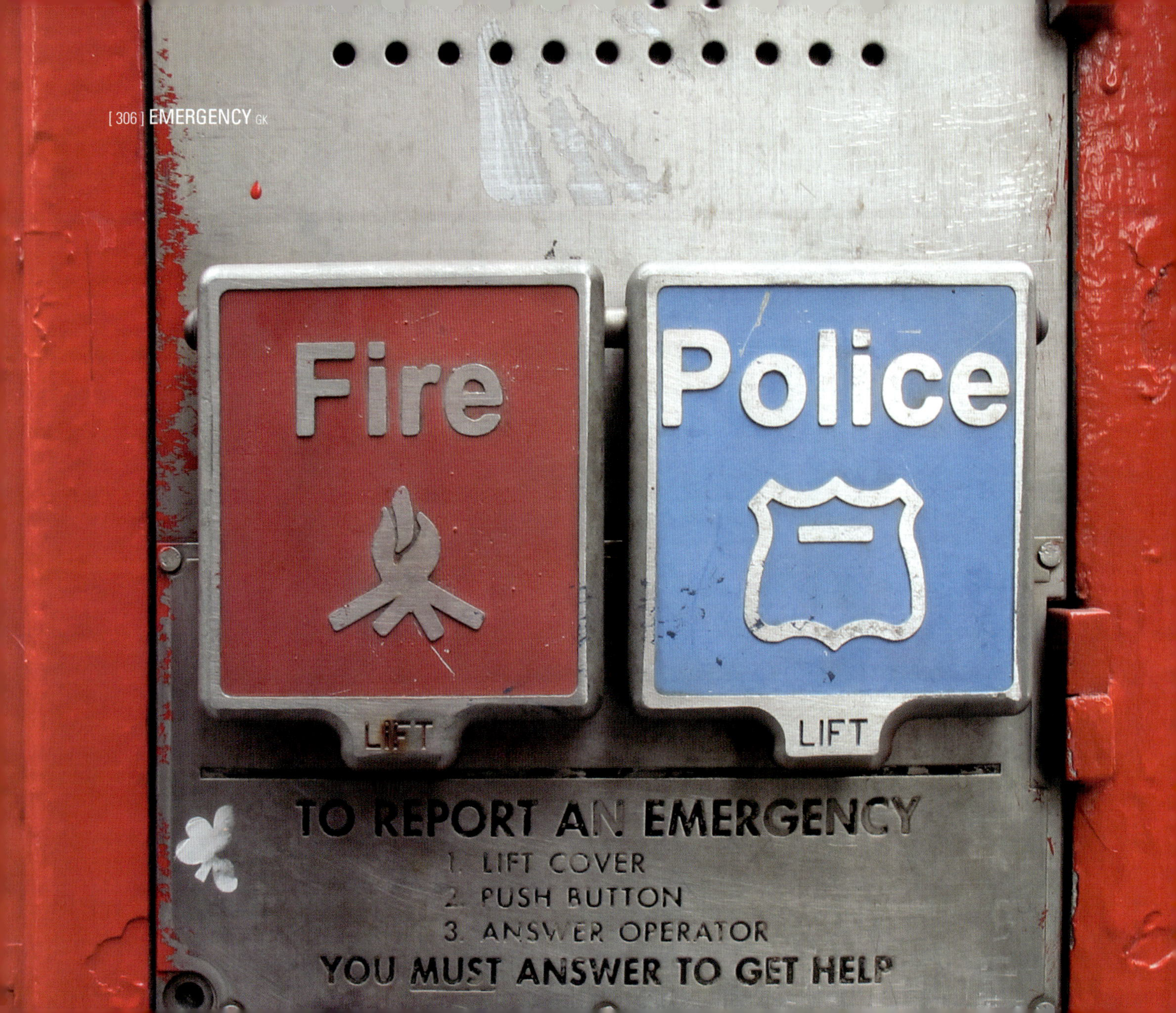
Fire
LIFT
Police
LIFT
TO REPORT AN EMERGENCY
1. LIFT COVER
2. PUSH BUTTON
3. ANSWER OPERATOR
YOU MUST ANSWER TO GET HELP

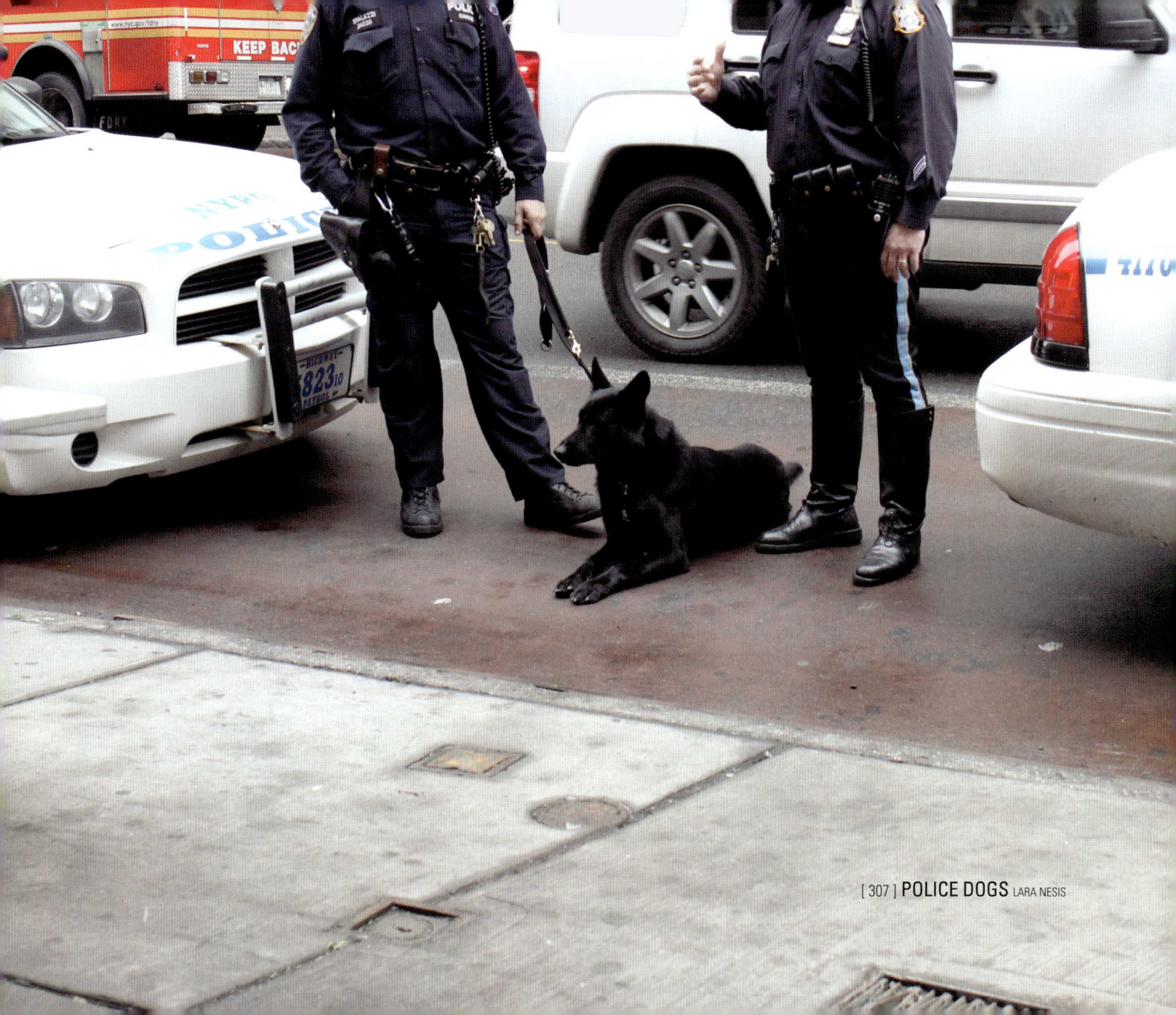

[307] **POLICE DOGS** LARA NESIS

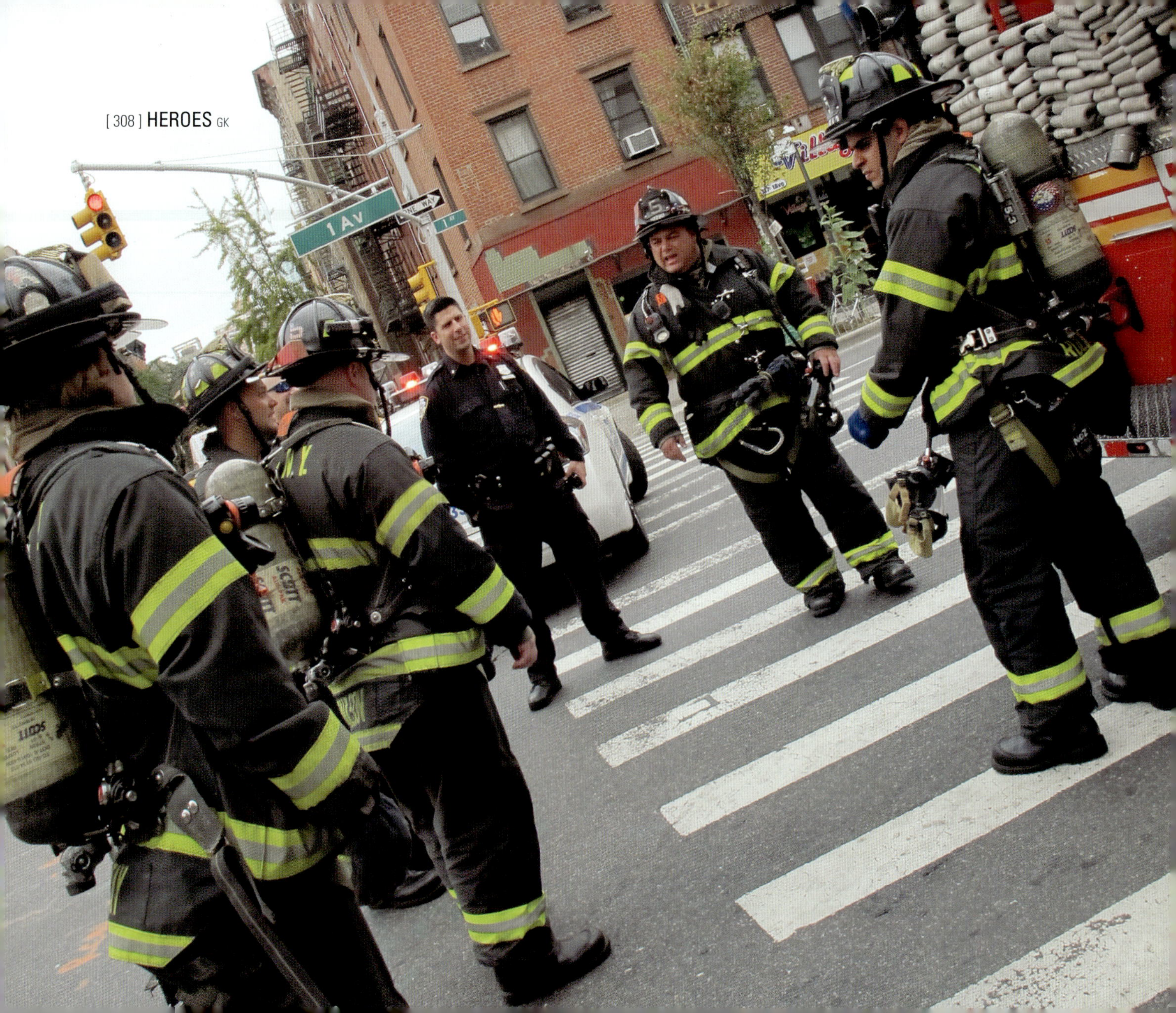
1 Av
ONE WAY
F.D.N.Y.

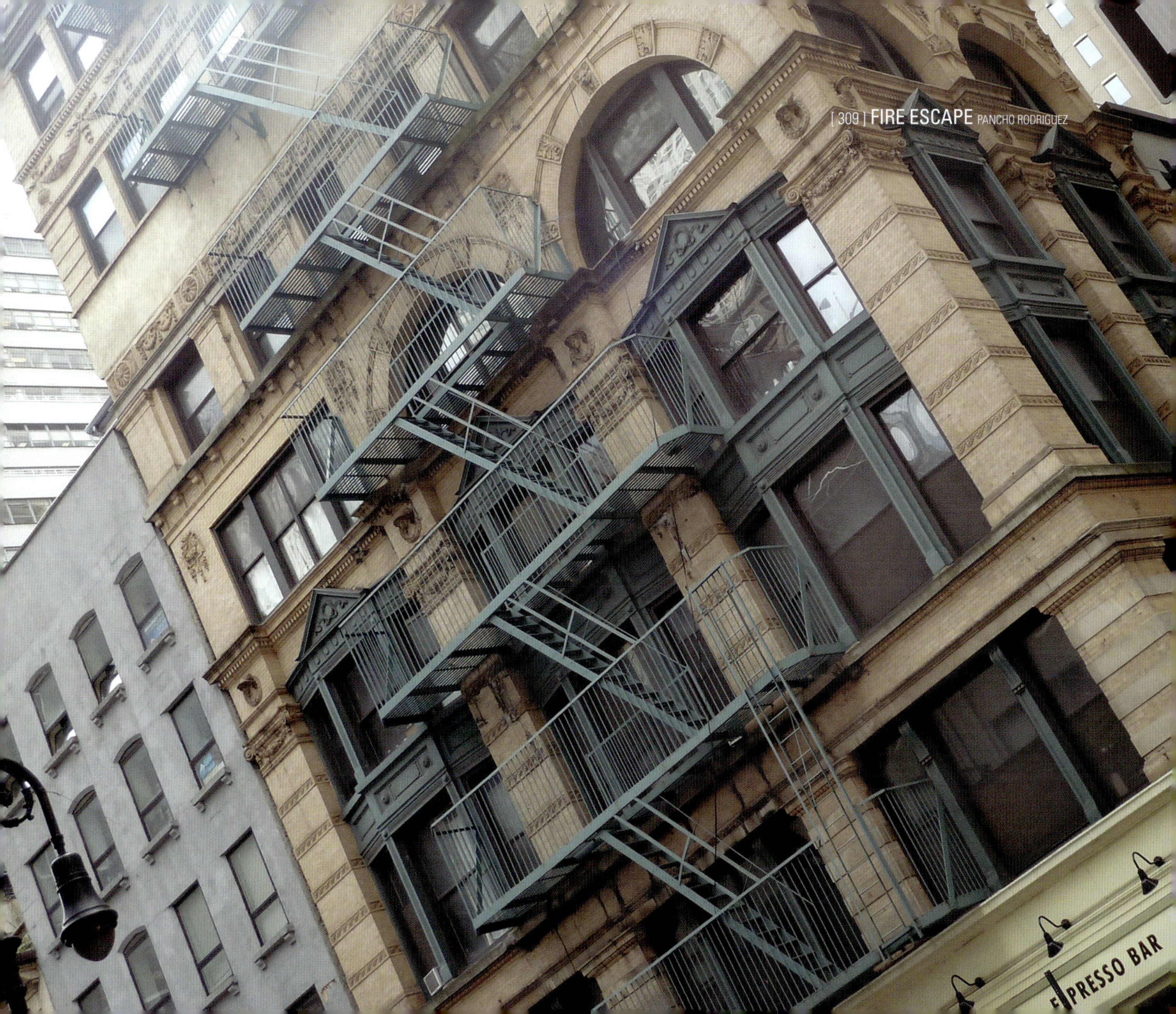

[309] **FIRE ESCAPE** Pancho Rodriguez

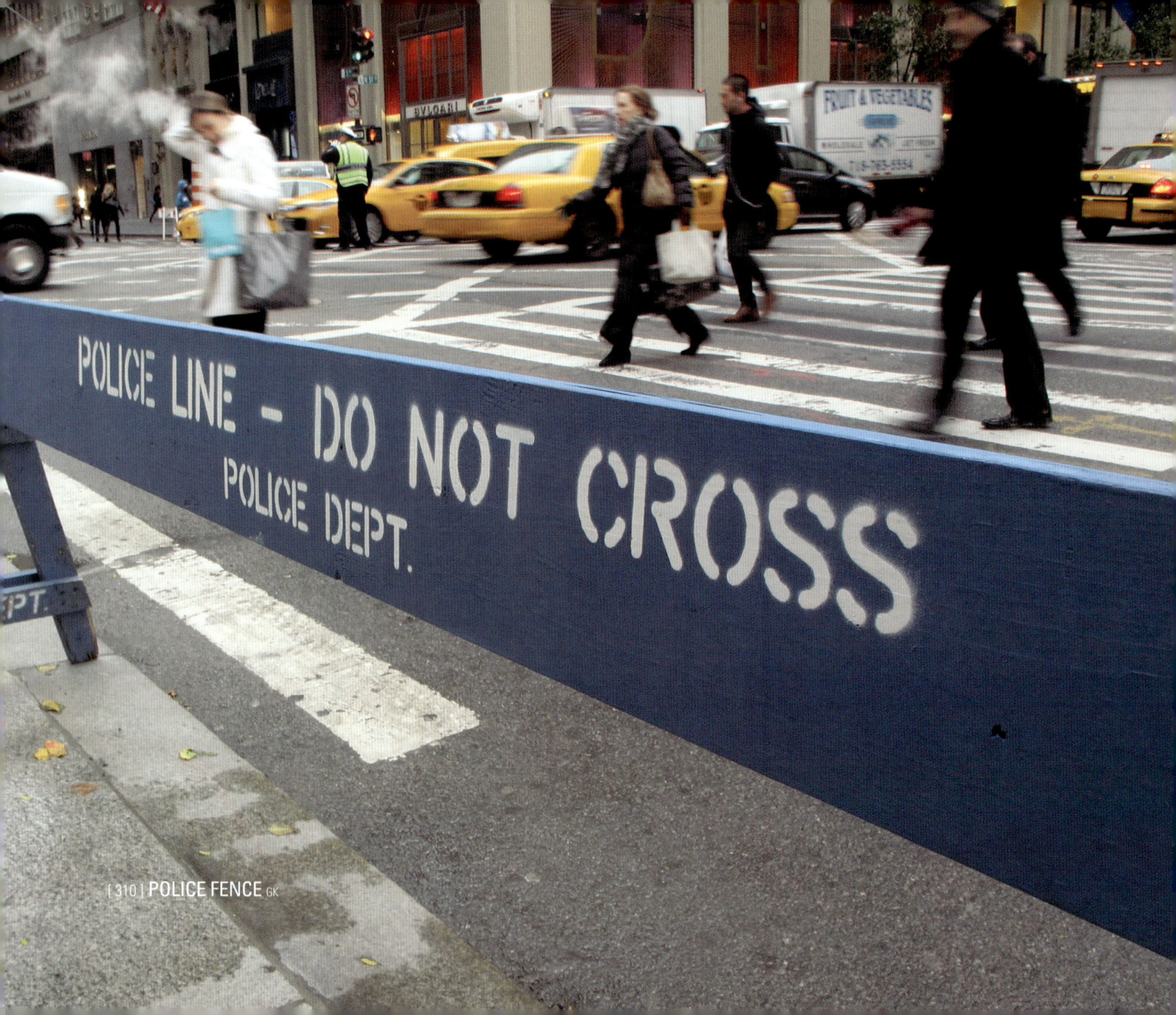

[310] POLICE FENCE GK

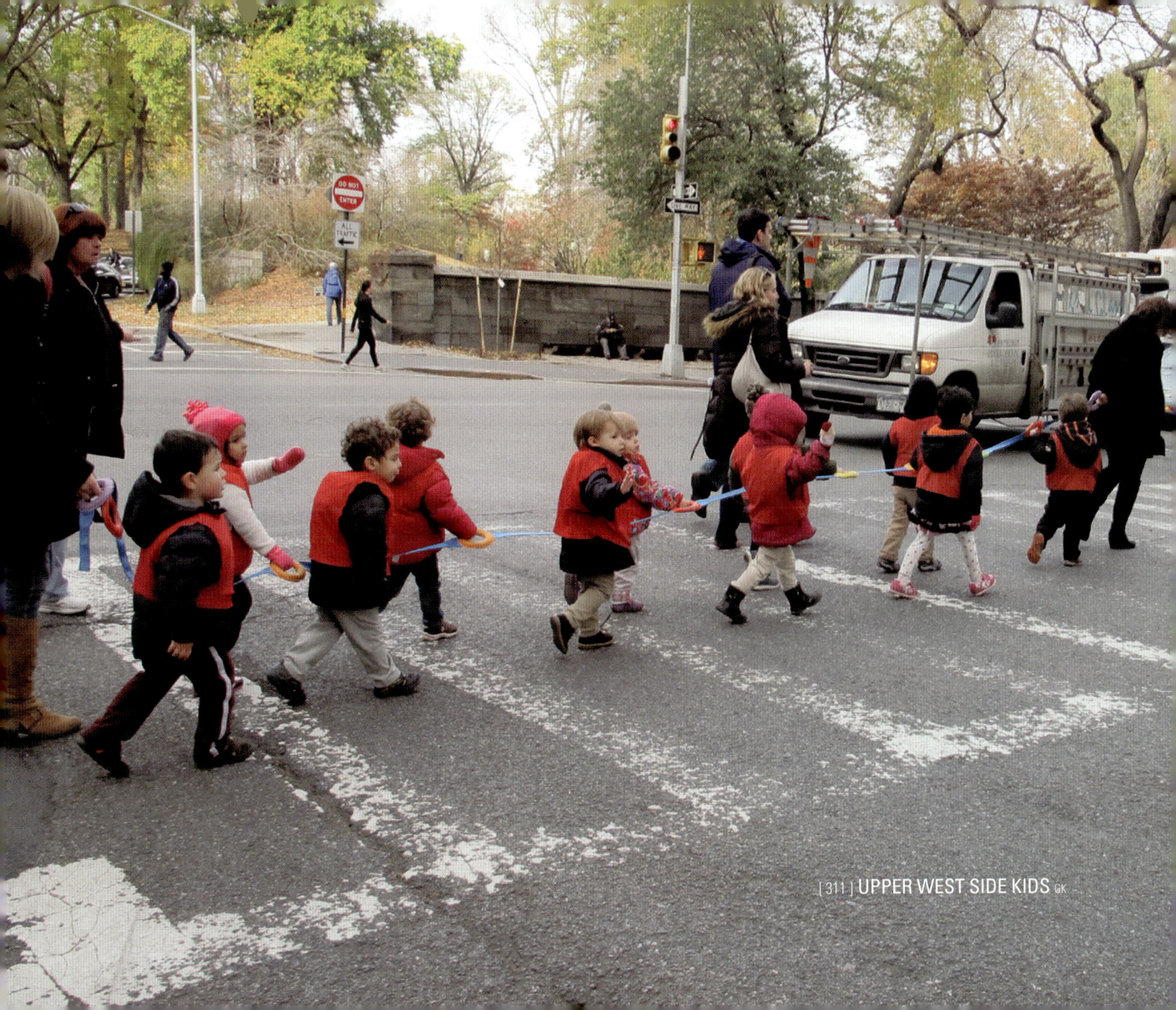

[311] UPPER WEST SIDE KIDS GK

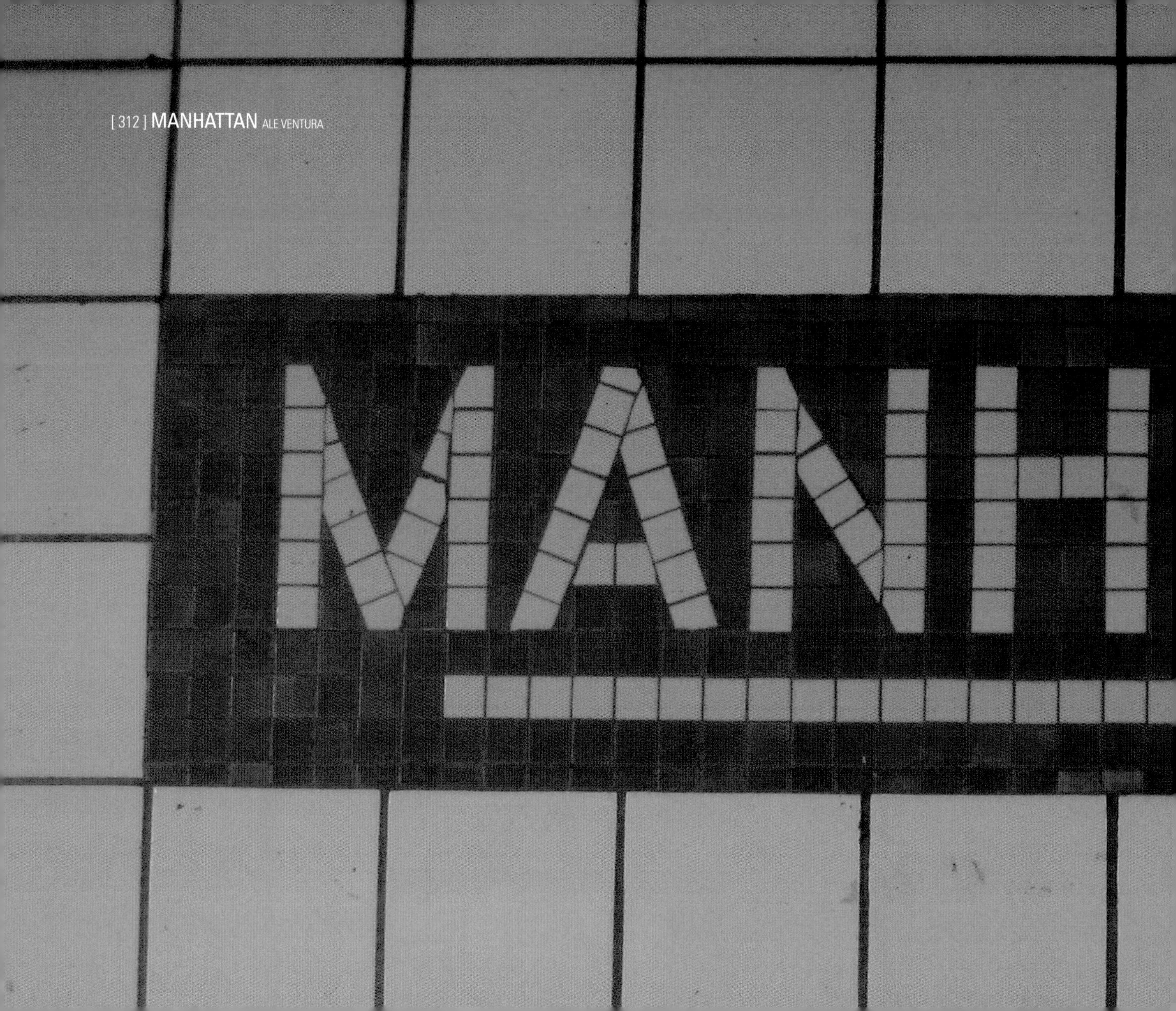

ATTAN

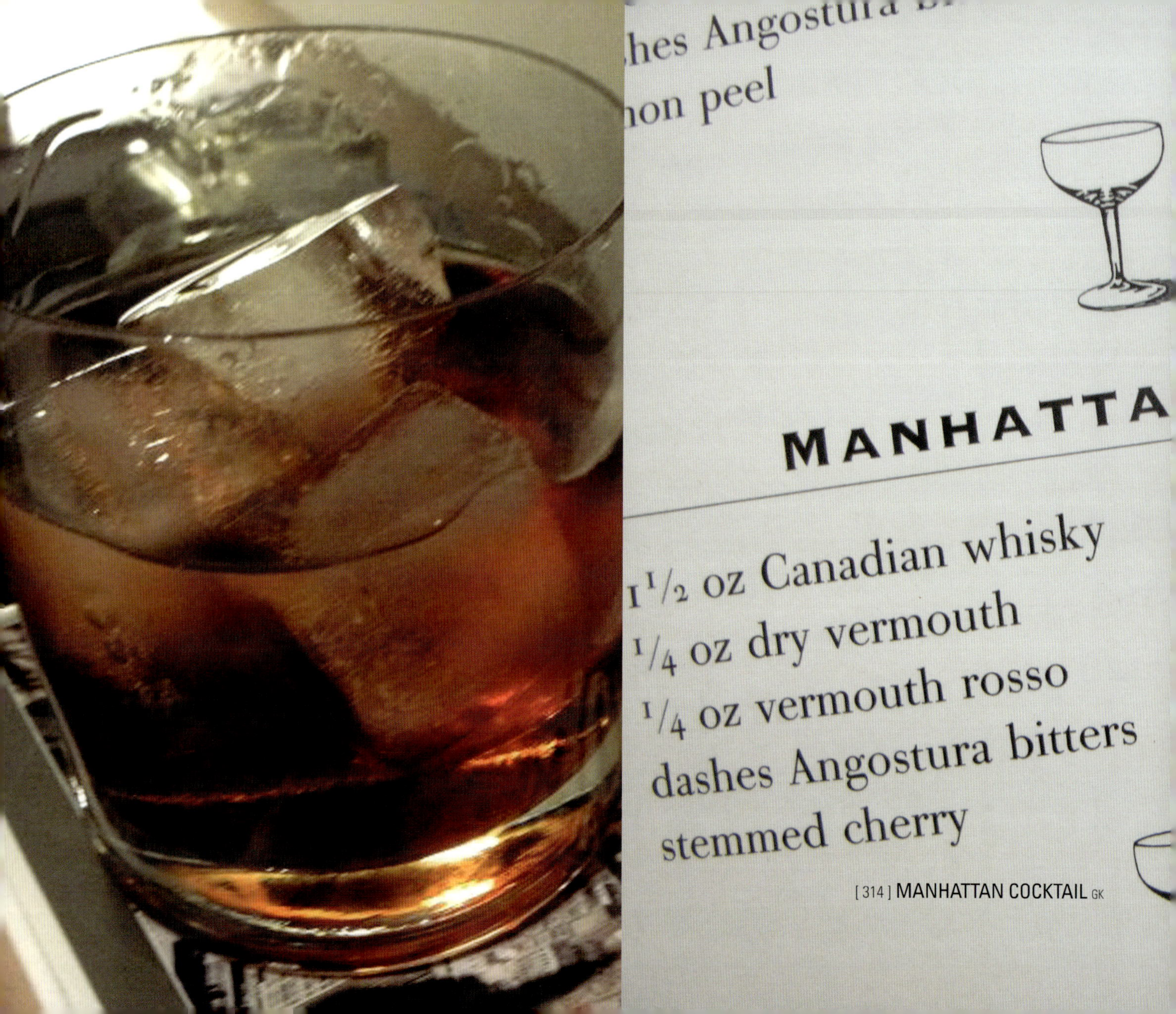

[314] MANHATTAN COCKTAIL GK

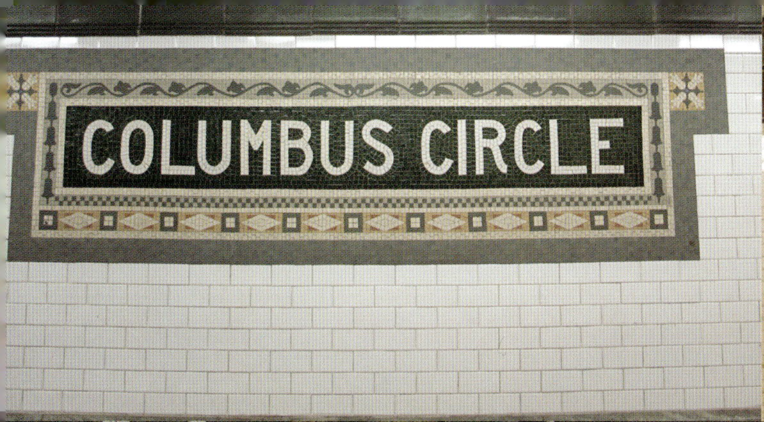
COLUMBUS CIRCLE

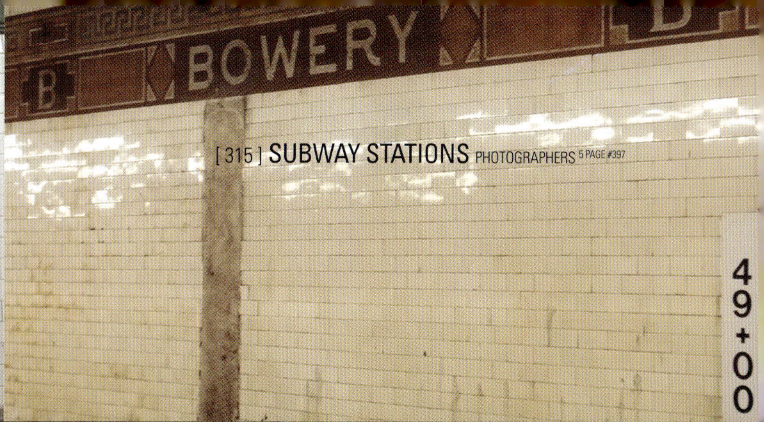
BOWERY
49+00

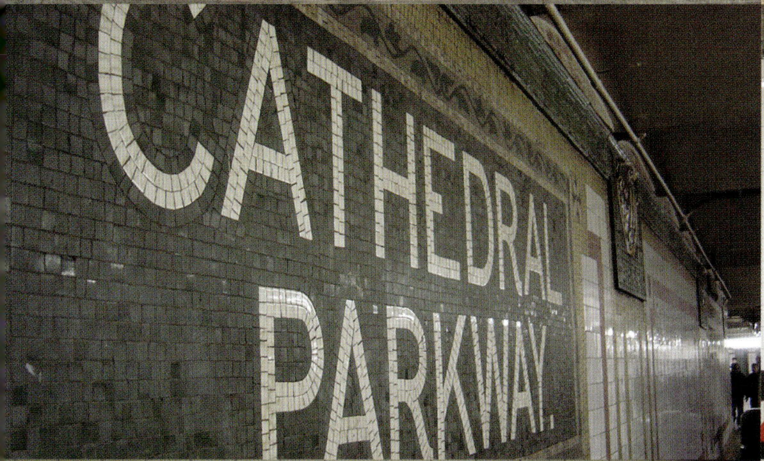
CATHEDRAL
PARKWAY.

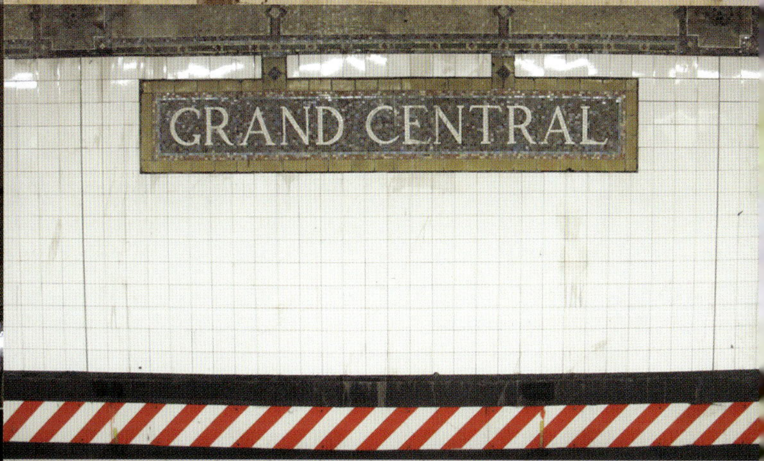
GRAND CENTRAL

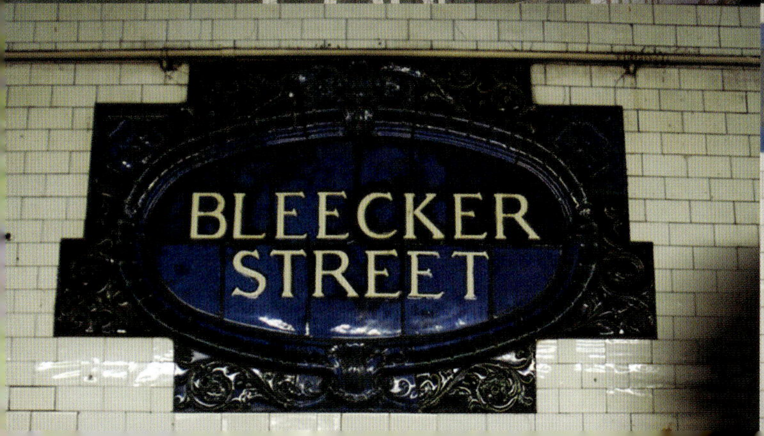
BLEECKER
STREET

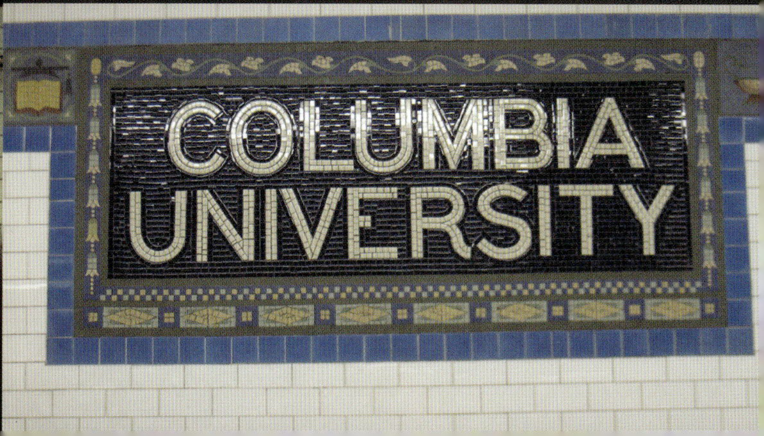
COLUMBIA
UNIVERSITY

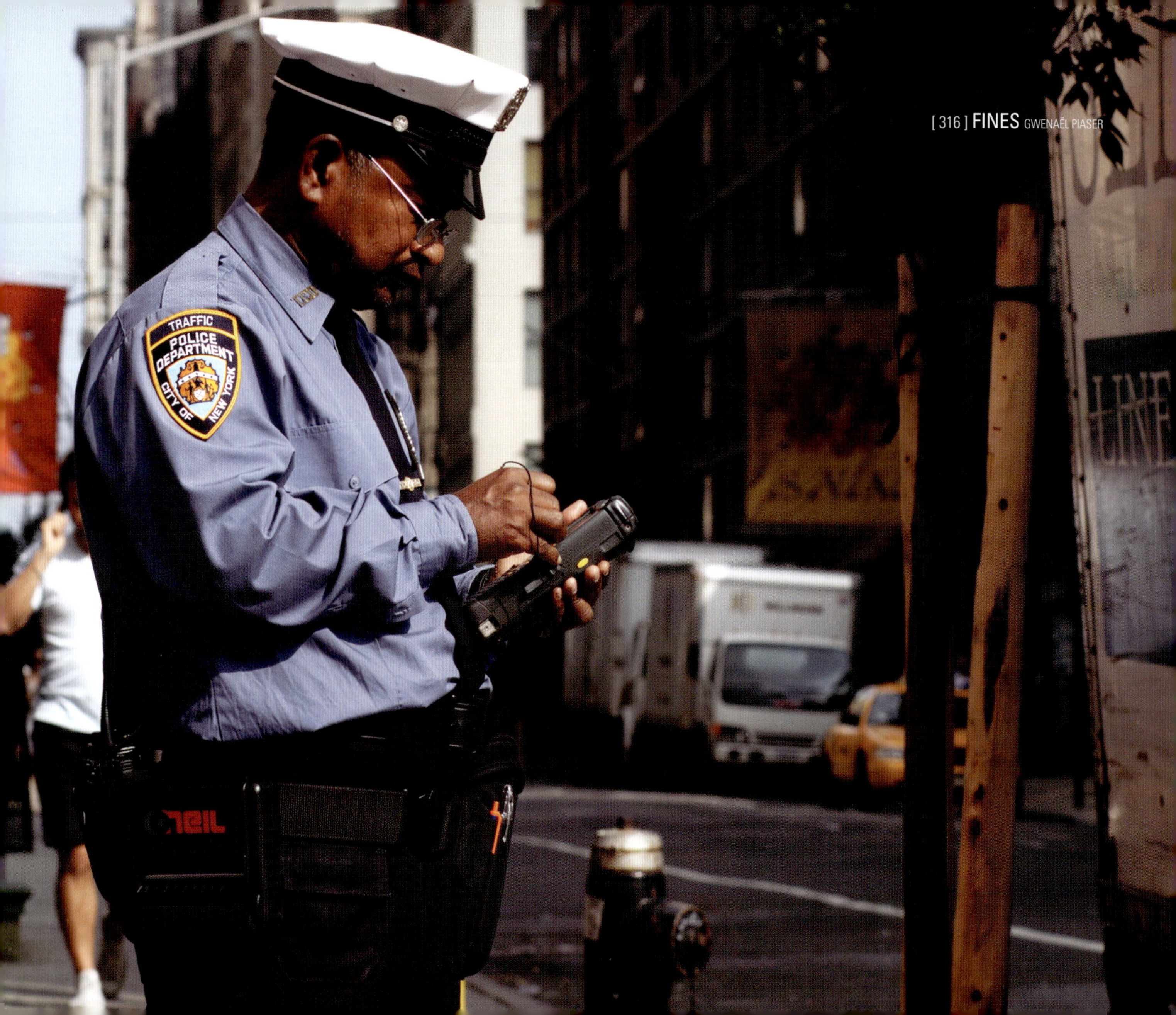
TRAFFIC
POLICE DEPARTMENT
CITY OF NEW YORK

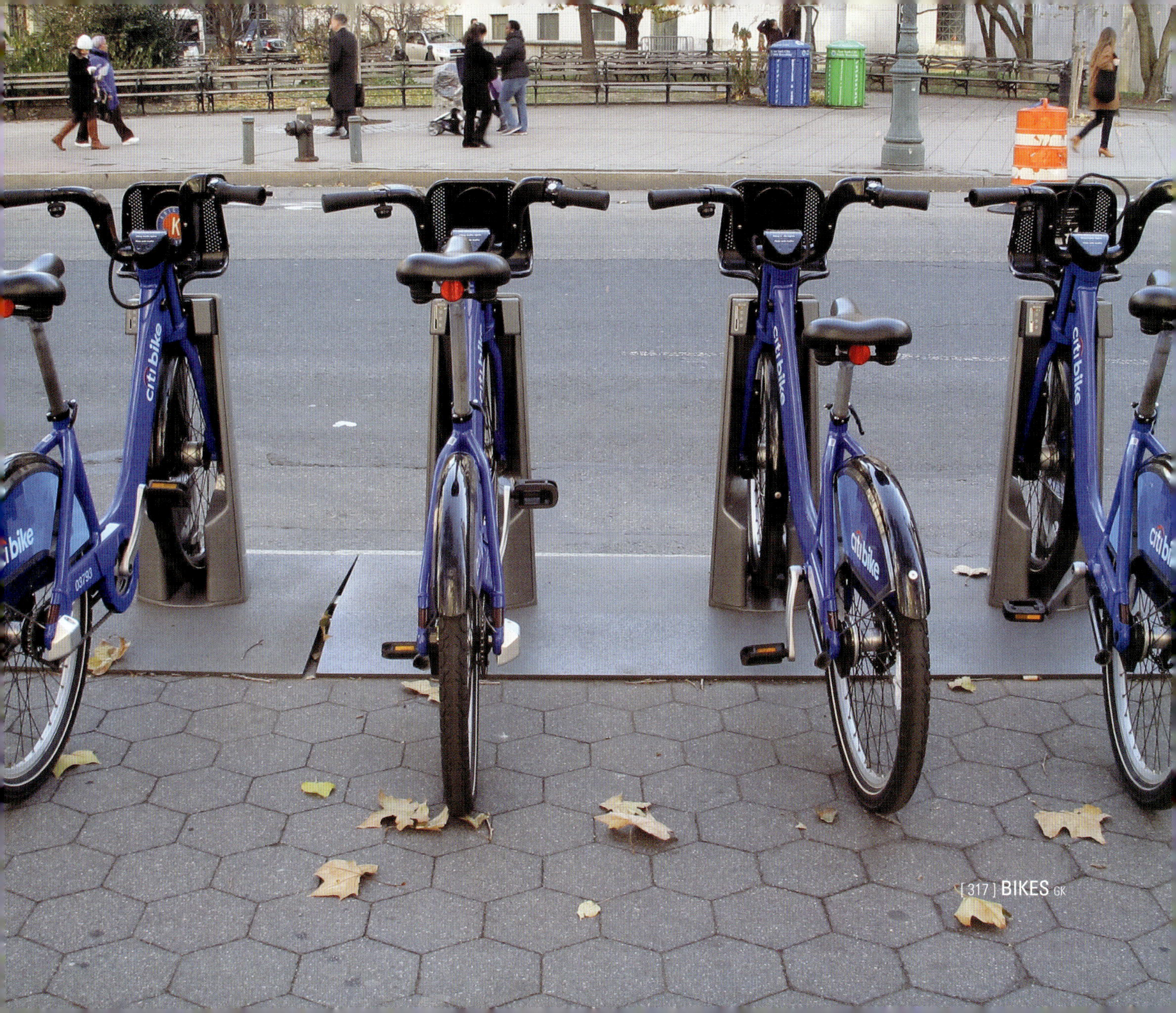

[317] BIKES GK

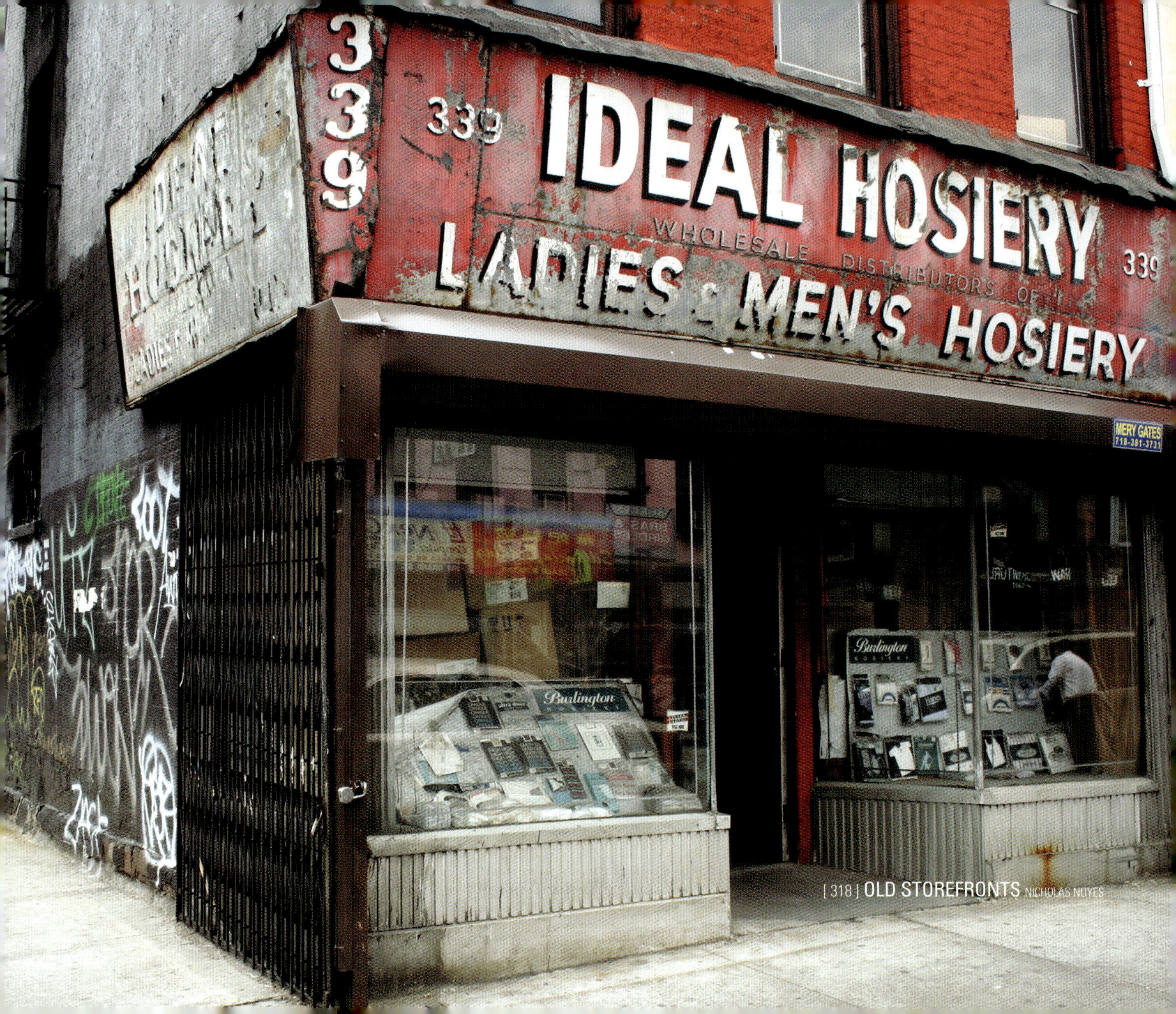
339
339
IDEAL HOSIERY
WHOLESALE DISTRIBUTORS OF
LADIES
MEN'S HOSIERY
339
MERY GATES
718-381-3731
Burlington
Burlington

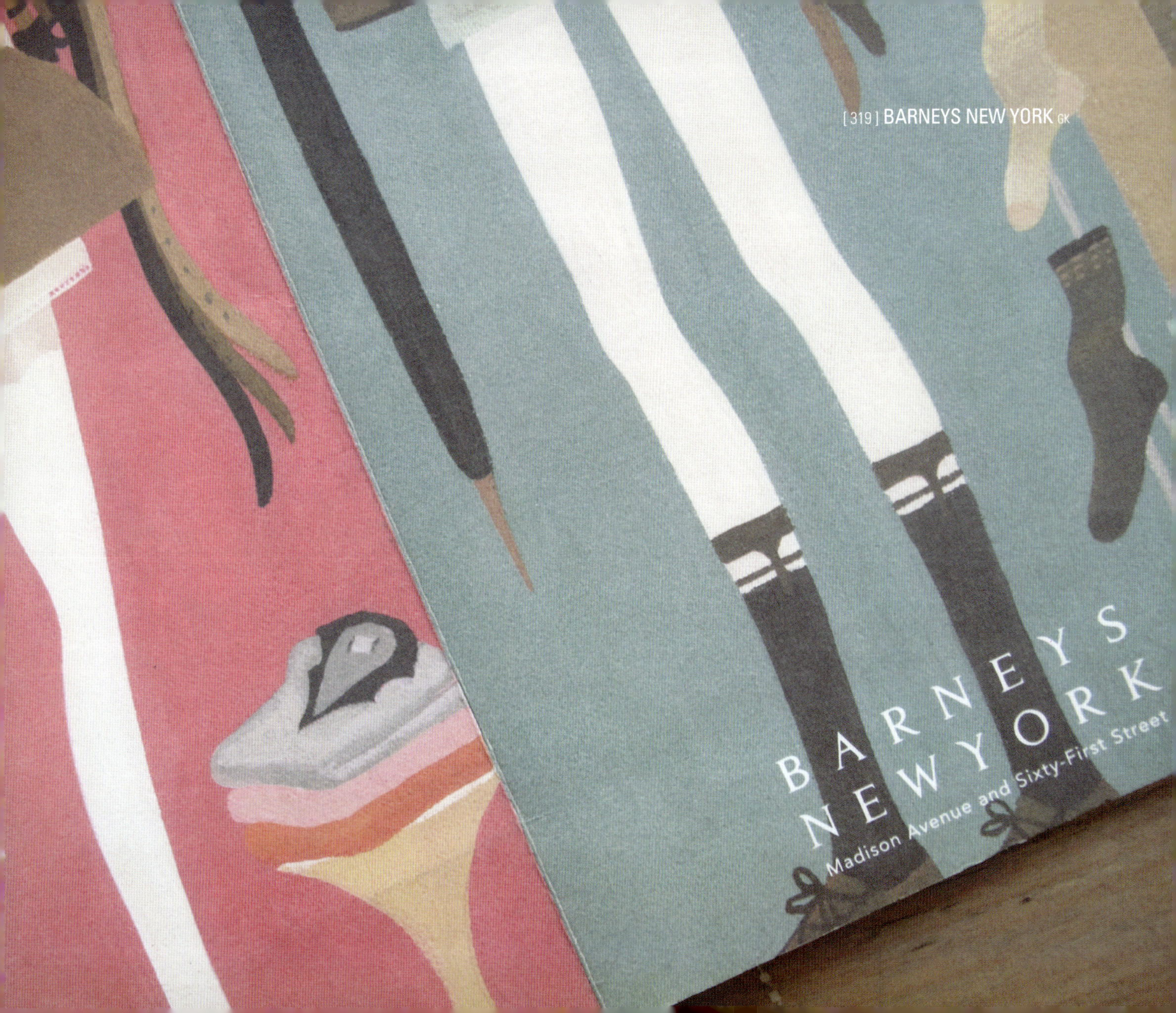

[319] BARNEYS NEW YORK GK

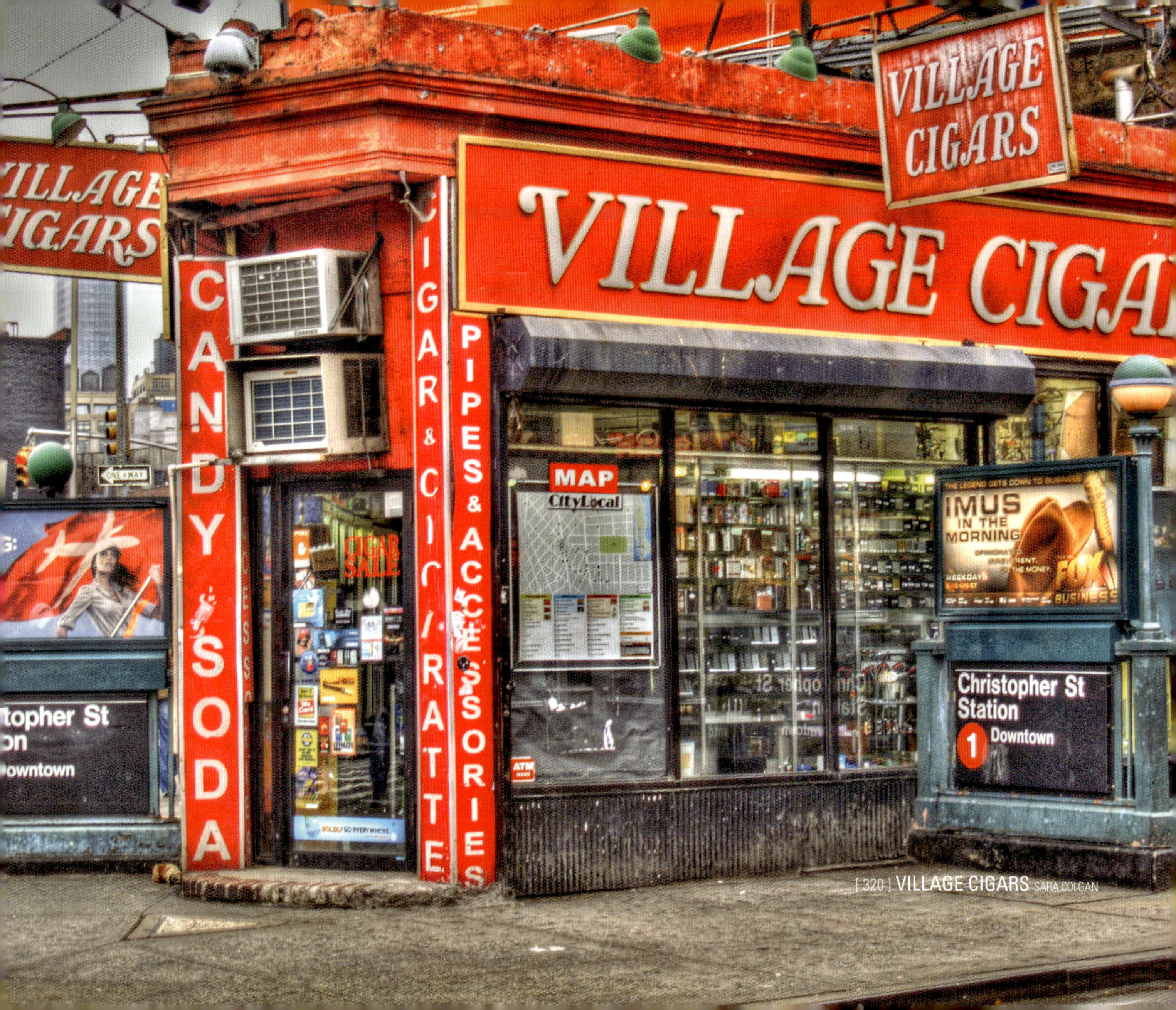

[320] VILLAGE CIGARS SARA COLGAN

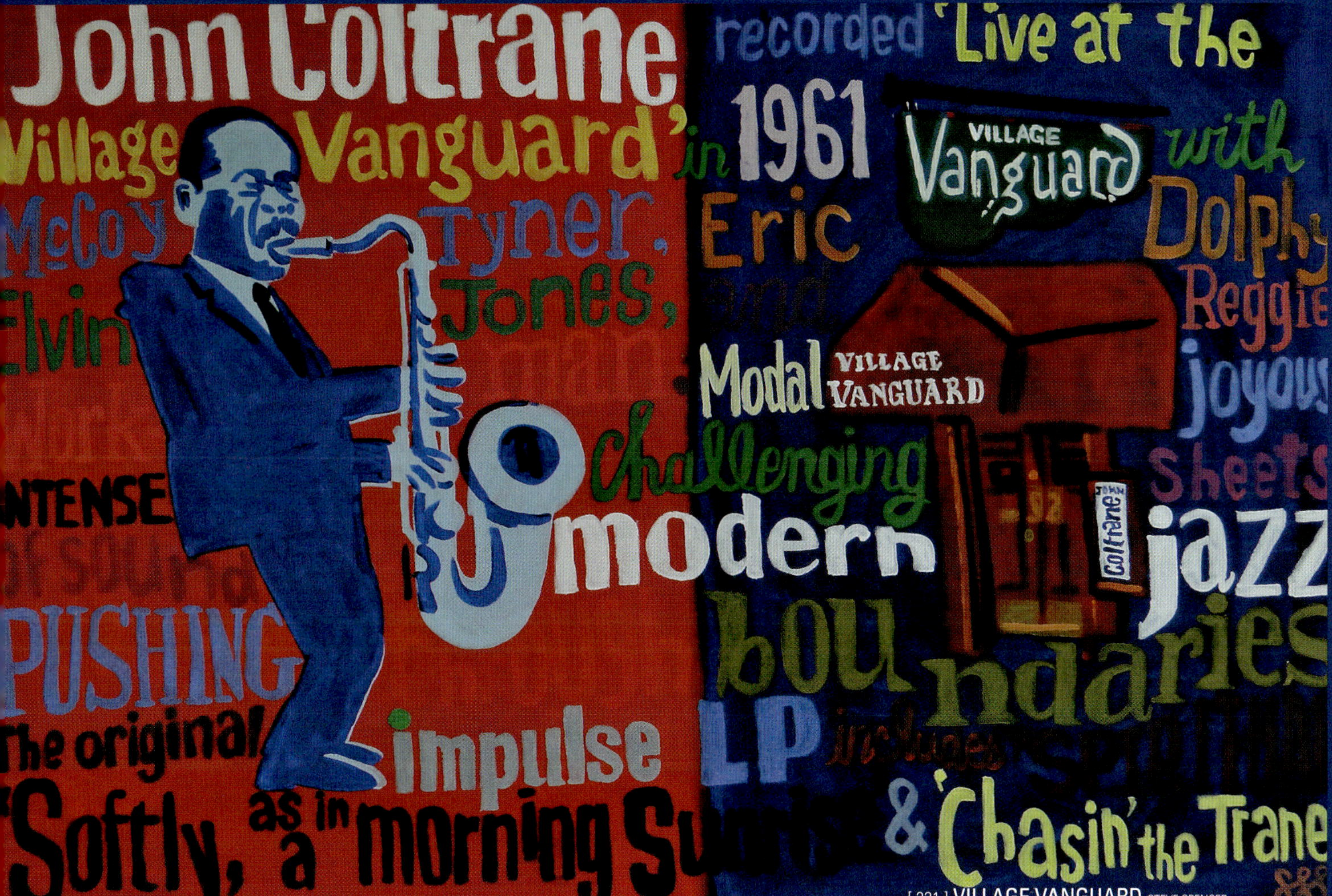

[321] VILLAGE VANGUARD STEVE SPENCER

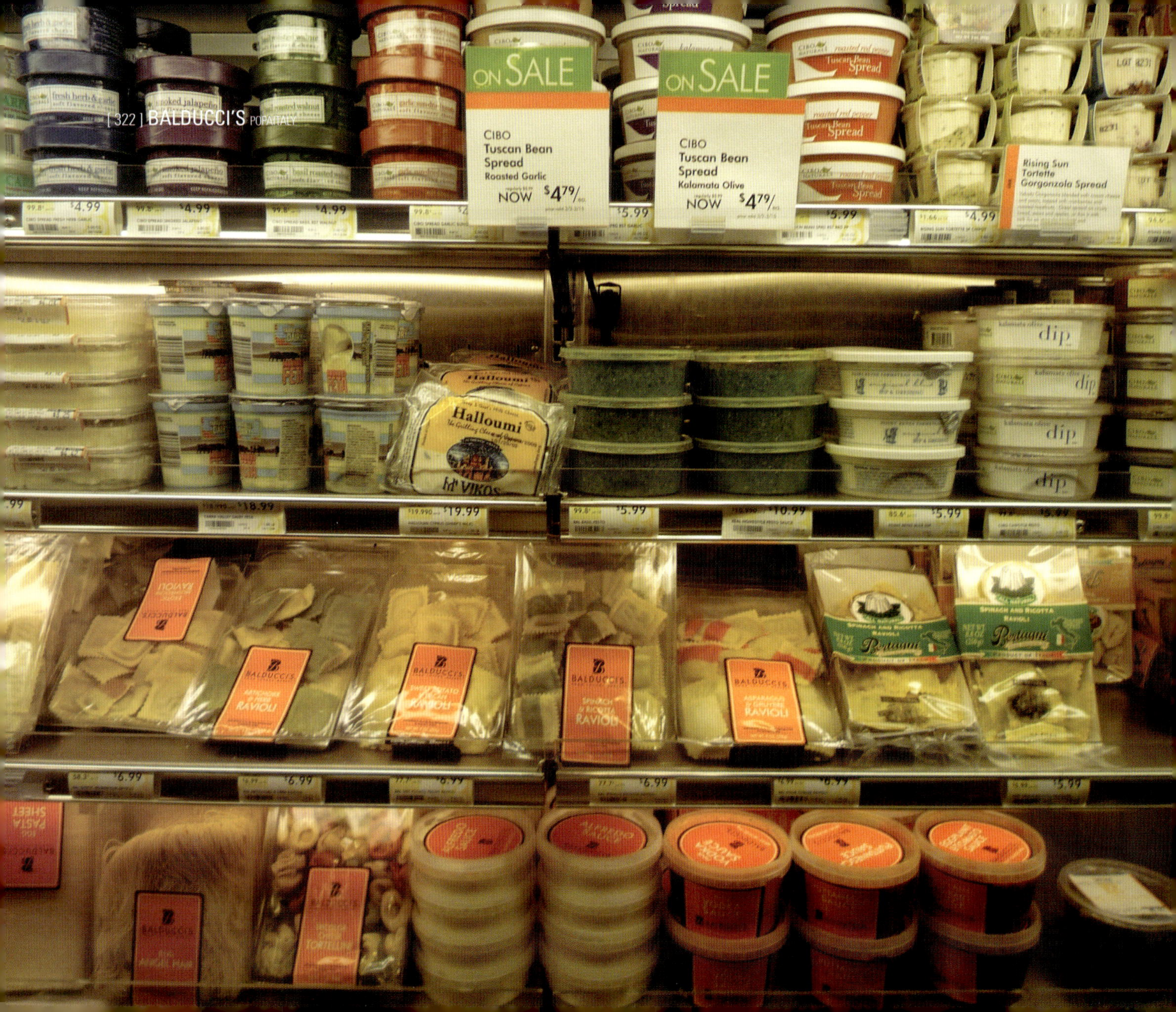
ON SALE
CIBO
Tuscan Bean
Spread
Roasted Garlic
NOW $4.79/ea.
ON SALE
CIBO
Tuscan Bean
Spread
Kalamata Olive
NOW $4.79/ea.
Rising Sun
Tortette
Gorgonzola Spread
Halloumi
dip
BALDUCCI'S
RAVIOLI

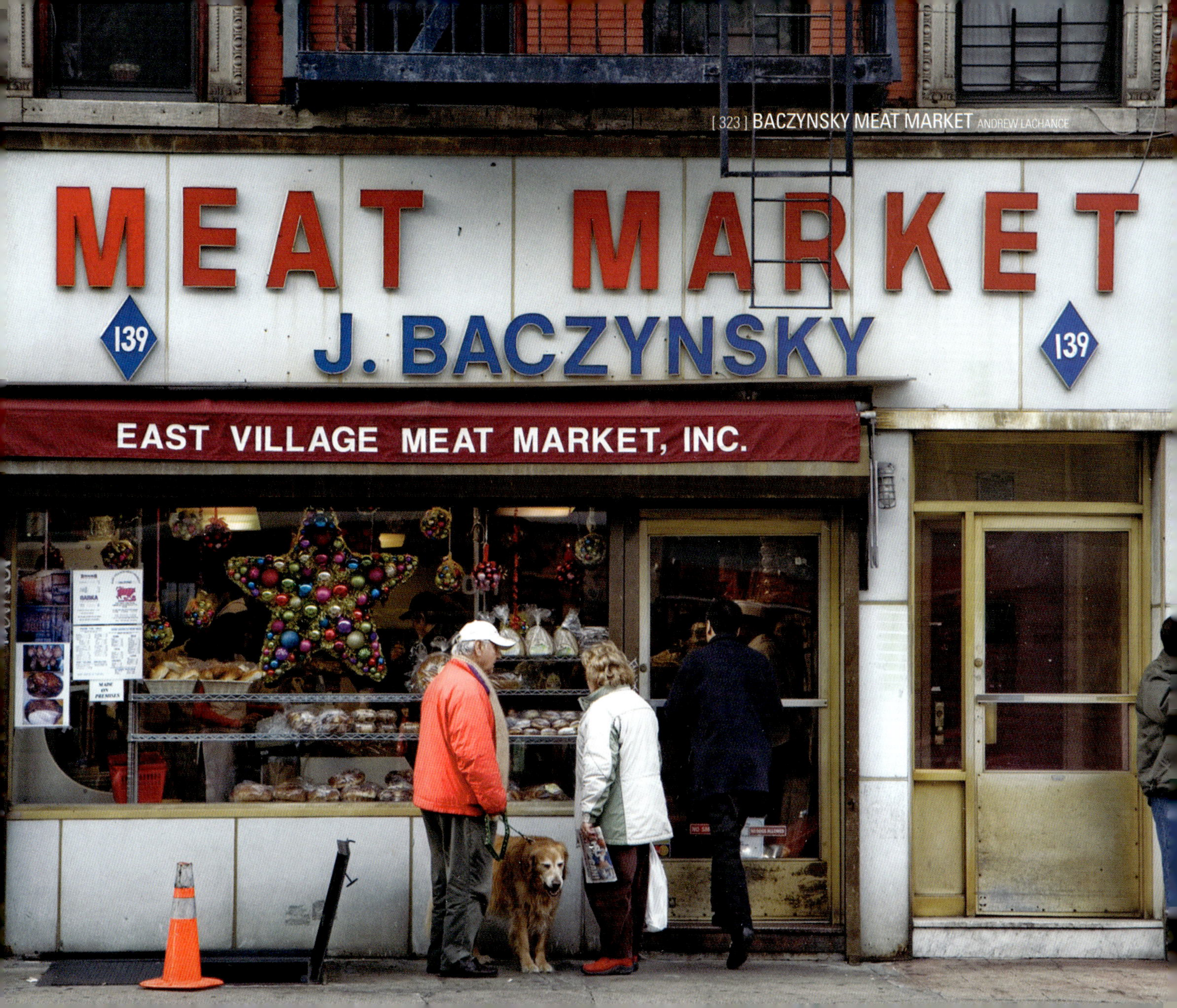

[323] BACZYNSKY MEAT MARKET ANDREW LACHANCE

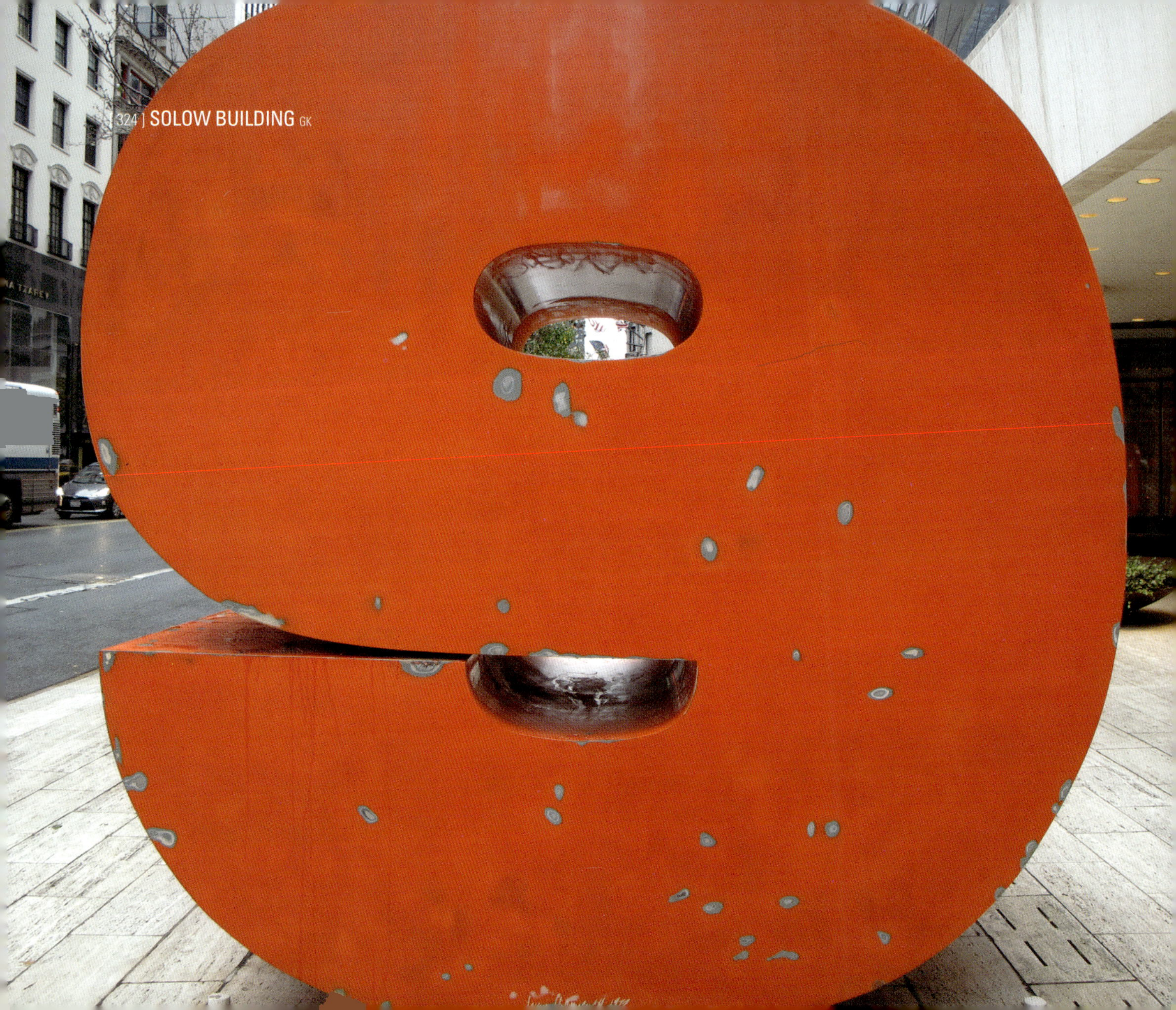

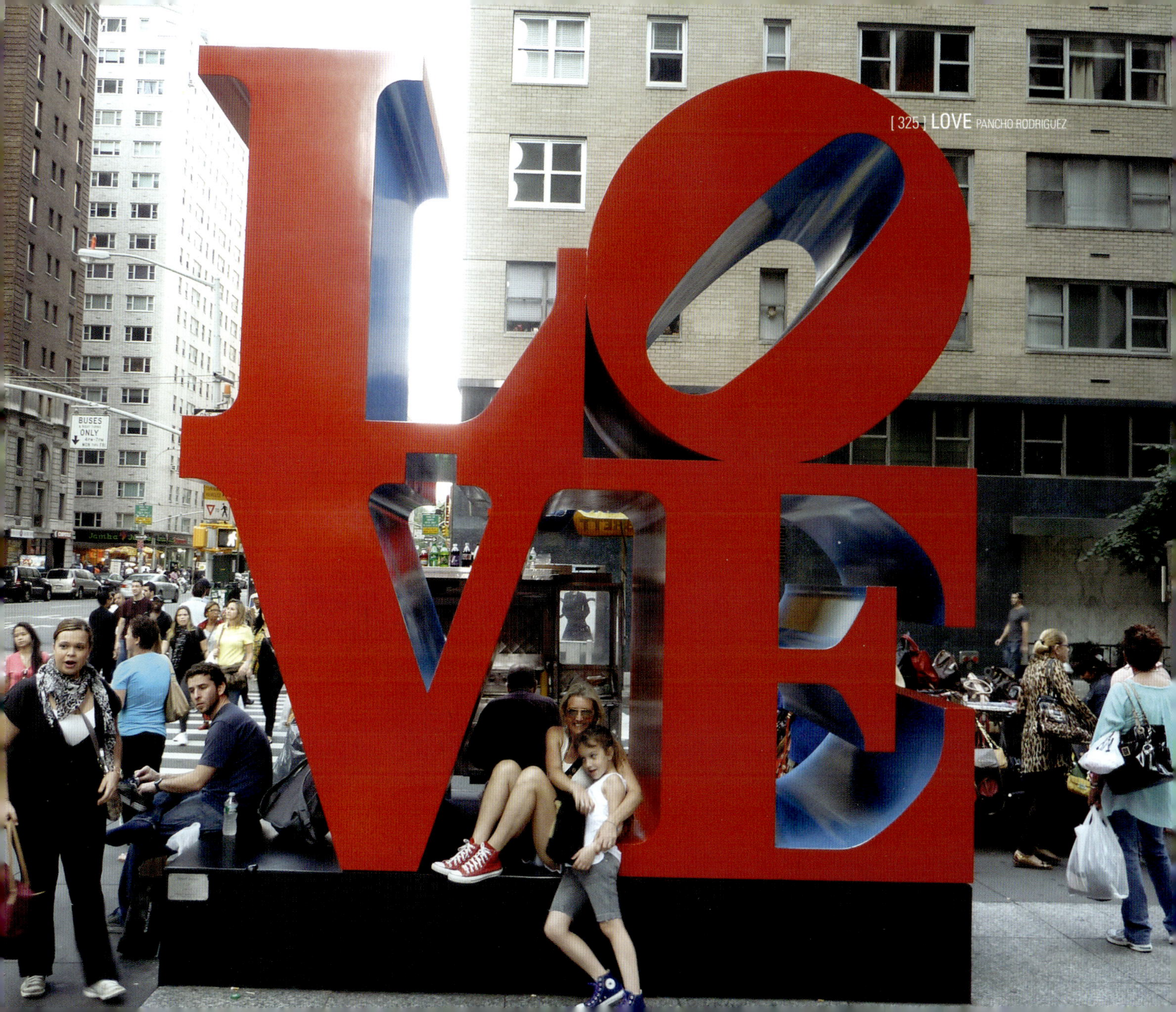

[325] LOVE PANCHO RODRIGUEZ

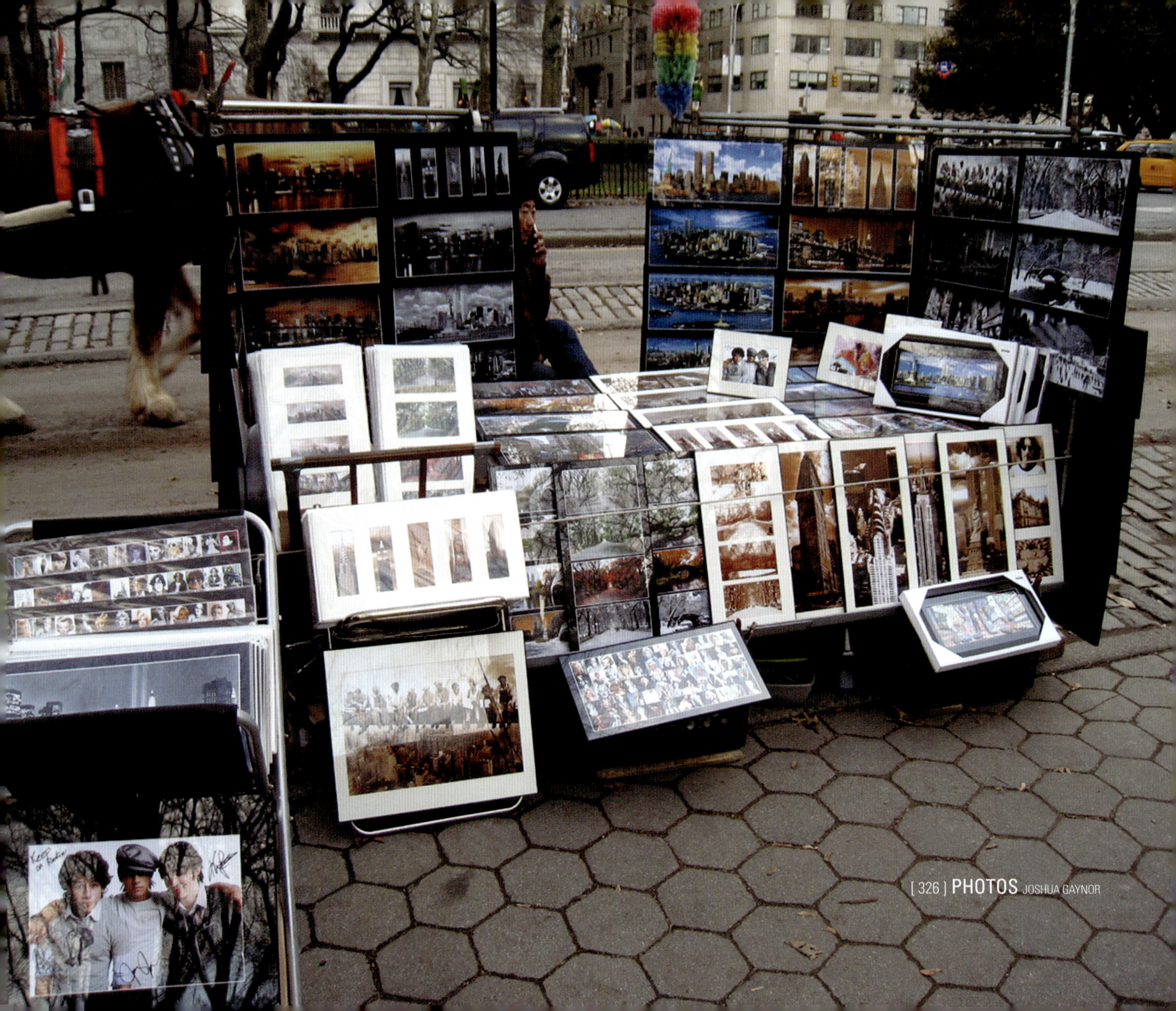

[326] **PHOTOS** JOSHUA GAYNOR

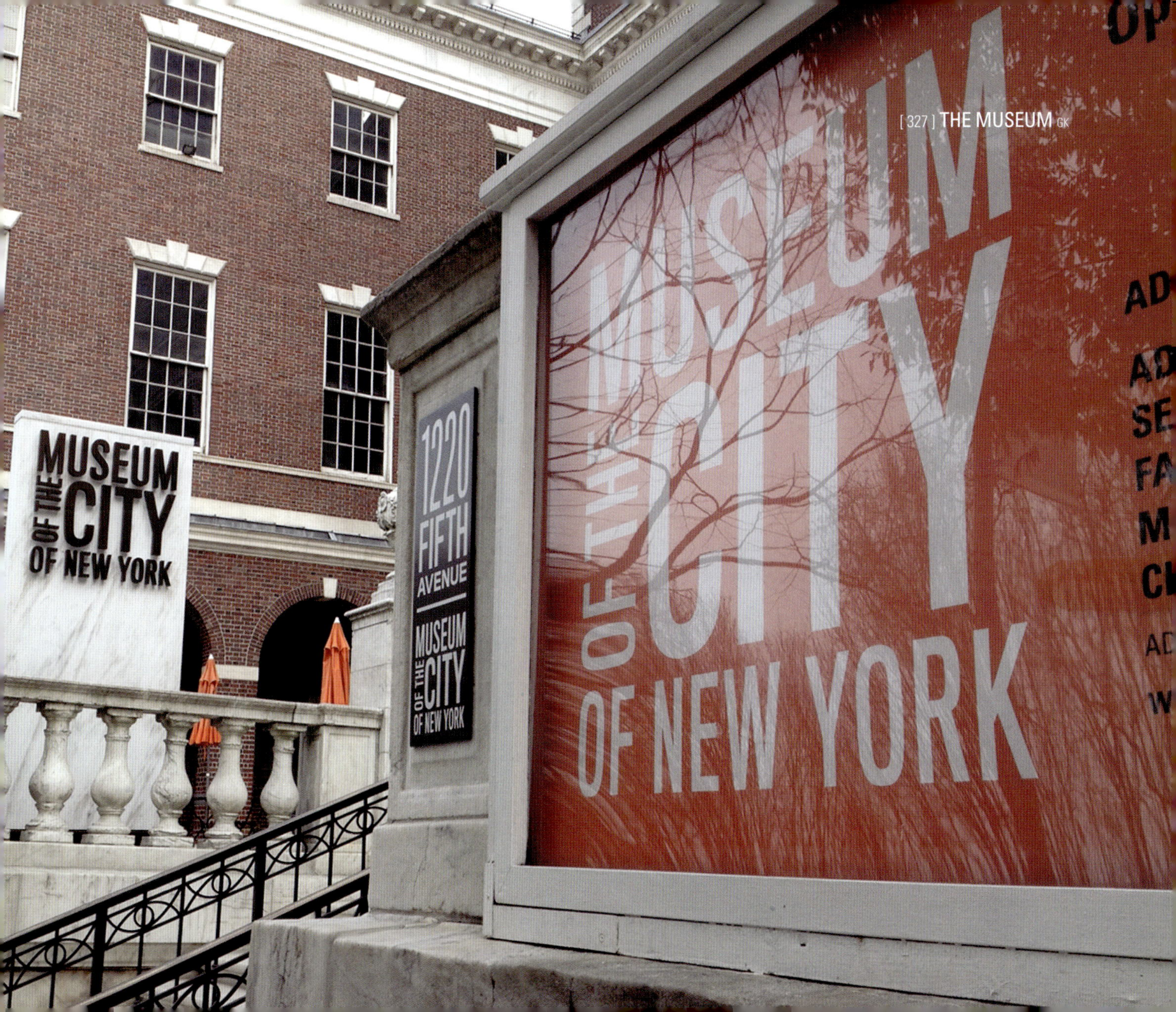
MUSEUM OF THE CITY OF NEW YORK
1220 FIFTH AVENUE
MUSEUM OF THE CITY OF NEW YORK
MUSEUM OF THE CITY OF NEW YORK

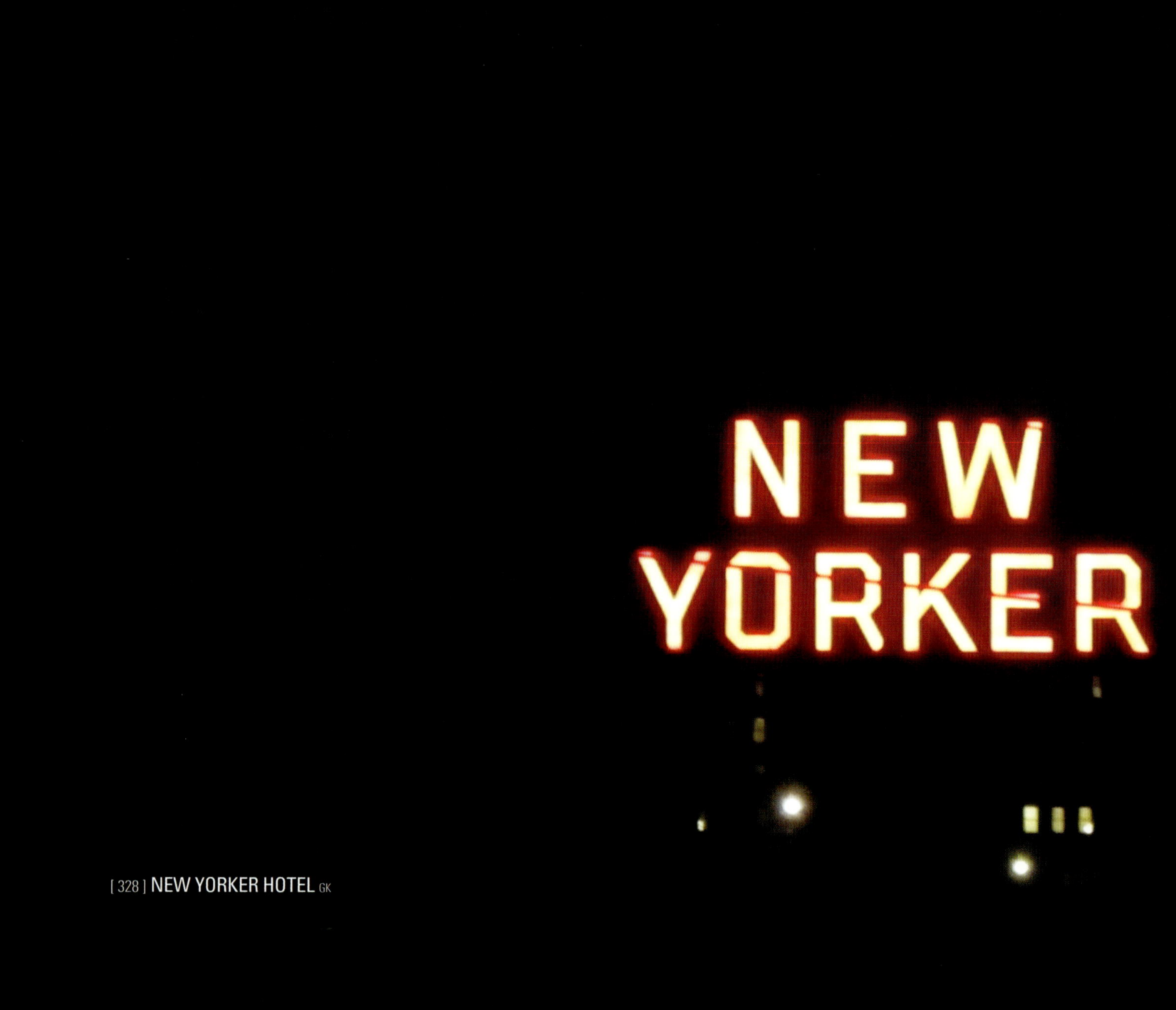

[328] NEW YORKER HOTEL GK

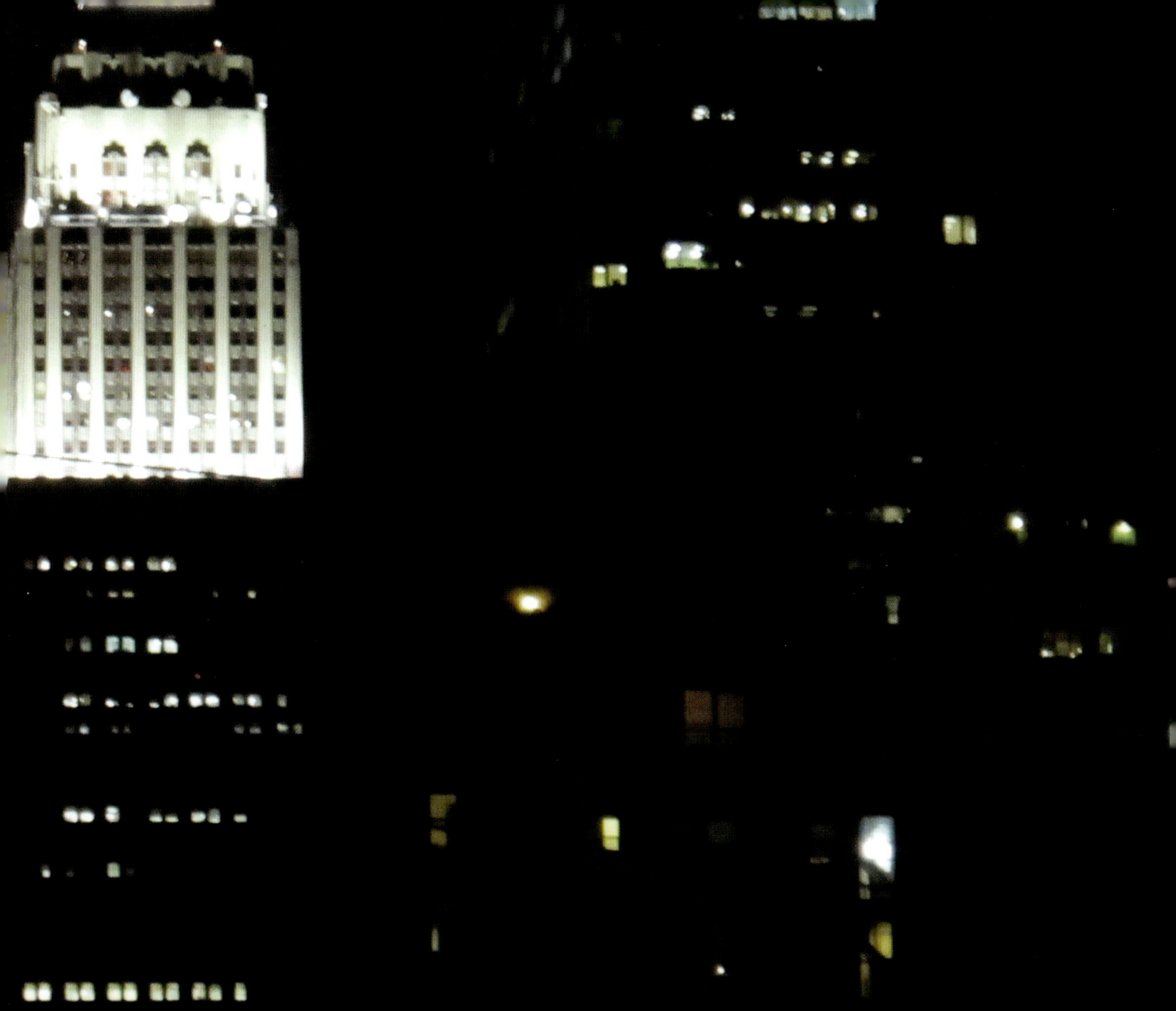

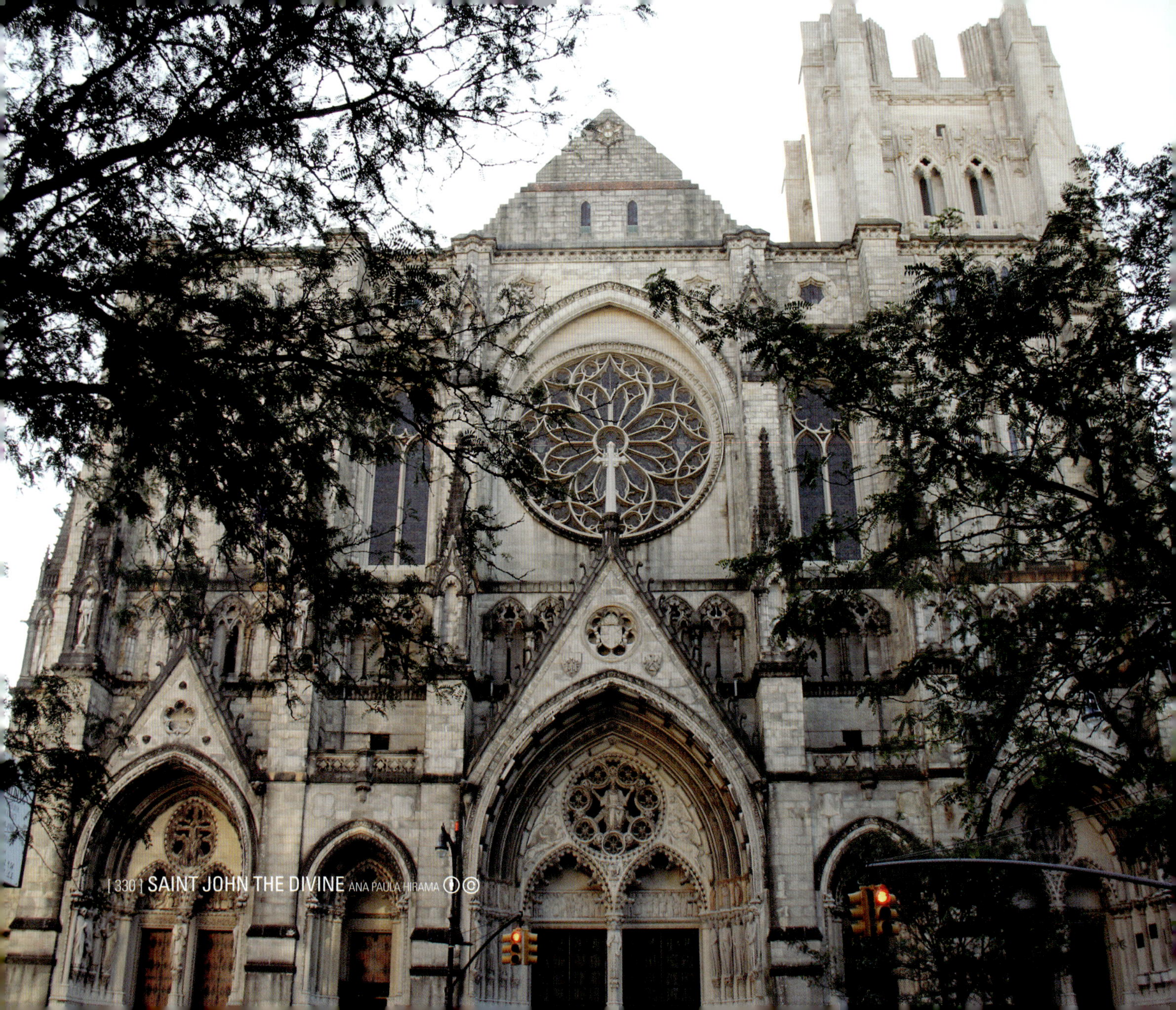

[330] SAINT JOHN THE DIVINE ANA PAULA HIRAMA

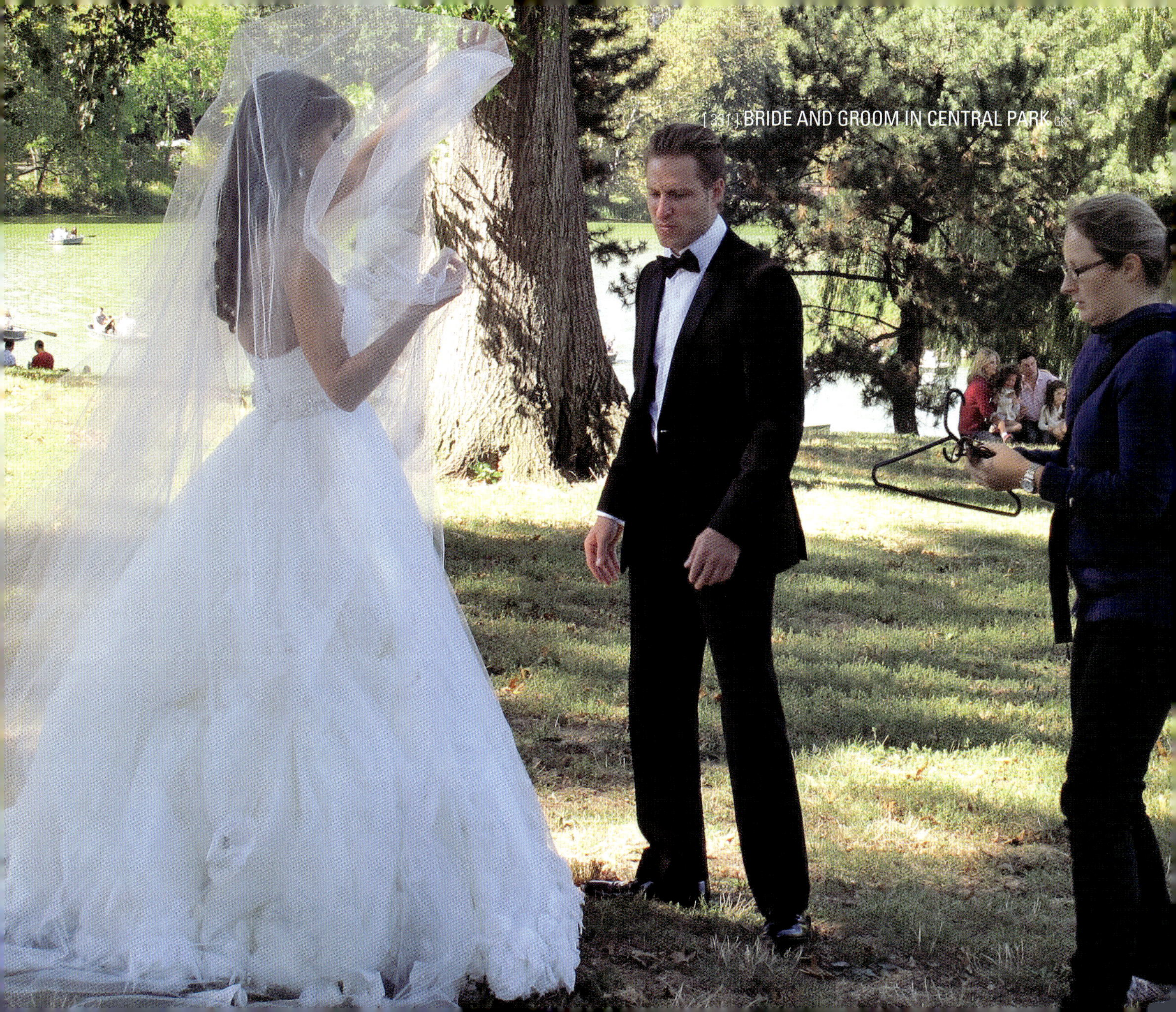

[331] BRIDE AND GROOM IN CENTRAL PARK GK

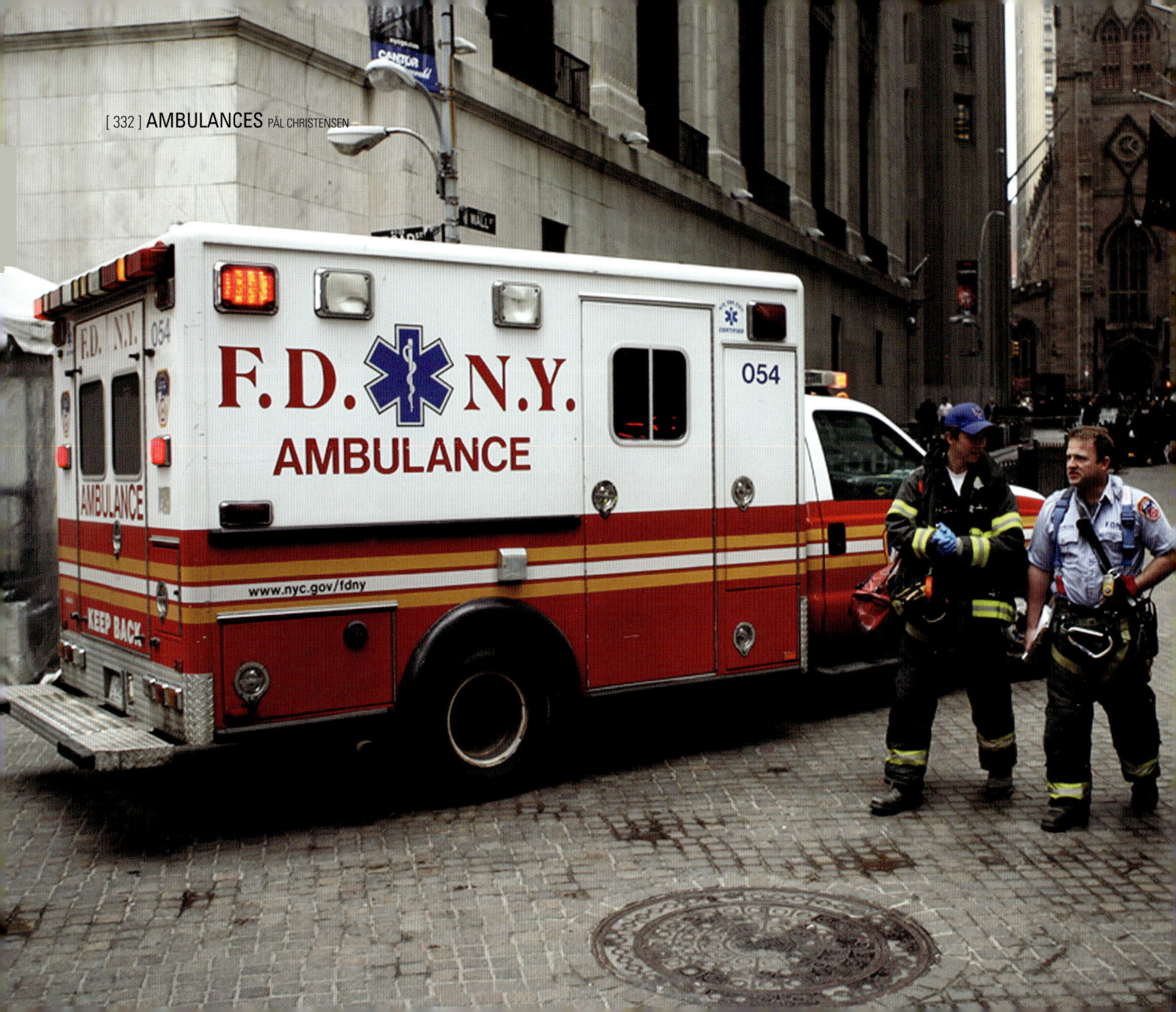
F.D. N.Y.
AMBULANCE
054
www.nyc.gov/fdny
KEEP BACK
AMBULANCE

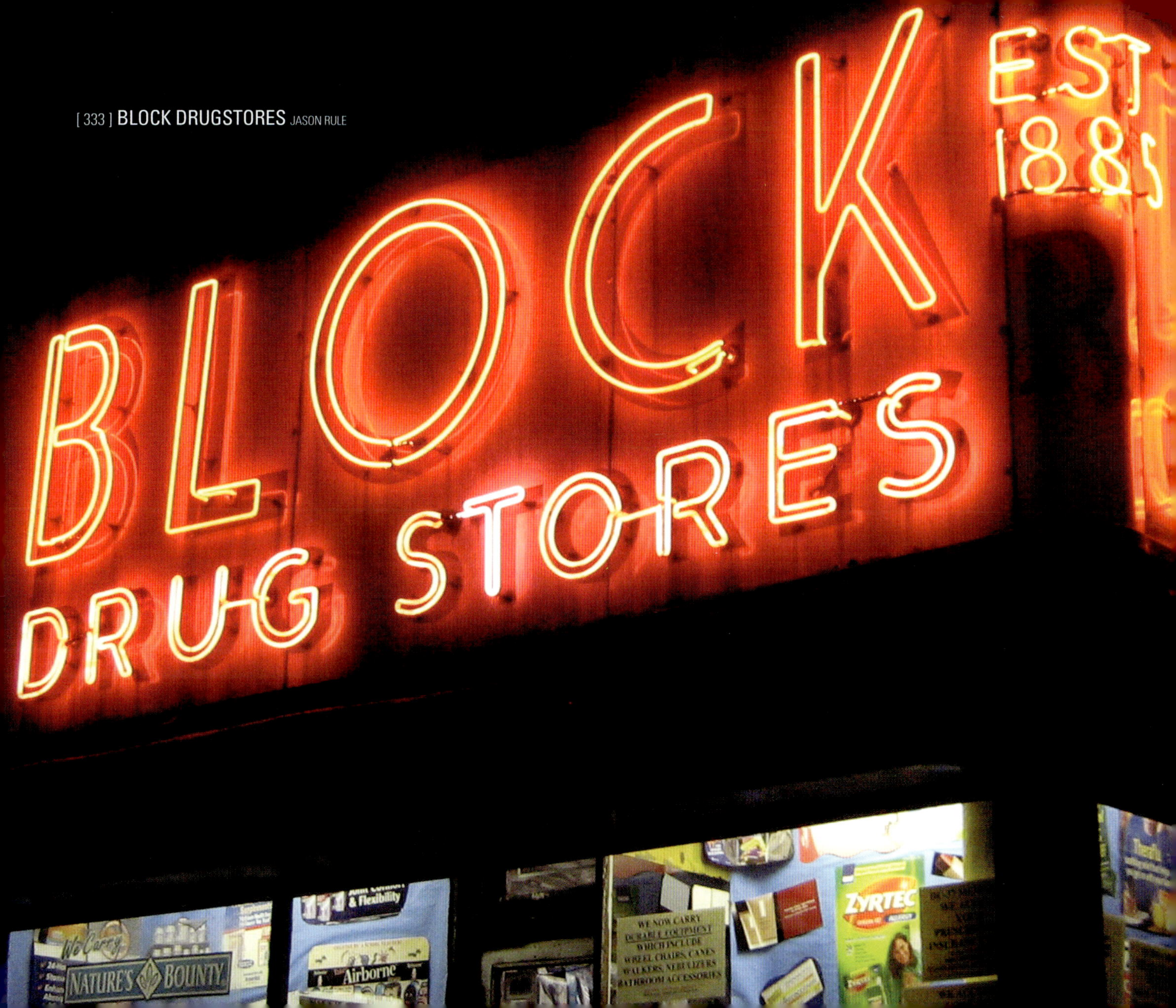

[333] BLOCK DRUGSTORES JASON RULE

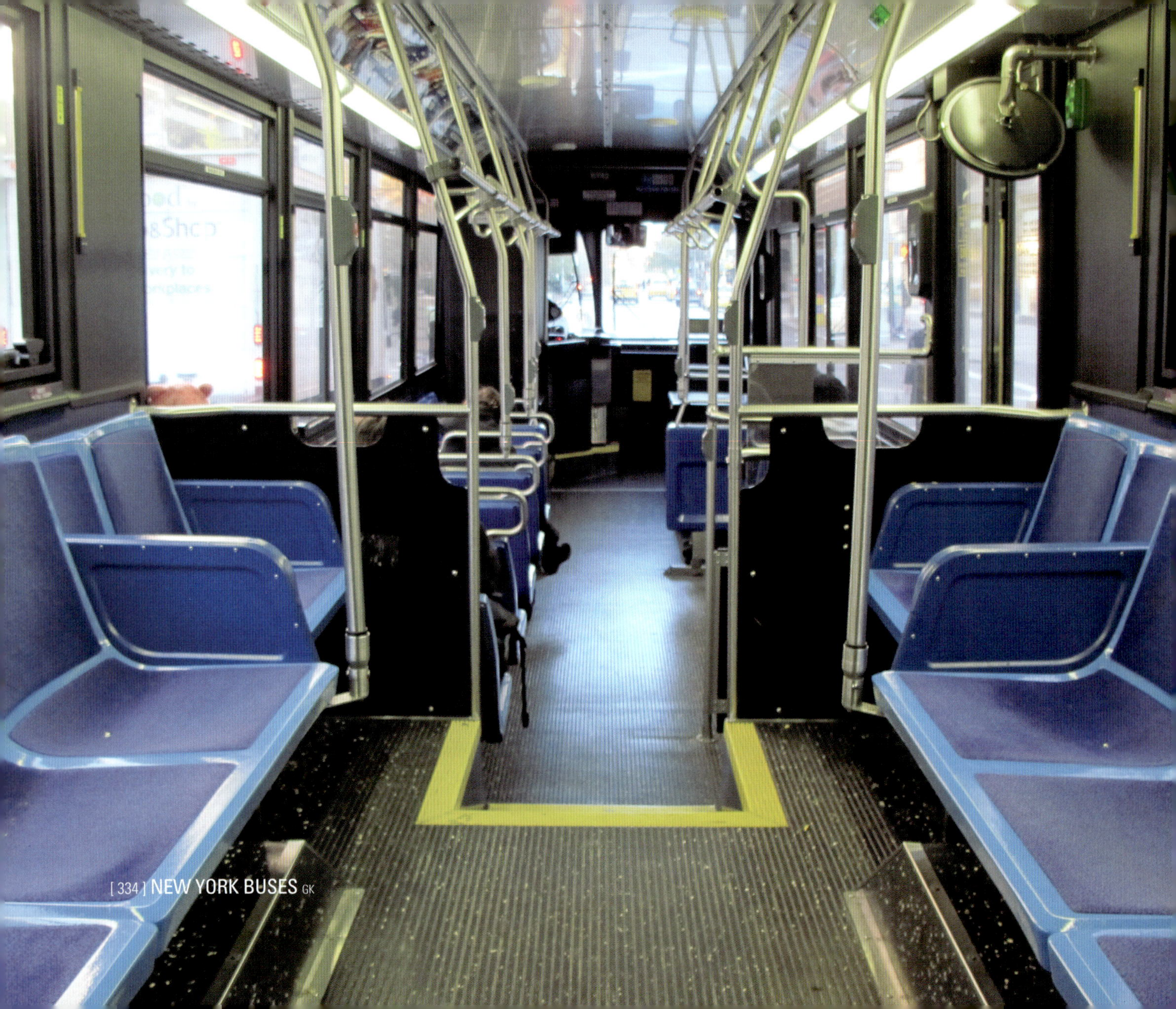

[334] NEW YORK BUSES GK

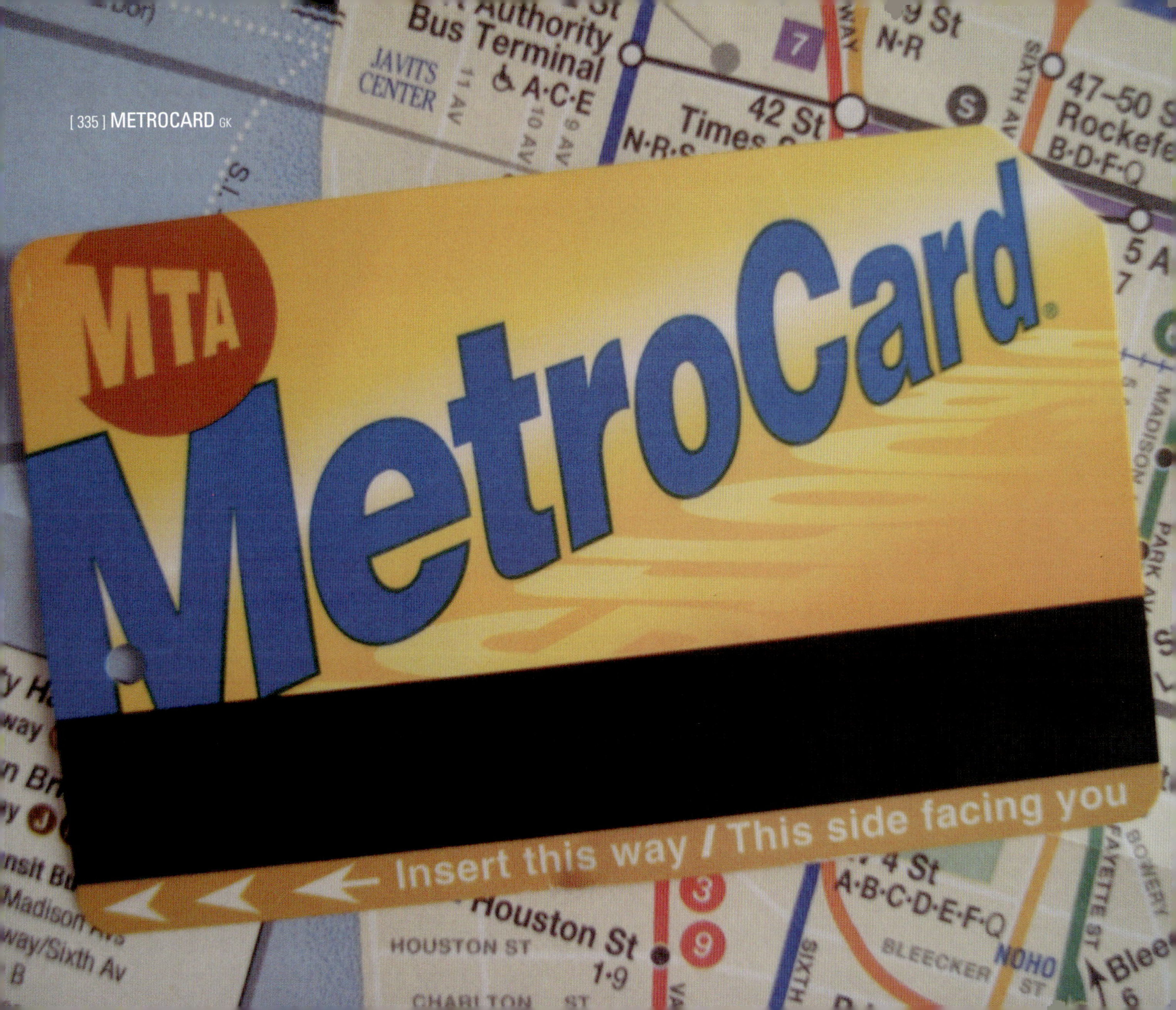
MTA
MetroCard
Insert this way / This side facing you
Bus Terminal
A·C·E
JAVITS CENTER
42 St
B·D·F·Q
Houston St
HOUSTON ST
A·B·C·D·E·F·Q
BLEECKER
NOHO

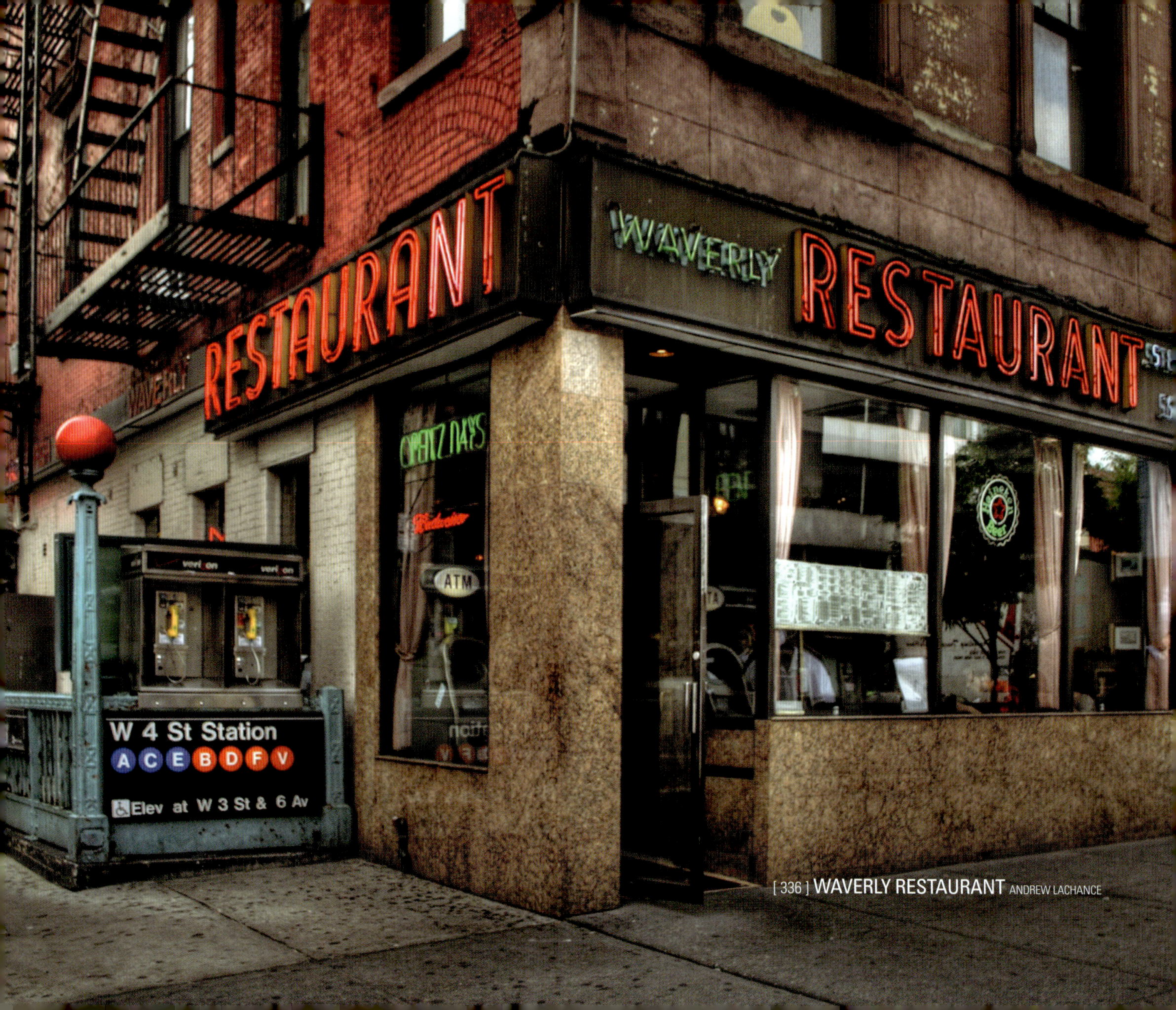

[336] **WAVERLY RESTAURANT** ANDREW LACHANCE

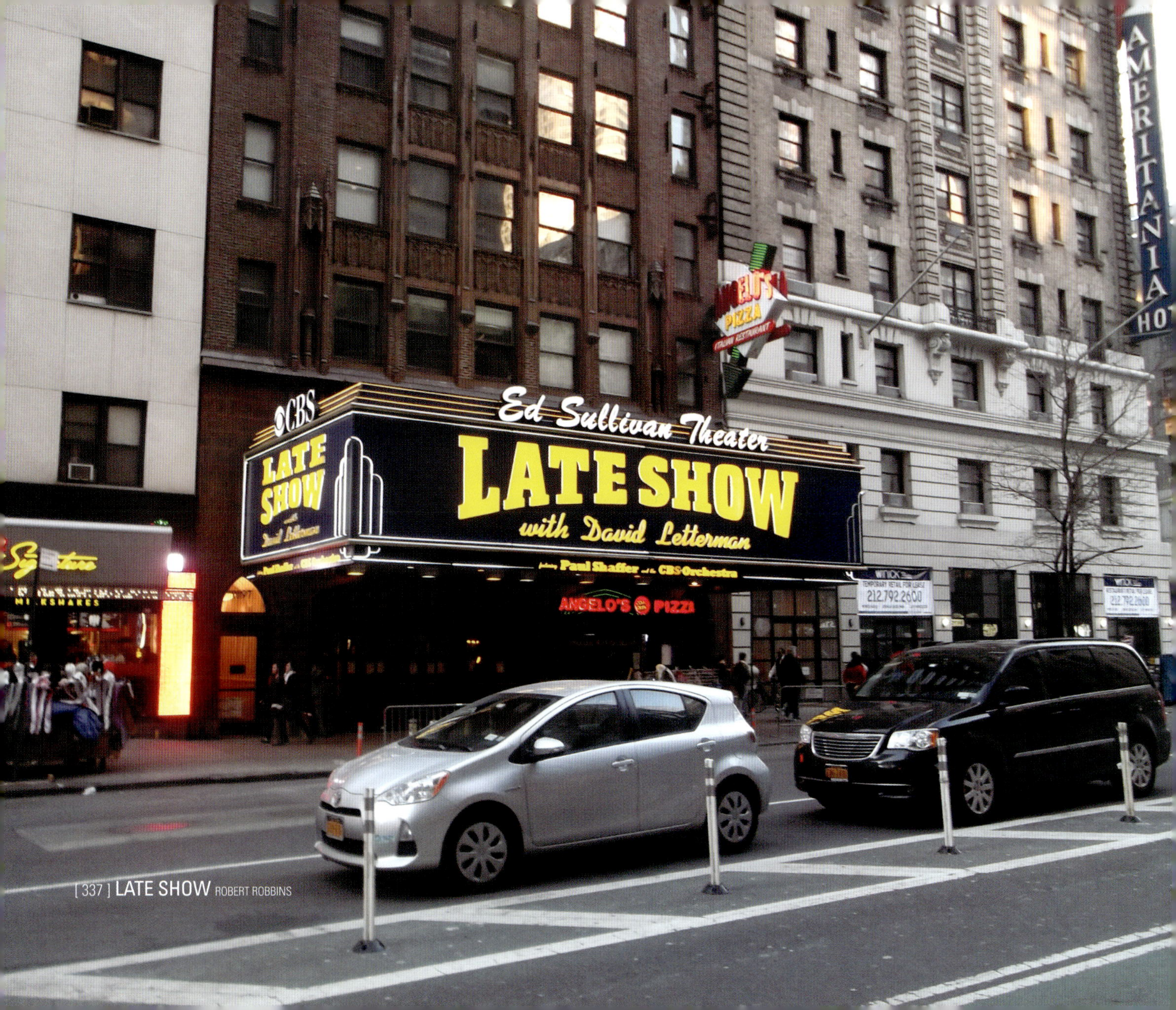

[337] LATE SHOW ROBERT ROBBINS

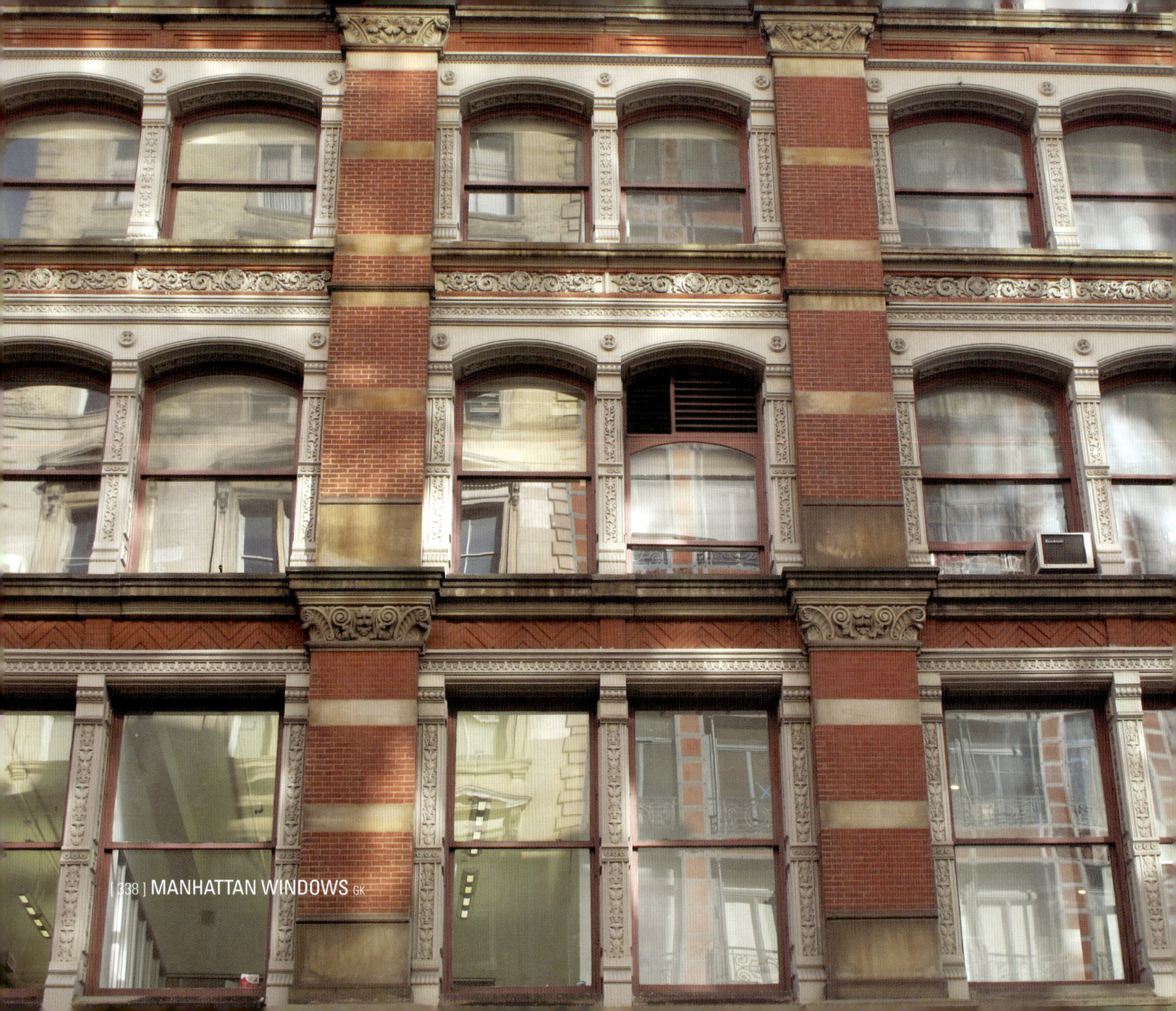

[338] MANHATTAN WINDOWS GK

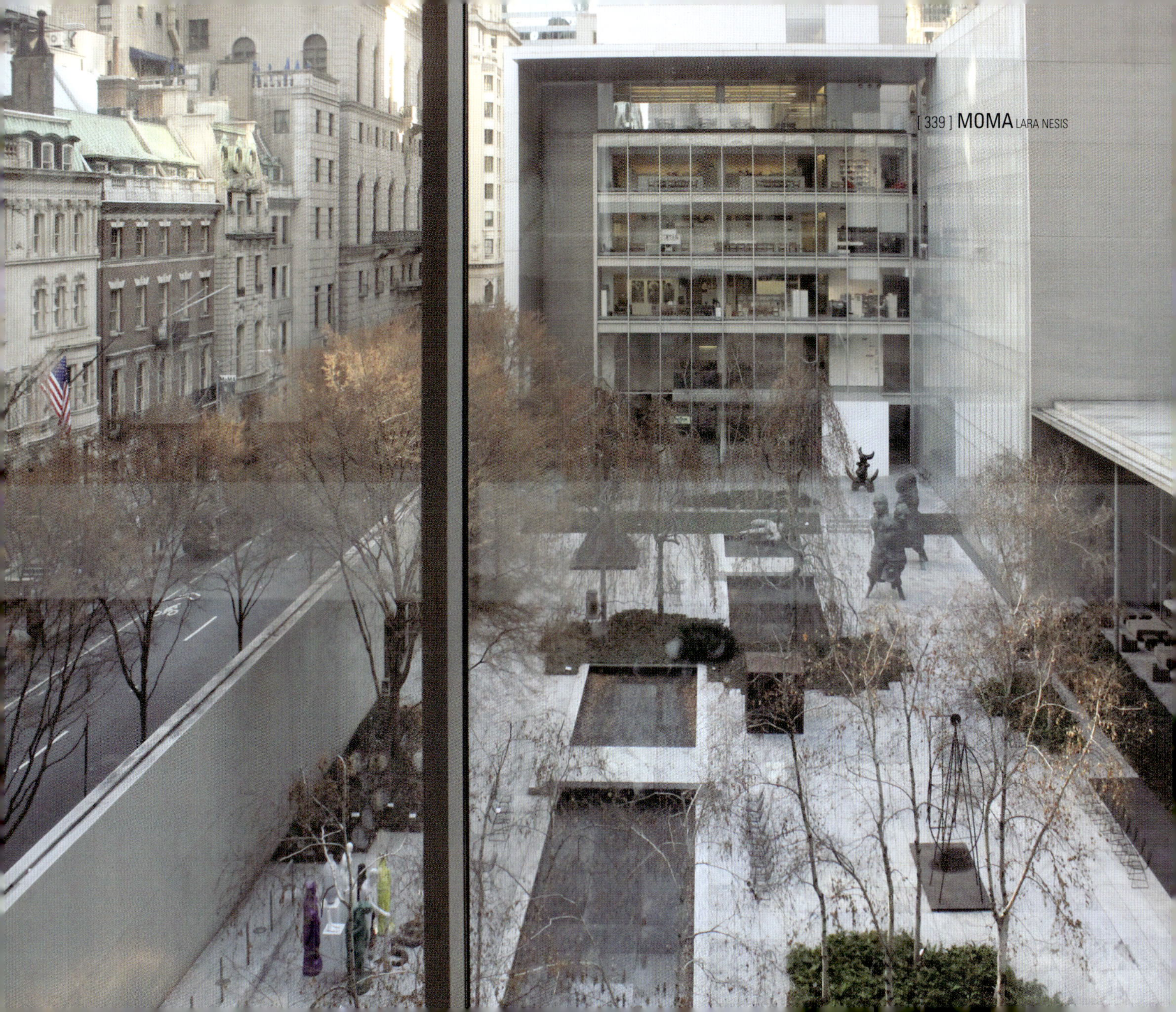

[339] MOMA LARA NESIS

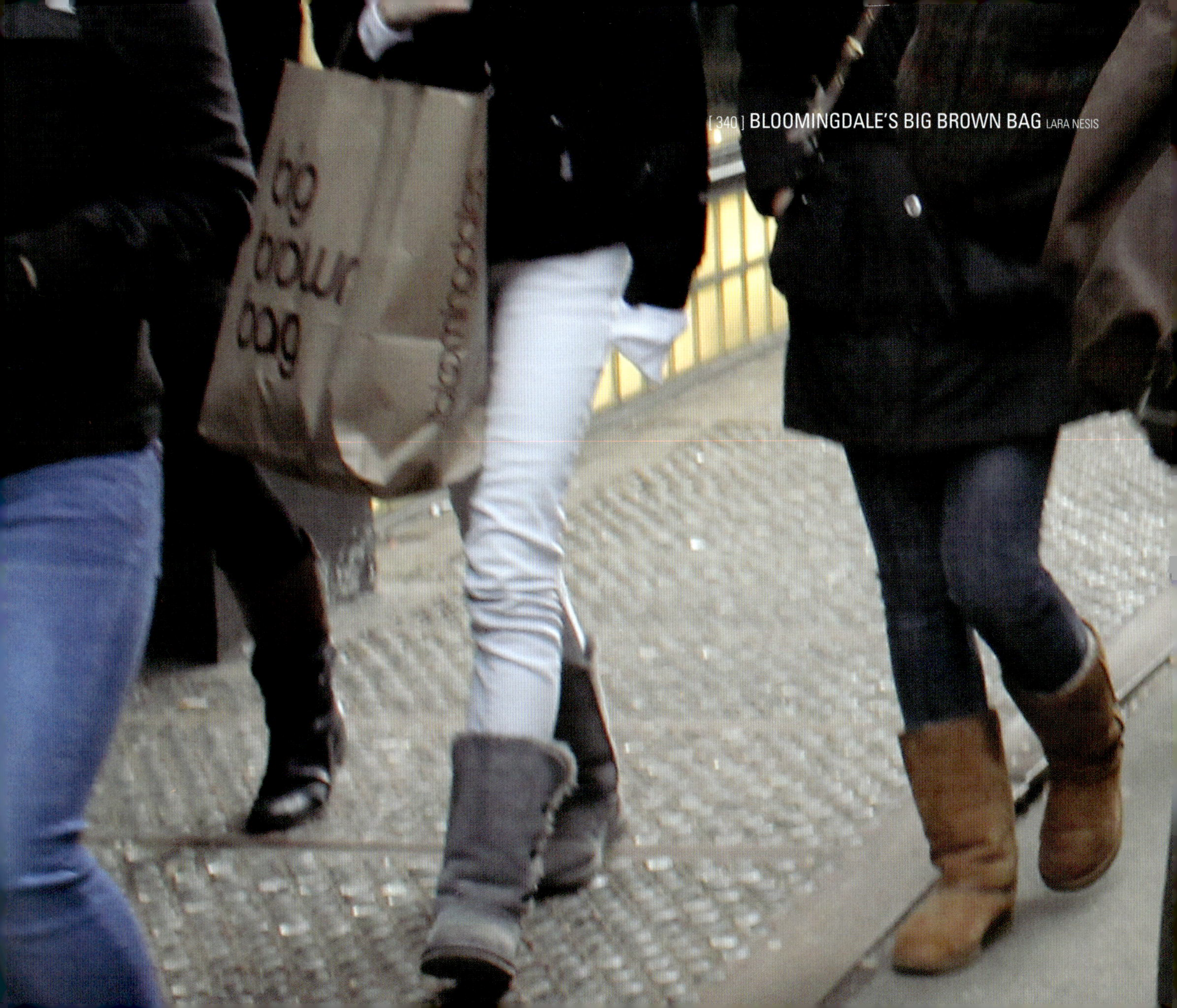

[340] BLOOMINGDALE'S BIG BROWN BAG LARA NESIS

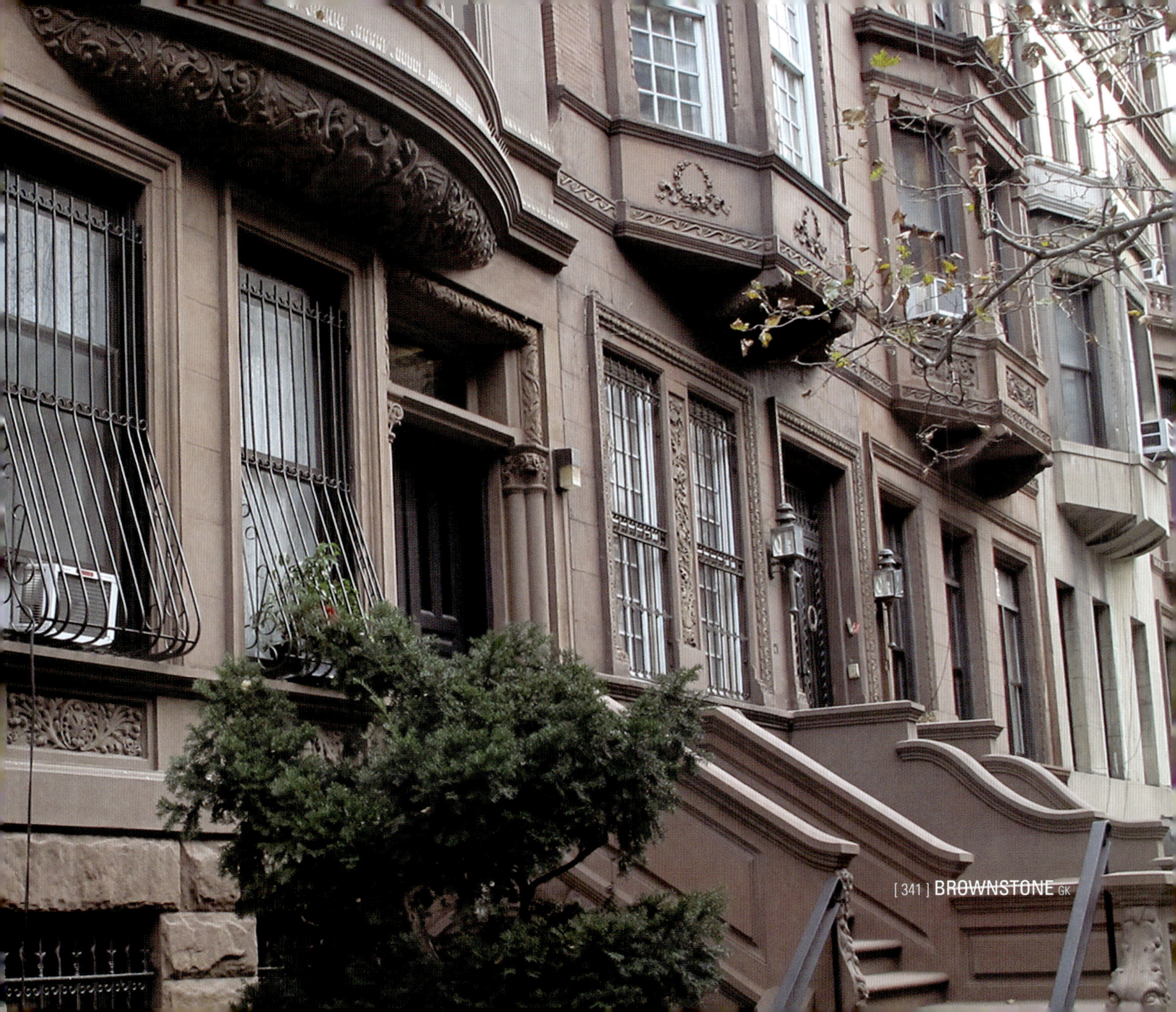

[341] BROWNSTONE GK

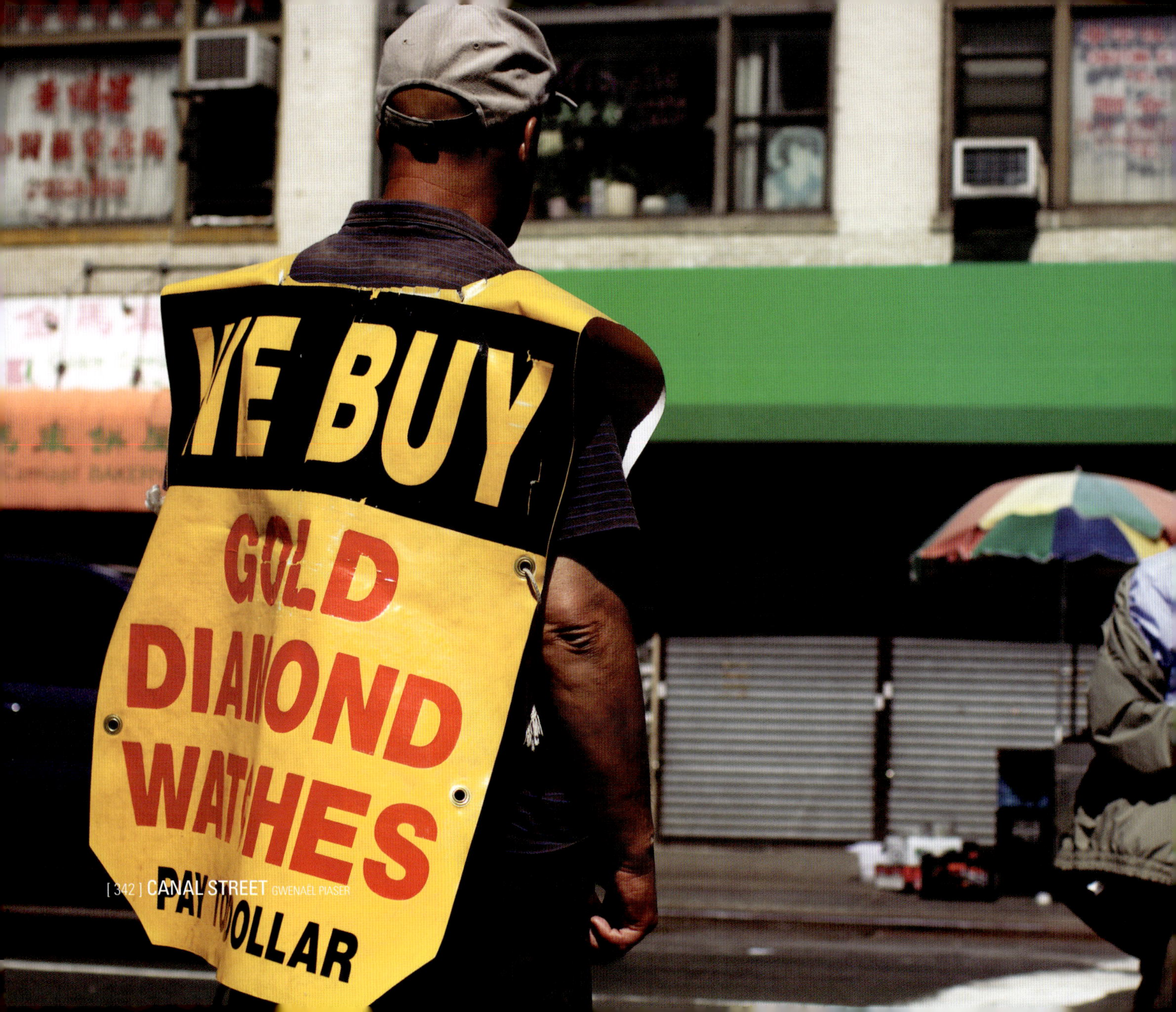
BUY
GOLD
DIAMOND

[343] STRAND MARK SUSINA

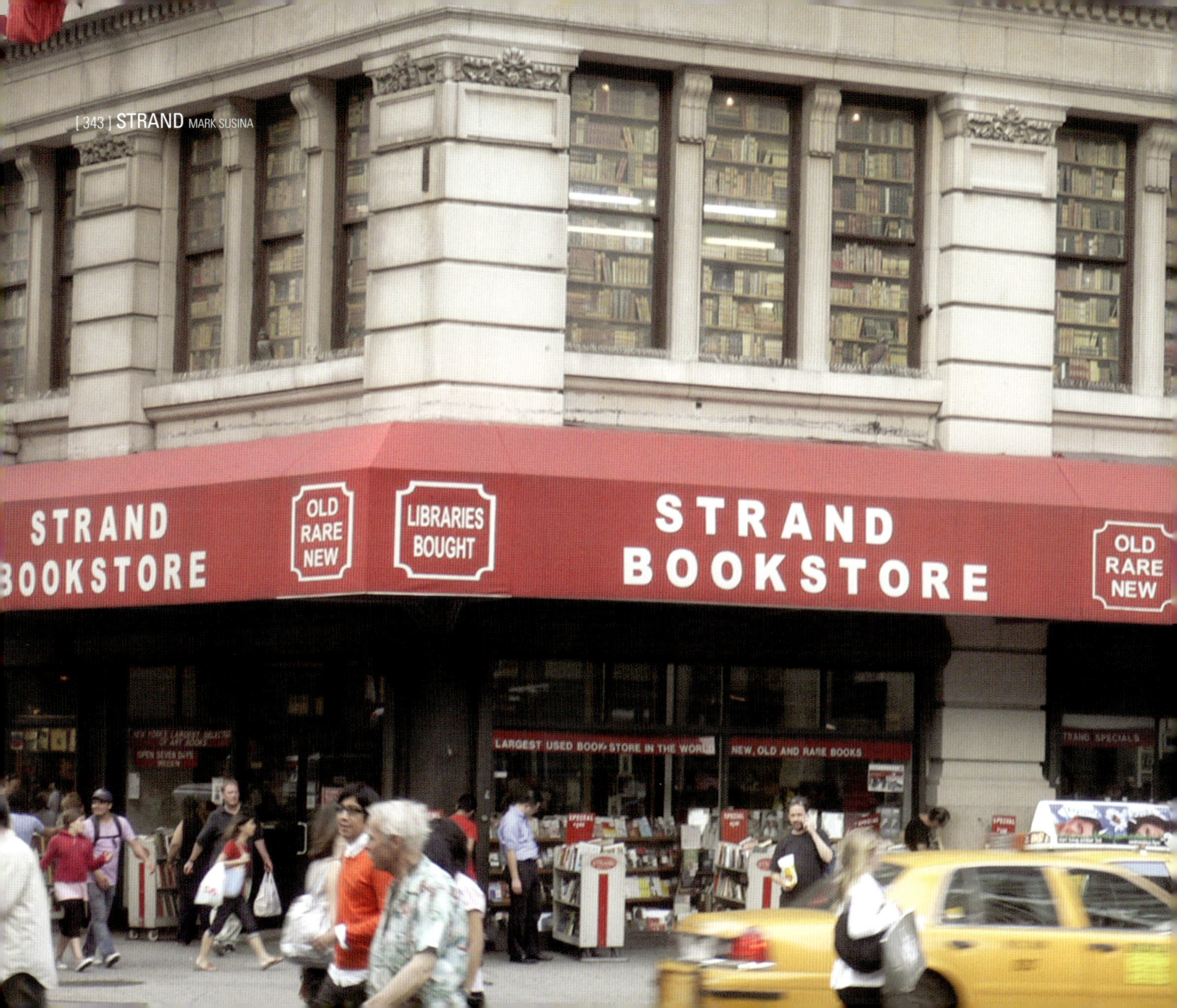

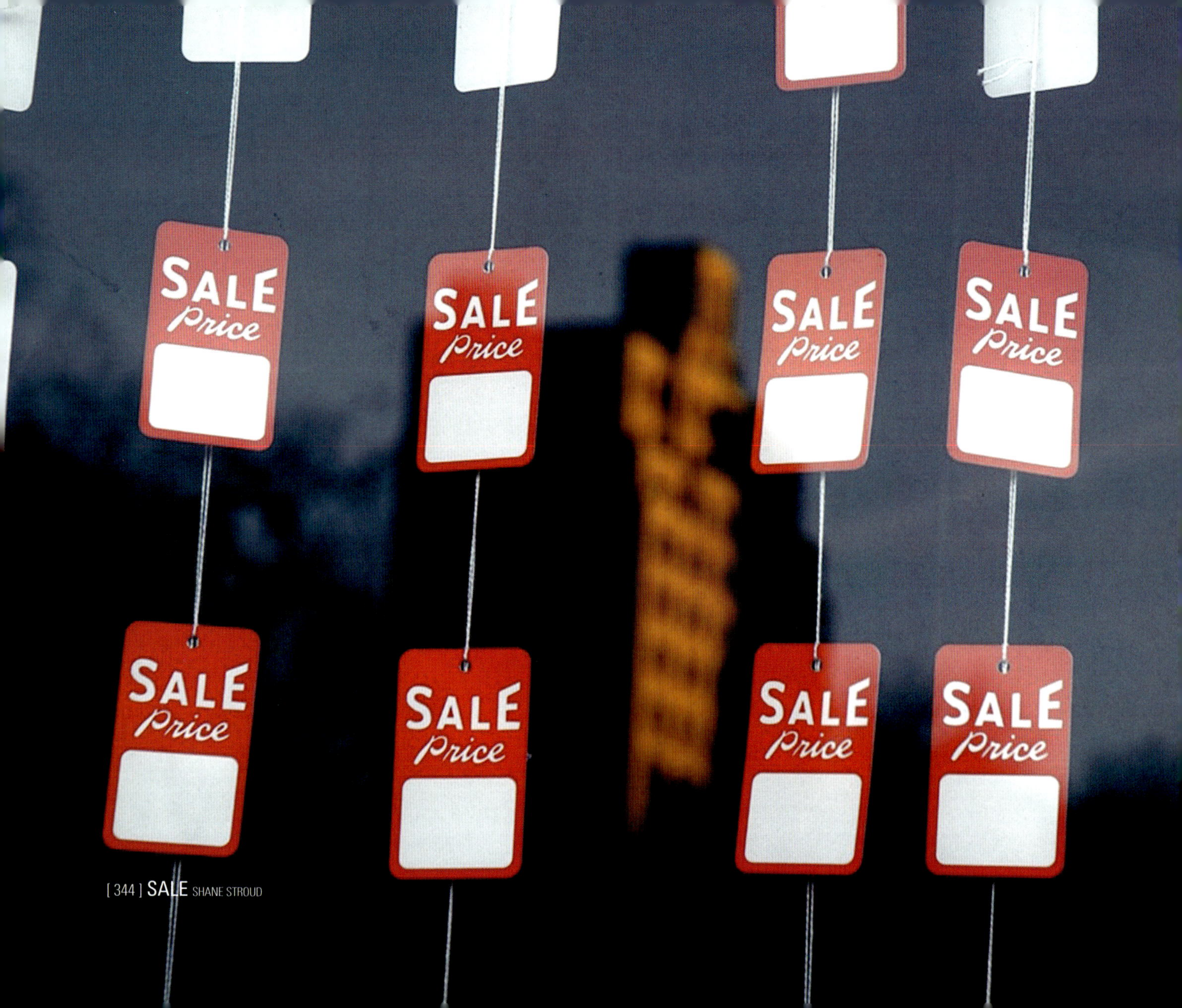

[344] SALE SHANE STROUD

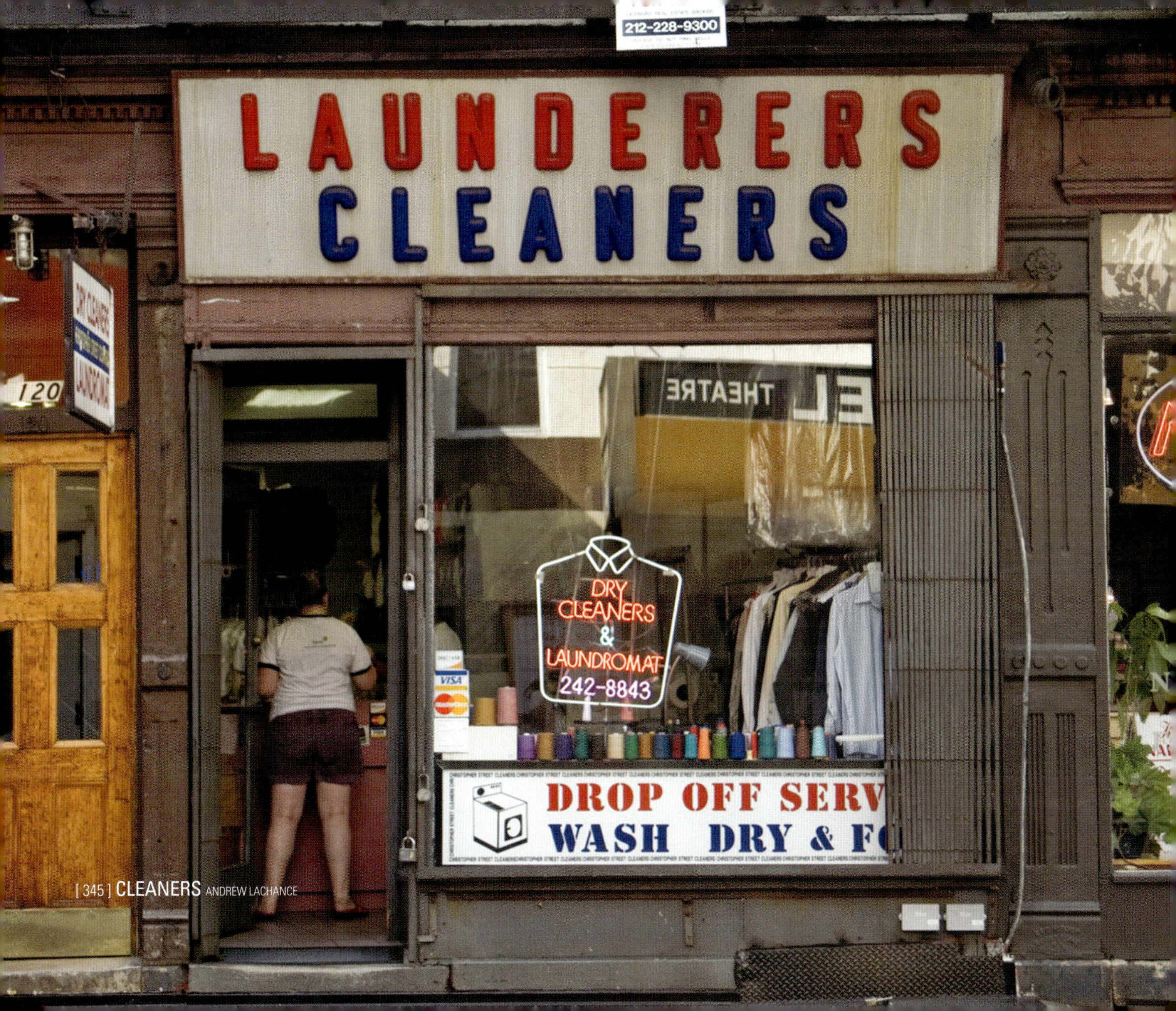

[345] CLEANERS ANDREW LACHANCE

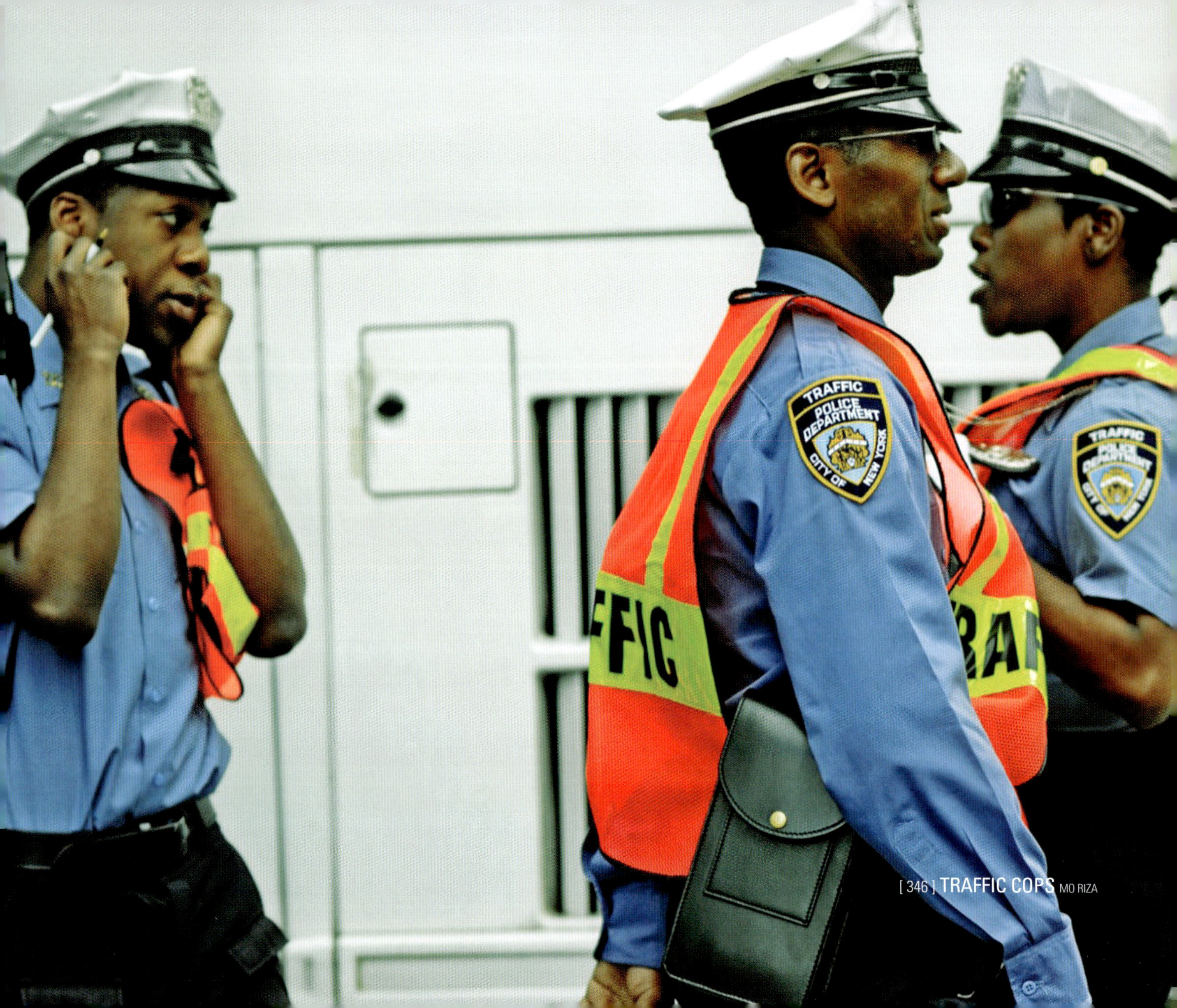

[346] **TRAFFIC COPS** MO RIZA

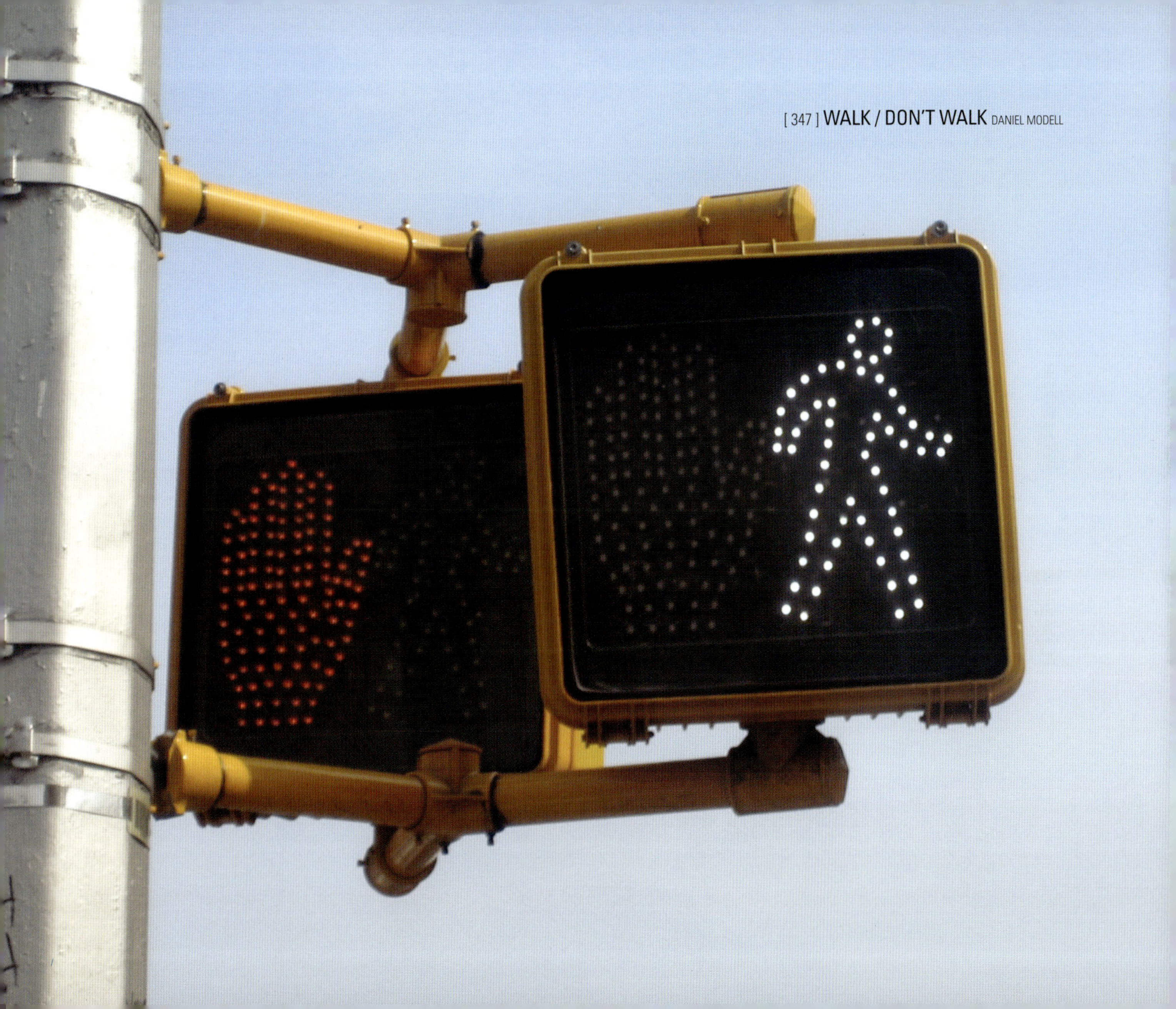

[347] WALK / DON'T WALK DANIEL MODELL

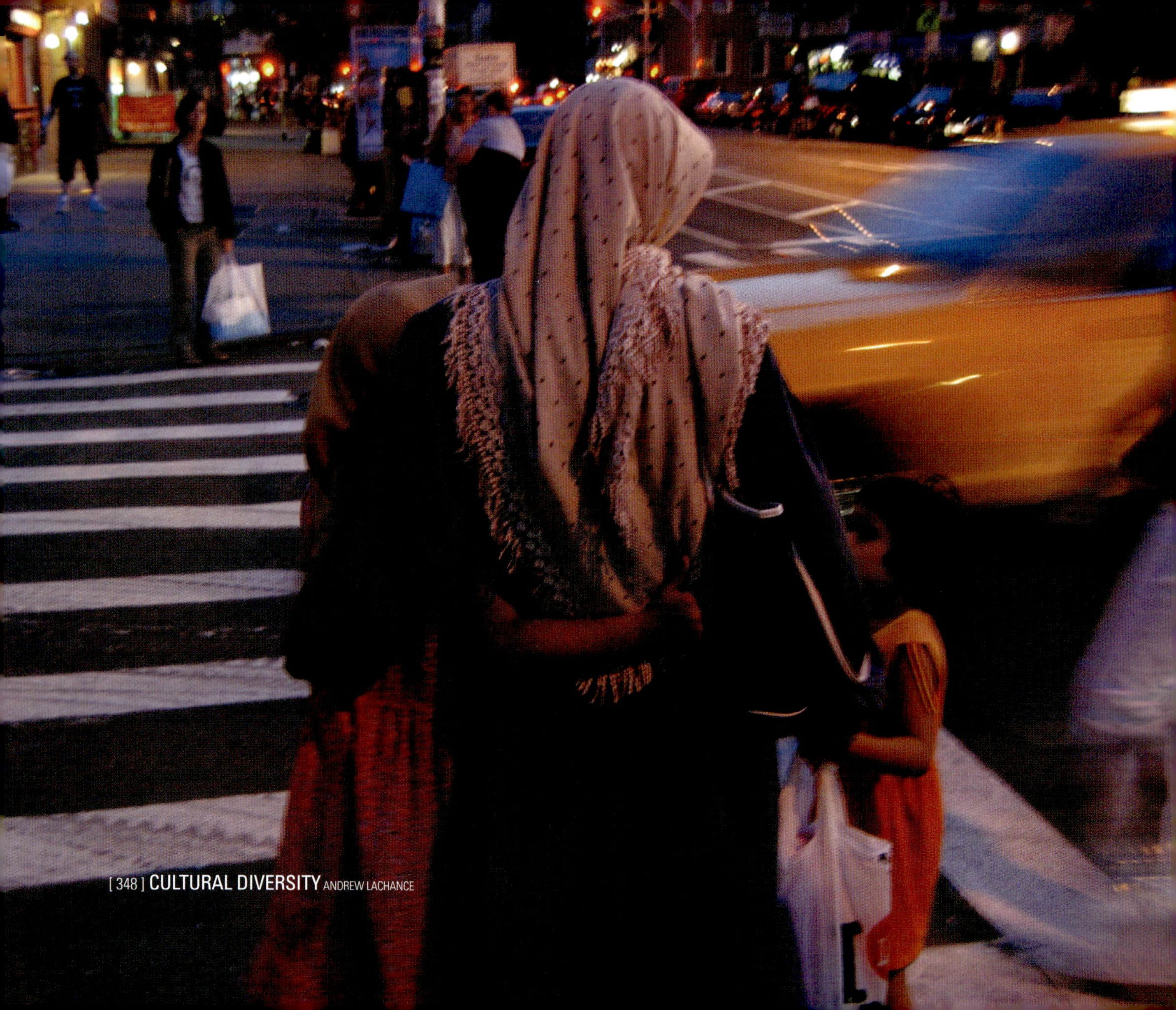

[348] CULTURAL DIVERSITY ANDREW LACHANCE

[349] THE UNITED NATIONS MARK SUSINA

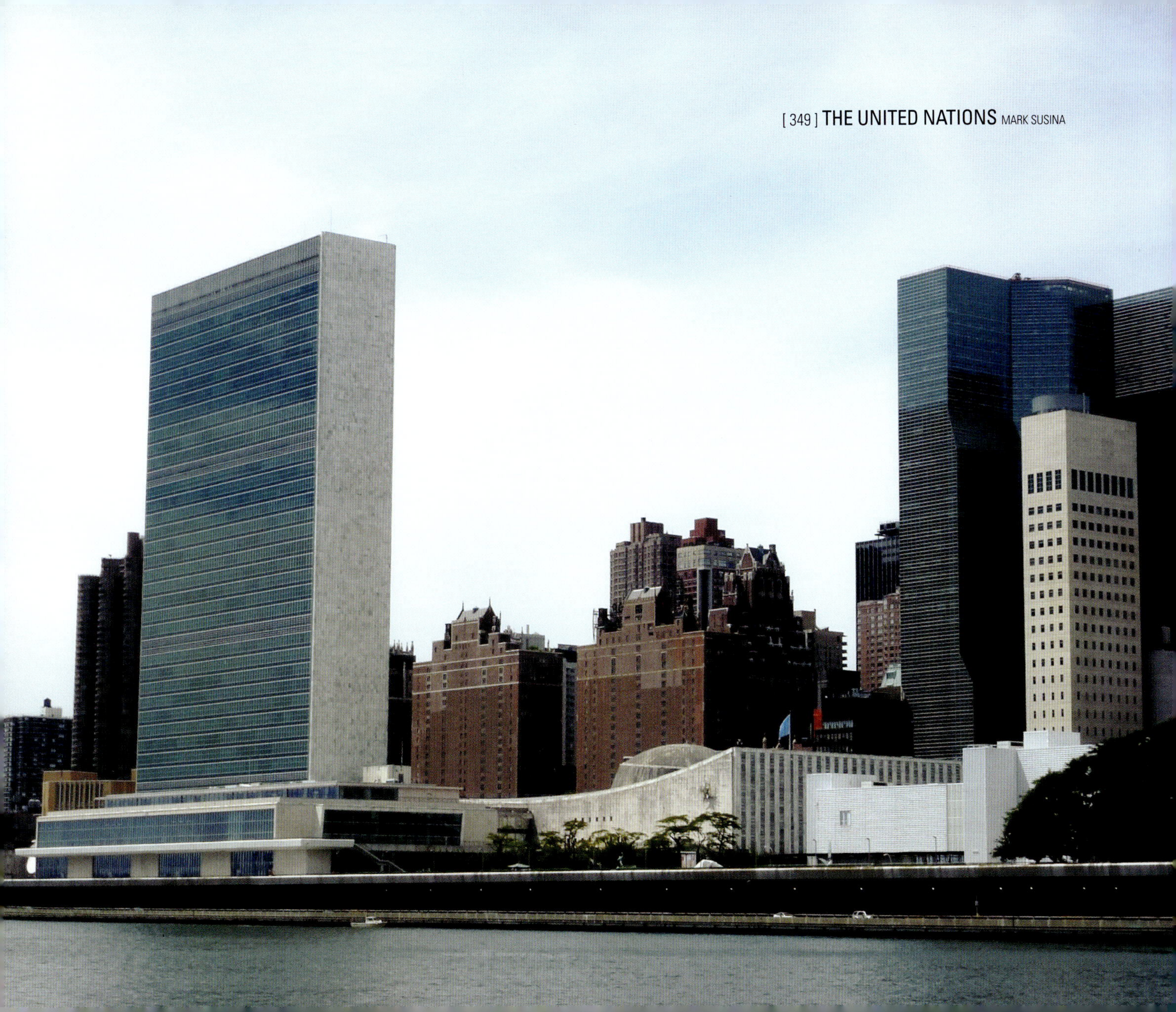

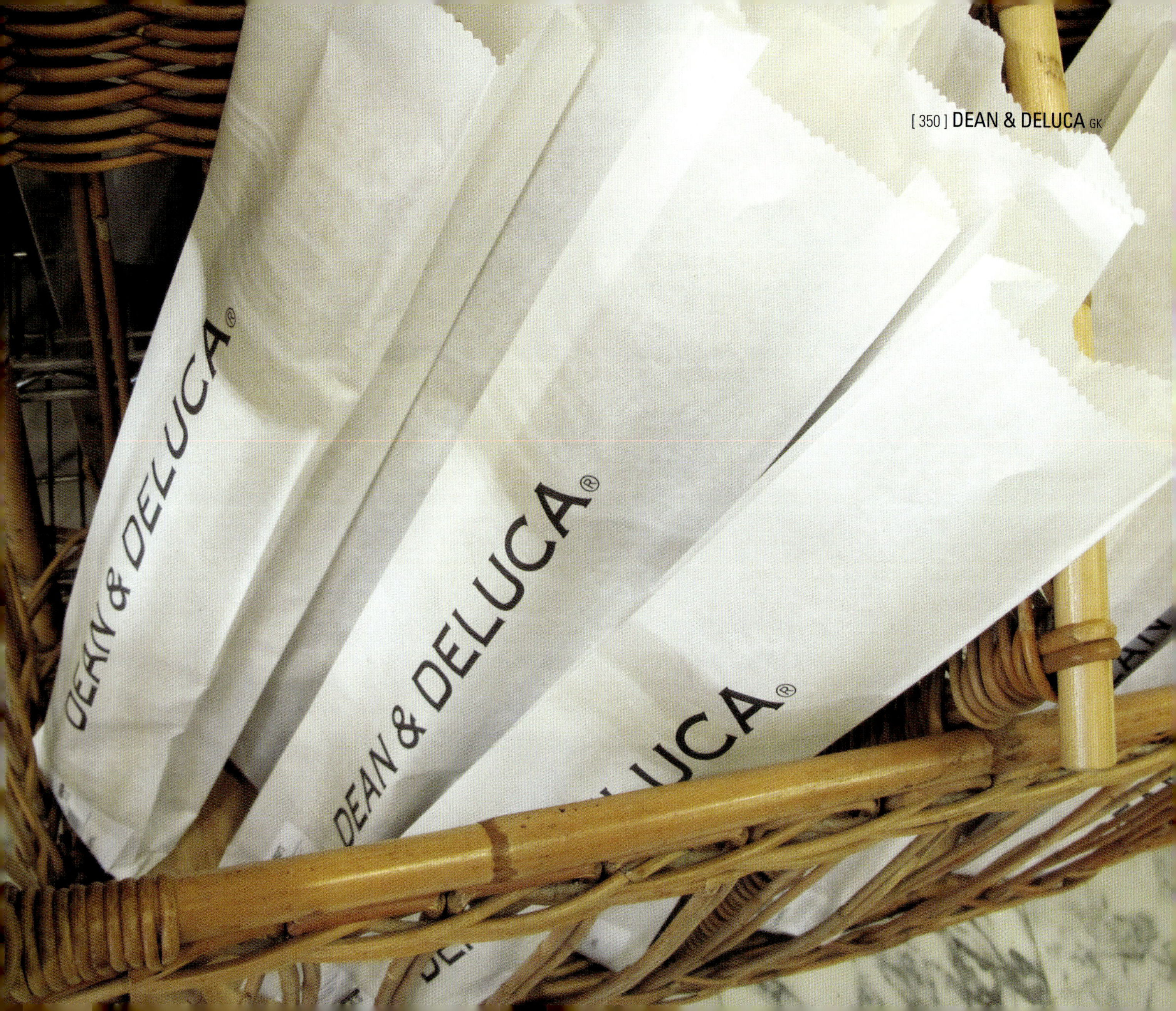

[350] **DEAN & DELUCA** GK

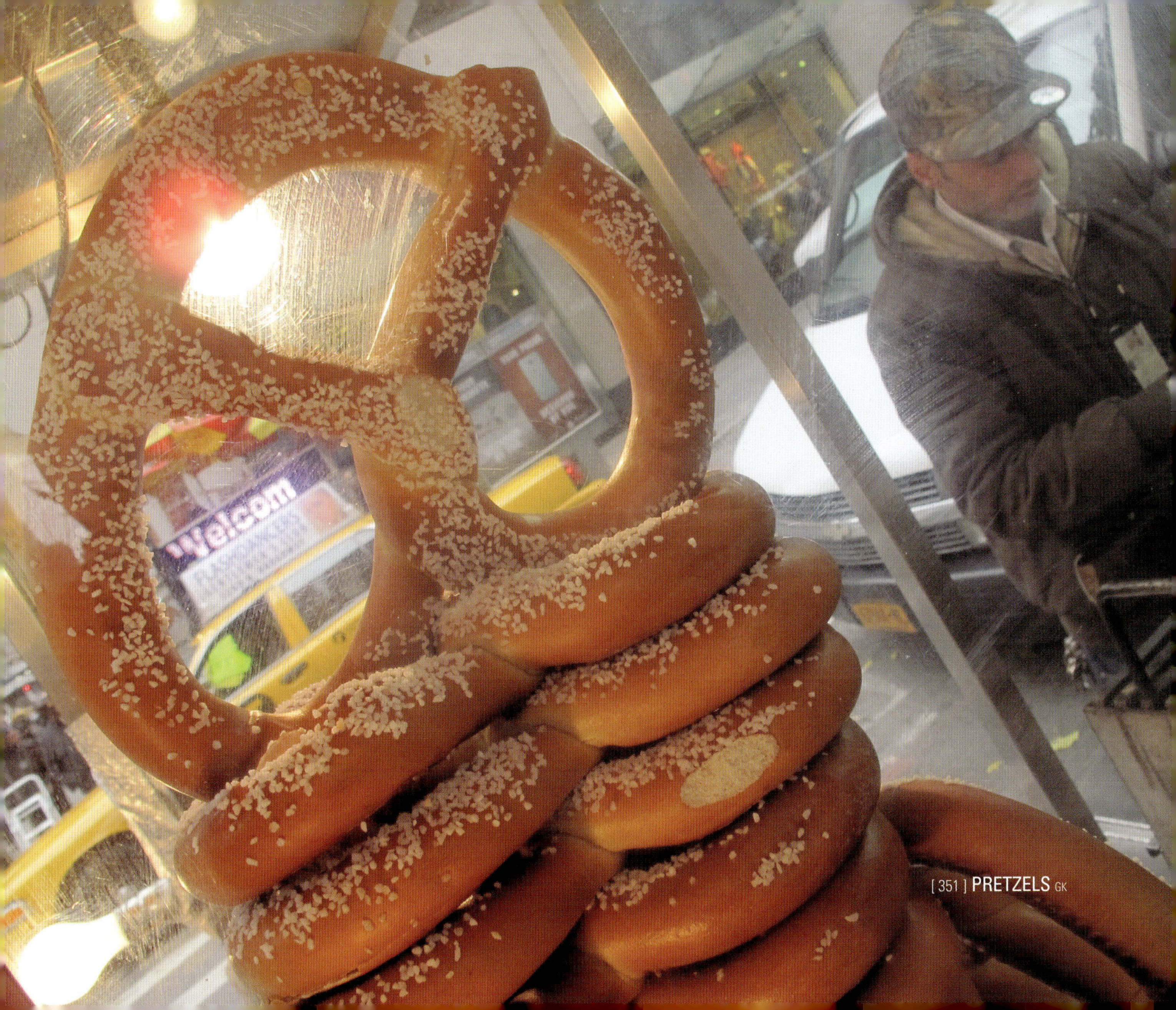

[351] **PRETZELS** GK

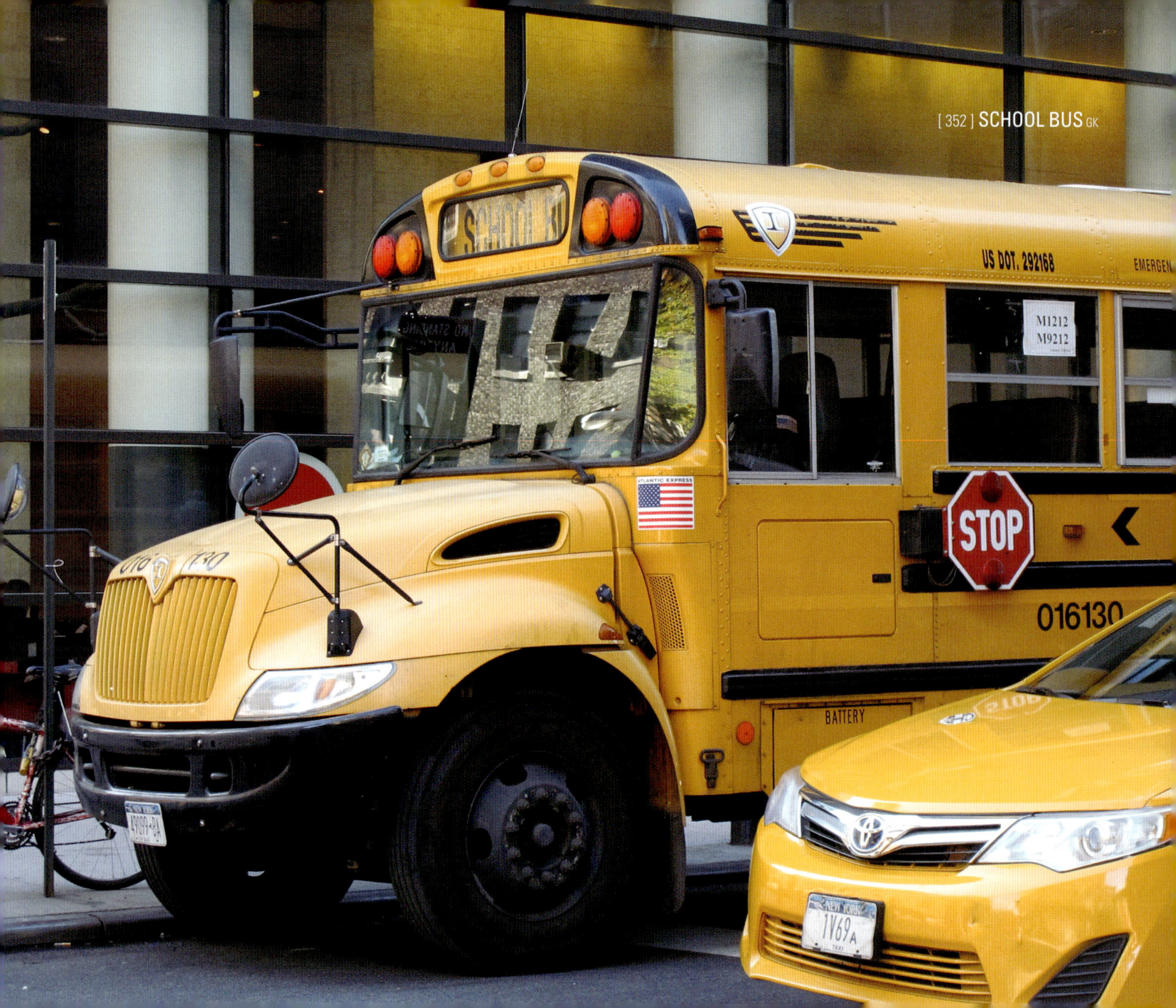

[352] **SCHOOL BUS** GK

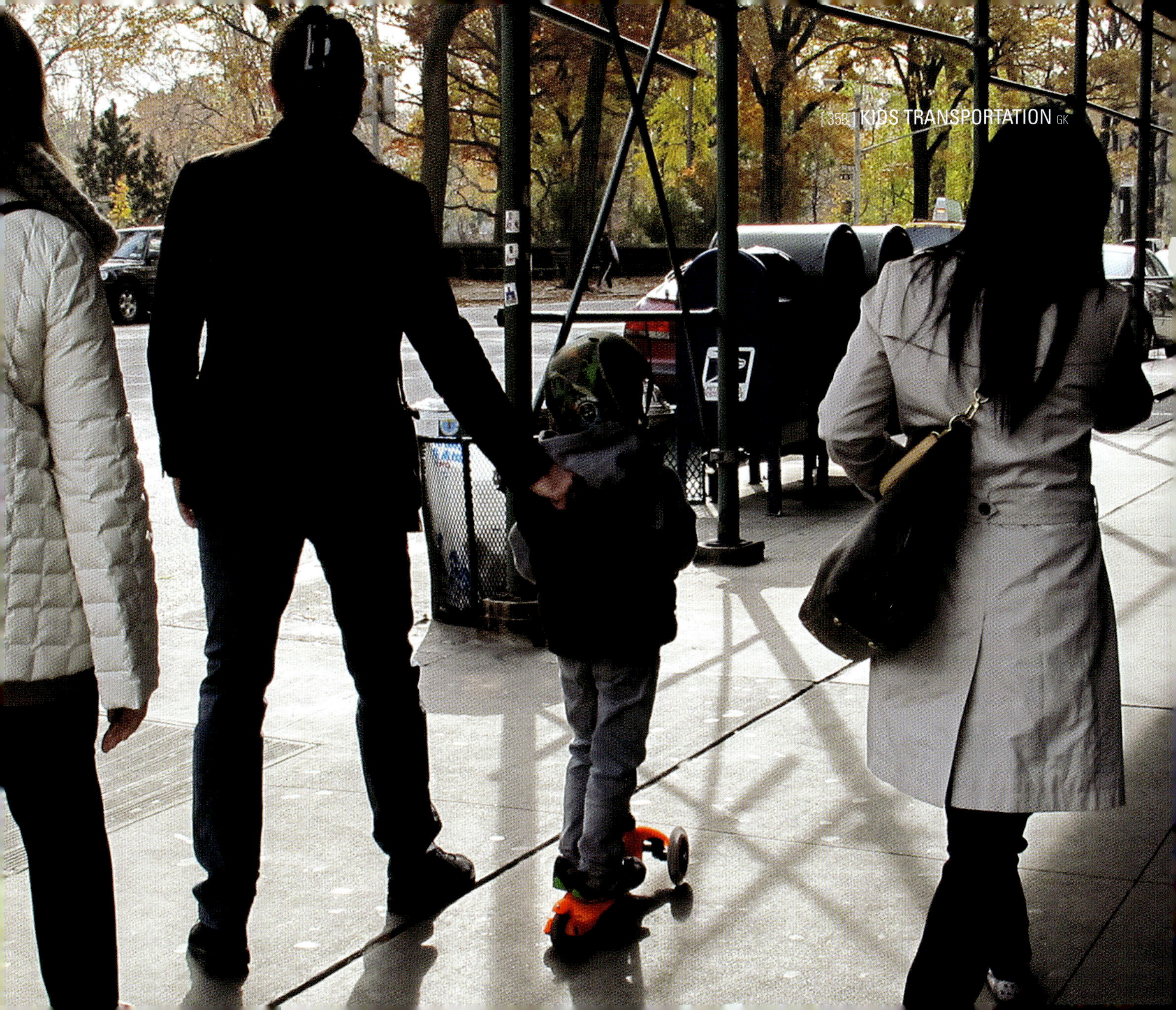

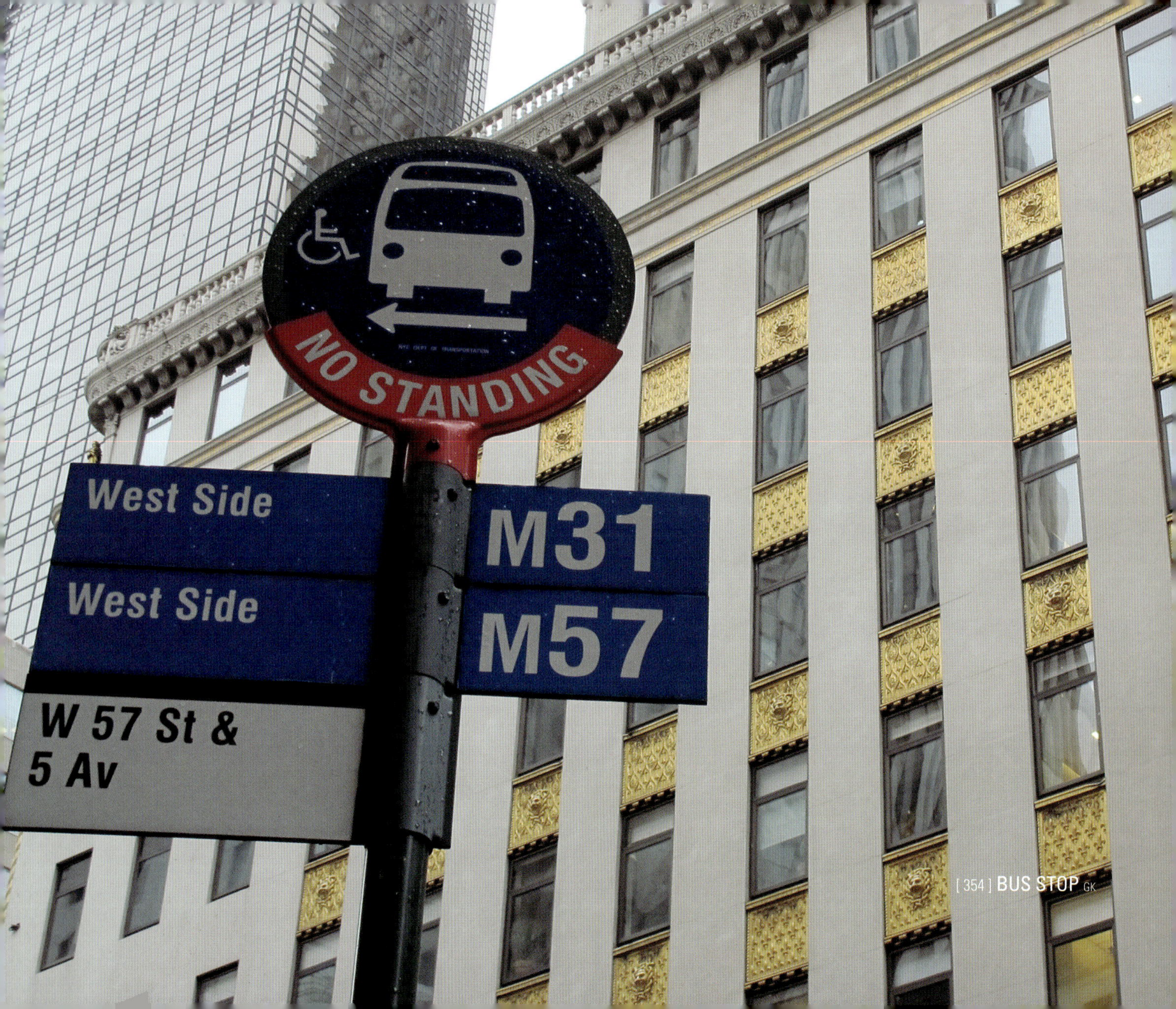

[354] BUS STOP GK

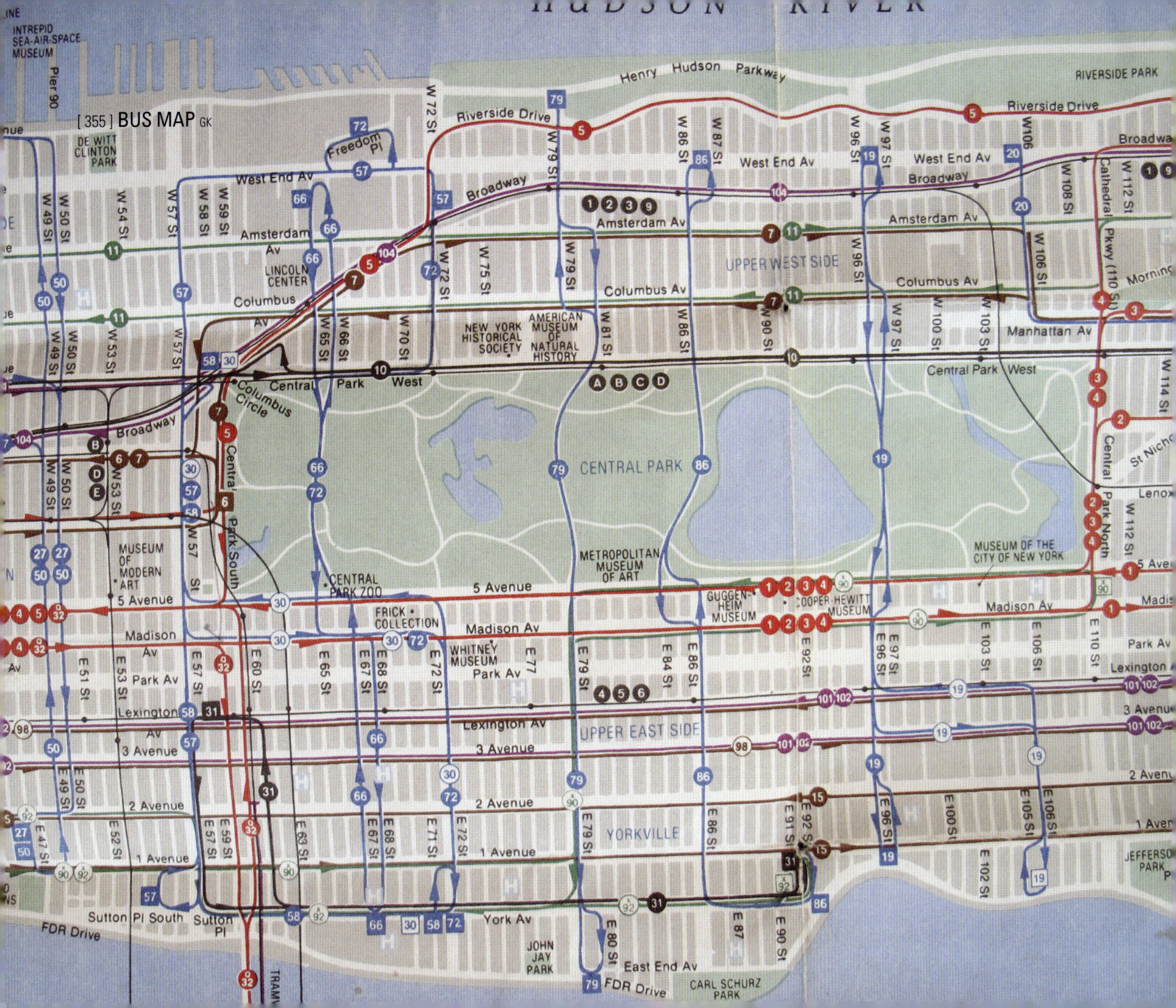
HUDSON RIVER
INTREPID SEA-AIR-SPACE MUSEUM
Pier 90
DE WITT CLINTON PARK
Henry Hudson Parkway
RIVERSIDE PARK
Riverside Drive
Freedom Pl
West End Av
Broadway
Amsterdam Av
Columbus Av
Manhattan Av
Central Park West
Columbus Circle
LINCOLN CENTER
NEW YORK HISTORICAL SOCIETY
AMERICAN MUSEUM OF NATURAL HISTORY
UPPER WEST SIDE
CENTRAL PARK
Central Park South
Central Park North
CENTRAL PARK ZOO
METROPOLITAN MUSEUM OF ART
GUGGENHEIM MUSEUM
COOPER-HEWITT MUSEUM
MUSEUM OF THE CITY OF NEW YORK
MUSEUM OF MODERN ART
FRICK COLLECTION
WHITNEY MUSEUM
5 Avenue
Madison Av
Park Av
Lexington Av
3 Avenue
2 Avenue
1 Avenue
York Av
East End Av
UPPER EAST SIDE
YORKVILLE
Sutton Pl South
Sutton Pl
FDR Drive
JOHN JAY PARK
CARL SCHURZ PARK
JEFFERSON PARK
Cathedral Pkwy (110 St)
St Nicholas
Lenox
Morningside
TRAMWAY

[356] NEW YORK AND TIMES SQUARE PANCHO RODRIGUEZ

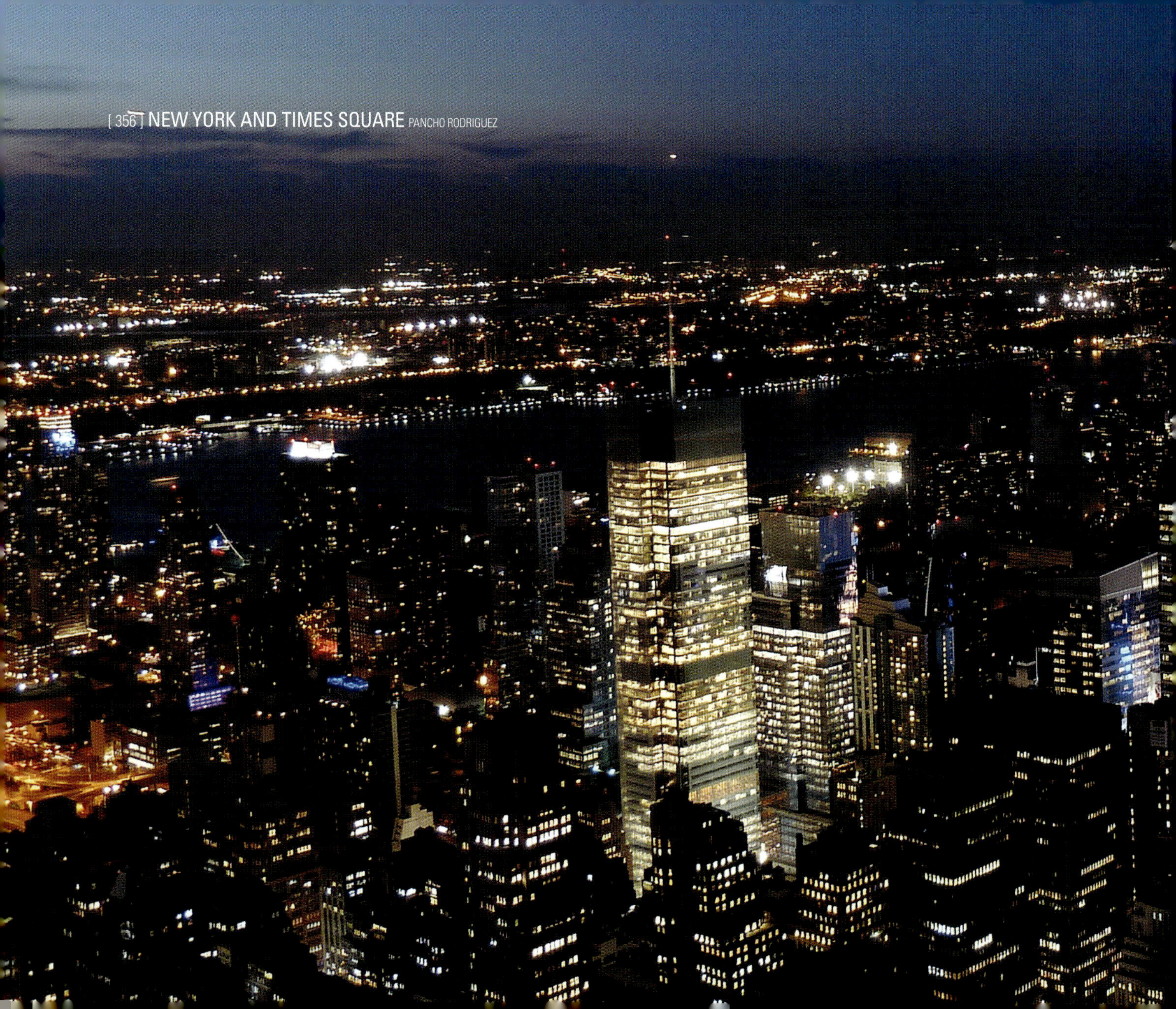

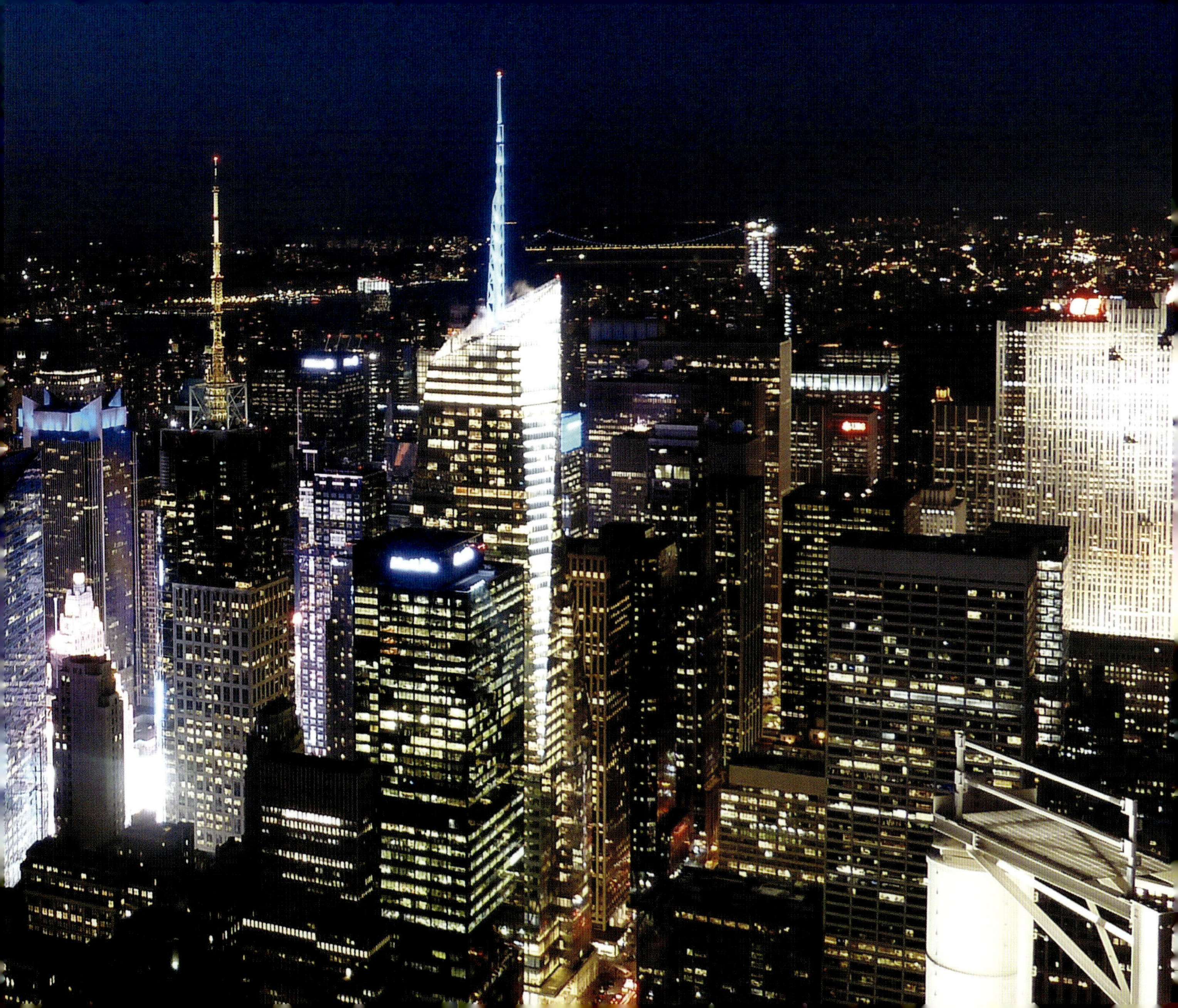

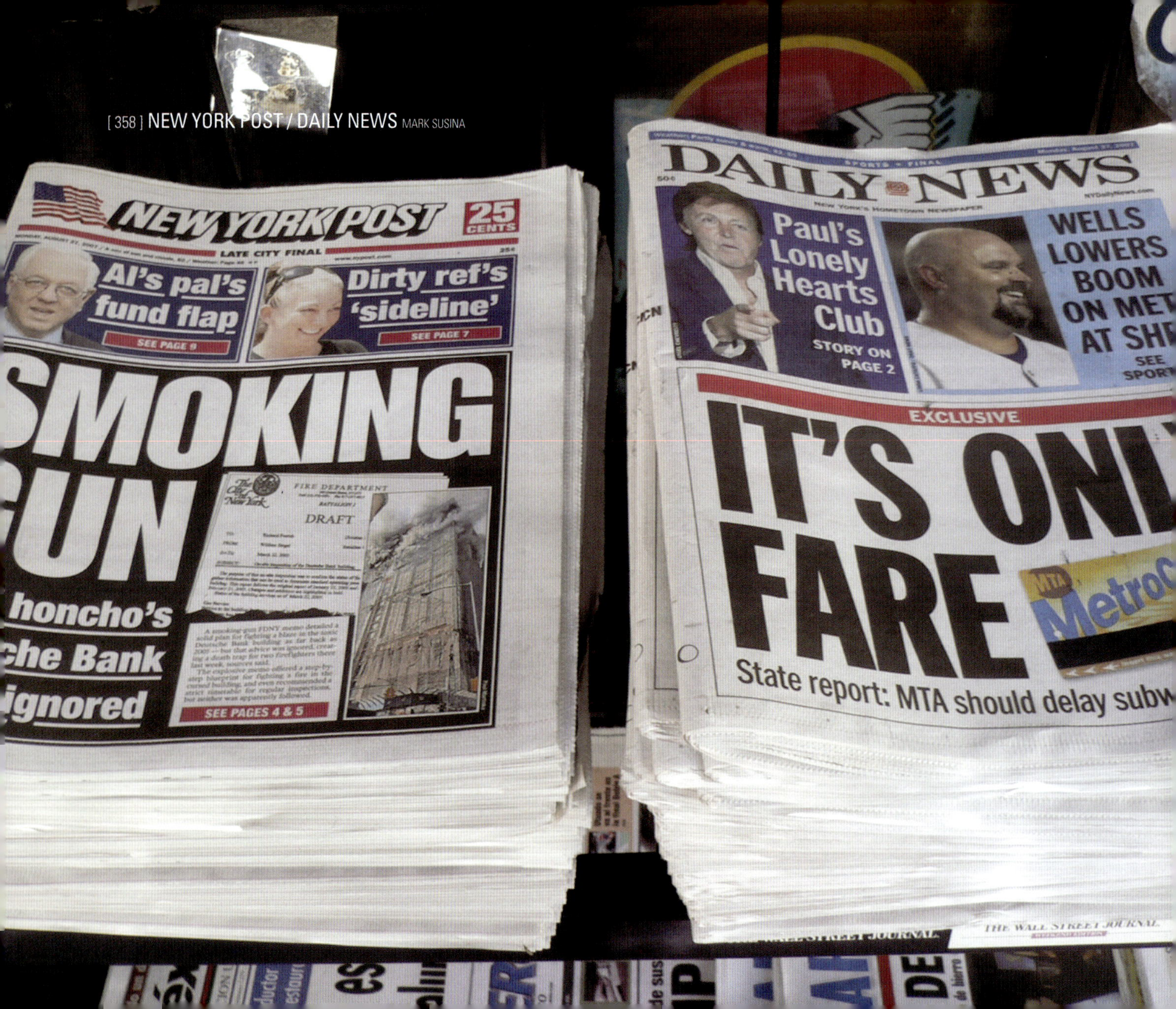
NEW YORK POST
25 CENTS
LATE CITY FINAL
Al's pal's fund flap
SEE PAGE 9
Dirty ref's 'sideline'
SEE PAGE 7
SMOKING
GUN
honcho's
che Bank
ignored
FIRE DEPARTMENT
DRAFT
SEE PAGES 4 & 5
DAILY NEWS
NEW YORK'S HOMETOWN NEWSPAPER
Paul's Lonely Hearts Club
STORY ON PAGE 2
WELLS LOWERS BOOM ON MET AT SH
EXCLUSIVE
IT'S ONL
FARE
MetroC
State report: MTA should delay subw
THE WALL STREET JOURNAL

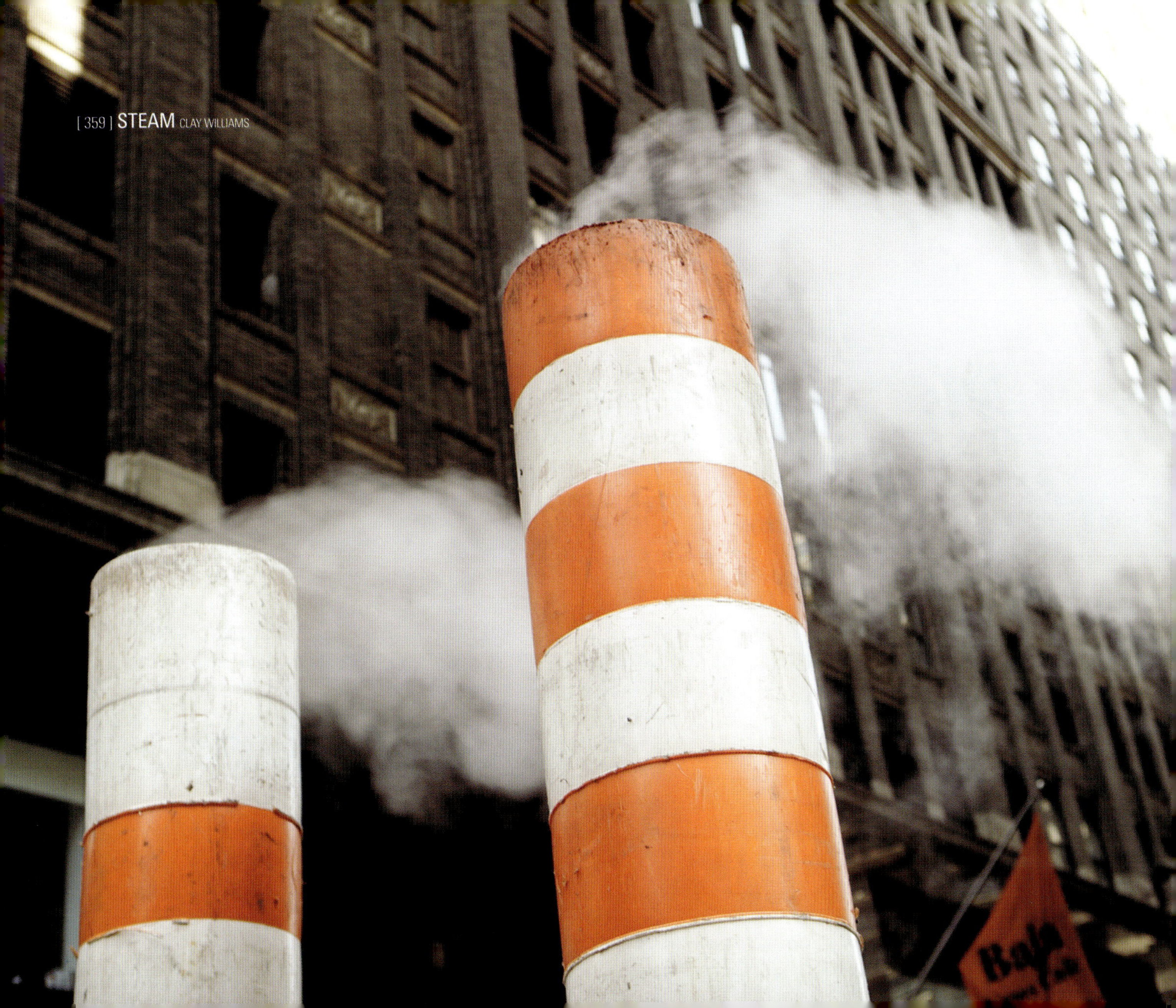

[359] **STEAM** CLAY WILLIAMS

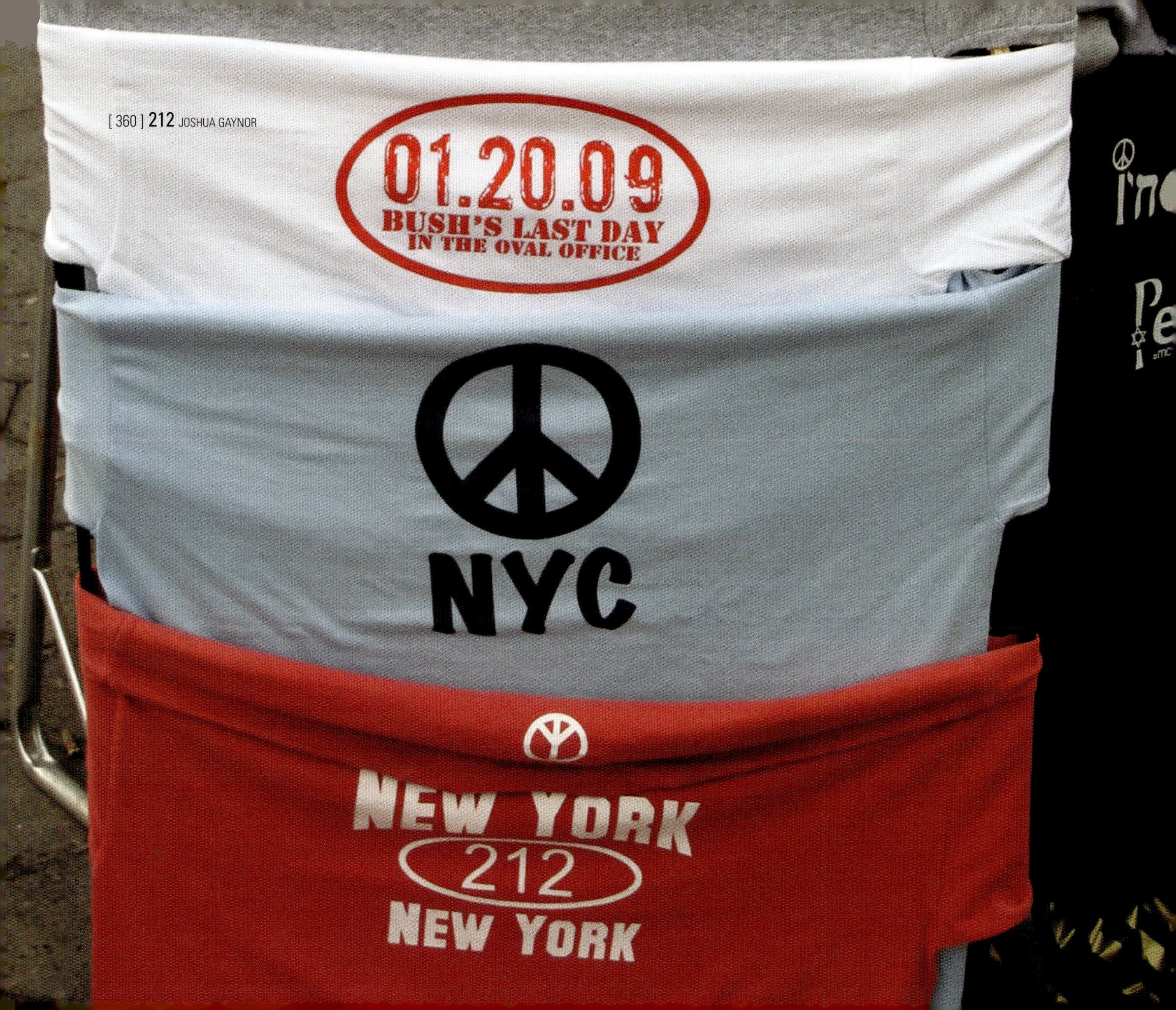
01.20.09
BUSH'S LAST DAY
IN THE OVAL OFFICE
NYC
NEW YORK
212
NEW YORK

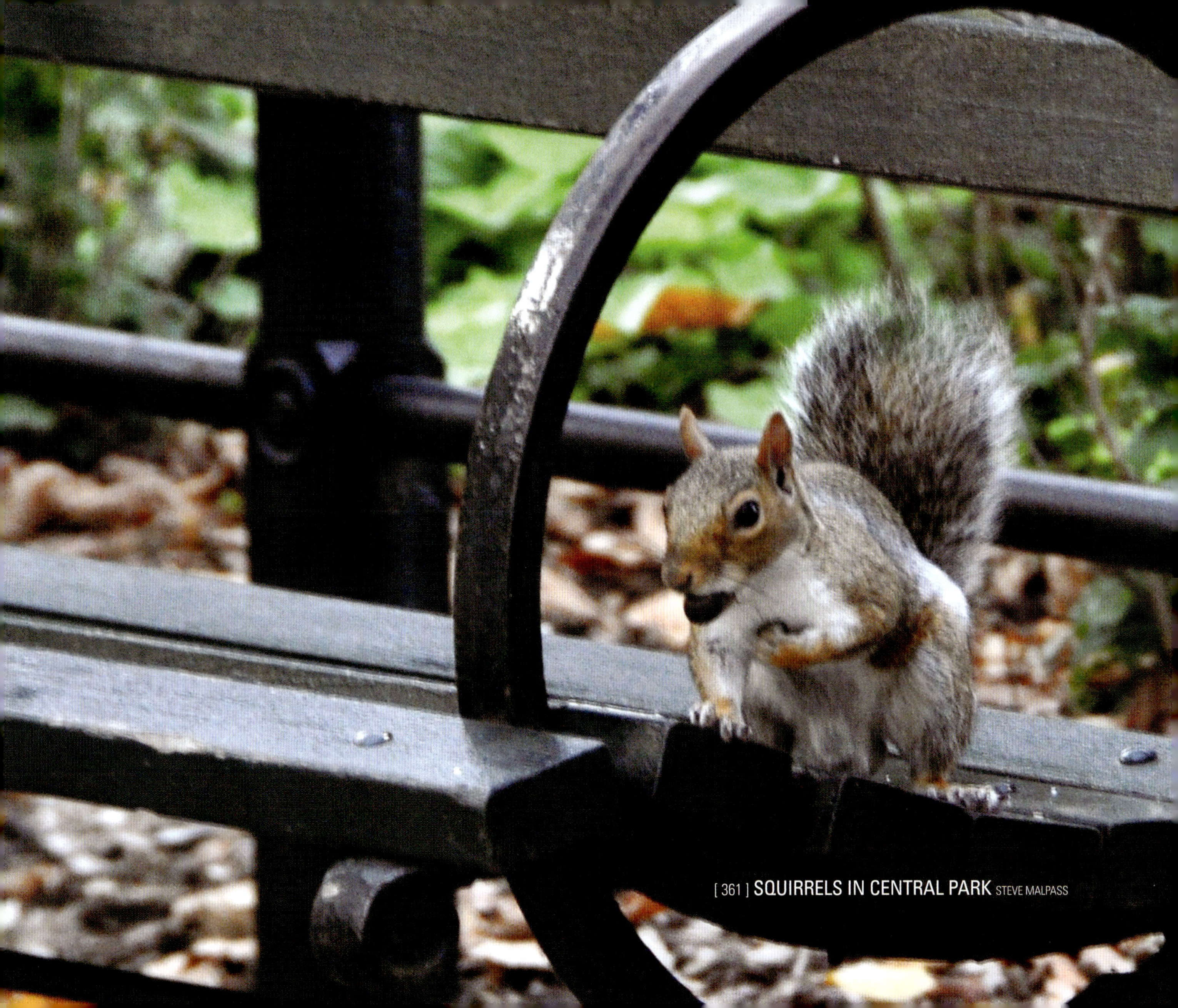

[361] **SQUIRRELS IN CENTRAL PARK** STEVE MALPASS

[362] FROM NEW JERSEY PATTY SMITH

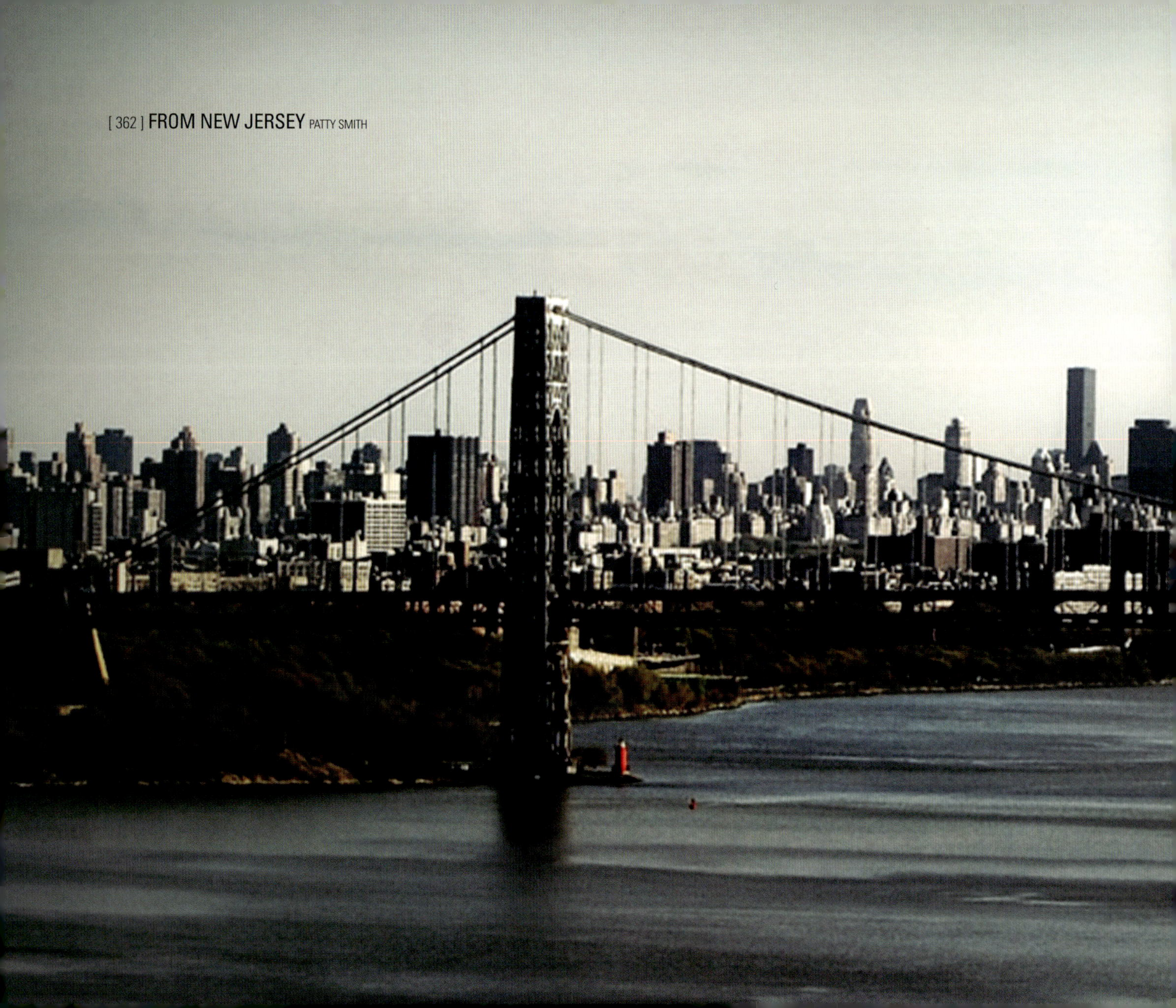

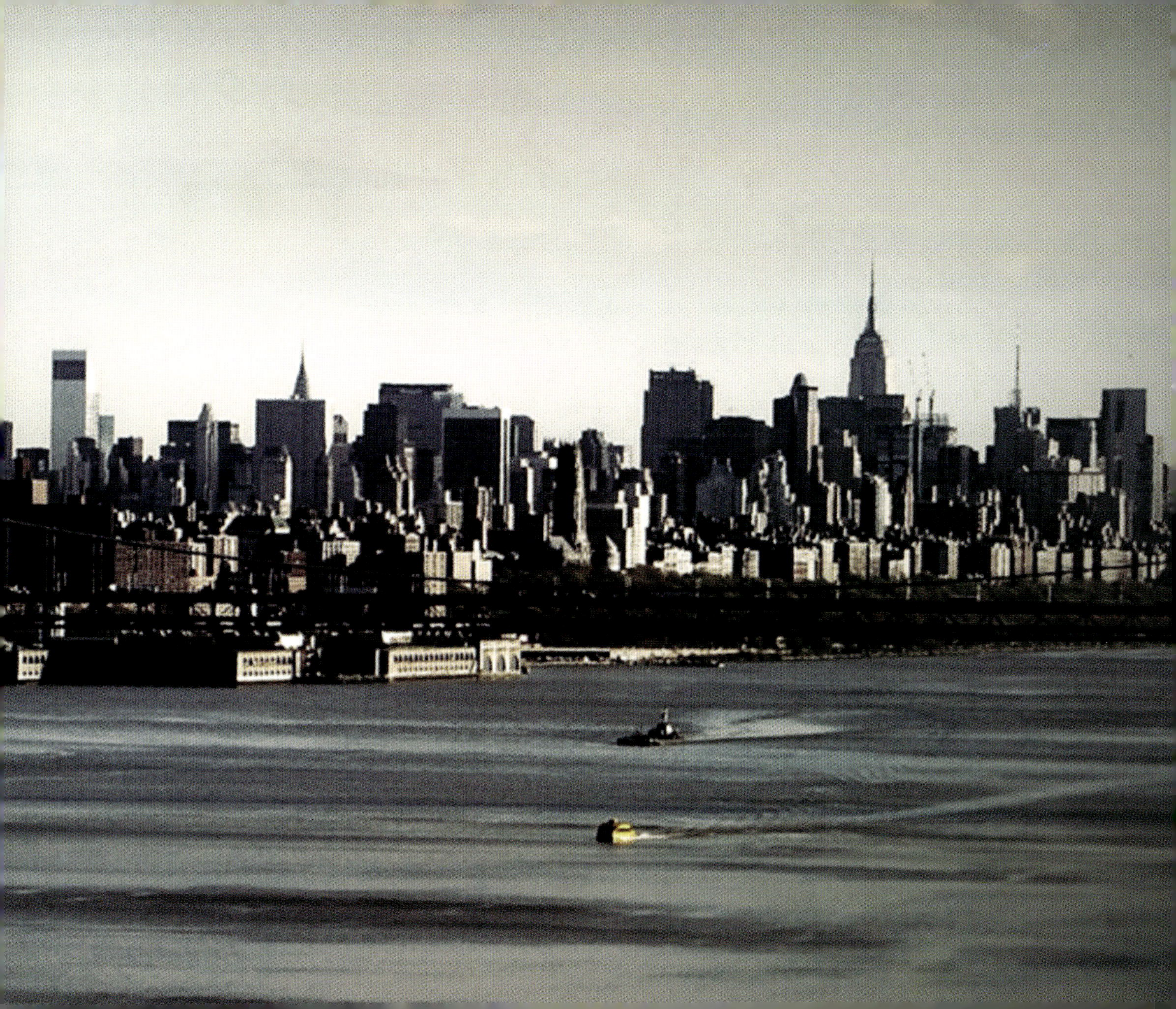

[364] THE TWIN TOWERS DANIEL MODELL

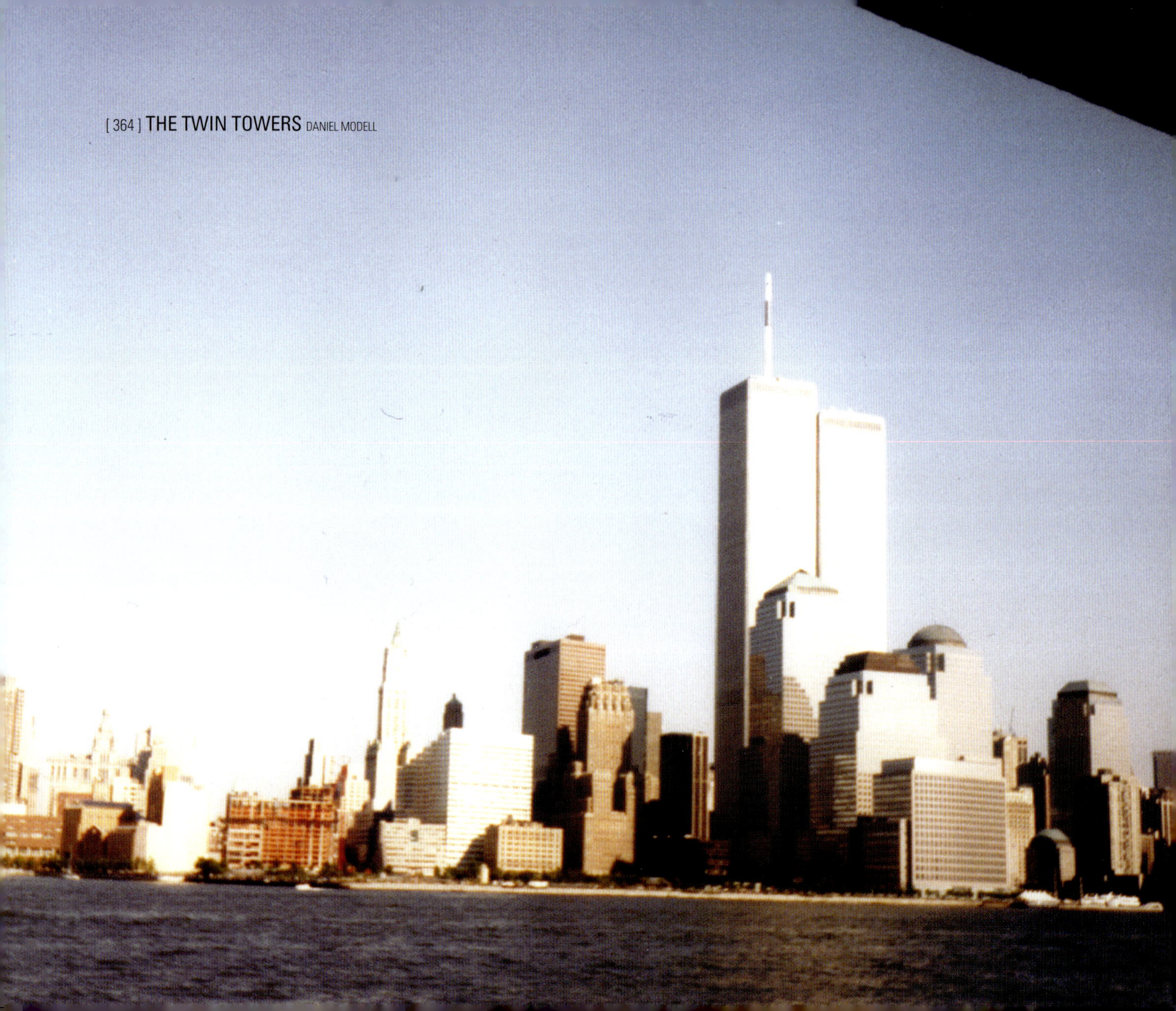

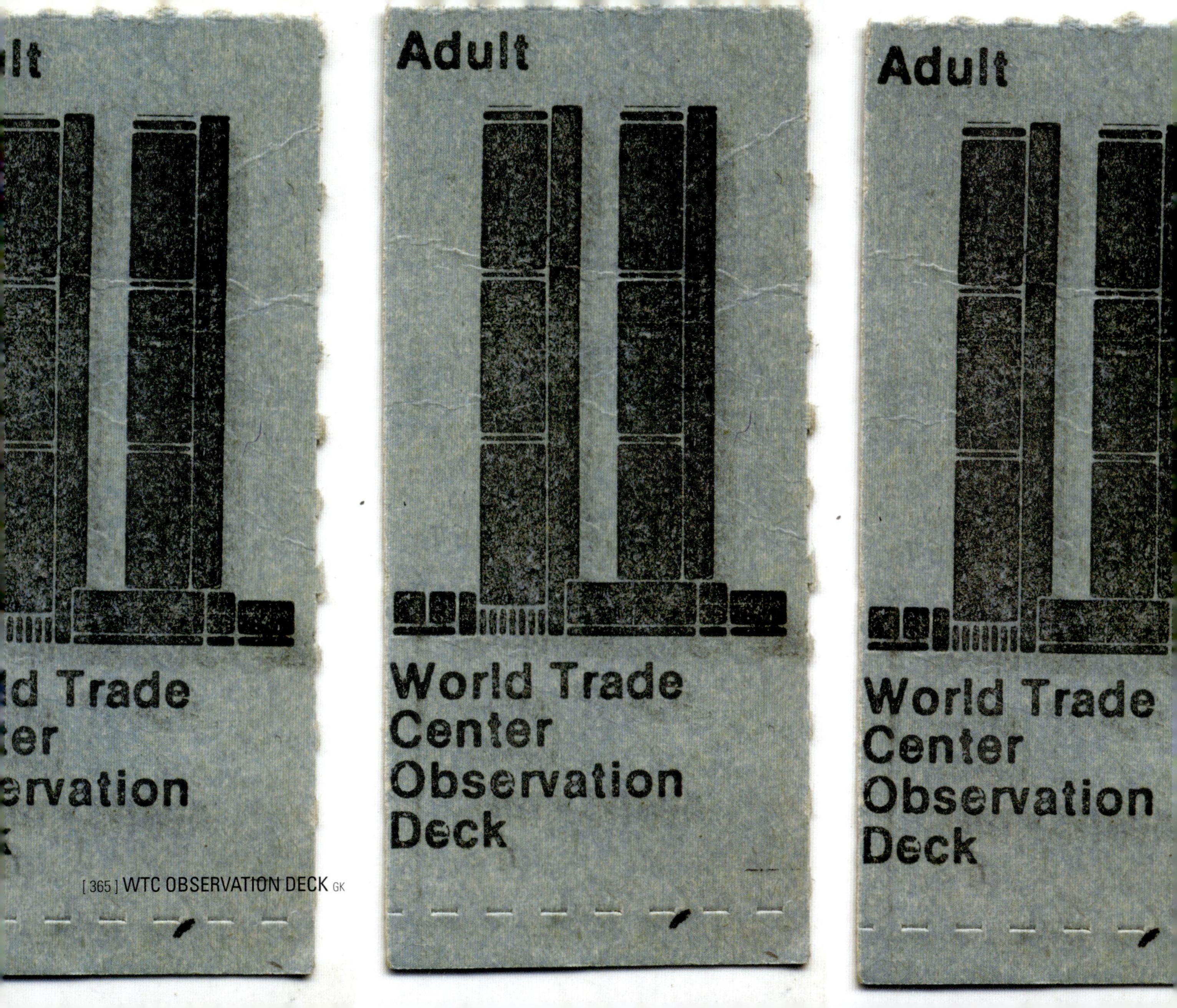

[365] WTC OBSERVATION DECK GK

[366] A CHANGED LANDSCAPE GK

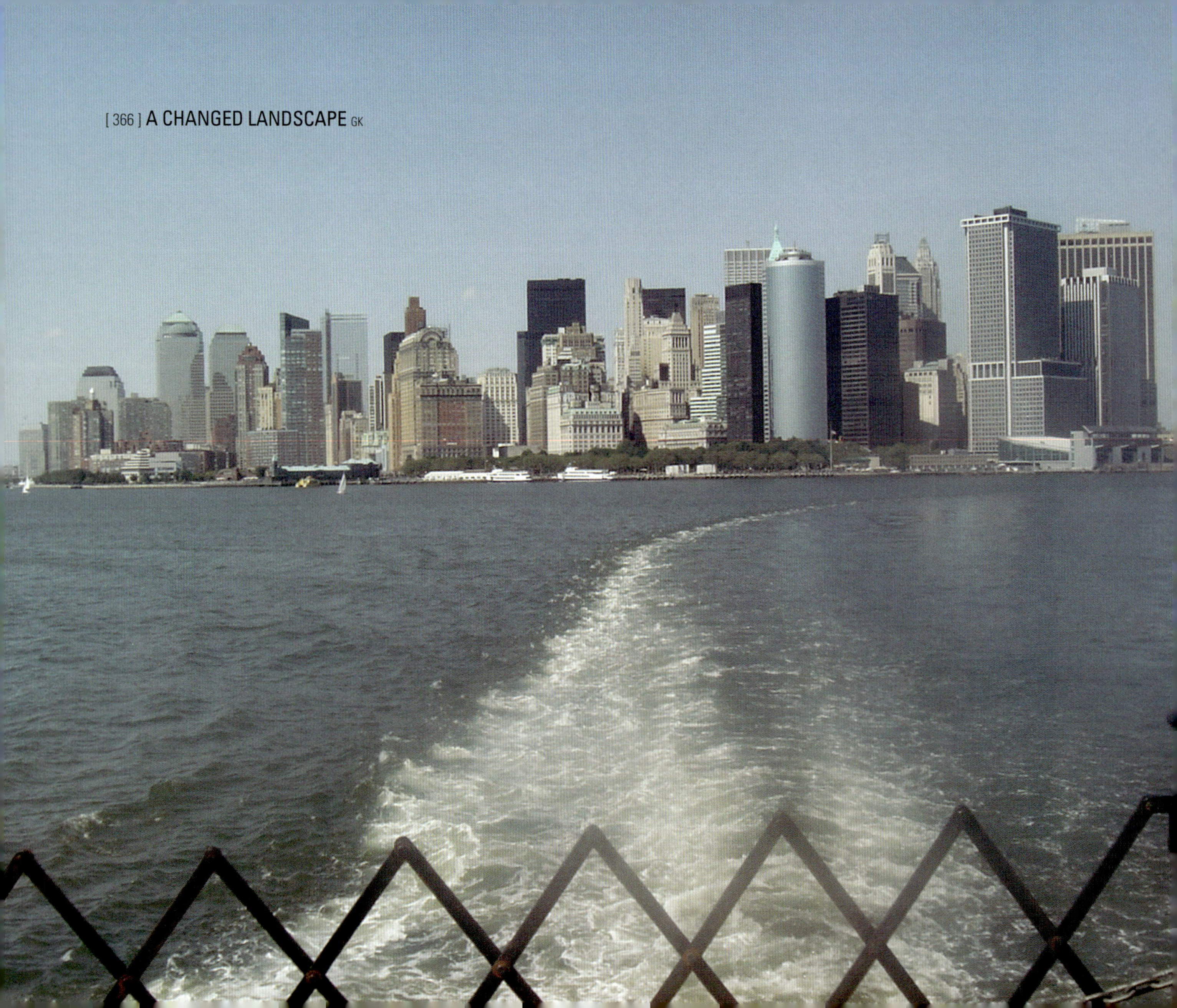

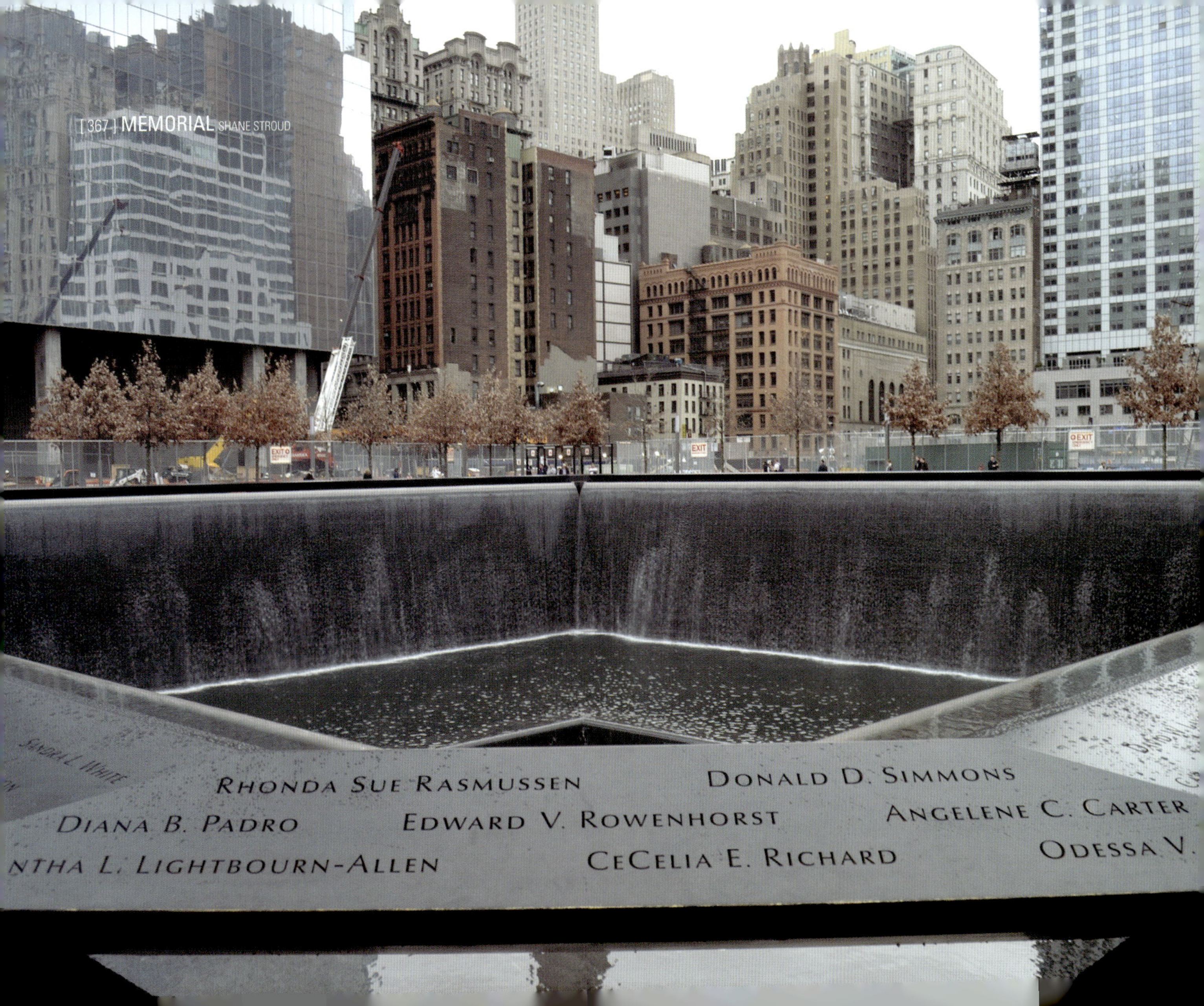

[367] MEMORIAL SHANE STROUD

[368] **FOREVER AND EVER** JOSEF PINLAC

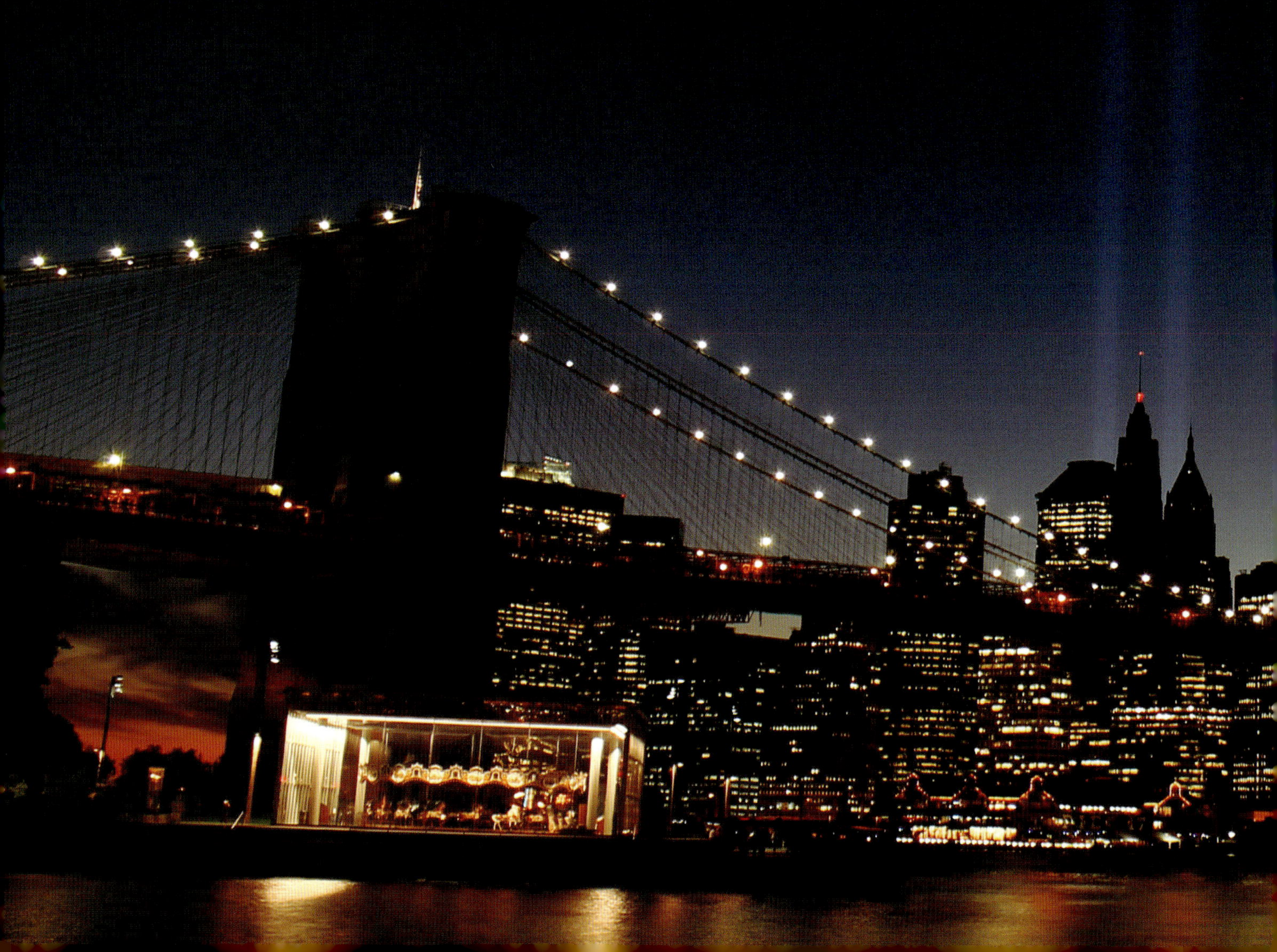

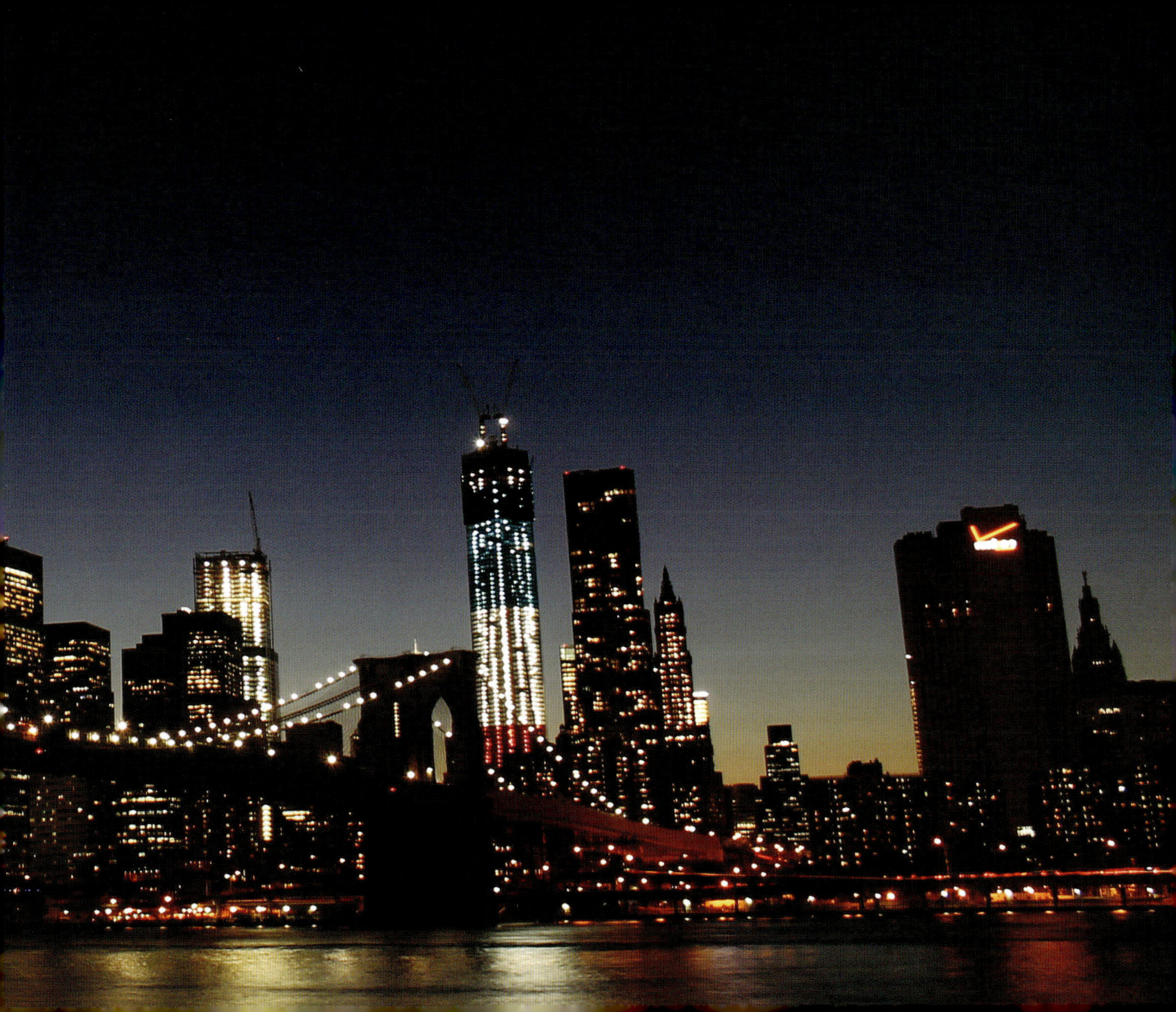

[370] ONE WORLD TRADE CENTER NICOLAS MIRGUET

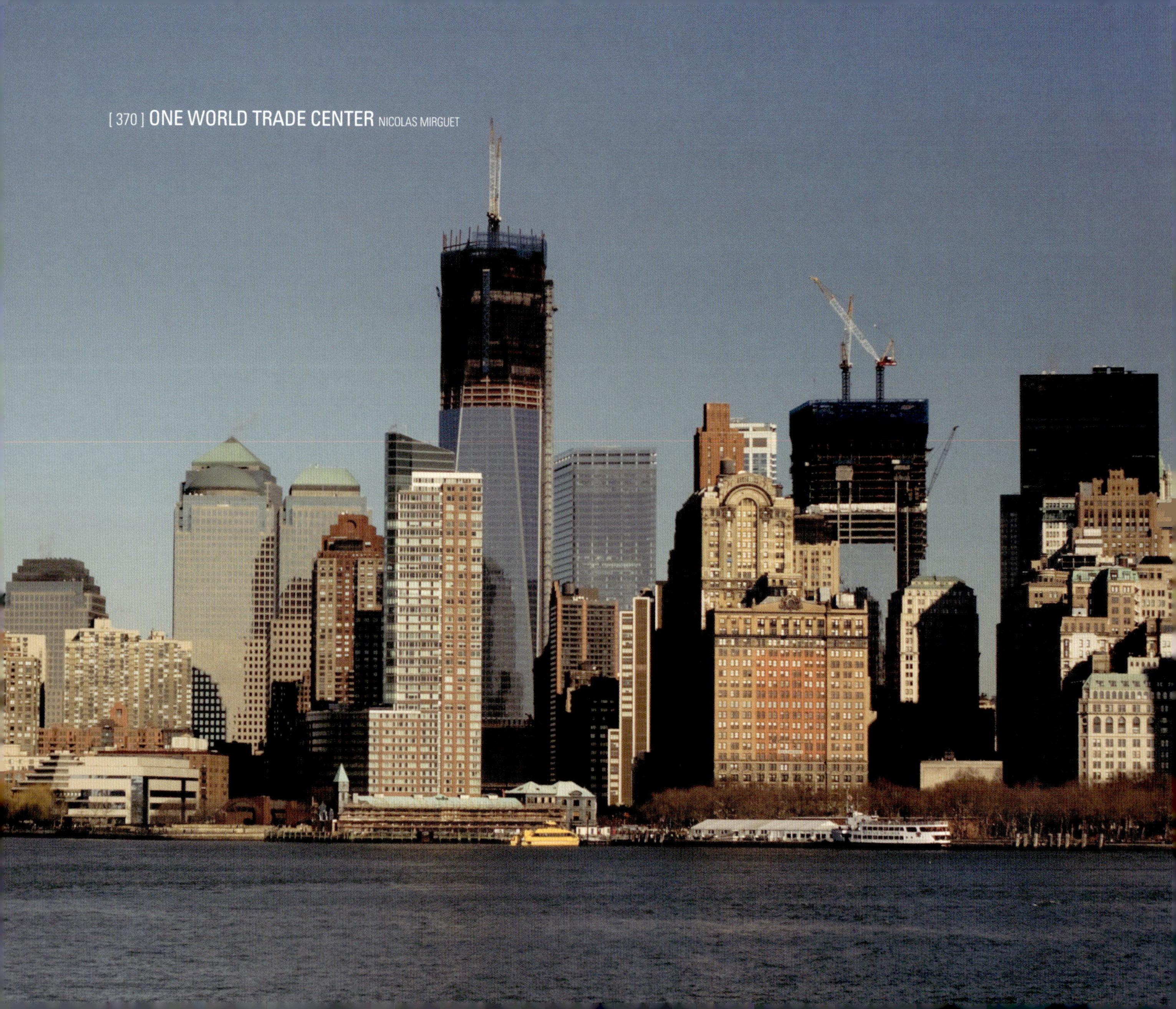

[371] FREEDOM TOWER PANCHO RODRIGUEZ

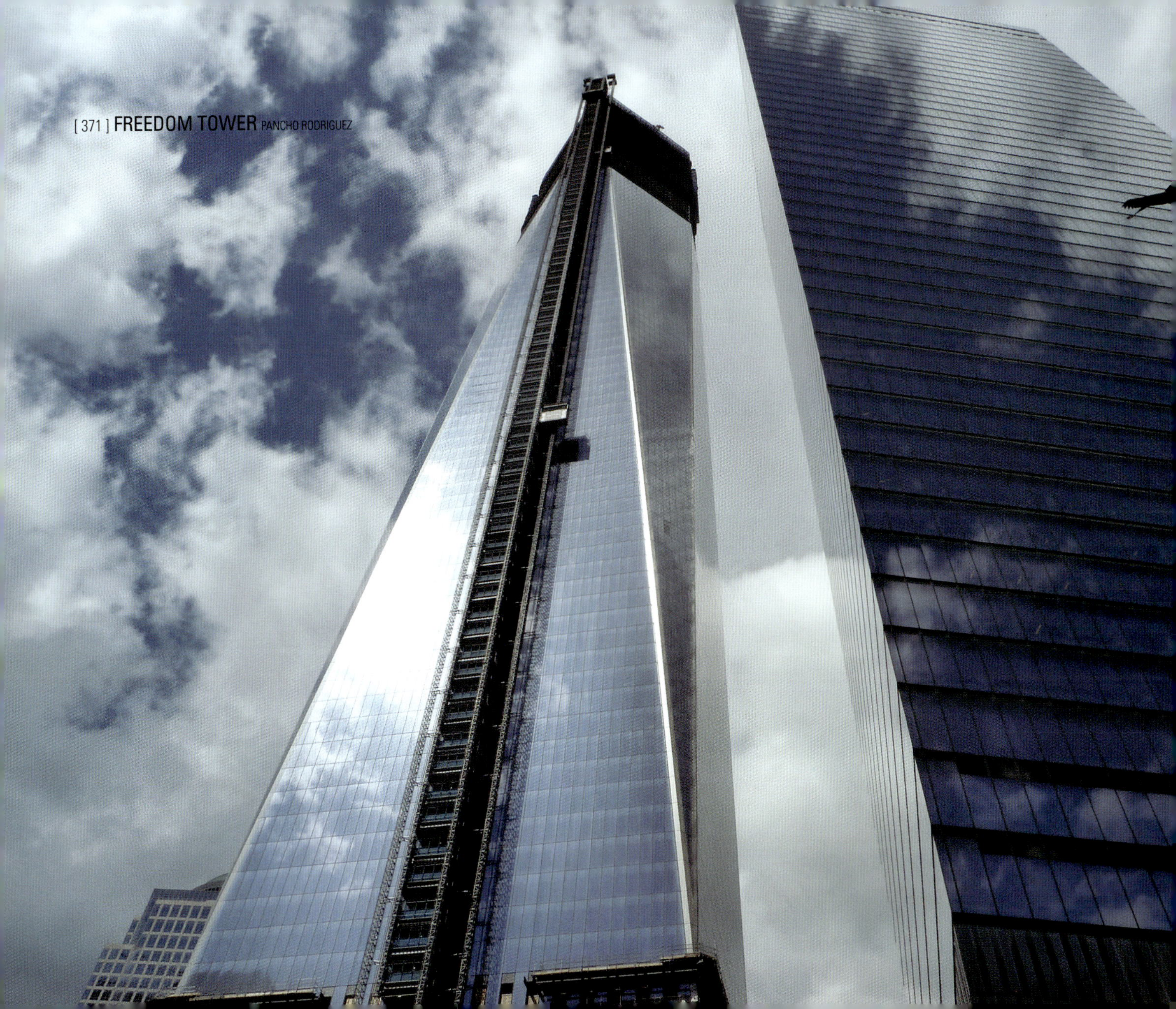

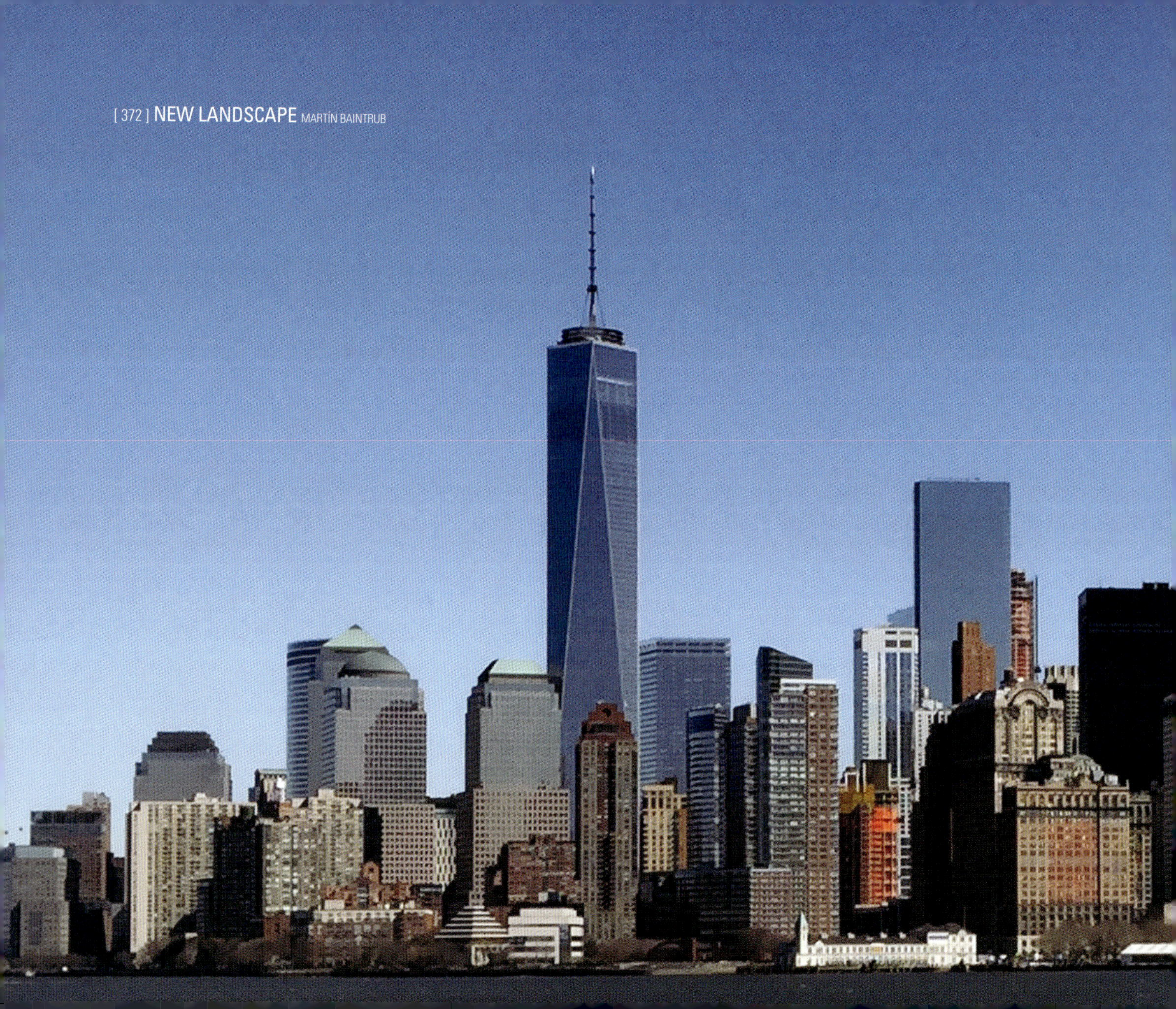

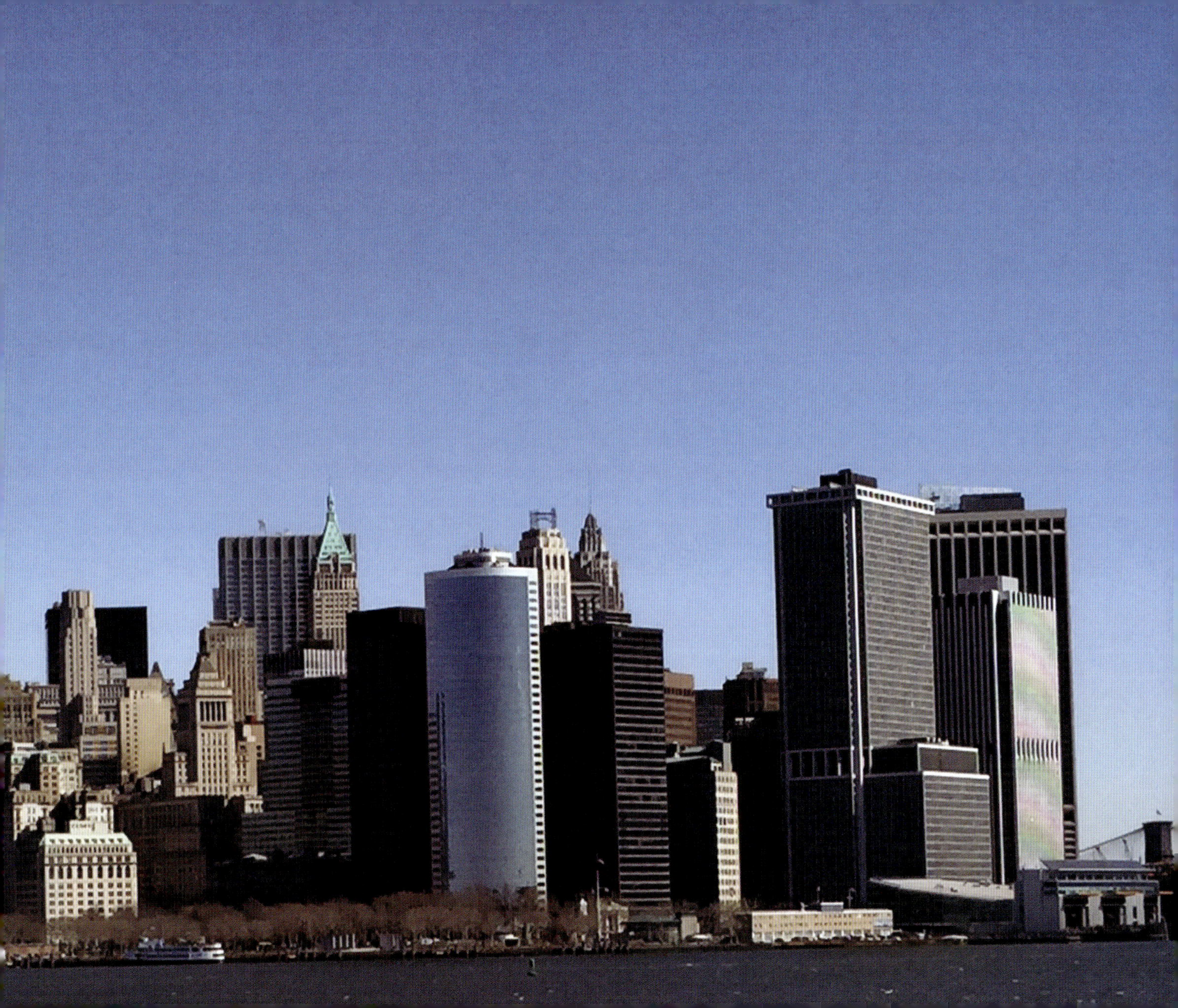

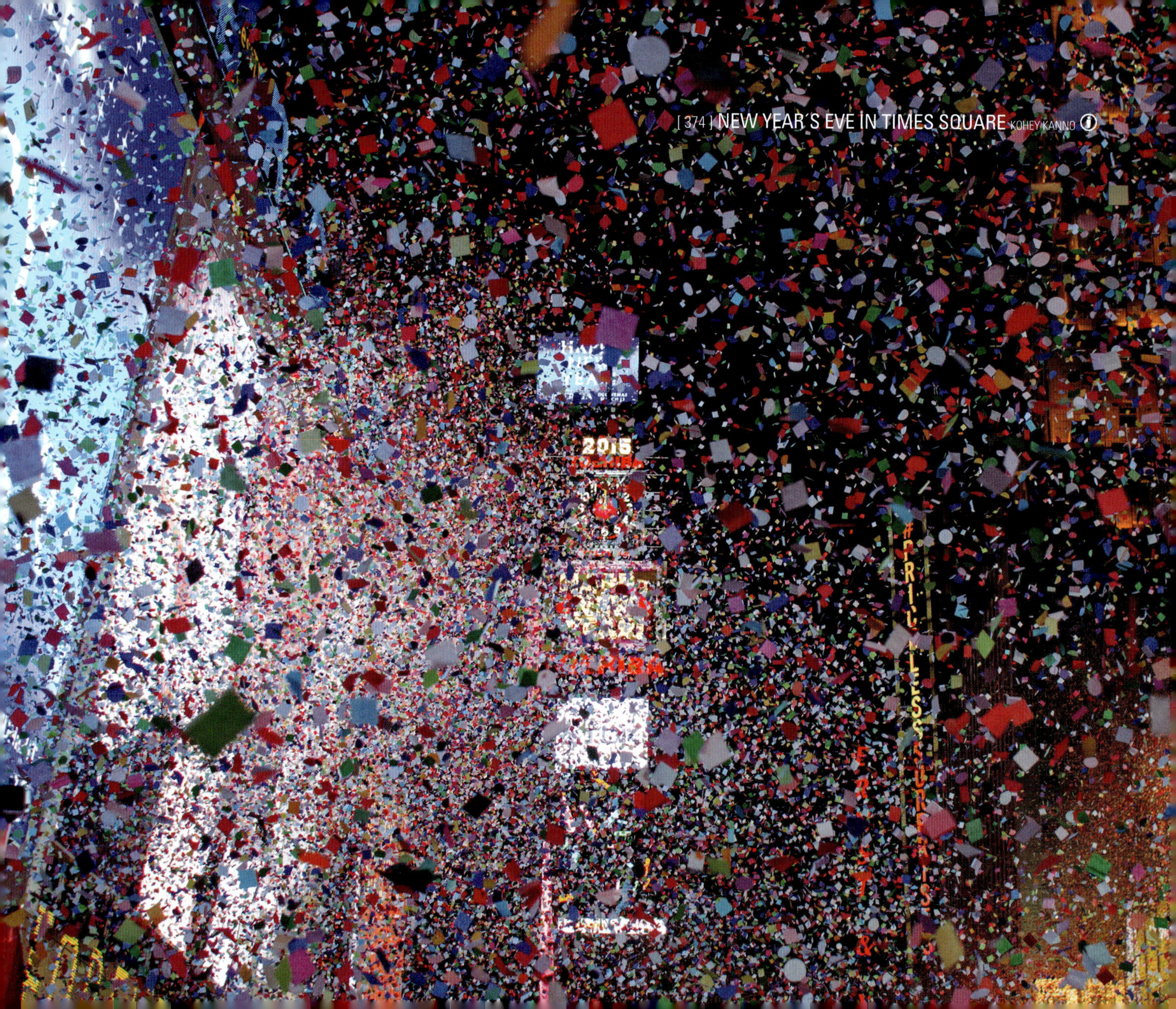

[374] NEW YEAR'S EVE IN TIMES SQUARE KOHEY KANNO

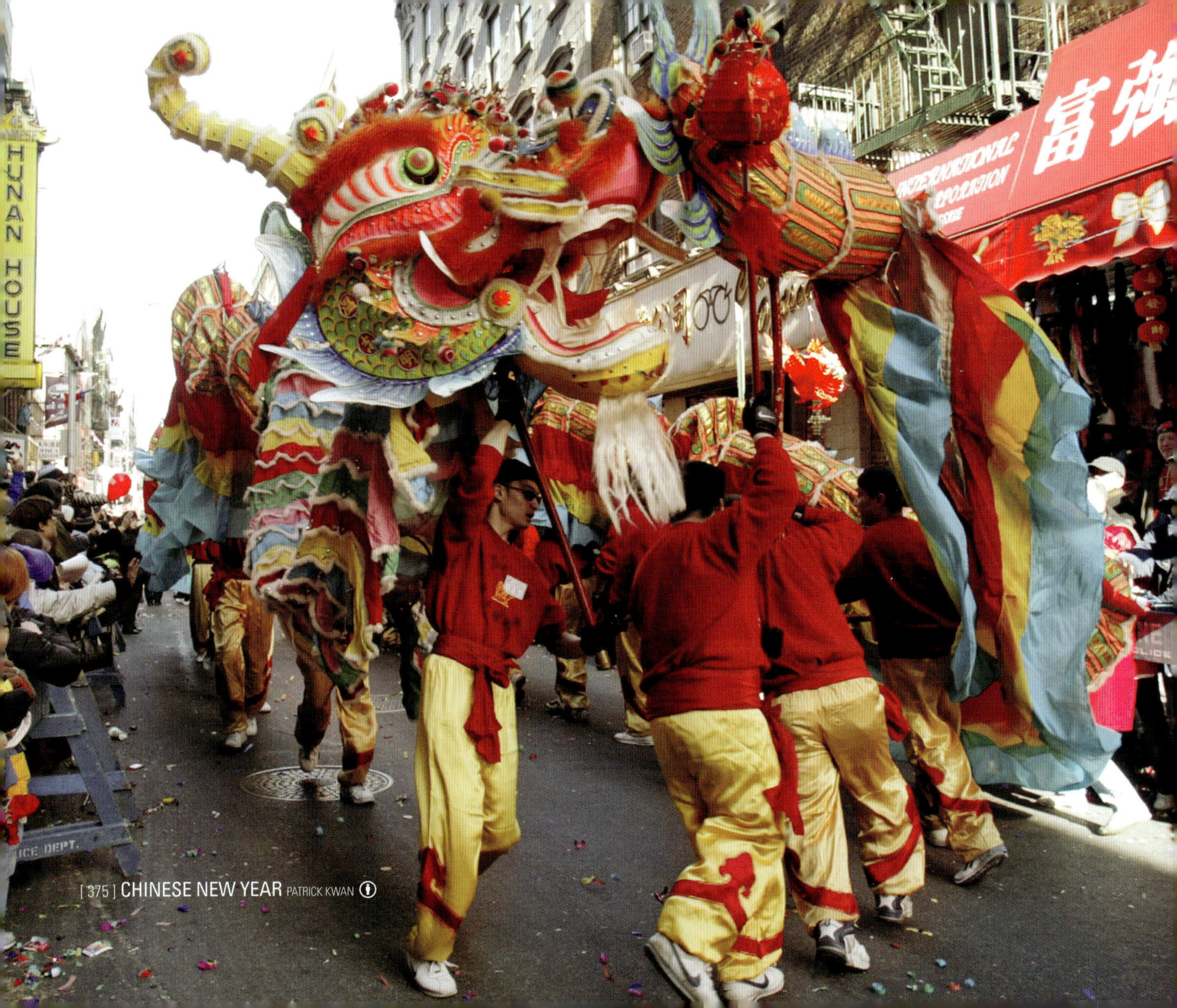

[375] CHINESE NEW YEAR PATRICK KWAN

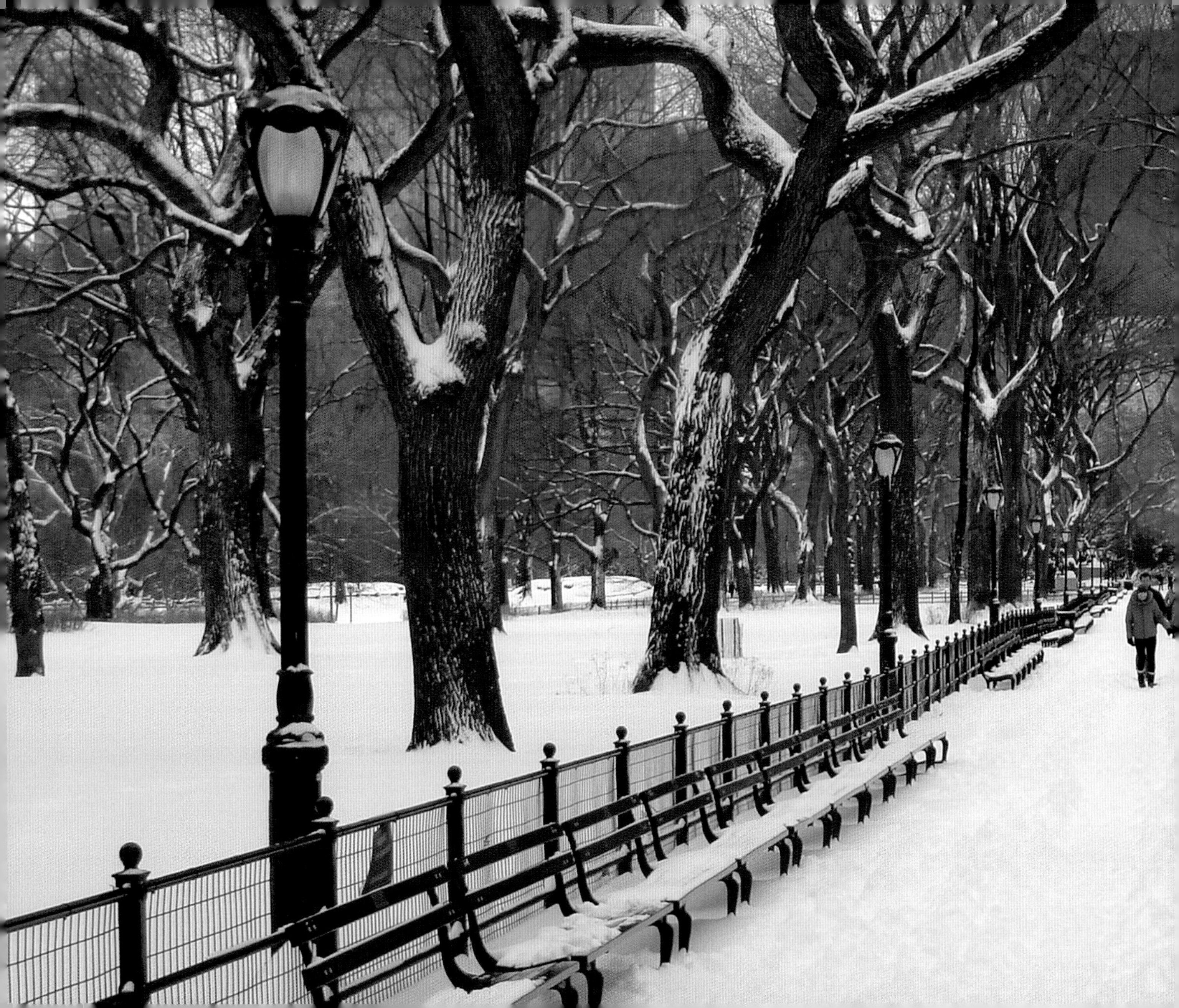

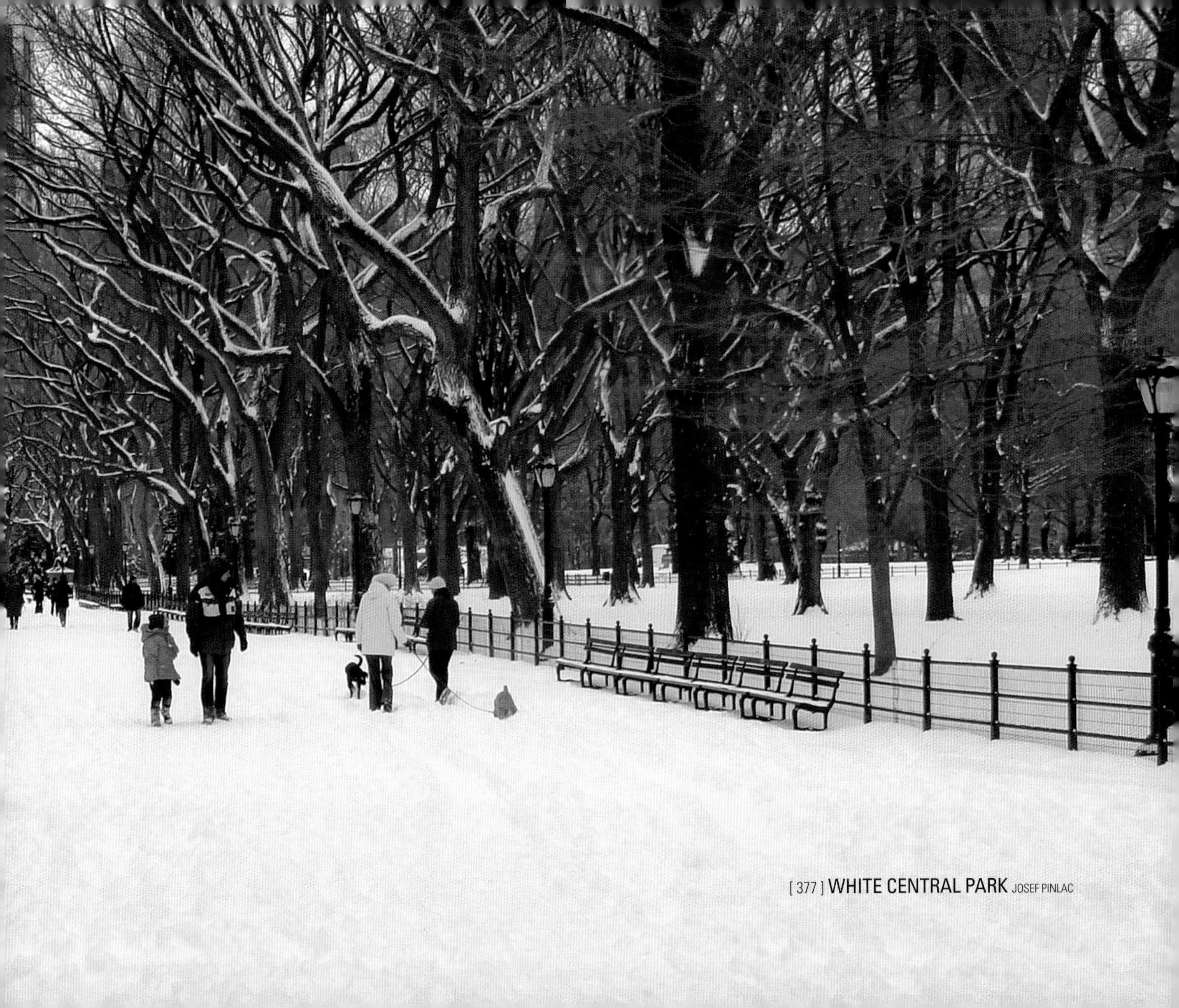

[377] WHITE CENTRAL PARK JOSEF PINLAC

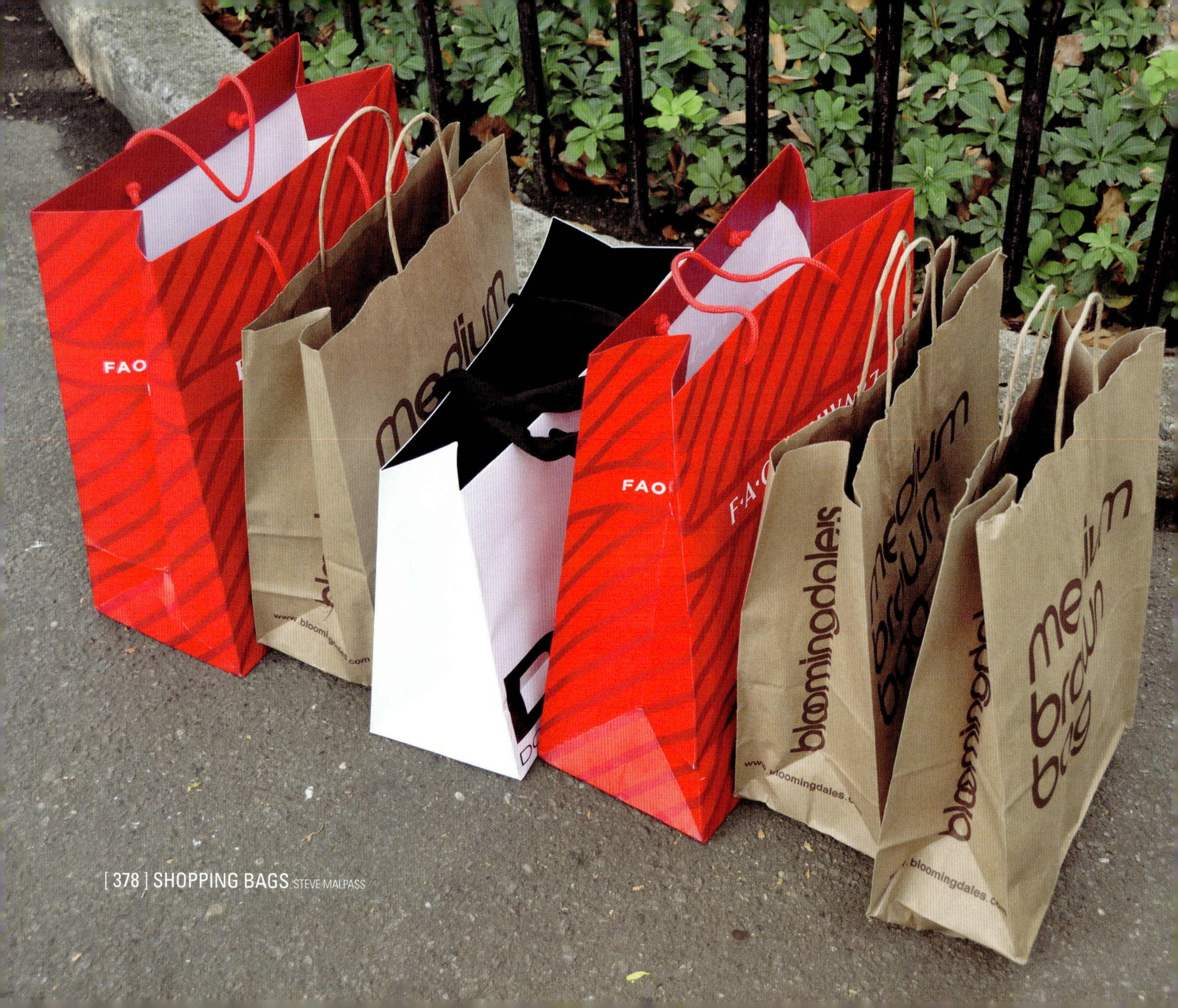

[378] SHOPPING BAGS STEVE MALPASS

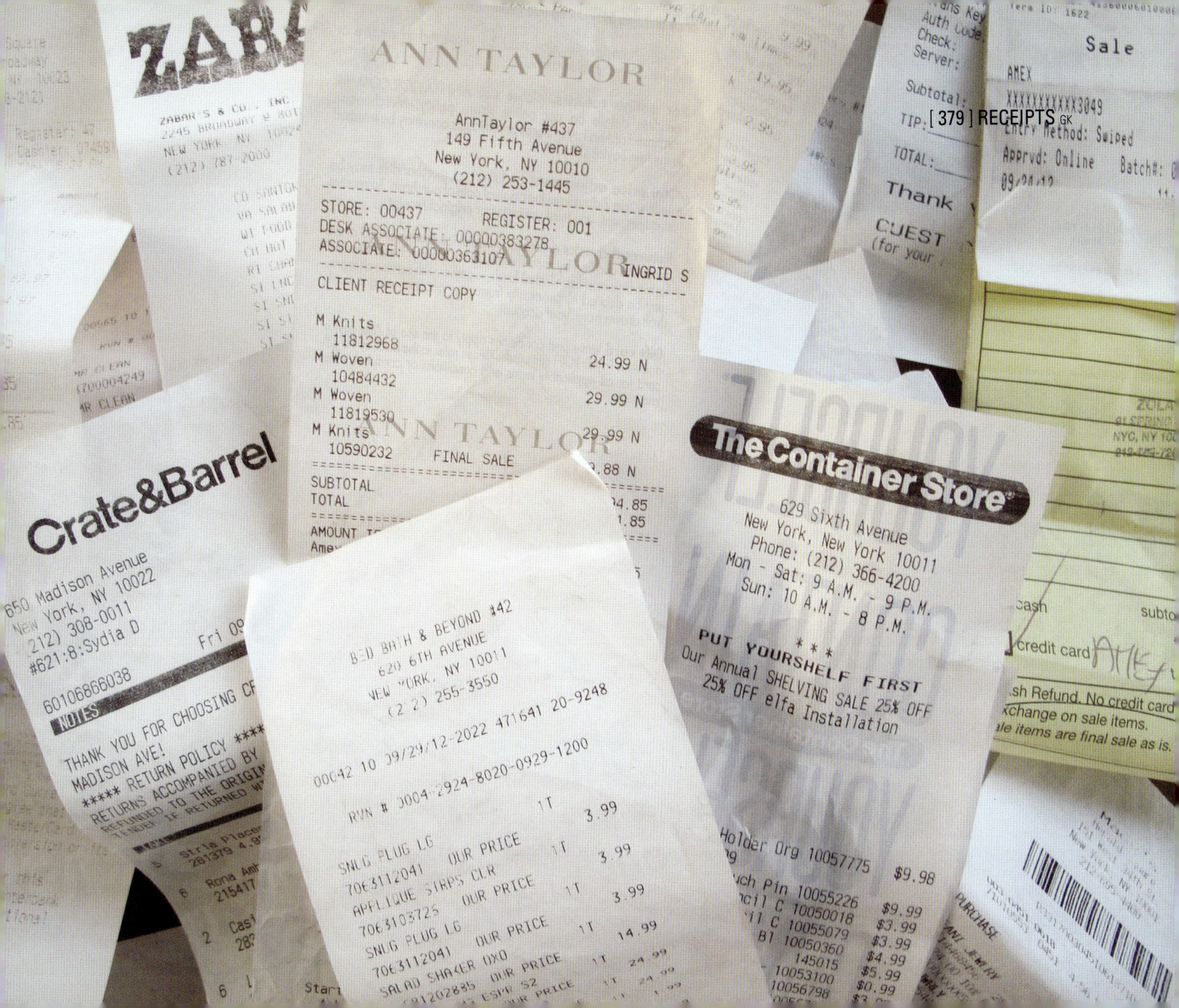
ZABAR'S & Co., INC.
2245 BROADWAY
NEW YORK NY
(212) 787-2000
ANN TAYLOR
AnnTaylor #437
149 Fifth Avenue
New York, NY 10010
(212) 253-1445
STORE: 00437 REGISTER: 001
DESK ASSOCIATE: 00000383278
ASSOCIATE: 00000363107 INGRID S
CLIENT RECEIPT COPY
M Knits
11812968
M Woven 24.99 N
10484432
M Woven 29.99 N
11819530
M Knits 29.99 N
10590232 FINAL SALE
SUBTOTAL
TOTAL
Sale
AMEX
XXXXXXXXXXX3049
Entry Method: Swiped
Apprvd: Online
Subtotal:
TIP:
TOTAL:
Thank
Crate&Barrel
650 Madison Avenue
New York, NY 10022
(212) 308-0011
#621:8:Sydia D
60106866038
NOTES
THANK YOU FOR CHOOSING CR
MADISON AVE!
***** RETURN POLICY
BED BATH & BEYOND #42
620 6TH AVENUE
NEW YORK, NY 10011
(212) 255-3550
00042 10 09/29/12-2022 471641 20-9248
00042 10 09/29/12-2022 471641 20-9248
RVN # 0004-2924-8020-0929-1200
SNUG PLUG LG 1T 3.99
7063112041 OUR PRICE
APPLIQUE STRPS CLR 1T 3.99
7063103725 OUR PRICE
SNUG PLUG LG 1T 3.99
7063112041 OUR PRICE
SALAD SHAKER OXO 1T 14.99
The Container Store
629 Sixth Avenue
New York, New York 10011
Phone: (212) 366-4200
Mon - Sat: 9 A.M. - 9 P.M.
Sun: 10 A.M. - 8 P.M.
PUT YOURSHELF FIRST
Our Annual SHELVING SALE 25% OFF
25% OFF elfa Installation
Holder Org 10057775 $9.98
cash
credit card
sh Refund. No credit card
xchange on sale items.
le items are final sale as is.

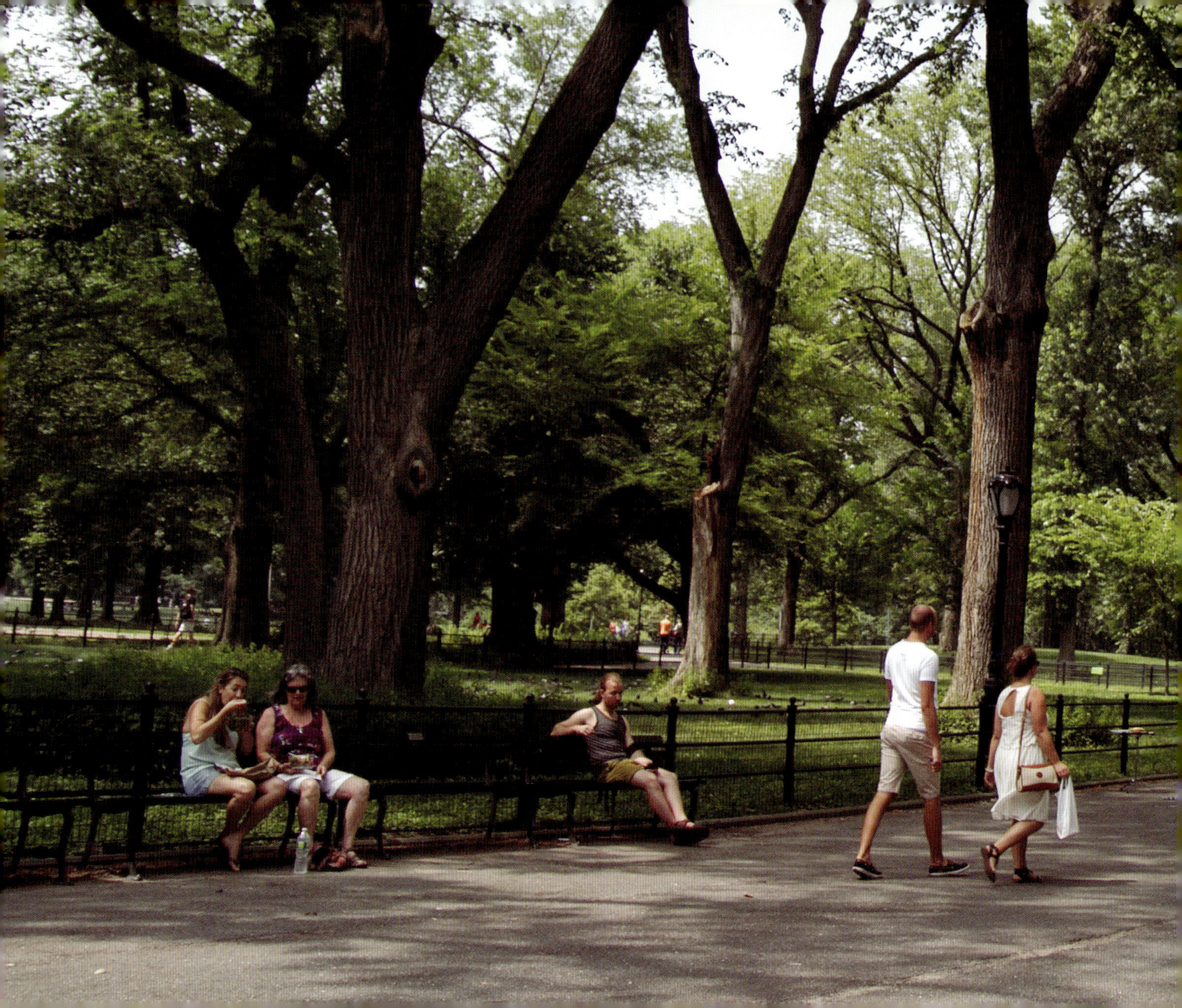

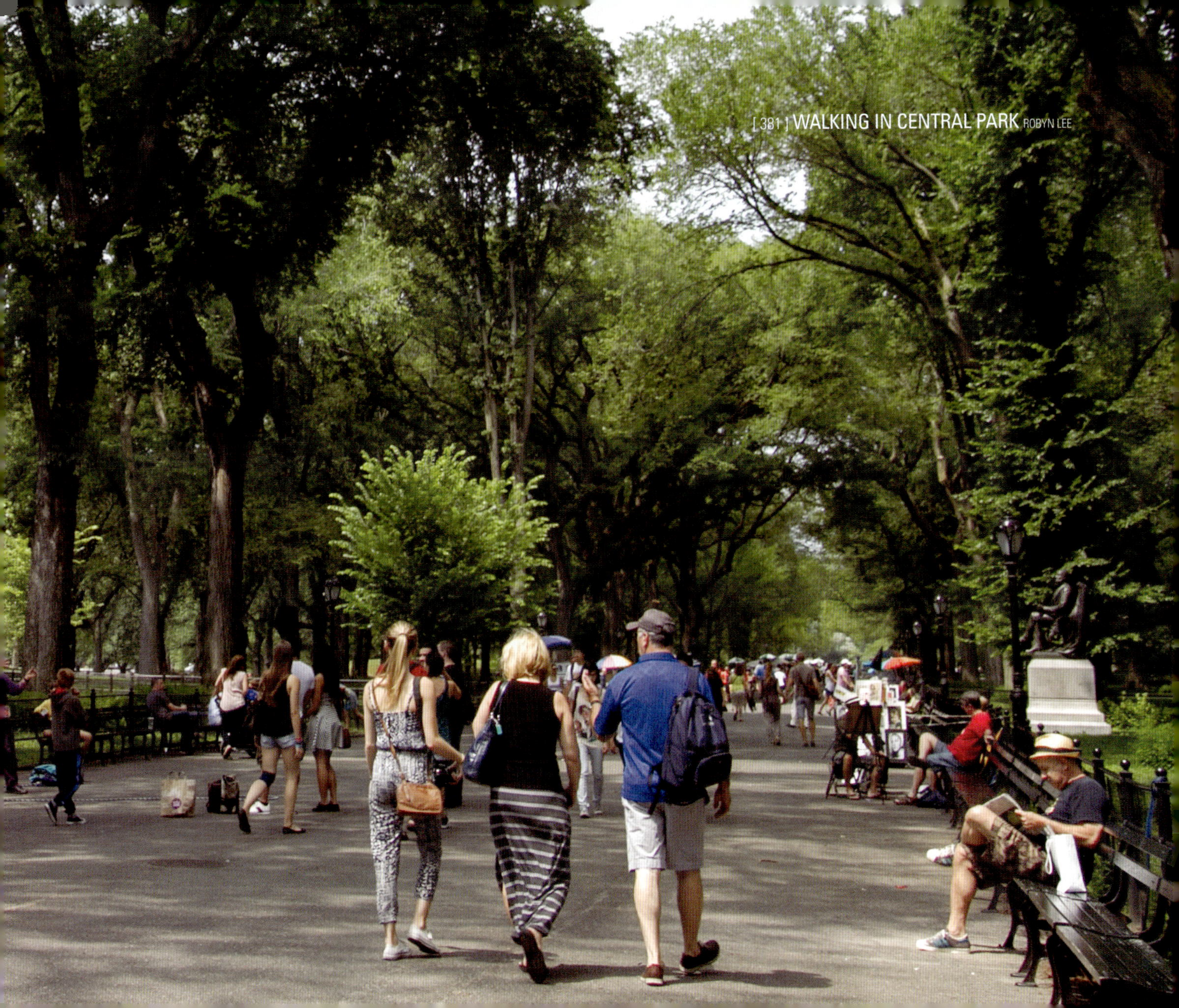

[381] WALKING IN CENTRAL PARK ROBYN LEE

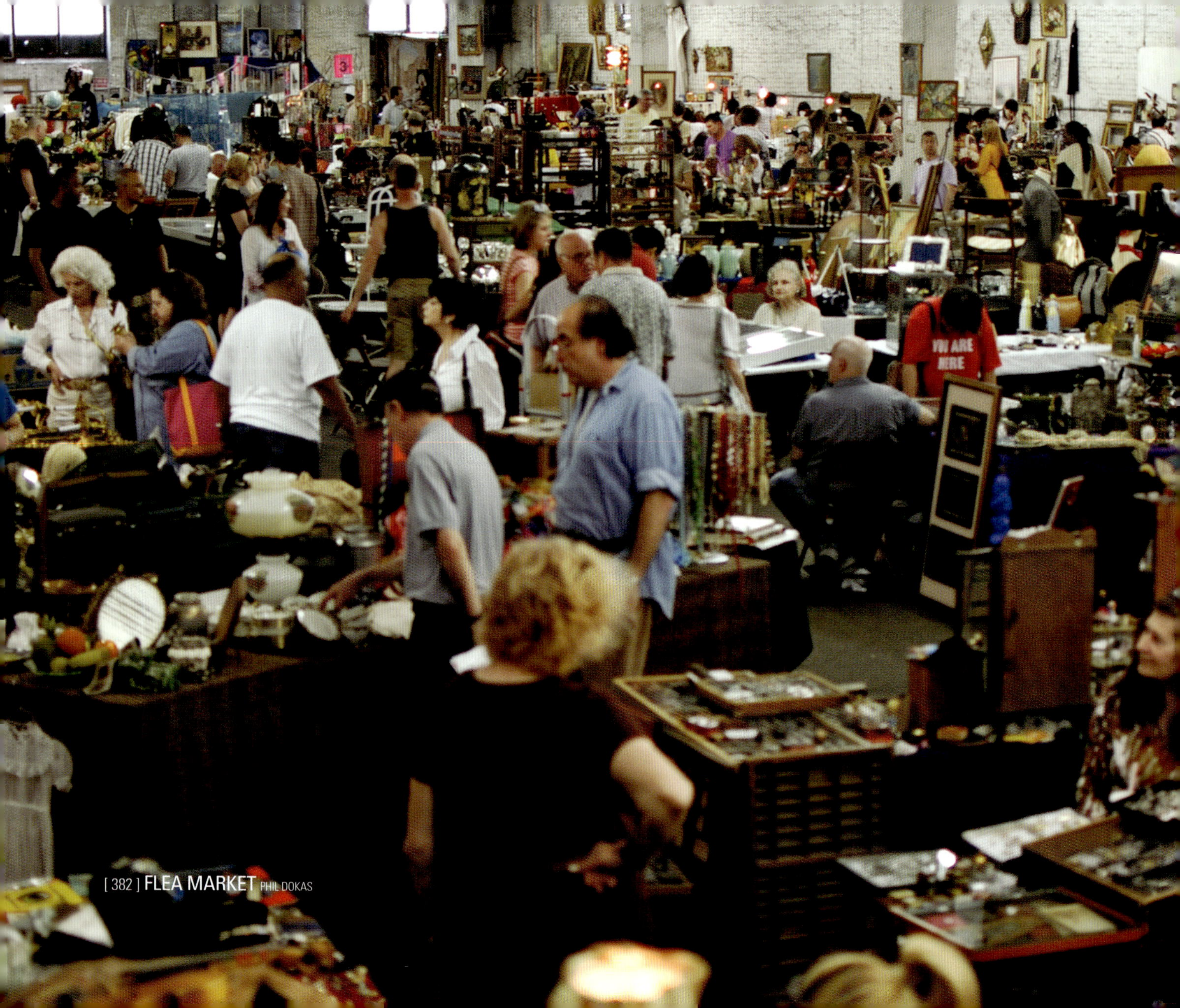

[382] **FLEA MARKET** PHIL DOKAS

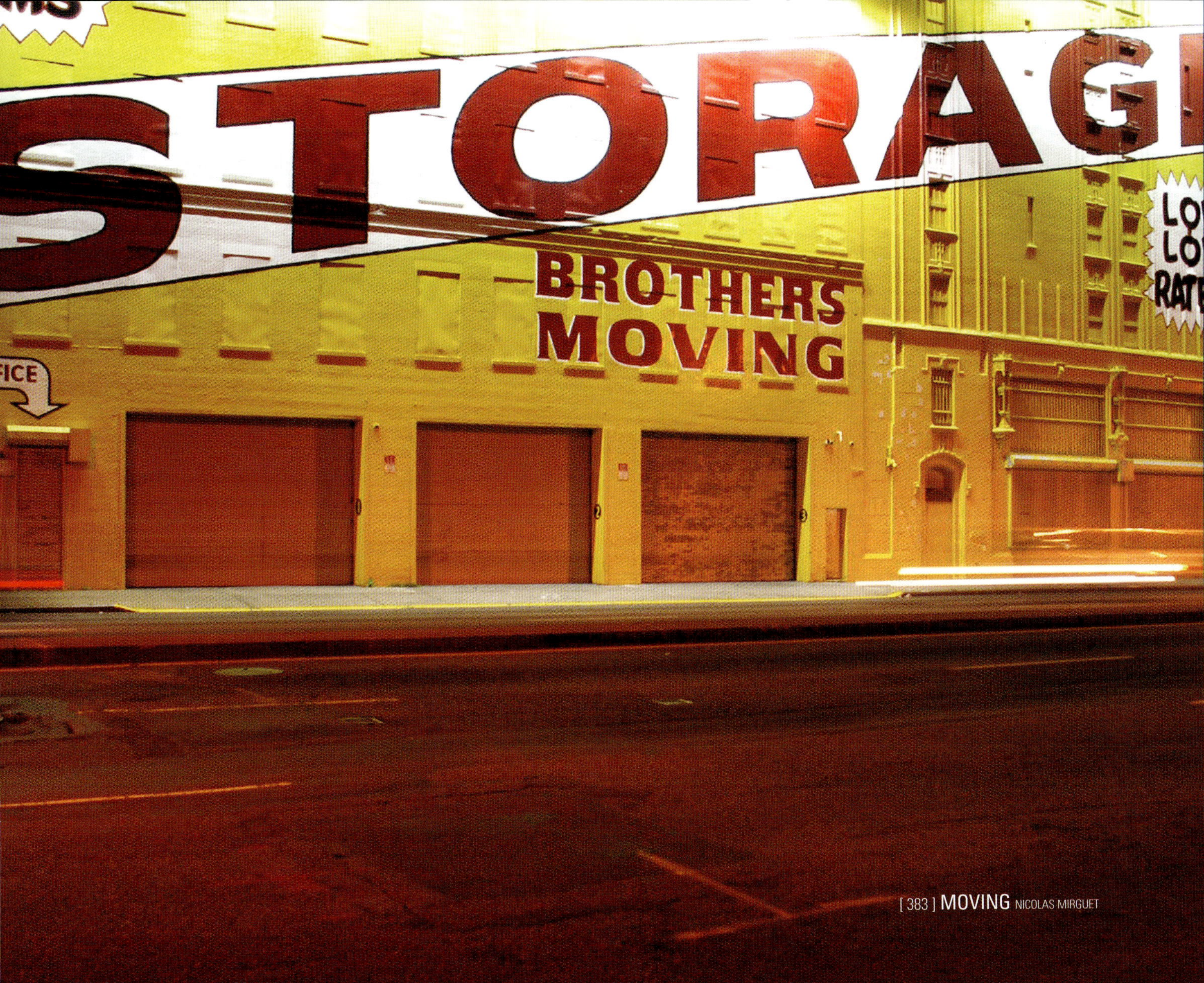

 MOVING NICOLAS MIRGUET

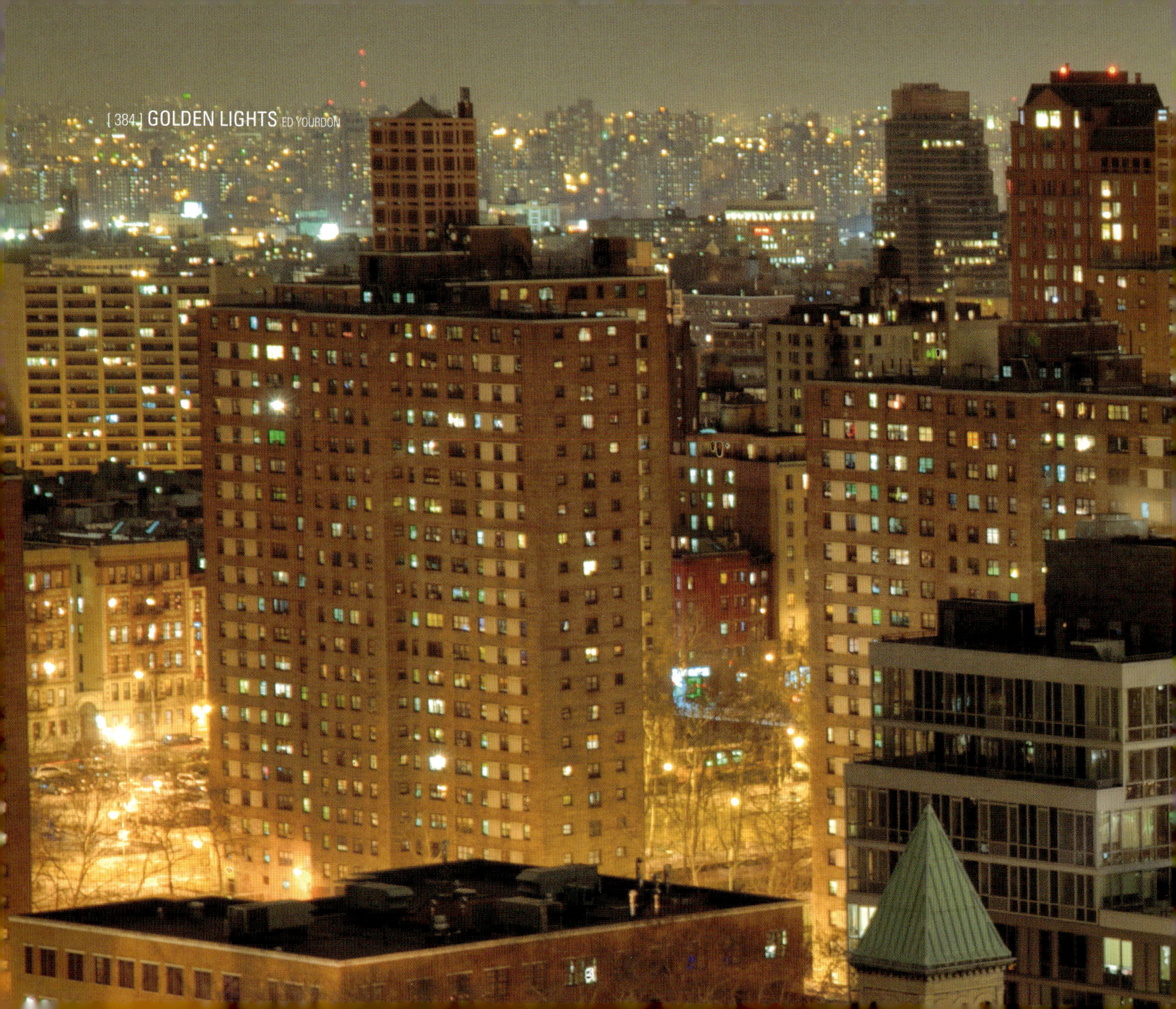

[384] GOLDEN LIGHTS ED YOURDON

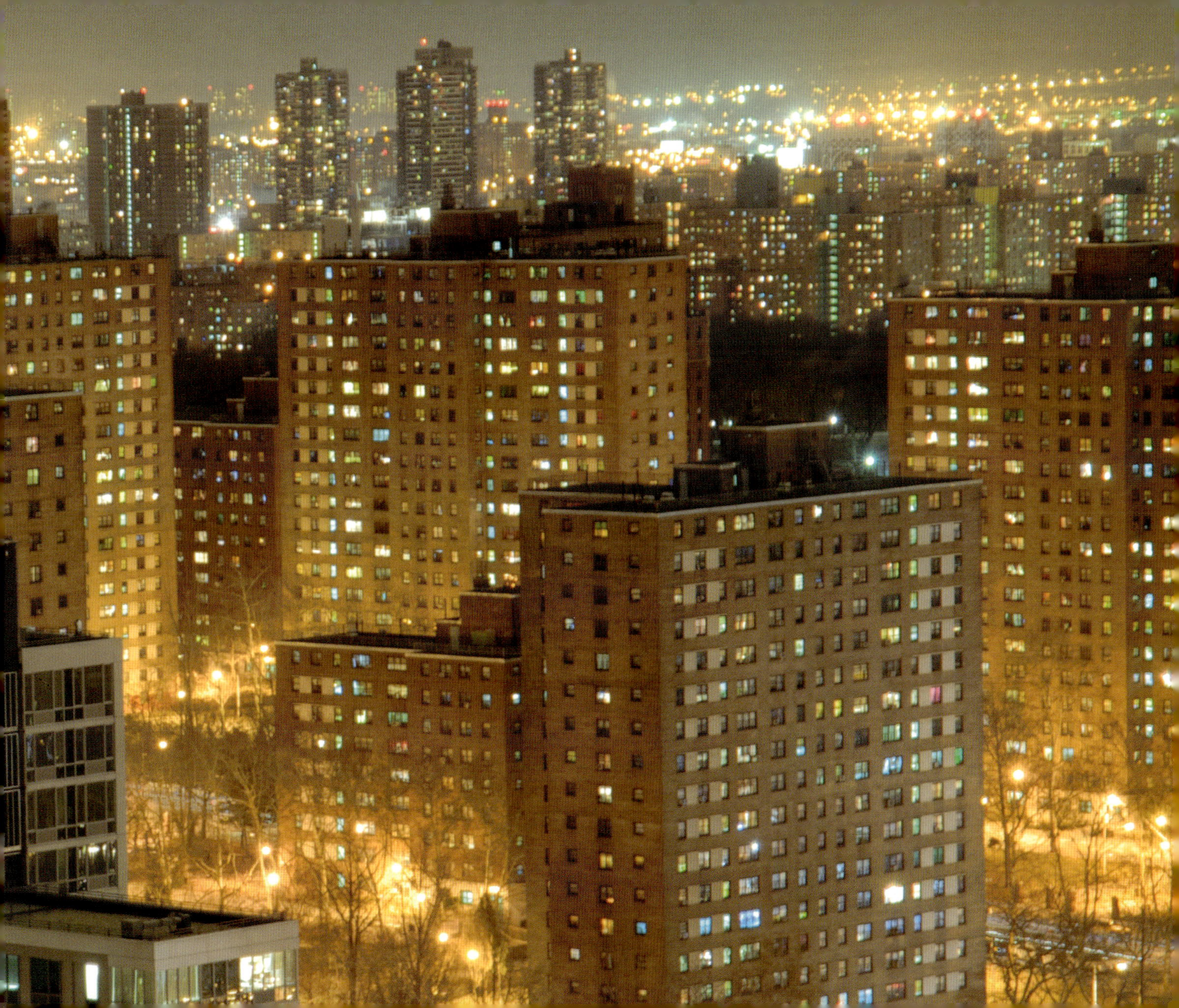

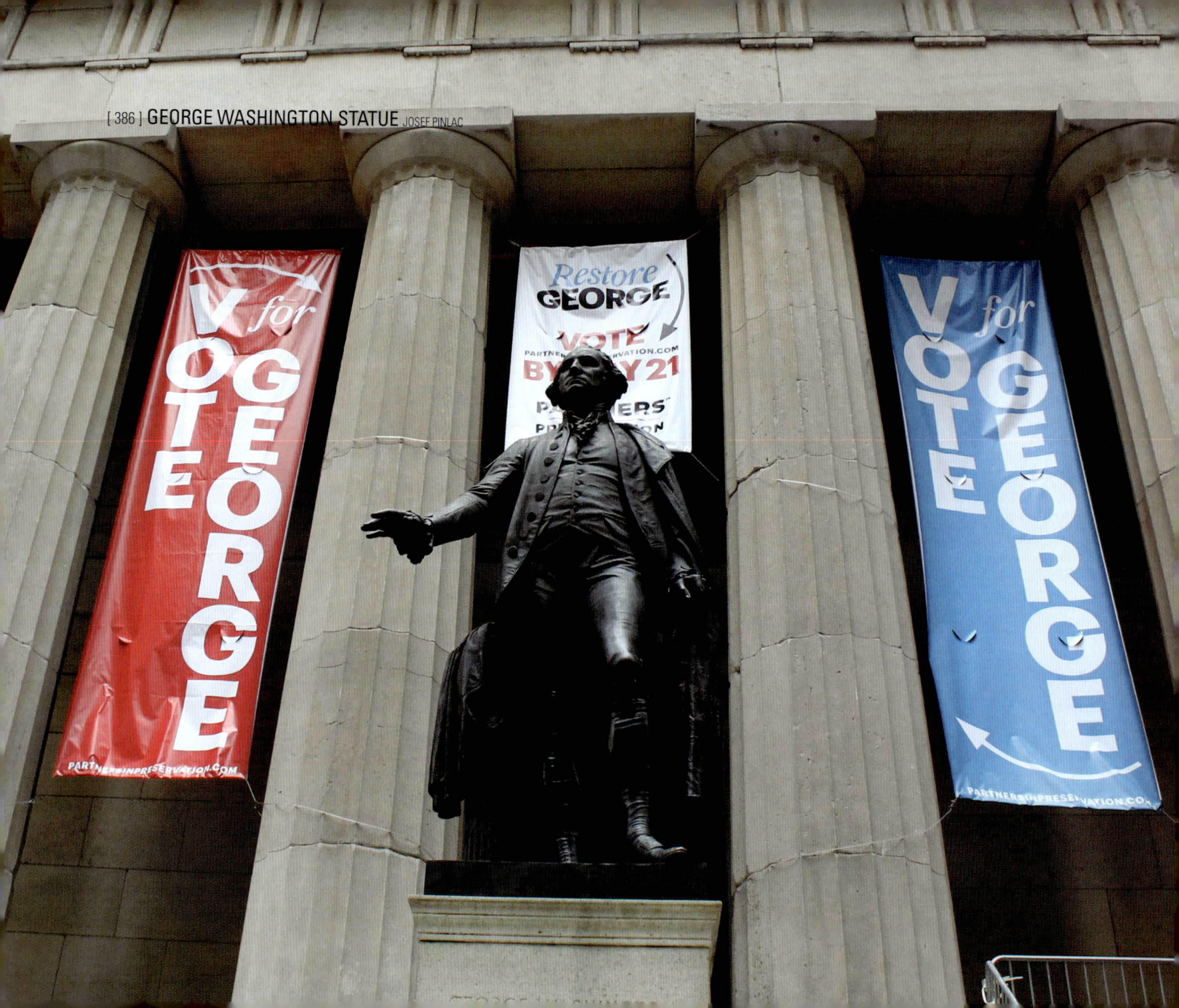

[386] GEORGE WASHINGTON STATUE JOSEF PINLAC

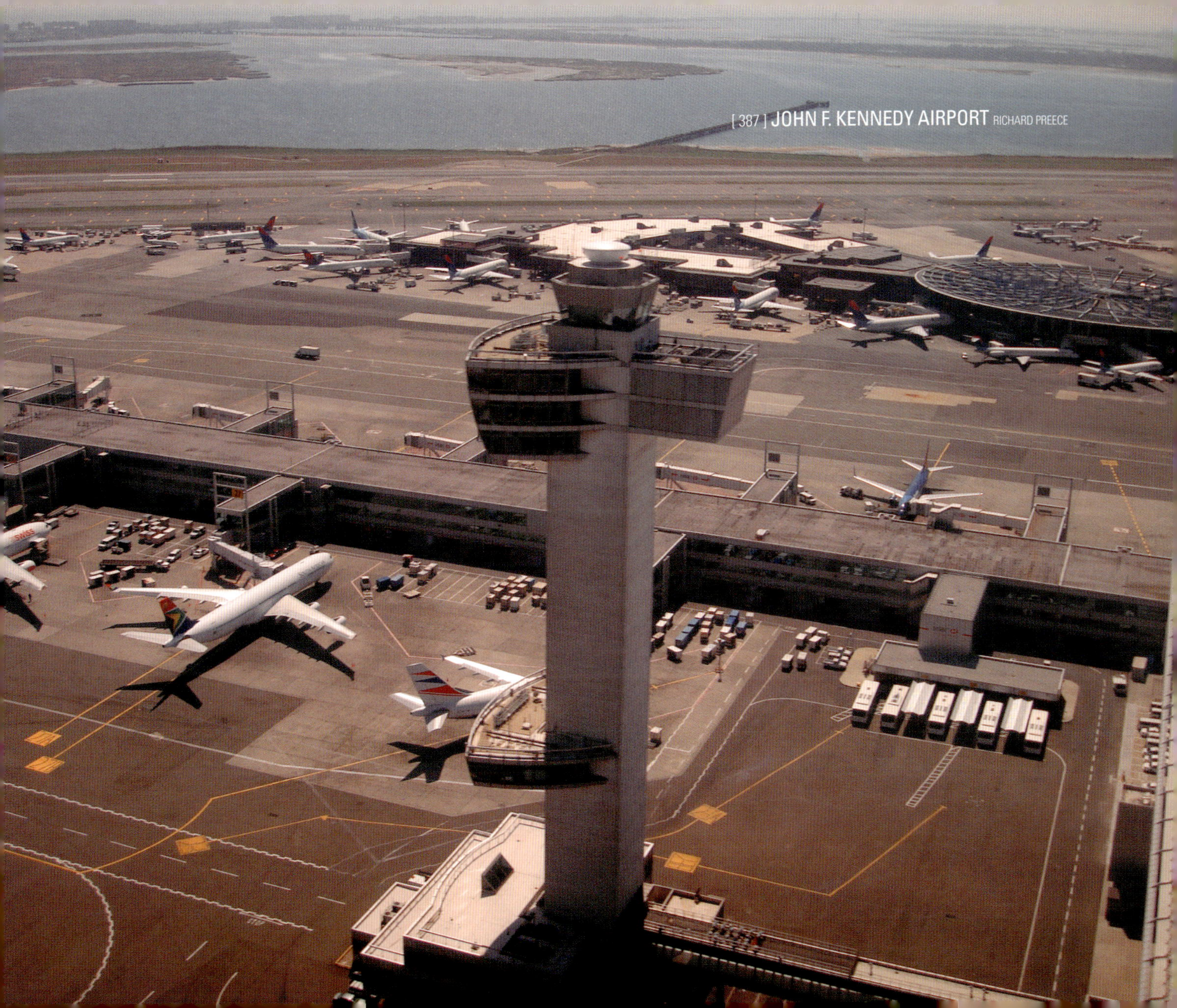

[387] JOHN F. KENNEDY AIRPORT RICHARD PREECE

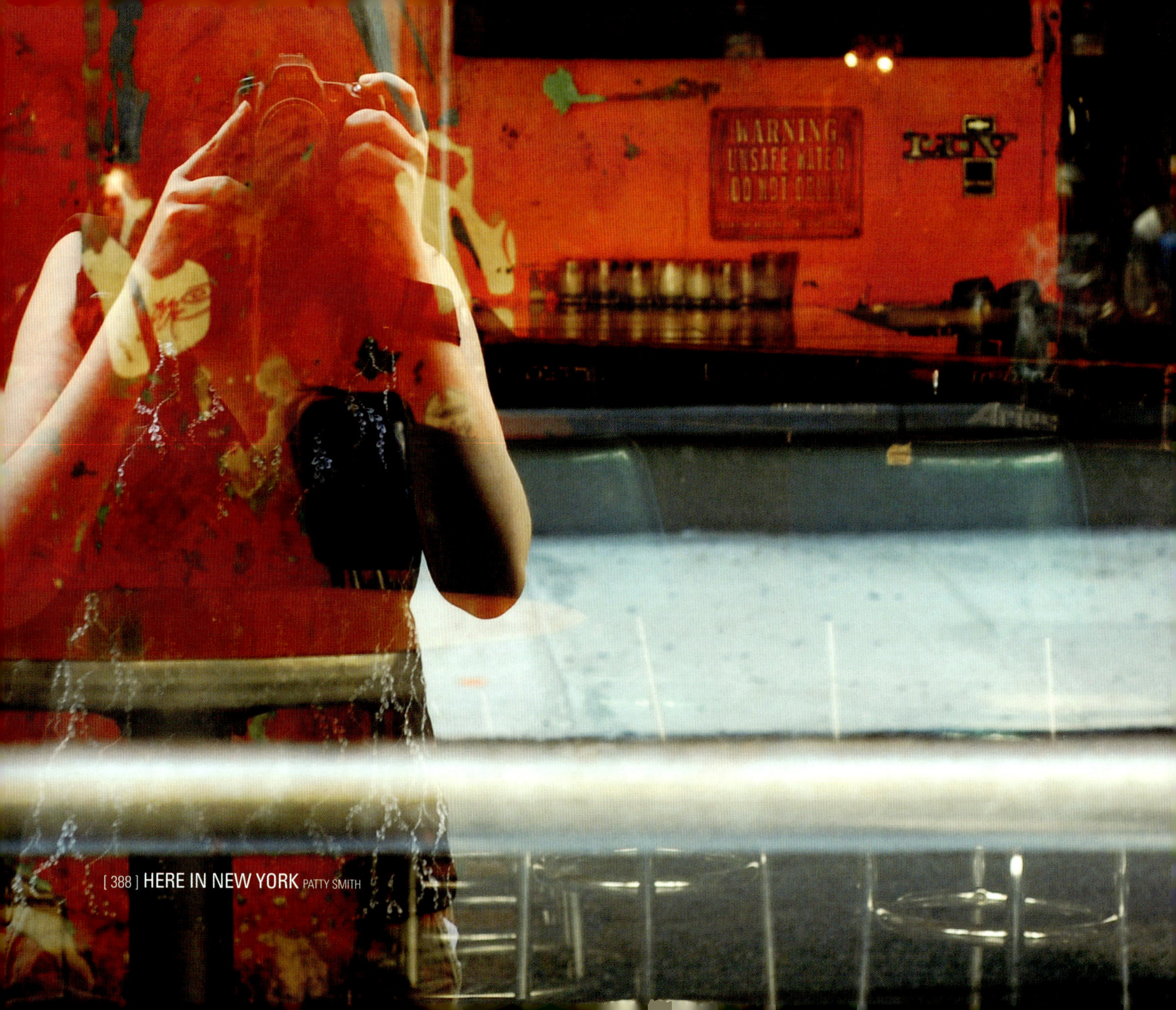

[388] HERE IN NEW YORK PATTY SMITH

If I can make it there I'll make it anywhere.
It's up to you, New York, New York.

[9] New York When Europeans first came to this land in 1524, it was inhabited by the Lenape tribe. In 1626, the Dutch arrived, and the written history of a city that many consider the most important in the world began. Thanks to its openness to both immigrants and new ideas, it is a destination for many seeking opportunity.
[10] Ellis Island From 1892 to 1954, some twelve million immigrants on their way to New York came through this checkpoint where their papers were inspected and they were given medical examinations. For many families, Ellis Island was a symbol of a new life.
[11] Flight to New York And so the journey begins…
[12] JFK tag This luggage tag means the beginning of a trip to New York.
[13] Moleskine New York A favorite of Hemingway, this edition of the traditional travel journal is perfect for recording your experience in New York. [Moleskine is a registered trademark of Moleskine SpA. All rights reserved].
[14] The Holland Tunnel Opened in 1927, the tunnel under the Hudson River connects New York and New Jersey. More than 35 million vehicles pass through it every year.
[15] 34th Street Station One of the city's major transportation hubs, there are direct lines from here to Penn Station, Madison Square Garden, Macy's, and the Empire State Building.
[17] View of Manhattan From Brooklyn Bridge Park, you can see emblematic downtown buildings such as the Woolworth Building and Trump Tower. This may be the single best view of Manhattan.
[18] From a taxi The most familiar view of New York is from the backseat of a cab. It's not as common in New York as it is in other cities around the world for passengers to converse with drivers. Always add a tip to the total fare.
[19] New York taxis Thanks to more than 13,600 yellow cabs—officially called medallion taxicabs—that circulate around the city, the cab is perhaps the number one New York icon. Started in 1897, the first taxicab company in New York made use of very basic electric cars. In 1907, Harry N. Allen founded The New York Taxicab Company. The cabs were originally painted red and green, but Allen repainted them all yellow to be visible from a distance.
[20] Registered trademark Even if the "I love NY" logo is a registered trademark, it belongs to everyone who loves New York City.
[21] Eleni's cookies Located in Chelsea Market, Eleni´s cookies partakes of the longstanding American tradition of cake and cookie decoration.
[22] Hotel Empire Ever since this hotel across from Lincoln Center opened its doors in 1923, its neon sign has been an essential part of the Upper West Side landscape.
[23] Empire State This building, which opened its doors in 1931, was the first building in the world with over 100 floors. A major symbol of New York, its observatory is visited by thousands of people every year.
[24] Newspapers The print run of the Sunday edition of *The New York Times* is over 1.5 million. Even though the online edition is growing, the print edition is a well entrenched local tradition.
[25] Newsstand Like everything that is both a good business and a mark of the city's identity, it's not easy to get a permit to run a newsstand. The newsstands in New York feature a wide range of international publications.
[26] *New York Illustrated* Since New York became one of the most important cities in the world, publications from all over have shown readers the architectural and technological advances that have emerged within its confines.
[27] Newspaper dispensers Dispensers containing free publications such as *The Village Voice*, a weekly essential to finding out what's happening on the city's cultural scene, can be found on corners throughout the city.
[28] 5th Avenue and 57th Street One of the most famous corners in the world.
[30] Alice in Wonderland One of the most popular statues in Central Park, it was created by Spanish sculptor José de Creeft. The figure of Alice sitting on an enormous mushroom is a favorite of children who, in the summertime, climb on the statue and play at its feet.
[31] The Plaza Hotel / Apple Store Two wonders of New York are located on 59th Street and 5th Avenue: the Plaza hotel, a New York icon and testament to timeless elegance that first opened its doors in 1907, and the Apple Store, the company's largest, which is open 24 hours a day and has become a major attraction.
[32] Bryant Park Located next to the New York Public Library, this park with tables and chairs is the place where many who work in the area eat lunch. It is also a magical place to read a book.
[33] Books in the Street It's common, especially in neighborhoods near universities, to display used books for sale on sidewalk tables.
[34] Psychic Reading There is something for everyone in New York.
[35] New York Public Library Located at 5th Avenue and 42nd Street where the water works once was, this building is a New York icon. It is one of the largest and most complete libraries in the world, with astonishing reading rooms and permanent and temporary exhibitions.
[36] Park Avenue The most beautiful avenue in New York is crossed by Grand Central Terminal, the dividing line between northern and southern Manhattan. The northern section of the city, where much of the local aristocracy lives, is a symbol of wealth and tradition.
[37] The Helmsley Building: Originally called the New York Central Building, this gem of Beaux-Arts architecture was constructed in 1929 as part of the Grand Central Terminal complex. Under it lies the viaduct that connects Park Avenue North to Park Avenue South.
[38] Shoeshine A New York tradition for men who like their shoes to gleam. Once, customers read the paper while getting a shine; today, they read on their cell phones.
[39] Barbershop Classic New York men still like to get a cut and a shave at a local barbershop.
[40] Brooklyn Bridge Before its construction, Manhattan and Brooklyn would be disconnected whenever the Hudson River froze over. In 1883, after thirteen years of construction, what is now one of the most famous symbols of New York was inaugurated. The requisite walk over the bridge affords one of the most beautiful views of the city.
[41] Platforms at Grand Central Terminal The train station with the largest number of platforms in the world (forty-four) is used by 500,000 people daily.
[42] Grand Central Terminal An icon of New York, Grand Central Terminal is a symbol of productivity and commerce. Originally built in 1871, the architectural gem we know today opened in 1913 with the boom in the railroad industry.
[44] Century 21 Founded in 1961, this store has great discounts on name-brand items. The location across from the Twin Towers was affected by the terrorist attack that destroyed the towers.
[45] Boro Taxis are a type of taxicab in New York City that are allowed to pick up passengers in outer boroughs and in Manhattan above East 96th and West 110th Streets. The color of boro taxis is apple green in contrast to the traditional yellow taxis in New York City.
[46] Pride New York restaurants like to be considered "the best" in something.
[47] Grand Central Market Strategically located for commuters, this market offers the best gourmet products available in the city.
[48] New York lights When evening comes, buildings light up and the New York skyline becomes one of the most attractive sights in the world.
[50] Breakfast A typical New York breakfast: pancakes with syrup and a cup of coffee.
[51] Tiffany & Co. A traditional jeweler founded in 1837, Tiffany & Co. and its little blue boxes are a symbol of status. The store located on 5th Avenue and 57th Street was the location for the film *Breakfast at Tiffany's*, based on the book by Truman Capote.

[52] The Juilliard School A performing arts conservatory founded in 1905 and located in Lincoln Center, The Julliard School is named for Augustus Julliard, a textile merchant who donated the funds that would turn it into one of the most prestigious academies in the country.

[53] Music in the subway Before being authorized to play music in a New York subway station, you must gain approval pursuant to the strict selection process sanctioned in 1987. Regardless, sometimes musicians just start playing on subway platforms.

[54] Auditions Thousands of actors from the world over come to New York for auditions; the lucky ones are cast in hit Broadway and theater productions.

[55] *West Side Story* With music by Leonard Bernstein, this classic—which is still performed on occasion—is one of the most famous Broadway musicals ever.

[56] Gray's Papaya The hot dogs sold at any of Gray's Papaya locations around the city are famous around the world for quality and price. The business, which was started by Paul Gray in 1973, has appeared in countless films, television series, and books that take place in Manhattan.

[58] Zabar's From the time Louis Zabar came to the United States from the Soviet Union in 1920, he was committed to offering his customers top quality goods. He soon specialized in smoked fish and other delicatessen items. An integral part of the Upper West Side for over seventy years, it is a New York tradition in the spring and summer to buy cold cuts at Zabar's and then walk over to Central Park for a picnic.

[59] Eataly This gourmet market, located at 5th Avenue and 23rd Street in the heart of the Flatiron district, is an invitation to celebrate the Italian tradition of good eating. With great products, restaurants, and a friendly atmosphere, it is ideal for those who understand that meal times are times of celebration.

[60] Entrance to the Dakota Building On December 8, 1980, John Lennon was murdered at the entrance to the Dakota Building on 72nd Street and Central Park West, where he lived with his wife Yoko Ono and their son Sean.

[61] Graffiti First popular in the New York subways in the 1970s, graffiti is now an aesthetic influence the world over. John Lennon loved New York; this world-famous image of him wearing a New York City T-shirt was taken by photographer Bob Gruen.

[63] Strawberry Fields Yoko Ono envisioned this place in Central Park as a memorial to John Lennon and as a place of reflection. The "Imagine" mosaic was donated by the city of Naples. Every day, people gather here to pay tribute to John Lennon by singing his songs.

[64] Dakota Building Construction on this building in what was then the largely vacant Upper West Side was finished in 1884. Celebrities such as Judy Garland, Leonard Bernstein, Rudolf Nureyev, and, of course, John Lennon have called its luxurious apartments home.

[65] Ansonia Building In 1899, William Earle Dodge Stokes commissioned architect Paul E. Duboy to design the largest hotel in Manhattan. A residential hotel until 1992, it has been home to New York celebrities such as Arturo Toscanini, Igor Stravinsky, and Enrico Caruso.

[66] Sheep Meadow The largest open field in Central Park, Sheep Meadow was originally used to shepherd sheep. New Yorkers love this spot for picnics and sunbathing.

[68] Pedicab A great way to explore Central Park. The pedicab owners, who have their own organization, must comply with certain New York City transit regulations.

[69] Running in Central Park Thanks to its views of the city and colorful vegetation that changes with the seasons, Central Park is one of the best places to go jogging in the world.

[70] Trash The New York City Sanitation Department—the largest department of its kind in any city—is in charge of the city's trash collection and recycling.

[71] Snack stands These carts, and a few eateries offering more elaborate dishes, are found throughout Central Park. There are constant reminders to help keep the park clean.

[73] Jacqueline Kennedy Onassis Reservoir + Eldorado The reservoir was built between 1858 and 1862 according to Frederick Law Olmsted and Calvert Vaux's design for Central Park. It was renamed in honor of Jacqueline Kennedy Onassis in 1994 to commemorate her contributions to the city. She enjoyed jogging in the area, which lay beneath the windows of her Fifth Avenue apartment. When frozen over in the winter, it forms part of a beautiful view of Central Park.

Construction on this gem of art deco architecture began in 1929. Eldorado is one of the most photographed buildings in New York, and has been a residence for many celebrities. It is one of the luxury buildings that line the west side of Central Park.

[74] Safety signs The city of New York has strict regulations on posting safety signs and marking construction sites.

[75] Subway entrance A MetroCard allows entrance into an underground world.

[76] Subway With more than 6,300 cars, the New York subway system has more cars than any other city in the world.

[77] Subway bench Typical seats on subway platforms.

[78] Window displays The window displays on 5th Avenue are a show in their own right.

[79] Reading New York is a city of readers who are comfortable opening a book or magazine just about anywhere.

[80] Tenement Museum On the basis of the museum's premises and the neighborhood around it, the Tenement Museum, located at the corner of Orchard and Houston, tells the story of how the thousands of families that immigrated to New York forged the identity of the city and of the country.

[81] Multicultural immigration New York City is home to hundreds of cultures.

[82] Murray's A part of the history of Greenwich Village, Murray's has specialized in cheese since 1940. Located on Bleecker St. between 6th & 7th Avenues

[83] Yonah Shimmel In 1890, a Romanian immigrant named Yonah Shimmel started selling his potato knishes from a pushcart he pushed around in the Lower East Side. In 1910, his cousin Joseph Berger opened this store at 137 E. Houston; it is still run by the family.

[84] Coffee on the go In the winter, it's common to see people drinking a hot beverage on the street to keep warm.

[86] Mother with twins Due to the increased use of different fertility treatments, twins have become a common sight in the city.

[87] Russ and Daughters After working for years as a street vendor selling Russian and Polish Jewish food, immigrant Joel Russ opened a shop in 1914. His daughters later joined the business and now, one hundred years later, it is one of the gems of New York.

[88] Odd jobs Especially in the Fashion district and Chinatown, occasional workers can be seen carting goods around at all hours.

[89] Basements The merchandise is brought in through doors that open onto underground storage spaces.

[91] Katz's Delicatessen Perhaps the most famous Jewish restaurant in the city, Katz's Delicatessen is located at Houston and Ludlow Streets in the Lower East Side. Founded in 1888, it is famous for their pastrami sandwich. Because the meat is cut to order, customers patiently wait their turn with tickets in hand.

[92] Williamsburg Bridge View from the M subway that crosses the East River above ground.

[94] Staten Island Ferry This means of transportation, immortalized by the film *Working Girl*, is used by those who live in Staten Island and work in downtown Manhattan. It offers a panoramic view of the skyscrapers in southern Manhattan.
[95] Photographing Manhattan New Yorkers love to cross the river to enjoy a spectacular view of the city.
[96] Flowers New York florists offer merchandise from around the world and brighten up the streets throughout the year.
[97] Shoe Repair Shoes are often a coveted item in New York, which means that shoemakers are typically held in high regard.
[98] Wind Due to the layout of the city and the rivers that surround it, strong gusts of wind sweeping the island from east to the west are commonplace.
[99] *New York* magazine Founded by Milton Glaser and Clay Felker in 1968, *New York* magazine is a weekly publication on life, culture, politics, and style with a special focus on the city of New York. [*New York* magazine is a registered trademark of New York Media LLC. All rights reserved].
[100] Radio City Music Hall The most famous theater in New York, Radio City Music Hall is part of Rockefeller Center. Opened in 1932, the venue, which can hold up to 5,933 people, is where many important award ceremonies are held.
[102] Ice skating at Rockefeller Center When fall begins, the sunken plaza at Rockefeller Center turns into one of the most famous skating rinks in the United States. With room for as many as 150 skaters, it is a popular tourist attraction.
[103] Wollman Rink Opened in 1949 and immortalized by the film *Love Story*, the cement floor of Wollman Rink doubles as a skating rink from October to April.
[105] The roof terrace at the Met With an unrivaled view of the park, the bar at this privileged spot in the city makes summer afternoons all the more pleasant.
[106] New York Mets The stadium of this New York baseball team is in Flushing, Queens. The New York Mets is a registered trademark of Sterling Mets,L.P.
[107] The stairs to the Met Meeting point, resting place, bleacher from which to watch street performances, and place to eat the excellent food sold at the trucks that line up in front of the museum.
[108] Museum Mile The stretch of 5th Avenue that goes from 82nd to 110th Streets is home to nine of the best museums in the world.
[109] Collectible Brochures The brochure industry is an important part of the New York cultural circuit. Brochures, which are often kept as collectors' items, are perfect for scrapbooks and photo albums.
[110] Carriage rides in Central Park Though the tradition of the horse-drawn carriage ride in the park has been a staple of New York for over 100 years, it is about to be replaced by electric cars. The drivers, though, will remain the same.
[111] Mounted police The NYPD mounted unit was created in 1871. Today, they maintain about 50 horses throughout the city.
[112] Saks Fifth Avenue In 1867, Andrew Saks opened a clothing store in Washington D.C. and, in 1924, he opened a flagship store in New York under the name that we know today. Saks Fifth Avenue now has fifty-four locations around the country.
[113-115] Traffic signs There are more than two million traffic signs on the streets of New York.
[116] Public phones After the advent of cell phones, more than 11,000 public phones in New York are now largely in disuse. A plan to turn them into free WiFi points is being considered.
[117] WiFi in the subway New York is very receptive to technological innovation. By 2017, the city's 277 subway stations will all have free WiFi service.
[118] The University Club This historic and exclusive New York club was founded in 1861 by alumni of the country's best universities in order to "[promote] Literature and Art by establishing and maintaining a Library, Reading Room and Gallery of Art, and by such other means as shall be expedient and proper for such purposes." Even today it represents the elite and the powerful.
[119] Columbia University The oldest university in the state of New York, it was founded in 1754 as King's College. One of the most prestigious universities in the world, it gives out the Pulitzer Prize and has more Nobel Laureates on its faculty than any other institution in the world. The university is the heart of the Upper West Side and its style makes itself felt throughout the neighborhood.
[120] I Love NY This logo, created by Milton Glaser in 1977 to promote tourism, was envisioned as part of a temporary campaign. It has since become the symbol of New York. The original sketch is housed at MoMA.
[121] Gay Pride March The march takes place in late June every year to commemorate resistance to a police raid on Stonewall Inn, a gay pub, in 1969. Gay pride marches, which are now held in thousands of cities across the globe, are a symbol of the struggle for the rights of LGBTI people.
[122] NYPD Helicopter The pilots of New York state police helicopters provide air support to police and emergency personnel throughout the state.
[123] Superman Though ostensibly this comic strip icon lives in the city of Metropolis, everyone knows his hometown is really New York. In this image from the streets of New York, Barack Obama, president of the United States, embodies the superhero.
[125] View of New York Central Park was not included in the Commissioners' Plan of 1811 which lay the city out on a grid. An interest in open outdoor spaces for recreation emerged in the mid-eighteenth century with new ideas about health and hygiene.
[126] USS *Maine* Designed by Harold Van Buren Magonigle, the monument to the USS *Maine* battleship at the southeastern entrance to Central Park shows the Columbia Triumphant. It is said that the bronze used for the statue came from the ship itself.
[127] Fire Pipes Ready to put out fires at any hour, there are fire pipes throughout the city, some of them so well polished that they are a source of pride and distinction.
[128] Seeing New York The city has many viewing points with binoculars for a closer look.
[129] Street Art Many murals painted by talented artists can be found throughout the city.
[130] Kid-friendly city New York, especially the areas near Central Park, is extremely kid friendly. If a store or restaurant has a policy on admitting children, it is generally posted in the entrance or reception area.
[131] FAO Schwarz In 1856, Frederick August Otto Schwarz came to the United States from Germany with the dream of opening the largest toy store in the world. The first toy store in the United States, Fao Schwarz now specializes in luxury toys.
[132] Big Apple Though sports journalist John J. Fitz Gerald first used this phrase in reference to New York in 1920, it was popularized in the 1970s by a tourism campaign.
[133] Piano at Fao Schwarz Thanks to the popular movie *Big* featuring Tom Hanks, any child who comes to New York wants to play this famous toy store's enormous piano.
[134] Reading on the bench A nice way to spend the morning.
[135] Reading in the subway In the hustle and bustle of New York, a ride on the subway provides an opportunity to read.
[136] Shoots Hundreds of films are shot every day on the streets of New York and each one is required to get a permit. Made in NY publishes online a complete list of the shows and films in production.

[137] No Parking If even on a good day it's hard to find a place to park in the city. Signs often spring up from one day to the next announcing that the street must be cleared for a special event.
[138] *The New York Times Magazine* The first issue of the Sunday magazine supplement to *The New York Times* was published on September 6, 1896; it contained the first photographs ever printed in a newspaper. [*New York Times Magazine* is a registered trademark of New York Times Company. All rights reserved].
[139] Made in NY This agency is responsible for issuing permits and providing assistance to film, television, and theater productions around the city.
[140] *The New York Times* Founded on September 18, 1851 by Henry Jarvis Raymond and George Jones, *The New York Times* is one of the most influential newspapers in the world. [*The New York Times* is a registered trademark of The New York Times Company. All rights reserved].
[141] MTA The Metropolitan Transportation Authority is the largest transportation network in the United States, serving a population of 15.1 million people in the 5,000-square-mile area fanning out from New York City through Long Island, southeastern New York state, and Connecticut.
[142] Variety and abundance The city's supermarkets offer a wide range of fruits and vegetables from the world over.
[144] Toys "R" Us When this business started in 1948 as the baby boom was getting underway, it sold only baby furniture. Its Times Square store is now the largest toy store in the world and a major attraction for all of New York's children.
[145] Columbus Park Regulars play traditional games at this park located in Chinatown.
[146] Chinatown It is said that over half the residents of New York speak a language other than English. Some eighty languages and dialects are believed to be spoken in the city.
[147] Doyers Street This street became famous as one of the favorite Chinatown settings of the mob in the 1930s. A typical Cantonese dim sum has been served at the Tea Parlor since 1920.
[148] Peking duck This traditional dish is often displayed in the windows of restaurants in Chinatown.
[149] Donuts While there are variations on the donut from around the world, almost everyone agrees that it originated in Central Europe. This fried dough with different types of glazes is typical of New York City.
[150] Russian Tea Room Located next door to Carnegie Hall, the Russian Tea Room was founded in 1927 by a member of the Imperial Russian Ballet Company. It is a favorite spot of politicians, artists, and bon vivants.
[151] American Ballet Theatre The most important ballet company in the country, the American Ballet Theatre was founded in 1937. Housed in the Metropolitan Opera House, the company features world-famous directors like Mikhail Baryshnikov.
[152] New York City Ballet When George Balanchine founded the New York City Ballet in 1948, he gave classical dance a breath of fresh air. The highly influential company is now a mecca for great dancers from around the world.
[153] Ballet classes Thousands of dance students come to New York City every year to take dance classes at leading institutions with excellent instructors.
[154] *The New York Review of Books* With a print run of over 135,000, *The New York Review of Books* is the most important independent publication on current events and literature in the world. [*The New York Review of Books* is a registered trademark of NYREV, Inc. All rights reserved].
[155] Books on New York A vast number of books on New York are available and most of the city's bookstores have a section dedicated to them.
[156] Storage The price of real estate in New York is among the highest in the world. Apartments are generally small so many people rent storage space.
[157] Parking In New York, people make the most of every last inch.
[158] Police meeting The NYPD is one of the oldest police departments established in the United States; tracing its roots back to the first Dutch eight man night watch in 1625, when New York City was New Amsterdam.
[159] Gotham City This nickname, which comes from the *Batman* comic, is one of the many used to refer to New York City.
[160] Between buildings The intermediate height provides a hypnotic view that makes you feel as if you are inside a video game.
[162] Glass of water New York's filtered drinking water system is fed with water from the Catskill Mountains. A glass of ice water is immediately served at any restaurant.
[163] Drinking Water Sampling Station These stations, where bacteriological inspections of drinking water are performed, can be found throughout the city.
[164] Ice cream truck To the delight of both young and old, ice cream trucks circulate through the city in summertime. Maps with daily routes are available online.
[165] Hydrants New York City's first fire hydrant was installed in 1808 at the corner of William and Liberty Streets. Today, they are a staple of the city's landscape as well as an essential tool for putting out fires. In summer, children use them to cool off.
[166] Firefighter in action While the team of firefighters gets ready to put out the fire, one of them is in charge of checking and turning on the water source. Firefighters are among the most respected individuals in the city.
[167] Water tanks A good early solution to the problem of water pressure and a means of ensuring water supply to fight fires, there are still between 10,000 and 15,000 water tanks on city rooftops, making them a part of the New York landscape.
[168] Licensed Taxicab There's plenty of paperwork to go through before receiving one of more than 13,000 licenses granted to become a New York cabdriver.
[169] Landmarks The city declares those buildings and businesses essential to its identity "landmarks."
[170] Edith Wharton (1862–1937) was the writer who best portrayed the upper-class society of old New York. Her best known book is the Pulitzer Prize-winning *The Age of Innocence.*
[171] *Sex and the City* By means of her character Carrie Bradshaw, Candace Bushnell revealed a different New York in a series that became a symbol of female friendship, the search for love, and life in the big city.
[172] Girls in NY The television show *Sex and the City* inspired thousands of women from around the world to visit the city. Andy Clark founded "Girls in NY," a Buenos Aires-based travel agency that organizes tours of the city.
[173] Collection of vintage New York postcards Old postcards have become decorative pieces and collectors' items.
[174] New York souvenirs No visitor goes home without a souvenir of some sort.
[175] Wintertime Cold New York winters often mean snowstorms that can bring the city to a standstill.
[176] New York pizza New York–style pizza has a large diameter, a thin crust, and tomato sauce and cheese on top. Since it doesn't break when folded, it is perfect to eat on the go.

[177] *Time Out* magazine A weekly first published in London in 1968, the New York edition of *Time Out* is essential to finding out what cultural events are taking place around the city. [*Time Out* is a registered trademark of Time Out Group Limited. All rights reserved].
[178] New York sightseeing bus Since 1926, Gray Line has provided tours of New York that stop at a number of interesting locations.
[179] Demonstrations In New York, like many US cities, you need a permit to hold a demonstration. But because New York has so many residents with such a wide range of concerns, orderly and peaceful demonstrations are always taking place somewhere.
[180] The Italian Empire State The top of the Empire State Building is lit up in different colors every day, depending on the occasion.
[181] The Italian flag The influence of Italian immigration is felt throughout the city.
[182] Little Italy Though it now blends into Chinatown, Little Italy was once the heart of the Italian immigrant neighborhood. It is still a culinary center and home to the Feast of San Gennaro. The mythical street of the mob, Mulberry Street has appeared in hundreds of films.
[183] Liquors Prohibition (1920–1933) meant a boom to illegal alcohol trade, speakeasies, and the mob. To this day a strict permit system regulates the sale of alcoholic beverages.
[184] Silvercup Studios sign Located in Queens, this iconic New York sign crowns the largest film and television complex in New York. This is where the popular series *The Sopranos* was filmed.
[185] Ferrara This café located at 195 Grand Street was founded by an Italian family in 1892. It is where the Great Caruso came for an espresso and cannoli after the opera. The line from *The Godfather* "Leave the gun, take the cannoli" is now famous.
[186] Petrossian When fleeing the Bolshevik Revolution, the Petrossian family took with it its most cherished belonging: caviar. A boom that began in Paris in 1920 later spread throughout the world. Today, Petrossian is a symbol of luxury. In 1984, it opened a restaurant in the historical Alwyn Court Building.
[187] Sanitary Inspection grade The NYC Department of Health and Mental Hygiene (DOHMH) inspects restaurants to post letter grades showing sanitary inspection results.
[188] The Metropolitan Museum of Art One of the largest and most important art museums in the world, The Met, which opened in 1872, has a collection of over two million pieces, including some of the most famous paintings in the world. A major tourist attraction, visitors are required to put on a pin that changes color every day of the week. [The Metropolitan Museum of Art is a registered trademark of the Metropolitan Museum of Art. All rights reserved].
[189] Magnolia Bakery Since its West Village location opened in 1996, Magnolia Bakery has become known all over the world for their delicious cupcakes.
[190] Demolition and reconstruction Due to the limited space available, old buildings are constantly being torn down to make room for modern constructions. In economic and architectural terms, the New York real estate business is a powerful force.
[191] The Waldorf Astoria Hotel The first Waldorf Hotel, which opened in 1897, was located on the lot where the Empire State Building stands today. Construction on the new building on Park Avenue was finished in 1931. It is an icon of New York style.
[192] Wall Street Bull The bronze sculpture by Arturo Di Modica that stands in Bowling Green Park near Wall Street is a symbol of aggressive financial optimism and prosperity.
[193] Business suits The men who work in New York's financial district are some of the most elegantly dressed in the world.
[194] **Wall Street** In 1652, the Dutch built a wall to mark the northern limit of New Amsterdam. It was taken down by the British in 1699 and made into a street. Today, Wall Street is the site of the New York Stock Exchange and the heart of the US financial system.
[195] *Wall Street Journal* This daily paper, focused on business and economic news, was published for the first time on July 8, 1889. Its current circulation is larger than that of any other paper anywhere. [*Wall Street Journal* is a registered trademark of Dow Jones & Company, Inc. All Rights Reserved].
[196] The New York Stock Exchange The New York Stock Exchange was created in 1817 when a group of brokers formed the New York Stock and Exchange Board to control the flow of stocks which, at that time, were traded freely, mostly on the sidewalks of Wall Street. It is currently the largest stock exchange in the world in terms of monetary value and number of businesses traded.
[197] Metropolitan Opera House Home to the Metropolitan Opera Company, this theater is located in Lincoln Center. Over 220 performances are held each year at what is considered a world-class opera house.
[198] David H. Koch Theater Located in Lincoln Center, the home theater of the New York City Ballet can hold as many as 2,713 people. Designed by architect Philip Johnson and opened on April 23, 1964, the theater is owned by the City of New York.
[199] Musicians in Central Park Because so many people walk through this open area near the Julliard School, Central Park is a favorite place for music students from all over the world to play.
[200] The Carlyle Hotel This building, located at 76th and Madison, houses hotel rooms and apartments. Designed by Moses Ginsberg, it was known as "the New York White House" because John F. Kennedy had an apartment there during his presidency.
[201] Woody Allen at Café Carlyle Since 1996, Allen and his jazz band have played at the café, which is known for murals by Marcel Vertes, on a weekly basis.
[202] The Statue of Liberty Perhaps the most famous monument in the United States shows Liberty enlightening the world. In 1886, France gave the statue to the US; it represents the hopes of those who arrive at the port of New York in search for a better life.
[204] Tom's Restaurant This classic New York restaurant has been around for over seventy years. Located on the corner of 112th and Broadway, it was frequented by Columbia students even before the television series *Seinfeld* made it famous.
[205] West Side Restaurant At the corner of Broadway and 69th Street, this is a traditional place for a perfect breakfast.
[206] Cheese Countless cheeses, both local and imported from the world over, are sold at Grand Central Market.
[207] New York–style cheesecake While traditional cheesecake may be Greek, the New York version was developed by William Lawrence in 1872. His recipe lives on.
[208] Andy Warhol's art One of the creators of Pop art, Andy Warhol is an iconic New York figure. His parties and social milieu were as famous and inspiring as his Art.
[209] Fanelli Café Located on the corner of Prince and Mercer in the heart of Soho, drinks have been sold here since 1847. During Prohibition, Fanelli, which has had that name since 1922, was a speakeasy.
[210] Actors Studio The Actors Studio is a non-profit organization for professional actors, directors, and playwrights founded in 1947. It provides a space for experimentation, study, and rehearsal. Many of the most famous actors in the US are members of this organization.

[211] Scripts Who in New York doesn't want to be an actor? Every corner of the city exudes theater and film. Thousands of aspiring actors who come to the city each year buy scripts from street vendors.
[212] Old Broadway tickets Because many of the plays that open on Broadway become classics, the tickets are treasured by collectors from around the world.
[213] Sardi's 234 West 44th Street. This traditional restaurant is famous for its caricatures of Broadway actors, who often dine here after debuts awaiting the reviews in the papers.
[214] R line After leaving Forest Hills, the R line travels through Queens and runs down the length of Manhattan to finally end in Bay Ridge, Brooklyn.
[215] Reflections line You can see this kind of reflection through all of Central Park.
[216] TKTS discount booth Located at the heart of Times Square, TKTS Discount Booth offers discounted tickets to same-day performances for Broadway, Off-Broadway, dance and music events. The lines start before noon and 12.5 million tickets are sold annually.
[217] *Playbill* A monthly theater magazine that has been published since 1884, *Playbill* also serves as a program for Broadway plays. Each theater adjusts the cover and contents according to its production. Many playbills eventually become collectors' items. [*Playbill* is a registered trademark of *Playbill*, Inc. All Rights Reserved].
[218] Times Square Station More people come through Times Square Station, where four different subway lines connect, than any other subway station in the city.
[219] Screen in Times Square A favorite tourist attraction, the screen occasionally shows images of passersby who look for themselves amid so many bright lights.
[220] New York bench Every city has a distinctive park bench and New York is no exception.
[221] Times Square A major symbol of New York, Times Square gets its name from the New York Times building that was at the intersection of 7th Avenue and Broadway. With its bright theater lights and advertising, Times Square is a show in and of itself, which is why stands have been put up as a meeting point and a place to take in the scene.
[222] Your story in the park The "adopt a bench" program is a way to support the conservation of Central Park. Since 1996, this program has provided a special way to pay eternal tribute to someone who loved the park or to immortalize a special moment.
[223] Essex House Construction on this hotel and residence began on October 30, 1929, the day after the stock market crash. Its roof holds one of the city's most iconic signs, a staple of the view of the New York skyline from Central Park. This is where Igor Stravinsky, among other famous figures, lived. It now belongs to the Marriott chain.
[224] Carnegie Deli Founded in 1937, Carnegie Deli on 7th Avenue at 55th Street is a true New York City landmark. Its pastrami sandwich and cheesecake are famous around the world.
[225] Carnegie Hall One of the most prestigious concert halls in the world, Carnegie Hall opened in 1891 with a concert conducted by Tchaikovsky. It was able to stay open thanks to the support of Isaac Stern, for whom the main hall is named.
[226] Downtown / Uptown Signs help to navigate around the New York subway system.
[228] Skateboarding Riding a skateboard around the city has become a popular, alternative means of transportation.
[229] Wheelchair accessible New York is very accessible to those with impaired mobility. It's common to see senior citizens getting around on their own.
[230] Elegance The elegance of older New York women is legendary.
[231] Diamond District Started in the 1920s by jewelers previously operating in the Bowery and on Canal and Fulton Streets, this one city block—47th Street between Fifth and Sixth Avenues—is where the most valuable diamond and jewelry trades in the world occur.
[232] Elevators In 1857, the first passenger elevator, designed by Mr. Otis, was installed in New York, making it possible to construct tall buildings and, eventually, skyscrapers.
[233] 8 Spruce Street More commonly known as Gehry Tower, this 76-floor building—the first skyscraper designed by Frank Gehry—is an interesting example of new architecture.
[234] Flatiron Building Construction on this building, originally the Fuller Building, was completed in 1902. It was admired not only for its height, but also for its triangular base that gives rise to the visual effects for which it gets its nickname. This building is so important that today the entire neighborhood is known as the Flatiron district.
[236] Trump Tower Along with its creator and owner Donald Trump, this building on 5th Avenue is a symbol of New York real estate.
[237] Real Estate Real estate has always been a major topic of discusion in the city.
[238] A New Era As the disappearance of Vinylmania attests, new trends and technologies are changing the city on a daily basis.
[239] Store for Rent It's expensive to rent store space in New York, particularly in certain neighborhoods, which indicates a high turnover rate.
[240] Off-duty taxi sign Since this signage system was confusing and hard to read, it was replaced, in 2013, by a sign that lights up when a cab is free.
[241] Taxi! At certain times of day, it is almost impossible to find a cab in New York. Regardless, people lift up their arms and hope for the best.
[242] Mitzvah Tank Since 1974, this bus belonging to the Jewish religious group Chabad-Lubavitch has circulated on the streets of New York to spread the idea of "the good deed of the day" and to act as a sort of mobile synagogue. Its daily route can be checked online.
[243] Macy's Thanksgiving Day Parade This traditional parade sponsored by Macy's department store since the 1920s is televised around the world.
[244] Madison Square Garden The world's most famous venue for sports and concerts can hold up to 18,200 people.
[245] The Knicks New York's first professional basketball team, originally called "The Knickerbockers," was founded in 1946.The New York Knicks is a registered trademark of MSG Holdings, L.P.
[246] B&H Due to its range of products and informed salespeople, this store on 34th Street and 9th Avenue is a destination for photographers both professional and amateur.
[247] I take photos Few cities in the world have been photographed as widely as New York.
[248] Orthodox Jews Over 1.5 millionJews live in New York City, and some 30 percent are Orthodox. Many of them live in the Williamsburg section of Brooklyn.
[249] Moishe's Since 1978, Moishe's Bake Shop, at 2nd Ave and 7th Street, has been providing the East Village with New York's tastiest kosher baked goods.
[250] Views There are a number of spots to get a panoramic view of New York. This one, from the 21st floor of a building, takes you into the heart of midtown Manhattan.
[252] Choices With so many options, it's hard to choose what to put on your bagel.
[253] Bagels A central European bread that arrived in New York with Jewish immigrants, the bagel is now one of the city's most deeply rooted traditions. You can eat a bagel plain or choose one of the countless options for toppings; the most traditional way to have a bagel is with lox and cream cheese.
[254] NBC Studios + Top of the Rock This building in Rockefeller Center houses two major New York icons: NBC studios, where shows such as *Saturday Night Live* and *The Today Show* are recorded, and the observation deck with the best view of northern New York.
[255] From above Looking at New York from above is a surreal experience that gives a sense of just how much goes on in the city.
[256] Apollo Theater Located on 125th street in Harlem, this theater opened its doors to African American audiences in 1934 and has since become famous for launching the careers of many major musicians such as Ella Fitzgerald.

[257] Jazz Thanks to its famous clubs featuring classic and avant-garde jazz and its excellent musicians, New York is heaven for jazz lovers.
[258] Rush Hour The expression "time is money" is palpable in New York, where people don't waste a second.
[259] The New York City Marathon Every November, thousands of professional and amateur runners from around the world flock to the city for the New York Marathon, one of the city's largest events. Training programs to help people achieve this feat are a year-long commitment.
[260] Houston and Bowery Wall This wall became famous for a mural that Keith Haring donated to the community in the late 1970s. There is now an ongoing program that invites artists such as Barry McGee to create works on this wall.
[262] Cup & Saucer Located at the corner of Canal and Eldridge, this restaurant with a window view and counter offers real American fare for breakfast and lunch. As authentic as it is delicious.
[263] Whitney Museum This museum of twentieth-century art from the United States is one of the best places in the world to get a sense of what is happening in contemporary art. It was founded by Gertrude Vanderbilt Whitney in 1931 on the basis of her private collection which had been rejected by the Metropolitan Museum of Art.
[264] *The New Yorker* Though the focus of *The New Yorker*, which was first published in 1925, is the New York social scene, it is famous around the world for the quality of its essays, literary criticism, and political writing. Since its founding, the contributors have been the leading writers, cartoon artists, and illustrators. Left cover: Garret Price, right cover, the Argentine illustrator, Liniers. [*The New Yorker* is a registered trademark of Condé Nast. All Rights Reserved].
[265] Christmas Trees Right after Thanksgiving, New York City begins getting ready for Christmas. The thousands of trees that flood in from specialized farms are sold in the streets in order to carry out a hundred-year-plus tradition.
[265] Christmas Trees Right after Thanksgiving, New York City begins getting ready for Christmas. The thousands of trees that flood in from specialized farms are sold in the streets in order to carry out a hundred-year-plus tradition.
[266] Chrysler Building The top of this art deco building at Lexington and 42nd Street is a symbol of New York. Until the Empire State was built seven months after the completion of the Chrysler Building in 1930, it was the tallest building in the world.
[267] Santacon A charitable organization with neither political nor religious affiliation, Santacon gathers thousands of Santa Clauses for a daylong pub crawl in New York City.
[268] Rockefeller Center Construction on this nineteen-building complex began in 1920 on a lot that Columbia University owned in midtown New York. Today it is a center of business and leisure, with some of the best stores and most popular events in the city, such as the lighting of the traditional Christmas tree that never fails to dazzle with its beauty.
[270] Baseball in Central Park Many baseball and softball teams practice in the park, which has twenty-six baseball diamonds that can be used with a reservation and permit.
[272] Apthorp Building Built between 1906–1908, this building is a landmark from the pre–World War I era. It is named for the owner of the farm that once stood on its terrain at Broadway and 79th Street. Due to its combination of design, luxury, and amenities, the Apthorp Building is a symbol of New York, especially the Upper West Side.
[273] Nora Ephron In her books and films, Nora Ephron (1941–2012) conveyed her infectious love of an ideal and romantic New York. Her home in the Apthorp Building was the location for the autobiographical film *Heartburn*.
[274] New York rooftop terraces On exclusive rooftop terraces, you can get some fresh air in the middle of one of the most beautiful cities in the world.
[275] Highline True proof of New York's ability to reinvent itself, this park that runs from Gansevoort Street in the Meatpacking district to West 34th Street between 10th and 11th Avenues was built on old elevated railway tracks that had been abandoned since 1980.
[276-277] Food carts Due to the wide variety of dishes available, street food in New York has its loyal fans and followers. There are even cell phone apps to find out where certain trucks stop, though many have a regular spot somewhere in the city.
[278] Subway entrance Every city has its distinctive subway entrance. In New York the forged iron railings have been painted the same shade of green for decades.
[279] Rizzoli Bookstore One of the most beautiful bookstores in the city, it specializes in books on art, architecture, design, and fashion. Founded in 1964 by Angelo Rizzoli, the bookstore–a pillar of New York culture–has moved to a new location at 1133 Broadway.
[280] No smoking Since 2003, smoking has been prohibited in all bars and restaurants in New York. This regulation was later extended throughout the country.
[281] Grocers From the morning paper to a salad for lunch, you can find anything you need at these stores. Local residents are often faithful customers.
[282] Saint Patrick's Cathedral When construction on this cathedral was completed in 1865, its neo-Gothic towers were intended to reign over the entire city. Located directly across from Rockefeller Center, it now cowers amid so many skyscrapers. Dedicated to Saint Patrick, the patron saint of Ireland, the cathedral is the center of the Saint Patrick's Day Parade held on March 17.
[283] Temple Emanu-El The largest synagogue in the world, temple Emanu-El is located at 5th Avenue and 65th Street. The Emanu-El community consists largely of the second wave of Jewish immigrants from Europe. After moving to a number of different locations, construction on this beautiful temple, which is now a staple of the Upper East Side, was completed in 1929.
[284] Rain It's a good idea to carry an umbrella in the city, as you never know when you'll get caught in the rain.
[285] Macy's One of the most famous department stores in New York, it first opened in 1858 and then, in 1902, moved to 34th Street to become "the largest store in the world." The red star on its logo has been around since the beginning.
[286] Blue Note Since it opened in 1981, it has become a temple for jazz lovers and a true Greenwich Village cultural institution. Located at 6th and McDougal, this is where jazz greats who come through New York play.
[287] *Porgy & Bess* An opera with music and lyrics by the Gershwin brothers, it opened at Carnegie Hall in 1935 and features the song "Summertime," which would eventually be recorded by jazz greats Louis Armstrong and Ella Fitzgerald.
[289] Washington Square This park, which housed a cemetery until 1825, was a gathering point for hippies in the 1970s, and scores of students from nearby New York University walk under its arch each day.
[290] Yankees One of New York's two major league baseball teams, the New York Yankees have been part of the city since 1903, with players such as Babe Ruth and Joe DiMaggio becoming baseball idols.The New York Yankees is a registered trademark of the New York Yankees Partnership.

[291] New York University Founded in 1831 by a group of eminent New Yorkers, NYU is one of the largest and most prestigious private universities in the world.
[292] Notices It's common for university students who come to the city for a few years to use notices as a way of communicating and offering services.
[293] Post No Bills Do not paste any posters or advertisements in this area.
[294] View from New Jersey Another vision of southern Manhattan.
[296] Demonstrations II New York is a city that values freedom of expression, resulting in protests about every conceivable issue.
[297] Books and Books There are thousands of books that discuss or take place in New York. Some of them have changed the history of literature and the way we look at the city.
[298] Signal to stop A system to let the driver know someone wants to get off the bus.
[299] Subway exit The same turnstile is used to get in and out of the subway.
[300] Curb your dog Thanks in part to signs announcing fines, the sidewalks of New York are largely devoid of dog excrement.
[301] New York dogs Many dogs in New York are privileged citizens that enjoy their own hair stylists and day care.
[302] Chelsea Hotel The tallest building in New York until 1902, it was converted into a hotel in 1905 and became a gathering point of artists and bohemians. Its rooms have seen the likes of Arthur Miller, Sid Vicious, and Dylan Thomas. This was the first building in the city to be declared a site of cultural and historical interest.
[303] The Pierre A luxury hotel on 5th Avenue at 61st Street, it was designed by Charles Pierre Casalasco, an immigrant who made the American dream come true. The hotel is a symbol of New York high society.
[304] Trash cans Littering, and the improper use of dumpsters, is not only considered anti-social, but also subject to heavy fines.
[305] Recycling The city of New York produces 23,000 tons of trash a day. There are strict and increasingly effective recycling programs.
[306] Emergency Around the city there are old posts where you can ask for help in the event of an emergency.
[307] Police dogs The New York police have two kinds of canines: detection dogs and patrol dogs.
[308] Heroes The New York City fire department dates back to 1648. Because there are so many wooden constructions in the city, fires are frequent. The department has more than 11,000 officers who are viewed as heroes, especially after the events of 9/11.
[309] Fire escapes Typical of old New York buildings, they are often used as balconies even though such use is strictly prohibited. Fire escapes have been the setting for hundreds of films, including Alfred Hitchcock's *Rear Window,* whose protagonist would sleep on one during summer nights.
[310] Police fence The New York police have these fences ready at strategic points around the city.
[311] Upper West Side kids Many nursery schools on the Upper West Side take their kids to Central Park to use the playground.
[312] Manhattan The island of Manhattan is one of the five boroughs that make up New York City. The name comes from the word Manna-hata, which means "island of many hills" in the language of the Lenape Indians.
[314] Manhattan cocktail According to legend, in 1874, Jennie Jerome, who would become Winston Churchill's mother, organized a party for New York governor-elect Samuel Tilden. She asked the bartender at the Manhattan Club to come up with a special cocktail for the occasion which was called the Manhattan.
[315] Subway stations The name of each station is written on the walls in mosaic without altering the original design.
[316] Fines New York City has an online system that makes it easier to pay fines.
[317] Bikes It is more and more common for New Yorkers and tourists alike to ride bikes around the city. A number of bike rental companies use innovative systems that make it easy to use this practical and sustainable method of getting around town.
[318] Old storefronts In a city where everything changes so fast, some businesses like this one at 339 Grand Street have been afforded protection by the city and become tourist attractions.
[319] Barneys New York Opened in 1923, this department store is famous for stocking the most exclusive brands.
[320] Village Cigars Located on the corner of Christopher Street and 7th Avenue since 1922 is this iconic Village business. The small mosaic triangle at the entrance marks the parcel of land that the original owner refused to cede to the city of New York.
[321] Village Vanguard This celebrated New York jazz club at 7th Avenue and 11th Street was founded in 1935. All the jazz greats that come through New York play here.
[322] Balducci's Thanks to its quality goods, this grocery store quickly became a model for gourmet markets around the city.
[323] Baczynsky Meat Market Located in the heart of the East Village, it opened its doors in 1970 to provide the best house-made smoked meats created from Polish and Ukrainian recipes.
[324] Solow Building Due to its curved facade and number nine statue, this building built in 1974 and located at 9 West 57th Street is a New York icon.
[325] LOVE In 1964, Robert Indiana—the creator of what is now one of the most photographed sculptures in New York—designed this Pop Art icon as a greeting card for MoMA (6th Ave. and 55th Street).
[326] Photos From certain angles, this beautiful city looks like an authentic work of art. Images of the city are sold in many New York parks.
[327] The Museum Founded in 1923, the Museum of the City of New York features collections, exhibitions, and historical and sociological accounts of how the city developed, all of which provide a more thorough understanding of this great metropolis.
[328] New Yorker Hotel First opened in 1929 and then reformed in 1994, this art deco hotel in midtown Manhattan provides the city with one of its most famous signs.
[330] Saint John the Divine The construction on Saint John the Divine—the cathedral of the Episcopal Archdiocese of New York located at Amsterdam Avenue and 111th Street—began in 1892. It appears to be endless.
[331] Bride and groom in Central Park It's a New York tradition to have your picture taken in the park on your wedding day.
[332] Ambulances The New York fire department employs over 3,000 paramedics.
[333] Block Drug Store Located at the corner of 6th Street and 2nd Avenue in the East Village, Block Drugstore opened its doors back in 1885. One of the oldest drugstores in New York, it is still in the hands of the original family.
[334] New York buses Currently over 300 bus lines circulate through the five boroughs 24 hours a day. Though slower than the subway, buses are a good way to observe the city above ground.

[335] MetroCard A rechargeable magnetic card that can be used to pay for different means of public transportation. You can make transfers on one swipe and take advantage of unlimited weekly passes. [Metrocard is a registered trademark of Metropolitan Transportation Authority. All rights reserved].
[336] Waverly Restaurant Open 24 hours, this restaurant on the corner of 6th Avenue and Waverly Place serves typical American fare.
[337] Late Show this television show is aired on CBS and produced by the Ed Sullivan Theater. It creates quite a stir at Broadway and 53rd.
[338] Manhattan windows Some of the most interesting things in New York can be seen by looking up and into windows.
[339] MoMA sculpture garden One of New York's treasures, the MoMA sculpture garden on 53rd Street contains abstract and figurative sculptures by Rodin, Calder, and others. The window that looks out onto the garden from inside the museum is one of the most photographed views in the city.
[340] Bloomingdale's Big Brown Bag Bloomingdale's first opened in 1861 when brothers Joseph and Lyman G. Bloomingdale began selling hoop skirts at their Ladies Notions' Shop on the Lower East Side. In 1886, they opened the current location on Lexington and 59th, helping to develop the neighborhood. Today, the store's big brown bag is a symbol of New York shopping.
[341] Brownstones Though technically a construction material, the term is used to refer to a typical New York style of housing. These once single-family homes were later subdivided by floor to be used as apartments.
[342] Canal Street You can buy anything that strikes your fancy on Canal Street, home to jewelers who buy gold and used watches only to resell them a few doors away.
[343] Strand Founded in 1927 on 4th Avenue in what was then called "Book Row"—an area that covered six city blocks and housed forty-eight bookstores—the Strand now carries over 2.5 million used, new, and rare books. The store on Broadway and 12th Street is a legendary location for book lovers.
[344] Sale There are sales all year-round in New York, but the most famous begin the day after Thanksgiving, known as Black Friday, the official beginning of the Christmas shopping season.
[345] Cleaners Many people live alone in New York City, which means it is often more convenient to send your laundry out to be cleaned and ironed by specialists than to wash it at home. Many cleaners offer delivery service.
[346] Traffic cops These officers play a vital role in keeping the streets of New York City safe and moving.
[347] Walk/ Don't walk These are the indications of traffic lights at pedestrian crossings.
[348] Cultural Diversity New York is a shining model of coexistence where people from different cultural traditions take part in the daily life of the city.
[349] The United Nations Based in New York, the United Nations—the largest international organization anywhere—was created in 1945, after World War II. At periodical meetings held year round, representatives of all the countries in the world decide on issues central to international relations.
[350] Dean and Deluca Now a chain of upscale grocery stores, the first one was established in New York City's SoHo district in September 1977. Its store at Broadway and Prince is one of the most traditional in the area.
[351] Pretzels One of the most typical street foods sold in New York, the pretzel first came to the city with Central European immigrants. Pretzels come in all sizes and are best eaten warm.
[352] School bus With its typical yellow school buses, the Office of Pupil Transportation (OPT) is the largest school transportation department in the country. More than 600,000 New York City students attending both public and non public schools located within the five boroughs and neighboring counties in New York, New Jersey, and Connecticut use these services.
[353] Kids' transportation No matter how New York kids get around town, the proper security measures are always taken.
[354] Bus stop Each bus line begins with the first letter of the borough in which it circulates.
[355] Bus map Bus maps are free and available at subway station ticket booths, though now there are very practical apps for cell phones with all the necessary information about New York buses and subways.
[356] New York and Times Square They say it takes as much energy to light up Times Square at any given moment as it does to fuel the entire continent of Africa. No one knows if it's true, but the power of the lights is striking.
[358] *New York Post / Daily News* The two most popular local dailies are the *New York Post*, founded in 1801, and the *Daily News* — which inspired the *Daily Planet* in the Superman comics — founded in 1919. [*New York Post* is a registered trademark of NYP Holdings, Inc. All Rights Reserved]. [*Daily News* is a registered trademark of NYDailyNews.com. All rights reserved].
[359] Steam The warm mist that rises from orange and white stacks is a result of the pressure exerted by the urban steam system that carries steam from the central generating stations under the streets of Manhattan to heat, cool, and deliver energy to large buildings and stores.
[360] 212 The traditional Manhattan area code is something of a trademark. Due to the rise of cell phones and the number of new lines, it became necessary to include new area codes such as 646 and 917, but none of them have the symbolic power of 212.
[361] Squirrels in Central Park The privileged inhabitants of Central Park, squirrels are a city icon loved by children.
[362] From New Jersey So many lovely views of the city can be seen from this neighboring state.
[364] The Twin Towers When they opened on April 4, 1973, the Twin Towers were the tallest buildings in the world, a distinction they kept for many years. Designed by Minoru Yamasaki and Associates (Troy, Michigan) and Emery Roth and Sons (New York) as a part of the World Trade Center, these 110-level skyscrapers were a symbol of North American economic might and a source of pride for the city of New York.
[365] WTC observation deck Since the September 11 attacks, any object related to the Twin Towers has become a treasure for collectors.
[366] A changed landscape It's hard to get used to the view of southern Manhattan without the towers.
[367] Memorial In August 2006, work began on the memorial to be erected where Tower 1 had stood. The project was designed by Israeli–North American architect Michael Arad of Handel Architects. Silence and reflection reign in this place of remembrance.
[368] Forever and ever The Twin Towers and the memory of those who lost their lives there are part of the city's landscape. They live on in the hearts of everyone who loves

New York.
[370] One World Trade Center After a great deal of controversy, construction began on the new building in 2006. The original design was by architect Daniel Libeskind, though later modifications were carried out by David Childs.
[371] Freedom Tower On May 10, 2013, the final piece was installed on the antenna above the tower, making One World Trade Center the tallest building in New York and the fourth tallest in the world. More importantly, though, the city showed its character and soul by building up from the ashes.
[372] New landscape This is the new skyline of southern Manhattan.
[374] New Year's Eve in Times Square Spending New Year's Eve in Times Square is a New York tradition that began in 1907. Over a million people gather here every year and many more watch the festivities on television.
[375] Chinese New Year When the Chinese New Year begins, Chinatown gets decked out for one of the most popular parades in the city.
[377] White Central Park Walking through a snowy Central Park in winter is a beautiful experience.
[378] Shopping bags Shopping bags have become a symbol of New York. Brands are well aware that their bags are fetish items for tourists and fashionistas.
[379] Receipts New York is a city meant for shopping. It is known for offering the best items available on the market at a wide range of price points. End-of-season sales attract New Yorkers and tourists from around the world.
[381] Walking in Central Park Every day, throughout the seasons, people enjoy walking through this park.
[382] Flea Market There are over twelve flea markets around the city. Most of them are held on Saturdays and Sundays. It is a New York tradition to visit flea markets where you can find treasures from around the world that have made their way to New York.
[383] Moving People move more often in New York than in most other cities, which means that moving and storage companies run by specialists are big business.
[384] Golden lights On misty nights, New York has a golden sheen all its own.
[386] George Washington Statue This bronze statue is located on the stairs to Federal Hall at 26 Wall Street. This was the first United States capitol building and the place where, in 1789, Washington was sworn in as president.
[387] John F. Kennedy Airport Better known by its code name: JFK, this is the US airport with the greatest volume of traffic: over 50,000 passengers come through every day.
[388] Here As the classic Sinatra song goes,"If I can make it there, I'll make it anywhere. It's up to you New York, New York."

Photographers:
ALBERTO NEGRIN - ALE VENTURA - ANA PAULA HIRAMA - ANDREW LACHANCE - ANDREW WERTHEIMER - ANDY CLARK - ANTONIO RUBIO - BEN HELMER - BEN SUTHERLAND - BILL SOISTMANN - BOSC D'ANJOU - BROADWAYTOUR.NET - BRUNO PEDEMONTI - CLARA SUÁREZ LASTRA - CLAY WILLIAMS - CORY DOCTOROW - DANIEL MODELL - DAREEN COOPER - DAVE NEWMAN - DAVID SALAFIA - DIANA SHUMATE - DIANA WILLIAMS MORGAN - DR SEARLS - DUEL RIS- ED YOURDON - EDENPICTURES - GARY CURTIS - GK: GABRIELA KOGAN - GWENAËL PIASER - IAN GRIEVSON - INGRID RICHTER JAN MARCINEK - JASON RULE - JAVIER DOREN - JOHANNA WOLF - JONATHAN GORANSKY JOSEF PINLAC - JOSHUA GAYNOR - KAMA GUEZALOVA - KOHEY KANNO - LACHLAND HARDY - LARA NESIS - LORI L. STALTERI - LUDOVIC BERTRON - MARK SUSINA - MARINA KOGAN - MARTÍN BAINTRUB - MO RIZA - NICHOLAS NOYES - NICK VOSNIADIS NICOLAS MIRGUET - ONUR KOCATAS - PÅL CHRISTENSEN - PANCHO RODRIGUEZ - PATRICK KWAN - PATTY SMITH - PHIL DOKAS - POPAITALY* - RAPHAEL RODRIGUEZ - REBECA ANCHONDO RICHARD PREECE - ROB BOUDON - ROBERT ROBBINS - ROBYN LEE - RUBÉN FERNÁNDEZ SARA COLGAN - SHANE STROUD - STEVE MALPASS - STEVE SPENCER - STEVEN SHOOK - SUSANA GALPERIN - TATSUO FUKUTOMI - THIMOTY KRAUSE - TOM DOLAN - VOX EFX BILLIE WARD

* POPAITALY is the trade association of the marketing at retail industry dedicated to serving its more than 1,700 members internationally by promoting, protecting, and advancing the broader interests of marketing at retail through research, education, trade forums, networking, and legislative efforts.

Photographers 1 pages #84-85 from left to right: GK, GK, ED YOURDON, GK, PATTY SMITH, GK, GK, GK.
Photographers 2 page #114: GK except NICOLAS MIRGUET (3rd of the 2nd line) page #115 from left to right: BOSC D'ANJOU, BEN SUTHERLAND.
Photographers 3 page #137 from left to right: DANIEL MODELL, BILLIE WARD.
Photographers 4 page #167 from left to right, line 1: STEVE MALPASS, NICHOLAS NOYES.Line 2: PHIL DOKAS, PATTY SMITH.
Photographers 5 page #315 from left to right, line 1: GK, MARK SUSINA. Line 2: GK, GK. Line 3: MO RIZA, JOSHUA GAYNOR.

The photographs in pages: 26, 80, 109, 173, 188, 212, 225, 263, 365 are collectible pieces from personal collections.

First published in the United State of America in 2015 by
Universe Publishing
A Division of Rizzoli International Publications, Inc.
300 Park Avenue South
New York, NY 10010
www.rizzoliusa.com

This book was produced by
ORO editions
31 Commercial Blvd. Suite F
Novato CA 94949
www.oroeditions.com

Edited and designed by Gabriela Kogan

2015 2016 2017 2018 / 10 9 8 7 6 5 4 3 2 1

ISBN: 978-0-7893-2940-0

Library of Congress Control Number: 2015933172

Printed in China

Jacket and Case Cover images
Front:
First line: ED YOURDON / GK / PATTY SMITH, GK, DIANA SHUMATE, GK
Second line: ED YOURDON, JOSEF PINLAC
Third line: GK, PATRICK KWAN, STEVE MALPASS, BILLIE WARD, GK
Fourth line: ED YOURDON, JOSHUA GAYNOR, MO RIZA, GK

Back:
First line: MO RIZA, GK, GK, GK
Second line: GK, SHANE STROUD, NICK VOSNIADIS, GK
Third line: DANIEL MODELL / BILLIE WARD, STEVE MALPASS, MO RIZA, GK, DANIEL MODELL / BILLIE WARD
Fourth line: PANCHO RODRIGUEZ, ALBERTO NEGRIN, SHANE STROUD, GK

Endpapers: ED YOURDON - PANCHO RODRIGUEZ

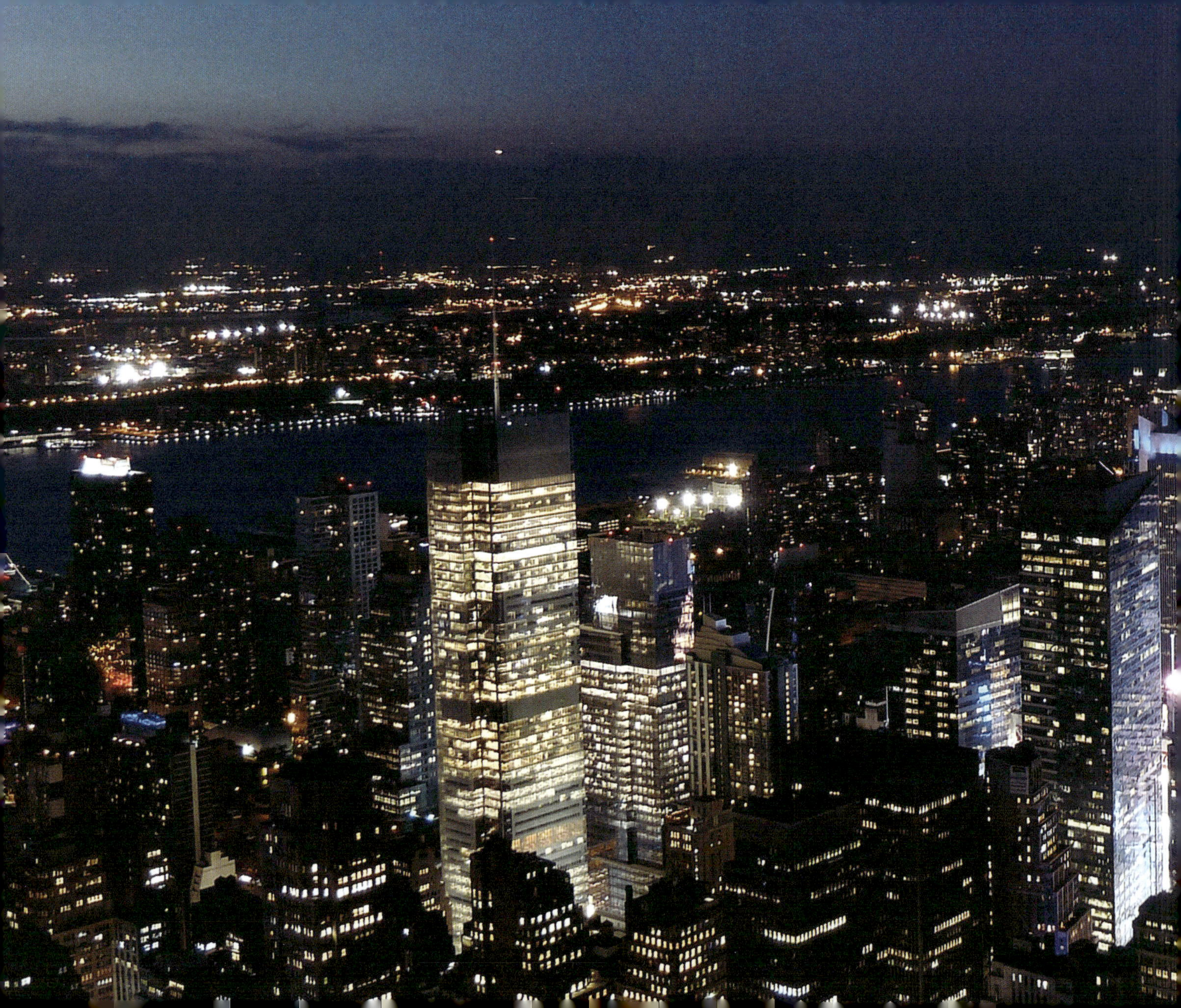